Business and Economic Statistics

Business and Economic
STATISTICS

By

WILLIAM A. SPURR, Ph.D.
PROFESSOR OF BUSINESS STATISTICS
GRADUATE SCHOOL OF BUSINESS, STANFORD UNIVERSITY

LESTER S. KELLOGG, M.A.
DIRECTOR OF ECONOMIC RESEARCH
DEERE & COMPANY

and

JOHN H. SMITH, Ph.D.
PROFESSOR OF STATISTICS, AMERICAN UNIVERSITY

REVISED EDITION

1961

RICHARD D. IRWIN, INC.
HOMEWOOD, ILLINOIS

© 1954 AND 1961 BY RICHARD D. IRWIN, INC.

ALL RIGHTS RESERVED. THIS BOOK OR ANY PART THEREOF MAY NOT
BE REPRODUCED WITHOUT THE WRITTEN PERMISSION OF THE PUBLISHER

Revised Edition

First Printing, September, 1961
Second Printing, September, 1963
Third Printing, May, 1964

Library of Congress Catalogue Card No. 61-14489

PRINTED IN THE UNITED STATES OF AMERICA

PREFACE

THIS BOOK is designed for basic courses in statistics in departments of business, economics, and general social science. It may be used in its entirety for a two-semester course, or it may be adapted to a one-semester course by omitting the more advanced sections.

Since the book is planned for the general student who needs to use statistics in his chosen field of work, the principal emphasis is placed on the use of statistical methods as scientific tools in the analysis of practical business and economic problems, rather than on theory or mathematical derivations. Nevertheless, the treatment is precise enough to meet the initial needs of those who plan to become professional statisticians.

The early chapters include the purposes of statistical analysis, collection of data from both library sources and sample surveys, and effective methods of presenting facts in tables and charts. Then follow three chapters on frequency distributions, averages, and dispersion, three chapters on statistical inference, two chapters on index numbers, and three on time series analysis. Finally, there are two chapters on correlation and regression, and a chapter on quality control.

Statistical analysis in business and economics is based on the same scientific principles as in other fields, but there is considerable difference in the emphasis placed on particular principles, the specialized techniques required, and the examples to which the principles are applied. In particular, many business and economic problems involve nonrandom variation. Thus, the economist is more interested in business cycles and economic growth than is the psychologist or biologist; so the subjects of index numbers and time series analysis receive more emphasis here than in a book on psychometric or biometric methods.

The treatment of each topic covers (1) *what* it is; (2) *why* it is measured; (3) *how* it is measured; and (4) how it is *interpreted* and applied in practice. Too many statistics books concentrate on (3) alone. Up-to-date practical examples in business and economics are offered as illustrations. Table and chart numbers are preceded by chapter numbers to aid in finding them. Thus Table 5–2 refers to the second table in Chapter 5. Problems and reading references are provided at the end of each chapter. In addition, a wide variety of problems and cases is provided in a Workbook that accompanies the text.

A distinctive feature of the text is the presentation of short-cut flexible graphic methods of analysis as well as mathematical techniques. Graphic analysis has several advantages: (1) it usually saves work; (2) it provides a continuing picture of the successive steps in analysis, as a useful teaching aid and a check on computations; and (3) it may provide more accurate answers than mathematical methods if personal judgment or flexibility plays an important role. Graphic methods are well developed in such fields as engineering, navigation, and architecture, but have only recently come into widespread use to supplement the traditional computational methods of statistics. In modern business, labor-saving devices are as essential in statistical analysis as on the production line. Elaborate statistical methods appropriate for theoretical study may be too cumbersome and time consuming for the business analyst. Graphic methods can also be used in conjunction with mathematical methods to utilize the advantages of each. Thus, a supervisor can sketch out a job in preparing a program for a computer, then check the results against his graphs.

The presentation has been simplified in two respects: (1) basic English is used, as far as possible, in place of the polysyllabic jargon so common in technical publications, and (2) the use of symbols and mathematical formulas is kept to a minimum. Symbols have been chosen to conform to modern common usage. The student should not be misled by the appearance of "higher mathematics" in the formulas used. They merely give instructions for performing operations in elementary algebra. A knowledge of first-year algebra is all that is essential for an understanding of basic statistical principles.

The second edition has been completely revised. Two new chapters have been added on statistical inference, with increased emphasis on the normal distribution, confidence intervals, and tests of hypotheses for means and proportions. The presentation of correlation has also been modernized, with primary emphasis on regression analysis and statistical inference as applied to economic data, including the forecasting of time series.

The treatment of basic, widely used methods has been expanded throughout the book, and examples have been updated to illustrate contemporary applications. At the same time, a number of traditional methods which are technically difficult and of limited use in business and economic analysis have been omitted.

The authors are greatly indebted to the following professors who contributed important sections to the more advanced chapters: Roy W. Jastram on statistical inference, Karl A. Fox and Oscar N. Serbein on correlation and regression, and Frank J. Williams and David S. Chambers on quality control. The authors also wish to express their appreciation to Professor Richard C. Henshaw, Jr. for the revision of problems and to Professor Charles P. Bonini for general review and numerous suggestions resulting from testing the manuscript in classes. William A. Spurr assumed the primary responsibility for coordinating these various contributions and for preparing the revised edition in its present form. It is hoped that the unusually thorough scrutiny and revisions of the text provided by both the co-authors and their collaborators will serve to achieve the purpose of combining simplicity and accuracy in presenting this subject.

WILLIAM A. SPURR
LESTER S. KELLOGG
JOHN H. SMITH

August, 1961

TABLE OF CONTENTS

CHAPTER   PAGE

1. STATISTICS IN BUSINESS AND ECONOMICS 1
   Statistical Analysis as a Scientific Method, 1. The Role of Statistics in Decision Making, 3. Statistics in Business, 4. Statistics in Economics, 6. Cautions in the Use of Statistical Data, 8.

2. USE OF RESEARCH SOURCES 18
   Defining the Problem, 18. Published and Unpublished Sources, 19. Collection of Data from Published Sources, 21. Ten Steps in Finding a Good Source, 22. Types of Source Materials, 24. The Correct Use of Data, 29.

3. COLLECTION OF ORIGINAL DATA 38
   Census versus Sample, 38. Personal Interviews versus Mail Questionnaires, 39. Preparation of Questionnaires, 42. Editing Schedules, 50. Preliminary Tabulation, 52.

4. METHODS OF SELECTING SAMPLES 64
   Samples and Inferences Concerning Populations, 65. Probability Sampling, 66. Nonprobability Sampling, 73. Recurrent Surveys and Panels, 76.

5. ACCURACY OF ECONOMIC DATA; RATIOS 82
   Accuracy of Economic Data, 82. Ratios, 87.

6. STATISTICAL TABLES 97
   Tables versus Charts, 97. Methods of Classifying Data, 98. Reference and Summary Tables, 100. Construction of Tables, 101.

7. HOW TO CONSTRUCT A CHART 113
   Basic Purposes of Charts, 113. Planning a Chart, 115. Constructing a Chart, 118. Telling a Story with Charts, 127.

8. COMMON TYPES OF CHARTS 130
   Bar Charts, 130. Circle Charts, 139. Ratio Charts, 140.

9. FREQUENCY DISTRIBUTIONS 155
   The Array, 156. Grouping into Broader Classes, 157. Charts of Frequency Distributions, 164. Types of Frequency Distributions, 170. Cumulative Frequency Distributions, 172.

10. AVERAGES 179
    The Arithmetic Mean, 179. The Median, 186. The Modified Mean, 189. The Mode, 190. The Geometric Mean, 191. Which Average To Use? 193. Characteristics of Averages, 194.

11. DISPERSION 200
    Purposes of Measuring Dispersion, 202. The Range, 203. The Quartile Deviation, 204. The Mean Deviation, 206. The Standard Deviation, 208.

CHAPTER	PAGE

Relation between Measures of Dispersion, 214. Measures of Relative Dispersion, 217. Skewness, 218. Uses of Measures of Dispersion, 219.

12. Statistical Inference: Arithmetic Means 224

The Normal Distribution, 225. How Sample Means are Distributed, 227. The Standard Error of the Mean, 233. Confidence Intervals, 238. How Big Should a Sample Be? 241.

13. Tests of Hypotheses 247

Type I and Type II Errors, 251. Operating Characteristic Curves, 255. Two-Tailed versus One-Tailed Tests, 257. Tests of Differences between Arithmetic Means, 260. Small Samples, 265.

14. Inferences Involving Proportions 271

The Standard Error of a Proportion, 272. The Confidence Interval for a Proportion, 272. The Test of a Hypothesis for a Proportion, 274. The Binomial Distribution, 275. The Test of a Difference between Two Proportions, 277.

15. Index Numbers 283

Advantages of Index Numbers, 283. Kinds of Index Numbers, 284. Basic Methods of Constructing Index Numbers, 287. Tests of a Good Index Number, 295. Adjustments in Index Numbers, 303.

16. Some Important Indexes 309

Wholesale Price Index, 310. Consumer Price Index, 313. Industrial Production Index, 318. National Income and Product, 320. Other National Indexes and Their Uses, 323. Regional Business Indexes, 327.

17. Analysis of Business Fluctuations 331

Types of Business Fluctuations, 331. The Problem of Time Series Analysis, 343.

18. Secular Trend 355

Purposes of Measuring Trend, 355. Period of Years Selected, 356. Methods of Measuring Trend, 357.

19. Seasonal and Cyclical Variations 389

Purposes of Measuring Seasonality, 389. Methods of Measuring Seasonal Variation, 391. Business Cycles, 410.

20. Simple Correlation and Regression 426

Preliminary Analysis, 426. Fundamental Concepts, 429. Regression Analysis, 430. Regression Analysis: Statistical Inference, 445. Coefficient of Correlation, 452.

21. Time Series and Multiple Correlation 464

Regression Analysis of Business and Economic Data, 464. Correlation of Time Series, 467. Multiple Correlation and Regression, 477. Linear Relationships, 478. Curvilinear Relationships, 486.

22. Statistical Quality Control 493

Types of Variation in Quality, 493. Control Charts for Variables, 495. Control of Attributes, 507. Acceptance Sampling, 510.

APPENDIXES

APPENDIXES	PAGE
A. Selected Sources of Business Statistics	519
B. Glossary of Symbols	531
C. Logarithms	533
D. Squares, Square Roots, and Reciprocals 1–1,000	538
E. Areas Under the Normal Curve	550
F. Values of t	551
G. Sums of Squares and Fourth Powers Used in Trend Fitting	552

INDEX

Index	555

1. STATISTICS IN BUSINESS AND ECONOMICS

STATISTICS in today's business and economics includes: (1) statistical data and (2) statistical analysis. The one is valueless without the other. Numerical data and methods of analysis are becoming increasingly important in business management and in every field of economics.

But what are statistical data? Not all numbers are statistical; logarithms, for instance, are merely abstract numbers. Statistical data are concrete numbers which represent objects—their counts or measurement. Statistics deals with numbers not merely as such but as expressions of significant relationships. It is not enough to collect and present the data, therefore; they must be carefully analyzed and interpreted as well, in order to make the best possible decisions based on the data. As Lord Kelvin put it,

> ... when you can measure what you are speaking about and express it in numbers you know something about it; but when you cannot measure it, when you cannot express it in numbers, your knowledge is of a meagre and unsatisfactory kind: it may be the beginning of knowledge, but you have scarcely, in your thoughts, advanced to the stage of *science,* whatever the matter may be.

STATISTICAL ANALYSIS AS A SCIENTIFIC METHOD

When masses of numerical information are to be analyzed, some means of summarization must be found which will reveal their major characteristics. Statistical analysis meets this need. Hence, in a broad sense, statistical analysis is a scientific method of studying quantitative data. It is a means of summarizing the essential features and relationships of the data, and then generalizing from these observations to determine broad patterns of behavior or future tendencies. Statistical analysis is therefore useful in any field of knowledge in which extensive numerical information is needed.

The social and biological sciences, in particular, require masses of facts in order to determine general behavior, because of the wide variation in individuals. In the physical sciences, on the other hand, precisely controlled laboratory experiments can be used instead, to a large extent. The physicist can estimate the speed of light by repeated trials, with a small error of measurement; whereas the market analyst who wishes to determine consumer preferences toward compact cars must deal with a sample of consumers who vary widely in their preferences. He must design a questionnaire, select an unbiased sample, and estimate the sampling error. Human and biological groups are more variable in behavior than are most physical phenomena, so their study requires a statistical approach even more than in the physical sciences. Statistical analysis is therefore the fundamental method of quantitative reasoning not only in business and economics but also in sociology, anthropology, psychology, education, medicine, public health, and biology.

Statistical theory is founded on the mathematics of probability, which provides the basis for determining not only general tendencies but also the reliability of each generalization. The whole process of reasoning from the specific to the general may be called *statistical inference,* as well as *generalization* or *induction.* The field of statistical analysis itself is also called *statistical methods* or merely *statistics.* The latter term is used here in the singular sense, as opposed to "statistics" in the plural sense which refers only to the observed data themselves.[1] Applications of statistical analysis in a particular field may be known under other names connoting the idea of *measurement* or *research,* such as econometrics, biometrics, psychometric methods, or forest mensuration; also business research, economic research, or marketing research methods.

The importance of the statistical approach to the solution of practical problems has gradually come to be realized during recent times. The progress in this direction is explained by several developments. Fundamentally, the tremendous growth of population, large-scale production, and trade that followed the Industrial Revolution has required the production and use of a vast volume of statistics in every sphere of social activity. Statistical knowledge has increased in quantity, quality, and frequency. The expanding needs of government have accelerated this growth. As a result, fact finding has become an integral part of economic progress.

---

[1] Note that the word "data" is plural; the singular is "datum."

Increasing public interest in and demand for social statistics rests, then, on the basic premise that the problems of society, as well as of natural science and technology, can be solved by the increase and diffusion of this especially matter-of-fact type of matter-of-fact knowledge. The whole world now seems to hold that statistics can be useful in understanding, assessing, and controlling the operations of society.[2]

Statisticians, too, have discovered new and more powerful analytical techniques which have increased the value of statistical methods of planning and control. The applied statisticians have also helped to dispel the aura of mystery which formerly surrounded the subject. This has been accomplished through a shift in teaching emphasis toward the applied side and through the publishing of textbooks and reference books which stress the simplicity of statistical application and avoid perpetuating the impression that one must be master of advanced mathematics in order to do statistical work.

THE ROLE OF STATISTICS IN DECISION MAKING

Statistical data are collected and analyzed not only for the purpose of adding to scientific knowledge in general but also for the purpose of helping the rational man to make decisions. One of the most important functions of the business executive, the government official, or the administrator in any field, is to make decisions. The function of statistics is to help decide what data are needed, and how the data shall be collected, tabulated, analyzed, and interpreted in such a way as to lead to the best possible decision. Unfortunately, the complete facts are not usually available, so incomplete data, or samples, must be used. Statistics then provides methods that help the executive make the best decision on the basis of these incomplete facts. Hence statistics has come to be defined as a group of methods for making wise decisions in the face of uncertainty.

Of course, statistical methods do not provide the only basis for decision making. There are many intangible factors—the business "climate," prospective government action, technological developments, or personnel relationships, for example—which make management an intuitive art rather than a science. Nevertheless, statistics provides the primary factual basis for reaching good decisions. The executive who masters the statistical approach to decision making will narrow the range of uncertainty, and increase his probability of making a correct decision.

---

[2] Solomon Fabricant, "Factors in the Accumulation of Social Statistics," *Journal of the American Statistical Association,* June 1952, p. 259.

As M. A. Girshick has said:

> All branches of statistics . . . deal with the same basic problem, namely, the problem of decision making in the face of uncertainty. All decision rules . . . must be evaluated by their consequences. These consequences are expressible in terms of risks, or more intrinsically, in terms of the probabilities of taking the various permissible actions which are induced by the experiment, decision rule, and the possible states of the system. In brief . . . not facts from figures but rather decisions from observations should become the main emphasis in elementary statistical observations.[3]

Faced with a business problem involving uncertainty, we can list the future events that may occur and the probability that each will happen, together with the various acts or decisions that may be taken, and the consequence (e.g., cost) of each combination of a given act and a resulting event. The best decision rule is then the one that minimizes the expected total cost, allowing for the probabilities involved. This procedure provides the executive with a better basis for decision making than he could have obtained from his unaided intuition. The introductory statistical methods presented in this book provide a useful foundation for the further study of statistical decision theory.

STATISTICS IN BUSINESS

The employment of statistical methods in the solution of business problems belongs almost exclusively to the twentieth century. At an earlier date when practically all business enterprises were small, management was able to comprehend its problems in detail by personal contact. The increased size of concerns in the present period has required more planning and greater regimentation of operations. At the same time, management has found it impossible to maintain personal contact with its problems. The alternative is control through the interpretation of numerical information. This chain of circumstances has led to the introduction of statistical methods of investigation as a primary aid in the performance of the function of management.

According to a study made by the Pacific Telephone and Telegraph Company:

> Today, management at all levels is guided quite generally by facts obtained through analysis of records rather than upon knowledge obtained merely through personal observation and experience. . . . Through application of appropriate statistical methods, current performance may be measured, significant relationships may be studied, past experience may be analyzed and probable future trends appraised.

---

[3] *Journal of the American Statistical Association,* September 1953, p. 646.

... The use of statistical methods and the performance of analytical work which is largely statistical in character—whether or not it happens to be carried on under the distinctive label of "statistics"—occupy a conspicuous place in the work of all departments of the company. . . .[4]

Statistical analysis is thus used as a basis for the control of many operations in a company and for planning or forecasting its activities. Through the aid of statistical reports the executive can gain a summary picture of current operations which improves his factual basis for making valid decisions affecting future operations.

The principal statistical activities of a typical large and progressive firm are as follows:

1. A central economic research or statistical department operates under the guidance of an "economist" or "chief statistician." This department analyzes general business trends and forecasts business activity, commodity prices, and other economic factors. It may co-ordinate the internal company statistics compiled by other departments and issue summary reports of operations to top executives. It also makes periodic comparisons of the company's performance with that of its competitors.

2. A marketing research staff makes surveys of consumer preferences and purchasing power and forecasts probable future trends in sales. It may prepare a detailed sales budget for the coming year, broken down by individual products and by months. Finally, it has the responsibility for setting salesmen's quotas by territories and products, based on past performance, income studies, and salesmen's estimates.[5]

3. The production department maintains a "quality control" staff that minimizes defective output by means of statistical checks, as described in Chapter 22. It prepares forecasts of production based on sales forecasts and other criteria, and checks actual production against these estimates. It also maintains an inventory control system and makes time and motion studies.

4. The controller's department combines statistical and accounting methods in making the over-all budget for the coming year—including sales; material, labor, and other costs; and net profits and capital requirements. It may maintain a standard cost system for controlling costs and setting prices of products.

5. The personnel department makes statistical studies of wage rates, incentive systems, the cost of living, employment trends, labor turnover rates, accident rates, and results of employee selection procedures.

---

[4] *Statistics in the Telephone Business* (March 1, 1951).

[5] See Frank D. Newbury, *Business Forecasting* (New York: McGraw-Hill Book Co., Inc., 1952), chaps. 1, 2, 15.

6. The investment department maintains security analysts who study individual stocks and bonds and the general outlook for the securities markets.

7. The executive department may include an "operations research" staff. This group consists of specialists, such as statisticians, mathematicians, and physicists, who apply scientific methods to the study of complex operations throughout the organization. The purpose is to provide top management with a factual basis for making policy decisions.

Some of the men and women who perform these functions are professional statisticians, but most of them have developed their knowledge of statistical analysis as an adjunct to their major specialties. In all departments of a business, personnel are concerned with the collection, classification, and presentation of statistics, even if their work requires no analysis. The general executive, too, must know some statistics as well as the basic principles of accounting, finance, business law, marketing, production management, and industrial relations in handling the various aspects of his job. He cannot depend entirely on specialists for his knowledge.

STATISTICS IN ECONOMICS

Economists and other social scientists are more concerned with conditions in the economy as a whole than with those in an individual concern, but they depend on statistics just as the business analyst does. Indeed, many of the statistical problems in economics are similar to, or identical with, those in business. Economists today are no longer content to theorize in abstract terms, citing statistics only as needed to buttress their arguments. Instead, they utilize the excellent data now available to build a sound factual foundation for their reasoning. Some of the uses of statistics in economics are as follows:

1. Extensive statistical studies of business cycles, long-term growth, and seasonal fluctuations serve to expand our knowledge of economic instability and to modify older theories.

2. Measures of gross national product and national income have greatly advanced over-all economic analysis and opened up an entire new field of study.

3. Statistical surveys of prices are essential in studying the theories of prices, pricing policy, and price trends, as well as their relationships to the general problem of inflation.

4. Financial statistics are basic in the fields of money and banking, short-term credit, consumer finance, and public finance.

5. Operational studies of public utilities, including the transportation and communication industries, require both statistical and legal tools of analysis. Such studies are necessary in connection with the federal and state regulation of these industries.

6. Analyses of population, land economics, and economic geography are basially statistical and geographic in their approach.

7. Studies of competition, oligopoly, and monopoly require statistical comparisons of market prices, costs, and profits of individual firms.

Statistical analysis is therefore carried on in every field of inductive economics—by individual professors, university economic research bureaus, chambers of commerce, trade associations, and such well-known research agencies as the National Bureau of Economic Research, the National Industrial Conference Board, the Twentieth Century Fund, and the Brookings Institution, to mention a few.

The most spectacular development of statistical analysis in economic research during recent years, however, has been in the federal government. As it has grown in size, the government has greatly expanded the scope of its statistical activities in every field of applied economics. Some agencies collect and publish statistics for their informational value to the public, while others compile data as a by-product of administrative or regulatory activities. Under the Full Employment Act of 1946 the President's Council of Economic Advisers and the congressional Joint Economic Committee employ many statistical indexes as guides in recommending to the President and Congress control measures designed to allay depression or inflation. Statistics has become as much a major tool of economic guidance and control by the federal government as it is an operational tool for individual concerns.

The world wars of the present generation have tremendously stimulated the government's need for statistical information in administering the great manpower and volumes of matériel involved. The pressures of war have also caused an accelerated development in statistical *methods*. Since the need for controls increases with the size of an enterprise, the federal government's wartime organization has required unprecedented numbers of statisticians in purchasing, logistics, operations research, and many other fields.

To conclude this introduction, we quote from M. J. Moroney's *Facts from Figures:*

> If you are young, then I say: Learn something about statistics as soon as you can. Don't dismiss it through ignorance or because it calls for thought . . . If you are older and already crowned with the laurels of success, see to it that those

under your wing who look to you for advice are encouraged to look into this subject. In this way you will show that your arteries are not yet hardened, and you will be able to reap the benefits without doing overmuch work yourself. Whoever you are, if your work calls for the interpretation of data, you may be able to do without statistics, but you won't do so well.

CAUTIONS IN THE USE OF STATISTICAL DATA

The beginner in statistical work is apt to have the attitude that numerical facts can be accepted without question. A few adverse experiences will usually dispel this initial trustfulness in favor of a healthy skepticism. The scientific attitude toward evidence is skeptical rather than either cynical or uncritically enthusiastic.

Many of the misuses that appear in statistical reports arise from failure of the authors to maintain a critical attitude toward their work. Even facts and statements that are true in some sense can be quoted out of context or presented in such a way that they are bound to be misinterpreted by most readers. As a result, the disillusioned have coined such slogans as: "There are three kinds of lies—lies, damn lies, and statistics," and conversely, "Figures don't lie, but liars figure." Many people use statistics as a drunkard uses a street lamp—for support rather than for illumination.

The scientific investigator must seek the *truth* above all. It is not enough to avoid outright falsehood; the investigator must be on the alert to detect possible distortion of truth. One can hardly pick up a newspaper without seeing some sensational headline based on scanty or doubtful data.

Several types of misuse are presented below. Some contain actual errors or falsification of facts, but others consist of entirely true statements taken out of context. All examples are taken from reputable publications, but many of the sources are omitted to avoid embarrassment.

Bias

Conscious or unconscious bias is very common in statistical work. It is easy to detect the conscious bias in an advertisement that quotes statistics to "prove" the superiority of a given product, while a competitor's ad quotes other statistics to "prove" the superiority of his own product. But many compilers of statistics have an ax to grind. A jewelers' association quotes figures purporting to show that the double-ring wedding has become "an accepted national custom." A labor organization claims that a cost-of-living index, on which wages are based, should be revised upward because it understates real costs, while an employers' association defends the index, pointing out components that overstate real costs. The source of the data must be considered, as well as the conclusions themselves.

Unconscious bias is even more insidious. Perhaps all statistical reports contain some unconscious bias, since the results of research must be interpreted by human beings, each of whom can judge only in terms of his own experience and his attitude toward the problem at hand. The investigator must disregard his preconceptions and avoid wishful thinking in order to attain an objective conclusion. If biased data must be used in the absence of better information, the nature and probable amount of the bias must be considered in interpreting the results.

Faulty Generalization

A basic error in statistical reasoning is to jump to a conclusion or generalization on the basis of too small a sample, or one which is not typical of the whole population to which the conclusions are applied. This subject is of such importance that several chapters in this book are devoted to methods of selecting samples and making statistical inferences.

As an example of using too small a sample, a national magazine reported that a group of Colorado schoolteachers had been given a test in history and failed with an average grade of 67, indicating that Colorado schoolteachers generally were deficient in history. An official of the Colorado Education Association retorted that only four teachers had been given the test, of whom three made the respectable average score of 83 and the fourth only 20, bringing the average of the four down to 67.

An extreme case of using too small a sample is that of generalizing from a sample of one, or citing only a single case. Thus, a typewriter manufacturer advertises that, "Tests by leading educators prove that students who use typewriters get up to 38% better grades."

Improper generalizations based on nontypical samples are more difficult to detect. Such samples may be adequate in size, but they differ from the total population in some essential characteristic; so the generalization is faulty. For example, a feature article in *Advertising Age* is entitled "Obits Show 'Average' Adman is Dead at 62," based on obituaries of 300 advertising men who died during the previous year. Perhaps the advertising game *does* kill men off young, but there may be two defects in the sample used: (1) Since many young men have entered this field in recent years, those who died during the past year were relatively young; the surviving ones who will live to a riper old age are of course not counted. (2) If advertising is a young man's game, as reputed, older men go into other fields and are counted there when they die. As an analogy, the average age at death of college students is about 20 years, but this does not indicate that college graduates die young.

Another example is a report in a business school alumni journal that the average graduate in the class of 1920 earned $87,049 in a recent year. This figure was based on 18 returns received from a questionnaire mailed to 62 class members. Unfortunately, the average income is not typical if a larger proportion of those with higher incomes return the questionnaire than do those with lower incomes, or if some respondents exaggerate their incomes, as is sometimes the case. Furthermore, if a few alumni have very high incomes, these figures greatly inflate the average.[6]

Faulty Deduction

Faulty deduction (in the sense that deductive reasoning is the opposite of inductive reasoning) occurs when a general statement is applied erroneously to a specific case.

Thus, an electric institute reported that "industry's generating capacity in December was 5.1 per cent above electricity demands." This statement was doubtless true of the country as a whole, but it would be faulty deduction to apply it to a specific region which might be short in generating capacity. Regions, such as the Far West, that have grown rapidly in population were in fact short of power at this time.

Similarly, an opponent of health insurance may say that families generally spend only 5 per cent of their total income on medical care— less than they spend on liquor or recreation. Nevertheless, medical care may be a crushing burden on an individual family in a particular year. The common error of faulty deduction arises fundamentally from the human tendency to apply a valid general rule as if it were an invariant mechanical law. Such a proposition should be stated as a general tendency instead, with allowance for individual differences.

Noncomparable Data

Comparisons are frequently made between two things that are not really alike. For example, certain airlines advertised that air travel was

---

[6] This example illustrates several misuses: (1) too small a sample, (2) nontypical sample, (3) spurious accuracy (see below), and (4) use of mean instead of median (see Chapter 10).

cheaper than first-class rail travel. The Southern Pacific Company in a series of advertisements entitled, "A short course in Railroading . . . for Airline executives," claimed that these figures were not comparable because (1) the one-way fares quoted did not make allowance for the greater reduction in round-trip fares on railroads, (2) the fares compared the cost of a chair on a plane with that of a bed or lower berth on a train, and (3) no allowance was made for the rails' carrying children free under five years of age and their extra baggage allowance.

A whisky manufacturer advertised that the price of his product (before taxes) had not increased appreciably during the past decade, without mentioning that the proportion of "grain neutral spirits" had been increased. Errors due to noncomparability affect price indexes generally, since the specifications of components vary from time to time.

A feature article in *Time* (October 28, 1957) praising West Germany's price stability, says: "In the U.S. the cost of living . . . has reached a record high of 121 (the 1948–49 average: 100). . . .

"In this global sea of inflationary troubles there is one major island where enterprise . . . has achieved a basic stability of consumers' prices. In West Germany the cost-of-living index was up a modest 16 points from 1950 levels." Here the base periods are not comparable, nor is the percentage comparison clear. Since the base period of the German index must be assumed to be 1950, its rise was 16 per cent, which just about equaled that in the United States, if computed from 1950 rather than from the 1947–49 base (erroneously reported by *Time* as 1948–49). In order to make a fair comparison between two things, it is essential that they have the same pertinent characteristics.

Errors in Semantics

Slanted or colored words are sometimes used to influence the reader or listener. Witness political campaigns. One common error is the use of "leading questions" in surveys, to suggest the desired answers. For example: "Why do you prefer our product?" One market analyst reports that even such a seemingly innocuous wording as, "Have you read ———— [the latest novel]?" brought a much larger proportion of favorable replies than when a similar group of people was asked the question, "Do you happen to have read ———— [the same novel]?" Note, too, the "record high" in United States prices as contrasted with the "modest" rise in German prices, in the *Time* article above. The impartial investigator must check his words, as well as his figures, for possible bias.

Assuming Causation from Correlation

This common fallacy of reasoning, sometimes called *non sequitur* ("it doesn't follow") by the pundits, means that because one thing precedes another in time, it is assumed to be the cause of the other. You get wet feet, then catch cold. The wet feet are then assumed to be the *cause* of the cold. A student writes a correspondence institute: "I am well pleased with the Law Course. A month after enrolling my salary was increased in the amount of 20 per cent." *Non sequitur.*

An article entitled "They Put a Parson on the Payroll" in the *American Magazine* states: "In just two years religion-on-the-job has accomplished several pretty wonderful things . . . labor turnover has dropped from 7.61 to 5.22% in two years, the accident rate has declined approximately 40% and absenteeism is much lower than it used to be." The assumption that the improvements in labor conditions were due to spiritual counseling does not appear to be justified in view of the many other factors that affect labor turnover and accident rates.

Many business cycle theorists in the past have found that some particular economic factor has correlated with general business activity, and hence have assumed that this factor is "the cause" of business cycles. Unfortunately, economic and business affairs represent a complex of interacting forces. The search for simple cause-and-effect relationships is naïve and unrealistic.

Similarly, large-scale studies have established a correlation between smoking and lung cancer. However, it is a matter of bitter dispute whether heavy smoking *causes* lung cancer, since so many other correlated factors (urban living, smog, tensions, etc.) may also affect cancer.

In general, if factors A and B fluctuate together, it may be that (1) A causes B, to be sure; but it might also be that (2) B causes A, (3) A and B influence each other continuously or intermittently, (4) A and B are both caused by C, or (5) the correlation is due to chance.

Oversimplification

A common error arises from oversimplifying a subject by omitting essential qualifications. The facts presented may be true in themselves; but if other pertinent facts are omitted, the reader may be misled. Many examples may be found in the pocket-size "quickie" type of magazine that abounds in fragmentary half-truths. A universal cure is claimed for a certain disease. The article does not mention that its sweeping statements are based on the inconclusive results of experiments on a fragmentary sample of patients, or that only partial cures were reported, or cures only in mild cases. An insurance company advertises low insurance rates without mentioning that these rates will double after five years. A household freezer is advertised as "featuring exclusive Amanamatic freezing, 2½ times faster!" Faster than what? Another advertisement says, "Dodge Sales Are Up 293% in the Bay Area." Since when?

A former president of the United States, in supporting a wage increase in the steel industry, cited the high profits of this industry without mentioning that these profits were quoted *before taxes.* Taxes actually took away two thirds of these "profits," so that only the remaining third was available for payment of wages.[7] Another former president announced that unemployment had declined from March to April 1960. This appears favorable, but he neglected to mention that the amount was less than the usual seasonal decline between these months. It is excellent practice to state one's conclusions in simple, nontechnical terms, but not at the expense of overlooking essential limitations and qualifications.

Spurious Accuracy

"The national debt on July 27, 1960 was $288,992,150,804.15." "China's population was 601,912,371 as of midnight June 30, 1953, according to Peiping's National Census Office." "The thirteen regional Shippers Advisory Boards estimated yesterday that railroad freight loadings . . . in the current quarter would be 8,146,723 cars." "A State Industrial Commission study found that a bachelor girl can live a 'single, healthy and moral' life on a minimum of $2,422.59 a year." (If she fails to receive that last $2.59, does her health or morals suffer, or both?) Certainly none of these figures is correct to the last digit. Such detailed figures are tiresome and suggest a degree of accuracy in counting or measurement that does not exist by any means. The accuracy of economic data is discussed in Chapter 5, where it is suggested that such data in general be rounded off to three or four significant figures.

Assumption of Stability in a Changing Economy

In forward planning, businessmen frequently assume that the most probable future level of activity will be that of the recent past. This is a fallacy; the normal condition is one of change. For example, an investor

---

[7] National City Bank of New York, *Monthly Letter on Economic Conditions,* May 1952, pp. 53–56.

buys a bond with the implicit expectation that the purchasing power of the bond will remain relatively stable during its life. If the probabilities point to an inflationary trend in prices, however, as during a war period, he makes a costly mistake in that the proceeds of his bond at maturity will probably buy fewer goods then than the same number of dollars would at the time of his investment.

Again, business executives tend to project the current stage of the business cycle into the future. If prosperity exists today, it is assumed to continue tomorrow. Depression today makes men cautious about future commitments. Yet past experience shows that prosperity is frequently followed by "recession," and vice versa.

These examples illustrate the need for forecasting. One of the basic purposes of statistical analysis is to provide a factual basis for planning future operations. Even a crude forecast is likely to be superior to the assumption that past conditions will continue. Applications of statistical analysis in forecasting will be emphasized in this book.

Errors in Percentages

Ratios and percentages seem quite simple, but they are frequently miscalculated through using the wrong base, failing to subtract 100 per cent in figuring increases, or misunderstanding the nature of the comparison. A textbook in office management states that "window envelopes cost around $1.00 less than regular envelopes, or $3.25, which represents a saving of 76.5 per cent." This should be 23.5 per cent—or 24 per cent to avoid spurious accuracy. A life insurance company reports a gain of insurance in force from 177 million to a billion dollars in 11 years, or "a gain of 565 per cent." This should be 465 per cent.

The Ways and Means Committee of the House of Representatives in 1951 considered raising personal income tax rates 3 percentage points "across the board." The tax scale, then graduated from 20 per cent up to 91 per cent, would be made to run from 23 to 94 per cent. Some critics attacked this as a "soak-the-poor measure, since a 3-point increase on the poor man's 20 per cent represented a 15 per cent jump, while 3 points on the rich man's 91 per cent was a mere nudge of 3.3 per cent. But other critics claimed that this was a "soak-the-rich" measure, since the poor man's take-home pay would be reduced from 80 to 77 cents on his dollar of income, or only $3\frac{3}{4}$ per cent, while the rich man's take-home pay would be cut from 9 to 6 cents, or $33\frac{1}{3}$ per cent! The Committee compromised by increasing taxes $12\frac{1}{2}$ per cent across the board. This expedient increased the minimum rate from 20 to $22\frac{1}{2}$ per cent reasonably enough, but unfortunately boosted the maximum rate from 91 to 102.4 per cent! It was subsequently cut to 94½ per cent.[8] This controversy illustrates the importance of the careful use of percentages. Chapter 5 presents an explanation of this deceptively simple topic.

SUMMARY

Statistical analysis is a scientific method of interpreting quantitative data. It is used to draw general inferences by induction from the behavior of variable data, whereas deductive reasoning applies general laws to specific cases. The statistical or inductive method is most effective in the social and biological sciences; the mechanical or deductive method is used more in the physical sciences. Statistical methods have become more important in recent times because of the growth of large-scale production and trade, the increasing scope of government, and improvements in statistical techniques themselves.

Statistical analysis is used in all branches of larger business organizations as a tool of planning and control. The principal statistical activities in business include general business analysis, marketing research, production control, budgeting, personnel and investment studies, and operations research.

Statistical analysis is also widely used in economics and social science generally, particularly in the study of economic fluctuations, social accounting, prices, finance, public utilities, economic geography, and related subjects. The growth of government activities, too, particularly in wartime, has required more and better statistics for central planning and administrative purposes.

The basic steps in statistical analysis include: (1) *collecting* the data from available sources or sample surveys; (2) *presenting* the results in tables and charts; and (3) *analyzing* and *interpreting* the figures by means of frequency distributions, index numbers, trend fitting, correlation, reliability measures, and similar techniques. These steps will be followed in this book in the usual order of a statistical investigation.

The true meaning of facts is easily distorted. The statistical investigator must therefore be on guard to avoid misrepresenting the facts and to detect misuses of statistics by others. A critical attitude is essential. The principal pitfalls in the use of statistics are: bias, either conscious or unconscious; faulty generalization due to reliance on too small a sample or on one that is not typical of the whole population; faulty deduction in applying a generalization to exceptional cases; comparisons

---

[8] National City Bank of New York, *Monthly Letter on Economic Conditions*, June 1951, pp. 66–67.

of noncomparable data; semantic errors such as the use of leading questions; the uncritical inference that correlation between two factors means that one is the cause of the other; oversimplification due to omission of essential qualifications; spurious accuracy; the assumption of future stability in a dynamic economy; and the misuse of ratios and percentages.

PROBLEMS

1. *a*) Explain the meaning of the term "statistics" when used in the singular sense as opposed to its use in the plural sense.
   b) Why does the employment of statistical methods in the solution of business problems belong almost exclusively to the twentieth century?
   c) Describe the principal statistical activities of a typical large and progressive firm.

2. Locate in the library and give the names of three major statistical journals together with the associations that publish them, and briefly describe the type of subject matter contained therein.

3. Visit an economic research agency or one of the seven types of statistical departments in a business organization mentioned in the text, and hand in a two- to three-page outline of its statistical activities.

4. What are some of the principal uses of statistics in economics?

5. Hand in a clipping illustrating an improper use of statistical data. Add a paragraph explaining the type of error presented.

6. Give an illustration of each of the following: (*a*) bias, (*b*) faulty deduction, (*c*) assuming causation from correlation, and (*d*) oversimplification.

SELECTED READINGS

GEE, WILSON. *Social Science Research Methods.* New York: Appleton-Century-Crofts, Inc., 1950.
   A survey of the principal types of scientific method used in social sciences, including statistical, case, historical, and experimental methods.

HUFF, DARRELL. *How to Lie with Statistics.* New York: W. W. Norton & Co., Inc., 1954.
   An amusing compendium of statistical misuses.

MORGENSTERN, OSKAR. *On the Accuracy of Economic Observations.* 2d ed. Princeton, N.J.: Princeton University Press, 1963.
   A stimulating discussion of types of errors in economic data.

NEISWANGER, WILLIAM A. *Elementary Statistical Methods.* Rev. ed. New York: Macmillan Co., 1956.
   Chapter 2 contains some excellent illustrations of errors in the use and interpretation of statistics.

NEWBURY, FRANK D. *Business Forecasting.* New York: McGraw-Hill Book Co., Inc., 1952.
   Statistical forecasting activities in a typical corporation are described in chapters 1, 2, and 15.
ROBERTS, HARRY V. "The New Business Statistics," *Journal of Business of the University of Chicago,* January 1960, pp. 21–30.
   Outlines the development of the decision-theory orientation of statistics.

2. USE OF RESEARCH SOURCES

THE FIRST step in statistical analysis is to find the necessary facts. Perhaps they are available in some published source. Or, they may be obtained from the internal records of a business firm. Again, the facts may not be available anywhere but must be collected firsthand in a special survey. For example, one may be asked: "Is the cost of living higher in Chicago than in New York?" "What is the rate of inventory turnover of our copper wire?" Or, "Would sales of our breakfast food be increased by redesigning the package?" The data needed to answer these questions may be obtained from published sources, internal records, and special surveys, respectively.

In nearly every investigation, fact finding is the first step, and may indeed be the most difficult one. It is nevertheless frequently the most fruitful kind of research. Hence it is important to know where to find the facts and how to compile them. This chapter describes how to plan a statistical study and seek out the existing data needed for economic analysis.[1] The next chapter describes how to collect, edit, and tabulate original data.

DEFINING THE PROBLEM

At the outset a rough statement of objectives and methods will serve to outline the scope of the problem. These preliminary ideas should

---

[1] The classification of data by source represents something of a departure from the usual classification found in textbooks. The customary division into primary and secondary data places the emphasis on the number of times the data have been recorded; i.e., primary data are those which are being recorded for the first time by the investigator who assembles them, whereas any subsequent recording of the data by others makes them secondary data.

The distinction between existing research sources and original sources places the emphasis on methods of procedure. One type of research is required to obtain information already available for general use, but quite a different type of work is required to collect data directly from the original source.

then be brought together in a more complete definition which will indicate the subject to be investigated, the exact objective of the study, and the limitations of its scope.

An example will demonstrate the difference between an incomplete and a complete statement of the subject for research. Suppose that as a company analyst you receive the following assignment: "What is the outlook for our raw material prices?" This statement does not in itself define the problem for research. Questions such as the following must be settled: "Are all raw materials to be included or only certain major ones?" "Is the investigation to be confined to evaluating the factors affecting the outlook for prices, or should a specific forecast be made?" "How much time is available for making the study?"

With questions of this sort settled, the problem might be restated as follows: "Estimate the domestic demand and supply situation of copper and steel scrap over the next six months, and forecast the average price of each commodity for this period. Have the report ready for the executive committee meeting to be held the first of next month." The purpose of the investigation is clear, and the limitations as to time and scope are definite.

In order to outline the scope of the plan properly, the entire program should be put in writing. There are several advantages to the investigator in doing this: It forces him to gain a proper perspective of the project. It permits him to pick up any loose ends in his plan. It gives him a complete statement for future reference if puzzling situations arise. It provides a preliminary outline for writing the final report.

PUBLISHED AND UNPUBLISHED SOURCES

A knowledge of any previous work that may have been done on a problem should be acquired as background before a new investigation is undertaken. The existence of earlier studies can be determined primarily through a search of library files. One may find that the problem has been investigated previously and that therefore any further analysis should be built upon the existing work. Such available studies may not only provide useful facts but also suggest effective techniques of analysis. Again, flaws may be found in the previous work which make it useless for the purposes in view. In fact, the chief value of studying such previous investigations may lie in discovering what *not* to do.

Library search may disclose that no similar statistical surveys have been published. But books and magazine articles may be discovered which give factual information on some phase of the subject or clues concerning methods of investigation. Library reading on the subject will aid the investigator in avoiding duplication of work already done, in avoiding the errors made in previous investigations, in discovering methods of approach and procedure, and in acquiring a broad perspective of his problem.

The reading which has been done on a problem should indicate fairly well whether the needed data are already available or whether they must be gathered directly. It will not serve merely to remember that some data on the subject were referred to in a book or magazine article. The data must be found and examined. Then several questions must be settled. Are the data in usable form? Are they up to date? Do they cover the proper geographic area? Are they expressed in the correct unit for the particular purpose? Are they reliable? If published sources should fail to provide all of the required data, the possibility of obtaining them directly must be explored.

At this stage the investigator should take some time for thoughtful consideration of his problem. Certain parts of his plan may need additional emphasis, and others should perhaps be discarded. New phases may enter as a result of the reading done. The knowledge which has been acquired by reading needs to be related to the particular problem at hand. The investigator should be able to visualize his entire procedure. Regardless of how efficient he may be, it is unlikely that he can foresee and provide for every contingency which may arise. The plan should therefore be sufficiently flexible to permit necessary adjustments to conditions as they develop.

The data needed for many statistical problems in business may be available in unpublished form. In particular, much information can be found directly in the internal records of the company concerned. Such records might include accounting ledgers, production orders, supply requisitions, idle equipment reports, individual employee records, and many other sources. Many business concerns have in recent years recognized the importance of information centers or central file units as a staff service to their employees. Since such centers or specialized libraries contain extensive collections of documents generated within the company—memoranda, reports, and correspondence—as well as material published elsewhere, they provide a valuable source of data for research projects. Managers of such services are specially trained in providing assistance in searching for data as well as in finding information on other related research projects.

Unpublished data for many industries can be secured from the Department of Commerce, the various trade associations, or other sources listed in this chapter. Even competitors' aid can sometimes be enlisted for a noncompetitive study. Unpublished material must generally be obtained by correspondence or personal contact directly from the individuals responsible for its maintenance.

Sometimes a combination of published and unpublished sources can be used. For example, in comparing wage rates in a particular community with similar rates in the entire country, it might be feasible to obtain the data for the nation from the reports of the U.S. Bureau of Labor Statistics, whereas the local data would have to be secured directly from business concerns in the community. In all such cases it is desirable to make full use of published sources.

The following discussion relates primarily to published sources, but the agencies described also have much unpublished data in their fields of specialization. Other unpublished sources, such as company records, are too varied to justify any general treatment. The researcher must depend on his own ingenuity in these fields.

COLLECTION OF DATA FROM PUBLISHED SOURCES

Published sources of business and economic data are for the most part current periodicals or yearbooks. Becoming familiar with the contents of these publications is a very real problem. A reference list of such sources and their contents is subject to constant changes. New publications appear and old ones disappear; new series are added, old series are discontinued; or the form of recording is altered. Regular users of published source material must therefore keep abreast of changes as they occur. A selected list of 92 principal sources of business statistics is given in Appendix A. The most important of these are starred (*) for easy reference.

Even the analyst who is well grounded in sources of information encounters many problems in ferreting out the data he seeks from existing publications. Offhand, one might expect the entire task of collecting data from published sources to consist of copying a quickly discovered list of figures from a book readily supplied by a library attendant. This is not what usually happens. Attendants versed in the intricacies of source materials are usually found only in highly specialized libraries. In most cases a library staff will be able to do little more than obtain requested books and magazines from the stacks.

Efficiency in collecting data from libraries comes only with long practice. It is a case primarily of learning what data to expect in different sources. While the beginner has no choice but to use what might be called the "shotgun" method—that is, to search until the desired data happen to be found—a seasoned investigator, using a process of elimination based on his previous experience, narrows his search to two or three likely sources. This might be called the "rifle" method, by contrast. If his selection has been accurate, the analyst will require very little time to find the data, obtain a clue to their location, or discover that they are not available at all.

TEN STEPS IN FINDING A GOOD SOURCE

There is a general sequence of steps which can be followed in searching for a desired set of business or economic data. The process is one of successive elimination, but some guidance in the order of procedure will facilitate the work. The following procedure is recommended:

Step 1. Consult one or more standard reference sources, such as the *Statistical Abstract of the United States; Survey of Current Business, Statistical Supplement; Monthly Labor Review; Federal Reserve Bulletin; Standard Trade and Securities, Current Statistics;* the National Industrial Conference Board's *Economic Almanac;* or any of the other general sources starred in Appendix A. Look in the indexes of these publications for the subject of the search. If the particular data can be obtained therein, the search is ended.

Step 2. If the data are not found, study the titles, headnotes, footnotes, and references of tables on the general subject to discover original sources which may contain more detail. In turn, study these detailed sources for references to collateral sources.

Step 3. If steps 1 and 2 have not led directly to a publication containing the information required, it is time to consult a bibliography of source material. The first nine references listed in Appendix A of this book provide useful guides to basic sources. Specialized bibliographies can be found by reference to the *Bibliographic Index* or to special business libraries such as those of the Newark and Cleveland public libraries.

Data in index number form can often be located by referring to Arthur H. Cole's *Measures of Business Change* or Richard M. Snyder's *Measuring Business Changes.* These books contain summary descriptions of hundreds of economic indicators.

Step 4. Check particularly the source books of federal government statistics, such as Hauser and Leonard's *Government Statistics for Business Use,* or the Bureau of the Budget's *Statistical Services of the United States Government.* Other government publications may be found in the *Monthly Catalog of United States Government Publications* and the *Catalog of U.S. Census Publications,* both published by the Superintendent of Documents. Andriot's *U.S. Government Statistics*

Documents Index is useful because it classifies these sources by subject, title, and issuing agency.

Step 5. If the data cannot be located, look up the subject of your inquiry in the library card catalog. References to nongovernment publications will probably come to hand quickest because government publications may be listed not under the main subject classification but under the author "United States" instead. Sublistings are by departments, bureaus, commissions, and offices.

Step 6. If the data are still elusive, or perhaps incomplete, go through the periodical indexes which are found in the library. The following are ordinarily available: *Bulletin of the Public Affairs Information Service, Business Periodicals Index, New York Times Index,* and the *Wall Street Journal Index.*

Step 7. Look through trade, financial, and technical magazines related to the subject. Many of these are listed in Appendix A. Check the statistical yearbooks and the review numbers of these journals.

Step 8. If access to the stacks of the library is possible, go to the section in which you have already found books dealing with the subject. Other publications in the same shelves may contain the desired data.

Step 9. If at this point the desired data have not been found, it is time to consult some specialist who may have knowledge of them. This person may be a research analyst, special librarian, corporation official, trade association secretary, or a government economist in a regional office. A number of such people may be called quickly by telephone. Even though the respondent may not have the desired information himself, he can usually refer the caller to the proper source.

Step 10. Finally, if the desired data cannot be found in published sources, it may be necessary to search for unpublished material from government or nongovernment agencies. Best results usually are attained through personal visits rather than through correspondence. The beginner should be warned that unpublished data are frequently on rough work sheets and often are made available only after persistent questioning.

A leading source of older unpublished records of the federal government is the National Archives in Washington, D.C. For historical studies in economics, business, sociology, and political science, and for detailed data on the two world wars, this storehouse of records is especially valuable. Information can be obtained by mail by those who cannot visit the Archives personally.

Only in the most difficult cases will it be necessary to employ all of the foregoing steps. Usually the first two or three will be productive.

After a few searches have been made, the general contents of the major publications will be sufficiently familiar so that in most cases the proper source can be selected immediately. The further one progresses in the use of published sources the less the need for formal methods and the greater the reliance on experience.

TYPES OF SOURCE MATERIALS

Published sources of data may be classified in a number of different ways. Four bases of classification are used in the succeeding discussion: (1) subject matter, (2) form of publication, (3) frequency of publication, and (4) publishing agency. The effective use of published sources requires a knowledge of these various approaches.

Subject Matter

In the first place, source material may be classified according to the type of data presented, as is done in the Dewey Decimal System used in libraries. This method, however, is not usually practicable in statistical research. Most source books of business or economic statistics deal with many types of data and are not confined to a single phase such as production of raw materials, manufacturing, or marketing.

The *Survey of Current Business* and *Federal Reserve Bulletin* are representative of the publications that cover many fields of economic activity. Even such specialized sources as the *Census of Manufactures, Monthly Labor Review,* and *Statistics of Railways* include numerous statistical series only indirectly related to the subject of their title.

Some source books may be classified according to their geographic scope, such as the entire United States, a particular state, city, local area, or several different countries. However, this method of classification is not definitive either, since most publications cover several types of areas. The *Statistical Abstract,* for example, is mainly devoted to national data; but many tables present statistics by regions, states, or individual cities as well.

Form of Publication

Statistical Source Books. Some publications consist almost entirely of statistical tables. Either the index or the table of contents can be used to find the data pertaining to a particular subject. Most publications of this kind come from governmental agencies, although in recent years there has been a great increase in the amount of such work done by private organizations. Examples of the latter are: *Standard Trade and Securities, Basic Statistics;* the *Commodity Yearbook* of the Commodity Research Bureau; and *Automobile Facts and Figures.*

Statistical Periodicals. The most convenient journals for use in finding current data are those that contain tables covering the same series of figures and appearing in the same section of the journal each issue. These tables have proper titles and footnotes showing sources of information and other explanations. *Survey of Current Business, Monthly Labor Review,* and *Dun's Review and Modern Industry* are examples of this type.

In other statistical periodicals, the form and contents of the tables will vary from one issue to the next. For example, *Railway Age* and *Steel* present whatever monthly or weekly data are available at the time of publication.

Auxiliary Sources. Publications which contain data that are incidental to other functions are more difficult to use. Figures may be scattered through the book or magazine in conjunction with articles to which they apply. This is the case with the *Commercial and Financial Chronicle, Business Week,* and *Barron's.*

In journals of this type, statistics are printed not only in tables but also in the text. Careful attention is necessary to detect data appearing in the body of the text, and caution must be exercised in using them because necessary explanations may be far removed from the related data.

Frequency of Publication

Daily. Daily papers such as the *Wall Street Journal,* the *Journal of Commerce,* and the financial section of the *New York Times* are invaluable in providing a great variety of up-to-the-minute information. Yet the very promptness of these publications tends to reduce accuracy; hence the data found in daily papers should be verified, if possible, in other sources before final use.

A number of valuable daily publications deal with particular subjects. Among these are the *Daily News Record,* the *Women's Wear Daily,* and the *American Metal Market.* There are also many daily reports issued by government agencies, such as the daily *Treasury Statement* and daily produce market reports issued by state departments of agriculture. Daily services such as the *Executive Letter* of the Bureau of National Affairs are issued only on a subscription basis, but they are widely read.

Weekly. Many types of economic statistics are now published on a weekly as well as a monthly basis, to meet the demands of businessmen for information that is as nearly current as possible. The demand is further evidence of the extent to which numerical facts have become useful in determining business policy. Data on railroad freight carloadings, bank debits, electric power production, and wholesale prices, for example, are available weekly. Leading weekly publications include the *Commercial and Financial Chronicle, Barron's, Business Week,* and the *Weekly Supplement* to the *Survey of Current Business.*

Monthly. Monthly publications provide a much broader coverage of economic data than the weekly journals. Among the most useful of the monthly issues are the *Survey of Current Business, Federal Reserve Bulletin,* and the monthly bulletins of certain private banks such as the First National City Bank of New York and the Cleveland Trust Company. Charts of leading indexes are published each month in *Economic Indicators* and the *Federal Reserve Chart Book on Financial and Business Statistics.* Regional data are covered in the monthly bulletins of the twelve Federal Reserve banks, the regional commercial banks, and university bureaus of business research, such as those of the University of Texas and Ohio State University.

Annually. Annual sources are more comprehensive than monthly publications because many figures are only available by years. Most important of these sources are the yearbooks which contain basic data, with some series running back for long periods. Since yearbooks require much preparation, the data may be several months old before the book is published. Examples are the *Statistical Abstract, Agricultural Statistics,* and the National Industrial Conference Board's *Economic Almanac. The World Almanac* and the *Information Please Almanac* are also in popular use because of their convenience and wide range of subjects.

Longer Intervals. The principal publications appearing at intervals of more than a year are the United States censuses. The *Census of Population,* for example, has appeared each ten years since 1790, while the *Census of Manufactures* appeared each five years from 1899 to 1919, then each two years until 1939, and then skipped to 1947 and 1954 before beginning another five-year cycle in 1958. These censuses provide extremely detailed data on the economy, and serve as "bench marks" to check the reliability of the incomplete annual or monthly data which are gathered between censuses.

Special Studies. Many valuable research reports appear only once, or at irregular intervals. These may have a unique value to the analyst, but sometimes can be discovered only after a careful search of library sources, as described earlier in the chapter. Examples of special studies are the various National Bureau of Economic Research studies on business cycles and national income. The *Census of Business* has been published at irregular intervals in the past. The Census Bureau also publishes a variety of special one-time studies on the regular censuses.

Press Releases. Recognizing the necessity of saving time, many government bureaus as well as private organizations release their more important data immediately after tabulation. In some instances the data contained in these releases are preliminary and may subsequently be revised in a regular publication. In other cases the data are not reprinted at any time.

For example, the Bureau of Mines issues each chapter of its *Minerals Yearbook* separately, in advance of the complete bound volume. The Bureau of Labor Statistics distributes special mimeographed releases on wholesale and retail prices and employment and payrolls, but the greater part of this material is reproduced in subsequent printed bulletins or in the *Monthly Labor Review.* The press release of the Consumer Price Index is now awaited by millions because of escalator clauses affecting wage rates. On the other hand, the Bureau of the Census releases information concerning the Census of Manufactures in both processed and printed form, much of which is never reprinted in the bound volumes. Knowledge of these various releases must be acquired by experience, since they are not always included in check lists of government publications.

Publishing Agency

Classification of sources by publishing agency has probably the greatest practical value in economic research, since publications are usually cataloged on this basis in libraries. Accordingly, the list of sources in Appendix A is arranged by publishing agency.

Sources of statistical data relating to the field of business and economics may be grouped in the following manner:

U.S. Government. The most important publishing agency in the world is the federal government. The manifold statistical activities of the government are described in *Federal Statistical Agencies,* by F. C. Mills and C. D. Long. The statistics themselves are surveyed in *Government Statistics for Business Use,* by P. M. Hauser and W. R. Leonard.

Some bureaus and offices in particular produce a tremendous amount of statistical data by the very nature of their work. In searching for data, one quickly becomes familiar with the Office of Business Economics and the Bureau of the Census in the Department of Commerce, the Bureau of Labor Statistics in the Department of Labor, the Agricultural Marketing Service and the Agricultural Research Service in the Department of Agriculture, the Bureau of Internal Revenue in the Department of the Treasury, the Bureau of Mines in the Department of the Interior, the Interstate Commerce Commission, the Federal

Trade Commission, the Board of Governors of the Federal Reserve System, and the Joint Economic Committee of the Congress.

In addition to regular government periodicals or yearbooks, there are often useful data in the annual reports of departments and of bureau and division heads. Some are available only as numbered documents of the Congress to which they were submitted, but others are published separately. Appendix A includes a number of these.

Finally, there are the special investigations made for congressional committees. They are usually detailed studies of a particular subject and as such are unique sources. They are likewise usually published as *Congressional Documents*. Excellent examples are the *Joint Economic Report* and other publications of the Joint Economic Committee.

State and Municipal Governments. In many cases the most complete sources of information concerning the individual states are the United States government publications that have already been mentioned. In addition, there is much material put out by the state governments themselves. Some states, however, are far in advance of others in furnishing statistical information to their citizens. A few have even begun the publication of yearbooks similar in plan to the *Statistical Abstract of the United States*. A useful compilation of regional income data is furnished in *Personal Income by States*, published by the U.S. Department of Commerce. This can be supplemented by consulting the library card catalog under the individual states. Information is likely to be found in the publications of the state departments of agriculture, banking and insurance, labor, and highways, as well as in those of the land grant colleges and other state institutions.

Very few source books are published by municipalities, but considerable local information is available in federal and state publications and in the reports of county planning boards.

Nongovernment. State and local information is also available through the publications of certain semipublic organizations. The best examples are the monthly reviews of business issued by the twelve Federal Reserve banks and statistical reports of the research bureaus of universities. The chambers of commerce of many states and cities also published detailed statistics for their areas.

In addition, there are many private agencies which publish statistical data for general use. In most cases the data are collected for the use of an interested group such as the members of a trade association or the subscribers to a service, but are made generally available through magazines and trade papers. Historically, private agencies preceded the government in supplying current data to the public. Among the pioneers in this field were *Dun's Review, The Commercial and Financial Chronicle, Moody's Investors Service,* and the National Industrial Conference Board.

The private agencies compiling and publishing statistical information may be classified as follows: statistical source books, general business periodicals, and specialized trade journals. The examples given in Appendix A include the principal nongovernment source books and general business periodicals. Many useful publications were necessarily omitted; hence the need for gradually expanding one's knowledge of them as progress is made in the use of source material.

Foreign and International. While the agencies already named provide most of the data needed for statistical work, there are occasions which call for the use of information from foreign countries or for world data. A large number of internationally comparable statistics extending back to 1928 can be obtained from the *Statistical Yearbook* published by the Statistical Office of the United Nations. The Dominion Bureau of Statistics is the principal source of information for Canada. Five of its publications are listed in Appendix A.

THE CORRECT USE OF DATA

The search procedure outlined above leads to the location of a given set of data in one or more sources. Before the data can be safely used, they must be tested for accuracy and for validity.

Testing for Accuracy

The data should be examined to detect discrepancies and verified by cross reference when several sources are available. Discrepancies in data are usually easy to detect but may escape the unwary collector. They may appear as a result of one or more of the following causes:

Changes in Unit. Changes may occur in the unit of measure, the definition of the unit, the nature of the unit, or the base period of an index number. Illustrations of all of these can be found in the *Statistical Abstract.*

An example of change in the unit of measure is shown in Table 841 in the 1951 volume, which presents "Cement—Production, by Kind: 1890 to 1949." Column 3 shows production of masonry, natural, and puzzolan cement. In 1921 and subsequent years the unit of measure is 376-pound barrels; but prior to 1921 it was barrels of 240, 265, and 320 pounds, in turn. The same column also illustrates changes in the definition of the unit. From 1890 to 1910 the data represented production; from 1915 to 1924, shipments; and from 1925 to 1949, production again. Thus the figures really represent two different things and cannot be regarded as single series even though they are printed in the same column.

Changes in the nature of the unit can be illustrated by Table 771 of the 1960 *Statistical Abstract,* showing the number of four-engine aircraft in commercial service from 1945 to date. Such a series has little significance in itself because of the great improvement in aircraft performance between the era of the DC-4 and that of the jet DC-8 or Boeing 707. The data must be used in conjunction with figures on available seats, speed, mileage, and the like.

Changes in the base period of an index number may be illustrated by the Bureau of Labor Statistics Wholesale Price Index, which was shifted from a 1926 base to a 1947–49 base in 1952.

Changes in Classification. Changes in time, space, coverage, or definition may also occur in statistical tables. An example of time changes appears in the *Statistical Abstract* for 1957, Table 1127, "Exports (including Re-exports) and General Imports of Merchandise, with Trade Balances: 1790 to 1956." Figures are for years ending September 30 from 1790 to 1842, for years ending June 30 from 1843 to 1915, and for calendar years thereafter.

Discrepancies due to changes in space classification may be illustrated by the widening boundaries of cities, which introduce errors into many kinds of urban data. For example, census reports of the increase in the population of many cities between 1950 and 1960 have been exaggerated because these cities annexed outlying areas in the 1950's so that the population of these areas was included in the 1960 figures but not in the 1950 figures. Another change in space classification occurred in the F. W. Dodge Corporation reports of construction contract awards, which were expanded in coverage from 37 to 48 states beginning January 1, 1957.

Changes in coverage or in number of reporting units affect many statistical series. Take, for example, the data on bank debits in "other reporting centers" reported in the 1953 *Statistical Abstract,* page 420. The figures represent from 121 to 131 cities in 1930 and 1935, but thereafter the coverage increased repeatedly until it included 201 cities in 1952. Clearly, the figures are not strictly comparable from 1930 to 1952.

Changes in definition appear in the *Censuses of Manufactures* for 1947 and 1954, which include a reclassification of establishments by industry in accordance with the *Standard Industrial Classification*

Manual, a redefinition of the minimum size limit for establishments included, and other changes in concept.

Revisions. An example of discrepancies due to revisions in data is found in the gross national product figures published in the *Survey of Current Business.* The component "changes in business inventories" for 1956 was first estimated in the February 1957 issue at $3.5 billion, but this figure was revised to $4.6 billion in the July 1957 national income number—an increase of 31 per cent. When the newspapers report a change of 1 or 2 per cent in gross national product accounts (or most other business indicators) as being significant, therefore, it must be remembered that such a change might easily be due to errors of estimate.

Since many statistics are first released in preliminary form and later revised as more returns are received, figures should always be taken from the latest available issue of a publication. For example, if it is necessary to obtain data from 1947 to 1960, and data from 1950 to 1960 are found in a recent issue of a publication, then the latest issue containing data from 1947 to 1950 should be used to complete the series. Data for 1950 appear in both issues and should be compared to insure that the same series is being reported throughout.

Occasionally the data may not agree in the two issues. Then two possibilities arise: (1) Explanations accompanying the tables may state the nature of the revision involved and indicate how to make the series comparable in the two issues. Or, the revised figures themselves might contain errors that may be discovered by comparison with earlier data. (2) If no explanation of the change is given, it may be necessary to find another source containing the same series in comparable form or a substitute series that will serve the purpose.

Difficulties in matching series in different issues of a source book occur most frequently as the result of shifting the base of an index. Adjustments can usually be made for such a revision by simple multiplication, as described in the chapter on index numbers, provided the two parts are of comparable nature.

Typographical Errors. Typographical errors occur in every newspaper, journal, or book, almost without exception. They may best be discovered by checking the figures with other data and by examining each statement critically, and asking the question, "Does this make sense?" rather than swallowing reports without benefit of mental mastication.

The *Survey of Current Business* for July 1957 (p. 29) reported gross national product for the fourth quarter of 1956 as being down sharply from the preceding quarter, though each of its four components had increased. To locate this typographical error, one could note that each of the components equaled the sum of its own parts, so the components' sum of 426.0 billion could be presumed correct, rather than the reported total of 406.0 billion.

Interruptions in Series. Breaks in the continuity of a series that has been published regularly create a problem for the user. For brief interruptions, such as that in steel ingot production caused by a steel strike, there is little loss in omitting the affected months. Protracted breaks in publication are more serious. For example, during World War II the publication of many series, particularly those concerned with foreign trade or strategic materials, was suspended as a security measure. In such a case other data must be sought or the entire period omitted.

Even a little experience will enable an investigator to recognize many of the inconsistencies in published data, but the detection of less obvious discrepancies requires varied experience in collection and the exercise of common sense—that is, a combination of experience, judgment, and figure perception.

Cross Reference. The comparison of data in several sources is known as cross reference. In many cases only one source of the data can be found and no verification by cross reference is possible. Frequently, however, similar data are collected by several agencies. In these instances, several sources should be checked to determine which is most complete, which contains the data in most usable form, and which has the best general record of reliability.

If several sources show the same figure, it may usually be considered to be accurate. If differences appear, they may be due to types of discrepancies enumerated in the preceding sections. On the other hand, if the inconsistencies cannot be explained, it may be necessary to search through collateral sources, or perhaps to write to the collecting agency for further information.

An example of the use of cross reference will demonstrate the method and its advantages. Suppose you wished to compare the volume of passenger traffic by rail, bus, and air in 1953.[2] You find the figures reported by three leading trade associations as shown in Table 2–1.

These figures are quite different! The largest figure for bus travel,

---

[2] This example is taken from *Management Methods,* December 1955, through courtesy of Management Magazines, Inc.

Table 2–1

PASSENGER TRAFFIC BY RAIL, BUS, AND AIR—1953

(Billions of Passenger-Miles)

	Source of Data		
	Association of American Railroads	National Association of Motor Bus Operators	Air Transport Association
Rail	32.7	27.5	26.9
Bus	28.4	21.3	19.7
Air	17.4	15.6	14.7
Total	78.5	64.4	61.3

for example, exceeds the smallest by 44 per cent. Yet all are issued by reputable organizations and are based on reports of the Interstate Commerce Commission and other government agencies.

Some of the discrepancies are due to a simple matter of timing. In July 1955 the ICC issued revised figures for 1953, taking into account certain types of travel which they had previously ignored. The AAR issued a mimeographed sheet in which they reported the revised series, but the other two associations had just released the annual editions of their statistical fact books, not so easily changed, and they were still issuing figures based on the older data.

But this doesn't explain the entire difference. The ATA did not include travel on the nonscheduled airlines, since their statisticians did not feel the figures were very reliable. *Bus Facts,* the NAMBO publication, included the travel of rail *commuters,* which the others did not, and it also added an estimate of chartered buses.

In other words, no two of the associations were really talking about the same thing. In general terms, of course, they were all discussing passenger travel, but each had its own special definition, which was just different enough to throw the figures off substantially.

In summary, then, the rule is to use the latest reliable source which is available and whenever possible verify it by cross reference, carefully investigating any discrepancies that cannot readily be explained.

Testing for Validity

Data derived from published sources must be tested not only for their accuracy, as described above, but also for their validity or reliability. In testing validity, the question to be asked is: "Are these data satisfactory for the purpose for which they are to be used?" The answer lies in understanding the background of the collection and in visualizing the collection process.

Understanding the Background. Data are gathered either directly for statistical purposes or as a by-product of nonstatistical activity. The Bureau of the Census and the Bureau of Labor Statistics, for example, collect data directly for statistical purposes. Every effort is made to make these figures as accurate as possible.

On the other hand, data are often secured merely as a by-product of some other activity, such as the gasoline consumed by motor vehicles and cigarette consumption data, both obtained by the Bureau of Internal Revenue in the course of collecting the taxes levied on these articles by the federal government.

Since by-product data are collected for some official or business purpose, the collectors have no primary interest in them once they have served that purpose. They may be kept in poor form; errors corrected for the major purpose may be omitted from the statistical record; overlaps and omissions may creep in because the record has not been adequately checked; and the data may not be in usable form for statistical purposes, although serving the major purpose well. Since the data from by-product sources are likely to contain such inaccuracies, it is desirable, wherever possible, to cross-check them in a direct statistical source.

Visualizing the Collection. Answering the question, "How were the data collected?" will furnish considerable insight into the difficulties that were encountered in collecting the data. Consequently, a fair basis may be obtained for judging their reliability. The description in Chapter 5 of the methods used in collecting data on world exports and on new building construction (pp. 84–85) provides examples of how to estimate the validity of data by visualizing the collection.

Another example of variable reliability is provided by the estimates of fertilizer consumption published in Table 794 of the *Statistical Abstract* for 1956. These figures are "based on tag sales, records of Government officials, etc." Perusal of the more detailed footnotes in earlier issues, however, yields the following qualifications: For some states the sales are determined by the number of tags addressed to consumers in that state by fertilizer manufacturers. If the counts are kept accurately, if the bags are all the same size, and if carload shipments sent to retailers near state boundaries are distributed mainly in the state in which the retailer resides, then the tag count may give fairly good results. For other states, estimates are made either by state authorities or by the National Fertilizer Association. Actual records of sales are compiled by state authorities for still another group of states. The reliability of these estimates therefore varies widely from state to state.

The detailed analysis of the notes accompanying such a table indicates the method of evaluating data in terms of the background and surrounding circumstances. Footnotes and headnotes should always be studied carefully; other sources should be consulted; and if necessary a letter should be written to the original collection agency to clear up any obscure points.

SUMMARY

A knowledge of research sources is essential in business or economic analysis. The first step in using these sources is to find the necessary materials. This may be done by consulting any of several types of sources, such as statistical reference books, bibliographies, card catalogs, periodical indexes, trade journals, library stacks, and experts in the field.

Research sources may be classified in four ways: (1) by subject matter; (2) by form of publication, such as the standard source books, statistical periodicals, and journals containing only incidental data; (3) frequency of publication, such as weekly or monthly journals or special studies; and (4) the publishing agency, such as the various federal bureaus, state governments, and private research agencies.

In collecting data from published sources, great care must be taken to test the figures for accuracy and for validity by noting any changes in the units in which the data are expressed, shifts in classification, revisions, typographical errors, or interruptions in the series. It is particularly useful to check several publications against each other and to study the method of collecting the data as a means of detecting errors and estimating the reliability of the results.

PROBLEMS

1. Each of the following is a statement of a problem for investigation. Rewrite any of them that fail to define the problem completely.
    a) Excise taxes have no adverse effect on the volume of long-distance telephone calls.
    b) Between 1956 and 1960 the movements of prices on the New York Stock Exchange can be explained largely by charting with them the Federal Reserve Index of Industrial Production.
    c) We (management) know that the change in the time of introducing new models of the Chord automobile from November to September has changed the sales curve, but we are in doubt whether the expected

decrease in the peak and trough of sales has occurred. Prepare a report on this question for the meeting of sales representatives on September 10.

2. A young stockbroker interested in general business conditions is planning a small library of statistical source material. The following list has been selected as adequate: *Economic Almanac,* current year; subscriptions to *Monthly Social Security Bulletin, Economic Indicators,* and *Wall Street Journal; Moody's Manuals,* most recent volumes; Volume I of the latest *Census of Agriculture.*
   a) Which of the foregoing would you retain?
   b) Name four others that should be included.
   c) Give reasons for your choice in (a) and (b).

3. Name the publications that correspond to the following descriptions:
   a) Published monthly by a banking agency in Washington, and containing some text material and detailed tables that are practically identical in form from month to month, chiefly on the subject of finance.
   b) A monthly publication of the congressional Joint Economic Committee which includes charts and tables on prices, employment, production, national income, purchasing power, and finance.
   c) An annual issue of a monthly magazine giving yearly estimates of personal income, and retail and wholesale sales for all counties in the United States. Useful in marketing studies.
   d) An annual volume containing general tables that show yearly quantity and value of mineral production by states; also employment and injuries. Separate chapters on each mineral give domestic production and shipments, prices, consumption, stocks, foreign trade, and world production by country.
   e) A series of volumes which present detailed data for 1947, 1954, and 1958 on manufacturing activities in the United States.

4. Name a source in which you think each of the following sets of data would be available. Explain your choice in each case.
   a) The number of tons of primary aluminum produced in the United States monthly during the past year, including the latest month available.
   b) The latest data on the number of employees on the payrolls of manufacturing concerns, by industries, in the United States.
   c) The amount of sales by apparel stores in the state of New York in 1954.
   d) The number of freight carloadings of livestock shipped in the United States during the last year.
   e) The index of industrial production in the United States for the most recent month.

5. The answer to each of the following questions is to be found in a commonly used *government* source. (a) Give exact reference to the source. (b) Describe the steps you followed in each case in order to locate the data.
   (1) The percentage of increase in population for New York and for Texas from 1950 to 1960.

(2) An index of consumer prices in Chicago during the most recent month and the same month last year.
(3) The wholesale price per gallon of No. 2 fuel oil at New York Harbor for the most recent week.

6. The answer to each of the following questions is to be found in a commonly used *nongovernment* source. (*a*) Give exact reference to the source. (*b*) Describe the steps you followed in each case in order to locate the data.
    (1) The number of new passenger car registrations for Ford and Chevrolet last year.
    (2) The number of business failures in manufacturing in the United States during the latest month available.
    (3) The percentage of foreign-made motor trucks sold in the United States each year since 1954.

7. Certain difficulties of collection occur in each of the following problems. Find as much information as you can in answering the question and explain the circumstances in the sources that make it difficult to secure complete and comparable data.
    a) An important measure of plant expansion in the steel industry is "capacity." Trace the changes in per cent of "capacity" since 1889.
    b) Compare the number of savings banks, depositors, and amount of savings in your own state with another state as of a recent date.
    c) Compare the changes in the number of employees in the chemical industry and in the automobile industry over the past 50 years.
    d) Compare the number of full-time employees in one-, two-, and three-store independent food stores in the United States with the number employed in chain food stores, in 1935 and in 1954.
    e) Select the five industries whose indexes of employment were lowest during the most recent month, and compare these indexes with their indexes in 1932.

SELECTED READINGS

See Appendix A

3. COLLECTION OF ORIGINAL DATA

CHAPTER 2 described how to find and use existing data in research sources. In case the figures are not already available, however, they may have to be collected directly by a survey of the original source. This chapter describes how to plan and carry out such a survey.

Most surveys are concerned with human populations. The sales manager of a business, for example, is interested in consumer preferences. General Motors polls the public to determine its likes and dislikes in car styling. The J. Walter Thompson Company maintains a consumer panel of selected families to check the brands of food products being purchased. Market research generally utilizes consumer surveys to measure the market acceptance of a product. Public opinion polls cover every possible topic. "The questionnaire is to our civilization what art and philosophy were to the Greeks, or law and sewers to the Romans—a natural form of self-expression."[1]

Many surveys, however, relate to nonhuman populations. The quality control supervisor of a manufacturing company samples its products to check for defective items. The purchasing agent does the same for goods being bought. The auditor samples a "population" of inventory items to check average costs. This chapter is primarily concerned with the collection of data from people, but the principles discussed apply to the collection of other types of original data as well.

CENSUS VERSUS SAMPLE

Some investigations require a complete enumeration, known as a "census." The United States Census of Population, for instance, is a complete enumeration. Other complete collections of data, such as the

---
[1] Dwight Macdonald in *The New Yorker,* November 22, 1958, p. 89.

statistics of imports, corporate incomes, cigarette consumption, and gasoline consumption, are by-products of the tax-collecting function of the government.

In contrast to these cases of complete collection of data are the great majority of surveys in which the census method is unfeasible or impossible. Instead of collecting all the information concerning a given subject, these investigations depend upon obtaining a sample which will be typical of the whole. The problems of sampling are so important that all of Chapter 4 is devoted to them. We are interested here merely in explaining how results representing a large population of items can be obtained by the use of a sample.

In constructing a wholesale price index, for example, no attempt is made to include the price at which every wholesale transaction is made, or even to sample the prices of every commodity sold at wholesale. The prices of only the most important articles are used. By proper selection and weighting, these prices can be made to reflect the behavior of a much broader group of commodities.

The use of a sample instead of a complete census saves much time and money and yields results that are usually quite accurate enough for the purpose.

PERSONAL INTERVIEWS VERSUS MAIL QUESTIONNAIRES

Original data are usually collected either through personal interviews or through questionnaires sent out by mail. These methods are compared below.

Personal Interviews

The principal advantage of personal interviews lies in the opportunity to secure nearly complete returns from the desired sample. Interviewers can usually reach nearly all of the people selected as a typical sample of the population to be surveyed.

When mail questionnaires are used, on the other hand, a large proportion of the recipients may disregard them. Furthermore, there is no assurance that those who reply are typical of the entire group to whom the questionnaires were mailed. Frequently, those who cannot give a favorable report on the information requested will not reply at all. Or, those with more education or more experience are likely to reply, whereas whole segments of the population which one wishes to reach may disregard the questionnaire entirely. Finally, questionnaires may be answered by a business subordinate or a junior member of a family rather than by the person to whom they are addressed. This situation creates an error quite apart from any tendency of respondents to give biased answers, a difficulty which the investigator faces in any case.

In the second place, personal interviewers can generally obtain accurate replies through explaining the questions, persuading the informant to provide the desired information, and judging the validity of the response. If the respondent appears uninformed or facetious, for example, the interviewer can discount his reply. Of course, the interviewers themselves must be carefully selected and trained to avoid introducing their own biases in phrasing the questions or recording the answers.

The advantages of personal contact are lost in the mail questionnaire. The form and tone of the latter must be designed therefore to supply as far as possible the missing personal element. It nevertheless remains an impersonal appeal for information and is likely to be treated as such. Not only will many questionnaires be discarded, but a number of those that are returned will have been misinterpreted or only partially completed.

Third, the personal contact of interviewers may be necessary to get replies to a long list of questions or to questions which require lengthy explanation. Mail questionnaires must ordinarily be limited to a few simple questions; otherwise, they will be filed in the wastebasket.

Mail Questionnaires

The principal advantage of obtaining information by mail is, of course, its economy. The cost of mailing, including return postage, is only a few cents per questionnaire, so that even if only a few replies are received, the cost per return will generally be less than that of personal interviews. Hence this method is used whenever the results are believed to be reliable.

Mail questionnaires are particularly economical if a large geographical area is to be covered. While interviewers may be employed economically within a single locality, their use may be too costly if extensive travel is required.

The use of mail questionnaires may also be preferable to that of interviewers in case the respondent requires considerable time to compile the data, as in reporting the operating results of retail stores. Interviewers ordinarily can only collect data that are immediately available. The fact that questionnaires can be answered at the respondent's convenience is a particular advantage if the corresponding interviews might have to be conducted under conditions when those interviewed are busy or distracted by business or household affairs.

In large surveys that would require numerous interviewers who cannot be thoroughly trained, a mail questionnaire has an advantage in avoiding the interviewers' bias. This was a factor in the Census Bureau's decision to use mail questionnaires extensively in place of interviews for the 1960 Census of Population.

Confidential information may sometimes be secured by mail more readily than by personal interviewers, as in the case of the Federal Reserve monthly surveys of department store sales or the U.S. Census of Manufactures. Some types of personal data, on the other hand, may be more easily obtained by skillful personal interviews, as in the case of the University of Michigan surveys of consumer buying plans.

Sometimes a "consumer panel" of typical families is selected by personal interview, and then these families are induced to report their brand purchases monthly by mail. The inducement may be money, merchandise, or stamps exchangeable for goods. This method combines the economy of mailing methods with the accuracy of a personally selected sample.

If mail questionnaires are used, they should be phrased so as to obtain the maximum number of replies. This may be done by reducing the list of questions to a minimum, using simple check marks or "yes-no" answers, securing the sponsorship of a well-known agency, and offering some incentive to reply, as described more fully in the following section on "Preparation of Questionnaires."

Mailing lists for questionnaires can be obtained from city directories, telephone books, Dun & Bradstreet's credit rating books, trade directories, city and county records such as lists of taxpayers, automobile registrations and building permits, the membership rolls of various organizations, and commercial mailing-list dealers. Of course, any such list must be checked to be sure that it is accurate, complete, and up to date before it can be used for economical or reliable results.

A practical example will illustrate the circumstances under which one method is more suitable than the other: A research bureau collects monthly data on retail food prices and on total sales from 25 identical grocery stores in a single city. The bureau uses agents to collect the price data but mail questionnaires to collect the sales figures. This is because an agent can get price data from the price tags or from the clerk at any time he appears at the store, whereas the monthly sales figures are not made up until the manager has time to prepare them. Further, the grocer would not be willing to write down the prices of the 42 articles which appear on the questionnaire, but he would agree to transfer a single sales figure from his ledger to the bureau's collection sheet.

Sometimes a questionnaire is sent to an entire mailing list; then, later on, interviewers are sent out to visit a number of the persons who did not reply. In this way it is possible to determine whether the replies of the nonrespondents differ from those of the respondents and, if so, in what respects. This combination method minimizes costs without sacrificing reliability. A variation of this method is employed when personal interviewers collect data in thickly populated centers and questionnaires are sent by mail to respondents in less accessible areas.

Use of the Telephone

The telephone has been used increasingly in some fields of sampling in recent years. Through its use, it is possible to obtain a large number of interviews quickly and at a relatively low cost. However, it is limited to telephone subscribers, who may not be typical of the entire population. Furthermore, only a relatively small amount of information can be obtained in each call. It is also difficult to obtain such data as age, economic condition, or occupation over the telephone.

The variety of methods used in collecting data may be illustrated by the four major services that rate TV shows by size of audience, according to an article in *TV Guide*. American Research Bureau sends "diaries" to some 2,200 homes; the families record their viewing and mail in reports weekly. *Pulse* sends interviewers (mostly women who are local residents) to people's homes; about 150,000 interviews are conducted monthly. *Trendex* uses the spot-check technique of telephone calls to some 1,000 TV homes in 15 cities. A. C. Nielsen Company has installed about 1,200 "Audimeters" on TV sets in homes scattered throughout the country. The audimeter records on tape the channel to which the set is tuned and the time it is turned on and off.

PREPARATION OF QUESTIONNAIRES

No matter how carefully the general plan of an investigation has been developed, there will be certain peculiarities which need to be discovered and provided for before starting the actual collection of data. If there are technical terms used in an industry, these should be known in advance. A knowledge of the form in which records are kept and the units in which data are recorded will aid in phrasing questions. The advice of specialists in the field will be useful in showing the proper method of approach to those who are to be canvassed.

A common practice is to test a preliminary draft of questions by submitting them to a small group of persons similar to those from whom the information is to be obtained. Such a "pretest" will aid in preparing the final draft of the questions, in providing the background for improved interview technique, and in creating advance good will for the investigation. For example, the Census Bureau in November 1954 pretested the questionnaire and procedures planned for later use in a national survey of smoking habits by conducting interviews in 400 Philadelphia households. Specifically, the pretest should check whether the eight rules below have been followed successfully and which of alternate questionnaires or operating procedures is more effective.

The success of a survey depends to a large extent upon the quality of the questions used. There will be considerable difference in the type of question included, depending upon whether interviewers or mail questionnaires are employed. Interviewers can generally obtain replies to questions which are more involved and more personal than those on mail questionnaires. In spite of this difference, the two types of questions can best be discussed together with separate explanations of the points that refer to one and not the other. There are eight rules that should be followed in preparing a questionnaire: (1) organize the questions carefully, (2) use clear wording, (3) define terms, (4) specify units, (5) be brief, (6) avoid offensive questions, (7) avoid bias, and (8) provide adequate instructions. These rules are discussed below.

1. *Organize the Questions Carefully*

In outlining the content of a questionnaire, the guiding principle is unity, in terms of the objective of the survey. Only those questions should be included which contribute directly to the objective. Further, the questions must be so planned that the replies can be tabulated to yield answers to the questions proposed at the outset of the study. This requires careful study of the ultimate goal of the investigation.

A survey was made in an eastern city to estimate the extent of the repair and modernization work needed in residential buildings throughout the area. The schedule of questions in Table 3–1 was prepared for the study. For multiple-family dwellings a form was to be filed for each dwelling unit in the building.

If questions 5 and 11 disclosed that the family had an automobile and no garage, or a single garage and two automobiles, presumably that family could be interested in garage construction. If question 15 showed that the house had no central heating system or had an antiquated system, perhaps the family would be interested in improved heating installation. If the answer to question 18 was a simple negative, further investigation of the house would be necessary to determine whether the deficiency was lack of paint, a leaking roof, defective plumbing, or other

Table 3-1

```
QUESTIONNAIRE USED IN A REAL ESTATE SURVEY
    OF NEEDED REPAIRS AND MODERNIZATION
 1. How many occupants? _____
 2. How many rooms? _____
 3. Basement? _____
 4. Stories? _____
 5. Single or double garage? _____
 6. Electric refrigerator? _____
 7. Rent? _____
 8. When was house built? _____
 9. Owner or renter? _____
10. How long has occupant lived in house? _____
11. Automobile? _____
12. Use auto for work? _____
13. How long to go to work? _____
14. How many in family are working? _____
15. What kind of heat? _____
16. Fuel used? _____
17. Single or double house? _____
18. Is house in good condition? _____
19. Who pays water rent? _____
```

needed repairs. Whatever the deficiency, the family could presumably be interested in remedying it.

Some of the questions, such as 6, 12, 13, 14, 16, and 19, are difficult to justify in this questionnaire; therefore in the revised form, Table 3-2, they have been omitted. The revision is designed to give more information concerning the repairs and modernization needed and to facilitate collection and tabulation. Interviewers using the revised form could save much time and effort and could make a better impression on the informant.

It is essential that the information be received in a form which facilitates tabulation and analysis. This is primarily a matter of visualizing the subsequent use of the data.

The sequence of the questions should be considered carefully in terms of the purpose of the study and the persons who will supply the information. Questions supplying identification and description of the respondent should come first, followed by major information questions. If personal or controversial opinions are requested, such questions are usually placed at the end of the list. Two different questions may be included on the same subject, to provide a cross-check on important points.

Table 3-2

REVISION OF REAL ESTATE QUESTIONNAIRE (TABLE 3-1)
ON NEEDED REPAIRS AND MODERNIZATION

House:
- (1) Address_____
- (2) Stories: 1 2 3 4 B A   (3) Single____ Double____ Other____
- (4) Year built_____   (5) Garage: 0 1 2 3 or more

Dwelling Unit:
- (6) Floor_____   (7) Years lived in by present occupant___
- (8) Owner___ Renter___   (9) Monthly rent_____
- (10) No. of rooms___ baths___   (11) No. of occupants___
- (12) No. of automobiles owned___
- (13) Heating equipment—central heat: Yes___ No___
- (14) Hot air___ steam___ radiant___
- (15) Any repairs needed: Yes___ No___

Repairs Needed:
- (16) House: (17) Equipment:
    - Paint   - Electric wiring
    - Porch   - Plumbing
    - Roof   - Heating system
    - Garage   - Other (specify)
    - Other (specify)

2. Use Clear Wording

When questionnaires in the hands of interviewers are used, as in the real estate survey just described, it is not necessary to word questions in so much detail as in a mail questionnaire. Since the interviewers are already familiar with the meaning of each question and the definition of terms, the abbreviated form shown in Table 3–2 is better than the sentence form of questions shown in Table 3–1. It is easier for the interviewer to check the answer wherever possible than to write several words, and uniform marking greatly facilitates tabulation. On the other hand, a mail questionnaire must be filled out by the respondent himself, so the questions must be complete sentences and must make their own appeal.

In either case it is especially important that the wording be clear. Each question should contain but one idea. It must be stated as simply as possible, so that there can be no doubt in the mind of the respondent what is wanted. For example, the 1950 Census of Population included a question on employment for persons 14 years old and over. Yet, the simple query, "Are you employed or unemployed?" could not be asked because it is ambiguous. Housewives, college students, temporarily unemployed persons, or those on leave from their work might classify themselves in either category. Again, the numbers of unemployed persons who are looking for work, are unable to work, or are retired have very different significance. The question was therefore phrased specifically as follows (in the follow-up questionnaire used for persons not at home when the agent called):

15. What were you doing last week? (Check each box that applies to you.)
   a) ☐ I worked at a job, or in my business or profession, or on a farm.
   b) ☐ I was looking for work.
   c) ☐ I had a job, profession, or business from which I was temporarily absent.
   d) ☐ I did housework in my own home.
   e) ☐ I am permanently unable to work.
   f) ☐ None of the above applies to me.

A questionnaire sent to state hospital superintendents included the question, "To what extent does overcrowding express itself in unsuitable sleeping quarters?" The phrase "to what extent" is indefinite. Such words as "unsuitable," "adequate," and "sufficient" as used in this questionnaire are meaningless unless related to definite standards. Questions should be objective rather than subjective.

3. Define Terms

In preparing a questionnaire, any word, phrase, or technical term which may lead to variation of interpretation should be defined. If a great amount of detailed definition proves necessary, the mail questionnaire should be avoided. Detailed definitions usually do not appear on the questionnaire forms used by interviewers but should be printed with the general instructions issued to them.

For either method of investigation, the definitions must be so precisely worded that (1) no ambiguity exists, (2) no limitations of terms are left indefinite, and (3) no technical uses of terms are unexplained. Some examples will show the necessity for careful wording and definition.

The treasurer of a department store submitted a list of questions to the department heads of the store. One of them read: "Have you been successful recently with promotions?" There may be no doubt as to what is wanted here, but it would be preferable to specify sales promotions rather than promotions of the staff.

If possible, the standard definitions and classifications issued by the

Bureau of the Budget should be used, so that the results will be consistent with data from other projects.[2] These standards include classifications of commodities and industries, definitions of metropolitan areas and production workers, and standard payroll-reporting periods.

4. Specify Units

The unit of numerical data must be carefully defined. The unit may be a person, a physical quantity such as a ton or a bushel, a dollar, or an abstract concept such as an order. In some cases the type of enumeration to be made immediately determines the unit to be used, as in counting population or recording sales. In other cases a choice of units is available, as in recording production of cement either in tons, barrels, or dollars of value. Once the unit has been selected, an exact definition will be required to avoid ambiguity.

Units can be divided into two kinds: (1) those with definition established by law or custom and (2) those for which the definition must be established separately wherever they are used. Examples of the first kind are the bushel, the dollar, or the hour. Each of these measures carries a standard definition which serves as an adequate description any time it is employed as a unit. On the other hand, when the unit used is a ship, a room, or a voter, it is necessary to explain what shall be counted and what shall be omitted during the enumeration. Thus a room in a dwelling is not a usable unit until many borderline cases such as closets, breakfast nooks, pantries, and sun rooms have been either included or excluded by definition. If a subsequent survey is made using a different definition of a room, the results of the two investigations cannot be compared although both use the unit "room" as the basis for counting. Similarly, in recording industrial accidents, a careful statement must be made of the kinds of injuries to be included as accidents.

The instructions accompanying a questionnaire included the statement: "Information to be secured for wage earners only." Trouble arose continually in determining exactly who were wage earners. Questions such as the following were brought in by the interviewers: "How about a physician who received a salary instead of fees?" "How about a daughter living at home and working for her father at a nominal salary?" "How about an insurance agent working on commission and receiving a fixed percentage of the annual profit?" The answers given to such questions as these depend upon the purpose of the investigation. But no matter how carefully any such unit as "wage earner" is defined,

---

[2] See *Standards for Statistical Surveys* (Washington, D.C.: Bureau of the Budget, March 28, 1952).

borderline cases will arise which will have to be settled arbitrarily by the director.

5. Be Brief

The use of a few easily answered questions in a questionnaire will increase the number of replies. Questions should be worded so that they can be answered by "yes" or "no," by numbers, or by a simple check to record choices, provided such answers are adequate.

The respondent should not be asked to make computations. Hence the question, "What is your annual remuneration?" is not a good one to ask a laborer, not only because the word "remuneration" may be foreign to his vocabulary but also because he may be unable to state his earnings except by the day or week. Requests for historical information should be avoided if possible, since this is often difficult to recall.

Make sure that no repetition of information is requested except in the case of "check" questions. The duplication adds to the length of the questionnaire and may antagonize the recipient, causing him to discard it. Examples of repetitious and overlapping questions in the following list were selected from a questionnaire sent to state hospitals by a social agency:

11. Do you need additional employees?
15. Do you have adequate hospital and medical facilities?
19. Do you have adequate facilities for giving your inmates instructive work and recreation?
21. Are your facilities for academic work sufficient?
22. Is your staff of teachers large enough?
28. Are inmates paroled whom you deem unfit to return to the community?
29. What are the outstanding needs of your institution?

Bed capacity	Medical equipment
Employees	Academic equipment
Teachers	Recreation facilities
Opportunities for work	Extended parole

The last question merely asks for information already covered by the preceding questions. Questions 15 and 19 each combine two separate ideas. There are other faults in the wording of these questions which will be referred to later.

6. Avoid Offensive Questions

Great care must be taken to avoid offense. For example, in small, closely held businesses, one cannot ask the question, "What was the dollar value of your net sales last year?" But the approximate data may be obtained by asking, "Please indicate in which of the broad groups below your net sales for last year would fall," followed by several sales classes arranged to give enough detail for use in the subsequent analysis. A question may not be personally offensive but may involve official complications. In the example quoted in the preceding section, a hospital superintendent might well hesitate to answer question 28, fearing to give offense to the parole board and to politicians. Questions concerning personal morality or religion should be avoided, if possible.

7. Avoid Bias

Bias may enter in two ways. First, the question may be phrased so as to suggest a certain answer. An example of a biased wording is: "Did the frozen codfish taste better to you than canned cod or shredded cod?" This is the notorious "leading question." It would be much better to list the three types of prepared fish and request that the user number them in the order of preference.

Second, estimates that are based on opinions rather than on actual figures may be biased. Suppose you were inquiring of a manufacturer of drugs whether his product was distributed at retail mainly through chain stores or independent stores. His direct contacts with the buyers of chain retailers might lead him to suppose that they were his chief customers, whereas a study of the sales records might well show the reverse.

If possible, ask questions only of well-informed persons. Otherwise, the result may be biased by guesswork, since the average man is usually willing to give an opinion on any subject whether he actually knows the answer or not. For example, the chamber of commerce of a western city asked a large number of businessmen what they thought the city's population was likely to be ten years in the future. The average of these estimates was then published as the chamber's forecast! Again, a business journal regularly surveys its readers' views on the business outlook, and publishes summaries of the results, although few of the readers are skilled forecasters. Quantity is no substitute for quality in survey design!

8. Provide Adequate Instructions

The instructions for interviewers must contain not only all definitions of terms and all fixed procedure for interviewing but also a description of cases to be included, boundaries of areas, time scheduling, and other pertinent details. The selection and briefing of interviewers is of extreme importance. Each one should be chosen for his ability to meet people, to inspire confidence, and to obtain information without offense. Those selected must be given rigorous training in all phases of the survey, including field training if necessary.

A mail questionnaire should be accompanied by a letter of transmittal containing a brief explanation of the purpose of the survey and providing some incentive for answering it, such as (1) an appeal for co-operation, (2) mutual interest in the results, (3) possible profit from the results, (4) obligation to the investigator, (5) prestige of position held by respondent, or (6) a gift of merchandise, stamps, or funds.[3] It is often desirable to include an extra copy of the questionnaire for the respondent's files.

Many questionnaires include a number of special questions designed to check the accuracy of the responses. For example, the Bureau of the Census in its monthly report received from manufacturers on production of farm machinery (Form M37B) includes five questions entitled "Checks for completeness and consistency in your report." One of these is: "Are the values reported on this form based on sales price, f.o.b. factory?" The questions are followed by boxes to be checked after making each test.

Follow-up Procedure

In some surveys, response to the first attempt to collect the information, whether by mail or personal interview, is insufficient for the purpose of the investigation and a follow-up procedure is needed. The extent of the follow-up is determined by the rate of response to the initial inquiry, the costs involved, and the precision required in the final results. Follow-ups may be conducted by a method that differs from that of the original survey, as in the case where persons failing to reply to a mail questionnaire may be interviewed in person.

EDITING SCHEDULES

As the returns from a survey come in they must be studied very carefully in order to detect any irregularities in the responses. Experience demonstrates that this step is necessary whatever the method of collection, although more errors will be found in mail questionnaires than in returns compiled by interviewers. Before any analysis is undertaken, these errors must be detected by an editor, and corrected if possible.

If the survey is a large one or the questionnaire form is complex,

---

[3] Examples of letters containing the various types of appeals may be found in M. A. Brumbaugh and L. S. Kellogg, *Business Statistics* (Homewood, Ill.: Richard D. Irwin, Inc., 1941), pp. 106–9.

two editors should go over the schedules independently. The second editor will find things which the first one overlooked.

The editor performs two functions: (1) detecting irregularities in the replies and (2) preparing the questionnaires for tabulation.

Editing for Irregularities

There is no fixed order in which the editing should proceed, but the following order will serve in many cases: (1) look for omissions, (2) verify check questions, (3) search for inconsistencies, (4) check computations, and (5) check for uniformity among questionnaires.

Look for Omissions. Each questionnaire should be complete. If the answers to any questions are missing, an attempt should be made to get the information either by mail or by a second interview with the informant. Failure to obtain the information by these means may require the editor to mark that part of the schedule "no report" or, if the missing information is vital, to discard the schedule.

Verify Check Questions. If the collection form includes answers to questions which should verify each other and these fail to check, the editor must search for other information that will indicate which of the responses is correct. For example, the age of a house may be stated as 30 years (in 1961), the date of construction as 1938, and the initial mortgagee as a bank which was liquidated in 1934. The date of construction has apparently been given incorrectly, but the editor must not guess about this. If no direct verification is possible, either the schedule should be returned to its author or the answers to these questions should be discarded.

Search for Inconsistencies. There will often be questions to which answers can occur only in certain combinations. The editor must test these combinations for consistency. For example, if a respondent in 1961 reports her age as 31 and later in the form lists her date of birth as 1924, the editor should suspect an error—probably an understatement in age!

Check Computations. Any additions or other calculations which are on the questionnaire should be carefully checked. Arithmetic errors can usually be corrected by the editor. There are some cases, however, in which errors of this kind will require a resubmission of the form to the maker.

Check for Uniformity among Returns. The editor should check for uniform interpretation of all of the questions. He is likely to find that certain questions have been misconstrued on some of the questionnaires. These things may not be evident in studying the returns individually but may appear when one question is studied on all of the returns. In an investigation of moving-picture attendance this question was asked: "How much did you spend for moving-picture admission last week?" One of the interviewers turned in reports showing expenditures well above the others. Inquiry revealed that he had asked for expenditures during the past *month*.

Preparing the Returns for Tabulation

After the various irregularities have been adjusted, some steps still remain before the questionnaires are ready for tabulation. The editor must first reclassify the items, if necessary, in the form in which they are to be tabulated. For instance, if the question, "What is your occupation?" appears on the questionnaire and no check list accompanies it, the answers will appear in a variety of forms. The editor must mark these replies according to the occupational classification to be used in tabulation. Again, the returns may show the state from which they come, whereas the tabulation is to be made by regions. These regions should be marked by the editor. This sort of editing adds to the speed and accuracy of the tabulation and makes it unnecessary to employ a highly skilled staff in the tabulation process.

The data on individual questionnaires are sometimes transferred to large work sheets by checking off each answer of a given return along a single row of the work sheet. The returns may be sorted by age, sex, or some other pertinent characteristic before filling out the work sheets. Totals can be shown in both the right-hand column and the bottom row.

In the 1950 Census of Population the census enumerators avoided the use of individual forms entirely by marking the original data on large sheets. Each sheet showed complete information for 30 persons, using only one line per person.

Sometimes the process of preparing the returns for tabulation involves an intermediate step known as *coding*. The best example of this occurs when mechanical tabulation is employed. Coding of information to be transferred to punch cards becomes one of the most important steps in the mechanical process, which is described in the next section.

PRELIMINARY TABULATION

The next step is to transfer the collected and edited information to preliminary tables. These are detailed tables which present for the first time a complete view of the data in an orderly classification. Out of these preliminary tables come the tables for analysis and presentation.

The former seldom appear in print, but the latter are usually a part of any complete statistical report. There are four principal methods of transferring information from the collection forms to preliminary tables. These are: (1) sorting-counting, (2) the use of tally sheets, (3) punch cards, and (4) electronic data processing.

Sorting-Counting

The sorting-counting process can be used to advantage when the data to be tabulated are relatively simple so that each case can be recorded on one card. The cards can be sorted and subsorted into piles according to any desired plan of classifying the data. The number of cards in each pile can then be recorded on a suitable form.

For example, an investigation of residential vacancies in a midwestern city was carried out by having a card filled out for each dwelling. The cards were edited and then sorted into five piles according to the number of residential units in the building. Each of these five piles was then sorted according to whether the dwelling was occupied or vacant. The cards in each of the ten piles were then counted, and the results entered in a table.

Tally Sheets

The use of tally sheets differs from sorting-counting in that the schedule cards or sheets are not separated into piles according to the various classifications. Instead, blank forms are made up to conform to

Table 3–3

RESIDENTIAL SURVEY, DISTRICT NO. 1

Number of Residential Units per Building	Number of Units Occupied	Number of Units Vacant	Total Units
1	HHT HHT /	//	13
2	HHT //	/	8
3	//	0	2
4	////	/	5
5 or more	0	0	0
Total	24	4	28

the classifications of the data. The information is then tallied on the form as it is read from the questionnaire. Table 3–3 shows a tally sheet for the residential vacancy survey described above.

If there is too much cross classification of the data, this method becomes cumbersome. It is then better to abandon the tally sheet and use sorting-counting, or machine tabulation as explained below. The tallying process may be simplified, however, by sorting the returns first into their major classifications and then tallying by subgroups. This preliminary sorting also aids in the detection of errors in reading or transcription. Errors can be localized in one of the piles and the rereading confined to that one, instead of having to reread all of the returns.

The tally sheet method is often the most desirable to use in taking information from a published source. For example, if one wished to classify the industries in the *Census of Manufactures* according to number of employees, the best method would be to make up a tally sheet with a classification by number of employees and tally the industries as they were read off.

Punch Cards

When a large number of questionnaires is to be analyzed, or when a great amount of cross tabulation is necessary, the task of tabulation becomes enormous. Under either of these circumstances the present practice is to use machinery designed for the purpose. At no other point is the statistician so much favored by the developments of the machine age as in tabulation. Equipment is available to perform quickly and accurately the steps of sorting, counting, cross tabulating, and recording in columnar form.

These advantages have led a great many business concerns to install "punch card" systems for maintaining records of current operations. The following are examples: bad-debt losses of members of a retail credit association; broker's record of security dealings with customers; merchandise control of a mail-order house; personnel records of an aircraft company; and stock control in the warehouse of a chain grocery company. Bank checks, too, are often printed as punch cards to facilitate the sorting and totaling operations.

Principles. The basic principle of punch card tabulation is that a hole punched in a card represents, by its horizontal and vertical position, a certain statistical fact. It becomes a permanent record that can be tabulated at any time by running the card through a machine. The first machine used in this operation is a "punch" in which the coded information is punched in the appropriate columns and rows. This is illustrated somewhat fancifully in Chart 3–1. A "gang punch" can be used to mark identical data, geographic regions, or the like in a number of cards simultaneously. A second operator then places the card in a verifier machine and repunches the code numbers. This machine will signal any error made in the initial punching process.

Once the cards are punched, they are fed into a "sorter," also shown in Chart 3-1. This machine sorts the punched cards into numbered compartments, each of which represents one set of information. By the addition of mechanical counters, sorting and counting may be accomplished in a single operation.

Chart 3-1*

PUNCH

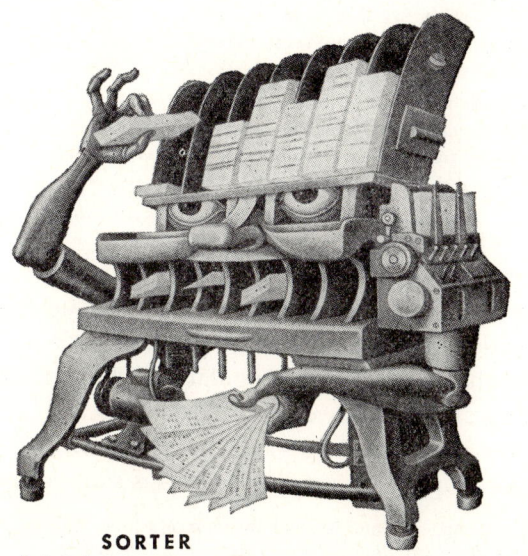

SORTER

* Animistic drawings by Artzybasheff, courtesy of Time, Inc.

The "tabulator" machine goes even further. After the cards have been sorted, the tabulator not only counts the various categories but adds the items in each and furnishes a printed record of the totals. For example, if cards were punched showing the weekly wage rates of a firm's employees, each card representing one employee, the tabulating machine could be set so that it would give a printed record of the number employed at each wage rate, the total earnings of each group, the total number of employees, and the total weekly payroll, with a single running of the cards. Other machines will select any card needed, make up duplicate cards, stamp out addressograph plates, or perform countless other operations.

Examples. The several steps in the punch card process are illustrated below. Table 3-4 represents a punch card used in an industrial market survey.[4] The information for this card is collected by a salesman of industrial equipment to provide the customer information needed in estimating future sales potentials. The customers are other companies that buy this equipment.

Table 3-4
STANDARD PUNCH CARD

The 80 columns of the card are grouped into fields of information, as shown in the headings. A code must then be set up to transfer descriptive information to the card. Thus, the salesman's branch office is coded "707," as shown by the rectangular punches in the first three columns. Numerical data, however, can be punched directly—e.g., 31,500 employees in columns 35-37. The completed card shows the branch office, sales representative, customer, his state, county, industry

---

[4] For further discussion, see International Business Machines Corporation, *Marketing Research by Means of the IBM Punched Card Method*, pp. 8 and 9.

and department of the company, the number of employees (to indicate the size of the company), and sales of the manufacturer's equipment lines A and B at various periods.

After similar cards have been punched for hundreds of customers, the cards can be quickly sorted and tabulated to show present and potential ("peacetime" in Table 3–4) sales classified by branch office, by sales representative, by customer, by lines (A and B), by industry, by state and county, or on whatever basis the data are needed.

Table 3–5

HAND-PUNCHED CARD

[card image showing questionnaire with following filled-in entries:]

(Metal Parts Mfg.)
1. Name *ABC Products* Code *3591*
2. Location *Brant St.*
3. No. Emp. & Dur. Max. *50/6* Min *30/1* Ave. *39/1*
4. Type jobs *Assembly and Prodn Workers, Machinists*
   Min. Wages *$1.25*
5. An. Pyl. '49 $ *179,000* 1st qtr. '50 $ *45,000*
6. Items 3 & 5 (above) (below) (same as) 1st qtr. '50
7. Union shop (yes) (no) peak prod. per *Jan. – June*
8. Val. prod. '49 $ *480,000* 1st qtr. '50 $ *130,000*
9. Val. raw mtl. used '49 $ *24,000* 1st qtr. '50 $ *65,000*
10. Type raw mtl. *Steel Shafting*
    From *S.F.* *S.F.*
    Transported *Tk* *Tk*
11. Waste prod. (yes) (no) Type *Scrap Steel*
    Amt. *2 Tons/Mo*
12. ...

For simpler surveys a different type of card, with holes around the edges, can be used. These are punched by hand with the desired information and are filed in a cabinet. They can then be sorted by inserting rods in the appropriate locations, and lifting, so that all slotted cards of a certain type drop down together.

Table 3–5 shows the top half of a 5 × 8-inch card used as a questionnaire by interviewers in an industrial survey conducted in Fresno County, California.[5] The interviewers wrote down the original answers on the center of the card, as illustrated. Later, the answers were coded

---

[5] Courtesy of Professor Arthur W. Gutenberg, University of Southern California.

and hand-punched around the edges for sorting and tabulation. For example, the punch or slot in the No. 23 space on the right margin indicates that the annual payroll of the ABC Company in 1949 (line 5) was in the fourth class interval, or between $100,000 and $150,000. Then all the companies of this size can be sorted by inserting a rod in the No. 23 space and letting the cards that are slotted there drop down.

The widespread industrial and governmental use of punch cards has made possible many statistical investigations that otherwise would not have been feasible. In other cases, results have been obtained in a few days that would have required many weeks of painstaking and relatively inaccurate hand tabulation. This feature is particularly important in industrial data that are soon out of date.

Electronic Data Processing

Electronic machines have been developed in recent years for high-speed calculations that will obviate the need for punch cards in many statistical operations. Electronic equipment can do everything the older equipment can do at much higher speeds with greatly expanded capacities, and in addition can perform the most intricate calculations. The cost, however, is sometimes prohibitive, so that punch cards are still preferable for certain purposes.

All necessary statistical data and instructions as to what to do with them are fed into these new machines, usually on magnetized tape or punch cards. Magnetized tape has much greater capacity and is, therefore, increasingly preferred to the use of the punch cards for this purpose. Chart 3-2 illustrates the difference in capacity: two fifths of an inch of tape a quarter-inch wide can carry the same information as a $3\frac{1}{4}'' \times 7\frac{3}{8}''$ card—that is, 80 alphabetical or numerical characters. The machines then sort, classify, and tabulate data, or perform series of calculations in a fraction of a second each by means of electronic impulses transmitted through intricate systems of transistors or tubes which can store or "remember" numbers and use them in successive operations.

In statistical and accounting work there are a number of general-purpose computing machines. Best known among them are the International Business Machines Corporation's Models 650 and 705 and Sperry Rand Corporation's UNIVAC. There are many other makes of computers, however, including a variety of specialized computer components which are now available for use by people competent to assemble them in "do-it-yourself" fashion.

A general-purpose electronic computer can perform a wide variety of functions in data processing: it can sort the information as desired, convert it into a different form, store it for future use, transfer it to other locations in the system, perform all types of arithmetic computations, and print the final results in readable form. All of this is done at high speeds in a completely integrated operation, with no human intervention. Furthermore, the machine can make simple decisions, as in reviewing payroll time sheets to determine whether employees are eligible for overtime pay. The versatility and speed of electronic data

Chart 3–2

RELATIVE SIZE OF STANDARD PUNCH CARD AND ⅔ INCH MAGNETIC TAPE —EACH WITH CAPACITY OF 80 CHARACTERS (SCALE REDUCED)

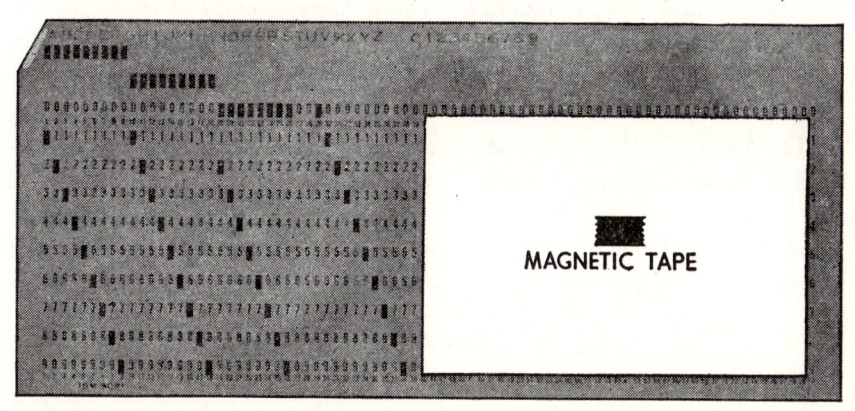

processing systems are therefore revolutionizing large-scale data handling and decision making in modern business.

According to Charles E. Becker, president of the Franklin Life Insurance Company:

We are convinced that the insurance field in general will not be able to keep up with the continued demand for its services without introducing electronic data processing equipment to handle the heavy volume of paper-work which future expansion will bring . . .

We have been in process of converting our procedures to electronic requirements for some time now. Four primary functions will go on to the UNIVAC first: premium billing and accounting, valuation, agents' commission calculating and accounting, and dividend accounting. Others will be added as we go along . . .

Another system, the ERMA (Electronic Recording Machine, Accounting), developed for the Bank of America by the Stanford Research Institute, handles all bookkeeping functions for 32,000 checking accounts. ERMA credits individual accounts with deposits, debits withdrawals, remembers details of all transactions, maintains correct balances, accepts stop payments and hold orders, prevents overdrawing of accounts, and sorts checks. The machine also verifies each accounting step automatically and immediately signals any error to the operator. There is an over-all balancing at the end of each day, plus a monthly recapitulation.

Other electronic data processing systems are used in handling airline reservations, controlling department store inventories, planning manufacturers' production schedules, and for many other purposes.

A detailed description of electronic data processing and computing is beyond the scope of this book. For a good nontechnical discussion of these systems from the management viewpoint, read George Kozmetsky and Paul Kircher, *Electronic Computers and Management Control*, or Richard G. Canning, *Electronic Data Processing for Business and Industry*. See also the monthly journals *Data Processing Digest* and *Automation*.

The business executive does not need to become an expert in electronics or mathematics in order to use electronic data processing. He can deal with the problems involved by acquainting himself with the general capabilities and limitations of these machines. For the actual programing he can rely on technical experts.

SUMMARY

The first step in statistical analysis is the collection of data. If the necessary figures cannot be found in published sources or in the internal records of a business, a special survey must be made. Such a survey need not be a complete census but can be restricted to a limited group if the respondents represent a typical sample of the entire population under study.

If personal interviewers are used, they can canvass the entire group to be sampled; they can explain questions carefully and evaluate the replies, thereby securing more reliable results than is possible by mail questionnaires. On the other hand, mail questionnaires are generally more economical, particularly if a wide area must be covered; so they are ordinarily used if the results can be made reliable. A combination of these two methods is sometimes used. Occasionally, too, interviews may be conducted by telephone.

In preparing questionnaires, it is essential to organize the questions carefully, to avoid ambiguities in the wording, to define all terms and units used, to avoid offensiveness and bias, to provide adequate instructions, and still be as brief as possible.

After the questionnaires have been filled in and returned, they must be edited for irregularities and prepared in proper form for tabulation.

The data compiled in simple projects can be tabulated by entering the necessary information on cards and sorting them by hand, or listing and totaling the figures on large tally sheets. For more complex investigations, the data can be coded and entered on punch cards. These cards are punched, checked, sorted, tabulated, and totaled by special machines. Simpler cards punched around the edge can be used for hand punching and sorting. Finally, electronic data processing machines have been developed in recent years for the high-speed tabulation and computation of complex data.

PROBLEMS

1. State in each of the following examples of collection whether personal interviews or mail questionnaires are preferable, and whether the census or sample method should be used. Give reasons for answers in each case.
    a) A retail dry goods association wished to study the distribution of operating expenses of its 61 members.
    b) A marketing research agency wished to inquire from the owners of a certain make of refrigerator whether they would purchase the same make again.
    c) A corporation president wanted information concerning how many of its 15,400 employees were homeowners, the value of their homes, the amount of mortgage, the interest rate paid, and the monthly payment on the mortgage.

2. What is the purpose of pretesting a questionnaire before starting a mail survey?

3. Cite the three most important rules, in your opinion, that should be followed in preparing a questionnaire on consumer attitudes toward color television. Give reasons for your choice.

4. Explain which of the following alternative wordings is preferable for a questionnaire and why:
    a) (1) What body style do you prefer for your next automobile?
       (2) Check the body style you prefer for your next automobile:
           4-door sedan_____   Station wagon_____
           2-door sedan_____   Convertible_____
           Hard top_____   Other (specify)_____
    b) (1) Do any of the following apply to your concern? (Check which.)
           Clerks poorly trained_____
           Clerical overtime pay too high_____
           Too many clerks_____
           Office management inefficient_____

(2) Which of the following would be most effective in reducing office expenses in your concern? (Check one.)
Additional training of clerical employees_____
Reduction of paid overtime for clerks_____
Reduction of clerical office force_____
Reorganization of office force_____

5. Define the following terms for use in a questionnaire. Be sure to provide for possible borderline cases: (*a*) a household, (*b*) a wholesaler, (*c*) an unemployed person, and (*d*) a drugstore.

6. *a*) List and give the reason for each of the steps in editing completed questionnaires for irregularities.
   b) What other steps does an editor follow in preparing the returns for tabulation?

7. The following card was returned to the interviewer by the editor. What do you think the editor found wrong, and what did he want the interviewer to do?

RESIDENTIAL VACANCY SURVEY

Serial No. _____

Address *324 Henkel Circle front and rear houses*
Ward _____ Tract _____ Enumeration District _____
No. of Dwelling Places in Building
   One_____   Two_____   Three_____
   Four_____   Over Four (give number) __5__
      Occupied __3__   Vacant __1__
      Residential __X__   Combination __X__
      Agent_____   R. A. Shawn

---

8. Which of the four methods of preliminary tabulation (sorting-counting, tally sheets, punch cards, or electronic data processing) would you use for each of the three surveys described in Problem 1 above? Explain your choice in each case. Assume the following number of returns: 1(*a*) 52 dealers; 1(*b*) 5,120 refrigerator owners; and 1(*c*) 1,200 employees.

9. Explain the function of the principal types of punch card machines, including at least two types not described in this textbook.

10. Visit a nearby electronic data processing installation and prepare a brief report on (*a*) description of the machine, (*b*) the types of operation performed, and (*c*) savings in costs, as compared with earlier methods.

SELECTED READINGS

Brown, Lyndon O. *Marketing and Distribution Research.* 3d ed. New York: Ronald Press Co., 1955.

Describes how to plan a survey, prepare a questionnaire, and edit and tabulate the results.

Canning, Richard G. *Electronic Data Processing for Business and Industry.* New York: John Wiley & Sons, Inc., 1956.

Explains in nontechnical language how to select and use modern electronic clerical systems; for the business executive.

Haskins & Sells. *Introduction to Data Processing.* 1957.

A short introduction to all types of processing methods, including manual calculators, punch card systems, and electronic data processing.

International Business Machines Corporation. *General Information Manual—FORTRAN.* 1961.

One of many IBM publications describing applications of punch card techniques in business.

Kozmetsky, George, and Kircher, Paul. *Electronic Computers and Management Control.* New York: McGraw-Hill Book Co., Inc., 1956.

Describes the fundamental characteristics of electronic data processing systems, the new methods of scientific analysis made possible, and their influence on management planning and control.

Mack, Mary L. *Statistics in the Making.* Columbus, Ohio: Ohio State University, Bureau of Business Research, 1958.

Subtitled "A Primer in Statistical Survey Method," this book covers the organization and operation of surveys, questionnaire construction, punch cards, and construction of tables.

Stockton, John R. *Business Statistics.* Cincinnati: Southwestern Publishing Co., 1958.

Chapter 3 presents a detailed account of internal business records and reports. Chapter 5 covers the collection and tabulation of external data.

U.S. Government, Bureau of the Budget. Circular No. A-46, Exhibit A. *Standards for Statistical Surveys.* March 28, 1952.

Presents standards for the planning and conduct of surveys, for guidance of federal agencies.

4. METHODS OF SELECTING SAMPLES

CHAPTER 3 outlined various methods of collecting original data. Such data are usually obtained from samples. An important problem in making a sample survey is to select the sample itself. This chapter describes the principal methods of planning a sample so that valid generalizations can be inferred from the results of the survey.

Sample studies are made in almost all types of business and economic research. For example, the Bureau of the Census estimates the number of cars and other products that American consumers plan to buy during the coming year from a sample of only 17,000 households out of the 53 million households in the country—only 1/30 of 1 per cent of the total.[1] Similarly, the U.S. Department of Agriculture uses a sample of two quarts of grain in a carload (57,600 quarts) to determine the grade of the grain; and the U.S. Bureau of Labor Statistics Consumer Price Index is based on prices of a few hundred commodities and services obtained from a relatively small number of stores and other respondents.

There are three basic reasons for the widespread use of sampling:

1. Sampling usually saves a great deal of time and money. Often when the cost of a complete census would be prohibitive, the necessary information can be obtained from a sample. The results of a survey need only be accurate enough to provide an adequate basis for decision making. Beyond a certain point the increase in information from additional data is not worth the increase in cost.

2. In many cases, a complete census is impossible, as, for example, in making a quick check of consumer preferences for an entirely new product, or in the destructive testing required to determine the breaking

---

[1] *Federal Reserve Bulletin,* September 1960, pp. 977–1003.

strength of steel rods, or in measuring the effectiveness of a new antibiotic.

3. Finally, sampling may actually yield more accurate results than a complete survey. A small group of interviewers can be selected and trained more rigorously to reduce the biases in a survey than a very large staff. Similarly, in testing materials, a few careful measurements may be preferable to a larger number of crude measurements. Because of these advantages and because of improvements in sampling techniques during recent years, the use of sampling has led to many important advances in modern business efficiency.

SAMPLES AND INFERENCES CONCERNING POPULATIONS

A *sample* is a group of units which is selected to represent a larger group called the *population* or *universe*.[2] (These terms here refer to inanimate objects as well as to living beings.) Sample surveys are usually concerned with some measurement or count, such as the average *amount* of money that consumers plan to spend on a new car, the total *number* of cars they plan to buy, or the *per cent* of consumers favoring foreign cars. The purpose of sampling is to estimate these same characteristics for the population from which the sample is selected. The population results are then used in decision making, as in a car manufacturer's decision as to the design of a new model.

The problem of estimating population values would be very simple if every sample were perfectly typical of its population, that is, if it were an exact small-scale replica of the whole group. For instance, if a shipment of 5,000 bolts contains 1,000 defectives, every perfectly typical sample of 50 bolts drawn from that population would contain exactly ten defectives. In practice, however, a sample is almost never a perfect replica of the population. Most well-chosen samples of 50 bolts from this shipment would contain more or less than ten defectives.

There are many effective methods of selecting samples, and these may be used in various combinations. The sample may be selected from the population as a whole, or it may be selected from certain parts or *strata* of the population. In either case, the sample may be selected at random, according to somebody's judgment, or by other methods. The individuals selected may be drawn one at a time or in clusters, such as the residents of selected city blocks. The clusters may be enumerated completely, or they may be subsampled by selecting, say, the head of every third household in the block. Since these procedures can be

---

[2] "Population" and "universe" are usually defined as being synonymous. The newer term "population" will be used in this discussion.

used in various combinations, they provide a great variety of methods for selecting samples.

In this chapter, only the most common sampling plans are presented; no attempt is made to mention all of the various combinations. There are two broad classes of methods of selecting samples: (1) *probability sampling*,[3] including simple random sampling, stratified random sampling, systematic selection, and cluster sampling; and (2) *nonprobability sampling,* including quota sampling and judgment sampling. These are discussed below.

PROBABILITY SAMPLING

Probability sampling includes all methods of sampling in which the sampling units are selected according to the laws of chance, so that the probability of being included is known (and not zero) for each member of the population. "Selected according to the laws of chance" means using some chance device such as a table of random numbers (described below), rather than personal judgment, to choose the items sampled. The "probability of being included" may be *equal* for all units in the population (as in simple random sampling), or it may be, say, "probability proportional to size" (e.g., a company with two million sales having twice the probability of being selected as one with one million sales). In any case, however, the probability must be *known,* and hence the population itself must be identifiable.

In probability samples one can estimate objectively the precision of the sample results or compare the precision of different types of samples. The *precision* of a sample is the difference between the sample result and that of a complete census theoretically taken under the same conditions. These advantages over nonprobability samples increase as the size of the sample increases. Hence, probability sampling is generally used, wherever feasible, in large-scale surveys.

Simple Random Sampling

A *simple random sample* of n units is one selected from a population in such a way that each combination of n units has an *equal* chance of being selected. Thus, in selecting a simple random sample of five bolts from a shipment, every combination of five bolts in the shipment must have the same chance of selection. The bolts could not be picked only from certain boxes, or just from the top of the pile.

---

[3] The application of probability sampling to statistical quality control is discussed in Chapter 22. This includes double sampling and sequential sampling plans (involving variable sample size) in acceptance sampling, which is used to determine whether to accept or reject industrial products.

This method is sometimes called "unrestricted" random sampling because units are selected from the population as a whole without any restriction; whereas procedures like stratification and clustering introduce restrictions (e.g., grouping the population before the sample is selected) which are designed to increase the precision of the sample, or reduce its cost.

Random sampling does not mean haphazard selection. Interviewing passers-by on a downtown street corner does not provide a random sample of a city's population because stay-at-homes have less chance of being interviewed than downtown shoppers or businessmen.

Simple random sampling is not often used alone in business and economic research, but it is important because it illustrates the fundamental principles of sampling, and is a basic part of more complex types of sample design that are widely used in practice.

Random selection is determined objectively by some equivalent of a game of chance. For example, the residents of a city block might be numbered from 1 to 72 and a roulette wheel could be spun ten times to determine the choice of ten persons to be interviewed. As in all probability samples, however, selections are usually made from a *table of random numbers.* Such a table is just as efficient as operating a game of chance, and is more convenient. In constructing a table of random numbers, the digits from 0 to 9 are drawn by some randomizing device so that each number is independent of any other. The RAND Corporation, for instance, programed an electronic data calculator so as to produce the random numbers listed in its book *A Million Random Digits.* Table 4–1 on page 68 is a section of another such table.

How to Use a Table of Random Numbers. To illustrate the use of this table, suppose you wish to select a random sample of six households from a city block of 78 households, as part of a market survey to determine brand preferences for frozen foods. First, list all households by address, and number them from 01 through 78. Second, take a page from a table of random numbers, and choose a starting point at any arbitrary point[4]—say, the thirteenth column, fifth row, in Table 4–1. This number is 43. Third, go down this column and the next columns to the right (or go in any predetermined direction) until you have selected six number between 01 and 78, with no repetitions.

Beginning with 43, the next number down is 93, but it is ineligible, being larger than 78, so continue with 74, 50, 07, 46, 86 (ineligible —larger than 78), 46 (ineligible—already selected), and 32—a total

---
[4] Ideally, the starting point should be selected by a game of chance. In practice, however, an arbitrary choice is generally considered satisfactory.

of six eligible numbers. Thus, the numbers of the households to be surveyed are 7, 32, 43, 46, 50, and 74.

If there are exactly 100 items in the population, read "00" as 100. If there are more than 100 items, combine adjacent columns as necessary to form larger numbers. Thus, in the upper-left corner of Table

Table 4–1
RANDOM NUMBERS

03	47	43	73	86	36	96	47	36	61	46	98	63	71	62
97	74	24	67	62	42	81	14	57	20	42	53	32	37	32
16	76	62	27	66	56	50	26	71	07	32	90	79	78	53
12	56	85	99	26	96	96	68	27	31	05	03	72	93	15
55	59	56	35	64	38	54	82	46	22	31	62	43	09	90
16	22	77	94	39	49	54	43	54	82	17	37	93	23	78
84	42	17	53	31	57	24	55	06	88	77	04	74	47	67
63	01	63	78	59	16	95	55	67	19	98	10	50	71	75
33	21	12	34	29	78	64	56	07	82	52	42	07	44	38
57	60	86	32	44	09	47	27	96	54	49	17	46	09	62
18	18	07	92	46	44	17	16	58	09	79	83	86	19	62
26	62	38	97	75	84	16	07	44	99	83	11	46	32	24
23	42	40	64	74	82	97	77	77	81	07	45	32	14	08
52	36	28	19	95	50	92	26	11	97	00	56	76	31	38
37	85	94	35	12	83	39	50	08	30	42	34	07	96	88
70	29	17	12	13	40	33	20	38	26	13	89	51	03	74
56	62	18	37	35	96	83	50	87	75	97	12	25	93	47
99	49	57	22	77	88	42	95	45	72	16	64	36	16	00
16	08	15	04	72	33	27	14	34	09	45	59	34	68	49
31	16	93	32	43	50	27	89	87	19	20	15	37	00	49

SOURCE: R. A. Fisher and F. Yates, *Statistical Tables for Biological, Agricultural and Medical Research* (London: Oliver & Boyd, Ltd., 1938), Table XXXIII, Random Numbers (I), p. 82. This is part of a much larger table.

4–1, the columns beginning 034 could be used for three-digit numbers, or those beginning 0347 for four-digit numbers.

Stratified Random Sampling

If a population is made up of fairly uniform parts or strata, the precision of sample results can be improved by *stratification.* That is, the population is first broken down into strata, such that the elements within each stratum are more alike than the elements of the population as a whole. Then an assigned part of the sample is drawn from each stratum by random selection (or by one of the nonrandom methods to be described later). Stratification is therefore only one step in the complete sampling method; it is always used in conjunction with other procedures.

As indicated above, the strata should be defined so that the significant elements within a stratum are more uniform than they are for the population as a whole. For example, in a study of household incomes a city can be divided into high- and low-income areas so that income varies less within each area than it does in the city as a whole. Here, geographic location provides a useful basis for stratification. In this case, the average income of a stratified random sample will probably be closer to the true average for the whole population than would that of a simple random sample of the same size selected from the city as a whole without stratification.

Stratification should usually be applied to *heterogeneous* populations, such as humans, since people can be divided into fairly uniform strata—by income, sex, age, or other criteria that affect the variable being studied (e.g., buying habits). Under these circumstances, stratification usually achieves greater precision for a given cost. On the other hand, stratification is unnecessary in *homogeneous* populations, as in measuring the diameter of ball bearings, where there are no discernible strata, such as differences in machine tools or operators, that affect the results.

Nonproportional Sampling. A stratified sample is either *proportional* or *nonproportional,* depending on whether the total sample is divided among the various strata in the same proportions as the population. In proportional sampling, for example, if the population of employees in a company is stratified by type of job, and salesmen are known to comprise 30 per cent of all employees, then salesmen should comprise just 30 per cent of the sample, and similarly with other classes of employees. The sample as a whole would then provide a good cross section of the population.

A stratified sample, however, need not necessarily be proportional. In either of the following cases, it is more efficient to use a *nonproportional* sample, in which certain strata are represented in larger proportion to the population than others. First, the individuals in some strata may be cheaper to sample than others. Thus, factory workers and traveling salesmen might each comprise 30 per cent of all employees, but if it is much cheaper to interview the factory workers at a plant than the scattered salesmen, it might be more efficient to interview twice the number of factory workers than salesmen, and adjust the results by the weights described below.

Second, if one stratum is more variable than another in the characteristic measured, a disproportionately large share of the sample should be taken from this stratum in order to improve the reliability of the whole sample. For example, in a survey of factory workers' wage rates, suppose that 50 per cent of the workers are nonunion and 50 per cent are unionized. Then, if nonunion workers varied much more in their wage scales than union workers, more nonunion workers should be sampled than union workers to improve the over-all estimate of average wages. To cite an extreme case, if all union workers received the same wage, a sample of one individual would suffice. A stratified sample should be nonproportional, therefore, when either the unit sampling cost or the variability of the characteristic measured differs greatly between strata, in order to achieve maximum precision at minimum cost.

Even when the sample is intended to be a proportional one, the investigator may receive too many returns from one part of the population and not enough from another—perhaps because some of the selected individuals failed to respond. In this case it is necessary merely to adjust the weights of the different parts to construct a weighted sample.[5] This gives a better picture of the population than does the original sample.

In general, the average value for the population is estimated in a nonproportional sample by weighting or multiplying the sample average in each stratum by the proportion of the population in that stratum. In the case of the nonunion and union workers, the average wage for each sample group should be multiplied by 50 per cent and added, to compute the average income of the whole population.

Systematic Selection

A systematic sample is one in which every kth item (e.g., every tenth item) is selected in a list representing a population or a stratum. The number k is called the *sampling interval*. The first number is chosen at random from the first k items, as described below. Systematic selection ensures that the items sampled will be spaced evenly throughout the population.

For example, suppose you wish to take a systematic sample of six households from a block of 78 households, as in the earlier example on random sampling. First, list and number the households as before. Then divide 6 into 78; this means that you should select every thirteenth house. Choose the first household at random from the numbers 1 through 13, using a table of random numbers. Say this is number 6. Now select every thirteenth house beginning with number 6—i.e., 6, 19, 32, 45, 58, and 71—to complete the sample.

Systematic sampling is often equivalent in its results to random sampling. However, systematic selection has an important advantage

---

[5] Of course, this is not the ideal solution to the problem of nonrespondents. Their number must be minimized in any survey, as emphasized in Chapter 3.

over simple random sampling if similar parts of the population tend to be grouped together, that is, if nearby elements resemble each other more than they resemble those at greater distances. For example, residents of similar incomes tend to be located close to one another. A systematic selection of a city's blocks, numbered in serpentine fashion as described below, would then include more nearly the same proportion of each income group than a simple random sample. Systematic selection serves somewhat the same purpose as stratification, therefore, in distributing the sampling units more evenly over the entire stratum or population.

Systematic selection should not be used, however, if there is some periodic variation in the population corresponding to the sampling interval. For example, in the case of sampling households in a block, if the block were laid out so that every eighth house were a large one on the corner, a systematic sample of every eighth house might include only large corner houses.

Systematic sampling has come into widespread use because it is easy to apply and it usually yields good results. For example, in the 1960 Census of Population every fourth person was asked several supplementary questions on housing. The cost of collecting and compiling information for this 25 per cent sample was small compared with that of a complete enumeration or of an independent 25 per cent sample survey. At the same time, the reliability of the information was sufficient for almost any purpose.

Cluster Sampling

Cluster sampling is the selection of sample units in two stages: In the first stage, certain groups or clusters called *primary sampling units* are selected from the population. These units might be companies selected from an industry. In the second stage, individual items called *elementary sampling units* are drawn from each of these clusters. These units might be employees—either a sample or all of the employees in a company. This second step in the sampling process is called *subsampling*. When each cluster is contained in a compact geographic area, cluster sampling is also called *area sampling*.

The main advantage of cluster sampling is that it reduces the cost per elementary sampling unit. It is extremely costly to select items at random from a population, or a large stratum thereof. A complete list of individuals is needed, with up-to-date addresses, if each one is to be readily accessible and have the same chance of being included in the sample. Even when such a list is available, the individuals selected at random may be so widely scattered that travel expenses would be excessive.

The use of cluster sampling permits grouping the observations for easier coverage. Lists of names need be prepared only for the sample clusters. Interviewers can also concentrate on these few clusters (e.g., blocks) and thus save travel time and expense.

On the other hand, the results of a cluster sample are usually *not* as precise as those of a random sample *of the same size*. They can be made equally or more precise only by taking a larger sample. The cost of conducting a survey, however, may still be lower. For example, instead of spending $10,000 to interview a random sample of 1,000 householders at an average cost of $10 each, one might get as good or better results for $9,000 with a cluster sample of 1,500 householders costing only $6.00 each.

Serpentine Numbering and Systematic Selection. A recommended method of selecting the clusters in area sampling is to number the primary sampling units in a *serpentine* sequence, following a winding path similar to that of a snake. (See Chart 4–1.) For example, in a study of household incomes, the numbering of city blocks should follow a sequence of blocks having about the same average household income. All blocks in such an area should be numbered before proceeding to a lower-income or higher-income area.

Chart 4–1
SERPENTINE NUMBERING OF CITY BLOCKS

1	2	3	4	5
10	9	8	7	6
11	12	13	14	15

After the block map has been numbered, the desired number of blocks should be chosen by *systematic* selection (e.g., every tenth block) with a random start, as explained previously.

This area sampling design achieves all of the advantages of the *geographic* stratification when blocks in one stratum are numbered before proceeding to another stratum. However, stratification by some other characteristic, such as block size, is sometimes advisable.

Subsampling. After the primary sampling units have been chosen, elementary sampling units are selected from each of these clusters. The selection may be a complete census of the cluster (e.g., all the houses in the block) or a random or systematic sample (e.g., every fifth house).

The cost per interview for a sample is higher than that for a complete census of the selected clusters. The choice between these alternatives depends in part on the complexity of the interview and the availability of lists. If the questionnaire is simple and no list of elementary sampling units (e.g., households) is available, it is usually cheaper to take a complete census of the selected clusters (e.g., blocks); when a lengthy interview is required, the advantages of subsampling justify the cost of listing and sampling the elementary sampling units.

NONPROBABILITY SAMPLING

Nonprobability sampling includes any method of sampling which does not satisfy all requirements of a probability sampling design. This may involve selection of a sample according to personal convenience (to minimize cost), or expert judgment (to increase precision in certain small samples), or under conditions where no complete list is available for objective selection (e.g., a survey of executives who influence corporate buying policy on industrial equipment). Nonprobability sampling methods are important in business and economic research despite the disadvantage that the precision of their results cannot be measured objectively. Two principal types of nonprobability sampling are *quota sampling* and *judgment sampling*.

Quota Sampling

A *quota sample* is one in which the interviewer is instructed to collect information from an assigned number, or quota, of individuals in each of several groups—the groups being specified as to age, sex, income, or other characteristic—much like the strata in stratified sampling. Subject to these controls, however, the individuals selected in each group are left to the interviewer's choice rather than being determined by probability methods.

For example, the McGraw-Hill Publishing Company, Inc., carries out numerous attitude surveys among executives who read industrial magazines, to aid the McGraw-Hill management in the conduct of its own publications. Readers are asked what journals and other sources of information they use, what topics interest them most, and similar questions. Interviews are conducted by "resident investigators"—mostly women living in the survey area. In one such survey, covering chemical process industries in 1960, the company's Research Department had a complete list of plants but no comprehensive list of individual executives. A stratified, systematic sample of plants was first selected in each area. Given this list, the investigator was instructed to locate and interview a specified number of engineers, production men, etc., who had some influence on the company's purchasing policy. The investigator would typically interview one to three engineers, etc., in each plant, and continue to other plants in the area until her quota was completed. This quota method is considered by the company to be the only feasible way of conducting an industrial survey when the population of respondents cannot be identified.

Quota sampling is popular in market surveys and public opinion polls because it is cheaper per elementary sample unit than random sampling and, when carefully controlled, has many of the advantages of stratified random sampling. However, it is subject to two important sources of error: (1) the quotas set for the interviewer represent a rather crude stratification plan for the population, being based on only a few broad criteria, such as age (young, middle-aged, or old) and income (low-, middle-, or high-income); (2) since the interviewer is free to select individuals within a quota, he may choose people in convenient locations who may not be typical of the class of the population they have been chosen to represent. For example, in a survey of the number of young children by households, the method of interviewing women who happen to be at home would be apt to yield a sample with too large a proportion of women with young children, because such women are more likely to be at home during the hours in which the interviewing is done than other women are. Interviewers therefore must be carefully trained to avoid such pitfalls.[6]

Quota sampling has been popular in pre-election polls since 1936 when quota samples yielded results far superior to those of a much larger mail questionnaire conducted by the *Literary Digest*. The larger poll was in error mainly because the sample was taken from telephone books and automobile registration lists, so that it contained too many voters from higher-income groups.

Most presidential pre-election polls have been successful since then, except in 1948, when they predicted a victory for Dewey rather than Truman. It is not certain to what extent this error is attributable to the quota sampling methods used or to other factors, such as improper interviewing techniques, the difference between what voters say and how they vote, or the shift of voters toward Truman after the pre-election polls closed. In 1960, most polls correctly predicted the close Kennedy victory. The Gallup Poll, for example, forecast his

---

[6] Sometimes the sample is chosen so that the *average* age, income, or other pertinent characteristic of the individuals selected is equal to the average for the population. This is sometimes called "controlled" or "purposive" sampling. However, this control does not necessarily mean that the sample will be typical in other respects, such as in buying habits. Furthermore, this method is more difficult to administer than the simpler quota method, so it is used less frequently.

margin at 52 per cent of the combined Kennedy-Nixon vote, as compared with the actual figure of 50.1 per cent.

It is often argued that all large-scale surveys should be based on a probability sampling design because of the greater objectivity of random selection. On the other hand, since a much larger quota sample can be taken for the same cost as a smaller random sample, and because population lists may be unavailable, quota samples are still favored in some circumstances.

Judgment Sampling

A judgment sample is one which is selected according to someone's personal judgment. A judgment sample may be superior to a probability sample (1) in very small-scale surveys, (2) in "pilot studies" which precede major surveys, or (3) in constructing index numbers. Also, they are often less costly than probability samples. Unfortunately, however, judgment samples may be biased, and there is no objective method of determining the validity of their results.

Examples of judgment samples in small-scale surveys include the choice of a single plant (i.e., a sample of one) in which to try out a new personnel policy, or the choice of a few typical cities in which to make a market survey. A recent survey of consumer preferences for shampoo was conducted in San Jose, California, since this city was considered to be typical of the western market for this product. Such a judgment selection was probably superior to choosing a single city at random from a list of all cities in the West.

This advantage of judgment selection, however, rapidly diminishes as the size of the sample increases, because there is a steady increase in the precision of a random sample, while the bias of the investigator persists in judgment sampling.

In pilot studies, which are designed to pretest a questionnaire to be used in any large survey, emphasis is placed on detecting unforeseen difficulties, which can be overcome by revising questions, rearranging the schedule, or training interviewers. For this purpose, respondents in a pilot study are often chosen on a judgment basis in such a way as to *overrepresent* types of individuals most likely to cause difficulties.

Another type of statistical work in which judgment selection is usually preferred to random selection is that of index number construction. Consider the problem of choosing a sample of foods to serve as the basis for an index number of food prices for the next several years. There should be sample items for each of several broad classes of food, such as meats and cereals. These items should be susceptible of precise description as to grade, weight, etc., in order that prices will be comparable from period to period. They should also be typical of their classes with respect to price movements and they should have some importance in themselves. In view of these and other similar difficulties, items used in the construction of index numbers are usually chosen according to the judgment of experts in the field. Probability selection in such cases is applied only to classes in which there are a great many items of the same order of importance.

Accordingly, judgment selection is recommended for samples which are too small for the advantages of more objective methods, for pilot studies in which certain types of bias may actually be desirable, and for the selection of components in index numbers. Objective methods of selection, however, are necessary to attain a high degree of reliability in most large samples.

RECURRENT SURVEYS AND PANELS

Certain types of surveys are repeated regularly in order to reveal *changes* in the population from time to time. In these cases, it is especially important that the samples in successive surveys should be comparable. Two examples will be described: employment surveys and consumer panels.

Employment Surveys

Certain data on employment can be obtained on a complete coverage basis; for example, employers report the number of their employees on social security tax reports made to the Bureau of Old Age and Survivors Insurance. Unemployment data, on the other hand, must be collected on a sample basis. The Bureau of the Census therefore makes monthly surveys of the labor force designed to collect unemployment statistics from a stratified random sample of individuals or households. Because of the lack of comparable data on a complete coverage basis, the objectivity associated with random sampling is especially important. At the same time, the respondents in successive surveys must be as comparable as possible. To satisfy both of these partially conflicting criteria, the Bureau of the Census retains each member of its sample for more than one survey, but in each survey it drops some of the respondents and replaces them with others selected at random from the same stratum. Thus, some of the advantages of comparability of an unchanging sample are retained, while biases which might develop through the effects of repeated questioning are minimized.

The employment data reported to the Bureau of Old Age and Survivors Insurance are reasonably complete, but the reports are not available for several months because of the processing time required. In order to get more up-to-date estimates of employment, therefore, the Bureau of Labor Statistics conducts a sample survey of a large number of companies each month, and applies the resulting percentage changes to the complete Bureau of Old Age and Survivors Insurance data available for an earlier month. The companies used in the Bureau of Labor Statistics sample must be identical from month to month for comparability. Unlike the census surveys of the labor force, however, it is unnecessary to drop some companies each month, since company reports are not subject to the biases that individuals may develop under repeated questioning.

Consumer Panels

A number of market research agencies maintain panels of consumers or retail outlets which report periodically. The sampling units may be selected originally by whichever method seems appropriate. The advantages of a practically unchanging sample are especially important in estimating short-run changes in market conditions. A typical large advertising agency maintains a carefully selected "consumer panel" whose members report all purchases of stated types of items every month, including prices, brand names, reasons for changing brands, and the like.

A. C. Nielsen Company uses a practically unchanging sample of consumers in its method of rating television programs by "Audimeters" attached to 1,200 television sets throughout the country; whereas Trendex uses a changing sample, since its interviewers dial telephone numbers at random to determine what TV programs are being watched. The sampling techniques of the rating services have such a powerful effect on television programming that they were scrutinized in detail by the Senate Committee on Interstate and Foreign Commerce in 1958.

Information supplied by a well-selected consumer panel is probably more useful in market research surveys than that collected from successive samples selected anew for each survey. Disadvantages arise, however, because some consumers are unable or unwilling to report their purchases in the detail required, so that those who agree to be panel members may not be typical of all consumers in their market behavior. Furthermore, it is possible that keeping detailed records and reporting the results may change the market behavior of a consumer after he has served on the panel for a while.

SUMMARY

Information obtained from samples is indispensable in modern business and economic research. It is important, therefore, to plan sample surveys in such a way as to obtain the desired information with maximum precision and minimum cost of time and effort.

Probability sampling includes all methods (such as simple random sampling, stratified random sampling, systematic selection, and cluster sampling) in which there is a known probability of being selected for each individual in the population. Nonprobability sampling includes all other methods, such as quota and judgment sampling. Probability sampling methods have a basic advantage in that the precision of their results can be measured objectively, and compared as between different sample designs. This is especially important in very large samples.

A *simple random sample* of n units is one selected from the population in such a way that each combination of n units has an *equal* probability of being selected. A table of random numbers is usually used to select items at random.

A *stratified random sample* is one in which the population is divided into fairly uniform groups, or strata. Then a random sample is drawn from each selected stratum. Whenever each stratum is more homogeneous than the population as a whole, a stratified sample yields more precise results than does a simple random sample of the same size. In case either the unit sampling cost or the variability within one stratum differs greatly from that of another, it is usually advantageous to use *nonproportional sampling,* in which the sample contains different proportions of the various strata than the population does. In this case each stratum average or other measure should be weighted in proportion to the size of the stratum in the population.

Systematic sampling is the process of taking observations at equal intervals in a list. When nearby parts of a population are alike, systematic sampling with a random start is superior to simple random sampling, in spacing the sampling units more evenly over the whole population.

Cluster sampling involves (1) selecting groups or clusters as primary sampling units; (2) taking a census or sample of "elementary sampling units" within these groups. Cluster sampling is called *area sampling* when the cluster falls in some geographic division, such as a city block. A cluster sample yields less precise results than a simple random sample of the same size, but the cost may be much less. The clusters are usually chosen by systematic selection from a map on which areas are numbered by *serpentine* order.

Nonprobability sampling (including quota sampling and judgment selection) is the selection of a sample according to personal choice, expert judgment, or under conditions where lack of data prevents a probability selection. It is sometimes recommended when probability sampling is not feasible.

In *quota sampling* the investigator may choose the respondents from a quota, or assigned number of individuals in each designated class. It is cheaper per unit than stratified random sampling, and is popular in market surveys and public opinion polls, despite the serious pitfalls inherent in this method.

Judgment sampling is the selection of a sample based on expert judgment. It is recommended for surveys in which the sample is very small, for pilot studies preceding larger surveys, and for most economic index numbers.

Recurrent surveys and consumer panels emphasize the *change* in important economic indicators from one survey to the next. Panel members are usually retained for more than one survey so that their reports will be comparable from time to time; but the membership must be changed gradually so that consumer behavior will not be affected by continued reporting on the panel.

PROBLEMS

1. Comment on the following statements:
    a) "Sampling errors are due to improper methods of selecting a sample."
    b) "Survey results may be made as accurate as necessary by increasing the size of the sample."
    c) "A complete census is always preferable to a sample, if time and money permit."
    d) "Probability sampling should be used in all large-scale surveys, to obtain valid results."
2. Distinguish between:
    a) Probability sampling and nonprobability sampling.
    b) Probability sampling and simple random sampling.
    c) Stratified systematic sampling and quota sampling.
    d) Proportional and nonproportional sampling in stratified samples.
    e) Primary and elementary sampling units in cluster sampling.

3. You wish to conduct a survey of students in a university to determine which facilities they prefer (e.g., swimming pool, bowling alley, cafeteria) in a new student union building that is being planned. Compare the advantages of each of the three pairs of sampling methods in Problems 2(*a*), 2(*c*), and 2(*d*) above, for this purpose.

4. As sponsor for a television program broadcast throughout the Chicago metropolitan area, you wish to compare the audience of your program with that of two competing programs at the same hour (Saturday, 8–9 P.M.). Judging results in terms of accuracy for a given amount of time and effort, which of the four methods described in Chapter 3, page 42 (i.e., American Research Bureau, *Pulse, Trendex,* and A. C. Nielsen), should be preferable and what improvements, if any, would you suggest?

5. Time, Inc., made a survey of college graduates to determine their success and satisfaction in life, as related to their education record, and various other characteristics that would aid *Time* in analyzing its readership. Using lists supplied by colleges, *Time* sent questionnaires to all 15,700 graduates of classes 1884 through 1947 whose names began with "Fa" (Farley, Farmer, etc.). Over 9,500 replies were received.
   a) What method of sample selection is this?
   b) What sources of error might distort the results?
   c) Suggest another method of selecting a sample of this size, that seems preferable to you, and show why this method should reduce the errors of response without greatly increasing the cost of the survey.

6. Each student is to select a sample of 25 values of a quantitative variable and compute the average by adding the values and dividing the sum by 25. To insure comparability of results obtained by the various members, the class should agree on choice of variable and method of selection to be used. Problems to be considered include:
   a) Are the data readily available?
   b) If values are recorded on cards, might the cards be shuffled to arrange them in random order?
   c) Are the values listed and numbered in order so as to facilitate selection by means of a table of random numbers?
   d) Would systematic selection be effective?
   e) What strata might be constructed for stratified sampling?

7. As a distributor of major household appliances, you wish to survey the potential market for new appliances in your town by interviewing a sample of householders. Plan a cluster sample of the area as follows:
   a) Secure an up-to-date map of the town, or one district of a larger city.
   b) Number the blocks, or equivalent areas, in serpentine fashion so as to follow a sequence of blocks having about the same household incomes.
   c) Choose a systematic sample, with random start, of 20 blocks on this map.
   d) Visit the tenth block selected (as an example) and list all house or apartment numbers around the block.

e) Select a random sample of six houses or apartments from this block, using a table of random numbers.

f) Comment briefly on the validity of this procedure for the problem at hand.

SELECTED READINGS

HANSEN, M. H.; HURWITZ, W. N.; and MADOW, W. G. *Sample Survey Methods and Theory.* New York: John Wiley & Sons, Inc., 1953.

Volume I is an authoritative and thorough treatment of sampling methods and applications.

KENDALL, M. G., and BUCKLAND, W. R. *A Dictionary of Statistical Terms.* New York: Hafner Publishing Co., 1957.

Provides definitions of the many terms used in the sampling field.

LORIE, J. H., and ROBERTS, V. H. *Basic Methods of Marketing Research.* New York: McGraw-Hill Book Co., Inc., 1951.

Contains much information in elementary language on methods of selecting samples.

PARTEN, MILDRED. *Surveys, Polls, and Samples: Practical Procedures.* New York: Harper & Bros., 1950.

Deals with practical problems of sample surveys. Sampling principles are discussed in chapters 4 and 7–9.

RAND CORPORATION. *A Million Random Digits with 100,000 Normal Deviates.* Glencoe, Ill.: The Free Press, 1955.

The first book "written" by an electronic calculator, this chaotic compilation contains the largest published list of random numbers, for use in drawing random samples.

RICHMOND, SAMUEL B. *Principles of Statistical Analysis.* 2d ed. New York: The Ronald Press Co., 1964.

Chapter 13 presents a brief but scholarly survey of basic sampling procedures.

TIPPETT, L. H. C. *Statistics.* 2d ed. London and New York: Oxford University Press, 1956.

Chapter 6 presents good nontechnical material on selecting samples.

YULE, G. U., and KENDALL, M. G. *An Introduction to the Theory of Statistics.* 14th ed., London: Griffin & Co., Ltd., 1950.

Chapter 16, "Preliminary Notions on Sampling," is an interesting discussion of fundamental concepts, with definitions of various methods of selection.

5. ACCURACY OF ECONOMIC DATA; RATIOS

THE LAST three chapters have covered the problems of *collecting* information. Before proceeding with the analysis and presentation of data, it is desirable to discuss certain fundamental concepts in the use of numbers.

A basic knowledge of arithmetic and elementary algebra is essential for work in statistics. Those who are rusty in these fields should review some text such as Helen M. Walker's excellent self-teaching manual, *Mathematics Essential for Elementary Statistics* (rev. ed.; New York: Henry Holt & Co., Inc., 1951), especially Part I. Higher mathematics, however, is not needed in most basic statistical operations.

This chapter covers two elementary topics of especial importance in economic and business statistics. These are: (1) methods of determining the accuracy of economic data and (2) the construction and interpretation of statistical ratios.

ACCURACY OF ECONOMIC DATA

The question of how many figures shall be retained in the result of a computation is particularly important in statistical work because many of the data employed are to some degree approximate. The economic analyst may deal with figures in the millions, but he must realize that only the first three or four figures are ordinarily significant. For example, Sears, Roebuck & Company on January 31, 1964 reported total assets of $3,668,621,951; but with all the difficulties of evaluating securities, real estate, and other accounts, only about four figures—3,669 millions—could be considered meaningful in appraising the company's balance sheet. The following rules for rounding off large numbers, therefore, will not only save labor in eliminating nonsignificant figures from calculations but will also safeguard one against the error of assuming that figures are accurate just because they contain many digits.

Rounding Off Numbers

Meaning. Precision work in a machine shop is seldom more accurate than to 1 part in 1,000. If the statistician dealing with economic data can achieve the same degree of accuracy as the machinist, the results will be amply satisfactory. Let us examine the meaning of data accurate to 1 part in 1,000. The average weekly earnings of factory workers in March 1961, according to the U.S. Department of Labor, was $90.71. This figure is an average obtained by dividing total weekly payrolls by number of workers employed, and it means that the result of the division was somewhere between $90.705 and $90.715. That is, the figure $90.71 is accurate to within ½ cent, or 1 part in 18,142.

This example illustrates the general principle that the rounding error in any figure quoted to four digits is not more than 1 part in 2,000; that is, the error in rounding off any figure to four places will be between ½ part in 1,000 and ½ part in 9,999. Hence, all the precision that is needed in most statistical work can be provided by maintaining accuracy to four digits, regardless of the relation of the four digits to the position of the decimal point.

Significant Figures. The digits that show the extent to which a number is accurate are called significant figures. The zeros used only to fix the position of the decimal point are not considered significant. All other zeros, and all digits other than zero, are significant. Thus, the number 108,000,000 has only three significant figures unless it is known from the surrounding circumstances that the zeros are accurate. The actual amount represented may be anything between 107,500,000 and 108,500,000, and the final zeros are not significant.

Likewise in a number less than one, zeros immediately following the decimal point are not significant. For example, 0.00042 has two significant figures, but 0.000420 has three significant figures because the final zero should be taken to mean that the operation was carried to three digits and the third one was found to be zero.

Method of Rounding Off. Whenever a reduction in the number of significant figures is desired, some consistent method of rounding off should be followed. The following rules are recommended:

1. When a number greater than five is dropped, increase the preceding digit by one.

2. When a number less than five is dropped, leave the preceding digit unchanged.

3. When the exact number five is dropped, increase the preceding digit by one if it is an odd number but leave it unchanged if it is an even number. That is, the rounded number is always even. This rule prevents cumulative errors in addition.

Examples (assuming four significant figures):

	Given Number	Rounded Number[1]
1.	1,267.56	1,268
2.	8,762.18	8,762
3.	5,863.50	5,864
4.	5,862.50	5,862

Counting and Measurement

Statistical data may be of two kinds: (1) those in which the units are counted and (2) those in which the units are measured. For example, the value of world exports in 1961 as reported by the Statistical Office of the United Nations was $133,150,000,000. The number of countries included in the report was an exact count, and any computations based upon it would not be subject to error. The value of exports, however, was obtained by totaling the reports of the several countries after converting the different monetary units to dollars. Owing to inaccuracies of reporting within individual countries, variations in methods of valuing exports, and the complication of applying exchange ratios to different monetary units, the figure for value of exports is at best only an approximation.

Measurement data, then, are subject to various errors of estimation. Sample data, as cited below, are also of this type. Even large counted numbers may be in error, as in the Census of Population, where some individuals may be overlooked in counting the total population of the country. Hence, in dealing with factual data, the first question that should be asked is: How accurate are the figures? Sometimes this question is answered specifically.

For example, in "Marital Status and Family Status: March 1960," the Bureau of the Census says:[2]

---

[1] Rounded numbers should be expressed in thousands, millions, or billions rather than in intermediate sized units. Thus 12,416,736 could be stated as 12,417 thousands if it were accurate to five digits; as 12.42 millions if it were accurate to four digits; or as 12.4 millions if it were accurate to three digits.

[2] *Current Population Reports—Population Characteristics*, November 2, 1960, pp. 6–7.

Since the estimates are based on a sample, they may differ somewhat from the figures that would have been obtained if a complete census had been taken . . . [for example, in March 1960] there were an estimated 1,023,000 rural-farm males from 45 to 54 years of age . . . The chances are about 68 out of 100 that the difference between a complete census count of the number of rural-farm males 45 to 54 years old would have differed from the estimate derived from the sample by less than 48,000.

This is followed by a table giving the sampling error for other sizes of estimate.

It is an excellent rule for the business analyst, similarly, to approximate the degree of error in any estimates he makes or uses, so that he may avoid being misled by unreliable data.

More commonly the error to be expected is not indicated. Thus the user of the data is left to judge the degree of accuracy which can properly be attributed to them. Judgments of this sort must be based upon a knowledge of the method used in obtaining the data and a background of information concerning the source. For example, the *Survey of Current Business* in March 1964 reported that the value of new building construction started in February 1964 was $4,272 million. This might appear to be an exact figure, but actually it represents estimates by more than a dozen collection agencies derived from hundreds of different sources of varying reliability. "Construction takes place on widely scattered sites and is carried on by tens of thousands of small contractors and by persons doing their own building and repair work,"[3] so that the above figure may be considerably in error.

These examples indicate the extent to which a knowledge of methods of collection is necessary in understanding the accuracy of data. False accuracy is common in published data, but it causes little difficulty so long as the background of the data is sufficiently familiar for users to be aware that more significant figures have been retained than is warranted.

Significant Figures in Computation

The emphasis up to this point has been on the number of significant digits to retain in figures pertaining to a single subject. We are now ready to develop methods of dealing with rounded numbers in performing computations. The rules applicable to each of the four fundamental operations will be explained in order.[4]

---

[3] F. C. Mills and C. D. Long, *The Statistical Agencies of the Federal Government* (New York: National Bureau of Economic Research, Inc., 1949), p. 60 and Chart 3.

[4] These rules are not applicable to accounting, where accuracy must be maintained to the nearest cent regardless of the number of significant digits retained in a particular figure.

In Addition. The total should include no more decimal places than the least accurate of the numbers added. In the example below, the land area of Asia is only reported to the nearest 100,000 square miles; so the total of all three continents is only correct to the same degree, and should be so indicated.

	Area in Square Miles
Europe	3,769,107
Africa	12,563,807
Asia	17,300,000
Total (incorrect)	33,632,914
Rounded total (correct)	33,600,000

SOURCE: *World Almanac, 1950,* p. 218.

In Subtraction. The rules for subtraction are the same as those for addition. There is a further pitfall in subtraction, however: a relatively small error in two large figures may produce a large percentage error in the difference. For example, *The Economic Report of the President* for January 1959 (p. 43) estimates total government receipts for the fiscal year 1960 at $77.1 billion and expenditures at $77.0 billion, leaving a surplus of $0.1 billion. However, if either of the first two figures is in error only $0.1 billion, or about ⅛ of 1 per cent, the corrected surplus will be 100 per cent above or below the preliminary estimate.

Similarly, the number of unemployed persons in the nation is sometimes estimated by subtracting the number employed from the total civilian "labor force" of those available for jobs. But an error of only 1½ per cent in each of these estimates might result in a 100 per cent error in the estimate of unemployment, as shown by the following figures:

Estimates of	Millions of Persons	Possible Error
Labor force	70 ± 1	1½ per cent
Employment	68 ± 1	1½ per cent
Unemployment	2 ± 2	100 per cent

This simple arithmetic accounts for the wide errors that frequently occur in estimates of unemployment, personal savings, net profits in corporate financial statements, and similar values obtained by the "residual" method.

In Multiplication. The product of two numbers has no more significant figures than the least number of significant figures in the numbers themselves. For example, in March 1961 there were 14,492 thousand factory workers, with average weekly earnings of $90.71. Total weekly earnings might then be estimated as the product, or $1,405,-279,320, a result which appears to have nine significant figures. But average earnings are only correct to four places. Therefore, total earnings should be stated as $1,405 million or $1,405,000,000. The reason for this approximation will be apparent from the two following computations, which show the different values that this product may take when the last significant figure of each number is given its maximum and minimum value.

	Minimum	*Maximum*
Workers..................	15,491,500	15,492,500
Average earnings...........	$90.705	$90.715
Total earnings.............	$1,405,156,508	$1,405,402,138

These products differ in the fifth significant figure; so nothing beyond the fourth figure is of any value.

In Division. The similar rule for division is: There should be no more significant figures in the quotient than the least number which appears in either the dividend or the divisor. Thus, $491,682 \div 72,000 = 6.8$. As another example, *Economic Indicators* reports net farm income at $11.8 billion in 1959, with an estimated 4.6 million farms, so that net income per farm (the quotient) is $2,565. However, if the number of farms is significant to only two figures, then only the first two figures in net income per farm are significant.

Squares and square roots, as special cases of multiplication and division, should contain no more significant figures than the original number. Thus, $(26.8)^2 = 718$, and $\sqrt{26.8} = 5.18$.

RATIOS

The ratio is an extremely useful and simple device for comparing one figure with another. Comparisons are often more significant than absolute values. Thus, if a company reports net profits of $10 million for the past year, this figure is not so meaningful in itself as a comparison with a related figure, such as a report that net profits were 5 per cent above the preceding year's. This section describes how to construct ratios that are accurate and meaningful for economic analysis, and how to interpret them.

The ratio of one number to another is a fraction in which the first number is the numerator and the second number is the denominator, or *base*. In other words, the ratio is obtained by dividing the first number by the second. Thus, the national debt on June 30, 1959 was reported as $1,607 per capita. The numerator of this ratio is $284.7 billion, the amount of the national debt, and the denominator is 177.1 million, the estimated population on that date.

Perhaps the simplest type of ratio is that in which the numerator and the denominator are expressed in the same units. Thus, if the net profits of a company are $12 million and sales are $100 million, the ratio of net profits to sales is found to be .12 or 12 per cent by dividing one dollar figure by another.

Various terms are used for ratios in which the terms are measured in different kinds of units. Thus, the birth *rate* is the number of births per thousand population; *density* of population is the number of persons in a region divided by its area; *per capita* national debt is the ratio of total debt to the number of persons in the country.

It is important to present a statistical ratio in such a way that the reader understands exactly what quantities are being compared, particularly when the units of the two terms of a ratio are different. When ratios are listed in a table, the exact units of both numerator and denominator should be indicated, usually in titles, or headings of rows and columns.

Selecting the Numerator and Base

The quantities selected for a statistical ratio should be related to each other in such a way that their ratio will be most meaningful for the problem at hand. Often, one or both of the quantities can be adjusted, or refined, so as to exclude any extraneous factors that would obscure the direct relationship between them. For example, the ratio "farm income per acre" in a given state would be more meaningful if the denominator were adjusted to exclude forests, deserts, and other non-farm land, to provide the ratio "farm income per acre of *arable* land."

In the same way, safety departments of manufacturing plants get an accident rate for each department by taking the ratio of employees injured to total number of operating employees, excluding office workers. Both the numerator and denominator of each departmental ratio are adjusted further in order to facilitate the study of accidents. The resulting ratio, known as the accident severity rate, is the number of days' work lost through accidents[5] divided by the number of equivalent full-time days worked,[6] per week, month, or year.

---

[5] The number of days' work lost can be counted for temporary accidents but not for death, permanent disability, or permanent impairment. Consequently standards have been established for each type of accident. Thus, according to one standard, 6,000 days are allowed for death, 4,000 days for loss of an arm, 1,200 days for loss of a thumb and one finger, etc., U.S. Bureau of Labor Statistics Bulletin No. 234, *The Safety Movement in the Iron and Steel Industry*, p. 278.

[6] The number of equivalent full-time days worked is obtained by dividing the total number of man-hours worked during a given period by the standard working hours per day.

The study of deaths in automobile accidents furnishes another example of the need for refining the figures used in computing ratios. Table 5-1, row 1, shows that the number of persons killed in motor vehicle accidents increased 6 per cent between 1950 and 1958. These figures suggest that the "automobile menace" is increasing. The increase may be due to the growth of population, however, so the number of deaths per 100,000 population has been computed, as shown in row 2. This ratio has *decreased* by 7 per cent. However, accidents are related more directly to the number of motor vehicles, which have increased more rapidly than the total population. The number of deaths per 100,000 motor vehicles, therefore, is shown in row 3. Now we see

Table 5-1

FATALITIES IN MOTOR VEHICLE ACCIDENTS, 1950 AND 1958

	1950	1958	Per Cent Change
1. Persons killed in motor vehicle accidents.	34,763	37,000	+6
2. Deaths per 100,000 population.	23.0	21.4	−7
3. Deaths per 10,000 motor vehicles.	7.1	5.4	−24
4. Deaths per 100,000,000 vehicle-miles.	7.6	5.6	−26

SOURCE: National Safety Council, *Accident Facts, 1959*, p. 59.

a 24 per cent decrease in this refined ratio. Finally, traffic deaths are related still more specifically to the number of vehicle-miles driven, and the average car was driven more miles in 1958 than in 1950. The number of deaths per 100,000,000 vehicle-miles is shown in row 4. The decrease is now 26 per cent! The more refined ratio therefore shows a much greater gain in safety, when the increased number of cars and mileage driven are taken into account, than when only the crude per capita ratio was used.

Which Item to Choose as Base

The base or denominator of a statistical ratio is always a standard with which the numerator is being compared. The numerator is the quantity on which the inquiry is focused; the denominator provides the basis for comparison. The following rules may be useful in selecting the base:

1. In comparing a part and the whole, the whole is always the base. Example: net profits to sales ratio = net profits ÷ sales.

2. In time comparisons of like items, the prior event is almost always taken as the base. Example: this year's sales as a per cent of last year's.

3. In comparing a cause and effect or an independent event with one at least partly dependent on it, the cause or the independent item is nearly always the base. Example: price-earnings ratio of a common stock = price ÷ earnings. (Exception: stock yield = dividend ÷ price.)

When either of two items is equally logical as a base, custom often determines the choice. Example: rate of inventory turnover = sales ÷ inventory.

The Number of Units in the Base. The base may be expressed as a single unit, 100 units, or some other multiple of ten, depending on which is customary, or most effective. Thus, the national debt of $1,607 per capita is expressed in terms of *one* denominator unit, or one person; an interest rate of 4 per cent means four dollars for every *hundred* dollars deposited; whereas the death rate may be reported as 9.0 per *thousand*. These cases are discussed below.

1. There are many examples in which the base of a ratio is expressed as a single unit. All per capita ratios use one person as the unit of the base. In agriculture, we use production per acre; in airlines, revenue per passenger-mile; in manufacturing, output per man-hour.

2. Most ratios used in statistics are expressed in terms of *per cents*. Thus we have a 4 per cent decrease in grocery prices, or a number of telephones in operation which is 105 per cent of the number a year ago. It is easier to picture 105 telephones in use now for every 100 a year ago than to visualize a fractional telephone in saying there are 1.05 telephones in use now for every *one* then. In each case the number stated as a per cent indicates how many numerator units there are for every hundred base units. Per cents are used only to compare identical units, however; comparisons of unlike quantities are expressed per base unit, such as gasoline consumption per 100 miles.

3. Any other multiple of ten may be used in the base. As shown in Table 5–1, the National Safety Council reports motor vehicle deaths per 10,000 motor vehicles, per 100,000 population, and per 100,000,-000 vehicle-miles. The larger numbers are used as a base so that the numerator can be reported mainly as a whole number rather than as decimal fractions.

Cautions in the Use of Ratios

Many of the errors in the use of ratios spring from failure to express the meaning of ratios correctly. Thus the value of construction contracts awarded in March 1961 was 142 per cent as great as in the previous month, or it might be said that construction was 42 per cent greater than in the previous month, but it would be incorrect to say that construction was 142 per cent greater. Similarly, an advertisement reads:

"In January 1955, there were only 330 [—Rent-a-Car] Offices. Today we opened our 1000th station—a growth of over 300% . . ." The increase from 330 to 1,000 was 670, a growth of only 203 per cent!

The following newspaper headline is another example of a careless statement: "Department Store Sales Jump Twelve Per Cent in August." Careful reading of the article discloses that the 12 per cent represented an increase over the sales in August of the preceding year and not from the preceding month of July as would be expected from the headline. A more explicit headline would read, "Department Store Sales in August Up Twelve Per Cent Over a Year Ago."

A further error in the use of per cents should be noted. The difference between two per cents, often called "percentage points," must not be interpreted as a per cent change. Thus, it is incorrectly stated that "average weekly earnings of factory workers in 1955 were 41 per cent above the 1948 level, but in May 1957, they had risen to 51 per cent, a 10 per cent increase." These are both per cents of the same base period, the 1948 level, but the per cent change is obtained by dividing the increase of 10 percentage points by the base level of 141, an increase of 7 per cent, not 10 per cent.

Especial care must be taken to distinguish between percentage difference and percentage relation in dealing with large differences. Thus, if two machines produce 40 and 320 gears, respectively, the production of the second machine is eight times as great, or 800 per cent as great as that of the first machine, but the production of the second machine is 700 per cent greater than that of the first. If the second machine is used as the base in the comparison, the production of the first machine is only 12½ per cent as great as that of the second machine, or 87½ per cent less than that of the second.

As has already been indicated, the base item in time ratios is practically always the earlier period. Failure to observe this rule leads to still further confusion in the expression of percentage increase or decrease, as illustrated in the following newspaper headline: "Liquor Prices Cut 200 Per Cent in Price War." Whatever the former price may have been, however, a cut of 100 per cent would reduce it to zero. Hence, any greater decline would mean that the retailers were paying the purchasers to take their wares! A decrease of a positive value can never exceed 100 per cent. What probably happened was that liquor formerly selling at $6.00 per quart was cut $4.00 and placed on sale at

$2.00. Dividing $4.00 by $2.00, the later price, gives 200 per cent; but this is the percentage by which the past exceeded the present, not the percentage decrease. The correct practice would have been to use the original price as the base of the ratio. That is, the cut was $4.00 ÷ $6.00 = 66⅔ per cent.

Finally, ratios should not be used if the original number used as base is very small. The report that one fourth of the bank tellers in a town have been indicted for embezzlement would be misleading if there were only four tellers to begin with. Similarly, a 1,000 per cent increase in profits over last year would hardly be significant if last year's profits totaled one dollar.

Importance of Including Original Data

Whenever possible, the data from which ratios have been derived should be shown with the ratios. The reader is rightly skeptical in accepting any statement of relationships that he cannot verify by making the computation himself. Table 5–2 contains a number of errors (in-

Table 5–2

OWNERSHIP OF U.S. GOVERNMENT SECURITIES, 1950 AND 1957
(Illustration of Errors)

Held by	January, 1950 Par Value in Billions	January, 1950 % of Total	March, 1957 Par Value in Billions	March, 1957 % of Total
U.S. government agencies and trust funds	$ 39.0	15.1	$ 5.42*	19.7
Banks	96.9	73.7†	89.4	32.5
Public	121.0	47.2	131.5	47.8
Totals	$ 56.9‡	100.0	$275.1	100.0

* Should read 54.2.
† Should read 37.7.
‡ Should read 256.9.

serted for purposes of illustration), but because the original data are also given, it is possible for the reader to detect the errors and to correct them, as well as to make his own interpretation.

Three of the errors in Table 5–2 are typographical, such as may often be found as a result of careless proofreading. First, the decimal point has been misplaced in the figure 5.42 for U.S. government holdings of securities in 1957. This may be detected either by checking the column total or by noting the large per cent of total figure. The second error is one of transposition in the per cent of total securities held by banks in 1950. In this case it is evident that since $121 billion is only 47.2 per cent of the total, $96.9 billion must be less than 73.7 per cent. The error may also be discovered by adding the per cent of total column, which, as printed, totals 136 instead of 100 per cent. The third error is that of omission in the total of the securities outstanding in 1950. Since the total of $56.9 billion is smaller than two of its components, the presence of the original data makes the error quite evident. In each of these cases the original data and the per cents provide a check on each other. When the per cents or ratios alone are given, it is impossible to determine where the error lies.

Two other minor faults in the table should be noted. The first is the "% of Total" heading, which is poor usage. It should be "Per Cent of Total." The second is the comparison of January figures in 1950 with March figures in 1957. If the data are subject to any seasonal influence, the figures for March 1950 would be more comparable with those of March 1957.

Sometimes additional relationships can be derived from a given set of data. If the original data are not shown, the reader is prevented from working out ratios which may be of more interest to him than those selected by the author.

SUMMARY

This chapter covers (1) the accuracy of statistical data and (2) ratios. These subjects are necessary prerequisites for further statistical work.

1. The accuracy of figures must always be considered. Statistical data are seldom accurate to more than three or four significant figures, so longer numbers should ordinarily be rounded off. The accuracy of any figure can be estimated by studying the method of collection.

The number of significant figures in computations is governed by the minimum number of significant figures in the data being processed. In subtraction, however, small errors in the original figures may produce a much larger error in the difference.

2. A statistical ratio is the quotient of two related values. The base, or denominator, is chosen as the standard with which the numerator is compared, and should be directly comparable with it.

Ratios should be refined, if possible, by adjusting the numerator or denominator to eliminate any extraneous factors obscuring their relationship. The base may be expressed in any convenient multiple of ten units, although the per cent form is most common.

BUSINESS AND ECONOMIC STATISTICS [Ch. 5

Ratios must be interpreted with care, particularly in distinguishing per cent change from the difference between two per cents. Ratios in tables should be accompanied by the original data to aid in checking figures and in making other comparisons.

PROBLEMS

1. Round each of the following numbers to (*a*) four significant figures and (*b*) three significant figures:

   (1) 395.890   (5) 547,550
   (2) 5,064.1   (6) 6,274.78
   (3) 75.682   (7) 594,681
   (4) 10,072   (8) 87.463

2. How many figures would you expect to be accurate in each of the following? Give reasons for your answer in each case. All examples were taken from the *Statistical Abstract of the United States, 1957.*
   a) The population of the United States was enumerated on April 1, 1950 as 150,697,361 persons.
   b) The population of the United States on March 1, 1957 was estimated by the Bureau of the Census as 170,270,000 persons.
   c) The Office of Education reports the enrollment in colleges, universities, and professional schools in 1954 as 2,514,712 students.
   d) The total assets of all member banks of the Federal Reserve System on December 31, 1956 were $52,909,812,000.
   e) The Department of Commerce estimates from a sample survey that the total retail sales of the United States in 1956 amounted to $191,471,-000,000.

3. Find the value of a wheat crop estimated at 3,500 bushels at a probable price of $2.16⅞ per bushel. Express the result to the correct number of significant figures.

4. For the year ended January 31, 1959, Sears, Roebuck & Company reported income before federal income taxes of $337,388,473, less provision for federal income taxes of $171,600,000, equals net income of $165,788,473, or $2.21 per share of stock. Express to the correct number of significant figures: (*a*) net income and (*b*) the estimated number of shares outstanding.

5. For each of the following pairs of items, compute the ratio and (1) state the relation in words, (2) give reasons for selecting the item you used as the base, (3) explain how the numerator and denominator are specifically related, and (4) justify the number of units used in the base. All figures are United States totals.
   a) Total steel produced, 1956 (short tons) 115,216,149
       Steel rails produced, 1956 (short tons) 1,301,369

b) Number of insured commercial banks reporting consumer installment paper in their portfolios, July 31, 1957 (approximate) 13,000
Amount of consumer installment loans held by these banks $12,492,000,000
c) Average weekly wage of steelworkers, 1949 .... $63.04
             1956 .... $101.83
d) Population, July 1, 1956 168,174,000
Estimated number of deaths from diseases of the heart, 1956 604,910

6. Given the following information concerning federal credit unions in 1956:

Area	Number of Associations	Thousands of Members	Loans Made during Year Number (000)	Loans Made during Year Amount (000)
United States............	8,350	4,502	3,300	$1,580,402
Pennsylvania............	843	433	300	129,306

a) Compute whatever ratios you consider necessary to analyze these data.
b) Write a statement of your findings.

7. The Aberthaw index of building costs in 1951 was 370 per cent of the 1914 base, and in 1956 was 422 per cent of the same base. What is:
a) The difference between the 1951 and 1956 figures in percentage points?
b) The percentage relation between costs in 1951 and 1956?
c) The percentage change from 1951 to 1956?

8. Given the following:

Month	Apparel Sales	Number of Days Store Was Open
February...............	$31,872	23
March..................	33,084	26

Find the per cent change in average daily sales from February to March.

9. The following is quoted from the report of an oil well servicing company to the stockholders: "Foreign operations [in 1956] including export sales, accounted for 15% of consolidated revenue, up from 12% in 1955; and net income was even higher in proportion, one reason being that the majority of the countries have less confiscatory income tax laws than the United States." What additional data would be needed in order to determine the importance of this report?

10. What refinement would you recommend in the denominator of each of these ratios?
    a) Employees killed in airplane accidents to total number of employees of airlines.
    b) The number employed in a community to the number of persons in the community.
    c) The number of Plymouth automobiles manufactured to the total number of motor vehicles sold in the United States.

11. The following data are computed from annual reports of the United States Steel Corporation:

	1949	1956
Output per man-hour............	$4.432	$8.410
Average wage per man-hour.....	1.775	2.926

Labor leaders argue from these ratios that labor has not received a fair share of its increased productivity. What further evidence should be introduced before reaching a conclusion on this point?

SELECTED READINGS

BARLOW'S TABLES. 4th ed. New York: Chemical Publishing Co., Inc., 1952.
These tables list the squares, cubes, square roots, cube roots, and reciprocals of all integer numbers up to 12,500.

GLOVER, JAMES W. *Tables of Applied Mathematics in Finance, Insurance, Statistics.* Ann Arbor, Mich.: George Wahr, 1951.
Parts III and IV contain a variety of probability and statistical functions, together with seven-place logarithmic tables.

MORGENSTERN, OSKAR. *On the Accuracy of Economic Observations.* 2d ed. Princeton: Princeton University Press, 1963.
A penetrating analysis of the *in*accuracies of economic statistics. Many such errors are shockingly large.

PEASE, KATHERINE. *Machine Computation of Elementary Statistics.* New York: Chartwell House, Inc., 1949.
A self-teaching manual for students learning the use of Friden, Marchant, or Monroe calculating machines.

U.S. GOVERNMENT, SMALL BUSINESS ADMINISTRATION. *Ratio Analysis for Small Business.* Washington, D.C.: Superintendent of Documents, 1957.
A popular survey of principal business ratios, sources of published ratios, and their analysis and evaluation.

WALKER, HELEN M. *Mathematics Essential for Elementary Statistics.* Rev. ed. New York: Henry Holt & Co., Inc., 1951.
Part I provides a particularly useful review of those elements of arithmetic and algebra that are most needed in statistics.

6. STATISTICAL TABLES

THE COLLECTION of data has been covered in previous chapters, together with some basic numerical concepts. This chapter and the two following describe the methods of preparing data for *analysis* and *presentation* in the form of tables and charts. The facts of business must be tabulated properly before they can be clearly interpreted. As the Research Institute of America expressed it in a recent report, "Setting the record straight, getting across the story of how business really works—how it bakes and divides the pie—is just part of an enormous human relations task confronting management today, but it is one of the first and basic steps." Too often the researcher loses his audience by presenting facts in awkward or confusing form. By following the simple rules suggested in this chapter on tables and in the two following chapters on charts, it should be possible to present statistical ideas with maximum effectiveness.

TABLES VERSUS CHARTS

The first problem of presentation is: Should data be presented in the form of a table or a chart?

Tables have several advantages over charts: (1) more information can be presented, (2) exact values can be read from a table, and (3) less work is involved in preparation. On the other hand, charts have the advantages of (1) attracting attention more readily with a graphic picture and (2) showing trends and comparisons more vividly than the abstract figures in tables. Most readers are visual-minded and prefer graphs to figures. As the Chinese proverb goes, "One picture is worth a thousand words."

In many corporate records, a chart and a table are placed together so that the executive can see both the general picture and the detailed figures. Thus, in Table 6–1 the Pacific Telephone and Telegraph Company Chief Statistician's Division presents monthly net operating income and cumulative income since the first of the year in tabular form, together with two charts showing the current trend of income and the year's total to date expressed as a per cent of a year ago.

Table 6–1

PACIFIC TELEPHONE AND TELEGRAPH COMPANY
NET OPERATING INCOME, JANUARY 1956–MAY 1957
(Thousands of Dollars)

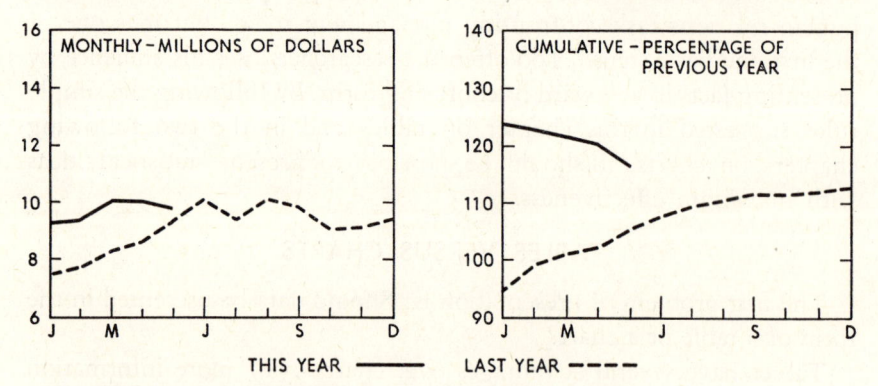

MONTH	MONTHLY 1956	MONTHLY 1957	CUMULATIVE 1956	CUMULATIVE 1957
JANUARY	7,530	9,340	7,530	9,340
FEBRUARY	7,767	9,472	15,297	18,812
MARCH	8,363	10,028	23,660	28,840
APRIL	8,622	10,003	32,282	38,843
MAY	9,459	9,759	41,741	48,602
JUNE	10,165		51,906	
JULY	9,486		61,392	
AUGUST	10,171		71,563	
SEPTEMBER	9,840		81,403	
OCTOBER	9,073		90,476	
NOVEMBER	9,122		99,598	
DECEMBER	9,473		109,071	

SOURCE: Chief Statistician's Division, Pacific Telephone and Telegraph Company.

In case there are only a few figures which can be expressed clearly in the text, neither a table nor chart may be necessary. Detailed data, however, should always be presented in a table or chart. If many figures are scattered through a written text, it becomes very confusing.

METHODS OF CLASSIFYING DATA

A statistical table is a classification of related numerical facts arranged in vertical columns and horizontal rows. Classification is the grouping of facts into classes that are distinguished by some significant characteristic. Sorting facts on one basis of classification and then on another basis is called cross classification. Tabulation is the process of recording classified data in a systematically arranged table. Thus a table is a report showing a systematic arrangement of data in keeping with a certain classification.

There are four common bases of classification: time, size, qualitative, and geographic. These are illustrated in Table 6–2, which shows the

Table 6–2

PERCENTAGE OF NONFARM FAMILIES OWNING HOMES
(Based on Survey of 2,604 Families in 1956 and 2,601 in 1955)

	1956	1955		1956	1955
All nonfarm families	57	55	D. Family money income before taxes in preceding year:		
A. Region:			Under $1,000	44	43
Northeast	52	46	$1,000–$1,999	41	45
North Central	60	59	$2,000–$2,999	50	39
South	59	58	$3,000–$3,999	46	46
West	57	60	$4,000–$4,999	56	54
			$5,000–$7,499	65	65
B. Occupation of head of family:			$7,500–$9,999	73	75
Professional and semiprofessional	60	58	$10,000 and over	80	
Managerial	64	65			
Self-employed	81	73			
Clerical and sales	54	55	E. Size of community:		
Skilled and semiskilled	58	56	Metropolitan area	49	46
Unskilled and service	34	40	Other city, 50,000 and over	46	51
Retired	69	65	Town or city, 2,500–49,999	64	56
C. Veteran status:			Town under 2,500	67	70
No veteran in family	42	43	Open country		68
One or more veterans	50	52			

SOURCE: Federal Reserve Board, "1956 Survey of Consumer Finances—Durable Goods and Housing," in *Federal Reserve Bulletin*, August 1956, p. 821.

percentage of American families owning their homes, as reported in a Federal Reserve Board Survey of Consumer Finances.

The rows showing both 1956 and 1955 data represent a *time* classification or time series. Time series may be further divided into (*a*) measurements taken at different points of time, like population, prices, or the data in Table 6–2; and (*b*) cumulative data that build up from zero in a given period, like monthly steel production or weekly retail sales. Methods specially designed for studying time series are presented in Chapters 17–19.

In sections D and E the families are classified by *size* or magnitude —in this case, by family income and by size of community. Similarly, families might be classified by number of children or by value of home owned. Size classifications will be discussed further in Chapter 9 on frequency distributions.

Classification based on *qualitative* differences is illustrated in sections B and C of the same table. Here the families are divided by occupation and by veteran status, respectively. The distinction is one of kind rather than of amount. Some of the other classifications based on qualitative differences are marital status, race, and employment status.

Finally, section A represents a *geographic* classification of families. This classification is essentially qualitative in nature, but is usually considered a distinct type. In a geographic classification, data may be listed by political subdivisions, such as states or counties, or by appropriate economic boundaries such as metropolitan areas.

REFERENCE AND SUMMARY TABLES

There are two principal types of tables, depending on the purposes for which they will be used. These are reference and summary tables. *Reference* tables are sometimes called general-purpose tables or repository tables. They are designed to present information for general use, without applying it to any particular problem. Such tables are to be found in the *Statistical Abstract of the United States,* the various censuses, and other government publications. Reference tables are frequently detailed so as to provide complete data for a variety of purposes; and they may include definitions, description of the collection process, and other information. They are not intended to be read through but are arranged for easy reference to the information they contain. Such tables are commonly found in the appendixes of business reports; their use in the body of a report should be avoided because they may be unduly cumbersome.

Summary tables are sometimes called special-purpose, derived, or text tables. They are designed to present specific figures for some particular use. These tables are usually short and appear in the body of a report to illustrate some point in the text. The tables in this chapter are of this type. Summary tables should be simple and attractive in form, to hold the reader's attention. They must be arranged so as to emphasize the most important figures presented and to point up significant comparisons.

A summary table is often abstracted from one or more reference tables. In the process of preparing a summary table from a reference table, it is often desirable to (1) select only the important figures, (2) use group totals instead of detailed data, (3) round off all numbers to three or four significant figures, (4) rearrange the data to place the most important item at the top left for emphasis, (5) place related figures next to each other for easy comparison, and (6) provide percentages, ratios, or averages to aid in summarizing and interpreting the results. This trimming and rearrangement will add greatly to the effectiveness of any summary table. Thus, Table 6–3 has been drastically condensed by the American Telephone and Telegraph Company from its detailed operating statistics, for more effective presentation to stockholders.

CONSTRUCTION OF TABLES

Certain principles of construction have proved useful in making effective tables. These rules should generally be followed, although occasionally some deviation from customary procedure may increase the effectiveness of a table. In all cases the use of good judgment is more important than the following of rigid rules.

Unity of Subject

The data contained in a table should pertain to one definite subject and should be confined to that subject. Summary tables should cover only a single phase of a broad subject. The classification of the data must also be pertinent to the topic at hand.

Different units may be used provided they all refer to one subject. The data in Table 6–3, for example, are given in four different units:

Table 6–3

BELL TELEPHONE SYSTEM OPERATING STATISTICS
1945–60

Year	Telephones (Millions)*	Phone Calls (Millions per Day)	Operating Revenues (Millions)	Employees (Thousands)*
1945	22.4	90.5	$1,931	475
1950	35.3	140.8	3,262	602
1955	46.2	168.9	5,297	746
1960	60.7	219.1	7,920	736

* December 31.
SOURCE: American Telephone and Telegraph Company, *Annual Report, 1960*, p. 31.

number of telephones, number of calls, dollars of operating revenue, and number of employees. However, all of them deal with the one subject—operations of the telephone company. Such ratios as number of calls per telephone, revenue per telephone, revenue per call, as well as indexes showing relative changes in each series, afford numerous possibilities for analysis.

Simple units may be replaced or supplemented by such measures as averages, percentage relationships, and compound units. An example of a compound unit is the "ton-mile," a measure of operating volume in railroading. It represents one ton moved the distance of one mile and is derived from the two simple units—"ton" and "mile." Similarly, in other lines of activity the units "man-hour" and "foot-pound" appear. These measures are often based upon different kinds of data, but if they all contribute to a single purpose, the table becomes a unified whole.

Many tables do not possess the unity found in Table 6–3. An example of heterogeneous data is shown in Table 6–4. The Federal Reserve in-

Table 6–4

RAIL AND WATER TRAFFIC, 1955–59

Year and Month	Freight Carloadings— Class I Railroads		Pullman Passenger-Miles (Millions)	Panama Canal Traffic (Thousands of Long Tons)
	Federal Reserve Index of Carloadings (1935–39 = 100)	Thousands of Cars Loaded		
1955: May	128	3,754	521	3,750
1956: May	130	3,835	491	4,045
1957: May	119	3,558	416	4,586
1958: May	97	2,730	345	4,072
1959: May	120	3,419	255	4,861

Source: *Survey of Current Business*. Several tables were combined to illustrate heterogeneity.

dex of freight carloadings, together with the number of freight cars loaded, forms a table complete in itself. Pullman passenger-miles and Panama Canal traffic are not related to each other, nor to freight carloadings, so there is no special purpose of combining them in a table. Several sets of unrelated information are justifiable only in reference tables in publications where space saving is a more important consideration than unity.

Cross Classification

The degree of classification employed in an investigation depends upon the nature of the data and the purpose for which they are collected. The extent to which it is necessary to study combinations of the several characteristics of the data will determine the degree of cross classification required in tabulation.

Simple classification is illustrated by General Motors sales in Table 6–5. This is a "one-way" table (ignoring for a moment the other companies) since General Motors sales are classified according to a single characteristic—body type.

If classification is desired according to two characteristics simultaneously, such as body type and manufacturer—they must be *cross-classified* in a "two-way" table. This requires listing in two directions so that one classification will appear horizontally and the other vertically. In Table 6–5, the manufacturers are listed horizontally across the top. These headings are known as the *caption*. Body types appear down the left side of the table. Any such vertical listing is termed the *stub*. The vertical lists of data beneath the several headings are referred to as *columns*, and the horizontal lists following the several items are called *rows*, as indicated in Table 6–5.

Table 6–5

AUTOMOBILE SALES, BY BODY TYPE
AND MANUFACTURER, 1961   ←*Title*

(Thousands of Cars)

Body Type	General Motors	Ford	Chrysler	Total
Sedans...........				
Hard Tops.......				
Other Types.....				
Total.......				

←*Caption*

←*Row*

↑ *Stub*   ↑ *Column*

When three or more orders of classification are desired, the problem becomes more difficult; a three- or four-dimensional relationship must be shown on a two-dimensional sheet of paper. This can be done by subdividing either or both of the first two classifications. For example, in the stub of Table 6–5, each body type could be subdivided into four-door and two-door models, as follows:

Body Type	General Motors	Ford	Chrysler	Total
Sedans:				
4-door.......				
2-door.......				
Hard Tops:				
4-door.......				
2-door.......				
Etc.				

This results in a "three-way" table. Note that each of the major classifications is subdivided in exactly the same way.

Next, either of these same classes could be again subdivided, or each of the classes in the caption could be subdivided to provide for a fourth classification, resulting in a "four-way" table. Thus, each caption heading, such as "General Motors," could be subdivided to show whether sales were made to dealers in this country or abroad, as follows:

GENERAL MOTORS		
Domestic Market	Exports	Total

Further cross classification would make the table even more complicated. Whenever the further subdivision of data leads to tables which are too complex to be read easily, it is preferable to increase the number of tables. Do not spend time devising ways of presenting multiple classifications in a single table; make two or more tables instead. A good, although not universal, rule is to confine a summary table to two or three classifications.

Table 6–6

TYPICAL INDUSTRIAL USES OF AIRPLANES
IN THE UNITED STATES

Operational Uses	Number of Operators	Number of Aircraft
Crop dusting.................	760	1,883
Crop spraying................	776	1,327
Seeding......................	423	1,077
Checking cattle..............	886	926
Hauling feed and equipment...	814	868

SOURCE: Abstracted from *Planes*, July 1950.

In any classification, the classes should be defined so as to be mutually exclusive if possible. Mutually exclusive classes are those whose limits do not overlap; hence an item cannot be included in two or more classes. The confusing effect of overlapping classes is illustrated in Table 6–6. Here it is uncertain how many of the aircraft engaged in crop dusting also did crop spraying and seeding. The total number of operators and aircraft engaged in industrial uses is also unknown. Finally, the period covered by the survey is not stated.

Title

The title must tell as simply as possible what is in the table. The wording must be perfectly clear so that the reader may at once grasp the contents and significance of the table. Several lines often are required to do this. Considerable ingenuity may be used in selecting appropriate wording, in getting each thought complete on a single line, and in varying type size.

Note, for example, that the title of Table 6–5 is clearer than if it were divided after "Body." Also, separate thoughts are on separate lines. Type size might also be varied to emphasize the important features. Sometimes a brief catch title in large type is used in the first line, followed by a detailed subtitle in smaller type.

The types of information required in a complete title are illustrated in Table 6–5. Ordinarily, the title should answer the questions: (1) *"What* do the data represent?" (automobile sales); (2) *"Where* are the data from?" (three American manufacturers); (3) *"When?"* (1961); and (4) *"How classified?"* (by body type and company).

The unit of measure should always be explicitly stated. Thus, "Thousands of Cars" appears under the title of Table 6–5. Similarly, other tables might be captioned "Per Cent of Total" or "Per Cent Increase over Last Year."

Sometimes a narrative catch title is effective in a summary table. This type of title should "tell the story," as in a newspaper headline. The other details—what, where, when, and how classified—then appear as a subtitle, or some of them may be omitted entirely. For example, Table 6–5 might have been titled: "Ford Leads in Sedan Sales." The reader could be expected to read from the table the other comparisons presented.

The storytelling title, however, is used more commonly in charts than in tables, as illustrated by Chart 7–8 (p. 126) in the following chapter.

Headnotes

Headnotes appear between the title and the body of the table. They are often necessary to show the units used, such as "Thousands of Cars," or to give some other explanation relating to the whole table. The following headnote and its preceding title will serve as an example:[1]

---

[1] From *Statistical Abstract of the United States, 1959,* p. 333.

PURCHASING POWER OF THE DOLLAR: 1935 TO 1958

[1947–49 = 100. Obtained by computing reciprocals of price indexes compiled by Department of Labor, Bureau of Labor Statistics; these reciprocals are expressed as percentages with average of base period 1947–49 = 100]

Footnotes

Anything in a table which cannot be understood by the reader from the title, captions, and stub should be explained in footnotes. These footnotes should contain statements concerning figures that are missing, preliminary, or revised, and explanations concerning any unusual figures or other features of the table that are not self-explanatory. A study of tables appearing in print will provide many illustrations of the use of footnotes. A footnote usually applies to a specific item within the table. Symbols such as an asterisk (*) or dagger (†) may be used to key the figures to footnotes. However, where several footnotes are needed, it is best to use small letters. Footnote numbers might be confused with the numbers of the table.

Reference to Sources

A table should always give exact reference to the source or sources from which the data were taken. There are three reasons for this: (1) the reader is given a sound basis for evaluating the data; (2) the reader is able to find further information if needed; and (3) the author gives proper credit to the source and places on it the responsibility for any error. He is, of course, not relieved of the responsibility for detecting obvious errors or inconsistencies. If a table contains data that have not been published previously, this fact should be stated in a note, which should include the name of the collecting agency. In general, the use of exact references is a method of guarding against the charge of inaccuracy.

Arrangement

The arrangement of a table on the page, the arrangement of data in the table, and the choice of ruling, spacing, and type face contribute to its effectiveness.

Fitting the Table to the Page. The size of the printed page determines the form of the table to a large extent. Hence the real problem of arrangement is to fit the table to the page so that it will be effective in that setting. The table should be planned to read from left to right. Tables which must be read from the right-hand side of the page, tables which cover two pages, and tables which must be unfolded should be used only when no combination of smaller tables will serve as well.

The proportions of the page may also determine which headings to use as stub and which as caption. In order to fit the usual page, the height of a full-page table must exceed the width. Furthermore, the space for each entry is wider than it is high (☐), and so there is room for more rows than columns. Therefore, in a cross classification the longer list of items ordinarily appears in the stub. Length of wording in the stub and caption is another factor to consider. It is better to use the longer wording in the stub, if possible, to avoid crowding the narrow column headings. In any case the most important figures to be compared should be placed in adjoining columns or rows.

Order of Items. The four bases of classification—time, size, qualitative, and geographic—have been discussed. A classification in any of these categories frequently results in a large number of items within each subgroup. These items must be arranged in some definite order.

Time series are listed in chronological order, usually beginning with the earliest period. When the major emphasis falls on the most recent events as in Table 6–2, page 99, a reverse time order may be used.

Size classifications or frequency distributions are arranged either from large to small, as in Table 6–2E, or from small to large, as in Table 6–2D, with the total at either end. An item such as "miscellaneous" or "other" is placed at the end of the list in any order of arrangement.

Classifications based on qualitative differences are usually listed in order of importance. Sometimes, however, custom or practice determines the order, as in the arrangement of occupations in Table 6–2B. For ease in locating any given item in a reference table, an alphabetical arrangement is preferable.

Geographic classifications are usually listed in alphabetic order for easy reference, particularly in reference tables. Sometimes the order is established by custom, such as in the traditional listing of the regions from Northeast to West shown in Table 6–2A. In a summary table, items may also be listed by *size* to emphasize the important elements, as in ranking the states by population.

Ruling, Spacing, and Type Face. These are devices for increasing the effectiveness of a table by concentrating emphasis on important entries and relieving the monotonous appearance of figures in rows and columns. Whenever rulings aid the reader in understanding the classifications of a table, they should be used. A double ruling or a single heavier line can be used to separate major divisions in a table.

In many printed tables there are no rulings. The separation between the columns and rows is accomplished by appropriate spacing. Successive indentations of items indicate the various degrees of subclassification. Boldface type, larger type, and italics are frequently used to set off totals or percentages from the other data or to emphasize important items.

Totals

Totals should be shown for any columns or rows that list parts of a whole expressed in the same unit. The sum total is useful both for its own sake and for comparison with the parts. The total is usually placed at the bottom of a column or at the right of a row as in Table 6–5, but when it is of primary importance the total might well appear first, in the position of prominence.

Significant Figures

In summary tables it is customary to use only three or four significant figures. More than four are seldom useful in statistical work (see Chapter 5), since too many digits would be apt to confuse the reader with meaningless figures. In rounding off, the decimal point should be located in the place of one of the former commas, to avoid confusion. Thus, 4,460,762 can be rounded to 4.46 millions or 4,461 thousands, but preferably not 44.6 hundred thousands.

Another problem occurs when rounded figures do not exactly equal the total, owing to rounding differences. In this case two alternatives are acceptable: (1) add a footnote saying that "components may not add to totals because of rounding," or (2) adjust one of the figures in the table to obtain the correct total. The figure to be changed should be the one least affected by the adjusted rounding. In no case should the correctly rounded total be adjusted to conform to the total of the rounded figures.

Review

Before a table is released it should be reviewed for form, content, validity, and clerical accuracy. It is difficult for the person preparing the table to make a thoroughly satisfactory check on the first three of these aspects. He has prepared the table and has done his best; he can hardly review it objectively now. He should, if possible, have his work reviewed by someone with experience.

In the case of a summary table the reviewer should read the accompanying text so that he can determine whether or not the table is satisfactory *for the present purpose*. He should ask himself the following questions: (1) Does the title clearly state what is in the table? (2) Are all the entries pertinent? (3) Is there unity of subject matter? (4) Are the classifications arranged so as to focus attention on the main comparisons? (5) Are the data arranged so as to emphasize important points? (6) Does the table include adequate interpretative figures such as totals, percentages, and averages? (7) Are there notations about peculiarities of the data? (8) Is the source stated properly? (9) Is the table in good form, so that it presents an attractive appearance?

An outside reviewer cannot be asked to verify the detailed computations. The analyst himself should re-add all columns and rows in the final form even though they were carefully checked in the original work sheets. This step often uncovers an error made in transcription and repeated in review.

SUMMARY

Data may be presented effectively in tables and charts by following the rules suggested in this chapter and in the two following chapters. Tables offer the advantages of showing more facts and more exact values with less labor of preparation than do charts, while charts serve to attract the reader's attention and show trends and comparisons more vividly than do tables.

A table is an orderly way of showing the significant relationships of data in vertical columns and horizontal rows. The data should be classified by a definite plan—usually by time, size, qualitative, or geographic differences. There are two principal types of tables: reference and summary tables. Reference tables are detailed and arranged for easy reference. They are usually placed in the appendix. Summary tables are short and are arranged to emphasize important facts and comparisons in the text. A summary table may be abstracted from one or more reference tables by omitting or grouping unimportant figures, rounding off numbers, rearranging the data for emphasis and comparability, and adding percentages, ratios, or averages.

The following principles should be followed in order to construct an effective table: (1) Confine the table to a single subject. (2) Cross-classify the data so as to bring out significant relationships, but do not use more than two or three classifications. The classifications should not overlap. (3) Have the title show "what, where, when, and how classified"; or let it tell the story as in a newspaper headline. (4–6) Include specific headnotes, footnotes, and reference to exact sources. (7) Arrange the table to fit the page, usually with more rows than columns.

List time series chronologically. List size classifications by magnitude. Arrange qualitative and geographic classifications in alphabetic or customary order in reference tables, or by magnitude in summary tables. Pay careful attention to ruling, spacing, and type face. (8) Include totals for parts of a whole expressed in the same unit. (9) Round off the figures in summary tables to three or four significant places. If these figures do not equal the rounded total, explain by footnote or round one of the figures the wrong way to get the total wanted. (10) Recheck computations, and ask someone else to review the final table for form, content, and validity.

PROBLEMS

The data concerning inspection of electric shavers contained in the five daily inspection reports reproduced below are to be used in preparing solutions to Problems 1–4:

1. *a*) Prepare a table of the number of electric shavers inspected, number accepted, number scrapped, and number salvaged each day.
   b) Prepare a table of per cents from the table of part (*a*), above.
   c) State some possible reasons for the day-to-day variations.

2. *a*) Prepare a table of the quality of work done by different operators.
   b) As a foreman, what use would you make of this information?

3. If some types of shavers are more complicated than others, then some should show a higher per cent of scrap and salvage than others. What can you find on this question?

4. *a*) Prepare a table showing the per cent accepted by individual operators in each of the five days.
   b) What information does this table show that the tables prepared for Problems 1(*b*) and 2(*a*) do not give?

5. The following statistics have been published for the United States Steel Corporation: In 1955, 25,506,000 net tons of steel products were shipped, and sales totaled $4,097,700,000. The following year, 23,911,000 net tons were shipped for an increase of $131.2 million in sales over the year before. In 1956 total expenses were $3,880,800,000, a total of $153.2 million more than the previous year. The number of employees declined from 272,646 to 260,646; they worked an average of 37.5 and 37.1 hours per week in the two years, respectively.
   a) Present this information in tabular form, taking account of all the points of established practice in table construction. Include any desirable ratios, percentages, or other derived figures.

SMOOTH-SHAVE COMPANY
Summary of Daily Inspection Reports

Date		Shaver No.	Machine Operator	No. of Shavers Inspected	No. of Shavers Accepted	No. of Shavers Scrapped	No. of Shavers Salvaged
Oct.	3	83	T.R.	2,680	2,650	30	....
		55	J.R.	1,207	1,200	7	....
		71	L.N.	2,950	2,150	800	....
		22	E.S.	1,893	1,780	113	....
		25	J.W.	1,350	1,350	...	....
	4	83	T.R.	2,545	2,500	45	....
		55	J.R.	1,712	700	62	950
		71	L.N.	2,600	2,075	525	....
		22	E.S.	1,703	1,550	153	....
		25	J.W.	1,979	1,180	350	449
	5	83	T.R.	1,888	1,850	38	....
		55	J.R.	1,514	1,500	14	....
		71	L.N.	2,850	2,500	350	....
		22	E.S.	1,320	1,320	...	....
		25	J.W.	383	250	28	105
	6	83	T.R.	3,835	2,000	35	1,800
		55	J.R.	1,804	1,800	4	....
		71	L.N.	2,295	2,075	220	....
		22	E.S.	1,236	1,150	86	....
		25	J.W.	694	427	177	90
	7	83	T.R.	2,727	2,700	27	....
		55	J.R.	1,665	1,583	82	....
		71	L.N.	2,920	2,600	320	....
		22	E.S.	1,463	1,360	103	....
		25	J.W.	1,280	1,280	...	....

b) Does your table or tables have unity? Explain. What degree of cross classification is present?

6. *a*) Consult Table 4, page 10, in the *Statistical Abstract* for 1953 or 1954; Table 4, page 9 in the 1955 edition; Table 190, page 158, in the 1956 edition; Table 195, page 158, in the 1957 edition; Table 200, page 160, in the 1958 edition; or Table 206, page 160, in the 1959 or 1960 editions.
(1) Explain the location of totals.
(2) Describe the type of classification used in the stub items.
b) In one of the *Statistical Abstract* tables listed on the next page:

Edition	Table	Page	Edition	Table	Page
1960	765	576	1955	701	577
1959	750	574	1954	680	586
1958	733	571	1953	655	563
1957	722	574	1952	638	528
1956	702	572	1951	617	521

(1) Describe the method of classification, the number of classifications, and the degree of cross classification. What is the order of arrangement within each classification?

(2) How many different units are there? Name them. Do you think it is justifiable to include all of them in one table? Why or why not?

(3) Discuss any desirable or undesirable features in the table.

7. *a)* Present a summary table in good form condensed from a recent census publication.

b) Explain specifically what information the table is intended to emphasize.

c) List the steps taken in condensation and rearrangement.

SELECTED READINGS

HALL, RAY O. *Handbook of Tabular Presentation.* New York: The Ronald Press Co., 1943.

Covers the principles of tabular construction, followed by illustrative tables and practice problems.

MACK, MARY L. *Statistics in the Making.* Columbus, Ohio: Ohio State University, Bureau of Business Research, 1958.

Part Three presents a detailed explanation of tabulation methods.

MYERS, JOHN H. *Statistical Presentation.* Ames, Iowa: Littlefield, Adams & Co., 1950, chap. 2.

A brief but clear exposition of the effective use of tables.

U.S. DEPARTMENT OF COMMERCE, BUREAU OF THE CENSUS. *Manual of Tabular Presentation.* Washington, D.C.: U.S. Government Printing Office, 1949.

An exhaustive 268-page manual of "theory and practice in the presentation of statistical data in tables for publication."

ZEISEL, HANS. *Say It with Figures.* 4th ed. New York: Harper & Bros., 1957.

An advanced book covering problems of classification, methods of numerical presentation, and principles of making tabulation decisions.

7. HOW TO CONSTRUCT A CHART

A CHART or graph[1] is the most vivid and forceful method of presenting statistical data. In this visual-minded age the popularity of picture magazines, movies, and television attests the value of pictorial presentation. The reader gains a clear and simple impression from a chart which he cannot get from reading the same material in a table or text. Thus the business executive follows a set of charts portraying his department's operating results or the trend of general business activity. The production man uses quality control charts, and the security analyst maintains elaborate graphs of stock market behavior.

With proper planning and execution a chart will give a truthful, clear, and attractive picture of the facts. A poor chart, on the other hand, may completely nullify the effect of an expensive statistical analysis. Yet how many poor charts there are! This chapter shows how to plan and construct an effective chart. These principles should be of value to the reader of charts as well as to the compiler, since only with this knowledge can he interpret a chart correctly. An understanding of form and structure is as important in judging the significance of a chart as in judging that of a painting.

BASIC PURPOSES OF CHARTS

Charts are designed to serve either of two major purposes: (1) analysis or (2) presentation of data.

Charts for Analysis

Charts may be used as working tools of analysis in any of the following ways: (1) As the first step in an investigation, a chart frequently

---

[1] "Graph" may be used in the same sense as "chart" to mean any representation of statistical data in pictorial form, or it may refer to a line or curve drawn upon a chart.

helps the analyst to evaluate the need for further study and to plan the next steps in research. (2) Later the chart provides him with a step-by-step picture of developments, thus aiding him in the use of his judgment. (3) A supervisor can use a graph as a visual guide in laying out a job to be performed by mathematical computation, and later in checking the accuracy and reasonableness of the results. (4) Graphic measurement may be used in place of mathematical computation to save time and labor, as in a ratio chart or nomograph. (5) Freehand curves may be fitted to data in more varied and flexible forms than mathematical curves, as in trend and correlation analysis.

Some types of charts are especially useful as analytic tools. In particular, the graph of a frequency distribution, a line drawing of a time series, and a scatter diagram of two related variables are all essential in statistical analysis. Such graphs are discussed in later chapters.

An analytic or work chart is usually drawn for the analyst's own use on large-scale graph paper, with careful attention to accuracy and the other basic principles of good charting. The finishing touches necessary for a final report or for reproduction purposes, however, need not be emphasized.

Charts for Presentation

Readers are more quickly attracted by a graph than by an equal amount of space devoted to text discussion or tables. Moreover, the main facts of an analysis can be effectively emphasized by charts, and relationships which might otherwise remain elusive become clear when graphically presented. Charts in this chapter will be discussed with these characteristics in mind, and the following questions will be answered: How can charts be made to attract the desired attention? How can they be constructed so that they will present the main facts or relationships most simply, accurately, and forcefully?

There are many kinds of pictorial diagrams, including lines, bars, circles, dots, and other forms, plotted on a variety of scales. The following principles of planning and constructing a chart will be illustrated by arithmetic-scale line graphs of time series, since this is the most prevalent type in business and economic literature. This type of chart shows a series of points connected by straight lines called a *curve,* with magnitude plotted on the vertical scale and time intervals on the horizontal scale. The same basic principles, however, apply generally to other kinds of charts. The distinctive features of bar charts, circle charts, and ratio-scale line charts will be described in the next chapter.

PLANNING A CHART

A chart should be planned so as to achieve simplicity, accuracy, adequate size, proper proportion, emphasis, and skilled execution. These requisites are described below, and illustrated in Chart 7–1.

Chart 7–1

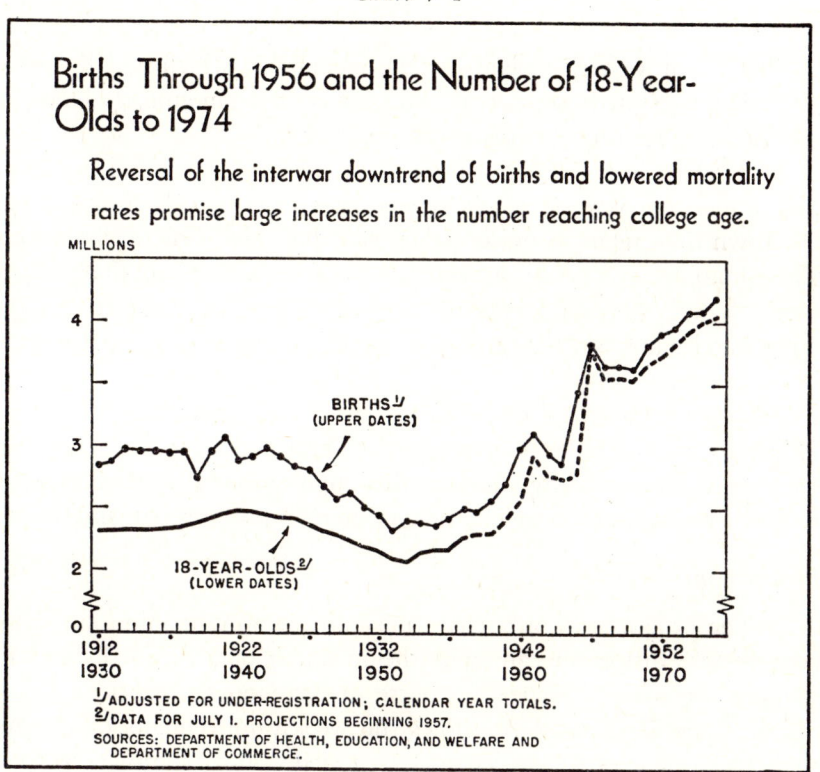

Births Through 1956 and the Number of 18-Year-Olds to 1974

Reversal of the interwar downtrend of births and lowered mortality rates promise large increases in the number reaching college age.

1/ ADJUSTED FOR UNDER-REGISTRATION; CALENDAR YEAR TOTALS.
2/ DATA FOR JULY 1. PROJECTIONS BEGINNING 1957.
SOURCES: DEPARTMENT OF HEALTH, EDUCATION, AND WELFARE AND DEPARTMENT OF COMMERCE.

SOURCE: *The Economic Report of the President, January, 1957*, p. 89.

Simplicity

A chart must be designed with its particular group of readers in mind: what is simple for one reader may be complex for another. In case of doubt, it is wiser to oversimplify a chart than to make it unduly complex. To achieve simplicity, there should not be too much information on any one chart. Also, technical terms should be avoided as far as possible.

Accuracy

Accuracy in graphics is more a matter of portraying a true picture to the reader than showing exact values. Hence, care must be exercised to avoid unconscious misrepresentation. In this connection, the selection of proper scales and the use of complete and accurate titles and legends are as important as precision of plotting.

Size

The size of a chart depends on the medium in which it will appear (whether a printed page, wall chart, etc.), the amount of detail involved, and the importance of the chart.

If the chart is to be included with text material, it should generally be limited to a page or less in size. A chart that is to be printed may be drawn half again to twice as large as the final printed dimensions. The photographic reduction will then eliminate any small imperfections. A wall or easel chart to be used before an audience, on the other hand, must be large and clear enough to be seen from any point in the room.

The amount of detail involved necessarily affects the size of a chart. When a chart includes a great deal of information, it must be large enough for easy reading. Finally, the importance of a chart may determine its size, since large charts look more important than small ones.

Proportion

Proper proportions in a chart may be even more important than size because distortion can twist the meaning of a finished diagram. Suppose we wish to chart the course of common stock prices during 1956. Chart 7–2, panel A, shows the weekly movements of the Associated Press average of 60 stocks, plotted with a complete vertical scale extending from 0 to 195. The market was apparently quite stable; the AP average began and ended the year at 180, and never departed from this level by as much as 7 per cent. But this picture is rather tame for a press release. By cutting off the unused vertical scale[2] below 170, and stretching the remaining scale about seven times, the Associated Press draftsman produced the chart shown in panel B. The market now appears to have experienced a succession of soaring booms and precipitous collapses! This is truly spectacular, but is it the truth?

Improper proportion distorts not only the meaning but also the ap-

---

[2] Breaking the vertical scale is a valid procedure provided the effect is not misleading, as explained under "Breaks in Vertical Scale" later in the chapter.

Chart 7–2
SCALE DISTORTION

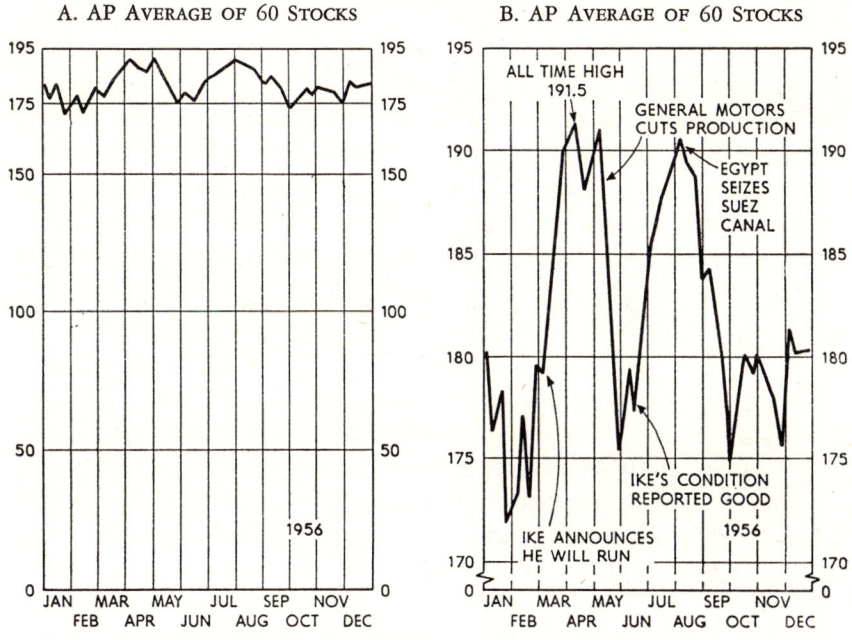

A. AP Average of 60 Stocks

B. AP Average of 60 Stocks

Source: Panel B reproduced from Associated Press release.

pearance of a chart. If the chart is too long and narrow, it has an awkward, stretched-out appearance. The chart as a whole is most attractive when the length is from 1¼ to 2 times the width.[3] Similarly, a curve slanted at 30° to 45° above the horizontal is more effective than one with very steep or flat slopes.

Emphasis

Proper emphasis is essential in effective graphic presentation. Since black and white offer the sharpest contrast of colors, and are cheapest to reproduce, this combination is most commonly used in printed graphs. Different types of lines can be used for maximum contrast, as shown in Chart 7–1. Colors, of course, can be used inexpensively and effectively when individual hand-drawn charts are to appear in the final report.

The curves representing the data should be much heavier than the background lines on the graph in order to stand out clearly. Where

---

[3] A chart of the proportions 1 to 1.414 (i.e., $\sqrt{2}$) can be divided into halves, each having the same proportions (0.707 to 1) as the original chart, a characteristic useful in grouping charts on a page.

there are several curves, the weight or type of line should indicate the relative importance of the curves. The usual order of the background lines is: border heaviest, followed by the zero or other base line, with the grid lightest or replaced by ticks along the inside margin of the chart.

The printing on a chart should be easy to read, but not so heavy as to detract from the diagram itself. Vertical letters and figures, drawn neatly in plain face, are most suitable for this purpose. The largest and heaviest lettering should be used for the title, a smaller size for the curve labels, scale values, etc., and probably the smallest and lightest of all for footnotes.

Skilled Execution

The materials available for effective graph making have improved greatly in recent years. Lettering guides are now manufactured in a wide variety of types and sizes, as are printed adhesive letters and "paste-up" titles. Conventional graphic forms and pictographs are also easily available. It is not necessary, therefore, to go to great cost to produce attractive graphs, provided skill in the use of available materials is developed.

Chart 7–1 illustrates the fundamentals of good presentation described above. The chart is *simple* in its detail and terminology, *accurate* in presenting a clear-cut picture with specific captions and explanatory title, large enough in *size* for easy reading, and properly *proportioned*. The two curves stand out clearly, and the type size is differentiated for proper *emphasis,* while lettering guides and other drawing aids have been used for *skilled execution.* The break in the vertical scale of this chart is discussed later in the chapter.

CONSTRUCTING A CHART

Nearly all charts have certain basic elements which should be considered in constructing or judging them. These features include axes, grid, scale divisions, titles, labels, legends, accompanying tables, references, and notes.[4]

Axes and Grid

There are two scales of measurement—the X scale measured along the horizontal axis and the Y scale on the vertical axis (see Chart 7–3). The axes cross at the *origin* or zero point. Plus values are meas-

---
[4] The principles in this section generally follow those suggested in *American Standard Time-Series Charts,* published in 1960 by the American Society of Mechanical Engineers.

Chart 7–3
AXES AND GRID

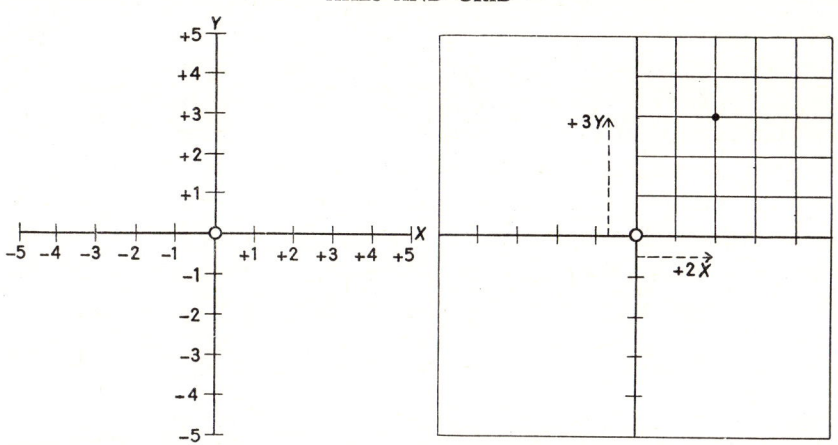

Charts use two scales of measurement: a horizontal or X scale, and a vertical or Y scale. Plus values are measured upward and to the right; minus values downward and to the left.

Each plotted point has a value on both the Y and X scales.

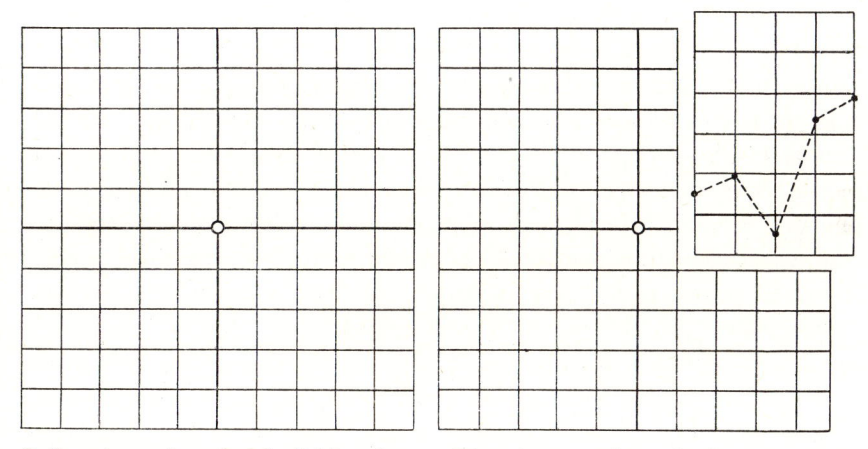

Rulings drawn through scale divisions form a co-ordinate surface or "grid."

Most charts are drawn in the upper right-hand portion of the co-ordinate grid.

ured from the origin to the right and upward; minus values to the left and downward.

Scale rulings drawn through the divisions of each of these scales form a co-ordinate field or *grid,* or which each point has both an X and a Y value, sometimes called an abscissa and an ordinate. Most charts show positive values only; so they include only the upper right-hand part or first quadrant of the grid.

In a time series graph the horizontal scale shows the time units from left to right, while the vertical scale measures the amount. In a frequency distribution the horizontal scale shows the size of each class, and the vertical scale the number in that class. These usages follow the convention that independent variables should be plotted on the X axis and dependent variables on the Y axis.

Grid lines are usually fine solid lines of uniform thickness, although the lines indicating the ends of years or other major divisions of the data may be emphasized. Frequently the grid is omitted entirely, as in Chart 7–1; or only the main guidelines are drawn, as in Chart 7–7 (p. 125), the other values being indicated by short ticks along the border scale. It is not necessary to indicate the numerical values of each of these ticks, but only enough of them to enable the reader to determine the value of any plotted point without difficulty.

Scale Divisions

The methods of marking intervals of time series require special attention in order to avoid confusion in reading the graph. There are two kinds of data: *point* data, taken at a specific instant of time, such as end of month or December 31; and *period* data, covering an interval of time, such as a yearly average or total. Theoretically, vertical rulings mark instants of time, and the spaces between rulings represent periods of time. Therefore month-end and year-end data should ordinarily be plotted on the line, and period data (as well as midmonth, or midyear point data) in the space. However, both types of figures are frequently plotted on the line to make the chart easier to read, especially since many readers persist in reading the curve where it crosses the vertical ruling regardless of the nature of the data.

In either case the time designation, such as "Jan." or "1960," should be centered directly under the vertical ruling, tick, or space on which the figure is plotted, to avoid ambiguity. One common type of ambiguity occurs when monthly averages or totals are plotted so that one value falls on the vertical line separating two years, as in Chart 7–4A. It is then uncertain whether this point represents December 1960, or January 1961. This may be remedied by labeling the line "Dec.," or by plotting the months in the center of each space, as in Chart 7–4B.

If space permits, it is desirable to label all months, as in Chart 7–4B, except in the case of an extended series showing long-term trends. Years should be printed out in full horizontally, below the monthly labels, in the center of the year's space.

Chart 7–4

PLOTTING PERIOD DATA ON A TIME SCALE

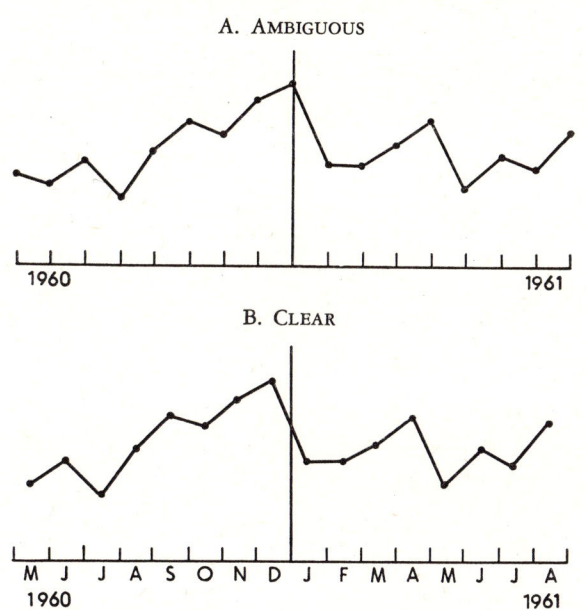

A. Ambiguous

B. Clear

Breaks in Horizontal Scale. As a general rule, the horizontal scale should be divided into regular intervals to depict the even progress of time. There are certain situations, however, which justify changes and breaks in the time scale.

In many business charts the main purpose is the presentation of current monthly or weekly data. Comparison with the past is a matter of only secondary importance. It has therefore become customary to use two time scales: one compressed to show historical data and one enlarged to show the current period, as illustrated in Chart 7–5. Sometimes the chart shows only the annual average for each of the earlier years, and monthly data for the current year. Either of these methods gives a more complete and continuous story than if several years were omitted entirely.

Naturally, when the earlier data are plotted on a compressed scale the slopes of the two parts of the curve cannot be compared directly. For the businessman who has become accustomed to these forms, however, there is no misrepresentation of facts. He has in compact form just the information he wants, and he is well aware that the current year is a sort of "slow motion picture" compared with the previous scale. However, these procedures are not recommended for general analysis. When they are used, the chart should be divided vertically

Chart 7–5

BANK DEBITS AND MANUFACTURING PAYROLLS
IN CLEVELAND, 1950–59

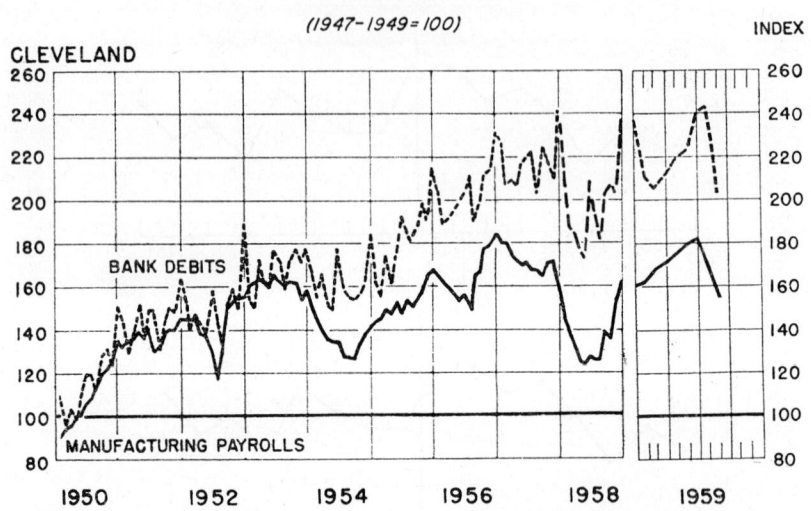

(1947–1949 = 100)

SOURCE: Ohio State University, *Bulletin of Business Research*, September 1959.

into two separate segments to emphasize the change in the time scale, as in Chart 7–5.

Breaks in Vertical Scale. Theoretically, there should be no break in the vertical scale of a time series chart any more than in the horizontal scale. However, the fluctuations of a curve are frequently of more significance than the distance above zero, and these swings can be expanded vertically for easier reading by omitting the unused part of the scale. Common practice, therefore, permits a "break" in the vertical scale below the lowest plotted point. Zero is indicated as the base; then a jagged line is drawn to break the vertical scale, as shown in Chart 7–1, page 115, and the scale is resumed above the break at any value required.

In graphs of index numbers, zero is frequently omitted altogether, since 100 is the base for comparison rather than zero. In Chart 7–5, for example, the significant feature is the relative growth in bank debits and payrolls since the 1947–49 base period, rather than the absolute levels of bank debits and payrolls; so the unused scale below 80 is omitted. The 100 per cent base line is always emphasized in index number charts.

Methods of Comparing Several Series

A problem arises in comparing two or more series that are recorded either in different units (such as number of employees and dollars of

Chart 7-6

SUPPLY OF ENERGY FROM COAL AND DOMESTIC OIL

FIVE-YEAR AVERAGES, 1901–1955

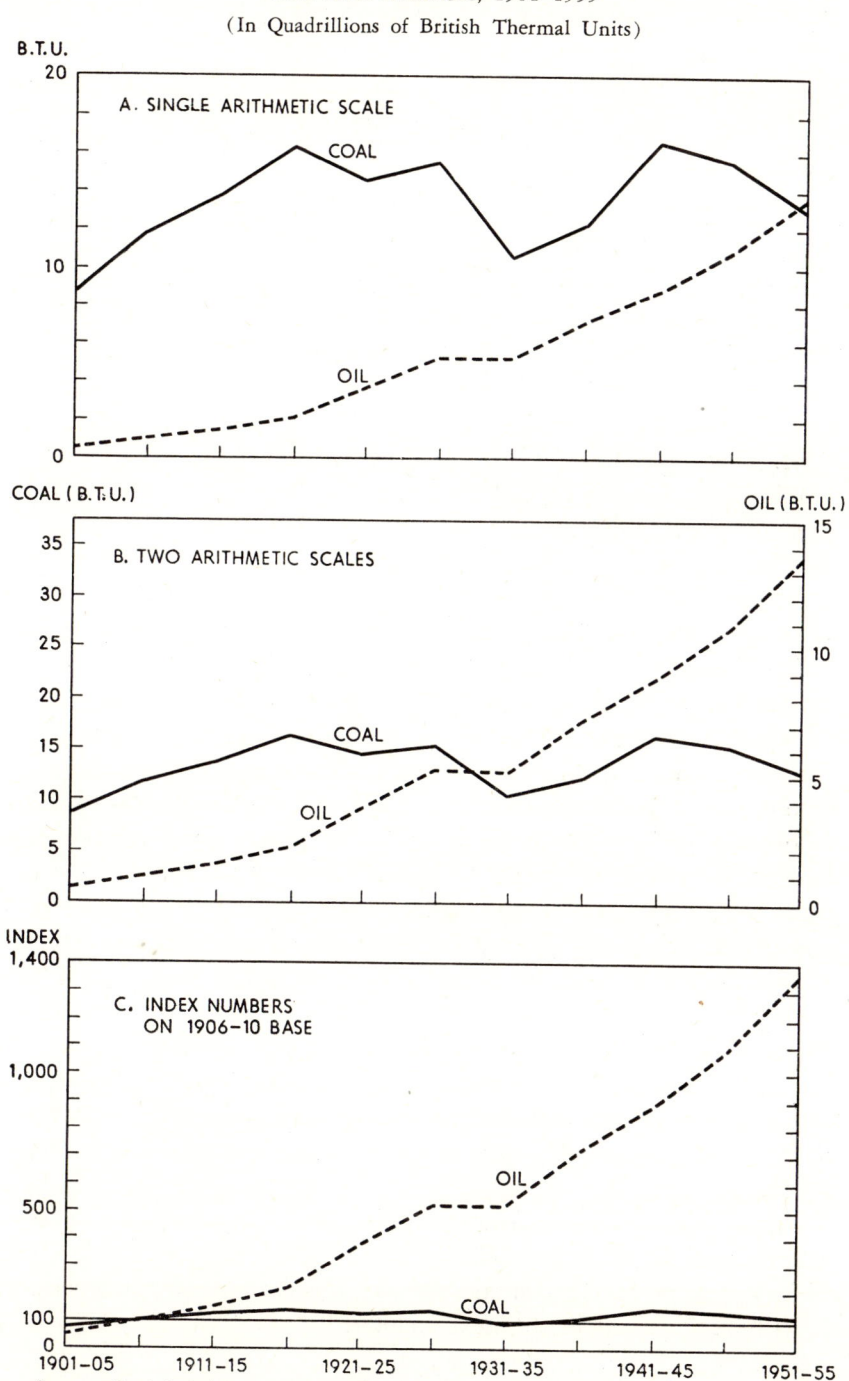

(In Quadrillions of British Thermal Units)

A. SINGLE ARITHMETIC SCALE

B. TWO ARITHMETIC SCALES

C. INDEX NUMBERS ON 1906–10 BASE

SOURCE: *Statistical Abstract of the United States.*

sales) or in the same unit at levels so far apart that it is difficult to use the same scale effectively for both (e.g., total industry sales versus sales of a small company). Chart 7–6 shows three ways of comparing two series on arithmetic scales.

Single Scale. If the two series are in the same unit and are not too far apart in size, a single arithmetic scale is best even though it minimizes the fluctuations of the smaller series. In this case, if the purpose is to show that coal has been the major source of power, as compared with domestic oil, prior to the 1950's, the top scale (Chart 7–6A) is the one to use.

Use of Two Scales. If the series are recorded in different units, or are widely different in size, they may be brought close together for easy comparison by plotting them on different scales. These scales should be selected so that the average level of the two is about the same. Thus by setting 2½ B.T.U.'s of coal equal to 1 B.T.U. of oil (!) in Chart 7–6B (since the average level of coal output has averaged about 2½ times that of oil for the period 1901–55), the curves are brought closer together. The timing and general direction of ups and downs can now be compared, but the amounts of change are not at all comparable. Although such charts are sometimes justifiable, this scale adjustment should be avoided if possible, because it may mislead the reader.

Index Numbers. When a comparison of relative changes of the variables is needed, they may be reduced to indexes, using the same base period in each case. Indexes are percentages obtained by dividing each series by its value in the base period. The 100 per cent or base line and the entire per cent scale will be common to the several series. Chart 7–6C compares the percentage variation of the two sources of power relative to the base period 1906–10. An index number chart affords valid comparisons between any period and the base period, but not necessarily with other periods when the indexes may be far apart. Thus, in 1941–45 coal scored a greater gain than oil over the preceding period both in B.T.U's and in per cent, but the index number chart shows oil rising more steeply, because of its higher level relative to the 1906–10 base. Index numbers will be discussed further in Chapter 15.

Ratio Scale. Perhaps the best method of comparing the relative changes in two dissimilar series is to plot them both on a ratio scale. This method permits percentage comparisons between *any* two periods. It will be described in the next chapter.

Shading

When it is desirable to emphasize changes in magnitude or in the different parts of a total, the area under a curve can be shaded by dots, lines, or other markings. Printed shadings of various designs can be purchased in sheets, and then cut out and pasted on charts as needed. The use of shading is illustrated in Chart 7–7. The area under the top line, which represents total farm income, is shaded in different de-

Chart 7–7

CASH RECEIPTS FROM FARM MARKETINGS

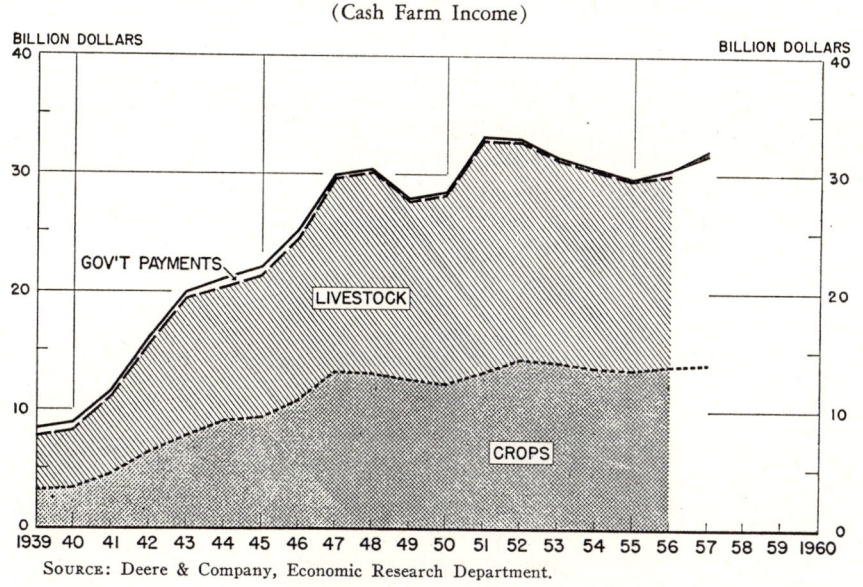

(Cash Farm Income)

SOURCE: Deere & Company, Economic Research Department.

signs to emphasize and distinguish the three principal components of income. In a chart of this kind, the vertical scale must not be broken, or the proportions will be distorted.

If it is desired to emphasize the *proportions* of each type of income to the total rather than the dollar amounts, the *percentages* of the total should be plotted on the vertical scale instead. Total income would then be represented by a horizontal line at the 100 per cent level.

Explanatory Material

Titles, subtitles, and scale headings (such as "Thousands of Tons") must meet the same requirements of clarity and precision that were

Chart 7-8

MEDICAL CARE PER PERSON HAS BEEN INCREASING RAPIDLY...

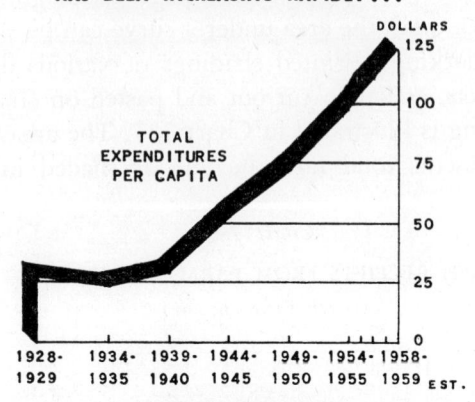

TOTAL EXPENDITURES PER CAPITA

DOLLARS: 0, 25, 50, 75, 100, 125

1928-1929, 1934-1935, 1939-1940, 1944-1945, 1949-1950, 1954-1955, 1958-1959 EST.

WITH HOSPITAL CARE IN THE FOREFRONT...

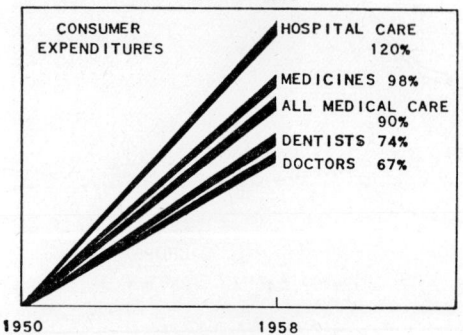

% CHANGE FROM 1950 TO 1958

CONSUMER EXPENDITURES

- HOSPITAL CARE 120%
- MEDICINES 98%
- ALL MEDICAL CARE 90%
- DENTISTS 74%
- DOCTORS 67%

1950 — 1958

AND INSURANCE COVERING MORE OF THE BILL

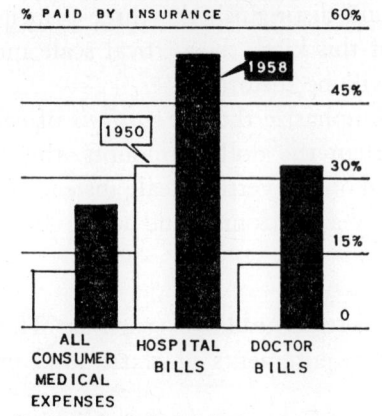

% PAID BY INSURANCE: 0, 15%, 30%, 45%, 60%

1950, 1958

ALL CONSUMER MEDICAL EXPENSES | HOSPITAL BILLS | DOCTOR BILLS

Source: Chase Manhattan Bank, *Business in Brief,* November–December 1959; data from Social Security Administration and Chase Manhattan Bank.

described in the chapter on tables (pp. 105–6). The narrative title is illustrated in Chart 7–8.

Curves may be identified by adjoining *labels,* or else by a *key* or legend which groups the labels in a separate area of the grid with a sample segment of each curve opposite its label. Labels adjacent to the curves are usually better than a key because they require less movement of the eye.

A label not only should identify the curve clearly but should be placed so as to help tell the story in an orderly manner. The label is usually placed in a horizontal position close to the curve and above it, but well clear of other curves and rulings, as in Chart 7–6. A diagonal pointer may be used if necessary, as in Chart 7–1 (p. 115).

When a table accompanies a chart to show exact numerical values, it should appear on the same page as the chart, or on the page facing it, and both should be read in the same direction.

The necessity for citing the source and noting any discrepancies in the data was explained in the discussion of tables (p. 106). The same rules apply to charts, although if the information is shown in an adjacent table, the chart need only refer to the table. Source and reference notes are usually printed in small type at the bottom of the chart, but an important note may be placed just below the subtitle or in the grid.

Anyone who wishes to draw graphs neatly and correctly will profit greatly from a course covering the use of drawing equipment. In the absence of such training, the study of a drawing manual or the instructions that come with ruling pens or lettering guides should help the novice in his first efforts in graphing. With a few hours of practice, anyone can learn to handle a ruling pen and lettering guides with good results.

TELLING A STORY WITH CHARTS

Increased emphasis in recent years on the requirement that a chart "tell a complete story" has led to the practice of combining a number of charts in a sequence so as to form a connected narrative.[5] A running narrative title is used to tie the charts together in a complete and unified exposition. This device is used widely in business journals and government reports. It is especially effective in the presentation of brief summary types of nonrecurring reports.

Any combination of charts may be used for telling a story. An illustration of the use of both lines and bars for this purpose is given in

---

[5] See J. A. Livingston, "Charts Should Tell a Story," *Journal of the American Statistical Association,* September 1945, pp. 342–50.

the three panels of Chart 7–8, which analyzes the increasing costs of medical care.

SUMMARY

If properly executed, charts can be used effectively for both the analysis and presentation of data. This chapter explains how to plan and construct a chart, specifically an arithmetic-scale line graph of a time series. The basic principles, however, apply to other types of charts as well.

In planning a chart one should consider six factors: (1) simplicity of form and terminology, (2) accuracy in portraying a true picture, (3) adequate size to be clearly read in the medium presented, (4) proper proportion to avoid distortion, (5) appropriate emphasis on the various curves and explanatory material, and (6) skilled execution through the use of drawing aids.

In constructing a chart the following procedure is recommended: (1) The conventional use of axes and grid should be followed. (2) Scale divisions must be drawn so as to avoid ambiguity in the time designations of plotted points. The time scale may be broken to emphasize recent trends, and the vertical scale may be broken to eliminate unused area and to expand the ups and downs of the curve, but distortion sometimes results. (3) Several series may be compared in any of four ways: on a single scale (if all are in the same unit); with two different scales (not ordinarily recommended); by expressing both as index numbers on a common base; or by plotting them on a ratio scale. (4) A chart may be shaded to emphasize changes in the magnitude of a curve or its component parts. These parts may be graphed either in absolute form or as percentages of the total. (5) Explanatory material, such as title, captions, source, and footnotes, must be clear and specific, following the rules laid down in the chapter on tables.

Finally, a series of charts may be grouped consecutively with running narrative titles in order to tell a complete story graphically.

PROBLEMS

1. *a*) For what purposes is graphic presentation superior to tabular presentation?
   b) In what ways is a chart an inadequate substitute for a table?
   c) How can the visual impression conveyed by a chart be distorted by the use of improper proportions?
   d) In graphic presentation what features of a chart should be emphasized and how may this objective be achieved?

2. *a*) How can you avoid ambiguity in plotting point data on a time scale?
   b) Why is there danger of misinterpretation if part of the area between zero and a time series curve is omitted on an arithmetic chart?
   c) What kinds of distortion may be caused by breaking the horizontal scale?
   d) What are the disadvantages of using different arithmetic scales in comparing several series?

3. *a*) Find a published chart which you consider is correctly and effectively drawn, and explain why you think so.
   b) Find a published chart which you consider incorrect or ineffective, and suggest changes that might improve it. Cite the exact source in each case.

4. Find (*a*) a component-part shaded chart and (*b*) a sequence of charts which have been put together to form a connected narrative from current business or economic publications (citing the exact issues and page numbers), and list the good and bad features of each.

5. Plan and construct a chart of a time series on a subject of interest to you from the *Statistical Abstract, Survey of Current Business, Federal Reserve Bulletin,* or other source for the last 15 months or 15 years, following the rules suggested in this chapter.

6. *a*) Plot the following data on three separate charts, corresponding to the three methods shown in Chart 7–6 (p. 123). Use 1956 as the base (100 per cent) for the index numbers (i.e., divide each value by 1956 value).
   b) Explain briefly what each chart shows.

SALES AND NET PROFIT OF A SMALL COMPANY, 1954–60

Year	Sales	Net Profit
1954	$21,000	$ 300
1955	28,000	500
1956	23,000	400
1957	31,000	900
1958	26,000	700
1959	47,000	1,500
1960	41,000	1,100

SELECTED READINGS
(See pages 153–54.)

8. COMMON TYPES OF CHARTS

THE PRINCIPAL types of charts used in business and economics are the following:

Arithmetic line charts consist of a series of points plotted on arithmetic scales and connected by straight lines. Line charts of time series and frequency distributions are discussed in Chapters 7 and 9, respectively.

Bar charts may consist of vertical bars called "columns," horizontal bars, or pictorial figures arranged as bars.

Circle charts and other geometric forms are useful in special situations.

Scatter diagrams consist of dots which show the relationship of two variables in correlation analysis. These charts are described in Chapter 20.

Ratio charts are a special type of line chart whose vertical scales are calibrated so as to show relative or percentage changes in the data rather than absolute changes. Ratio charts are particularly useful in the analysis of time series, as explained in Chapters 18 and 19.

This chapter will describe the basic characteristics and uses of bar charts, circle charts, and ratio charts. Many variations of these and other types may be found in the books listed at the end of the chapter.

BAR CHARTS

While the arithmetic line chart described in Chapter 7 is the most important type for the presentation of data, various geometric forms are also in common use for popular portrayal of simple comparisons. These forms may be of one dimension, such as bars of uniform width which *vary only in length;* two dimensions, such as rectangles or circles; or three dimensions, such as cubes, spheres, or other solid objects.

Of these forms, bars usually give the most accurate impression of size, since in two- or three-dimension figures the reader is uncertain whether to compare the diameters or the areas or the volumes, as the case may be. If the diameters denote the true comparison, then the areas or volumes exaggerate it. Chart 8–1, for example, indicates that the need for "avionics" engineers (i.e., those who develop control systems for aircraft) is expected to nearly double in the next five years. The right-hand silhouette is therefore drawn about twice the height

Chart 8–1

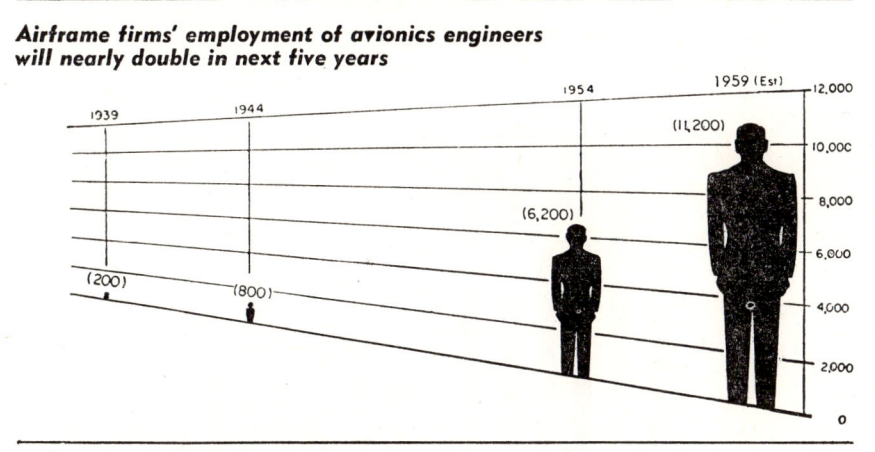

Airframe firms' employment of avionics engineers will nearly double in next five years

SOURCE: *Aviation Week*, December 27, 1954, p. 42.

of the adjoining one. However, this engineer of the future is about *four* times as big as his predecessor in area, and nearly *eight* times as big in weight—since this is a three-dimensional measure. At the other extreme, the figures representing employment in the two earliest years are so tiny as to be almost invisible. The drawing thus greatly exaggerates the increase in the demand for engineers. (The increase is still further exaggerated by drawing the chart in perspective.) For this reason the use of two- and three-dimension drawings of different size should generally be avoided.

Bar versus Line Charts

Bar charts may be preferable to line charts in portraying a relatively few values of one or two series. Line charts are preferable where there are many values or several series. Bars emphasize the individual amounts, while lines emphasize the general trend. Bars are also effective for showing the component parts of a whole. Bars and lines may be combined, as in a time series, where bars may represent yearly averages for earlier years and a curve shows the more recent monthly movements.

Vertical versus Horizontal Bars

Most bar charts in business and economic literature represent time series, as in the case of line charts; but other types of data can be shown as well. The bars are usually *vertical* in time and size distributions and *horizontal* in qualitative and geographic comparisons.

Chart 8–2

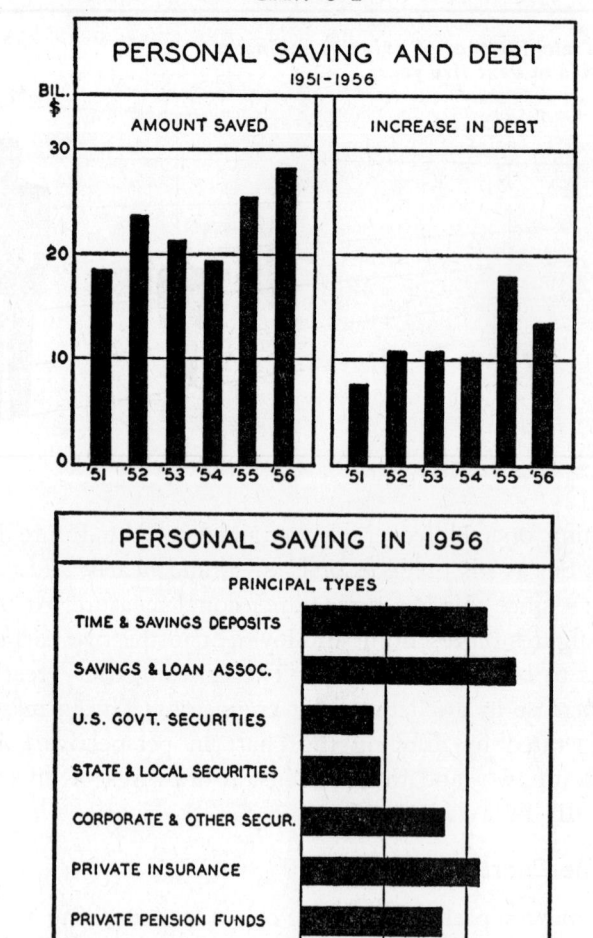

PERSONAL SAVING AND DEBT
1951–1956

PERSONAL SAVING IN 1956
PRINCIPAL TYPES

SOURCE: Cleveland Trust Company, *Business Bulletin*, July 16, 1957, p. 4; data from Securities and Exchange Commission.

In Chart 8–2, for example, *vertical* bars, or columns, are used to represent two *time* series: the changes in personal savings and debt each year from 1951 to 1956. The use of vertical bars in *size* distributions is illustrated in Chapter 9.

In other classifications of data, *horizontal* bars are customarily used. The lower panel of Chart 8–2, for example, represents a *qualitative* comparison of the different types of savings in 1956. In showing a qualitative comparison of this kind, or a *geographic* comparison (such

Chart 8–3

CHANGES IN PLANTED ACREAGES OF MAJOR CROPS
1957* VERSUS 1956

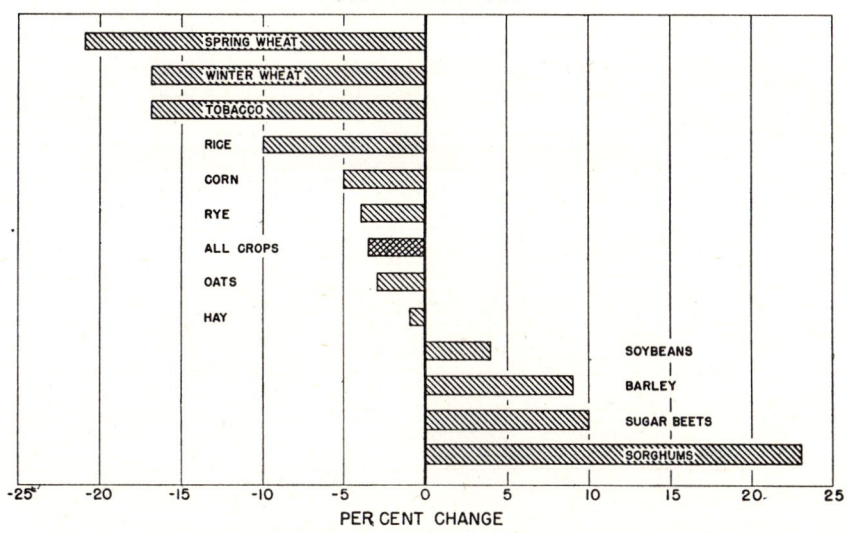

* Based on March 1 planting intentions and December 1 estimates (for wheat and rye).
Source: Deere & Company, Economic Research Department, April 30, 1957; data from U.S. Department of Agriculture.

as personal savings by regions), the categories are usually listed down the left side of the page, and the amounts are represented by bars extending from a vertical base line horizontally to the right, if positive, or to the left, if negative.

A common form of the latter is the per cent (or amount) change chart, such as Chart 8–3, which shows the shifts from the previous year in acreages planted in various crops, arrayed in order of their percentage growth or decline. The bars could also have been arranged in some other logical order, such as alphabetically, or in some customary sequence, as in the lower panel of Chart 8–2.

Horizontal bars are also used to show actual performance of any kind as compared with a standard or quota represented by a horizontal space, as in Gantt and quota charts.

Scales and Spacing

Since bars represent magnitudes by their lengths, the zero line must be shown and the arithmetic scale must not be broken, in order to present a true comparison.[1] The bars would be shortened by the same amount, to be sure, but their proportional difference would be increased. Note the scale in Chart 8–4, which is taken from a newspa-

Chart 8–4

COMPARE OCTANE RATINGS OF LEADING WESTERN PREMIUM GASOLINES				
	97	98	99	100-OCTANE
GASOLINE A				
GASOLINE B				
GASOLINE C				
GASOLINE D				
GASOLINE E				
GASOLINE F				
GASOLINE G				

per advertisement for "Gasoline A" (the brand name has been changed). By omitting the scale values from 0 to nearly 97, the octane rating of Gasoline A is made to appear 200 per cent greater than that of Gasoline B—about 100 times the true difference of 2 per cent! Occasionally, one excessively long bar in a series of bars may be broken off at the end and the amount shown directly beyond it, without distorting the general trend of the other bars, but this practice is not recommended.

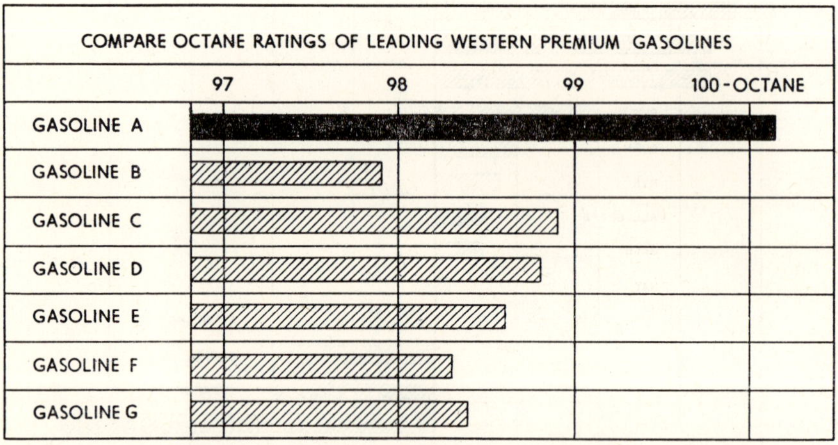

The time scale should also remain intact. That is, if certain years are omitted, the bars should be spaced accordingly.

Scale values are usually included (see Charts 8–2 and 8–3) but may

---

[1] An exception is the range chart, such as that in which vertical bars depict high and low stock prices. Here zero is not a factor.

Ch. 8]   COMMON TYPES OF CHARTS   135

be omitted if the values are lettered inside each bar. The only grid lines shown are the principal ones crossing the bars, and even these may be denoted merely by ticks at the scale numbers, as in Chart 8–6.

Bars are most effective when shaded to stand out against the white background. They should ordinarily be separated by spaces, usually about half as wide as the bars themselves. Occasionally, however, the bars are connected to give a continuous shaded effect. In Chart 8–5, for

Chart 8–5

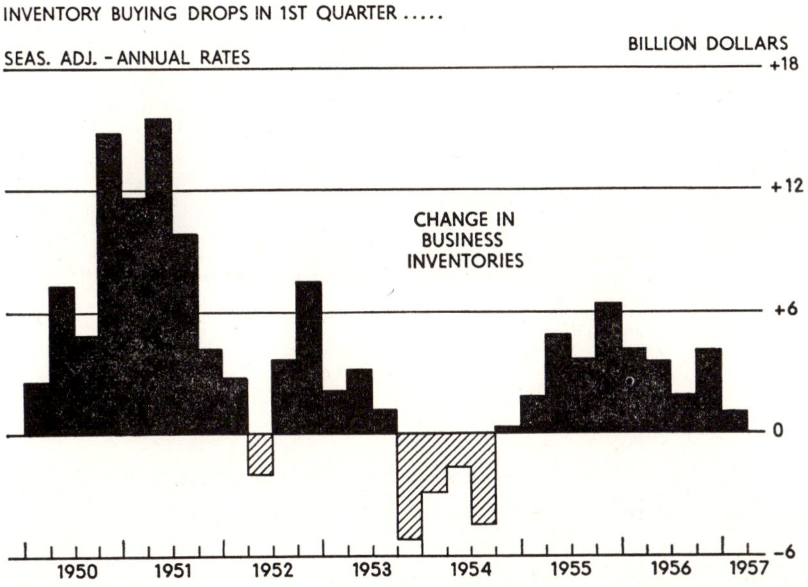

INVENTORY BUYING DROPS IN 1ST QUARTER .....

SEAS. ADJ. – ANNUAL RATES   BILLION DOLLARS

SOURCE: Chase Manhattan Bank, *Business in Brief,* April 1957, p. 1; data from U.S. Department of Commerce.

example, the bars are connected to emphasize the trends in inventory buying over recent years. In charts of size distributions the bars are also connected, to show a continuous range of values, as illustrated in Chapter 9.

Groups of Bars

Bars may be grouped to show two, and sometimes three, subclassifications. In this case, each type of bar is distinguished by a different texture (stippled, lined, crosshatched, or black in most cases) and identified by a label or key. The groups are spaced well apart. Only one scale can be used, since the bars would not be comparable in length if measured in different units.

In Chart 8–6, for example, adjoining pairs of bars compare changes in days of labor required to buy a farm machine (the main classifica-

Chart 8–6
DAYS OF LABOR REQUIRED TO BUY VARIOUS FARM MACHINES

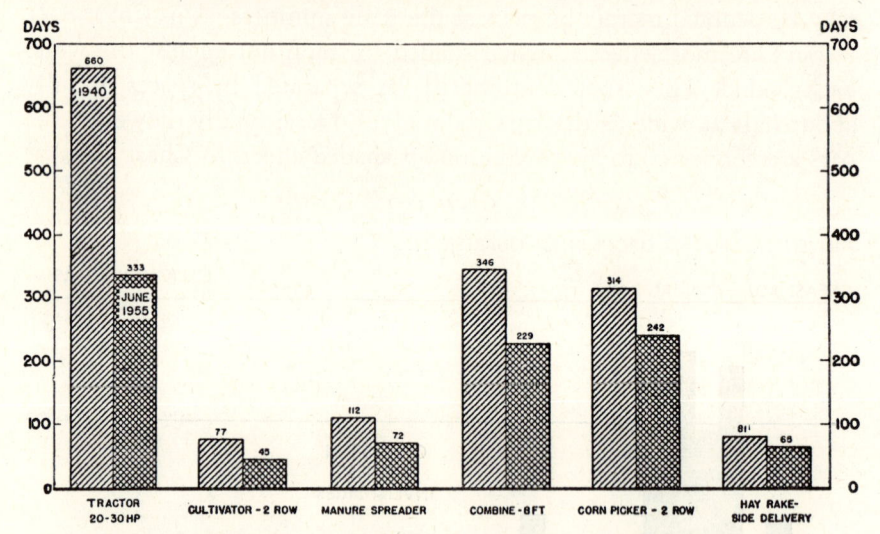

[Bar chart showing days of labor for 1940 and June 1955:
- TRACTOR 20-30 HP: 660 (1940), 333 (1955)
- CULTIVATOR - 2 ROW: 77, 45
- MANURE SPREADER: 112, 72
- COMBINE - 6 FT: 346, 229
- CORN PICKER - 2 ROW: 314, 242
- HAY RAKE-SIDE DELIVERY: 81, 65]

SOURCE: Deere & Company, Economic Research Department, January 1956; data from J. C. Bottum and J. O. Dunbar, Purdue University.

tion) in 1940 and 1955, subclassified by six different types of machines shown by separate pairs of bars, on a single scale.

Pictographs

Pictographs show rows of identical figures, such as workers or tractors, the length of the row indicating the amount in the same way as a bar does. This is an attractive device for dramatizing approximate comparisons and gives a fair picture so long as the figures are of uniform size and are readily identifiable.

Section A of Chart 8–7 illustrates the proper use of pictographs to show a doubling in number of employees, along with a vertical pictorial comparison of wages represented by piles of coins. Section B, on the other hand, illustrates how not to draw a pictograph. Some of its errors are: (1) figures of people are inappropriate to represent electric power; (2) no scale or other values are given; (3) figures are apparently drawn proportional to their heights, and so exaggerate differences in over-all size; (4) no indication is given as to whether supply refers to actual output or capacity, or in what year; (5) the areas

Ch. 8] COMMON TYPES OF CHARTS 137

Chart 8-7

PICTOGRAPHS
A. Good

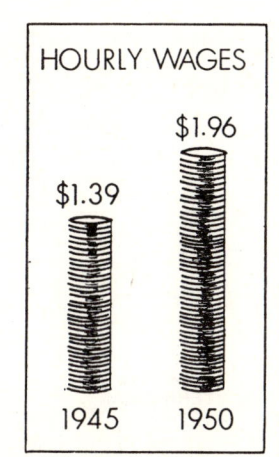

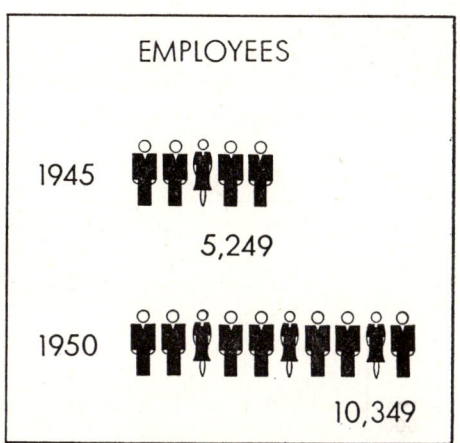

HOURLY WAGES	EMPLOYEES
$1.39 (1945) $1.96 (1950)	1945: 5,249 1950: 10,349

Source: *Willys-Overland Motors Annual Report, Year Ended September 30, 1950.*

B. Bad

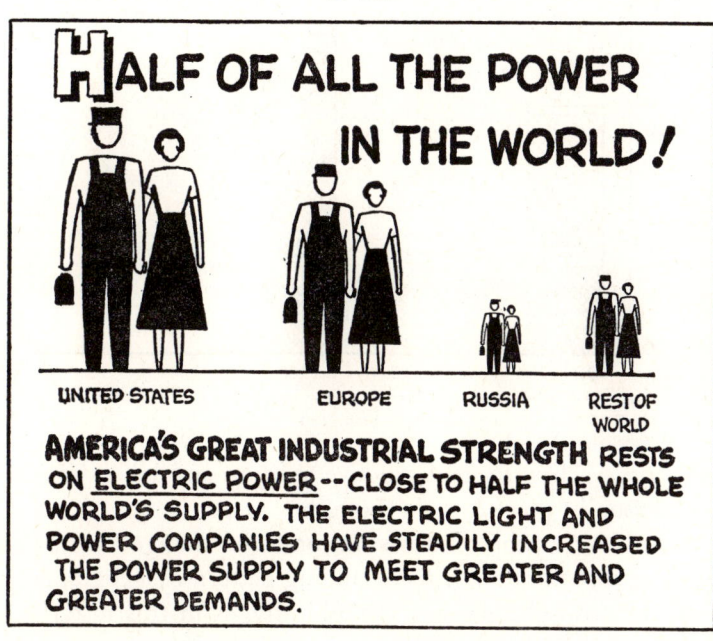

HALF OF ALL THE POWER IN THE WORLD!

UNITED STATES   EUROPE   RUSSIA   REST OF WORLD

AMERICA'S GREAT INDUSTRIAL STRENGTH RESTS ON <u>ELECTRIC POWER</u>--CLOSE TO HALF THE WHOLE WORLD'S SUPPLY. THE ELECTRIC LIGHT AND POWER COMPANIES HAVE STEADILY INCREASED THE POWER SUPPLY TO MEET GREATER AND GREATER DEMANDS.

of Europe and Russia are not mutually exclusive; and (6) no source of data is shown. (The source of this chart itself has been omitted to avoid embarrassment.)

Component Part Bars

Bar charts may be used effectively to show component parts of a total as well as the total itself. The bars are subdivided into relatively

Chart 8–8

AMERICAN TRAVEL EXPENDITURES IN FOREIGN COUNTRIES
(Excluding Fare Payments)

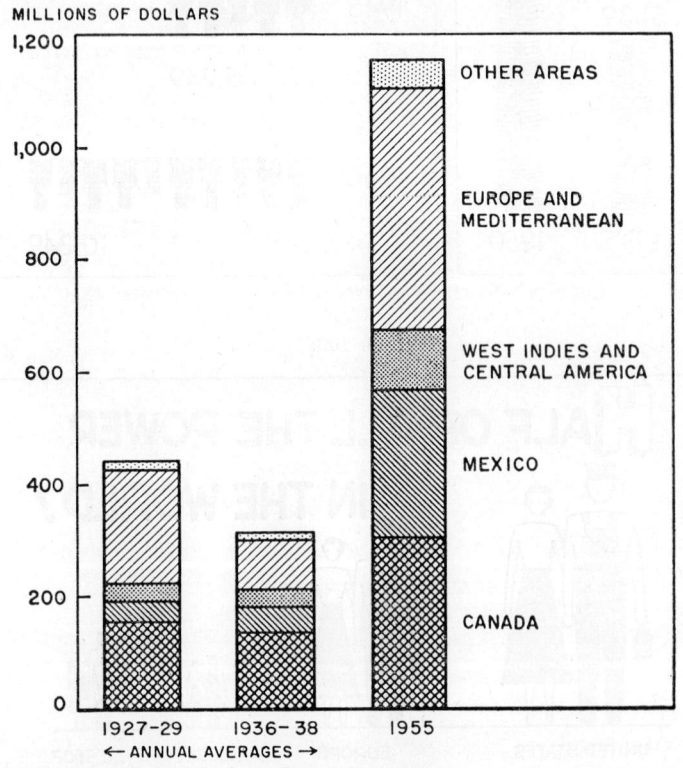

SOURCE: *Survey of Current Business,* June 1956, p. 17.

few segments, each with its distinctive shading and label. The darkest shading is usually placed at the bottom.

Chart 8–8, for example, shows not only the changes in total travel expenditures abroad but also the changing pattern by geographic areas. These can be arranged either geographically, as in this instance, or in order of size, with the most important area at the bottom.

Divided bars may show either absolute amounts or proportions of the total as 100 per cent. If actual values are more important, the original units are shown on the scale and the bars are of varying lengths. If, on the other hand, a relative breakdown is desired, the scale is in per cents, and all bars have the same length—100 per cent.

When the parts of only one total are to be compared, each one may be laid off from the zero base line as a separate bar for better part-to-part contrast, instead of being stacked cumulatively in one divided bar; but for several totals this arrangement would be confusing.

CIRCLE CHARTS

Another method of showing the component parts of a whole is to plot them on a circle or pie chart, as in Chart 8–9. Each part is ex-

Chart 8–9

PERSONAL CONSUMPTION EXPENDITURES
IN THE UNITED STATES, 1958
(Per Cent of Total)

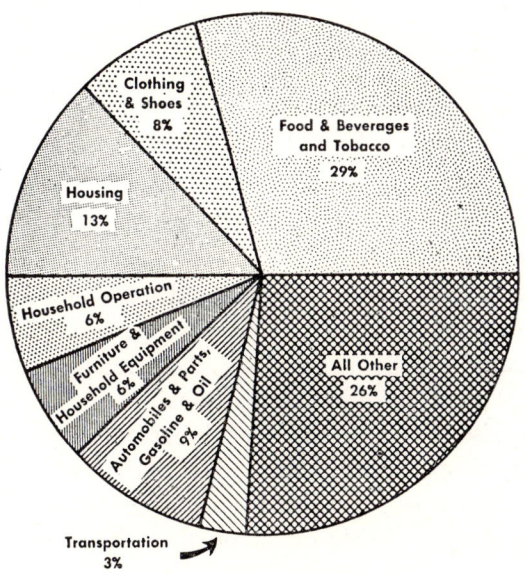

- Clothing & Shoes 8%
- Food & Beverages and Tobacco 29%
- Housing 13%
- Household Operation 6%
- Furniture & Household Equipment 6%
- Automobiles & Parts, Gasoline & Oil 9%
- All Other 26%
- Transportation 3%

SOURCE: *Survey of Current Business,* March 1959, p. 21.

pressed as a per cent of the total and is plotted by a protractor (1 per cent = 3.6°) as a sector around a circle whose total circumference represents the whole, or 100 per cent. The sectors may be plotted clockwise in order of size, starting from one of the cardinal compass points; but usage is not uniform in this respect. The proportions are the same whether actual amounts or percentages are labeled in the appropriate sectors.

In a breakdown of dollar values, the circle can be pictured as a silver dollar, and the parts represented as so many cents on the dollar instead of percentages, to present a more vivid picture. Many corporation stockholders' reports show the distribution of the sales dollar into various types of costs, dividends, and net profits in this way. Several circles of equal size are often used to show the breakdown of sales for past years as well.

Circles of different size, however, cannot properly be used to compare the size of different totals. This is because the reader does not know whether to compare the diameters or the areas (which vary as the squares of the diameters), and he is likely to misjudge the comparison in either case. Usually the circles are drawn so that their diameters are in the correct proportion to each other; but then the area comparison is exaggerated, as in the figures portrayed in Chart 8–1 (p. 131). Divided *bars* should be used to show totals of different size, since their one-dimension lengths can be easily judged not only for the totals themselves but for the component parts as well. Circles can, therefore, show proportions properly by variations in the angles of sectors but not by variations in diameter.

RATIO CHARTS

Arithmetic scales are satisfactory for showing absolute changes in the data but fail to reveal clearly what is often of more importance—the relative or per cent changes. For example, it is ordinarily not so significant that a company's sales increased more dollars over a given period than those of its smaller competitor as that its *percentage* increase was greater. For many purposes, then, relative comparisons are more important than absolute comparisons.

Some comparisons can be made arithmetically by simple division, such as in ratios, per cents, and index numbers. Division can be performed by the use of logarithms, since numbers may be multiplied or divided by simply adding or subtracting their logarithms. These computations may also be done mechanically by a slide rule, whose two sliding scales are calibrated with the logarithms of numbers. The ratio scale on a chart is the same as that on a slide rule. What logarithms can perform arithmetically and the slide rule mechanically, therefore, the ratio chart performs graphically. In addition, the ratio chart has a time scale which gives a visual picture of changing trends and comparisons, thus greatly extending the scope of this analytic device.

The ratio chart is consequently coming into widespread use not only for the analysis of data but for the presentation of relative changes and comparisons in many different fields. Such charts are even being used for presentation to the general reader who may be unfamiliar with the technical nature of this grid. To quote one leading journal:

Barron's uses ratio charts almost exclusively in plotting stock market prices whether of individual stocks or averages, because an investor is interested in comparing percentage rather than absolute changes. To him, a rise in the price of a stock from 5 to 10 is just as important as from 25 to 50, or 200 to 400, because in each case it means a capital appreciation of 100%.

The ratio chart is not ordinarily used for very simple exhibits, however; nor when absolute magnitudes are of primary interest; nor when zero or negative values appear (which it cannot show). Sometimes an arithmetic and a ratio chart of the same data are presented together to show both rate of change and amount of change, as in Chart 8–14 (p. 148).

Characteristics of the Ratio Chart

The term "ratio chart" means that the chart shows ratios in their true proportion, that is, equal ratios or percentages cover equal spaces on the vertical scale. The ratio chart is also called a "semilogarithmic" or "semilog" chart because the natural numbers are plotted on the vertical scale at distances from the "1" bottom line proportional to their logarithms, while the horizontal scale is arithmetic. A ratio chart should be so labeled;[2] but if not, it may be identified in a publication by the fact that the vertical scale numbers get closer together as the scale rises (Chart 8–10). In particular, the vertical distances between 1 and 2, 3 and 6, and 5 and 10 are all the same, since these distances all represent the same ratio of 1 to 2 irrespective of their position on the chart.

The horizontal axis shows time on the usual arithmetic scale. Two different time scales cannot be used if the slopes of curves in the two segments are to be compared. The plotted points are connected by straight lines; bars or shadings are inappropriate. The principles of planning and constructing a ratio chart are otherwise the same as for the arithmetic time series line chart already described; and the same rules regarding layout, titles, captions, and the like, apply.

In the ratio chart (as the term is generally used), only one scale is logarithmic. The double logarithmic chart, on the other hand, is one in which both scales are logarithmic. This chart has more specialized analytic applications; so it will not be discussed here. One use of the double logarithmic chart is in scatter diagrams showing the relationship between two variables, as illustrated in Chart 20–4.

---

[2] An explanatory caption such as "Ratio Chart: Straight trends shows constant per cent rate of growth; parallel lines represent same per cent increase" may be placed in the top of the grid for further explanation.

Chart 8–10

ONE-CYCLE RATIO OR SEMILOGARITHMIC CHART
With Per Cent Measuring Scale

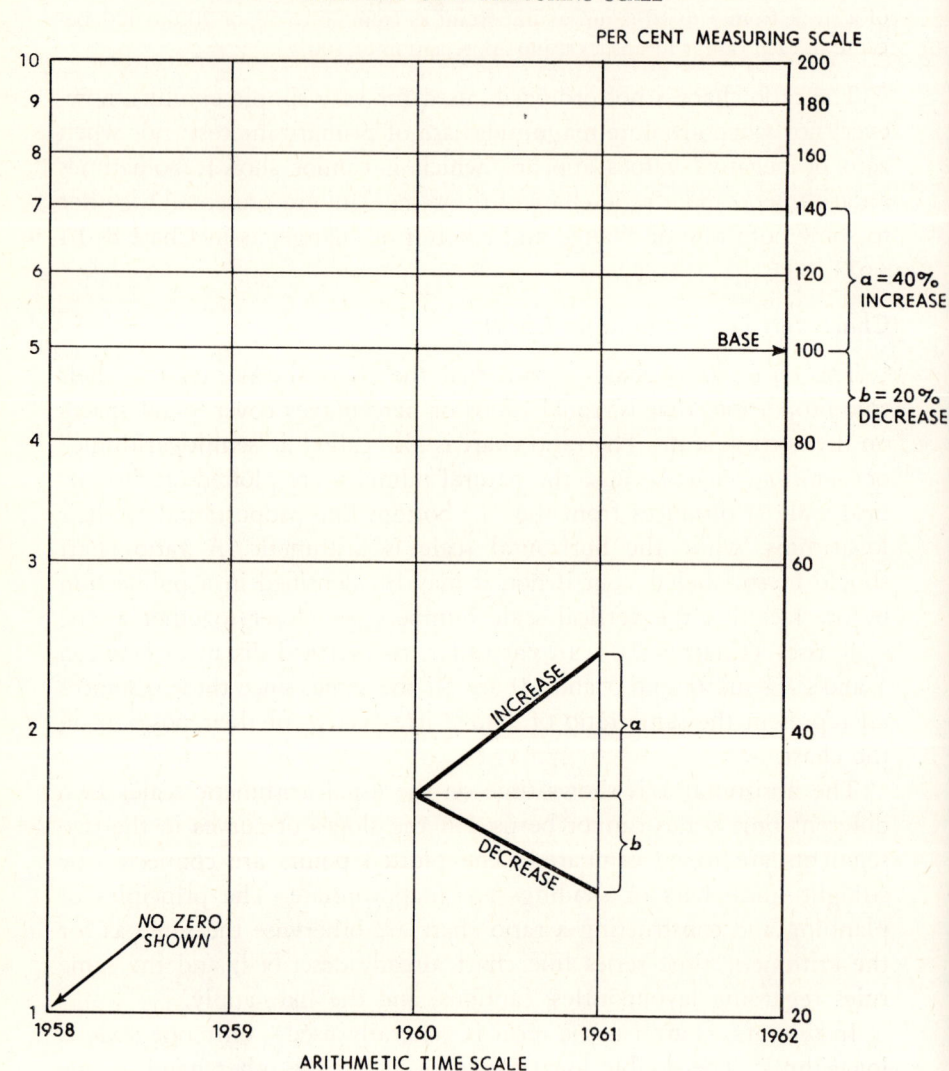

A log scale is said to have one *cycle* if the scale numbers extend only from 1 to 10 (or multiples thereof); two cycles if the scale is divided into two equal parts covering the ranges 1 to 10 and 10 to 100, respectively; three cycles if divided into three equal parts ranging from 1 to 10, 10 to 100, and 100 to 1,000; and so on. The scale can also be extended downward indefinitely to 0.1, 0.01, 0.001, etc., but can never reach zero. Hence the log scale cannot be used for a series that includes zero or negative values.

Construction of the Ratio Scale

The ratio scale may be constructed by laying off the logarithms of the numbers 1, 2, 3, etc., vertically from the bottom line (or horizontally from the left) in some convenient unit of distance, and marking these points with their natural values. Thus, in Chart 8–10, the scale number "1" is at the bottom (since $\log 1 = 0$) and the top number 10 is one unit above (since $\log 10 = 1$), the unit being 5 inches in this diagram. The "2" is marked .301 of the way up the graph (since $\log 2 = .301$ in Appendix B), or 1.5 inches up; "3" is marked .477 of the way up; and so on.

Another method is to place a slide rule on a blank sheet and mark off and label the divisions of one of its basic scales (the *A–B* two-cycle scale or the *C–D* one-cycle scale), as on the rule.

Chart 8–11

EXPANDING A RATIO SCALE

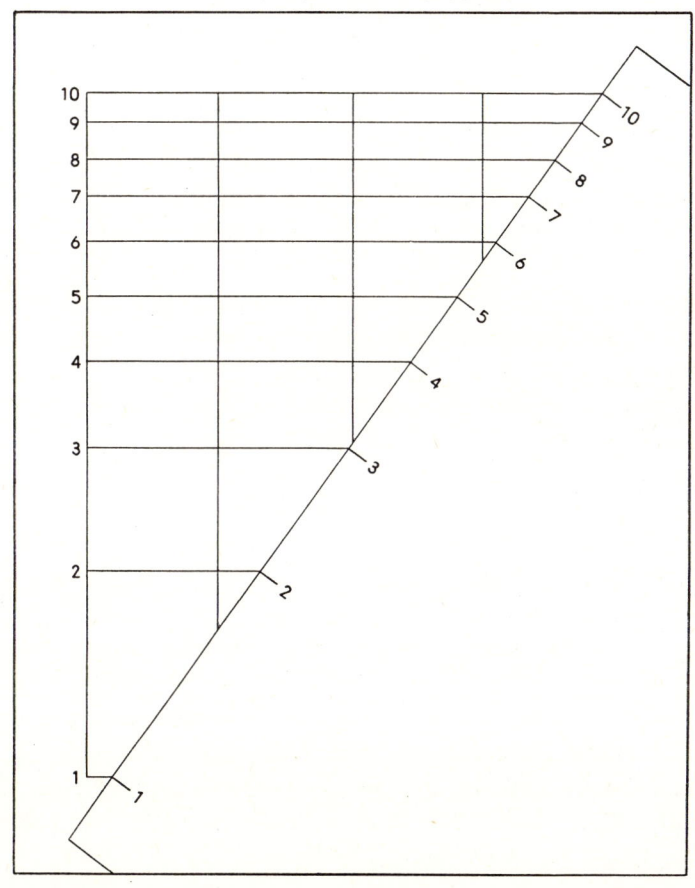

For most purposes, however, it is simplest to purchase the printed sheet at a graphic supply store, where many types of logarithmic grids made by Keuffel and Esser, Dietzgen, Codex, and other manufacturers are available. Hence, it is no more necessary to know logarithms in using a ratio chart than in using a slide rule. If a blank sheet is to be marked with only the main grid lines for reproduction, it may be placed over the printed grid, on a glass with a light beneath if necessary, to facilitate plotting.

If a large exhibit is needed, such as a wall chart, the blank sheet may be placed diagonally on the printed grid, the angle determining the size of the enlargement, and the scale divisions marked off on the sheet, as shown in Chart 8–11. This device is useful for enlarging any type of diagram or map. Conversely, the scale may be contracted by placing the printed grid diagonally on a blank sheet and marking off the scale divisions similarly.

How to Plot

The first problem in plotting data on a ratio chart is to choose between one-, two-, and three-cycle paper. If the largest value in a series is less than ten times the smallest, one-cycle paper is usually preferable, because this has the largest scale. Only the portion of the scale that is used in plotting need be shown in the finished chart, since there is no zero or other base line from which heights are measured. For the same reason, the scale need not be marked with a break to indicate omitted values.

The printed log scale begins with 1, rather than 0, at the bottom. In order to plot data most easily, mark the bottom line with one of the numbers 1, 2, 4, or 5, followed or preceded by any number of zeros, such as 0.01 million persons, 20 dollars, 4,000 tons, or 5 per cent. If some other value, such as 3 or 75, were placed at the bottom, it would complicate plotting, since the minor grid lines would represent odd amounts. If there is a choice of two numbers, select the one that will best center the curve on the chart.

Once the bottom value is selected—say $20—multiply this by the printed scale figures 1, 2, 3 . . . and mark them accordingly (20, 40, 60, . . .) until the top of the cycle is marked with a value ten times the bottom (200). This is a *must*. If the printed figures 1, 2, 3, were labeled 20, 30, 40, for example, the logarithmic proportions would be lost and the graph would be meaningless as a ratio chart.

As an example, suppose the data to be plotted range from 78 to 413 pounds. Since 413 is less than ten times 78, one-cycle paper can be used. The nearest starting point (1, 2, 4, or 5) below 78 is 50; so the scale numbers 1, 2, 3, . . . 10 may be marked 50, 100, 150, . . . 500 pounds. As a check, the top scale value must be ten times the bottom on one-cycle paper, one hundred times on two-cycle paper, and so on.

Special care must be taken in plotting data because some printed grid lines are omitted as the scale contracts in the higher values. All plotted points should also be rechecked. Note that the natural values themselves are plotted; logarithms are not used in any way.

Different scales can be used to compare series of disparate size or those expressed in different units. For example, the relative growth of a large and a small company, or of coal production in tons and oil in barrels, may be fairly gauged because the slopes of the curves register percentage changes, which are comparable even if the original units are not. Thus the incompatible are made compatible.

The scales should be selected so as to bring the series close together for easy comparison, with the more important series on top for appearance's sake. The choice of scale affects only the height of a curve above the bottom line, which is not significant; it does not affect the shape or slope of the curve in any way.

Uses of the Ratio Chart

The slope of a line on a ratio chart indicates the percentage change between two points of time. A continuing line of the same slope or two parallel lines therefore represent the same relative movement. The steeper the slope, the greater the per cent rate of change. A given vertical distance corresponds to the same percentage difference anywhere on the chart. These characteristics give ratio charts the unique advantages described below:

Constant Relative Rate of Growth as a Straight Line. A series growing or declining by the same percentage each year, such as a sum of money at compound interest, or sales increasing 10 per cent a year, appears on the ratio chart as a straight line.[3] If the series curves away from the straight line, it denotes a corresponding change in the rate of growth or the rate of decline, as shown in Chart 8–12. Many young industries expand at about a constant percentage rate each year until they mature, when the rate of growth tends to taper off, as in

---

[3] This "logarithmic straight line," also called an exponential curve or compound interest curve, fits any geometric progression, such as 1, 2, 4, 8, 16. It should not be confused with a line representing a constant *amount* of change, or arithmetic progression, such as 1, 2, 3, 4, 5, which appears as a straight line on an *arithmetic* grid.

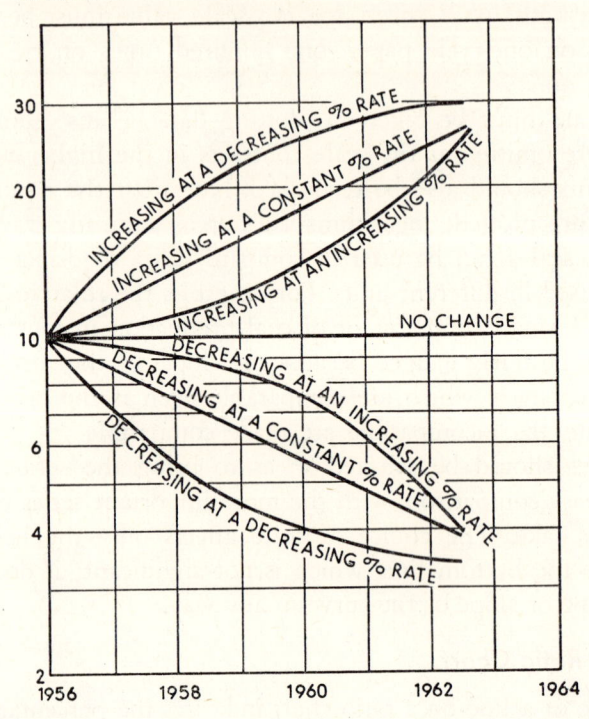

Chart 8–12
MEANING OF CURVE SHAPES ON RATIO CHART

the top curve of Chart 8–12. Thus the oil production curve in Chart 8–13 is nearly straight from 1900 to 1925 but bends over to the right thereafter, while the older coal industry grew at a decreasing rate until about 1920, and then turned down.

By watching a company's production curve on a ratio chart, therefore, the analyst can determine whether or not it is maintaining its past rate of gain. Furthermore, if historic factors of growth may be expected to persist, the analyst can project past trends in order to forecast future output. This method is described in Chapter 18.

Comparison between Two Curves. The relative growth or decline of two or more curves can be seen at a glance by comparing their slopes on a ratio chart. Parallel lines indicate the same rate of change. If the slopes differ, the steeper is changing at a faster percentage rate. Thus in Chart 8–14, panel B, if the atomic energy curve rises more steeply than total industrial use of energy, this means that its per cent growth is greater, irrespective of the size of the two series or the units in which they are measured. Hence there is better comparability of relative changes than in the case of arithmetic charts.

An arithmetic graph of two series on a single scale always emphasizes the growth of the larger one, as in Chart 8–14, left panel. A 10 billion kilowatt-hour rise in atomic energy use—from 10 to 20 billion, for example—is a 100 per cent increase; but a much larger arith-

Chart 8–13

SUPPLY OF ENERGY FROM COAL AND DOMESTIC OIL
FIVE-YEAR AVERAGES, 1901–55
(In Quadrillions of British Thermal Units)

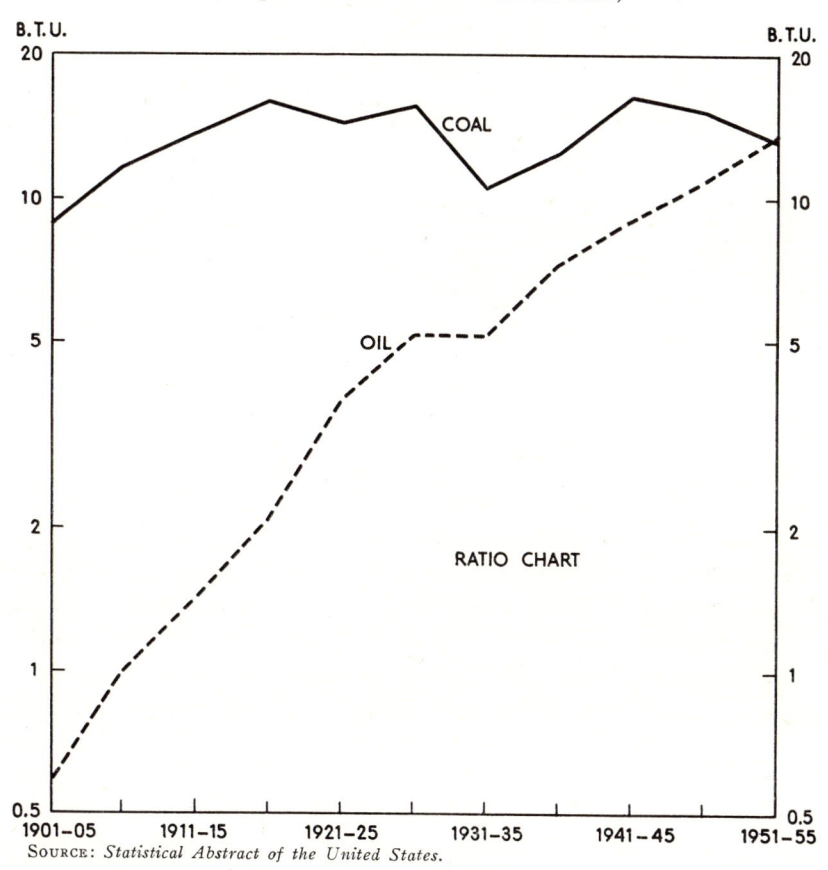

SOURCE: *Statistical Abstract of the United States.*

metic rise of 50 billion in total industrial use of energy—say from 200 to 250 billion—is only a 25 per cent increase. Or, if two different scales are used to bring the curves together, the relationship is arbitrarily distorted. Even index numbers only afford easy comparison with one base level. The ratio chart affords true relative comparisons between any two points on the grid, and yet absolute values can be read from the scale, unlike the case of index numbers.

Chart 8–14

ATOMIC ENERGY USE VERSUS TOTAL INDUSTRIAL USE
OF ENERGY, 1948–55, ON ARITHMETIC AND RATIO SCALES
(Billions of Kilowatt-Hours)

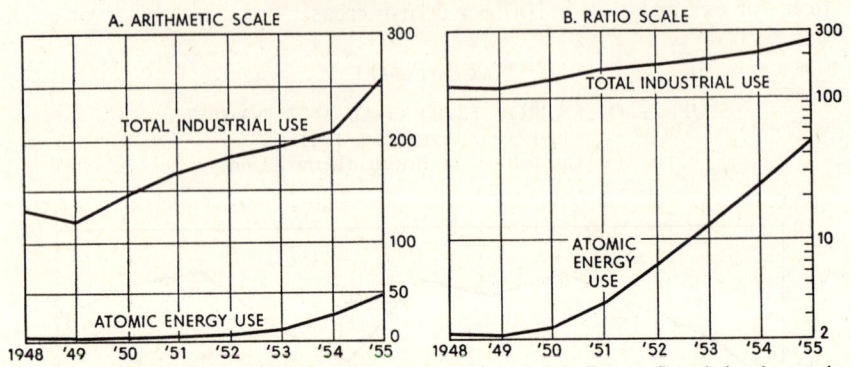

Note: Atomic energy use is primarily electricity sold to Atomic Energy Commission for use in the federal government's atomic energy plants.
Source: *Electrical World*, September 17, 1956.

The arithmetic graphs of oil and coal production (Chart 7–6, p. 123) do not show the relative rates of growth. The index numbers in the bottom panel do show the per cent changes from one base period; but if some earlier period had been taken as the base, the relative increase in the use of oil would have been much greater because of the smaller base. On the ratio scale (Chart 8–13), however, the relative rates of growth are indicated at a glance by the slopes of the two curves. These may be compared either in a single period or over the long run. Oil has gained at the expense of coal in every five-year period since 1900 except between 1936–40 and 1941–45, when oil was rationed because of war needs.

In Chart 8–15, too, the ratio scale makes the rates of change in truck transport comparable with those in all other freight, although they differ widely in size. The rates of change in trucking are also comparable with those in passenger car travel, though one is expressed in ton-miles and the other in vehicle-miles. For example, the chart shows that trucking has scored greater relative gains than either of the other two forms of transport over the period 1939–55.

The relative severity of depressions or seasonal fluctuations in different industries is also apparent at a glance from the vertical range of fluctuation on a ratio chart. Thus, passenger car travel suffered a greater percentage drop than did truck transport between 1941 and 1943, according to Chart 8–15.

Performing Calculations on a Ratio Chart. Percentages or ratios may be read directly from a log scale in this way:

Chart 8–15
TRENDS IN MOTOR VEHICLE TRAVEL AND FREIGHT TRANSPORT

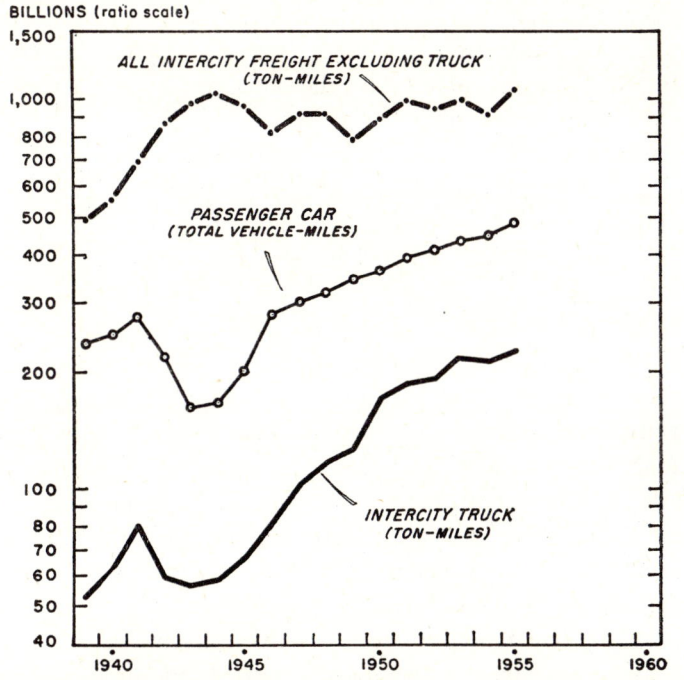

SOURCE: *Survey of Current Business,* December 1956, p. 21; data from Bureau of Public Roads and Interstate Commerce Commission.

1. Mark a per cent measuring scale as shown on the right column of Chart 8–10, page 142. That is, on a one-cycle chart, multiply the printed scale numbers by 20, so that the scale extends from 20 per cent to 200 per cent. On a two-cycle chart, mark the center line "100 per cent," and so on, so that the vertical scale extends from 10 per cent to 1,000 per cent.

2. Mark the *vertical* distance between any two points on the edge of a blank strip of paper, or take it off on a pair of dividers (e.g., the increase *a* or decrease *b* between 1960 and 1961 on Chart 8–10).

3. Lay off the increase upward, or the decrease downward, *from the 100 per cent base point* of the measuring scale, and read the value of the second point as a per cent in terms of the first point as 100 per cent. The per cent *change* is this figure minus 100. Thus, on Chart 8–10, the 1960–61 increase *a* is read off as 40 per cent, while the decrease *b* is 20 per cent.

The relationship between any two points at the same time (such as the ratio of net profits to sales in 1960) can be read off in the same way.

Instead of transferring the vertical distances on a chart to its own per cent measuring scale, a separate strip of the graph paper marked with a per cent scale may be placed vertically on the chart to measure percentages or ratios directly. (The *slope* of the line, rather than its vertical projection, could also be measured on a protractor, but this method is more awkward.)

The use of a log scale as a calculator leads to various methods of averaging percentage deviations and rates of growth, as in the graphic determination of seasonal indexes and logarithmic straight line trends. These methods will be discussed in later chapters.

Limitations of Ratio Charts

Ratio charts have certain limitations in the presentation of data which restrict their use accordingly: (1) They do not give a visual idea of absolute magnitude as a distance above the base line, although these magnitudes can be read from the scale. (2) They are difficult for the layman to understand, and so should not be used for simple illustrations which an arithmetic chart could show as well. (3) They cannot show zero or negative values. (4) Finally, they are sometimes mistakenly used to contract a wide range of absolute values into a small space. This is legitimate if relative movements are of interest, but if a picture of absolute changes is needed, one or more arithmetic scales must be used.

SUMMARY

The principal forms of charts are arithmetic line charts, bar and circle charts, scatter diagrams, and ratio charts. Bar and circle charts and ratio charts are discussed in this chapter; the others are presented elsewhere.

Bar charts are usually preferable to two- and three-dimension geometric forms, such as circles and solids, for showing simple comparisons. They may also be used in place of line charts for portraying a relatively few values or for representing the parts of a whole. Since bars denote size by their length, the scale should not be broken. Shading and spacing of bars are also desirable. Bars may be grouped to show subclassifications, with appropriate shading and labeling.

Vertical bars or columns are usually employed for time and size comparisons, and horizontal bars for geographic and other qualitative classifications, including per cent changes of various categories. Pictographs are animated bars that are effective for illustrating rough comparisons if the figures are self-explanatory and of uniform size. Bar charts may be divided to show the changes of component parts either in absolute amounts or relative to the total as 100 per cent, whichever is more significant.

Circle charts are also useful for showing component parts of a whole as sectors of different angular size, like slices of pie; but circles of different diameter are apt to misrepresent the true comparison.

Arithmetic charts are suitable for showing absolute amounts but do not show relative comparisons as well. *Ratio* or *semilogarithmic* charts make data comparable by means of a vertical logarithmic scale, with an arithmetic time scale to picture dynamic changes. Or, a double logarithmic scale can be used to compare any two variables. The ratio graph is thus an invaluable tool of analysis. Ratio chart paper with a variety of printed grids can be purchased in graphic supply stores. A ratio scale can also be constructed by plotting natural numbers at distances from the bottom line proportional to their logarithms, or by marking slide-rule divisions on a blank sheet. A printed grid may be enlarged by marking its divisions on a sheet placed diagonally on it.

Data should be plotted on one-cycle paper for maximum enlargement if the range is within the 10 to 1 ratio. The bottom of the scale should be marked 1, 2, 4, or 5 (with appropriate zeros and unit) and this value multiplied by the printed scale figures to get the other values. Different scales may be used to bring series of diverse sizes and units together for easy comparison.

The ratio chart is useful for three types of comparison: (1) It shows a constant per cent rate of growth as a straight line; so changes in this rate are denoted by curvature of the line, and trend forecasts can sometimes be made. (2) The relative growth or fluctuations of two curves may be compared more accurately than in arithmetic charts, since parallel lines indicate the same per cent rates of change anywhere on the chart and steeper slopes indicate higher rates. (3) Percentages or ratios may be read directly from the vertical scale and applied toward further graphic analysis.

Ratio charts, however, should not be used to give a visual picture of absolute amounts or to contract a wide range of such values, nor for very simple illustrations, nor for data including zero or negative values.

PROBLEMS

1. Compare the merits of—
    a) Line charts and bars.
    b) Circles and bars.
    c) Pictographs and bars.

2. a) Plot the following data in good form (see Chapter 7) on any of the four types of charts listed in Problem 1.
    b) Defend your choice of chart.

152 BUSINESS AND ECONOMIC STATISTICS [Ch. 8

Year	Natural Gas Marketed Production, United States (Billion Cubic Feet)
1930	1,943
1935	1,917
1940	2,660
1945	3,919
1950	6,282
1955	9,405

SOURCE: *Statistical Abstract.*

3. *a*) Draw a per cent change chart of the following data.
   b) Explain your order of arrangement.

SALES IN A COUNTRY GENERAL STORE BY TYPE OF GOODS, 1950 AND 1960

Type of Goods	1950	1960
Groceries	$20,713	$22,014
Meats	519	857
Shoes	1,584	721
Rubber footwear	607	862
Dry goods	1,583	1,430
Notions	1,921	981
Hardware	1,025	1,129
Drugs	254	153

4. *a*) Prepare a circle chart and a bar chart showing absolute amounts or proportions of the total, whichever is appropriate, for the following data. Arrange the automobile companies in an effective order.

PRODUCTION OF PASSENGER CARS IN THE UNITED STATES

(In Thousands of Units)

Company	Full Year 1956[1]	Jan.–Sept. 1957[2]
American Motors	104.2	73
Ford	1,669.2	1,486
Chrysler	870.3	966
Studebaker-Packard	95.8	53
General Motors	3,062.4	2,105
Total	5,801.9	4,683

SOURCES OF DATA:
[1] Standard & Poor's Industry Surveys, "Autos," p. A 105, June 6, 1957.
[2] Estimated from data in the *Wall Street Journal*, October 4, 1957, p. 8.

b) Which type of graph is better here—circles or bars; absolutes or relatives? Why?

c) Justify your arrangement of companies.

5. *a*) Discuss the relative advantages of arithmetic and logarithmic vertical scales for time series charts.

   b) How would you label the bottom and top of a printed ratio sheet for data having the following ranges: 390 to 1,400 tons; 65 to 3,200 million passenger-miles; $0.16 to $55.50; 89,000,000 to 180,000,000 population? How many cycles does your ratio sheet have in each case—1, 2, or 3?

6. *a*) Plot the data in Chapter 7, Problem 6, on a ratio chart.

   b) What does this chart show about trends in sales and net profit, contrasted with what the arithmetic charts reveal?

7. *a*) Draw a ratio chart of the data given below.

   b) Interpret the facts shown by your chart.

PRODUCTION OF GRAPEFRUIT IN THE UNITED STATES, 1929–54

Year	California	Florida	Texas	Arizona	Total
1929	1.0	8.2	1.5	0.4	11.2
1934	2.2	15.2	2.8	1.2	21.4
1939	2.0	15.8	13.9	2.9	34.6
1944	3.8	22.3	22.3	3.8	52.2
1949	2.5	24.2	6.4	3.4	36.5
1954	2.4	34.8	2.5	2.5	42.2

Production (Millions of Boxes)

Source: *Agricultural Statistics.*

8. *a*) Compare the growth of two industries or companies since 1947 by plotting their annual production or sales curves on a ratio chart.

   b) Compare the per cent rates of change in different years for one of the curves.

   c) Compare the relative growth of the two curves during this period.

   d) Mark a per cent measuring scale on the chart. Show the per cent change in each series between the first and last years by measuring the vertical difference on this scale.

SELECTED READINGS

AMERICAN SOCIETY OF MECHANICAL ENGINEERS. *Time-Series Charts.* New York, 1960.

This manual focuses on design, as it affects a chart's meaning.

AMERICAN STANDARDS ASSOCIATION. *Illustrations for Publication and Projection.* New York: American Society of Mechanical Engineers, 1959.

A standard manual covering preferred practice for the preparation of charts.

HUFF, DARRELL. *How to Lie with Statistics.* New York: W. W. Norton & Co., Inc., 1954.
   Chapters 5, 6, and 9 illustrate some common misuses of charts.
LUTZ, R. R. *Graphic Presentation Simplified.* New York: Funk & Wagnalls Co., 1949.
   A detailed description of many types of simple charts used for presentation.
MODLEY, RUDOLF, and LOWENSTEIN, DYNO. *Pictographs and Graphs.* New York: Harper & Bros., 1952.
   Explains how to make and use pictorial charts.
MYERS, JOHN H. *Statistical Presentation.* Ames, Iowa: Littlefield, Adams & Co., 1950.
   A concise and readable manual on the construction of effective tables and charts.
SCHMID, CALVIN F. *Handbook of Graphic Presentation.* New York: The Ronald Press Co., 1954.
   A complete, readable treatment of graphic techniques and their use in designing the principal types of charts, with many illustrations.
SPEAR, MARY E. *Charting Statistics.* New York: McGraw-Hill Book Co., Inc., 1952.
   A book on practical graphic presentation, depicting many types of charts and their uses in economics.
U.S. GOVERNMENT, DEPARTMENT OF AGRICULTURE. Agriculture Handbook No. 128. *Graphic Analysis in Agricultural Economics.* Washington, D.C.: Superintendent of Documents, 1957.
   Applies graphic methods of analysis to frequency distributions, time series, correlation, linear programing, and many other fields of statistics.
WELD, WALTER E. *How to Chart.* Norwood, Mass.: Codex Book Co., 1947.
   Describes when and why to use each kind of business chart. Includes three chapters on the ratio chart.

9. FREQUENCY DISTRIBUTIONS

PRIOR chapters have described the methods of collecting statistical information and presenting the results in tables and charts. Beginning in this chapter, the principal methods of analyzing data are discussed. The first step is to reduce large masses of raw figures to a simple form. Then computed measures, such as averages and measures of dispersion, can be used to summarize the important characteristics of the data.

Many types of data are classified according to size. Examples are: rents paid for houses, weights of cattle marketed, and wages of workers. In each case the original data are measurements or values of a variable (e.g., rent, which varies from house to house) which will be called X. These are classified by assigning each value to the size class or *class interval* to which it belongs. The number of values of X in each interval is called the *frequency,* and the whole table of frequencies is called a *frequency distribution.*

A *frequency distribution* therefore is a table in which values of a variable are classified according to size. It is a valuable laborsaving device for summarizing figures that are too extensive for treatment in ungrouped form. Through the use of this device, a maximum of information can be presented with a minimum of data.

In order that the analysis of a frequency distribution may be meaningful, it is necessary that the data be *homogeneous,* that is, sufficiently alike to be comparable for the purposes of the study. This concept of homogeneity is important in all types of research.

Homogeneity may be illustrated by a study of gasoline prices in Rockford, Illinois, conducted for the Standard Oil Company of Indiana in 1955. Here, the prices for the regular grade at major-brand service stations varied from 30.3 to 31.7 cents a gallon, while the prices at private-brand or "cut-rate" stations varied from 27.4 to 29.9 cents.

Hence each of these homogeneous groups was analyzed separately. If all stations had been combined, the resulting distribution would have been *heterogeneous,* and would have concealed important differences in pricing policy of the two types of station. This distribution would have revealed its heterogeneity, however, because of the two points of concentration in the price data. It is nearly always preferable to separate data into groups that are homogeneous in characteristics that affect the variable being studied (e.g., the type of service station affects prices) than to combine disparate groups into a single frequency distribution.

THE ARRAY

Sometimes it is convenient to arrange the values of the variable in an *array,* as a preliminary step. An array is a listing of values arranged in order of *size*—either from smallest to largest, or vice versa. The values can be listed individually, but if there are many duplicate numbers, it is more convenient to group them on a tally sheet.

Table 9–1, for example, shows the over-all dimension of 63 gears, taken from a quality control measurement. The raw data in panel A are too awkward to handle directly, so they have been *arrayed* in panel

Table 9–1

RAW DATA AND ARRAY
Dimensions of 63 Gears as Illustrated (Inches)

SOURCE: Marchant Calculators, Inc., *Statistical Quality Control,* 1954, p. 17.

B by means of a tally sheet. That is, the possible values of the dimension are first listed, and each item from panel A is then tallied in panel B opposite its size—each fifth mark crossing the preceding four marks for ease in counting. The tally sheet thus presents an array in which identical values appear as successive tally marks, rather than by repeating the figures themselves.

The array in Table 9-1, panel B, not only shows the data in simpler form than in panel A but reveals at a glance certain salient characteristics—the highest value (.4270), the lowest (.4235), and the most frequent size (.4250). Also, in this simple case where no further grouping of values is needed, the array is already in the form of a usable frequency distribution, with class intervals .0005" wide—the number of marks opposite each dimension indicating the frequency with which this measurement occurred.

GROUPING INTO BROADER CLASSES

Most types of data, however, have so many different values that an array is excessively detailed. The figures must then be grouped into broader classes. The methods for doing this are illustrated below with data adapted from a U.S. Bureau of Labor Statistics survey of straight-time hourly earnings of 214 machine tool operators in machinery manufacturing plants in an eastern city. Studies of this type are needed for industrial relations analysis, labor-union wage negotiations, and many aspects of welfare economics.

Table 9-2 presents an array of these hourly earnings in the form of a tally sheet, with the number of operators at each earnings level noted in the column headed "f" (for frequency). This table still has too many separate values for easy analysis and presentation. The earnings situation can be more readily grasped after the data are grouped into broader intervals. For this purpose, class intervals 10 cents wide were chosen, beginning with $2.25 as the lower limit of the first interval. The *class interval* is the range of values for each class. This is effectively the difference between the lower limits, or upper limits, of two consecutive classes.

The resulting frequency distribution is shown in Table 9-3. The reasons for this choice of intervals are as follows: The number of classes (eight) is large enough to show the general distribution of earnings and small enough to simplify analysis and presentation. The class limits ($2.25, $2.35, etc.) are multiples of 5 cents, which are simple round numbers, while the midpoints ($2.30, $2.40, etc.) are at the popular rates at multiples of 10 cents. This permits easy interpretation and minimized errors of grouping. Finally, the intervals

158   BUSINESS AND ECONOMIC STATISTICS   [Ch. 9

Table 9–2

MORE DETAILED ARRAY
STRAIGHT-TIME HOURLY EARNINGS OF 214 MACHINE TOOL OPERATORS, CLASS A, IN MACHINERY MANUFACTURING PLANTS IN AN EASTERN CITY
(In Dollars per Hour)

Earnings	Operators Tally	f	Earnings	Operators Tally	f	Earnings	Operators Tally	f
2.30	|	1	2.55	⊮	5	2.80	⊮	5
2.31			2.56	⊮ |	6	2.81	|	1
2.32	|	1	2.57	|||	3	2.82		
2.33			2.58	||||	4	2.83		
2.34			2.59	⊮	5	2.84		
2.35	||	2	2.60	⊮ ⊮ |	11	2.85	|	1
2.36	||	2	2.61	||||	4	2.86	|	1
2.37			2.62	|||	3	2.87	|	1
2.38	|||	3	2.63	⊮ ⊮ ⊮ ⊮	20	2.88		
2.39	||	2	2.64	||	2	2.89		
2.40	⊮ ||	7	2.65	⊮ ||||	9	2.90		
2.41	|	1	2.66	||	2	2.91		
2.42			2.67	|||	3	2.92		
2.43	|	1	2.68	||	2	2.93		
2.44	⊮	5	2.69	|||	3	2.94		
2.45	||||	4	2.70	⊮ ⊮ |||	13	2.95		
2.46	|||	3	2.71	|||	3	2.96		
2.47	⊮	5	2.72	⊮ |	6	2.97	|	1
2.48	|||	3	2.73	|	1	2.98	|	1
2.49	||	2	2.74	|||	3	2.99		
2.50	⊮ ⊮ ||	12	2.75	⊮ ⊮ |	11	3.00		
2.51	⊮	5	2.76	⊮	5	3.01		
2.52	|	1	2.77	|	1	3.02	|	1
2.53	⊮ ⊮ ||	12	2.78			3.03		
2.54	||	2	2.79	||	2	3.04	|	1

Table 9–3

FREQUENCY DISTRIBUTION
HOURLY EARNINGS OF 214 MACHINE TOOL OPERATORS

Hourly Earnings	Midpoint	Number of Operators f
$2.25 and under $2.35	$2.30	2
$2.35 and under $2.45	2.40	23
$2.45 and under $2.55	2.50	49
$2.55 and under $2.65	2.60	63
$2.65 and under $2.75	2.70	45
$2.75 and under $2.85	2.80	25
$2.85 and under $2.95	2.90	3
$2.95 and under $3.05	3.00	4
Total	....	214

($2.25 and under $2.35, etc.) are defined clearly and unambiguously. These principles are discussed below.

Number and Width of Class Intervals

The number and width of the class intervals must be decided simultaneously because the narrower the intervals the greater their number must be to cover the range of values.

In general, it is advisable to divide the data into from 6 to 15 classes. If the number of classes is too small, important characteristics of the data may be concealed by grouping in intervals that are too broad. At the other extreme, it is rarely necessary to preserve so much detail that more than 15 classes are needed. Also, if there are too many classes, there may be a confusing zigzag of frequencies, and some classes may contain no values of X at all. This is the case in Table 9-2, which lists 75 one-cent intervals.

The number of classes sometimes depends on the number of items in a sample, too, since small samples often have zigzag frequencies because of sampling errors. These will be smoothed out in larger samples, provided the distribution in the population itself is smooth. Hence, more classes can be used in larger samples without incurring zigzag frequencies.

Once the approximate number of classes has been chosen, the exact number is determined by the width of the interval. This interval is usually selected as a convenient round number located so that clusters of data occur at its midpoints, as described in the next section. To find the number of classes, then, divide the range of values by the interval width and take the next larger integer. Thus, dividing the range of machine tool operators' earnings ($3.04 − $2.30 = $0.74) by the 10-cent interval width gives 7.4 or 8 as the number of classes. Conversely, the approximate width of interval required could be found by dividing the range by the desired number of classes.

In case of doubt, try out various combinations and make a choice among them according to your best judgment. The trial-and-error method of selecting the number of classes in a frequency distribution is preferable to the use of a formula for this purpose.[1]

---

[1] Some writers have given arbitrary rules for determining the desirable number of intervals from the total number of values of X. For example, H. A. Sturges, in the *Journal of the American Statistical Association*, March 1926, pp. 65–66, suggests that for n values of X the number of class intervals should be k, where 2^k is the smallest power of 2 larger than n. This formula would require 28 classes for grouping the 180 million population of the United States, since $2^{28} = 268$ million! Other writers suggest from 6 to 15 classes for presentation but from 15 to 25 classes for accuracy in computations.

Choice of Midpoints

The midpoint of a class interval is halfway between its limits. The exact location of the class limits depends on the method of reporting the original data and subsequent rounding, if any. For example, in population censuses, ages are reported to the *last* birthday. Here, the five-year interval "20–24" includes all persons from their twentieth birthday to the eve of their twenty-fifth birthday. In this case, therefore, the midpoint is halfway between 20 and 25, or 22.5. On the other hand, when ages are rounded off to the *nearest* birthday, as in life insurance practice, the class interval "20–24" is interpreted as 19.5 up to, but not including, 24.5. Thus the midpoint is 22.

The midpoint of an interval in a frequency distribution is used to represent the average value of all the items in the class. This usage involves *errors of grouping*, which are similar to *errors of rounding off* numbers in general. For example, in rounding off the age 22.4 to 22, the error is 0.4. It is important to minimize the errors of grouping in choosing the midpoints and limits of the intervals to be used.

There would be no errors of grouping if all values of X were exactly at midpoints. Although this condition is rare, there are often points around which values tend to cluster. For example, retail prices or wage rates often cluster about multiples of 5 and 10 cents. Points at which this type of clustering occurs are called *points of concentration*. In Table 9–2 the points of concentration actually occur at multiples of 10 cents (e.g., $2.40, $2.50), which are used as midpoints in Table 9–3.

Location of Class Limits

Class limits should be located in such a way as to minimize errors of grouping. Also, if possible, both the midpoints and limits should be simple round numbers. In Table 9–3, for example, midpoints are multiples of 10 cents and class limits are odd multiples of 5 cents.

Errors of grouping are not serious when the average of the values of X in each interval is roughly equal to the midpoint, that is, when grouping errors approximately offset each other. The most important practical point, however, is to locate intervals so that the points of concentration are at midpoints.

In the case of the 214 hourly earnings, there are major points of concentration at multiples of 10 cents and minor clusters at odd multiples of 5 cents. Thus the location of the intervals in Table 9–3 places major points of concentration at midpoints at the cost of having minor points of concentration at lower limits. It would be possible to have all of these points of concentration at midpoints by using intervals 5 cents wide beginning with "2.275 and under 2.325." It is doubtful, however, whether the slight increase in accuracy is worth the use of odd figures as class limits and the additional work required by the larger number of classes. Another possibility is that of combining pairs of the 5-cent intervals just considered to obtain 10-cent intervals beginning with "2.275 and under 2.375." The latter choice would not place any point of concentration at a midpoint, but it would place pairs of points of concentration symmetrically about each midpoint. This choice of interval would be satisfactory if all points of concentration were about equally populous, but it has little or no advantage in the distribution of hourly earnings because the major points of concentration are so pronounced.

Designation of Classes

Location of classes must be stated precisely to avoid ambiguity. Any of several methods of designating classes may be used, depending in part on the nature of the data. The four common methods illustrated in Table 9–4 represent beginning monthly salaries of college graduates. Intervals chosen are $50 wide with multiples of 50 at or near the midpoints.

Of these methods, the one shown in column A is the poorest, for it may be ambiguous; it is not clear whether $325 is included in the first or the second class. Nevertheless, this form is occasionally used, and the first class is interpreted to mean $275 and *under* $325.

Sometimes only the midpoints of the classes are indicated, as in column B. This method is concise and explicit as to the important midpoints themselves. It would be appropriate for data expressed to the nearest dollar except that it is ambiguous in Table 9–4 with respect to the location of limiting values such as $325.

If monthly salaries are rounded to the nearest dollar and upper limits are excluded, the listing in column C is preferable. Here $325 clearly falls in the second class; and the next lower possible salary, $324, falls in the first class. However, if salaries were paid in dollars and cents, such as $324.50, the class limits in column C would have to be carried out to the same number of decimals, such as $275.00–$324.99, to locate such values precisely. The midpoint of such an interval is also an awkward figure ($299.995 instead of $300.00), although this difference can usually be ignored as trivial. The column C method is the one used in the Northwestern University survey of starting salaries for college men, as quoted in Problem 4, page 176.

The class limits in column D are suitable for data which, like time or length, can vary continuously. Data which are not continuous are said to be *discrete*. Discrete data have distinct values, with no intermediate values. Thus, the number of children in a family can be 2 or 3, but not 2.7. The class limits in column D are appropriate also for data which have been rounded prior to being grouped in the frequency distribution, but this rounding must be taken into account when locating midpoints. For example, if the data were rounded by dropping the odd cents, the midpoint of the first class would be $300. On the other hand, if the data were rounded to the *nearest* dollar, the precise limits would be $274.50 and $324.50, so the midpoint would be $299.50. The class limits in column D do not indicate specifically the number of significant figures for rounded data and they require more space than columns A, B, and C. Nevertheless, they are considered to be the clearest designation of the four.

Table 9–4
METHODS OF DESIGNATING CLASSES
For Beginning Salaries of College Graduates
(In Dollars per Month)

A Overlapping (Ambiguous)	B Midpoint (Ambiguous)	C Possible Value Limits (For Discrete Data)	D Upper Limit Excluded (For Continuous Data)
275–325	300	275–324	275 and under 325
325–375	350	325–374	325 and under 375
375–425	400	375–424	375 and under 425
425–475	450	425–474	425 and under 475
475–525	500	475–524	475 and under 525

Uniformity in Width of Class Intervals

It is highly desirable that all intervals used in a frequency distribution have the same width because frequencies are easier to interpret and averages are easier to compute. Intervals of varying width are confusing and awkward to use in analysis. For some types of data, however, unequal intervals must be used in order to cover a wide range of data or to maintain their confidential nature. If intervals of different widths must be used, all widths should be multiples of the smallest one, if possible. Unequal intervals are often necessary in grouping incomes, such as:

Under $ 2,000
$ 2,000–$ 3,999
$ 4,000–$ 5,999
$ 6,000–$ 9,999
$10,000–$19,999
$20,000 and over

In such cases, it is rather common to have two *open-end classes* at the extremes, with the lower limit of the smallest class and the upper limit of the largest class not shown, e.g., "under $2,000" and "$20,000 and over." This open-end type of frequency distribution is sometimes needed to include a few extremely large or small values without adding a number of extra classes. The sum of the values in such open-end classes should be indicated, if possible, to aid in further computations. The absence of limiting values, however, like the use of intervals of unequal width, is a handicap to subsequent analysis.

Percentage Frequency Distributions

It is often desirable to divide the number of items in each class by the total number in order to show each frequency as a percentage of the total. A percentage frequency distribution is illustrated in Table 9–5. The use of percentages has three advantages: (1) It permits comparisons of the individual frequencies with each other and with the total on a common 100 per cent base. (2) It facilitates comparisons between two frequency distributions having different numbers of

Table 9–5

PERCENTAGE FREQUENCY DISTRIBUTIONS
HOURLY EARNINGS OF CLASS A AND CLASS B
MACHINE TOOL OPERATORS

Hourly Earnings	Number of Operators		Per Cent of Operators	
	Class A	Class B	Class A	Class B
$2.05 and under $2.15	..	2	..	3
$2.15 and under $2.25	..	10	..	15
$2.25 and under $2.35	2	26	1	39
$2.35 and under $2.45	23	16	11	24
$2.45 and under $2.55	49	6	23	9
$2.55 and under $2.65	63	4	29	6
$2.65 and under $2.75	45	2	21	3
$2.75 and under $2.85	25	1	12	1
$2.85 and under $2.95	3	..	1	..
$2.95 and under $3.05	4	..	2	..
Total	214	67	100	100

items, provided they have identical class limits. (3) It permits one to make inferences from sample data regarding the population, provided the sample is carefully selected. For example, it might be inferred from Table 9–5 that about 29 per cent of *all* Class A machine tool operators in the area earn from $2.55 to $2.65 an hour.

CHARTS OF FREQUENCY DISTRIBUTIONS

A frequency distribution may be presented as a chart designed to picture its main characteristics. Thus, in Table 9–1 (p. 156), we could place the gears in adjoining piles according to size. The .4250" gears would be piled highest, and so on. Bars or lines are ordinarily used instead of pictographs, however, as described below.

To construct a chart of a frequency distribution, measure the variable X along the horizontal scale and label either the class limits or midpoints. Then, at the midpoint, plot the frequency of the class on the vertical scale (assuming classes of equal width). Both the horizontal and vertical scales are the ordinary arithmetic type. The vertical scale must always begin at zero, but the horizontal scale need only include the range of X values and one extra interval at each end. The two most common frequency diagrams of sample data are the histogram—a vertical bar chart—and the frequency polygon—a line chart. The smooth frequency curve, used to describe the distribution of values in a population, is discussed later in the chapter.

The Histogram

A histogram is a set of vertical bars whose *areas* are proportional to the frequencies represented. When the class intervals, or bar widths, are equal, the *height* alone can be used to represent the frequency in that class. The height of the bar thus shows frequency *per unit width*. The bars may be separated to show the breaks in discrete data, but they should adjoin to represent continuous data.

In Chart 9–1, for example, the histogram represents the earnings of the 214 machine tool operators listed in Table 9–3. This chart shows at a glance how the earnings are distributed.

The class which contains the greatest concentration of earnings figures is called the *modal class*. It stands out in the chart as the tallest bar. On either side, the bars taper off in height, showing that the farther the earnings are from the modal class, the fewer are the number of workers. Many types of economic data have this type of distribution—approximately symmetrical with a modal class near the center.

If there are two separate modal classes in a histogram, the data

Chart 9-1
HISTOGRAM
HOURLY EARNINGS OF 214 MACHINE TOOL OPERATORS

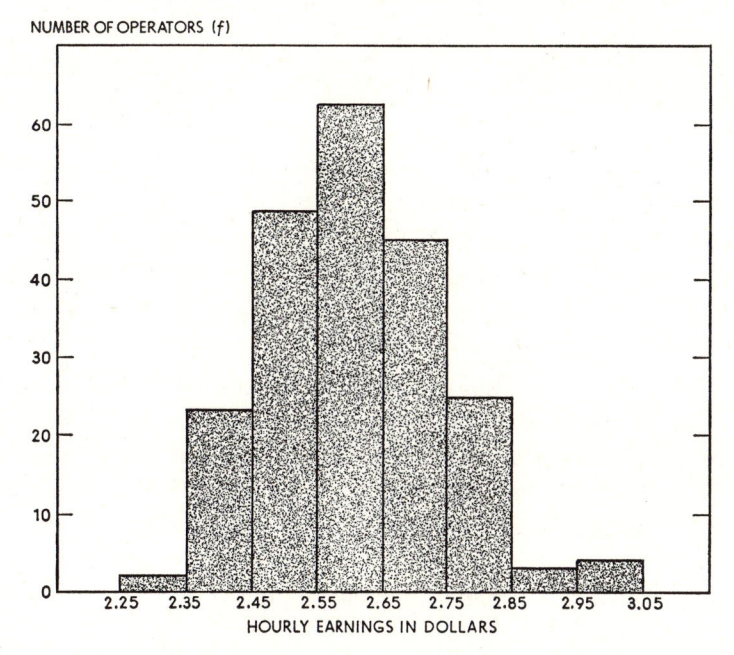

may prove to be heterogeneous (e.g., foremen might have been included with operators). In this case, the figures should be separated into homogeneous groups before being analyzed.

The height of each bar of a histogram is equal to the frequency of the class when intervals are equal in width; but when the width varies, frequency is represented only by *area* rather than by height. So if two class intervals have the same frequency but one is half as wide as the other, the first bar should be twice as high as the second.

To visualize this, consider the bars in Chart 9-1 to be made up of flat blocks, one for each operator. The right-hand bar, on the base $2.95–$3.05, is made up of four blocks as pictured in Chart 9-2A. Now double this interval so that it covers the range $2.95–$3.15. Two pairs of blocks must be laid side by side to fill the wider space, as in Chart 9-2B. The height of this bar (2) is then only half the corresponding frequency (4). The *area,* however, is 2 × 2 = 4, which is still equal to the frequency. To make this double-width bar 4 units high, as in Chart 9-2C, would exaggerate the size of this class. Of course, one need not make this distinction between height and area of bars when all class intervals are of the same width. This is one of the advantages of having equal-sized intervals.

Chart 9-2

AREA OF BAR IN HISTOGRAM MUST BE PROPORTIONAL TO FREQUENCY

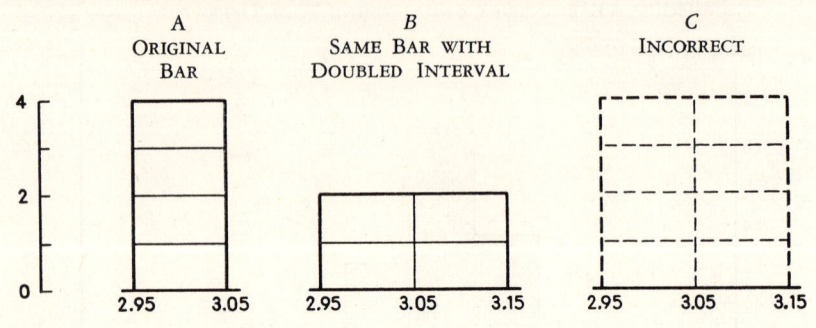

A	B	C
Original Bar	Same Bar with Doubled Interval	Incorrect

The Frequency Polygon

The *frequency polygon* is a line chart based on the same data and plotted on the same scales as a histogram. To draw a polygon, plot each frequency on the vertical scale over the midpoint of the interval on the X axis (assuming classes of equal width). Then connect these points with straight lines, and extend them to an interval of zero frequency at each end.

As shown in Chart 9-3, the frequency polygon could be constructed

Chart 9-3

FREQUENCY POLYGON
HOURLY EARNINGS OF 214 MACHINE TOOL OPERATORS

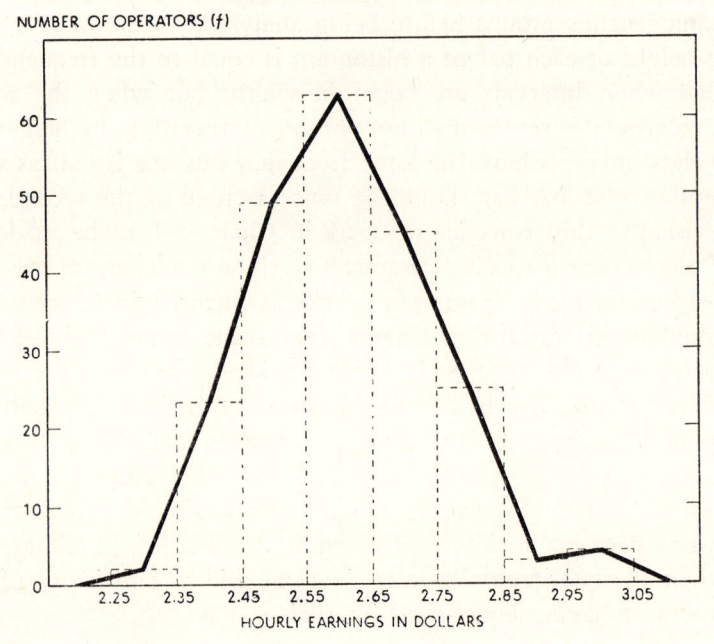

equally well from the histogram in Chart 9-1 (which is lightly blocked in as background) by connecting the midpoints of the bar tops, including one bar of zero height at each end. This line, together with the base line, forms a polygon enclosing an area equal to that of the histogram.[2] Although the areas are thus shifted slightly from the classes to which the frequencies belong (as compared with the histogram), the frequency polygon has the virtue of substituting a gradual increase and decrease in concentration of cases for the more abrupt steps of the histogram. In many cases, if a sample of continuous data is enlarged and the class intervals are made smaller, both the histogram and frequency polygon of the enlarged sample will approach the smooth frequency curve which describes the distribution in the population from which the sample was drawn.

Histograms versus Frequency Polygons

The histogram has the following advantages over the frequency polygon: (1) each bar represents the exact number of values of X in a class, whereas the corresponding area under the polygon does not; (2) the individual classes stand out more clearly than in a frequency polygon; (3) a histogram of unequal class intervals is more accurate than a frequency polygon, which does not preserve total area; and (4) separated bars may be used to emphasize gaps in a discrete distribution.

Frequency polygons have these advantages: (1) they are simpler than bar charts, having fewer lines; (2) they resemble the smooth curve which describes the population better than does the histogram; and (3) they make fewer confusing intersections when two frequency diagrams are compared.

Histograms are usually preferable when classes are few; frequency polygons when classes are numerous. Either type of chart, however, can ordinarily be used.

Frequency charts have an advantage that is characteristic of all charts—they provide a quick and simple method of summarizing and presenting facts. An apparel manufacturer or retailer, for instance, can use this type of diagram in controlling his purchases and inventory. From his sales records he can prepare frequency charts showing the sizes of clothing, shoes, and other merchandise characteristic of his customers, to serve as guides in future purchasing and inventory control.

---

[2] This follows from the fact that each pair of adjoining triangles formed by the top lines of the polygon and the histogram in Chart 9-3 are equal in area. Similar areas are not equal, however, when intervals are of unequal width.

Comparison of Two Frequency Distributions

It is often helpful to compare graphs of two frequency distributions on the same chart. For example, it might be necessary to contrast the wages of machine tool operators in New York for two different years, or wages of New York and Chicago operators for the same year. Polygons should be used for such comparisons because bars of histograms overlap, thus blurring the picture. The class limits of the two distribu-

Chart 9–4

COMPARISON OF FREQUENCY DISTRIBUTIONS
HOURLY EARNINGS OF CLASS A AND CLASS B MACHINE TOOL OPERATORS

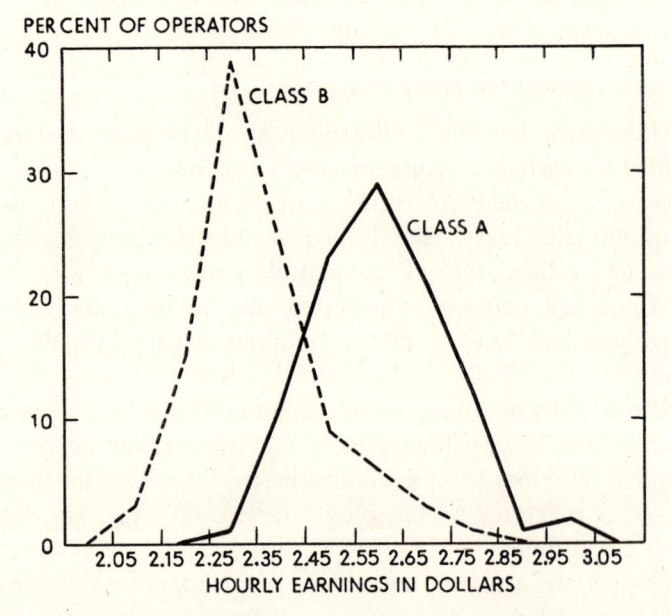

tions should be the same. Finally, if the number of values differs in the two groups, percentage frequencies should be used to give comparable ordinates.

To illustrate, Chart 9–4 compares the earnings of our Class A machine tool operators with those of Class B operators, as listed in Table 9–5. The two frequency polygons are in percentage form. Comparison of the two curves shows that (1) Class A operators earn more than Class B operators for the most part; (2) the most frequent earnings rates are in the $2.25–$2.35 bracket for the Class B workers, as compared with $2.55–$2.65 for the Class A men; and (3) there is a much greater concentration of Class B earnings than Class A earnings in these modal classes, as shown by the relative heights of the two curves.

Frequency Curves

A smooth curve can be drawn to portray the frequency distribution of a *population* of continuous data. This is the limiting form of either the histogram or frequency polygon as the number of values in the sample becomes infinitely large, and the class intervals become infinitely small. A frequency curve smooths out sampling errors which are particularly evident in small samples—and provides a frequency value for *every* value of X, rather than just one value for each class interval. Smooth curves cannot be used, however, for data that cluster around certain values, such as the machine tool operators' earnings in Table 9–2.

Chart 9–5

FREQUENCY DISTRIBUTION
LAYING MASH: PRICES REPORTED BY FEED DEALERS, SEPTEMBER 1949

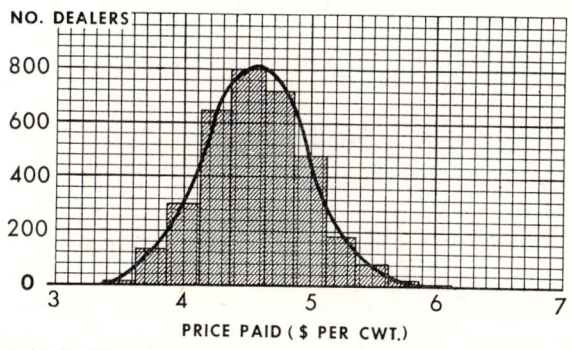

SOURCE: Frederick V. Waugh, *Graphic Analysis in Economics,* U.S. Department of Agriculture, Agricultural Handbook 128 (1957), p. 3.

Chart 9–5 shows a histogram of the prices charged by 3,395 dealers throughout the United States for laying mash. The height of each bar shows the number of dealers reporting prices within that price interval. A smooth curve has been drawn by Frederick A. Waugh of the U.S. Department of Agriculture to show "the general nature of the distribution." Such curves may be fitted either graphically, on a judgment basis, or by mathematical methods. A careful study of the data is necessary in either case to assure a realistic fit. In the graphic method, the curve should be drawn in such a way that *the area cut from each bar is approximately equal to the area added to that bar* by the curve. Chart 9–5 deviates from this rule slightly in the case of the two tallest bars in order to follow a "normal curve." This type of curve is described below.

TYPES OF FREQUENCY DISTRIBUTIONS

The principal types of frequency distributions are illustrated by frequency curves in Chart 9–6. The most important of such curves is the bell-shaped *normal curve* shown in Charts 9–5 and 9–6, panel A. This curve describes the distribution of many kinds of measurement in the physical, biological, and social sciences. Thus, the prices of laying mash in Chart 9–5 vary with freight rates, differences in ingredients, dealers' markup, etc., but nevertheless form a nearly normal distribution. The normal curve is particularly important, moreover, because it reflects variations due to *chance,* such as the errors in random sampling. This curve will be used in the later chapters in studying the reliability of sample measures, and in making inferences about populations.

The two curves in panel B of Chart 9–6 are symmetrical like the normal curve, but one is more peaked, with longer tails; and the other is more squat, and with shorter tails than the normal curve. The peaked curve might represent prices of gasoline in a city where most service stations charged about the same price, but a few prices were widely scattered. The squat curve would show that prices were distributed more evenly over a limited range, but without being concentrated at one point.

Curves C and D represent distributions that also have a "central tendency" as shown by the peak near the center of the curve, but the two branches of the curve are unequal or "skewed." Curve C, with the longer branch to the left in the negative direction, is called "skewed to the left" or "negatively skewed." This type of curve commonly results from a distribution having a fixed upper limit but a more remote lower limit, as in the case when test scores cluster closer to the perfect score than to zero. Curve D, which is skewed to the right, or positively skewed, is the most common type encountered in business and economic data. Distributions of personal earnings, commodity prices, or assets of companies, for example, tend to cluster closer to the lower limit of zero than to the indefinite upper limit. An appropriate test given to a uniform group of job applicants might produce a symmetrical grade distribution, whereas a more difficult test would produce scores lower on the average and skewed to the right, while an easier test would produce scores higher on the average and skewed to the left.

Chart 9–6
TYPES OF FREQUENCY CURVES

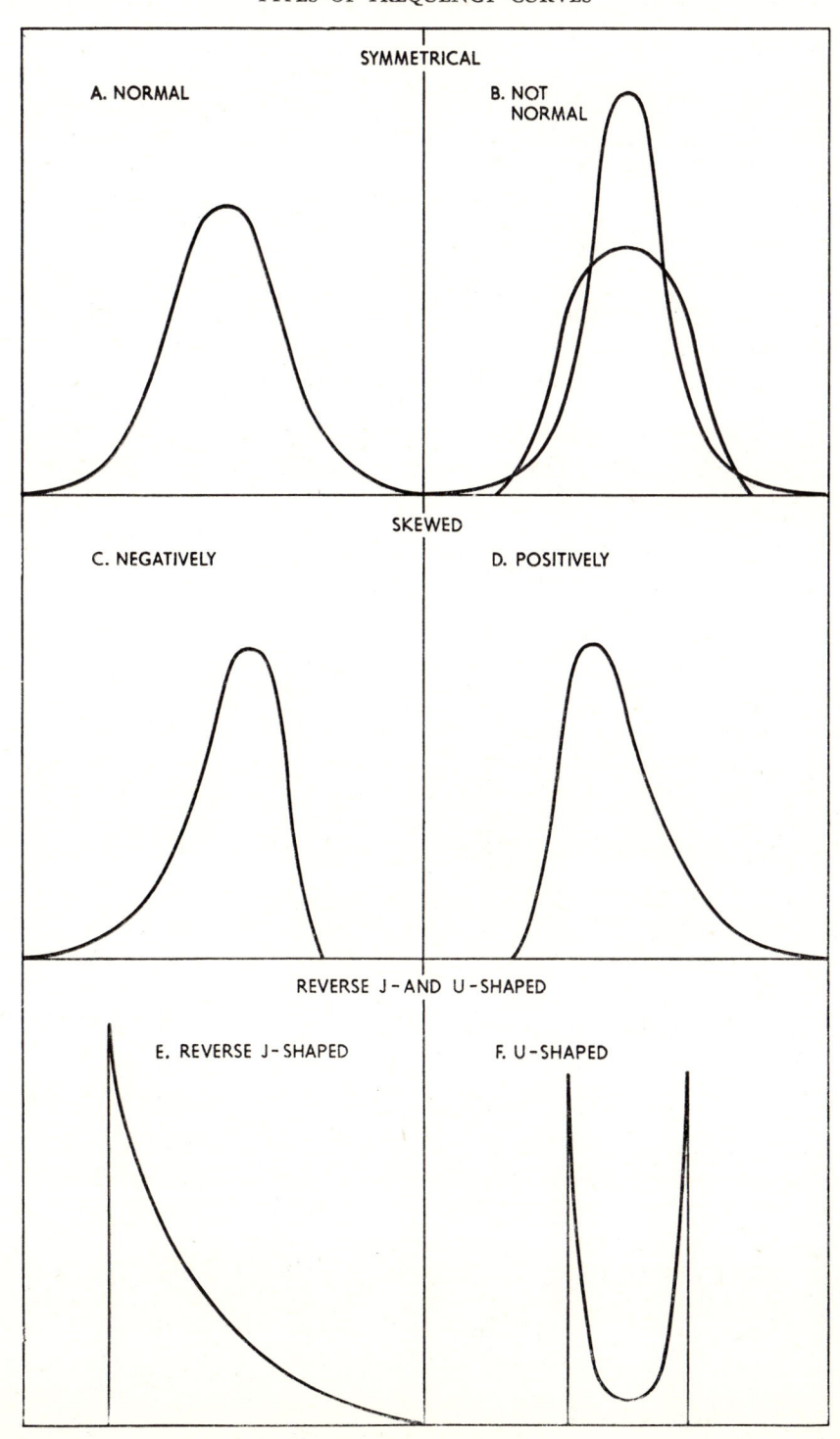

SYMMETRICAL

A. NORMAL

B. NOT NORMAL

SKEWED

C. NEGATIVELY

D. POSITIVELY

REVERSE J- AND U-SHAPED

E. REVERSE J-SHAPED

F. U-SHAPED

Curves E and F are less common. The reverse J-shaped curve occurs in some distributions, such as income tax payments, where the smallest returns are most numerous and the number of returns (on the Y axis) drops off sharply at first and then more gradually as the size of payment (on the X axis) increases. The U curve may be illustrated by the number of houses classified by per cent of mortgage debt to house value, where many houses have no debt or a heavy debt, while relatively few have a middle-sized debt in relation to house value.[3] The averages and measures of dispersion discussed in the next chapters apply especially to curve types A, B, C, and D, which have a pronounced central tendency; types E and F cannot be summarized so easily.

CUMULATIVE FREQUENCY DISTRIBUTIONS

Sometimes one needs to know the answers to questions like: "How many operators earn less than $2.75 an hour?" If so, it is convenient

Table 9–6

CUMULATIVE FREQUENCY DISTRIBUTIONS
HOURLY EARNINGS OF 214 MACHINE TOOL OPERATORS

(1) Hourly Earnings	(2) Number in Class with Lower Limit Shown	(3) Number Earning Less	(4) Number Earning as Much or More
$2.25	2	0	214
2.35	23	2	212
2.45	49	25	189
2.55	63	74	140
2.65	45	137	77
2.75	25	182	32
2.85	3	207	7
2.95	4	210	4
3.05	0	214	0
Total	214		

SOURCE: Table 9–3.

to add the frequencies cumulatively, beginning with the lowest-paid class, and list the resulting subtotals in a table called a *cumulative frequency distribution,* as in Table 9–6, column 3. The frequencies can also be cumulated in the opposite order, as in column 4.

Table 9–6 shows at a glance how many operators earn *less than*

[3] As an example, see *Federal Reserve Bulletin,* September 1959, p. 1108.

any amount listed, or that amount *or more*. Thus, 182 operators earn less than $2.75, while 32 earn $2.75 or more. Columns 3 and 4 could also be expressed as percentages of the total number of operators (214) for better comparability with other groups of different size.

The graph of a cumulative frequency distribution is called a cumulative frequency curve or an *ogive* (pronounced ō′jīve) because its shape resembles that of an ogive or rib of a Gothic arch. The data in Table 9–6 are graphed in Chart 9–7. The per cent scale at the right is

Chart 9–7

CUMULATIVE FREQUENCY CURVES
Hourly Earnings of 214 Machine Tool Operators

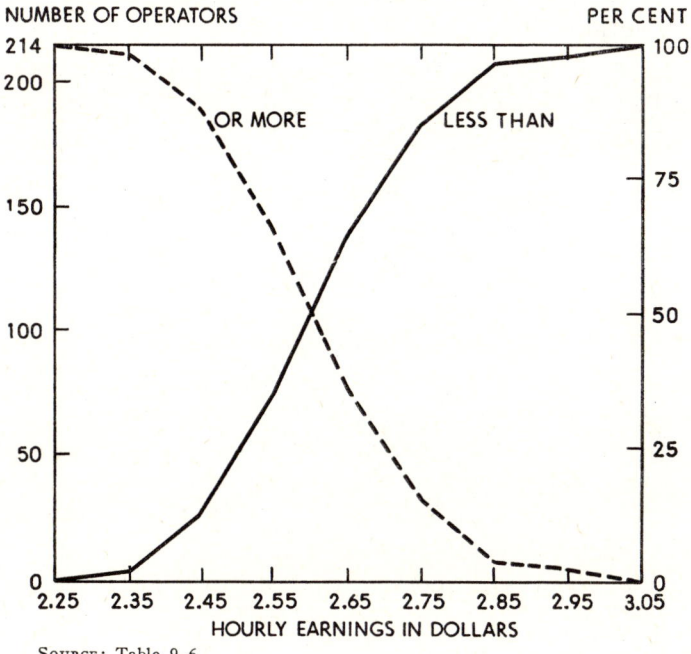

Source: Table 9–6.

made so that 100 per cent corresponds to 214 operators on the left-hand scale. The ogives then show graphically what number or per cent of the operators earn less than the amounts listed in Table 9–6, and those amounts or more.

In addition, the ogives permit easy interpolation for finding values between the plotted points. For example, the upward ogive shows that 25 per cent, or about 53 operators, earn less than $2.51, while the downward ogive shows that 25 per cent earn $2.70 or more. The intersection of the two curves at the 50 per cent horizontal line indicates that about half the workers earn $2.60 or less, and half more. These three earnings figures are the quartiles and median, to be discussed in the next chapter.

The same percentages can be used to make inferences about *all* comparable machine tool operators, provided the group of 214 is a good sample of the population. In this case, the sample was carefully selected; so it can be inferred that about 25 per cent of *all* such operators earn less than $2.51, etc.

An ogive can also be drawn as a smooth *curve* through the plotted points, with the aid of a French curve, rather than as a series of straight lines. The use of the curve implies *gradual change* in degree of concentration—often a more realistic assumption than that the values are *uniformly* distributed over each class interval.

The slope of the ogive denotes the concentration of X values. The steepest part of the curve marks the modal class, where the concentration is greatest. The mode is described in the next chapter.

SUMMARY

In many types of problem, values of a variable X are classified by size at a point in time and summarized in a *frequency distribution* to facilitate presentation and analysis. The range of the variable is divided into intervals, and only the number of values of X in each class is shown, thus sacrificing some detail for conciseness.

The values of X are first *arrayed* by listing them individually or marking them on a tally sheet in the order of their size. The figures are then *grouped* into from 6 to 15 classes so as to show the important characteristics of the data, but without undue detail. Class limits are chosen so that points of concentration, if any, are at midpoints or symmetrical about such points, in order that each midpoint will approximate the average value of X in the class interval. The intervals should be equal in size, if possible. The limits of the classes must be specified unambiguously. Frequencies may be expressed as percentages of the total number to facilitate comparisons.

Frequency distributions may be charted by plotting frequencies on the Y scale above the class midpoints on the X axis. Either a *histogram* (bar chart) or a *frequency polygon* (line chart) may be used. Two frequency distributions may be conveniently compared by plotting the percentage frequencies as polygons on the same horizontal scale. A smooth curve drawn through a histogram or frequency polygon of a continuous distribution approximates the frequency curve for the population from which the sample was drawn, provided the sample is carefully selected, and the data do not cluster at certain points.

Frequency distributions may assume a *normal* bell-shaped curve or some other symmetrical form; they may be skewed or asymmetrical either to the left or right; or in extreme cases, they may assume the shape of a reverse **J** or **U**.

Finally, frequencies may be cumulated and plotted as a cumulative frequency curve or *ogive* to show the number or proportion of values less than or greater than a given amount.

PROBLEMS

1. Define and give the purpose of (*a*) the tally sheet, (*b*) percentage frequency distribution, (*c*) frequency polygon, (*d*) ogive, and (*e*) normal curve.

2. Indicate which of the following are correct statements and amend any that are incorrect:
    a) Points of concentration are always present in an array and should be considered in preparing a frequency distribution.
    b) All frequency distributions should have at most fourteen class intervals.
    c) Class intervals of unequal width should never be used.
    d) Class limits should be established so that the average value of the items in each interval is approximately equal to the midpoint of the interval.
    e) In presenting a distribution of continuous data, the best way to designate the classes is by listing the class midpoints.

3. State wherein each of the following meets or fails to meet the principles of constructing a frequency distribution.

(*a*)

Income	Average Monthly Rent
Under $2,000	$62.70
$2,000–$2,900	55.40
$2,900–$4,000	55.00
$4,000–$4,900	61.10
$5,000–$6,500	73.50
etc.	

(*b*)

Age (Years)	Thousands of Persons
All ages	5,390
Under 4	335
Under 2	87
4–9	602
10–15	721
16–25	1,358
26–35	1,483
etc.	

4–6. A survey of typical starting salaries offered college men by 185 companies in 1957 showed the following results:

176   BUSINESS AND ECONOMIC STATISTICS   [Ch. 9

| | FIELD ||||
Starting Salary*	Engineering	Accounting	Sales	General Business Trainees
300 and under 325*	0	4	5	6
325 and under 350	0	9	18	16
350 and under 375	4	28	20	27
375 and under 400	11	40	22	29
400 and under 425	25	26	14	19
425 and under 450	77	8	12	6
450 and under 475*	20	1	2	1
475 and under 500*	4	0	0	0
500 and under 525*	3	0	0	0
Number of companies reporting	144	116	93	104

* The class limits and data in the end classes have been modified slightly in order to facilitate analysis.

Source: Frank S. Endicott, *Trends in the Employment of College and University Graduates in Business and Industry*, Northwestern University, 1957.

NOTE: These data will be used also in Chapters 10 and 11.

4. *a*) Plot histograms for two fields in the above table as assigned, using separate graphs.
   b) Plot frequency polygons for the same two fields, using either one or two graphs.
   c) Compare the merits of the histogram and the polygon in this case.

5. *a*) Compute a percentage frequency table for the two fields assigned in 4(*a*) above. Use these computations to construct two percentage frequency polygons on the same graph.
   b) What is the reason for using percentage frequencies in comparing two distributions?
   c) In what situation would percentage frequencies be unnecessary for comparing two distributions?

6. *a*) Construct a "more than" cumulative frequency table and ogive for one of the fields in the above table as assigned.
   b) Construct a "less than" table and ogive for the same field.
   c) How many companies offered starting salaries to college men in this field of $375 and more; of $425 and more?
   d) How many companies offered starting salaries to college men in this field of less than $450; of less than $400?

7. *a*) Make a frequency table, using the 112 items in the 4 columns assigned to you from the following table (see numbered assignments below table).
   b) Give reasons for your choice of class limits and width of class intervals.
   c) Draw a graph showing your frequency distribution.

d) What information concerning earnings of women in this plant can be derived from your table and graph?

NOTE: This problem will be continued in Chapters 10 and 11.

DAILY EARNINGS OF 168 WOMEN IN AN ELECTRONIC ASSEMBLY PLANT, IN DOLLARS

(a)	(b)	(c)	(d)	(e)	(f)
15.20	18.00	11.20	16.00	20.00	13.60
11.60	14.00	12.00	11.30	12.20	12.00
8.00	12.00	17.60	15.60	8.50	8.00
12.80	12.80	9.50	12.00	14.50	10.00
14.00	11.80	12.00	10.60	16.00	12.60
6.40	9.20	14.00	12.00	12.60	14.00
12.00	7.60	12.00	15.00	12.00	6.50
12.40	14.80	8.20	6.00	8.00	16.00
24.00	18.00	28.00	8.00	19.00	14.00
14.60	16.80	16.80	16.00	22.00	14.60
9.00	14.20	14.40	17.20	15.20	19.20
16.50	12.00	21.20	14.40	10.00	12.30
20.00	12.00	20.00	12.50	14.00	11.60
18.00	21.00	23.00	20.00	16.00	16.40
14.10	8.00	14.00	18.80	16.40	16.00
22.50	16.00	16.10	12.00	12.00	20.00
12.00	24.00	19.90	12.00	23.80	21.40
20.80	19.60	12.90	8.40	28.40	24.00
16.00	27.00	24.00	23.50	17.30	28.80
18.00	20.00	16.00	20.00	18.00	15.20
7.20	10.40	8.00	21.60	14.00	25.00
14.00	15.50	11.80	24.40	11.40	12.00
26.00	21.80	15.00	14.00	24.50	20.40
16.00	14.00	16.00	16.20	6.00	17.60
16.00	6.00	12.40	28.00	20.00	8.80
12.00	16.00	18.40	16.90	16.00	16.00
19.40	12.40	15.50	13.00	12.00	18.00
10.00	16.00	6.00	14.00	13.20	12.00

Assignments:

No.	Columns	No.	Columns	No.	Columns
1.........a	b c d	6........a	b e f	11........b	c d e
2.........a	b c e	7........a	c d e	12........b	c d f
3.........a	b c f	8........a	c d f	13........b	c e f
4.........a	b d e	9........a	c e f	14........b	d e f
5.........a	b d f	10........a	d e f	15........c	d e f

8. U.S. family personal incomes in 1962 were distributed as follows, according to the *Survey of Current Business* (April 1964):

178 BUSINESS AND ECONOMIC STATISTICS [Ch. 9

Income	Per Cent	Income	Per Cent
Under $2,000	6.9	$ 6,000–$ 7,499	16.0
$2,000–$2,999	6.2	$ 7,500–$ 9,999	18.6
$3,000–$3,999	8.2	$10,000–$14,999	14.8
$4,000–$4,999	9.8	$15,000 and over	8.7
$5,000–$5,999	10.8	Total families	100.0

a) Criticize the choice of class intervals and class limits.

b) Plot a histogram of this distribution. Then draw a smooth curve to approximate the true continuous distribution of incomes. What type of frequency curve is this—normal, negatively skewed, etc.? (See pp. 169–71.)

9. An automobile advertisement lists the following distribution of gas mileage reported by owners of its new cars:

Miles per Gallon	Per Cent	Miles per Gallon	Per Cent
15 and under 16*	6	19 and under 20	14
16 and under 17	10	20 and under 21	18
17 and under 18	16	21 and under 22*	12
18 and under 19	24	Total owners	100

* Open-end classes have been assigned arbitrary limits to facilitate later computations.

a) Plot a histogram of gas mileage, and draw a smooth curve through it to iron out sampling irregularities and approximate the continuous distribution of mileage performance for the whole population of car owners. What type of frequency distribution is this? (See pp. 169–71.)

b) List a cumulative frequency distribution and draw an ogive showing the per cent of owners reporting a given gas mileage or more. From this curve, half the owners get what gas mileage or more? The most economical fourth of the owners get what gas mileage or more? (Give results to nearest tenth of a gallon.)

SELECTED READINGS

MILLS, FREDERICK C. *Statistical Methods.* 3d ed. New York: Henry Holt & Co., Inc., 1955, pp. 40–85.
   A clear discussion of distributions, including methods of smoothing.

NEISWANGER, WILLIAM A. *Elementary Statistical Methods.* Rev. ed. New York: Macmillan Co., 1956, chap. 8.
   A careful analysis of frequency tables and graphs.

WAUGH, FREDERICK V. *Graphic Analysis in Agricultural Economics.* Washington, D.C.: U.S. Department of Agriculture, 1957, pp. 2–7.
   Describes graphic methods of smoothing histograms and ogives.

10. AVERAGES

A BASIC purpose of statistical analysis is to develop concise summary figures that will describe unwieldy masses of raw data. The initial stages in this analytic process have already been described—that is, appraising the accuracy of data, reducing related figures to ratios, classifying facts for tabulation and graphic presentation, and condensing a long list of separate values into a frequency distribution.

An important type of summary measure needed in statistical analysis is the *average*.[1] Averages are familiar to everyone in such examples as average weekly wages, average prices of securities, a man of average income, a medium-sized house, and the usual rate of interest charged a bank's customers. Careful analysis of these examples shows that they involve several different concepts of "average" which should be distinguished from each other. No single average can be used indiscriminately. In fact, different methods of computation are required for each of several different types of averages.

The most common averages are: (1) the arithmetic mean, (2) the median, and (3) the mode. The first is determined by calculation, the second by its position in an array, and the third by finding the point about which values of the variable cluster most closely. These will be described in turn. Other calculated averages, such as the modified mean and the geometric mean, have important special uses but will not be emphasized in this chapter.

THE ARITHMETIC MEAN

The most common average is the arithmetic mean or, more simply, the mean. The term "average," when used alone, usually refers to the

---

[1] An average is sometimes called a "measure of central tendency" because individual values of the variable usually cluster around it. Averages are useful, however, for certain types of data in which there is little or no central tendency.

mean. The *mean* of any series of values is found by adding them and dividing their sum by the number of values. In terms of symbols to be used in this chapter, the mean of n values of a variable X is calculated by adding X values and dividing the sum by n.

Ungrouped Data

The general method of computing the mean is the same whether the data are ungrouped or grouped in a frequency distribution, but the formulas look a little different. As an example of ungrouped data, consider a man working at piece rates who earns $2.80, $3.05, $3.00, and $3.15 in four successive hours. His mean hourly earnings is found by adding his earnings for the four hours and dividing by 4. The earnings total $12.00, so the mean is $3.00. This process is generalized by the following formula:

$$\overline{X} = \frac{\Sigma X}{n}$$

where $\overline{X}$ (read "X bar") is the symbol for the mean of the variable X (hourly earnings in dollars); Σ is the Greek letter capital sigma (corresponding to our S), which means "the sum of"; and n is the number of values.[2]

The formula thus provides a shorthand statement of how to compute the mean—namely, to add the n individual values of X (to find ΣX) and to divide by n, the number of values. Visualizing the meaning of symbols in this way should make it easier to understand formulas expressed in terms of symbols. These will become increasingly helpful as the formulas become more complex. A Glossary of Symbols is presented in Appendix B.

When a variable has a number of identical values, multiplication can be used as a short cut for addition in totaling X. Thus, to find the average dimension of the 63 gears in Table 9–1 (p. 156) one could add the 63 figures in panel A, but it would be easier to multiply each dimension in panel B by its *frequency,* and add the products as follows: $1(.4270) + 4(.4265) + 10(.4260) + \cdots$. Specifically, since there are ten gears measuring .4260, it is simpler to multiply 10 by .4260 than to add .4260 ten times. The whole process is summarized by the formula

---

[2] Strictly speaking, the symbols $\overline{X}$ and n apply only to *sample* data. In later chapters, μ (the Greek letter mu) will be used to designate the mean of an entire population and N the number of values in the population. Hence $\mu = \Sigma X/N$.

$$\overline{X} = \frac{\Sigma fX}{n}$$

where f is the symbol for frequency, and ΣfX means that each different value of X is multiplied by its frequency and the products (fX) are then added. Using either formula,

$$\overline{X} = \frac{26.7820}{63} = .4251, \text{ the mean dimension in inches.}$$

The Weighted Mean. In many types of problems, the values to be averaged are of different degrees of importance. In such cases, each value is multiplied by a numerical weight based on its relative importance, and the total is divided by the sum of the weights. The result is called a *weighted mean*. The weights are handled just as if they were frequencies. Hence a weighted mean can be computed by the above formula—taking f as the weight and n as the sum of the weights.

Thus, an aptitude score may be based on an English test with weight 2 and a Mathematics test with weight 1. The weights total 3. If a person makes 90 and 60 on these tests respectively, his combined aptitude score is

$$\overline{X} = \frac{\Sigma fX}{n} = \frac{2(90) + 1(60)}{3} = \frac{240}{3} = 80$$

Weighted means are used extensively in the construction of index numbers, to be described in Chapter 15.

All means can be regarded as weighted in some way, either explicitly or implicitly. From this point of view, the "unweighted" mean is one in which the weights are all equal. In computing any mean therefore it is important to use appropriate weights. In averaging the ratios of profits to sales for 30 retail grocers, for example, the total profits for all 30 grocers can be divided by their total sales to allow the larger firms more weight in the results; or the firms may be weighted equally by taking a simple average of the 30 ratios.

Weighted averages in general will be larger than simple averages if the heavier weights are applied to the larger values, and smaller if the heavier weights are applied to smaller values. Thus, if the larger grocery stores are more profitable than the smaller ones, the weighted mean profits-to-sales figure will exceed the unweighted mean.

Grouped Data

The mean of data grouped in a frequency distribution is computed in the same way as described above. In a frequency distribution, however, the *midpoint* of each interval is used to represent all values of X in the interval. Accordingly, each midpoint is multiplied by the number of values in that class. The sum of these products is then divided by the total number of values of X to find the mean.

The formula for computing the arithmetic mean from a frequency distribution is therefore:

$$\overline{X} = \frac{\Sigma fX}{n}$$

where

$\overline{X}$ = the arithmetic mean computed from a frequency distribution,
X = the midpoint of each interval,
f = the frequency (number of values of X) in that interval,
fX = their product,
ΣfX = the sum of these products, and
n = the total number of values or the sum of the frequencies.

In calculating the arithmetic mean for the earnings of machine tool operators shown in Table 10–1, the midpoint of each interval is used to

Table 10–1

DIRECT METHOD OF COMPUTING THE ARITHMETIC MEAN FROM A FREQUENCY DISTRIBUTION

HOURLY EARNINGS OF 214 MACHINE TOOL OPERATORS

Hourly Earnings (Dollars)	(1) Class Midpoint X	(2) Number of Operators (Frequency) f	(3) Frequency × Midpoint fX
2.25 and under 2.35	2.30	2	4.60
2.35 and under 2.45	2.40	23	55.20
2.45 and under 2.55	2.50	49	122.50
2.55 and under 2.65	2.60	63	163.80
2.65 and under 2.75	2.70	45	121.50
2.75 and under 2.85	2.80	25	70.00
2.85 and under 2.95	2.90	3	8.70
2.95 and under 3.05	3.00	4	12.00
Total		214	558.30

SOURCE: Table 9–2.

represent all earnings figures in that interval. The total earnings for the two operators in the first class is thus computed to be 2.30 × 2 =

4.60. Applying this procedure to the other classes yields the products listed in column 3, for which the grand total is 558.30. Then dividing this total by 214, the number of operators, the arithmetic mean is found to be $2.609 per hour. That is,

$$\overline{X} = \frac{\Sigma fX}{n} = \frac{558.30}{214}$$
$$= 2.609$$

The mean computed from a frequency distribution is subject to a slight *error of grouping,* since all values are rounded off to the nearest class midpoint. This error would be nil if the mean of the values in each class were equal to the midpoint, or if the plus and minus errors of grouping in the various classes offset each other. The error can be minimized by placing the midpoints of class intervals at points around which the data tend to cluster, or midway between such points within intervals. Grouping errors of opposite sign often tend to offset each other, so that the grouped mean is usually very close to the ungrouped mean, particularly if the number of values is large and the distribution is nearly symmetrical. Thus, the arithmetic mean of $2.609 per hour obtained from the frequency distribution is only $.003 greater than the exact mean of $2.606 per hour computed from the original figures.

The arithmetic mean and other statistical measures are often computed from a frequency distribution rather than from ungrouped data despite minor errors of grouping because (1) it is much easier to calculate the mean from grouped data when the number of original values is large, and (2) many types of data are available only in the form of frequency distributions.

Short-Cut Method. The direct method of computing the arithmetic mean from a frequency distribution is simple when all numbers involved are simple integers. However, it sometimes requires multiplication of many pairs of large numbers and laborious addition of their products. If class intervals are of equal width, the computations can be simplified by using a short-cut method, and chances for mistakes will be minimized.

The short-cut method is illustrated in Table 10–2. Although at first this method may not appear shorter, a little practice will demonstrate that much time and labor can be saved because the multipliers are reduced to small whole numbers.

Table 10-2

SHORT-CUT METHOD OF COMPUTING THE ARITHMETIC MEAN FOR GROUPED DATA

HOURLY EARNINGS OF 214 MACHINE TOOL OPERATORS

(1) Hourly Earnings (Dollars)	(2) Class Midpoint X	(3) Number of Operators (Frequency) f	(4) Deviation from Assumed Mean d	(5) Frequency × Deviation fd
2.25 and under 2.35	2.30	2	−3	− 6
2.35 and under 2.45	2.40	23	−2	−46
2.45 and under 2.55	2.50	49	−1	−49
2.55 and under 2.65	2.60	63	0	0
2.65 and under 2.75	2.70	45	1	45
2.75 and under 2.85	2.80	25	2	50
2.85 and under 2.95	2.90	3	3	9
2.95 and under 3.05	3.00	4	4	16
Total		214		19

The steps for computing the mean by the short-cut method are as follows:

1. List the class limits (if desired), the midpoints, and the frequencies, as shown in columns 1 to 3.
2. Select any midpoint as the "assumed mean" ($\overline{X}_a$), preferably the midpoint of one of the middle intervals. In Table 10-2 the assumed mean is taken as $2.60.
3. List the deviation (d) of each class midpoint from the assumed mean in units of the class interval, as in column 4. Thus a zero is written opposite 2.60, the next larger midpoint is marked +1, the next smaller −1, and so on in whole numbers, 1, 2, 3, etc. Be sure to mark the deviations of the larger midpoints "+" and the smaller midpoints "−," irrespective of which end is listed first in the table. If there were a gap and then some values, say in the "3.15 and under 3.25" class, that class would have a deviation of 6, not 5, class units from the assumed mean.
4. Multiply the frequency in each class by its deviation and list the product (fd) in column 5, being sure to include the sign.
5. Total these products (Σfd), multiply this total by i, the width of the interval in original units, and divide by the number of items (n) to obtain $i\Sigma fd/n$. This correction term is used to adjust the assumed mean in step 6 below.

6. Add the adjustment obtained in step 5 to the assumed mean to obtain the correct mean.

The formula for the arithmetic mean computed by the short-cut method is

$$\overline{X} = \overline{X}_a + \frac{i\Sigma fd}{n}$$

where

$\overline{X}$ = the arithmetic mean,
$\overline{X}_a$ = the assumed mean placed at any class midpoint,
i = the width of the interval (measured from the lower limit of one interval to the lower limit of the next),
f = the frequency or number of items in each class,
d = the deviation of a midpoint from the assumed mean in class interval units,
Σfd = the sum of f times d for each class (not Σf times Σd), and
n = the total number of items.

In Table 10–2, therefore,

$$\overline{X} = \overline{X}_a + \frac{i\Sigma fd}{n}$$

$$= 2.60 + \frac{.10(19)}{214}$$

$$= 2.60 + .009$$

$$= 2.609, \text{ or } \$2.609 \text{ per hour}$$

The short-cut method of computing the arithmetic mean yields *precisely* the same result as $X = \Sigma fX/n$, the formula for the direct method. In either case, the mean of grouped data is slightly less exact than that computed from the original data by means of the formula $\overline{X} = \Sigma X/n$, because in the formulas containing f, all values are rounded off to the class midpoints and are thus affected by errors of grouping.

Method for Classes of Unequal Width. In case the intervals in a frequency distribution vary in width, the direct method, $\overline{X} = \Sigma fX/n$, should be used. Special care must be exercised in selecting the midpoints (X) because of their irregular spacing. The short-cut method might be used if the difference between each class midpoint and the assumed mean were expressed in units of some common factor (i), but this is an awkward procedure, and it is not recommended for general use.

Open-End Distributions. On some occasions it is necessary to compute the mean from a frequency distribution having open-end classes whose lower or upper limit is not indicated, such as a salary class "$325 or less." Although open-end intervals should be avoided ordinarily, it is possible to compute the mean from open-end distributions provided either the individual values, their average, or their total is available for each open-end class to supply the missing data. Otherwise, the mean can be computed only by guessing at these values. In such instances the median, modified mean, or mode should be used in preference to the mean, since they do not depend on extreme values.

THE MEDIAN

The median of any set of data is the middle value in order of size if n is odd, or the mean of the two middle items if n is even. When there are a few very large or small values, the median is often superior to the mean as an average. For example, the *Monthly Labor Review* reports median wages and salaries by occupations, and *Dun's Review and Modern Industry* reports median operating ratios for small samples of business firms because the median represents the typical middle man or firm undistorted by large values that so greatly affect the mean. To cite a specific case, the median income of American families in 1960 was $5,600, whereas the mean was $6,900, according to the *Survey of Current Business* for May 1961.

The median can sometimes be found when other averages are not defined because individuals are not measured quantitatively. For example, employees in a plant can be rated by arranging them in order of merit without assigning a numerical grade to each individual. To find the value of the median under these conditions, only one or two individuals need be measured or graded. The median can also be computed in an open-end frequency distribution, while the mean cannot, if the end values are unknown.

Ungrouped Data

In ungrouped data, the median is most easily found when the values are arranged in an array. Consider the price-earnings ratios 9.6, 7.3, 9.2, 4.0, and 19.9 (i.e., common stock prices divided by earnings per share) for five steel companies. Arranged in order of size, the five ratios are:

$$4.0, 7.3, 9.2, 9.6, \text{ and } 19.9.$$

The median is then the middle value, or 9.2. If a sixth ratio, 20.0, were added, the median would be the mean of the two middle items 9.2 and 9.6, or 9.4. In general, the median in an array is not computed from a formula but is selected as the value whose rank or "order number" is $n/2 + 1/2$, counting from the lowest value. Thus, for the six ratios above, the order number of the median is $6/2 + \frac{1}{2} = 3\frac{1}{2}$, i.e., halfway between the third and fourth values.

This example illustrates an important advantage of the median over the mean. The ratio of the price of a stock to the earnings per share is sometimes very large when the earnings are abnormally small, as in the case of the 19.9 ratio above. Because of this figure, the mean (10.0) exceeds any of the other four ratios. The median is often more reliable than the mean in samples from populations in which such extreme deviations occur, because the reliability of the mean is greatly affected by extreme deviations while the reliability of the median depends chiefly upon the degree of clustering about the median of the population.

Grouped Data

When data are grouped in a frequency distribution, the median falls in the class interval whose frequency is the first to make the cumulative frequency greater than $n/2$. It is convenient to call this the median class. The median may then be located within the median class by means of the interpolation formula

$$Md = L + \frac{i(n/2 - F)}{f}$$

where

Md = the median,
L = the lower limit of the median class,
i = the width of the median class,
f = the frequency for the median class,
F = the cumulative frequency for all classes below the median class,
n = the total number of values of X (the sum of all frequencies).

In applying this formula to the earnings data of Table 10–2 above, the first step is to locate the class that contains the middle value, i.e., the one ranked $n/2 = 214/2 = 107$.[3] By cumulating the f column, the successive subtotals are found to be 2, 25, 74, 137, etc. The first subtotal to exceed $n/2$ is 137. Accordingly, the *fourth* class is the median class. Its lower limit is $L = 2.55$; its frequency is $f = 63$; the cumulative frequency for X less than L is $F = 74$; and the interval is $i = .10$. Substituting these values in the formula, the median is:

---

[3] The middle value interpolated over a continuous range is at the exact midpoint $n/2$ in rank, rather than $n/2 + 1/2$ as in discrete data.

$$Md = L + \frac{i(n/2 - F)}{f}$$
$$= 2.55 + \frac{.10(107 - 74)}{63}$$
$$= 2.55 + .052$$
$$= 2.602, \text{ or } \$2.602 \text{ per hour}$$

This value is only an approximation to the median of the original ungrouped data, since it is interpolated on the assumption that values of X in the median class are *evenly distributed* over that interval. In this case the true median, taken from the original data in Table 9–2, page 158, is exactly $2.60, because the earnings around the median cluster at this point.

About half of the 214 earnings are smaller than the median of $2.60 and about half are larger. The proportion on each side of the median is exactly one half when the median is between the two middle values. In fact, a vertical line at the interpolated median always divides the histogram into two parts whose areas are equal. Nevertheless, the proportion of items on each side of the median is sometimes more or less than one half. In ungrouped data, one or more values may be equal to the median so that the proportion of values smaller (or greater) than the median may be considerably less than one half—it can never be greater. In grouped data, more than one half of the original values may be on one side of the interpolated median because of uneven distribution of values within the median class. For these reasons, it is better to say that the proportion of values on each side of the median is only *approximately* equal to one half.

Open-End Distributions. Since the median is not affected by the size of extreme values, it can be determined in an open-end distribution such as that of the prices of houses presented in Table 10–3. The per cent figures here can be treated as ordinary frequencies, and the median is found to be $11,429. This indicates that in 1954–56 about half of the houses purchased cost more than $11,429, and about half cost less.

Graphic Interpolation. The median in a frequency distribution can be obtained graphically from a cumulative frequency curve or ogive. For example, the median hourly earnings of the 214 machine tool operators can be found from either ogive in Chart 9–7 (p. 173). A horizontal line is drawn from the 50 per cent ordinate on the right vertical scale (107 or $n/2$ on the left scale) until it intersects the ogive. (The two ogives in Chart 9–7 intersect at the same point.) The X value of this point, which is read as $2.60 on the bottom scale, is the median. The graphic method yields the same result as the interpolation formula of the preceding section, except for errors in plotting and reading the scale.

Table 10–3

PRICES PAID BY PURCHASERS OF HOUSES IN 1954–56
(Based on Sample of about 450 New and Existing Nonfarm Houses)

Price of House	Per Cent of Houses	Cumulative Percentage
Under $5,000	14	14
$5,000–$7,499	12	26
$7,500–$9,999	14	40
$10,000–$14,999	35	75
$15,000 and over	25	100
Total	100	

SOURCE: "1957 Survey of Consumer Finances," *Federal Reserve Bulletin*, June 1957, p. 630.

$$Md = L + \frac{i(n/2 - F)}{f}$$

$$= 10,000 + \frac{5,000(50 - 40)}{35}$$

$$= 11,429$$

THE MODIFIED MEAN

A modified mean is the mean of a central group of values in an array or frequency distribution, omitting any very large and small values that are so extreme and atypical as to distort the over-all mean. Indeterminate items in open-end classes may also be omitted. The analyst must use his judgment as to how many values to discard. Usually the same predetermined number of items is omitted at each end of the array or distribution, as in seasonal analysis (described in Chapter 19), but there are many variations. The National Bureau of Economic Research in averaging business cycles omits certain extreme values that are judged to be erratic, but does not exclude indiscriminately any fixed number of items at both ends of an array.[4]

---

[4] Arthur F. Burns and Wesley C. Mitchell, *Measuring Business Cycles* (New York: National Bureau of Economic Research, 1946), p. 496.

As more and more end items are omitted until only the middle one or two are left, the modified mean becomes the median. There is thus a whole family of modified means, of which the mean itself includes the maximum and the median the minimum number of central values in an array. The intermediate means are, therefore, compromises between the mean and the median, selected to combine the best features of both.

THE MODE

The *mode* in statistics means just what it does in the dictionary—the prevalent or most frequently encountered thing. More precisely, the mode is defined as the *value which occurs most often* or the value around which there is the *greatest degree of clustering*. The modal wage is the one received by the greatest number of workers. The modal interest rate for bonds is the one that occurs more often than any other. If the most common or usual value is the one needed for a business decision, the *mode* is the appropriate type of average to use.

It is particularly important that the data used to determine the mode be homogeneous or enough alike to be comparable. Wage data that include skilled and unskilled workers, men and women, or industrial and farm workers may be so diverse that the modal wage would have little meaning. Such data might also have two or more modes of about equally high frequency. The mode is ordinarily meaningful only if there is a marked concentration of values about a single point.

Ungrouped Data

The mode can occasionally be determined directly from ungrouped data. When a large proportion of values are equal, no process of grouping could dislodge this value from its modal position. This is especially true of discrete data having only a limited number of possible distinct values. For example, if a bank charges the general run of its customers $4\frac{1}{2}$ per cent interest on commercial loans, then $4\frac{1}{2}$ per cent is the mode of interest rates, irrespective of what rates apply in special cases. Similarly, a survey indicates that more parents prefer to have three children than any other number. Thus, three is the modal family size preferred by parents.

Grouped Data

Most types of data, however, must be grouped in a frequency distribution in order to locate the mode. To illustrate, in the array of hourly earnings listed by cents in Table 9–2 (p. 158), the most frequently occurring rate is $2.63, but $2.70 is almost as popular; and there are other scattered points of concentration, such as $2.50 and $2.75, which cause doubts as to where the major area of concentration really is. By grouping the earnings as in Table 10–2, however, there appears only a single mode. This occurs in the $2.55–$2.65 interval. The modal interval can be described by saying, "More earnings fall in the $2.55–$2.65 class than in any other."

The value of the mode within this interval may be estimated graphically in a continuous distribution by drawing a smooth curve through the histogram so that the area cut from each bar is about equal to the area added to that bar by the curve, as described on page 169. The mode is then the X value at the peak of the frequency curve. Thus, in Chart 9–5 (p. 169) the modal price of laying mash is about $4.57 per hundredweight.

Interpolation formulas are also used to locate a "single-valued" mode within the modal interval.[5] More simply, the midpoint of the modal interval could be taken as the mode, but this is recommended only if values cluster at this point. Ordinarily, a single-valued estimate of the mode is neither accurate nor necessary in practice. In the relatively rare cases in which the mode is needed, it is usually enough to cite the modal interval.

The modal interval itself is only a rough estimate, since it depends on the choice of class limits. Grouping the data in different class intervals will produce different values of the modal interval. In some types of data, therefore, the mode is practically indeterminate. Hence the mode or modal interval should be used only if the problem specifically requires the most usual or common value as an average rather than the middle or the mean value.

THE GEOMETRIC MEAN

The geometric mean is sometimes appropriate for averaging index numbers, percentages, and other ratios. It may also be a good type of average for frequency distributions of absolute data that are skewed to the right (see Chart 9–6D, p. 171), provided the distribution of

---

[5] See the first edition of this book, pages 208–10, for a description of the most common method. The mode may also be estimated from the mean and median, as follows:

$$\text{Mode} = \text{Mean} - 3(\text{Mean} - \text{Median}).$$

This formula is based on the tendency of the median to fall roughly one third of the way from the mean toward the mode in a continuous distribution of only moderate skewness. Unfortunately, frequency distributions of economic data are seldom smooth enough to justify the use of this formula in estimating the mode.

logarithms is more nearly symmetrical. Moderately symmetrical distributions of absolute values with only a few extreme items, however, can best be averaged by a median rather than by the geometric mean.

The geometric mean has certain disadvantages that have limited its use. It is difficult to compute and to interpret. Hence the arithmetic mean is actually used for computing index numbers (Chapter 15) and other averages of ratios for which the geometric mean might seem more appropriate. Also, the geometric mean cannot be computed if any of the values is zero or negative. Profit and loss data, for example, could not be averaged in this manner.

The geometric mean is computed in exactly the same way as the arithmetic mean, except that the logarithms of the numbers are averaged to find the logarithm of the geometric mean. The geometric mean of X may thus be defined as the antilogarithm of the arithmetic mean of log X.[6] Therefore, except that log X is used in place of X, the main formulas used to find the geometric mean are the same as the corresponding ones for the arithmetic mean.

Ungrouped Data

For ungrouped data,

$$\log G = \frac{\Sigma \log X}{n}$$

where G is the geometric mean.

The geometric mean of the price-earnings ratios for five steel stocks is computed in Table 10–4.

Table 10–4

GEOMETRIC MEAN OF FIVE PRICE-EARNINGS RATIOS

Common Stock	Price-Earnings Ratio (X)	Logarithm of Price-Earnings Ratio (log X)
A	9.6	0.9823
B	7.3	0.8633
C	9.2	0.9638
D	4.0	0.6021
E	19.9	1.2989
Total	50.0	4.7104

---

[6] The geometric mean may also be defined as the nth root of the product of n values ($G = \sqrt[n]{X_1 \cdot X_2 \cdots X_n}$), but this form is not popular because one would usually find the result by logarithms anyway and this approach leads to that explained in the text.

Substituting in the formula:

$$\log G = \frac{\Sigma \log X}{n} \qquad G = \text{antilog } (\log G)$$

$$= \frac{4.7104}{5} \qquad\qquad = \text{antilog } 0.9421$$

$$= 0.9421 \qquad\qquad\qquad = 8.8$$

For comparison, the arithmetic mean of these five ratios is 10.0. The geometric mean is always less than the arithmetic mean for a series of different values.

Grouped Data

The geometric mean may be similarly computed from a frequency distribution by multiplying the logarithm of each class midpoint, log X, by the class frequency, f, before averaging the results. That is,

$$\log G = \frac{\Sigma f \log X}{n}$$

This formula will not be illustrated here, since its practical use is somewhat limited.

WHICH AVERAGE TO USE?

Much of the chapter thus far has been devoted to methods of computing the various types of averages. In the course of the several explanations, the distinctive features of the measures have been set forth in some detail but in incidental fashion. At this point, the reader may well ask, "Which of these various averages should I use?" or "When ought I to use one or the other of the averages described?"

There is no arbitrary single answer that can be given to these questions. The selection of the proper average depends upon three main factors:

1. The concept of the typical value required by the problem. Is a composite average of all absolute or relative values needed (arithmetic or geometric mean), or is a middle value wanted (median), or the most common value (mode)?
2. The type of data available. Are they badly skewed (avoid the mean), gappy around the middle (avoid the median), or lacking a major point of concentration (avoid the mode)? In particular, the choice between the arithmetic mean and median of a sam-

ple depends on the shape of the frequency curve for the population. Refer to Chart 9–6 (p. 171). If the distribution is normal (panel A) or flat-topped with few extreme values (panel B, lower curve), the mean has a smaller sampling error than the median. That is, the mean of the sample is likely to be closer to the true mean of the population than the median of the sample is to the true median. On the other hand, if the distribution is sharply peaked around the median and includes some extreme values (panel B, higher curve), the median has the smaller sampling error. This is because the clustering around the population median makes the sample median more accurate, and extreme values make the sample mean erratic.
3. The peculiarities or characteristics of the averages themselves. These will be summarized below, under "Characteristics of Averages."

As a rule of thumb, the arithmetic mean should ordinarily be used as a simple, widely understood average which gives due weight to all values. For certain types of ratios, however, the geometric mean may be preferable. If the items are few in number or erratic in value, a modified mean is desirable. In any case, the short-cut method is recommended for frequency distributions having classes of equal size. The median is commonly preferred to the mean if a simpler, middle value is needed—particularly if the data are badly skewed, as is common in economic measurements. Finally, the mode may be used if the most usual or common value is wanted.

CHARACTERISTICS OF AVERAGES

The arithmetic mean, median, and mode have the same value in a symmetrical "normal" distribution. If the distribution is skewed, the mode remains under the highest point of the curve, the arithmetic mean is pulled out in the direction of the extreme values, and the median, which is affected by the *number* of extreme items but not their *value,* tends to fall between the mean and the mode. The mean, median, and mode thus rank in the order given. The geometric mean, which gives less weight to large absolute values, is smaller than the arithmetic mean in either case.

Chart 10–1 shows the relation of the arithmetic mean, median, and mode in a positively skewed distribution—by far the most common type in business and economic data. Here the arithmetic mean is the largest value, and the mode is the smallest. Thus, family incomes in

Chart 10-1

RELATIONSHIP OF ARITHMETIC MEAN, MEDIAN, AND MODE IN A POSITIVELY SKEWED DISTRIBUTION

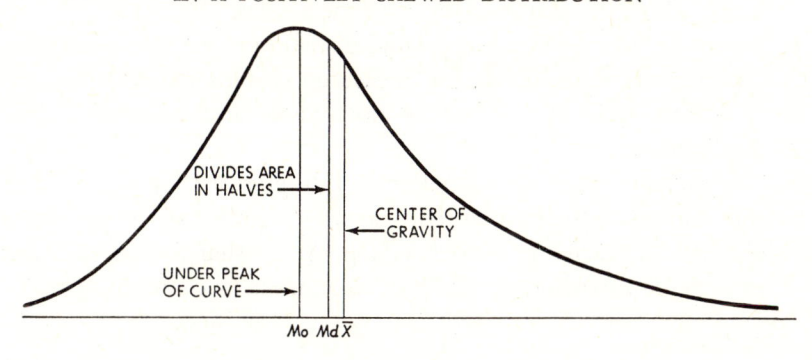

[Chart showing a positively skewed distribution curve with labels: "DIVIDES AREA IN HALVES", "CENTER OF GRAVITY", "UNDER PEAK OF CURVE", and x-axis markers "Mo Md $\bar{X}$"]

1960 had a mean value of $6,900 and a median of $5,600, as cited above, but the mode was only $4,820. The mean is the X value of the center of gravity. That is, if the area under the curve were a solid piece of metal, a fulcrum under $\bar{X}$ would balance it. (The logarithm of the geometric mean would balance the area under a frequency curve of logarithms.) The median divides the *area* under the curve (i.e., the total frequency) into two equal parts. The mode is the value of X under the highest point of the curve.

The characteristics of the individual averages are listed below:

Arithmetic Mean

1. The arithmetic mean is the most widely known and widely used average.
2. It is, nevertheless, an artificial concept, since it may not coincide with any actual value.
3. It is affected by the value of every item, but
4. It may be affected too much by extreme values.
5. It can be computed from the original data without forming an array or frequency distribution, or from the total value and number of items alone.
6. Being determined by a rigid formula, it lends itself to subsequent algebraic treatment better than the median or mode.
7. It is less affected by sampling errors than the median, in a normal or flat-topped distribution.

Median

1. The median is a simple concept—easy to understand and easy to compute.

2. It is affected by the number but not the value of extreme items.
3. It is widely used in skewed distributions where the arithmetic mean would be distorted by extreme values.
4. It may be located in an open-end distribution, or one where the data may be ranked but not measured quantitatively.
5. It is unreliable if the data do not cluster at the center of the distribution.
6. The median will have a smaller sampling error than the mean if the data *do* cluster markedly at the middle or if there are abnormally large or small values. Such sharply peaked and long-tailed distributions are fairly common in economic data.

Modified Means

1. Modified means are compromises between the arithmetic mean and the median, so they combine the characteristics of both.
2. Any one of several modified means may be used, depending on the number of items selected by the analyst.
3. Modified means are particularly adapted to a small or erratic group of values in which neither the mean nor the median is satisfactory.

Mode

1. The mode can best be computed from a frequency distribution, unless one value predominates in an array.
2. It can be located in open-end distributions, since it is not affected by either the number or value of items in remote classes.
3. The mode is erratic if there are but few values or zigzag frequencies—particularly if there are several modes, or peaks.
4. It is affected by the arbitrary selection of class limits and class intervals.

Geometric Mean

1. The geometric mean averages ratios or percentages in the same way that the arithmetic mean averages absolute values, so it is also characterized by points 2 to 7 under "Arithmetic Mean," above, as applied to the logarithms of numbers.
2. The geometric mean is a difficult concept, and hence is not widely understood.
3. It cannot be computed if the series contains zero or negative values.

SUMMARY OF FORMULAS

Since the characteristics of the various averages have been summarized above, the chapter may be concluded by listing the principal formulas used:

Type of Average	Ungrouped Data	Grouped Data
Arithmetic mean	$\bar{X} = \dfrac{\Sigma X}{n}$	$\bar{X} = \dfrac{\Sigma fX}{n}$ $= \bar{X}_a + \dfrac{i\Sigma fd}{n}$
Median	Value # $n/2 + \frac{1}{2}$ in an array	$Md = L + \dfrac{i(n/2 - F)}{f}$
Modified mean	Same as $\bar{X}$, for central values	
Mode	Most common value	Same
Geometric mean	$\log G = \dfrac{\Sigma \log X}{n}$	$\log G = \dfrac{\Sigma f \log X}{n}$

PROBLEMS

1. In the "dollar-averaging" method of investment, the same amount of money is invested each month in a variable number of shares of common stock. Thus, $50 will buy one share of a stock selling at $50 a share in one month, but two shares of that stock if it sells at $25 in another month. The three shares then cost $100, or an average of $33⅓ per share, as compared with the average market price of $37½ in the two months [(50 + 25) ÷ 2], irrespective of whether the market is rising or falling. Explain this apparent anomaly in terms of the two types of averages represented.

2. An investor owns three stocks on which he receives the following dividends in 1960 and 1962:

Stock	1960 Investment	1960 Dividend	1960 Yield	1962 Investment	1962 Dividend	1962 Yield
A	$ 8,000	$ 480	6%	$ 5,000	$300	6%
B	5,000	200	4	12,000	480	4
C	6,000	480	8	2,000	160	8
Total	$19,000	$1,160		$19,000	$940	
Average yield			6.11%			4.95%

a) How are the average yields obtained?
b) Inasmuch as none of the individual yields has changed, how do you explain the decrease in average yield?

3. From Chapter 9, Problem 7:
   a) Compute the arithmetic mean from your frequency distribution by the short-cut method. (Indicate all computations in this and following problems.) Discuss the grouping errors that affect this value.
   b) Find the median both from the original data and from your frequency distribution. If these values differ, explain why.
   c) What does the comparison of the mean and median reveal about the shape of the distribution?
   d) State the modal interval. Which of the three averages is most meaningful in this case? Why?

4. a) Compute the mean starting salary offered to college men by 185 companies, shown in Chapter 9, page 176, the table preceding Problem 4, in the field of (1) engineering, (2) accounting, (3) sales, or (4) general business trainees, whichever is assigned, using two different methods. Compare the merits of these two methods.
   b) Is this mean more or less accurate than one computed from the original ungrouped salary data? Why?
   c) From the shape of the distribution and the value of the mean, describe the distribution of starting salaries in whichever field is assigned.

5. a) Find the median starting salary for whichever field was assigned in Problem 4 above.
   b) Give the modal interval for the same field.
   c) Explain the difference in the meaning of these two averages.
   d) If the last three classes had been grouped into one class and labeled "$450 and over" which measure or measures would have been affected—the mean, median, or mode? Why?

6. The durations of nine business cycles in the United States from 1919 to 1958, measured from trough to trough, were 27, 36, 40, 64, 63, 88, 48, 58, and 44 months, respectively, according to Table 17–1.
   a) List the mean, median, and all possible modified means of these periods.
   b) Which of these averages is preferable? Why?
   c) What is the difficulty in computing the mode for these figures?

7. Under a wages-and-hours law it is considered desirable that the number of hours of work per week should be standardized for some 250 establishments, all now operating under similar conditions except with respect to hours of work. What should be the standardized number of hours (a) if the object is to keep the total hours of work the same and (b) if the object is to change as few establishments as possible?

8. a) Compute the geometric mean for the business cycle data in Problem 6.
   b) Is this value preferable to the arithmetic mean as a measure of average cycle length? Explain.

9. Regarding the dimensions of 63 gears in Table 9–1, p. 156:
   a) Is this distribution discrete or continuous? Symmetrical, or skewed to the right or left?
   b) Find the mean and median to the nearest .0001 inch.
   c) Which type of average is usually the best estimate of the corresponding population value, for a distribution of this kind? Why?

10. Chapter 9, Problem 8 (p. 177), reports the distribution of family incomes in 1962. The mean income was stated as $8,151.
    a) Estimate the median income. What is its significance?
    b) Give the modal interval.
    c) Explain why the mean, median, and mode differ so widely in value. Which is the best measure of typical family income? Why?

11. In Chapter 9, Problem 9 (p. 178):
    a) Compute the mean mileage per gallon.
    b) Interpolate to estimate the median mileage.
    c) What does the difference between the mean and median indicate about the skewness of this distribution?

SELECTED READINGS

BURNS, ARTHUR F., and MITCHELL, WESLEY C. *Measuring Business Cycles.* New York: National Bureau of Economic Research, 1946, pp. 46, 380–83, 491–503.
   Presents empirical comparisons of weighted and unweighted means, modified means, and the median.

CROXTON, FREDERICK E., and COWDEN, DUDLEY. *Applied General Statistics.* 2d ed. New York: Prentice-Hall, Inc., 1955, pp. 173–211.
   Discusses the geometric mean, and comparative formulas for the mode.

NEISWANGER, WILLIAM A. *Elementary Statistical Methods.* Rev. ed. New York: Macmillan Co., 1956, pp. 254–300.
   A good discussion of the meaning of the various averages.

SMITH, JOHN H. "Some Properties of the Median as an Average," *American Statistician,* October 1958, pp. 24 f.
   Analyzes characteristics of the median that are inadequately treated in current textbook literature.

YULE, G. UDNY, and KENDALL, M. G. *An Introduction to the Theory of Statistics.* 14th ed. London: Charles Griffin & Co., Ltd., 1950, chap. 5.
   A comprehensive nonmathematical treatment of averages.

11. DISPERSION

IN THE TWO preceding chapters, attention has been centered on two basic methods of describing a set of data: first, the frequency distribution, which groups a large number of values into a few classes; and second, the average, which summarizes the typical value. These devices are useful and important, but they do not describe all of the important characteristics of the figures. Other measures are needed to show how the data vary about the average, because this variation is sometimes as important as the average itself.

There are four important characteristics of a distribution of values which may be described by summary measures:

1. Average—typical size.
2. Dispersion—variation, spread, or scatter.
3. Skewness—asymmetry or lopsidedness.
4. Kurtosis—peakedness or relative influence of extreme deviations.

These four characteristics are illustrated in Chart 11–1, below, by smooth frequency curves. A frequency curve as defined in Chapter 9 portrays the frequency distribution of a population of continuous data in which the area under any segment of the curve corresponds to the number of values in that interval. Chart 11–1 is drawn so that the total area under each curve is unity and the area within any interval is equal to the relative frequency for that interval.

Suppose these curves represent the distribution of wage rates in a large factory. Panel 1 then shows that wages in department A *average* lower than those in department B, although both have the same dispersion. In panel 2, department A has a wider variation or *dispersion* of wages than department B, although both have the same average. The curves in both panels are symmetrical and normal. Panel 3 illustrates

Chart 11–1

FOUR SUMMARY MEASURES OF A FREQUENCY DISTRIBUTION

1. Average Is Small (*A*) or Large (*B*)

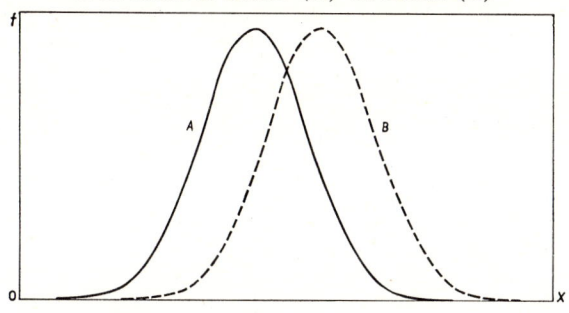

2. Dispersion Is Wide (*A*) or Narrow (*B*)

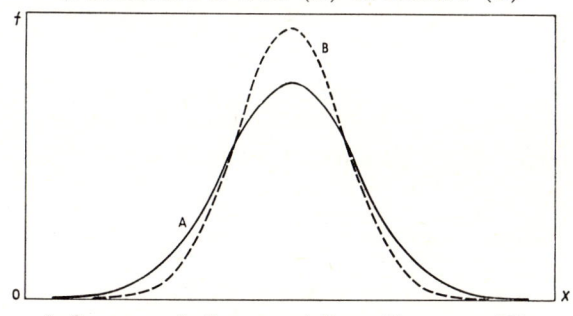

3. Skewness Is Positive (*A*) or Negative (*B*)

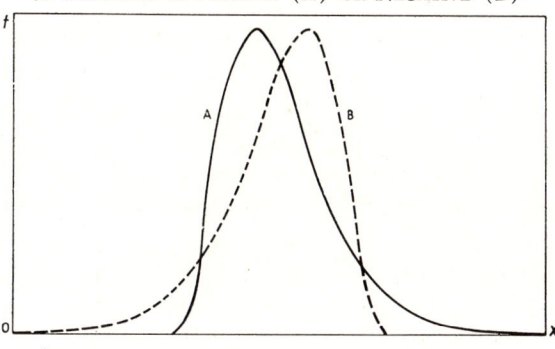

4. Kurtosis Is Peaked (*A*), Flat-Topped (*B*) or Normal (*C*)

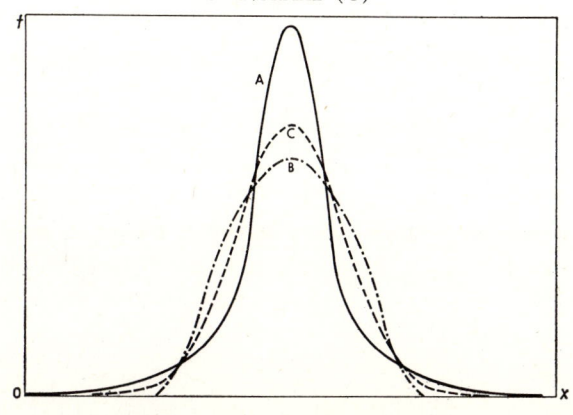

skewness. Here most of the wages in department A are near the minimum rate, although some are much higher (i.e., skewness is positive or to the right); while in department B most of the wages are near the maximum (skewness is negative or to the left). Finally, panel 4 shows different types of *kurtosis* in three symmetrical distributions having the same average and the same dispersion (as measured by the standard deviation, to be explained later). The distribution in department A is peaked, since most of the workers receive about the same wage with few very high or low wages; while the distribution in department B is flat-topped, indicating that the typical wages cover a wider spread with fewer extreme deviations; and in department C the distribution is normal, as if it had been determined by chance.[1]

Averages and measures of dispersion are the most important of these four kinds of summary measures. Dispersion will be described at length, and skewness very briefly, in this chapter. Kurtosis will be omitted, except for nontechnical references to the effects of extreme deviations.

PURPOSES OF MEASURING DISPERSION

Dispersion is the variation, or scatter, of a set of values. Measures of dispersion are needed for two basic purposes: (1) to gauge the reliability of averages and (2) to serve as a basis for control of the variability itself.

To illustrate the first purpose, suppose a company analyst is measuring the cost of living in a large city as one factor determining whether wages should be raised. If in five filling stations selected at random, he finds that the price of standard gasoline varies between 33 and 34 cents per gallon, he might be justified in using the mean of as few as five prices, say 33.4 cents, to represent the price of gasoline. That is, the mean of five prices represents closely the price at each station, and it provides a reliable estimate of the mean price of all standard-grade gasoline sold in the city. On the other hand, prices of a certain type of woman's dress might vary from $9.95 to $24.95 in five stores. The mean of so few prices would then be highly unreliable as an estimate of the mean price of all such dresses in the city, but a measure of dispersion is needed to reveal this fact. To summarize the facts in most cases, therefore, *both an average and a measure of dispersion must be presented.*

When dispersion is small, the average is a typical value in that it

---

[1] Curves *A, B,* and *C* are called leptokurtic, platykurtic, and mesokurtic, respectively.

closely represents the individual values, and it is reliable in that it is a good estimate of the corresponding average in the population. On the other hand, when the dispersion is great, the average is not so typical and, unless the sample is very large, the average may be quite unreliable (see Chapters 4 and 12).

The second basic purpose of measuring dispersion is to determine the nature and causes of variation in order to control the variation itself. In matters of health, variations in body temperature, pulse beat, and blood pressure are basic guides to diagnosis. Prescribed treatment is designed to control their variation. In industrial production, efficient operation requires control of quality variation, the causes of which are sought through inspection and quality control programs. Thus, measurement of dispersion is basic to the control of causes of variation.

Measures of dispersion include: (1) the range, (2) the quartile deviation, (3) the mean deviation, and (4) the standard deviation. These measures are analogous to the averages described in Chapter 10, both in their characteristics and methods of calculation.

THE RANGE

The range is the difference between the largest and the smallest values of a variable. It is the simplest of all measures of dispersion. For the gasoline prices varying from 33 to 34 cents per gallon, the range is 1 cent. The range can be easily computed in an array, but it cannot be determined accurately from a frequency distribution unless the high and low values in the end classes are known.

Sometimes the range is indicated merely by citing the largest and smallest figures themselves. Quotations of stock prices and commodity prices include the high and low for the day. Weather reports state the maximum and minimum temperatures. If the high and low values are not widely separated from the other values, as in these cases, the range may be a fairly good measure of dispersion. In particular, the range is the basic measure of variation used in quality control, as described in Chapter 22.

However, if the two extremes are erratic, the range is unreliable and misleading because it gives no hint of the dispersion of the intervening values. In the distribution of prices paid for cars, for example, the range might extend from a custom-built Rolls-Royce at $20,000 to a Jeep at $800; this would give little information about the variation in prices paid by the majority of consumers. In general, if the population contains a few extreme deviations, the range obtained from a random sample is more unreliable than any other measure of dispersion. For these reasons, the range is not recommended for general use.

The influence of extreme deviations on a measure of dispersion can be reduced by excluding a specified proportion of values at each end of the array and using the range of the remaining central values as the measure of dispersion. The simplest and most useful of these measures is the quartile deviation, which is explained below.

THE QUARTILE DEVIATION

The quartile deviation (Q) is defined by the formula

$$Q = \frac{(Q_3 - Q_1)}{2}$$

where Q_1 and Q_3 are the first and third quartiles, respectively. The quartiles are the three points which divide an array or frequency distribution into four roughly equal groups.[2] That is, the first or lower quartile, Q_1, separates the lowest-valued quarter of the total number of values from the second quarter; the second quartile, Q_2 (almost always called the median), separates the second quarter from the third quarter; and the third or upper quartile, Q_3, separates the third quarter from the top quarter. Consequently, the quartile range, Q_3–Q_1, includes the middle half of the items. The quartile deviation is half this range.

The quartiles are widely used as measures of dispersion. *Dun's Review and Modern Industry,* for example, reports the medians and quartiles of 14 operating ratios in each of 12 types of retail stores. Thus, the quartiles of net-profits-to-sales ratios for 78 dry goods stores in 1958 were .65 per cent and 12.66 per cent, as compared with the median of 2.17 per cent.[3] This means that while the "typical" dry goods store earned 2.17 per cent on sales, about one fourth of the companies earned less than .65 per cent and one fourth earned over 12.66 per cent, indicating a wide spread of profitability in this field. Similarly, the National Industrial Conference Board's *Management Record* reports the median and quartile salaries for various occupations by cities. In these cases, the quartiles themselves are reported rather than the quartile deviation.

---

[2] The groups are rarely exactly equal, for reasons described under the median and because n is seldom a multiple of 4.

The term "quartile" is sometimes applied to an entire range of values rather than to a point. Thus, a score might be said to fall "in the upper quartile" (i.e., between the top value and the upper quartile partition point). Such a range, however, should be called "quarter" to avoid confusion with "quartile," which should refer only to a point.

[3] *Dun's Review and Modern Industry,* October 1959, p. 82.

Ungrouped Data

The first and third quartiles are found in an array just as is the median or second quartile. They are the values whose ranks or order numbers are $n/4 + 1/2$ and $3n/4 + 1/2$, respectively, counting from the lowest value. Fractional order numbers are interpolated between neighboring values in the array.

In the case of the hourly earnings of 214 machine tool operators listed in Table 9–2 (p. 158), the value of Q_1 is the earnings whose rank is $214/4 + 1/2$, or 54. This is the earnings of the 54th man,[4] the middle man of the lower-paid half of the operators. Similarly, the value of Q_3 is the earnings of the man who is 161st from the bottom or 54th from the top, the middle man of the upper half. The values of Q_1 and Q_3 are found to be \$2.50 and \$2.70, respectively, from the original ungrouped data in Table 9–2. This means that about one fourth of the operators earn less than \$2.50, one fourth exceed \$2.70, and the middle half fall between these values. The quartile deviation is then $(2.70 - 2.50) \div 2$, or \$0.10.

Grouped Data

The quartiles can be estimated for a frequency distribution in the same way as the median by these analogous formulas:

$$Q_1 = L + \frac{i(n/4 - F)}{f} \qquad Q_3 = L + \frac{i(3n/4 - F)}{f}$$

where L is the lower limit of the class containing the quartile, i is the class width, f is the frequency or number in that class, F is the cumulative frequency below that class, and n is the total number of values. In these formulas, it is assumed that values of X are spread evenly over each interval, as explained in connection with the median.

For the machine tool operators' earnings grouped in Table 11–1, Q_1, the 54th value, falls in the third class ($L = \$2.45$, $f = 49$, $F = 25$); and Q_3, the 161st value, falls in the fifth class ($L = \$2.65$, $f = 45$, $F = 137$). Therefore,

$$\begin{aligned} Q_1 &= 2.45 + .10\,(53.5 - 25) \div 49 \\ &= 2.45 + .10\,(.58) \\ &= 2.508 \text{ dollars per hour} \end{aligned}$$

$$\begin{aligned} Q_3 &= 2.65 + .10\,(160.5 - 137) \div 45 \\ &= 2.65 + .10\,(.52) \\ &= 2.702 \text{ dollars per hour} \end{aligned}$$

---

[4] If there were 215 operators, Q_1 would rank $215/4 + 1/2$, or $54\frac{1}{4}$, i.e., one fourth of the way from the earnings of the 54th man to that of the 55th man from the bottom.

The quartile deviation is then $(2.702 - 2.508) \div 2 = .097$ dollars per hour. These three estimates check fairly closely with the exact values already obtained from the ungrouped data.

The quartiles can be located graphically from a cumulative frequency curve, or ogive, in the same manner as the median. To de-

Table 11-1

INTERPOLATION FOR QUARTILES
IN A FREQUENCY DISTRIBUTION

HOURLY EARNINGS OF 214 MACHINE TOOL OPERATORS

Lower Limit of Class (L)	Number in Class (f)	Number Earning Less (F)	Location of Quartiles
$2.25	2	0	
2.35	23	2	
2.45	49	25	$Q_1 = \#54$
2.55	63	74	
2.65	45	137	$Q_3 = \#161$
2.75	25	182	
2.85	3	207	
2.95	4	210	
3.05	0	214	
Total	214		

termine Q_1, for example, draw a horizontal line from $n/4$ on the Y axis to the "less than" curve; then drop a perpendicular and read off the value of Q_1 on the X axis. This method is illustrated in Chart 9-7 (p. 173).

The quartile deviation is relatively unaffected by extreme deviations. On the other hand, since the quartile deviation depends entirely upon the values of the quartiles Q_1 and Q_3, its reliability depends on the degree of concentration at the quartiles of the population from which the sample is selected. In particular, if there are gaps in the population around the quartiles, the quartile deviation is unreliable. The measures of dispersion which follow differ from the quartile deviation in that they take into account the deviation of *every* value from the average.

THE MEAN DEVIATION

The mean deviation, sometimes called the average deviation, is excatly what its name implies. It is simply the mean of the absolute deviations of all the values from some central point, such as the arithmetic mean or median. The deviations must be averaged as if they were all positive, since the mean of plus and minus deviations would be zero (if measured from the mean), or nearly so. The mean deviation theoretically should be measured from the median since it is then smallest, but it is usually more convenient to measure the deviations from the mean, as described below. There is little difference in the results.

The mean deviation is a concise and simple measure of variability. Unlike the range and quartile deviation, it takes every item into account, and it is simpler and less affected by extreme deviations than the standard deviation, which will be described in the next section. It is therefore often used in small samples that include extreme values. The National Bureau of Economic Research, for example, computes mean deviations to show how different business cycles vary in duration, intensity, and other respects: "The average deviations . . . bring out what we consider one of the most important aspects of cyclical behavior. Some economic processes are fairly uniform in their movements from cycle to cycle, and so have relatively small average deviations; most factors show wide diversity of movement, and so have large average deviations."[5]

Ungrouped Data

The formula for the mean deviation (measured from the arithmetic mean) in a set of ungrouped data is:

$$\text{M.D.} = \frac{\Sigma |x|}{n}$$

where x is the *deviation* of each item X from the mean $\overline{X}$; i.e., $x = X - \overline{X}$. The blinkers | | mean that the signs are ignored. Then the sum (Σ) of the absolute deviations $|x|$ is divided by the number of values (n) to find the mean deviation (M.D.).

The mean deviation is computed in Table 11–2 for the price-earnings ratios of five steel stocks, whose mean is 10.0.

This means that while the five price-earnings ratios averaged 10.0, there was a wide variation among them, since the average departure from the mean was 4.0. Furthermore, the sample includes only five stocks. Therefore, the average ratio of 10.0 must be considered rather unreliable as an estimate of the typical price-earnings ratio for steel stocks generally, assuming a large population of such stocks.

---

[5] Arthur F. Burns and Wesley C. Mitchell, *Measuring Business Cycles* (New York: National Bureau of Economic Research, 1946), p. 381.

Table 11–2

COMPUTATION OF MEAN DEVIATION
FOR UNGROUPED DATA

PRICE-EARNINGS RATIOS OF FIVE STEEL STOCKS

Common Stock	Price-Earnings Ratio (X)	Deviation from Mean $\|x\|$
A	9.6	0.4
B	7.3	2.7
C	9.2	0.8
D	4.0	6.0
E	19.9	9.9
Total	50.0	19.8
Mean	$10.0 = \overline{X}$	$4.0 = $ M.D.

$$\text{M.D.} = \frac{\Sigma |x|}{n} = \frac{19.8}{5} = 4.0$$

Grouped Data

The mean deviation can be computed from grouped data by the formula

$$\text{M.D.} = \frac{\Sigma f |x|}{n}$$

where $|x|$ is the absolute deviation of the class midpoint (X) from the arithmetic mean, ignoring signs, and f is the frequency in that class.[6] This formula will not be illustrated here, since its practical use is limited. The mean deviation has certain logical and mathematical limitations, such as disregarding plus and minus signs in averaging deviations. Consequently, the standard deviation is usually used instead for large distributions of grouped data.

THE STANDARD DEVIATION

The standard deviation is found by (1) *squaring* the deviations of individual values from the arithmetic mean, (2) summing the squares, (3) dividing the sum by ($n-1$), and (4) extracting the square root. Like the mean deviation, the standard deviation is based on the deviations of all values, but it is better adapted to further statistical

---

[6] For a short-cut method of computing the mean deviation for grouped data, see the first edition of this book, pp. 227–28.

analysis. This is partly because squaring the deviations makes them all positive, so that the standard deviation is easier to handle algebraically than the mean deviation. The standard deviation is therefore of such importance that it is, in fact, the "standard" measure of dispersion.

Ungrouped Data

The basic formula for the standard deviation of ungrouped data is:

$$s = \sqrt{\frac{\Sigma x^2}{n-1}}$$

where s is the standard deviation; $x = X - \overline{X}$, the deviation of any value of X from the arithmetic mean $\overline{X}$; Σx^2 is the sum of the squared deviations; and n is the number of items in the sample. The deviations may be squared most easily by referring to a table of squares, such as Appendix D or *Barlow's Tables*.

The square of the standard deviation is called the *variance*. This is an important concept in statistical inference, to be considered later.

The above formula is now commonly used in statistics because it provides the best estimate of the standard deviation of the population from which the sample was drawn. An alternative formula for the standard deviation is $\sqrt{\Sigma x^2 / n}$, which measures the dispersion of the sample itself but tends to understate the dispersion of the population. Since we usually take a sample in order to estimate population values, we will use $n - 1$ in our equations for s, the sample standard deviation,

Table 11–3

COMPUTATION OF STANDARD DEVIATION
FOR UNGROUPED DATA

PRICE-EARNINGS RATIOS OF FIVE STEEL STOCKS

(1) Common Stock	(2) Price-Earnings Ratio (X)	(3) Deviation from Mean ($x = X - \overline{X}$)	(4) x^2	(5) X^2
A	9.6	− .4	.16	92.16
B	7.3	−2.7	7.29	53.29
C	9.2	− .8	.64	84.64
D	4.0	−6.0	36.00	16.00
E	19.9	9.9	98.01	396.01
Total	50.0	.0	142.10	642.10
Mean	10.0			

and will regard s as an estimate of σ (small sigma), the population standard deviation. However, n may be substituted for $n-1$ if desired; it makes little difference when n is large, as in most economic data.

For the five price-earnings ratios listed in Table 11–3, column 2, the deviations from the mean of 10.0 are shown in column 3 and the squares in column 4. Their sum (Σx^2) is 142.10, and $n = 5$ stocks. The standard deviation is then

$$s = \sqrt{\frac{\Sigma x^2}{n-1}} = \sqrt{\frac{142.10}{4}} = \sqrt{35.52} = 6.0$$

Short-Cut Method. While the above formula *describes* the standard deviation succinctly, it is usually easier to *compute* its value directly from the original data, without finding the deviations from the mean. The following formula can be used to give exactly the same result as the one above:

$$s = \sqrt{\frac{\Sigma X^2 - (\Sigma X)^2/n}{n-1}}$$

In Table 11–3, column 5 shows the original X values squared for use in this formula; columns 3 and 4 are not needed. Then,

$$s = \sqrt{\frac{642.10 - (50.0)^2/5}{4}}$$

$$= \sqrt{\frac{642.10 - 500}{4}}$$

$$= \sqrt{35.52}$$

$$= 6.0$$

The standard deviation is larger than the mean deviation of 4.0. This is always true because the squaring of the deviations puts more emphasis upon the extreme items.

Grouped Data

In a frequency distribution the midpoint of each class is used to represent every value in that class. The basic formula for the standard deviation therefore becomes

$$s = \sqrt{\frac{\Sigma f x^2}{n-1}}$$

where x is the deviation of the class midpoint (X) from the arithmetic mean and f is the frequency in that class.

Short-Cut Methods. The computation can be simplified by using the class midpoints (X) themselves rather than their deviations (x) from the mean, as follows:

$$s = \sqrt{\frac{\Sigma fX^2 - (\Sigma fX)^2/n}{n - 1}}$$

These two formulas are the same as those for ungrouped data except for using X as the class midpoint and f as the class frequency. A brief illustration is given in Table 11–4, which shows the prices of a transistor radio in six stores. The mean price is $26.

Table 11–4

COMPUTATION OF STANDARD DEVIATION
FOR GROUPED DATA (TWO METHODS)

PRICES OF A TRANSISTOR RADIO IN SIX STORES

(1) Price in Dollars (Class Midpoint) X	(2) Number of Stores (Frequency) f	(3) Deviation from Mean (Dollars) x	(4) fx^2	(5) fX	(6) fX^2
27	2	1	2	54	1,458
26	3	0	0	78	2,028
25	0	−1	0	0	0
24	1	−2	4	24	576
Total	6		6	156	4,062

Using the first formula,

$$s = \sqrt{\frac{\Sigma fx^2}{n-1}} = \sqrt{\frac{6}{5}} = \$1.10$$

Using the "short-cut" formula (which isn't really shorter in this simple case),

$$s = \sqrt{\frac{\Sigma fX^2 - (\Sigma fX)^2/n}{n-1}} = \sqrt{\frac{4,062 - (156)^2/6}{5}}$$

$$= \sqrt{\frac{4,062 - 4,056}{5}} = \sqrt{\frac{6}{5}} = \$1.10$$

The results of the two formulas are thus identical. These methods are not discussed further because in practice the standard deviation of grouped data is usually computed by a still shorter method, similar to that used for the arithmetic mean in Chapter 10.

The shortest method of computing the standard deviation of data grouped in equal intervals is to use the formula

$$s = i\sqrt{\frac{\Sigma fd^2 - (\Sigma fd)^2/n}{n-1}}$$

where

$i =$ the width of the class interval,
$f =$ the frequency or number of items in each class,
$d =$ the deviation of a class midpoint from the assumed mean in class interval units,
$\Sigma fd^2 =$ the sum of f times d^2 for each class (not Σf times Σd^2), and
$n =$ the total number of items.

The method is illustrated in Table 11-5. The first four columns of

Table 11-5

SHORT-CUT COMPUTATION OF STANDARD DEVIATION FOR GROUPED DATA

HOURLY EARNINGS OF 214 MACHINE TOOL OPERATORS

(1) Class Midpoint (Dollars) X	(2) Frequency f	(3) Deviation from Assumed Mean in Classes d	(4) fd	(5) fd²
2.30	2	−3	−6	18
2.40	23	−2	−46	92
2.50	49	−1	−49	49
2.60	63	0	0	0
2.70	45	1	45	45
2.80	25	2	50	100
2.90	3	3	9	27
3.00	4	4	16	64
Total	214		19	395

this table are identical with those used in Table 10-2 (p. 184), to find the arithmetic mean by the short-cut method. The steps are listed on pages 184-85. The last column (fd^2) may be computed by multiplying d by fd, i.e., col. 3 × col. 4. [This is *not* $(fd)^2$.] Since the d's are small integers, columns 4 and 5 can usually be computed mentally. Then the column totals are substituted in the formula as follows:[7]

$$s = i\sqrt{\frac{\Sigma fd^2 - (\Sigma fd)^2/n}{n-1}}$$

$$= .10\sqrt{\frac{395 - (19)^2/214}{213}}$$

$$= .10\sqrt{\frac{395 - 1.69}{213}}$$

$$= .10\sqrt{1.85}$$

$$= .136 \text{ dollars per hour}$$

The result of this formula is the same as for the two other formulas given, but the computations in columns 3, 4, and 5 are simpler. In any case, the standard deviation for grouped data is slightly less exact than that computed from the original data, since in formulas containing f the values in each class are rounded off to the class midpoint.[8]

If the widths of class intervals in a frequency distribution are unequal, the class deviations must be adjusted to uniform units (such as the smallest interval or the highest common factor) in order to apply the short-cut formula. Otherwise the preceding formula

$$s = \sqrt{\frac{\Sigma fX^2 - (\Sigma fX)^2/n}{n-1}}$$

should be used. If the distribution has an open end, neither the mean deviation nor the standard deviation can be computed, unless the missing end values can be estimated. If the end classes were simply omitted, as in computing the modified mean, either measure of dispersion would be reduced arbitrarily.

---

[7] If n is used instead of $n-1$ in this formula, the result is still $.136, since the substitution of 214 for 213 does not affect the first three significant figures of the answer.

[8] The three formulas for grouped data would be exact if every value of X were equal to its class midpoint. In case the concentration of values tapers off on both sides of the mean, as in a normal distribution, it is appropriate to adjust for grouping errors by subtracting $i^2 \div 12$ from the variance. This is called *Sheppard's adjustment*. This adjustment is not generally recommended, however, because (1) when major points of concentration occur at midpoints the unadjusted formula is more nearly appropriate, (2) when values of X are evenly distributed over the intervals the one-twelfth adjustment should be *added*, not subtracted. Hence the unadjusted formula is not only appropriate for one assumption but is also the mean of results obtained from two other assumptions. Finally, (3) errors of grouping are often small in comparison with other types of errors.

RELATION BETWEEN MEASURES OF DISPERSION

In a normal distribution there is a fixed relationship between the three most commonly used measures of dispersion. The quartile deviation is smallest, the mean deviation next, and the standard deviation, σ, is largest, in the following proportions:[9]

$$Q \cong 2/3\sigma$$
$$\text{M.D.} \cong 4/5\sigma$$

where the sign $\cong$ denotes approximate equality.

These relationships can be easily memorized because of the sequence 2, 3, 4, 5. The same proportions tend to hold true for many distributions that are not quite normal. They are useful in estimating one measure of dispersion when another is known, or in checking roughly the accuracy of a calculated value. In the case of the machine tool operators, for example, $Q = \$.097$, M.D. $= \$.103$, and s, the estimate of $\sigma, = \$.136$. Here σ could be estimated roughly from Q as $\sigma = 3/2Q = \$.145$; or, more accurately from M.D., as $\sigma = 5/4\text{M.D.} = \$.129$. If the computed standard deviation differs very widely from its value estimated from Q or M.D., either an error has been made or the distribution differs considerably from normal.

Another comparison may be made of the proportion of items that are typically included within the interval of one Q, M.D., or σ measured both above and below the population mean μ (small mu in Greek). In a normal distribution:

$\mu \pm Q$ includes 50 per cent of the items,
$\mu \pm$ M.D. includes 57.51 per cent of the items,
$\mu \pm \sigma$ includes 68.27 per cent of the items.

These relationships are shown graphically in Chart 11–2. Note that the standard deviation is the distance between the mean and the point of inflection on the normal curve, i.e., the point where the curve changes from being concave downward to being concave upward, and where it is steepest.

For the machine tool operators, the interval around the sample mean $\overline{X} \pm Q$ is $\$2.609 \pm \$.097$, or from $\$2.512$ to $\$2.706$ per hour. This interval actually includes about 50 per cent of the workers, and so the distribution is nearly normal in this respect. The proportions within the intervals $\overline{X} \pm$ M.D. and $\overline{X} \pm s$ are also nearly normal for the hourly

---

[9] More precisely, $Q = .6745\sigma$ and M.D. $= .7979\sigma$.

earnings, since they contain 53 per cent and 67 per cent of the workers, respectively.

The proportions of items typically falling within 1, 2, and 3 standard deviations of the mean are also widely used in statistical analysis. In a normal distribution:

$\mu \pm \sigma$ includes 68.27 per cent of the items,
$\mu \pm 2\sigma$ includes 95.45 per cent of the items,
$\mu \pm 3\sigma$ includes 99.73 per cent of the items.

These relations are also shown graphically in Chart 11–2. The interval $\overline{X} \pm 2\sigma$ thus includes about 19 out of 20 of the items, while $\overline{X} \pm 3\sigma$

Chart 11–2

PROPORTIONS OF AREA OF NORMAL CURVE INCLUDED IN INTERVALS BASED ON COMMON MEASURES OF DISPERSION

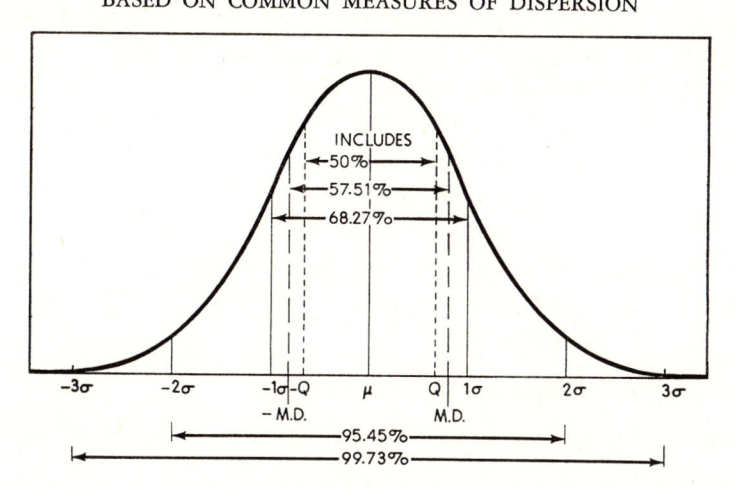

includes nearly all of them. In the case of the machine tool operators, the interval $\$2.609 \pm (3 \times \$.136)$, or from $2.201 to $3.017, includes 212 out of 214 workers (Table 9–2, p. 158). In general, so long as the departure from symmetry is only moderate, an interval of 3σ on both sides of the average will give the practical limits of the distribution.

Which Measure of Dispersion to Use?

As in the case of averages, the selection of the proper measure of dispersion depends on three main factors:

1. The concept of dispersion required by the problem. Is a single pair of values adequate, such as the two extremes or the two quartiles (range or Q)? Or is a simple average of all absolute deviations from the mean or median needed (i.e., mean devia-

tion)? Or an average (the standard deviation) that is better adapted for further calculations?
2. The type of data available. If they are few in number, or contain extreme values, avoid the standard deviation. If they are generally skewed, avoid the mean deviation as well. If they have gaps around the quartiles, the quartile deviation should be avoided.
3. The peculiarities of the dispersion measures themselves. These are summarized under "Characteristics of Measures of Dispersion," below.

As a rule of thumb, the median and quartiles may be used as simple, easily understandable summary values for rough or skewed data, as in a distribution of personal incomes, but the over-all range should be avoided.[10] The mean deviation is commonly used to give equal weight to all deviations where n is small and in ungrouped data, even if the distribution is somewhat erratic, as in time series. But if n is large and the distribution is fairly symmetrical, and if more refined analysis is needed, such as the study of inference or correlation, the standard deviation should be used instead. A major reason for the widespread use of the standard deviation is that it has the smallest sampling error of any dispersion measure when the distribution is normal; that is, the sample value tends to deviate from the population value by the smallest percentage.

Characteristics of Measures of Dispersion

The characteristics of the individual measures of dispersion are summarized below:

Range:

1. The range is the easiest measure to compute and to understand, but
2. It is often unreliable, being based on two extreme values only.

Quartile Deviation:

1. The quartile deviation is also easy to calculate and to understand.
2. It depends on only two values, which include the middle half of the items.
3. It is usually superior to the range as a rough measure of dispersion.

---

[10] An exception is the use of the range in quality control, to be discussed in Chapter 22.

4. It may be determined in an open-end distribution, or one in which the data may be ranked but not measured quantitatively.
5. It is also useful in badly skewed distributions or those in which other measures of dispersion would be warped by extreme values.
6. However, it is unreliable if there are gaps in the data around the quartiles.

Mean Deviation:

1. The mean deviation has the advantage of giving equal weight to the deviation of every value from the mean or median.
2. It is therefore a more sensitive measure of dispersion than those described above, and ordinarily has a smaller sampling error.
3. It is also easier to compute and to understand, and is less affected by extreme values than the standard deviation.
4. Unfortunately, it is difficult to handle algebraically, since minus signs must be ignored in its computation.

Standard Deviation:

1. The standard deviation is usually more useful and better adapted to further analysis than the mean deviation.
2. It is more reliable as an estimator of the population value than any other dispersion measure, provided the distribution is normal.
3. It is the most widely used measure of dispersion and the easiest to handle algebraically.
4. However, it is harder to compute and more difficult to understand, and
5. It is greatly affected by extreme values that may be due to skewness of data.

MEASURES OF RELATIVE DISPERSION

The measures of dispersion so far described are expressed in original units, such as dollars. These values may be used to compare the variation in two distributions provided the variables are expressed in the same units and are of about the same average size. In case the two sets of data are expressed in different units, however, such as tons of coal versus cubic feet of gas, or if the average size is very different, such as executives' salaries versus laborers' wages, the absolute measures of dispersion are not comparable and measures of *relative* dispersion should be used instead.

A measure of relative dispersion is the ratio of a measure of absolute dispersion to an appropriate average, and is usually expressed as a per cent. It is sometimes called a *coefficient of dispersion* because "coefficient" means a ratio or pure number that is independent of the unit of measurement. A coefficient of dispersion may be computed from either the quartile or mean deviation,[11] but is usually expressed as the ratio of the standard deviation to the mean, $s/\overline{X}$.

Thus, for the machine tool operators' earnings, the coefficient of dispersion is

$$s/\overline{X} = .136/2.609 = 5.2 \text{ per cent}$$

That is, the standard deviation is 5.2 per cent of the mean earnings. If a group of foremen had a standard deviation of $.160 and mean earnings of $4.00 an hour, their earnings would vary more than those of the operators in dollars, to be sure ($.160 versus $.136); but they would vary less relative to their average earnings ($.160 \div 4.00 = 4.0$ per cent versus 5.2 per cent). The *relative* measure is the more significant comparison.

Standard Deviation Units

Individual deviations from the mean ($x = X - \overline{X}$) may also be reduced to comparable units by dividing them by the standard deviation (s). Thus, for a machine tool operator earning $2.80 an hour, or $.191 above the mean of $2.609, $x/s = .191/.136 = 1.40$. His wage is, therefore, 1.40 standard deviations above the mean, a value which is comparable with, say, his output in units produced, which may be 2.20 standard deviations above the mean. Perhaps he rates a raise in pay!

The values of x/s will vary from approximately $+3$ to -3 for any set of data, since this spread includes nearly all the items in a normal distribution. The interval $\overline{X} \pm 3s$ therefore provides the practical limits of variation used in quality control and other applications. Variation greater than these limits indicates the presence of abnormal forces that must be isolated and eliminated.

SKEWNESS

Skewness means the lack of symmetry in the shape of a frequency curve. The extent of this lopsidedness is another important characteristic of a frequency distribution.

The simplest measure of skewness is based on the spread between the arithmetic mean and median. They are identical in a symmetrical distribution. In a skewed distribution, however, the mean is pulled out in the direction of the extreme values while the mode remains under the highest point of the curve, and the median, which is affected by the number of extreme values but not their value, tends to fall about

---

[11] The formulas are $(Q_3 - Q_1)/(Q_3 + Q_1)$ and M.D. $/\overline{X}$, respectively.

one third of the way from the mean toward the mode, provided the skew is moderate.

A *coefficient of skewness* may therefore be defined as follows:

$$Sk = \frac{3(\overline{X} - Md)}{s}$$

where $\overline{X}$ is the mean, Md is the median, and s is the standard deviation.

The numerator $3(\overline{X} - Md)$ is used instead of $(\overline{X} - \text{Mode})$ because the mode is often difficult to locate accurately. Dividing by s expresses the measure in standard deviation units, so that it is comparable as between distributions that differ in unit of measurement or in average size. If the mean exceeds the median the skewness is positive; otherwise it is negative.

The formula will not be illustrated here because of its limited practical use. The accurate measurement of skewness requires more advanced techniques. In elementary analysis, skewness is ordinarily treated in descriptive terms rather than being summarized by a single measure.

USES OF MEASURES OF DISPERSION

As the student gains experience with the analysis of data, he will perceive opportunities for the use of measures of dispersion other than those which have just been described. The following summary briefly indicates these various applications.

Aid in Description

The simplest and most common use of a measure of dispersion is in the description of data. Averages are typical values, but measures of dispersion indicate the scatter of the data. The extent and direction of skewness should also be noted.

Comparison of Dispersion

The average values of two sets of data may be very similar, while the range and pattern of scatter differ greatly. If the data are generally alike, the measures of dispersion can be compared in absolute units to determine how the data differ in their variability. When several sets of data are expressed in different kinds of units or in similar units of widely different size, comparisons based on measures of relative dispersion are usually more appropriate.

Provision of a Standard

By the use of measures of dispersion, particularly the standard deviation, it is possible to compare the variation in a given group of data with that of the normal curve as a standard. It has been pointed out that approximately 68 per cent of all the items in a normal distribution are included between one standard deviation above the mean and one standard deviation below the mean. When characteristics of a variable are expressed in standard deviation units, its distribution can be compared with a normal distribution. This use is at the very heart of studies of reliability of sample averages, quality control programs in industrial production, and other applications of statistical methods.

Measurement of Sampling Errors

Reliability of sample averages is an important part of statistical analysis. Averages vary by chance from sample to sample in the same population. In order to evaluate the reliability of the average in a single sample, we must know more about the variation of that average in all possible samples. The standard deviation is ordinarily used in this type of study, as explained in the next chapter.

SUMMARY OF FORMULAS

Since the characteristics of the various measures of dispersion and skewness have been summarized above, the chapter may be concluded by listing the principal formulas used:

Measure	Ungrouped Data	Grouped Data
Range	Subtract end values	Same
Quartile deviation	$Q = \dfrac{Q_3 - Q_1}{2}$	Same
	Q_1 is #$n/4 + 1/2$*	$Q_1 = L + \dfrac{i(n/4 - F)}{f}$
	Q_3 is #$3n/4 + 1/2$*	$Q_3 = L + \dfrac{i(3n/4 - F)}{f}$
Mean deviation	$\text{M.D.} = \dfrac{\Sigma\|x\|}{n}$	$\text{M.D.} = \dfrac{i\Sigma f\|x\|}{n}$
Standard deviation	$s = \sqrt{\dfrac{\Sigma x^2}{n-1}}$	$s = \sqrt{\dfrac{\Sigma f x^2}{n-1}}$
Shortcut	$s = \sqrt{\dfrac{\Sigma X^2 - (\Sigma X)^2/n}{n-1}}$	$s = i\sqrt{\dfrac{\Sigma f d^2 - (\Sigma f d)^2/n}{n-1}}$
Relative dispersion	Divide measure of absolute dispersion by appropriate average	
Skewness	$Sk = \dfrac{3(X - Md)}{s}$	Same

* In an array, counting from lowest value.

PROBLEMS

1. Cite actual or hypothetical illustrations, not given in the text, of each of the following:
   a) Two main purposes of measuring dispersion.
   b) Positive and negative skewness.
   c) Narrow dispersion and peaked kurtosis.

2. The values below show the number of hours of operation before repairs were required for eight power lawn mowers:

$$\begin{array}{c} \textit{Number of Hours} \\ 21 \\ 27 \\ 29 \\ 35 \\ 29 \\ 21 \\ 27 \\ \underline{35} \\ \text{Total} = 224 \text{ hours} \end{array}$$

   Compute and explain briefly the meaning of:
   a) The third quartile.
   b) The mean deviation.
   c) The standard deviation.
   d) A measure of relative dispersion, using the standard deviation.
   e) The largest value (35) expressed in standard deviation units.

3. In Chapter 9, Problem 7:
   a) Find the range and quartile deviation from your original list of 112 items.
   b) Interpolate the quartiles and compute the quartile deviation from your frequency distribution of these data.
   c) Why do the quartile values differ in (a) and (b)?

4. Using your frequency distribution in the problem above:
   a) Compute the standard deviation.
   b) Explain the meaning of this measure in terms of electronic workers' earnings.
   c) Should this value of s differ from the following? Give reasons.
      (1) The s of the original ungrouped data.
      (2) The s for the other formulas containing f.
   d) Estimate the mean deviation from the standard deviation, assuming a nearly normal distribution.

5. Answer the same questions as in Problem 4, above, for the starting salaries in engineering, accounting, sales, or general business, whichever is assigned, in Chapter 9 (p. 176), the table preceding Problem 4.

6. A purchasing agent obtained samples of incandescent lamps from two suppliers. He had the samples tested in his own laboratory for length of life, with the following results:

Length of Life in Hours	Samples from— Company A	Samples from— Company B
700 and under 900	10	3
900 and under 1,100	16	42
1,100 and under 1,300	26	12
1,300 and under 1,500	8	3
Total	60	60

a) Which company's lamps have the greater average length of life?
b) Which company's lamps are more uniform?

7. *a*) What ratio is M.D. to Q, in a normal distribution?
b) The interval $\mu \pm 3\sigma$ includes nearly all the items in a normal distribution. Express this range in Q units.
c) If you compute the standard deviation to be .612 pounds, and note as a rough check that the over-all quartile range ($Q_3 - Q_1$) is 36 pounds, what is the most obvious type of error you might have made?
d) In a normal distribution of text scores with $\mu = 60$, $\sigma = 9$, what percentage of scores exceeds 33? 51? 78?

8. If a test of 100 pieces of cotton thread shows a mean breaking strength of 15 pounds and a median breaking strength of 14.8 pounds, with a standard deviation of 3 pounds, about what number of pieces of thread in the lot should have a breaking strength between 12 and 21 pounds?

9. Regarding the dimensions of 63 gears in Table 9–1, p. 156:
a) Estimate the standard deviation of the whole lot from which this sample was drawn.
b) Check your result against the rough estimate of σ as one sixth the range (since the interval $\overline{X} \pm 3\sigma$ includes practically all items in a normal distribution).
c) How far does the largest gear (.4270) differ from the mean in standard deviation units?

10. In Chapter 9, Problem 8 (p. 177):
a) Compute whatever measure of dispersion you think most appropriate, and explain its significance.

b) If there are any dispersion measures you cannot compute from these data, name them and indicate why you cannot.

11. In Chapter 9, Problem 9 (p. 178):
    a) Compute the standard deviation.
    b) Find the estimated variance for all such cars. Explain its significance.
    c) If you get 14 miles per gallon with this car, how many standard deviations are you below the mean of 18.82 m.p.g.?

SELECTED READINGS

BURNS, ARTHUR F., and MITCHELL, WESLEY C. *Measuring Business Cycles.* New York: National Bureau of Economic Research, 1946, pp. 33–34, 380–81, 503–6.
  Stresses the virtues of the mean deviation as a measure of dispersion.

FREUND, JOHN E., and WILLIAMS, FRANK J. *Modern Business Statistics.* Englewood Cliffs, N.J.: Prentice-Hall, Inc., 1958, chap. 4.
  Presents a clear explanation of the standard deviation, including the choice of n or $n-1$ in its computation.

KELLEY, TRUMAN L. *Fundamentals of Statistics.* Cambridge: Harvard University Press, 1947, pp. 230–33.
  Recommends the 10.90 percentile range as having a smaller sampling error than other positional ranges.

MILLS, FREDERICK C. *Statistical Methods.* 3d ed. New York: Henry Holt & Co., Inc., 1955, chap. 5.
  Presents alternative methods of computing M.D. and the standard deviation, and characteristics of various dispersion measures.

YULE, G. UDNY, and KENDALL, M. G. *An Introduction to the Theory of Statistics.* 14th ed. London: Charles Griffin & Co., Ltd., 1950, chaps. 6 and 7.
  A good discussion of measures of dispersion, skewness, and kurtosis.

12. STATISTICAL INFERENCE: ARITHMETIC MEANS

THE ABILITY to make valid generalizations and predictions from sample data is an important step forward in scientific knowledge. The sampling methods useful in making such inferences were described in Chapter 4. Chapters 9–11 presented the necessary tools of analysis—frequency distributions, averages, and measures of dispersion. These basic concepts can now be brought together in the further study of statistical inference.

Statistical inference is the process by which we draw a conclusion about some measure of a population based on a sample value. The measure might be the arithmetic mean, median, standard deviation, range, or proportion, or some other characteristic. The population measure is called a *parameter,* while the sample measure is called a *statistic.* We will first consider the problem of estimating the *arithmetic mean* of a population from the mean of a sample. This is called a *point estimate,* since it endeavors to provide the best single estimated value of the parameter. An *interval estimate,* on the other hand, proceeds by specifying a range of values. Thus, after testing a sample of steel rods, we may make a point estimate that the mean breaking strength of all such rods is ten pounds; but we might also make an interval estimate that the mean for all rods probably lies in the interval from 8 to 12 pounds, as described later.

The following methods apply strictly to simple random samples, but they can be adapted to other types of probability sampling as well. The term "sample mean" in this chapter will therefore refer to the arithmetic mean of a simple random sample.

The following symbols will be used:

Ch. 12] STATISTICAL INFERENCE: ARITHMETIC MEANS 225

	Sample	Population
Arithmetic mean	$\bar{X}$	μ
Standard deviation	s	σ
Standard error of the mean	$s_{\bar{x}}$	$\sigma_{\bar{x}}$
Number of items	n	N

The first step is to explore the normal distribution, or normal curve of error.

THE NORMAL DISTRIBUTION

The normal distribution was described in Chapter 9 as a continuous frequency distribution represented by a symmetrical bell-shaped curve (see Charts 9–5, 9–6, 11–1, and 11–2). It is useful for two purposes:

1. It portrays the distribution of a population of certain types of measurements, such as the prices of laying mash in Chart 9–5, page 169.
2. More important, it describes how certain measures, such as the mean, vary from sample to sample because of *chance*. That is, the normal curve portrays the frequency distribution of all possible means of large samples that might be drawn from almost any kind of population. In this chapter we will show how a distribution of sample means follows this pattern, so that we can estimate the *sampling error*.

Table of Areas under the Normal Curve

In order to estimate the sampling error, we must first be able to determine the proportion of items in a normal distribution that fall within certain intervals. The table in Appendix E, page 550, shows the proportion of total frequencies, or of the total area under a normal curve, which lies under a segment between the mean and any other point along the horizontal axis above the mean. The deviation x ($x = X - \bar{X}$; or $x = X - \mu$) must be divided by the standard deviation, σ, to express it in standard deviation units. The value x/σ is called the *standard normal deviate*. For any value of X, the normal deviate tells the number of standard deviations X is away from the mean and in which direction.

The left-hand stub and the heading of Appendix E show the values of these deviations (x/σ) from .0 (the mean itself) to 5.0, a point far out under the tail of the normal curve. The body of the table shows the proportion of the total area between the mean and any given value of x/σ. Since the normal curve is symmetrical about the mean, the table can be used for points either above or below the mean.[1]

To illustrate, suppose a large number of job applicants take an aptitude test given by the personnel department of a company. The scores on the test form a normal distribution[2] with an arithmetic mean of 80, and standard deviation of 4. Now consider the following cases. These are illustrated in Chart 12–1, panels A–D, respectively.

Chart 12–1

FINDING AREA UNDER A NORMAL CURVE
IN APPENDIX E

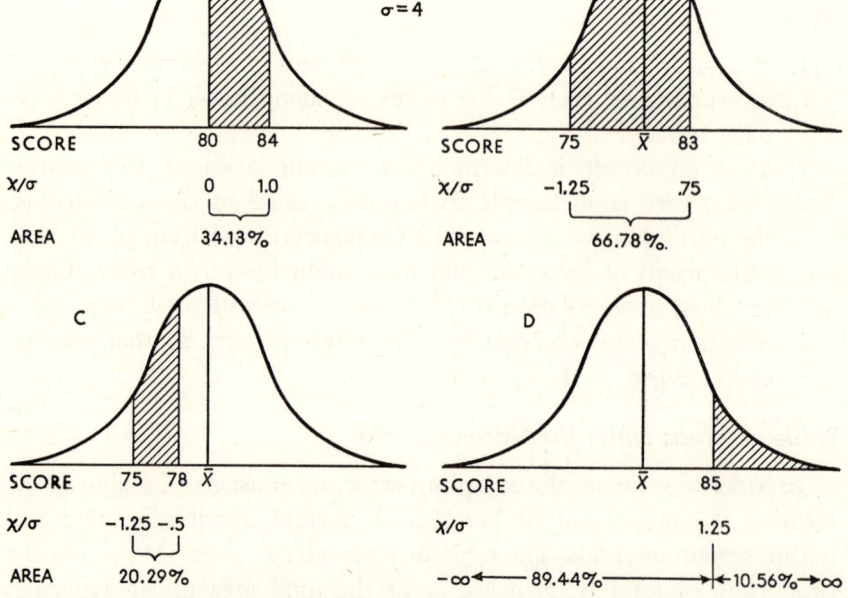

A. What proportion of applicants should score between 80 and 84? The deviation of the point 84 from the mean 80 is 4, so in standard deviation units, $x/\sigma = 4/4 = 1.0$. Looking in Appendix E opposite $x/\sigma = 1.0$, the proportion of the total area in this segment is .3413, or 34.13 per cent. The table shows relative frequencies, while the chart shows relative areas. The two are equivalent, since the area under any segment of the curve is proportional to the frequency. The

---

[1] Theoretically, the curve extends indefinitely on each side of the mean without touching the X axis. However, only a negligible part of the area lies more than four or five standard deviations from the mean, so the infinite tails can be ignored.

[2] The distribution of scores may be treated as continuous, since differences between successive scores are small.

proportion of scores that fall between the mean and one standard deviation on *both* sides of the mean is twice 34.13 per cent, or 68.26 per cent—the same value that was given for $\mu \pm \sigma$ on page 215 except for a slight error in rounding.

Many intervals do not terminate at the mean. These may be broken down, however, into intervals that do terminate at the mean, as shown below. Hence Appendix E can be used for any interval.

B. What proportion of scores should fall between 75 and 83? Since these points fall on both sides of the mean, the areas between the mean and each point must be added. For the score 83, $x/\sigma = (83-80)/4 = .75$. In Appendix E, look down the x/σ column to .7 and across to the column headed .05; the area is .2734. Similarly, for 75, $x/\sigma = (75-80)/4 = -1.25$, and the area is .3944. The combined area is then $.2734 + .3944 = .6678$, or 66.78 per cent.

C. What proportion of scores should fall between 75 and 78? Since both points are on the same side of the mean, the areas between each point and the mean must be subtracted to get the area between them. For 75, the area is .3944 as above. For 78, $x/\sigma = -.5$ and the area is .1915. The area between 75 and 78 is then $.3944 - .1915 = .2029$, or 20.29 per cent of the total area.

D. What proportion of scores should *exceed* 85? This is 50 per cent —the entire segment above the mean—minus the proportion of scores between the mean and 85, or 39.44 per cent (for $x/\sigma = 1.25$). The answer is then 10.56 per cent. Similarly the proportion of scores *below* 85 (the unshaded part of panel D) is $50 + 39.44 = 89.44$ per cent.

The table of areas under a normal curve thus serves to show the proportion of the total number of items under any segment of the curve. It will also be used to measure probabilities. When in doubt as to how to apply this table, draw a rough diagram, as in Chart 12–1, to picture the areas needed.

HOW SAMPLE MEANS ARE DISTRIBUTED

The normal distribution is especially useful in making inferences about the mean of the population from which the sample was selected. Such inferences are usually made from a single sample. However, we can best understand the principle involved by selecting a large number of samples from the same population and studying the behavior of the means obtained from these samples. The means themselves are treated as *individual values,* and are grouped in a frequency distribution—a certain number of means falling into each class interval. This is called the *sampling distribution of the mean.* The mean and standard deviation of this distribution will describe the behavior of the sample means.

An Experiment

To illustrate the sampling distribution of the mean when the population is known, consider the following experiment:

A manufacturer of electrical equipment receives shipments of ball

Table 12–1

SAMPLING THE DIAMETERS OF 565 BALL BEARINGS

	Number of Ball Bearings in—						
Diameter*	Population	1st Sample	2d Sample	3d Sample	4th Sample	5th Sample	Five Samples Combined
(1)	(2)	(3)	(4)	(5)	(6)	(7)	(8)
−6	1	......	......	1	......	1	2
−5	4	......	......	1	......	2	3
−4	15	......	2	1	1	......	4
−3	38	2	1	1	4	3	11
−2	70	8	7	5	3	10	33
−1	97	9	7	12	7	11	46
0	115	12	11	11	10	6	50
1	97	9	11	10	8	7	45
2	70	5	4	6	9	4	28
3	38	1	5	1	4	4	15
4	15	4	2	......	3	2	11
5	4	......	......	......	1	......	1
6	1	......	......	1	......	......	1
Number of ball bearings	565	50	50	50	50	50	250
Average diameter*	0	+.14	+.20	−.18	+.52	−.42	+.05

* Difference from specification (.25 inches) in thousandths of an inch.

bearings from a steel company for use in electric fans. Specifications call for these balls to average one quarter of an inch in diameter, and none of them must deviate from the specification by more than a given tolerance. Since it is not feasible to measure every ball bearing, it is necessary to depend on sample inspection to avoid acceptance of unsatisfactory shipments.

The inspection supervisor wished to illustrate the sampling principles involved as part of the training program for inspectors. Accordingly, he selected one shipment of 565 ball bearings as the population. He then had the whole lot measured with automatic calipers. The results are shown in Table 12–1, columns 1 and 2. Thus, only one of the 565 balls was six thousandths of an inch below specification, four balls were five thousandths below, and so on; the average of all the balls (last row) was exactly equal to the specification.

Samples of 50 steel balls each were then selected at random from the bin containing the shipment, and their diameters were measured. After each 50 were selected, they were returned to the bin and thoroughly mixed so that the next sample could be selected from the same population as the first sample. In all, 100 samples of 50 balls each were selected.

The results of the first five of the 100 samples are shown in columns 3–7 of Table 12–1. Each of these samples differs from the others, and none of them is a perfect replica of the population. The mean diameter for each sample is shown in the last row.

The Three Distributions. It is important to distinguish the three different distributions illustrated by this experiment. They are shown in Chart 12–2. First is the distribution of ball-bearing diameters (X) in the population itself—curve A. The figures are taken from Table 12–1, column 2. Frequencies are plotted as percentages of the total, on the Y axis, for comparability with curve B. (The curve would have been smooth if the ball bearings had been measured exactly rather than to the nearest .001 inch.) This population is normal, with its mean μ equal to zero. Other populations may be skewed or otherwise irregular.

Second is the distribution of the X values in a sample drawn from this population, such as the fourth sample in Table 12–1, shown in curve B. The sample distribution has somewhat the same general shape as the population, but it is more irregular, and its mean ($\overline{X}$) differs from the true mean (μ) because of sampling errors. As the sample size increases (e.g., Table 12–1, col. 8), the shape of the sample distribution approaches more and more closely that of the population distribution, whether the latter be skewed or what not. Both the mean and the standard deviation of the sample also approach the population values.

Third is the sampling distribution of the *means* ($\overline{X}$) of a great many samples (curve C) of size n that can be drawn from this population. This curve shows the distribution of 100 sample means. It has been drawn with a smaller area than that under the other curves; other-

Chart 12-2
THE THREE DISTRIBUTIONS INVOLVED IN ESTIMATING THE MEAN
BALL-BEARING DIAMETERS (TRUE MEAN = 0)

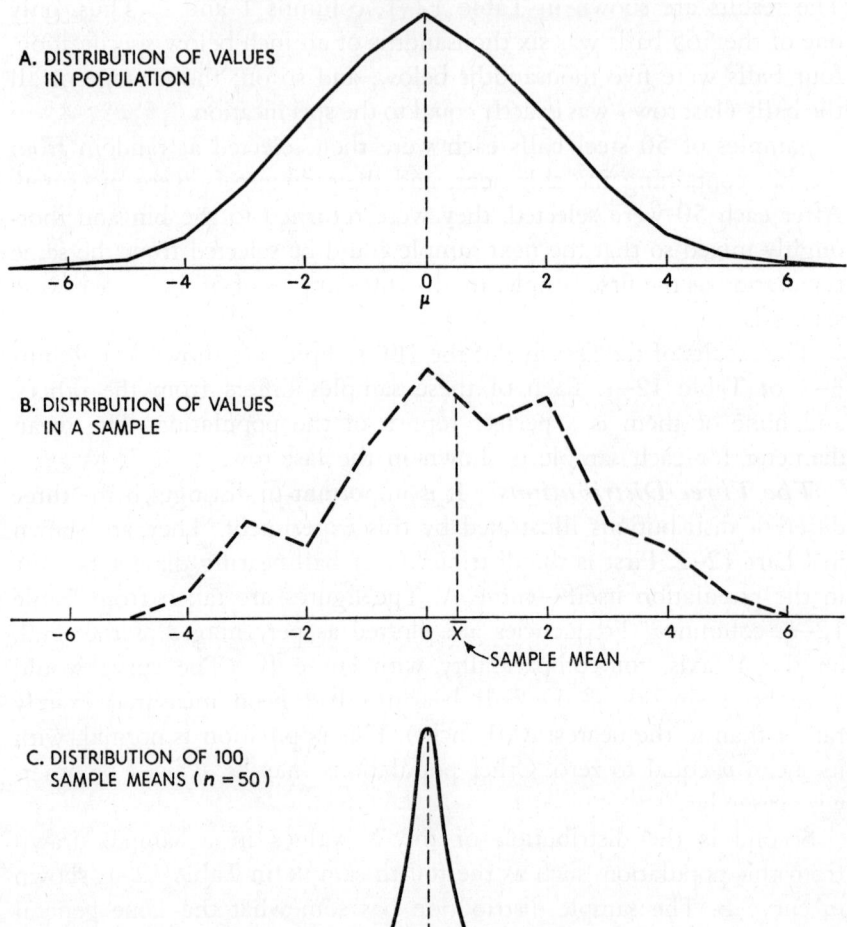

A. DISTRIBUTION OF VALUES IN POPULATION

B. DISTRIBUTION OF VALUES IN A SAMPLE

C. DISTRIBUTION OF 100 SAMPLE MEANS ($n = 50$)

Unit: Thousandths of an inch differences from specification.
SOURCE: Table 12-1 and related data.

wise it would be awkwardly tall. The five sample means shown in the bottom row of Table 12–1 fall well within the range of curve C. The mean of this distribution is very close to that of the population, and its dispersion or standard deviation is much less than that of curve A or B. If all possible samples of size 50 were drawn from this population, the distribution shown in curve C would be smoother, and nearly normal.

As the sample size increases, the distribution of sample means becomes still narrower in spread, and more normal in shape, as described below. Chart 12–3 shows how the sample means from a normal population tend to cluster more closely about the population mean as the sample size increases. The three curves in Chart 12–3 have the same area and are all normal, but they differ markedly in dispersion.

Sampling Concepts. The ball-bearing experiment illustrates several concepts in sampling:

1. Each of the means is approximately, but not exactly, equal to the population mean. Of the 100 samples selected in the larger study (not

Chart 12–3

SAMPLING DISTRIBUTIONS OF THE MEANS OF SAMPLES OF SIZE $n = 4$ AND $n = 25$, COMPARED WITH DISTRIBUTION OF A NORMAL POPULATION

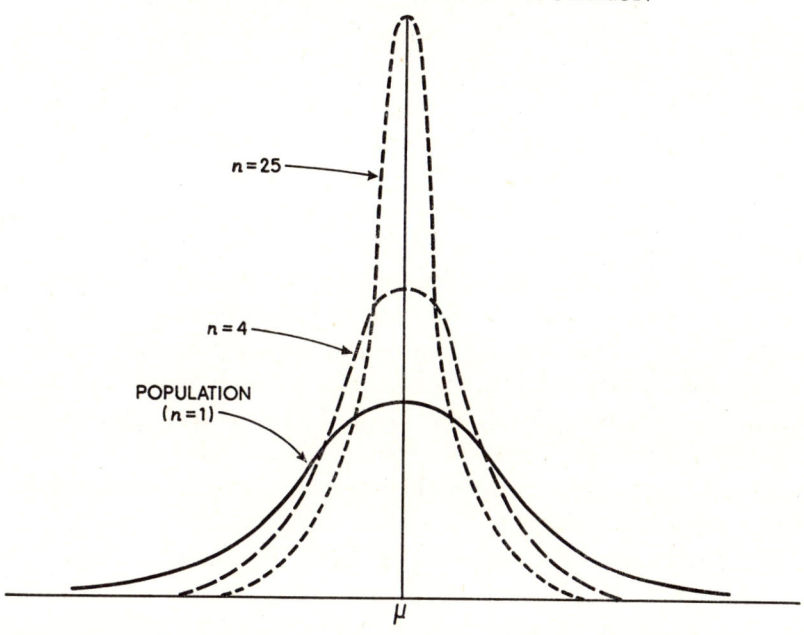

reported here in detail) only five exactly equaled the population in mean diameter, while 53 were above and 42 were below it.

2. The sample means cluster much more closely about the population mean than do the original values. Thus, the means in the last row of the table vary only from −.42 to +.52, while the individual diameters (cols. 1 and 2) range from −6.0 to +6.0. Hence the standard deviation of the sample means is much smaller than the standard deviation of the original values.

3. If larger samples were taken, their means would cluster still

more closely around the population mean since the positive and negative errors of sampling tend to offset each other. This is illustrated by combining the five samples shown to obtain the larger sample of 250 balls listed in column 8. The mean of this larger sample is $+.05$, a result which is much closer to the population value (0) than is any of the means of the five samples of 50. The over-all average of the 100 sample means proved to be $+.02$, which is closer yet to the population mean.

Thus, *the larger the sample, the closer its mean is likely to be to the mean of the entire population,* and the greater the precision of the sample mean. It can be shown that if all possible samples of a given size are drawn from a population, the arithmetic mean of the sample means will equal the population mean.

4. The distribution of sample means follows a normal curve. More precisely, if a number of random samples of size n are drawn from a given population, their means tend to form a normal distribution, provided (1) the size of sample is large[3] and (2) the population is not unduly skewed. If the population is skewed, the distribution of sample means will be much less skewed, in inverse proportion to the size of the sample. Thus for samples of size 50 the distribution of means will only be $1/50$ as skewed as the population (i.e., $n = 1$).[4]

The arithmetic mean therefore tends to be normally distributed as n increases in size, almost regardless of the shape of the original population. This principle is called the *central limit theorem*. It applies to the distribution of most other statistics as well, such as the median and standard deviation (but not the range). The central limit theorem gives the normal distribution its central place in the theory of sampling, since many important problems can be solved by this single pattern of sampling variability.

The distribution of sample means being normal, or nearly so, it can be completely described by its mean and its standard deviation. Furthermore, these values may be estimated from a single large random sample, as described under "The Standard Error of the Mean" below.

The Sample Mean as an Unbiased, Efficient Estimator

When we select a statistic such as the mean or median to estimate the population value, we ordinarily expect it to satisfy two criteria:

---

[3] In many cases a size of 30 is large enough, but no exact number can be given; it depends in part on the population distribution.

[4] See F. E. Croxton and D. J. Cowden, *Applied General Statistics* (2d ed.; New York: Prentice-Hall, Inc., 1955), p. 627.

1. The statistic should, on the average, give the "correct" answer—the population value. That is, the mean of a distribution of all possible means for a given size of sample—called the *expected value*—should equal the population value. Such an estimate is said to be *unbiased*. Means in random samples are unbiased estimators. Thus in Table 12–1, the expected value is the over-all mean of all possible sample means, each representing 50 ball bearings. This is zero, the same as the population mean. The mean of an individual sample, then, whatever its value, is said to be an unbiased estimator. The median is also unbiased if the population is symmetrical.

2. The second criterion states that the sampling distribution of the statistic be concentrated as closely as possible about the true population value. Such a statistic is said to be *efficient*. It can be shown that the sample mean is a more efficient estimator than the sample median in a normal population, since the sample values cluster more closely about the population value. In Chart 12–2, panel C, a distribution of sample medians would have a wider spread than that shown for the means.[5] (The median may be more efficient, however, for sharply peaked, long-tailed distributions, as emphasized in Chapter 10.) The arithmetic mean, therefore, is said to be an *unbiased* and *efficient* estimator of the population mean, in populations that are nearly normal.

THE STANDARD ERROR OF THE MEAN

The standard deviation of the distribution of sample means is called the *standard error of the mean*. (The word "error" is used here in place of "deviation" to emphasize that variation among sample means is due to sampling errors.) The standard error measures the *precision* of the sample estimate, that is, how closely the sample value is likely to approach the true value.[6] The smaller the standard error, the greater the precision. Where the population is large in relation to the sample size, the formula for the standard error of the mean is:

$$\sigma_{\bar{X}} = \frac{\sigma}{\sqrt{n}}$$

where σ is the standard deviation of X in the population and n is the size of the sample.

---

[5] The standard error of the median is 1.25 times that of the mean in a normal population.

[6] "Precision" or "reliability" as used in statistics means how closely we can reproduce from a sample the results that would be obtained if we took a complete census, using the same methods of measurement, interview procedures, etc. The "accuracy" of a survey takes into account these sampling errors as well as nonsampling errors arising from methods of measurement, questionnaire design, etc., that would affect the census as well as the sample. We can only measure precision, but it is the over-all accuracy that we attempt to maximize in designing surveys.

Thus, in the ball-bearing example the standard deviation of the population (Table 12–1, col. 2) is:

$$\sigma = \sqrt{\frac{\Sigma f x^2}{N}} = \sqrt{\frac{2{,}190}{565}} = 1.969 \quad (\text{Unit} = .001'')$$

Then, for samples of size 50, the standard error of the mean is

$$\sigma_{\bar{x}} = \frac{\sigma}{\sqrt{n}} = \frac{1.969}{\sqrt{50}} = .278$$

and for samples of size 250,

$$\sigma_{\bar{x}} = \frac{1.969}{\sqrt{250}} = .124$$

The standard error of the sample means, therefore, varies directly with the standard deviation of the population σ, and inversely with $\sqrt{n}$. By increasing the sample size, the standard error of the mean can be reduced to any desired level. However, the reduction is not pro rata. The sample size must be quadrupled to cut the standard error in half.

Finding the Standard Error of the Mean When σ Is Unknown

In practice, the standard deviation of the population (σ) is usually unknown, but it can be estimated as being equal to the standard deviation of a single large sample (s). That is, instead of $\sigma_{\bar{x}} = \sigma/\sqrt{n}$, we can say

$$s_{\bar{x}} = \frac{s}{\sqrt{n}}$$

where $s_{\bar{x}}$ is the standard error of the mean estimated from a single sample, and s is the standard deviation of the sample.[7]

Thus, for the first sample in Table 12–1,

$$s = \sqrt{\frac{\Sigma f x^2}{n - 1}} = \sqrt{\frac{161}{49}} = 1.81$$

---

[7] Sometimes n is used instead of $n - 1$ in the formula for s, e.g., $s = \sqrt{\Sigma f x^2 / n}$. In this case use $s_{\bar{x}} = \dfrac{s}{\sqrt{n - 1}}$ to achieve the same result as above. That is, by combining the two formulas, $s_{\bar{x}} = \sqrt{\dfrac{\Sigma f x^2}{n(n - 1)}}$ in either case. (Omit f in formulas for ungrouped data.)

and

$$s_{\bar{x}} = \frac{s}{\sqrt{n}} = \frac{1.81}{\sqrt{50}} = .256$$

This estimate of the standard error of the mean differs by 8 per cent from the true $\sigma_{\bar{x}}$ of .278.

Again, for the combined sample of 250,

$$s = \sqrt{\frac{1,017}{249}} = 2.021$$

and

$$s_{\bar{x}} = \frac{2.021}{\sqrt{250}} = .127$$

For the larger sample, the estimated standard error of the mean differs by only 2 per cent from the true $\sigma_{\bar{x}}$ of .124. This illustrates the principle that the standard error of the mean can be estimated satisfactorily from the standard deviation of a single large sample (the larger the better) when the standard deviation of the population is unknown.

Effect of Population Size. The above formulas for $\sigma_{\bar{x}}$ and $s_{\bar{x}}$ are correct if the population is infinitely large, or if the sampling is carried out with replacement, which amounts to the same thing. Sampling with replacement means that after an item is selected it is replaced and has a chance of being selected again. These formulas are also substantially correct when the sample is a small percentage—say less than 5 per cent—of a finite population. Thus far, the ball-bearing experiment has been treated as if its population were infinite.

Where the sample comprises a large proportion of the population and is done without replacement, the expression $\sigma/\sqrt{n}$ should be multiplied by $\sqrt{(N-n)/(N-1)}$, or approximately $\sqrt{1-n/N}$, where n is the sample size and N is the population size. That is,

$$\sigma_{\bar{x}} = \sqrt{1 - \frac{n}{N}} \frac{\sigma}{\sqrt{n}} \text{ for finite populations.}$$

The term $1 - n/N$ is the proportion of the population not included in the sample, and is called the finite multiplier.[8] Its use always reduces the standard error.

---

[8] See M. H. Hansen, W. N. Hurwitz, and W. G. Madow, *Sample Survey Methods and Theory* (New York: John Wiley & Sons, Inc., 1953), Vol. I, pp. 122–24; and W. A. Wallis and H. V. Roberts, *Statistics, A New Approach* (Glencoe, Ill.: The Free Press, 1956), pp. 368–71. The finite multiplier is also called the finite population factor, finite population correction, and finite sampling correction.

For example, since each sample of 50 ball bearings in Table 12–1, columns 3–7, was drawn without replacement from the population of 565 balls, we should have:

$$\sigma_{\bar{x}} = \sqrt{\frac{565-50}{565-1}} \; \frac{1.969}{\sqrt{50}}$$
$$= .957 \times .278$$
$$= .266$$

instead of .278 for sampling with replacement.

Thus the precision of the sample estimate, measured by $\sigma_{\bar{x}}$, is determined not only by the absolute size of the sample but also to some extent by the proportion of the population sampled. This is in accordance with common sense. A 10 per cent sample certainly seems more reliable than a 5 per cent sample.

In most actual surveys, however, the sample is such a small percentage of the population that n/N is negligible, and $\sigma_{\bar{x}}$ is virtually equal to $\sigma/\sqrt{n}$. Hence the reliability of a sample usually depends almost entirely on the absolute size of the sample, and *not* on the percentage of the population sampled. In planning a market survey of consumers in a large city, one should ask questions like "Is a sample of 1,000 big enough?" and not "Is a 10 per cent sample big enough?" The size of city makes little difference.

How $\sigma_{\bar{x}}$ Is Used

The standard error of the mean in the ball-bearing example is .278 thousandths of an inch for samples of size 50. Since .278 is the standard deviation of all possible means of size 50, and the distribution of means of large samples is normal, we can say what proportion of the sample means lies within any given interval of the true (population) mean. In this case the true mean is known ($\mu = 0$). Then 68.27 per cent of the sample means fall within one standard error ($\sigma_{\bar{x}}$) of the true mean, i.e., from $+.278$ to $-.278$. Similarly, 95.45 per cent fall within twice this range, and 99.73 per cent fall within the $3\sigma_{\bar{x}}$ limits. This means that there is a *probability* of about 68 per cent—or 68 chances out of 100—that a *single* sample mean will fall within the interval of $\mu \pm \sigma_{\bar{x}}$, or $\pm .278$; and so on for any other degree of probability desired. The table of areas under the normal curve therefore shows *probabilities* as well as frequencies.

These figures also show just how much more closely the sample means cluster than do the individual ball-bearing diameters. While 68 per cent of the *means* lie within $\sigma_{\bar{x}}$ or .278 thousandths of an inch from the true mean, the same percentage of individual ball bearings lie within σ or 1.969 thousandths of the true mean—a far wider spread.

If the distribution of the population is not normal, the above figures are still approximately correct for larger samples. In an experiment at the University of California, Berkeley, some 3,000 independent samples of 30 items each were drawn at random (using a table of random numbers) from a skewed population consisting of 200 weekly earnings figures for a group of wage earners and clerical workers in the San Francisco Bay Area. The population values ranged from $17.50 to $116.91 a week, and averaged $57.95. The arithmetic mean, the standard deviation, and the approximate standard error of the mean $s_{\bar{x}}$ were computed for each sample. The question then arose: What percentage of the 3,000 sample means fell within various multiples of the standard error around the true population mean, μ, of $57.95? The results were as follows:

	$\mu \pm s_{\bar{x}}$	$\mu \pm 2s_{\bar{x}}$	$\mu \pm 3s_{\bar{x}}$
Theoretical expectancy	68.27%	95.45%	99.73%
Experimental results	68.4 %	95.2 %	99.6 %

This shows a remarkable agreement between fact and theory, despite the fact that (1) the sample size was but 30 items; (2) the sample standard deviation s was used, instead of the true population value σ; and (3) the population was not normally distributed. The theory therefore works well in practice. For smaller samples, however—say when n is under 30—the above values may have to be adjusted, as will be described in Chapter 13.

The corresponding results for any other probability or interval in the sampling distribution of means can be found in Appendix E, just as we previously did for individual values. For example, within what interval will exactly 95 per cent of the sample means fall in the ball-bearing case ($n = 50$)? Since the proportion .95 lies on both sides of the population mean, look up half this amount, .475, for the proportion on one side of the mean, in the body of Appendix E. The interval is then $\pm 1.96\sigma_{\bar{x}}$ or $\pm .545$ thousandths of an inch.

It is customary to state probabilities in such round numbers as 95 or 99, so the following relationships in a normal distribution are important:

Mean $\pm 1.96\sigma$ includes 95.0 per cent of the area.
Mean $\pm 2.58\sigma$ includes 99.0 per cent of the area.

These are often used instead of the statements that the mean $\pm 2\sigma$ includes 95.45 per cent and $\pm 3\sigma$ includes 99.73 per cent of the area.

When the population mean is *not* known, and we use a sample mean to estimate it, we can only say that 68 per cent of the sample means lie within one standard error of the true mean, wherever that may be, and similarly for other intervals. Nevertheless, we will see in the next section how this information about the spread of sample means around the unspecified true mean can be used to make satisfactory estimates of the true mean.

CONFIDENCE INTERVALS

It is often necessary to estimate the unknown mean (or other parameter) of a population. To do so, we need both the sample value and a measure of the margin of error to which this value is subject. This may be done as follows:

1. Find the mean $\overline{X}$ and its standard error ($s_{\overline{x}} = s/\sqrt{n}$) from a large random sample as point estimates of the population values.
2. Specify a zone based on $\overline{X}$ and $s_{\overline{x}}$ within which we may be confident that the true population mean does lie. This is called a *confidence interval*. The end points of this interval are called *confidence limits*.
3. State the probability—say 95 or 99 per cent—that such a zone will include the population mean. This probability is called the *confidence coefficient* or *level of confidence*. It must be set in advance. Each confidence interval that may be chosen has an associated probability of including the population mean—the wider the interval the greater the probability. Thus, the zone $\overline{X} \pm 1.96\,\sigma_{\overline{x}}$ is the "95 per cent confidence interval." This relationship is based on the fact that 95 per cent of all sample means tend to fall within $1.96\,\sigma_{\overline{x}}$ of the population mean, where $\sigma_{\overline{x}}$ is the true standard error of the mean. Similarly, the zone $\overline{X} \pm 2.58\,\sigma_{\overline{x}}$ is the "99 per cent confidence interval." The zone for any other confidence coefficient may be found in Appendix E. The selection of the appropriate confidence coefficient is discussed on pages 240–41.

For example, we wish to estimate the mean diameter of the population of ball bearings in Table 12–1, which is assumed to be unknown. We take sample No. 1 (col. 3) and proceed as above. (All units are in thousandths of an inch.)

$$\overline{X} = +.14$$

$$s_{\overline{x}} = \frac{s}{\sqrt{n}} = \frac{1.81}{\sqrt{50}} = \frac{1.81}{7.07} = .256$$

Use this value as an estimate of the true standard error of the mean $\sigma_{\bar{X}}$. The error involved is a minor one for larger samples.

Compute $\bar{X} \pm 1.96 s_{\bar{X}}$ as the 95 per cent confidence interval for the population mean:

$$\bar{X} + 1.96 s_{\bar{X}} = .14 + 1.96(.256) = .14 + .50 = +.64$$
$$\bar{X} - 1.96 s_{\bar{X}} = .14 - 1.96(.256) = .14 - .50 = -.36$$

Our best point estimate of the population mean is therefore the sample mean, $+.14$, but this estimate is subject to a margin of error defined by the 95 per cent confidence limits of $+.64$ and $-.36$. Such a probability statement needs careful interpretation. For any particular sample, the confidence interval either includes the population mean or it does not—we don't know. The probability is either 100 per cent or zero. (In this case it does, since we know the population mean is zero.) The statement means that if a very large number of samples of size n are drawn, and the confidence interval is computed for each, 95 per cent of these intervals will include the population mean.

Chart 12–4 shows the means and confidence limits for this sample and for the other four samples of 50 ball bearings listed in Table 12–1.

Chart 12–4

NINETY-FIVE PER CENT CONFIDENCE LIMITS FOR THE POPULATION MEAN OBTAINED FROM SIX SAMPLE MEANS OF BALL-BEARING DIAMETERS ($n = 50$)

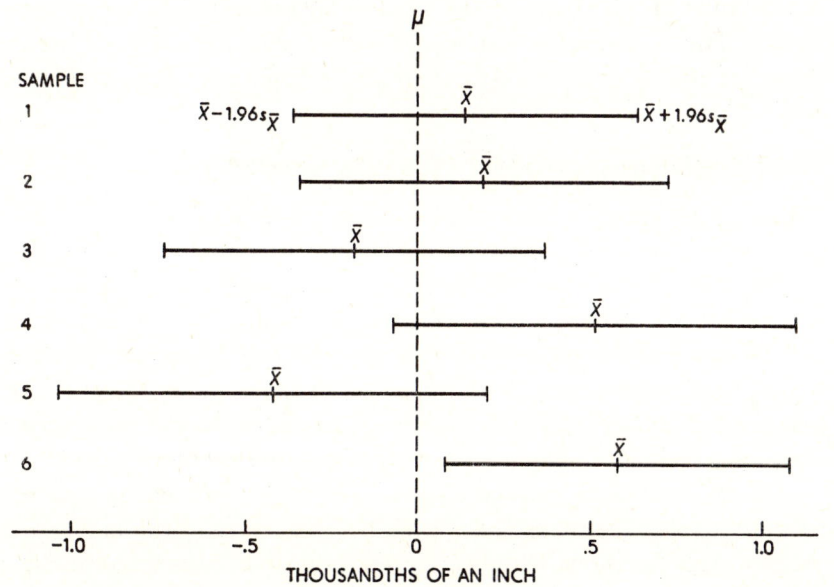

Source: Table 12–1 (except sample 6).

The means and intervals all vary, but the latter all include the population mean, μ, shown as a dashed line. The confidence interval for a sixth sample, however (not shown in Table 12–1), fails to include the true mean. Of all such possible confidence intervals, then, 95 per cent include the population mean.

The confidence interval around a sample mean might be likened to a quoit aimed at a peg—the population mean. Then 95 per cent of the quoits will ring the peg. If a bigger quoit is used—say the wider 99 per cent confidence interval of $\overline{X} \pm 2.58\, s_{\overline{x}}$—then 99 per cent of the quoits will be ringers.

We can say, therefore, that "the probability is 95 per cent of being correct in asserting that μ lies between $-.36$ and $+.64$." It is *wrong* to say, as is commonly done, "The probability is 95 per cent that μ lies between $-.36$ and $+.64$." The population mean is a fixed value and has no probability distribution, so no statement can be made about its probability of lying within a given interval.

A 99 per cent confidence interval can be computed as $\overline{X} \pm 2.58\, s_{\overline{x}}$ and similarly for any other confidence coefficient, using the table of areas under the normal curve. The 99 per cent interval for ball-bearing sample No. 1 is:

$$\overline{X} \pm 2.58 s_{\overline{x}} = +.14 \pm 2.58(.256) = +.14 \pm .66$$

Hence, we can say that the population mean lies between the confidence limits of $-.52$ and $+.80$, with a 99 per cent chance of being correct. The fact that we can make such a statement with a specific degree of confidence is an outstanding contribution of statistical inference.

Which Confidence Coefficient Should Be Selected?

Raising the confidence coefficient from 95 to 99 per cent increases our degree of assurance that the confidence interval contains the population value, but it also makes our estimate less precise, since the confidence interval itself has been widened by 32 per cent (i.e., from 1.96 to 2.58 standard errors). A too-wide interval may be useless. In selecting the confidence coefficient for a given size of sample, therefore, we may choose greater confidence with less precision, or greater precision with less confidence. The choice depends on the problem. While any confidence coefficient may be chosen, the 95 per cent level is widely used in the social sciences and the 99 per cent level in the natural sciences where precision is higher. In addition, it is customary to use 3 sigma limits in statistical quality control, with a confidence coefficient of 99.73 per cent, as described in Chapter 22. The choice of these figures, however, is rather arbitrary.

Any economic or business report that cites the mean (or other statistic) of a probability sample should give the reliability of this value in terms of a confidence interval or some other use of $\sigma_{\bar{x}}$ as a measure of the sampling error. For example, the Census Bureau's *Monthly Report on the Labor Force* cited in Chapter 5 says, "The chances are about 19 out of 20 that the difference between the estimate and the figure which would have been obtained from a complete census is less than the sampling variability indicated below" (followed by a table showing various sample sizes and the corresponding 95 per cent confidence intervals). A statistic having a large sampling error may be useless; at any rate, the error should be stated. The report should also point out that this reliability measure does not include the effect of bias due to nonsampling errors in sample design, incomplete coverage of sample, bias of respondent, etc. These errors should be discussed in qualitative terms.

Errors in Confidence Intervals. The confidence intervals just described may be inaccurate because: (1) the standard error of the mean estimated from a single sample is not equal to the true standard error and (2) the sample means may not be quite normally distributed. These errors are appreciable in small samples, but they become insignificant in larger samples. Thus, in the example cited above, increasing the sample size from 50 to 250 reduced the discrepancy in the standard error of the mean from 8 to 2 per cent.

HOW BIG SHOULD A SAMPLE BE?

In planning a sample survey, is it necessary to sample 100 items? 1,000? Or all we can afford? The answer depends mainly on two factors: (1) the precision required for a correct management decision and (2) the cost of sampling. These will be considered in turn.

The relation between precision of the sample mean and size of sample is:

$$\sigma_{\bar{x}} = \frac{\sigma}{\sqrt{n}}$$

To estimate how big n should be, there are three steps:

1. Determine how small the standard error of the mean, $\sigma_{\bar{x}}$, must be in order to obtain the necessary precision. The precision depends on how the results are to be used, and is for management to decide.

2. Take a random sample of any convenient size and compute the sample standard deviation s as an estimate of σ, the population standard deviation.
3. Substitute the desired value of $\sigma_{\bar{x}}$ and the estimated σ in the above equation and solve for n. This size of sample will give the necessary precision. If a larger sample is then taken, its standard deviation can be used to provide a revised estimate of σ and hence $\sigma_{\bar{x}}$.

The size of the population is usually a negligible factor, as pointed out earlier. However, if the sample makes up more than 5 or 10 per cent of the population, the finite multiplier should be applied to the above equation.

As an example, suppose it is necessary to measure ball-bearing diameters so precisely that $\sigma_{\bar{x}}$ must be no more than .1 thousandths of an inch. (That is, if the 99 per cent confidence level is chosen, 2.58 $\sigma_{\bar{x}}$ must not exceed .258 thousandths.) Then take a sample of convenient size and compute s as an estimate of σ, e.g., sample No. 1 in Table 12–1 where $n = 50$ and $s = 1.81$. Now, substitute these values in the equation $\sigma_{\bar{x}} = \sigma/\sqrt{n}$ and solve for n:

$$.1 = \frac{1.81}{\sqrt{n}}$$

Transposing, $\sqrt{n} = 18.1$

Squaring both sides, $n = 328$

Therefore a sample of about 328 ball bearings (including the original 50) should be tried. After sampling 250 diameters, as in Table 12–1, column 8, we could recompute s, which is now 2.02. Substituting in the same equation, we get a better approximation of sample size:

$$.1 = \frac{2.02}{\sqrt{n}}$$

$$n = 408$$

The actual σ for the population of 565 ball bearings is 1.97, which would call for a sample of 388 (with replacement) to make $\sigma_{\bar{x}} = .1$.

The cost of a survey includes a constant factor—for setting up the project, overhead, etc.—and a variable factor—so much per item sampled. Suppose it costs $300 to set up the ball-bearing inspection and $1.00 per measurement. Then the total cost (C) in dollars is:

$$C = 300 + 1n$$

The executive can then compare the cost with the precision of the sample result for various possible sizes of sample, in order to choose among them. Thus, for the ball-bearing example:

n	$s_{\bar{x}}$*	Cost
50	.256	$350
250	.127	550

* In thousandths of an inch.

Since the cost increases directly with the size of sample, and reliability increases only with the square root of sample size, there are diminishing returns, and at some point the slight increase in reliability will not justify the added cost of sampling.

Consumer surveys conducted by personal interview may cost many dollars per schedule, but where important decisions are at stake, the necessary precision may justify a costly survey. As a case in point, the Elgin National Watch Company suffered from foreign competition in the late 1950's and lost over $8,000,000 in 1957-58. The company then spent $50,000 for market surveys. According to *Time* (May 2, 1960),

> The surveys showed that Elgin simply was not making what buyers wanted. Men were found to prefer round watches (most of Elgin's were rectangular), to like functional stainless steel, water- and shockproof cases (Elgin's were mostly yellow gold), to want sweep second hands (only 15% of Elgin's had them). . . .

The surveys also showed that consumers wanted cheaper watches. The company introduced new, competitively priced models, and in the year ended March 1, 1960 made net profits of $815,000. Obviously, if a business decision as important as revising a product line depends on the results of market surveys, high precision is required and high cost is justified.

The reliability and cost of a survey depend not only on the size of sample but also on the sampling plan itself. The principal plans were discussed in Chapter 4. For example, instead of a simple random or systematic sample, the reliability of a given-sized sample can be increased by stratification, or the unit cost can be reduced by cluster sampling. See M. H. Hansen, W. N. Hurwitz, and W. G. Madow, *Sample Survey Methods and Theory* (New York: John Wiley & Sons, Inc., 1953), Vol. I, for a further discussion of this subject.

SUMMARY

Statistical inference is the process of making a generalization or prediction about a population value, called a *parameter,* based on a sample value, called a *statistic*. This may be a single-valued *point estimate*, or a range of values designated as an *interval estimate*. The process is first described for the mean of a simple random sample.

If all possible means of large samples are drawn from a population, the sampling distribution tends to follow a *normal curve*. The proportion of items that fall within a given area under the normal curve may be determined from Appendix E. This proportion represents *relative frequencies*, or the *probability* that a single item (e.g., a sample mean) will fall within the segment.

An experiment is presented to show how sample means cluster about the population mean—the cluster being closer and hence the precision greater for larger samples. The sampling distribution of the mean must be clearly distinguished from the distribution of individual values in the population or the somewhat similar distribution of individual values in the sample itself (Chart 12–2). The tendency of the sampling distribution of the mean to form a normal curve as n increases in size, whatever the type of population, is called the *central limit theorem*.

The sample mean is said to be an *unbiased* estimator of the population mean because its *expected* value equals the population value. The expected value is the mean of a distribution of all possible means for a given size of sample. The sample mean is also said to be *efficient* because its sampling distribution usually clusters more closely about the population value than does, say, the median.

The *standard error of the mean* (i.e., the standard deviation of all possible sample means) measures the precision of the sample estimate. It is related to the population standard deviation and the sample size as follows: $\sigma_{\bar{x}} = \sigma/\sqrt{n}$. However, since σ is usually unknown, the standard error of the mean can be estimated from the standard deviation of a single large sample by the formula $s_{\bar{x}} = s/\sqrt{n}$. This expression should be multiplied by $\sqrt{1 - n/N}$, the "finite multiplier," if the sample size n is more than about 5 per cent of the population size N.

Since sample means are normally distributed, the *probability* is 68 per cent that a single sample mean will fall within the interval $\mu \pm \sigma_{\bar{x}}$. The probability for any value of $x/\sigma_{\bar{x}}$ can be found in Appendix E.

We can estimate that the population mean falls within a certain *confidence interval*, based on the sample mean and standard deviation, with a predetermined probability—say 95 or 99 per cent—of being correct. Thus $\bar{X} \pm 1.96\,\sigma_{\bar{x}}$ is the 95 per cent confidence interval for the mean —that is, if we state that the population mean falls within this zone, we will have a 95 per cent chance of being correct. We can increase the confidence coefficient—say to 99 per cent—but only at the cost of making the estimate less precise by widening the confidence interval. The choice depends on the problem. In any case, the confidence interval and coefficient should be stated in reporting the results of sample surveys.

The size of a sample can be determined by solving the equation $\sigma_{\bar{x}} = \sigma/\sqrt{n}$ for n, where $\sigma_{\bar{x}}$ measures the required precision, and σ is estimated from a trial sample. Since precision increases with $\sqrt{n}$ and the cost of sampling increases with n, the precision and cost should be contrasted for several sizes of samples, in order to select the optimum sample size.

PROBLEMS

1. Explain the following concepts:
    a) Point estimate of the mean.
    b) Sampling distribution of the mean.
    c) Central limit theorem.
    d) Standard error of the mean.
    e) Confidence interval for the mean.

2. a) A machine, when in adjustment, produces parts that are normally distributed and have a mean diameter of .300 inches with a standard deviation of .040 inches. If only parts between .250 and .350 inches are acceptable, what proportion of the parts will be *unacceptable* when the machine is in adjustment?
    b) If the machine were to go out of adjustment and produce parts that had a mean diameter of .270 inches with the same standard deviation of .040 inches, what proportion of the parts would be *acceptable?*

3. a) If the machine described in Problem 2(a) is in adjustment, what is the probability that the *mean* value of a random sample of four parts will fall between .290 and .304 inches?
    b) What would happen to the standard error of the mean if we increased the sample size from 4 to 16?

4. A random sample of 144 building bricks has a mean weight of 7.1 pounds and standard deviation of .30 pounds. Is it likely that this sample comes from a brickyard that produces bricks with a mean weight of 7 pounds?

5. "A sample of 40 from a population of 40,000 will give nearly as precise an estimate of the population mean as a sample of 40 from a population of 4,000, provided the standard deviations of the populations are the same." Is this statement reasonable? Give figures to support your answer.

6. A random sample of 64 is drawn from the records of daily output of a large group of employees in order to estimate the population mean. The sample

shows a mean of 136 units and a standard deviation of 24 units. Calculate a 98 per cent confidence interval for the mean output of all employees.

7. A random sample of 400 accounts receivable is selected from the 2,000 accounts due a firm. The sample mean is found to be $165.50, with standard deviation of $26.00. Set up a 95 per cent confidence interval as an estimate of the population mean. Interpret the meaning of this interval.

8. A survey is planned to determine the average annual family expenditures for medical expenses of employees in a given company within $50, at the 90 per cent confidence level. A pilot study provides an estimate of $334 as the standard deviation of medical expenditures. How large a random sample is needed to yield an estimate with the necessary precision?

9. The average grade on an examination taken by a large number of students is 80. The standard deviation of the grades is 6. The instructor wishes to award A's to 10 per cent of the class. Assuming grades are approximately normally distributed, above what numerical grade would he give an A?

10. The haddock catch in Seaport A over the past 10 years has averaged 100 million pounds annually, with a standard deviation of 5 million pounds. For Seaport B over the same period, the mean has been 10 million pounds, with a standard deviation of 2 million pounds. If in one year the Seaport A catch is 108 million pounds, how large must the Seaport B catch be that year to be just as exceptional? (Assume normal distributions.)

11. The controller of a department store takes a sample of 64 monthly statements to be mailed to credit card holders, and finds that the average amount owed is $28, with standard deviation of $12. How many accounts should he sample, in total, if he wishes to estimate the mean amount owed within a dollar, with only 1 chance in 20 of being outside that range?

SELECTED READINGS

(See Chapter 14.)

13. TESTS OF HYPOTHESES

WE CAN make a statistical inference either by estimating that the population mean (or other parameter) lies within a certain *confidence interval* or by *testing a hypothesis*. The sampling error $\sigma_{\bar{x}}$ is used in either case. Confidence intervals were considered in Chapter 12. In testing a hypothesis we first set up a hypothesis concerning the true population value of the mean μ, or some other parameter. Then we decide on the basis of a random sample whether to accept or reject this hypothesis. If the sample value is close to the hypothetical value, we accept the hypothesis; otherwise we reject it.

An Example

Consider a specific example: In the manufacture of safety razor blades the width is obviously important. Some variation in dimension must be expected due to a large number of small causes affecting the production process. But even so, the average width should meet a certain specification. Suppose that the production process for a particular brand of razor blade has been geared to produce a mean width of .700 inches. Production has been under way for some time since the cutting and honing machines were last set, and the production manager wishes to know whether the mean width turned out is still .700 inches, as intended.

This may be treated as a problem in statistical inference. It would be possible, of course, actually to measure all of the hundreds of thousands of blades turned out and to ascertain the mean width directly. But this would be expensive and very time consuming. A better alternative would be to reason in terms of a sample. The statistical population of blade widths covers *all* the blades coming from the production line in the future under given technical controls. Since the production process was initially set up to give a mean width of .700 inches, the statistical hypothesis is posed that the true mean of this population is .700 inches. But the process could have gotten a little out of line, and management wishes to know whether .700 inches is still the mean width of all blades. We can take a mere sample, and on the basis of the evidence which it offers evaluate the truth or falsity of the hypothesis that the mean width of all such blades is .700 inches.

Rejecting the Hypothesis. Suppose we draw a simple random sample of 100 blades from the production line. We measure each of these carefully and find the mean width in the sample to be .703 inches. The standard deviation in the sample turns out to be .010 inches.

We then have the following evidence from the sample:

$$n = 100$$
$$\bar{X} = .703 \text{ inches}$$
$$s = .010 \text{ inches}$$

and we wish to test the hypothesis that the population mean is .700 inches (i.e., the hypothetical mean $\mu_h = .700$ inches). The hypothesis in effect states that this sample mean of .703 inches was drawn from a *sampling distribution* of all possible sample means whose over-all mean is .700 inches.

Now the important question arises: If the true mean of the population *really* were .700 inches, how likely is it that we would draw a random sample of 100 blades and find their mean width to be as far away as .703 inches or farther? In other words, what is the probability that a value could differ by .003 inches or more from the population mean *by chance alone?* If this is a high probability, we can accept the hypothesis that the true mean is .700 inches. If the probability is low, however, the truth of the hypothesis becomes questionable.

To get at this question, compute the standard error of the mean from the sample:

$$s_{\bar{X}} = \frac{s}{\sqrt{n}} = \frac{.010}{\sqrt{100}} = .001 \text{ inches}$$

Since the difference between the hypothetical mean of .700 inches and the actual sample mean of .703 inches is .003 inches, and the standard error of the mean is .001 inches, the difference is equal to three standard errors of the mean (i.e., $.003/.001 = 3$), as shown in Chart 13–1.

Now if .700 inches really were the population mean, we know from Appendix E that 99.7 per cent of all possible sample means, for random samples of 100, would fall within three standard errors around .700 inches. (See wide bracket in Chart 13-1.) Hence the probability is only .3 per cent that we would get a sample mean falling as far away as ours does.

Chart 13-1

SAMPLING DISTRIBUTION OF MEANS OF
RAZOR-WIDTH SAMPLES OF SIZE 100
(Hypothetical Mean = .700 Inches)

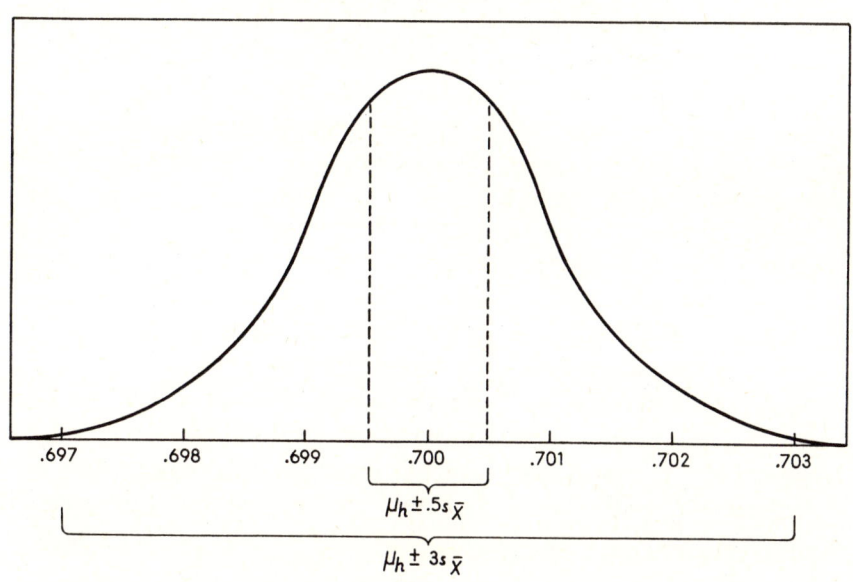

[Chart showing normal distribution curve with x-axis from .697 to .703, with brackets indicating $\mu_h \pm .5 s_{\bar{x}}$ and $\mu_h \pm 3 s_{\bar{x}}$]

We have two choices:
1. We may continue to accept the hypothesis (i.e., leave the production process alone), and attribute the deviation of the sample mean to chance.
2. We may reject the hypothesis as being inconsistent with the evidence found in the sample (hence, correct the production process).

Either of two things is true: the hypothesis is correct, and an exceedingly unlikely event has occurred by chance alone (one which would be expected to happen only 3 out of 1,000 times); or the hypothesis is wrong. We have to make a decision between the two.

In this case we would probably make choice 2, and conclude that the mean width of blades from that production line was not really

.700 inches. We would reject the hypothesis as being inconsistent with the evidence found in the sample. We would then be wrong only when the hypothesis was actually true and by chance alone a sample mean fell as far away as three standard errors. But on the average this would occur only 3 in 1,000 times.

Accepting the Hypothesis. Suppose that we adopt the conclusion, strongly indicated above, and shut down the production process to look for the trouble. The trouble is corrected, and the machines are again set to yield an average blade width of .700 inches.

Later, after production has gone on for some time, the query again arises: Is it reasonable to believe that the true mean width of blades produced remains .700 inches? Since the process was readjusted to yield that figure, the hypothesis seems reasonable. We could then test it by taking another random sample of 100 blades. This time the standard deviation is still .010 inches, so the standard error of the mean is still .001 inches; but the mean is only .7005 inches.

In order to test the hypothesis that the true mean of the population is .700 inches, we again go through the same line of reasoning. If the true population mean really were .700 inches, how likely is it that we should draw a random sample of 100 blades and find their sample mean to be as far away as .7005 inches?

Since the difference between the hypothetical mean and the observed sample mean is .0005 inches, and the standard error of the mean is .001 inches, the difference is equal to .5 standard errors. By consulting Appendix E, we find that the area within this interval around the mean of a normal curve is $.19 \times 2 = 38$ per cent, so that $100 - 38 = 62$ per cent of the total area falls *outside* this interval. (See dashed lines in Chart 13-1.) If .700 inches were the true mean, therefore, we should nevertheless expect to find that about 62 per cent of all such possible sample means would, *by chance alone,* fall as far away as $.5s_{\bar{x}}$ or farther. Therefore the *probability* is 62 per cent that our particular sample mean could fall this far away.

Remembering that we had substantial reason to accept the hypothesis in the first place—the process having been adjusted to yield a population mean of .700 inches—we should continue to hold to the hypothesis and attribute to mere chance the appearance of a .7005 inches mean in a single random sample of 100 blades.

The Choice between Accepting and Rejecting the Hypothesis. A legal analogy may help in understanding the reasoning involved. In a sense, the hypothesis is on trial and is considered innocent until proved guilty. The evidence is found in the random sample. Before the hypothesis is condemned, the evidence must prove it guilty—not with absolute certainty, but beyond reasonable doubt. The particular form which the evidence takes is the probability that a value as different as the sample mean could have been drawn if the hypothesis were true. If this probability is high, we can accept the hypothesis. On the other hand, if this probability is low, the hypothesis is doubtful. The lower the probability, the progressively greater is the doubt that the hypothesis could be correct. Finally, if the probability is so low that it appears unacceptable to believe that a value as different as the sample mean could have arisen solely by chance, the hypothesis is rejected. It is judged guilty beyond reasonable doubt.

In the second example just considered, the probability was quite high (62 per cent) that a discrepancy of .0005 inches could be attributed to mere chance. Therefore, we accepted the hypothesis, particularly since we had pretty good reason to believe in it before the sample was drawn. We could easily view the hypothetical mean of .700 inches as compatible with the findings of the sample *and* the operations of chance. But in the first example given ($\overline{X} = .703$ inches) the probability was so low (.3 per cent) that such a large difference could arise by chance, that the hypothesis ($\mu_h = .700$ inches) was rejected as being untrue.

TYPE I AND TYPE II ERRORS

Understandably, the question can be raised: what critical value should we select for the probability of getting the observed difference ($\overline{X} - \mu_h$) by chance, above which we should accept the hypothesis and below which we should reject it? This value is called the *critical probability*. The answer to this question is not simple, but to explore it will throw further light on the nature and logic of statistical inference.

Only four possible things can happen when we test a hypothesis. We may be wrong because we:

1. Reject a true hypothesis (a "Type I" error) or
2. Accept a false hypothesis (a "Type II" error).

Or, we may be right because we:

3. Accept a true hypothesis, or
4. Reject a false hypothesis.

The types of errors noted as possibilities 1 and 2, respectively, are known either as Type I and Type II errors, or as errors of the first kind and errors of the second kind.

Type I Errors

In a long run of cases in which the hypothesis is in fact *true* (although we do not know it is true, else there would be no need to test it), we will necessarily either be wrong as in 1 or right as in 3. That is to say, if we make an error it will have to be Type I. Suppose we should adopt 5 per cent as the critical probability, accepting the hypothesis when the probability of getting the observed difference by chance exceeds 5 per cent and rejecting the hypothesis when this probability proves to be less than 5 per cent. This amounts to the decision to accept the hypothesis when the discrepancy of the sample mean is less than 1.96 standard errors, and to reject the hypothesis when the discrepancy is more than 1.96 standard errors. Using this value as the critical probability, we would expect to make a Type I error 5 per cent of the time. This is because even when the hypothesis is true, 5 per cent of all possible sample means still lie farther away than 1.96 standard errors. And whenever by chance we got one of these, and the hypothesis was true, we would make the mistake of rejecting a true hypothesis.

Or, we might choose 1 per cent as the critical probability, which would correspond to a discrepancy between hypothesis and the sample mean equal to 2.58 standard errors. When the hypothesis is in fact true, only 1 per cent of all possible sample means would lie farther away than 2.58 standard errors. We would make a Type I error only when by chance alone we happened to draw one of these. Which is to say, we would now make an error of the first kind only 1 per cent of the time.

Clearly, then, the proportion of cases in which we would make an error of the first kind, that of rejecting a true hypothesis, can be made as small as we wish simply by reducing the value for the critical probability. In fact *the percentage of cases in which we would expect to make an error of the first kind is precisely equal to the critical probability adopted.*

Sometimes references will be made by statisticians to "the 5 per cent level of risk," or to "the 1 per cent level of risk," or to some other number associated with a risk level. When they do so, in this connection, they are referring to the risk they are willing to accept of committing a Type I error.

Type II Errors

So far we have concerned ourselves only with the first kind of error. But there is also the second kind—the possible error of accepting a false hypothesis. The lower the value we set for the critical probability, in general the fewer the hypotheses we will reject. But the chances are then increased of accepting more hypotheses which are false. We can buy safety in one direction only at the expense of danger in the other.

Unfortunately, it is impossible to predict in general the percentage of times we should expect to commit an error of the second kind on the basis of any particular value adopted for the critical probability. The reason for this is that the chance of accepting a false hypothesis depends also upon *how* false the particular hypothesis happens to be. Remember that sample means tend to cluster around the true means of the populations from which they are drawn. If the hypothetical mean is far away from the true mean, it is unlikely that a sample mean will be drawn which appears consistent with the hypothesis. If the hypothetical mean is false but not far from the mark, an error of the second kind is much more likely to be made.

In a long run of instances in which hypotheses are actually false some will be farther from the true mean than others. Therefore, it is impossible to predict in general the probability of accepting false hypotheses. We can appreciate, however, that the chances of accepting false hypotheses are increased as fewer hypotheses are rejected due to the use of a lower value for the critical probability.

Balancing Type I against Type II Errors

In using statistical tests of hypotheses for decision making, then, we face two dangers: that of rejecting a true hypothesis and that of accepting a false hypothesis. The danger of committing a Type I error can be made as low as we please by reducing the value chosen for the critical probability; but this can be done only at the expense of increasing the danger of committing a Type II error. In practice, the final choice of the value for the critical probability represents some compromise between these two risks. It must be arrived at by balancing the consequences of a Type I error against the possible consequences of a Type II error. The more serious an error of the first kind, relative to an error of the second kind, the lower the critical probability should be placed, and conversely.

In any actual case the specific meaning of the two kinds of error is usually apparent. In the razor-blade example a Type I error would mean falsely condemning the accuracy of a production process which was in fact operating as intended. A Type II error would mean continued production of a product which in fact was not meeting specifications. The economic penalty of the Type I error might be an expensive shutdown to look for a nonexistent trouble. The economic consequences of the Type II error might be the loss of consumer goodwill as the customers later found the product unsatisfactory. (They might get razor burn with undue frequency, or find that the average blade did not fit into the razor.) With these potential economic consequences in mind, it would be up to management to set the value for the critical probability where, in its judgment, the best compromise is reached between risks of incurring the two types of errors.

This is another example of a general truth. In recent years tremendous advances have been made in statistical analysis, and in its application to business decisions. But statistics cannot make a business decision for us. They can only give us a rational basis on which to make the decision ourselves. In the present case statistical methods can inform us how to reduce the dangers of rejecting a true hypothesis—that is, by lowering the critical probability chosen—and they warn us that the chances of accepting a false hypothesis are thereby increased. Where we set the critical probability depends ultimately upon our judgment as to the relative degrees of risk we wish to assume of making these respective kinds of error in any actual case.

What Critical Probability to Use. The 5 per cent and 1 per cent values for the critical probability are in common use—the choice depending on the risk to be assumed of rejecting a true hypothesis. These correspond to observed discrepancies between hypothesis and sample mean equal to 1.96 $s_{\bar{x}}$ and 2.58 $s_{\bar{x}}$, respectively. Nevertheless, the analyst should not choose one of these conventional values slavishly. He should make his own judgment, in each case, along the lines discussed above. Testing the average strength of parachute cords is far different from testing the average strength of binder twine.

Effect of Sample Size on Probability of Errors

So far the discussion of hypothesis testing has been in terms of some particular size of sample. So long as a given sample size is assumed, the risk of a Type I error can only be reduced at the expense of increasing the risk of a Type II error. There is, however, a way of reducing the chance of accepting a false hypothesis without at the same time increasing the chance of rejecting a true hypothesis. By taking a larger sample the *combined* chance of committing either error can be reduced.

As the size of the sample drawn is increased, $\bar{X}$ will tend to fall closer to the actual value for μ, since $s_{\bar{x}}$ is decreased. With any particular value for the critical probability, Type I errors will be made with the same relative frequency whatever the sample size. But as $\overline{X}$ is pulled in closer to μ (as is the tendency in taking a larger sample) $\overline{X}$ will in fewer instances appear consistent with a value other than μ, i.e., with a false hypothesis regarding μ.

Thus, by taking a larger sample, the chance of a Type II error (accepting a false hypothesis) is reduced, while the chance of rejecting a true hypothesis can be held constant by using a constant value for the critical probability. The combined chance of error will be smaller if we can reduce one component while we hold the other chance component constant. Just as we might expect, fewer over-all mistakes of statistical inference will be made the larger the size of sample used.

OPERATING CHARACTERISTIC CURVES

The exact probability of making a Type II error depends upon how far the true mean μ of the population is away from μ_h, the hypothetical mean. This can best be illustrated by an *operating characteristic curve* or *OC* curve, as shown in Chart 13–2.

Chart 13–2A

PROBABILITY OF ACCEPTING THE NULL HYPOTHESIS
FOR ALL POSSIBLE ALTERNATIVE MEANS
(Operating Characteristic Curves)

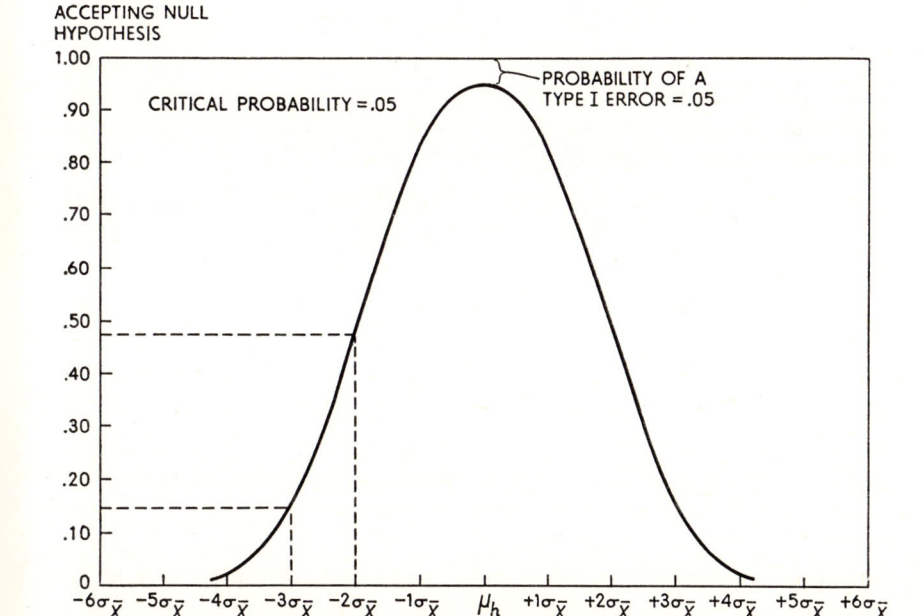

Chart 13-2B

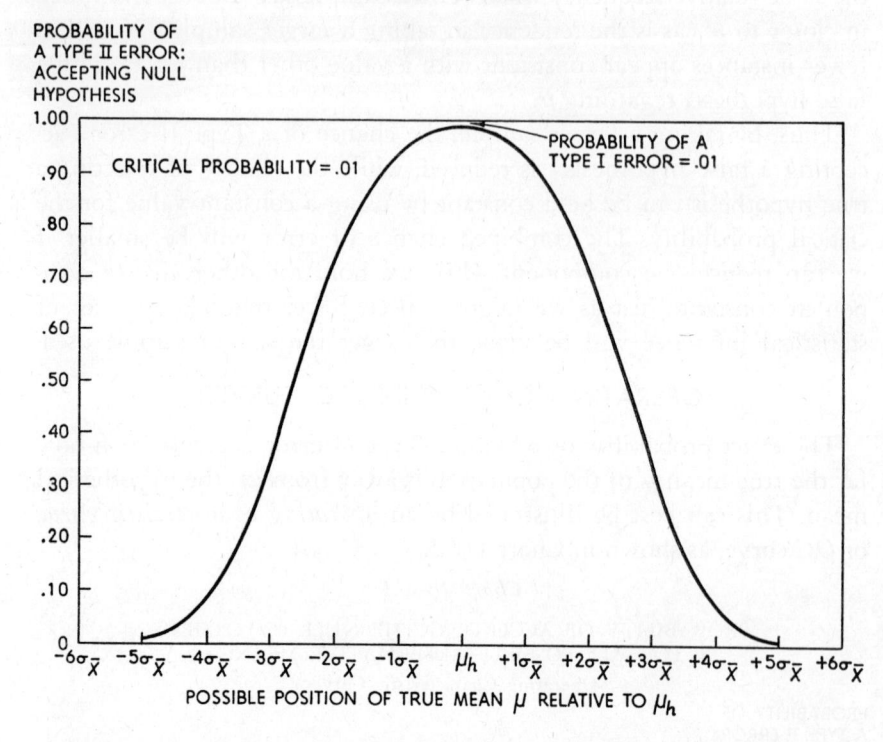

PROBABILITY OF
A TYPE II ERROR:
ACCEPTING NULL
HYPOTHESIS

CRITICAL PROBABILITY = .01

PROBABILITY OF A TYPE I ERROR = .01

POSSIBLE POSITION OF TRUE MEAN μ RELATIVE TO μ_h

The vertical scale of Chart 13-2 shows the probability of committing a Type II error (i.e., accepting the null hypothesis when it is false). The horizontal scale shows all possible values for the true mean of the population, relative to the hypothetical mean μ_h. Thus if the true mean were one standard error less than μ_h, it would be at the point $-1\sigma_{\bar{x}}$ on the horizontal axis. Panel A represents the use of a critical probability of .05, and panel B a critical probability of .01. In either case, the probability of a Type II error can be found for any possible value of the true mean. Thus in Chart 13-2A, if the true mean were three standard errors below the hypothetical mean ($-3\sigma_{\bar{x}}$), the probability of a Type II error would be .15, as shown by a dashed line. Similarly if the true mean were two standard errors below the hypothetical mean ($-2\sigma_{\bar{x}}$), the probability of a Type II error would be .48.

When the true mean is exactly at the hypothetical mean ($\mu = \mu_h$), a Type II error is impossible. Then the distance from the top of the curve to 1.0 represents the probability of a Type I error. Thus, since .95 is the probability of accepting the hypothesis when $\mu = \mu_h$, .05 is the probability of rejecting it (when it is true), that is, of committing a Type I error.

There are two additional points to be noted:
1. The more stringent the critical probability, the higher will be the probability of a Type II error. This can be seen by comparing the two curves in Chart 13–2. The probabilities on Chart 13–2B (with the more stringent critical probability of .01) are higher at every point than on Chart 13–2A.
2. Increasing the sample size affects the *OC* curve in the following manner. When the sample size is increased the standard error becomes smaller. Thus each possible value of the true mean moves a larger number of standard errors away from μ_h, and the further away from μ_h, the smaller is the Type II error. Thus increasing the sample size has the effect of decreasing the probability of a Type II error at every point.

The probability of a Type II error thus depends on the critical probability, the size of sample, and how far the hypothesis is from the truth. If it is far, a Type II error is unlikely; but if $\mu - \mu_h$ is small, it is more difficult to discriminate, and the probability of a Type II error becomes very large.[1]

TWO-TAILED VERSUS ONE-TAILED TESTS

In the form of testing hypotheses so far discussed the probability has been calculated of getting a discrepancy as large as or larger than that observed by adding together the two "tails" of the sampling distribution beyond the number of standard errors corresponding to $(\overline{X} - \mu_h)$. This is referred to as "testing in both directions" or as a "two-tailed test."

Two-Tailed Tests

In the first example the probability of .3 per cent was attached to the likelihood of getting a discrepancy as large as or larger than that observed ($3 s_{\overline{x}}$), regardless of the sign of the discrepancy, i.e., whether it might have arisen by $\overline{X} \geq .703$ inches or $\overline{X} \leq .697$ inches. In the second example the probability of 62 per cent was calculated for the

---

[1] "An analogy may be drawn with the use of a lie-detector machine. Such a test depends, in part, upon the extent to which the suspect's pulse rate increases above his normal rate, e.g., 72, when answering pertinent questions. There are many reasons why any individual's pulse rate may rise above his norm. Therefore, some rate *above* this norm (72) must be regarded as being significantly different. What happens if this rate is set too close to 72? Then many honest people may be unjustly accused of lying, that is, many Type I errors are made. What happens if we set the rate well above 72? Then some liars may go undetected and a Type II error is made. Our courts willingly risk making the latter error." [C. Frank Smith and D. A. Leabo, *Basic Statistics for Business Economics* (Homewood, Ill.: Richard D. Irwin, Inc., 1960), p. 155 n.]

chance of getting a difference equal to or exceeding that observed ($.5s_{\bar{X}}$), whether that difference be above or below .700 inches.

There are three related reasons for testing in both directions when testing a single numerical value (such as .700 inches) as being the true mean of the population:

1. The hypothesis is formed before the sample is drawn, hence we don't know in advance whether the observed discrepancy between μ_h and $\bar{X}$ will have a positive or a negative sign.
2. An observed discrepancy of any particular size would be equally harmful to the hypothesis whether it had a positive or a negative sign.
3. A hypothesis must not be rephrased to incorporate any of the information found in the very same sample which is used to test it.

The last point requires a bit of expansion. The hypothesis that the mean width of blade is .700 inches is a single-valued hypothesis; it says not greater than that, not less than that. If, on finding $\bar{X}$ equal to .703 inches, we had calculated only the probability of getting by chance a sample mean as large as or larger than .703 inches, we would have subtly shifted our initial hypothesis to the hypothesis that the population mean is *not greater than* .700 inches. Implicitly, we would have wound up testing a different hypothesis than the one intended, and simply because of the sign of the discrepancy which was found after the sample had been drawn.

In the razor-blade case it seemed quite appropriate to test the single-valued hypothesis of .700 inches, i.e., to test in both directions, since presumably we would be just as concerned about blades being too wide as being too narrow.

One-Tailed Tests

In other cases, however, it might be appropriate to test in one direction, only; that is, to test what can be called a multi-valued hypothesis.

If we were concerned with the strength of parachute cords, we would not be worried about their being too strong; we would worry only about their being too weak. If for safety's sake they were designed, let us say, to have a mean breaking point of 1,000 pounds we would be interested in the hypothesis that the true population mean was *not less than* 1,000 pounds. Correspondingly, we would test the multi-valued hypothesis that the true mean had a value of 1,000 pounds or some larger value.

Should a sample mean greater than 1,000 pounds be found in a random sample drawn, it would immediately be accepted as consistent with the hypothesis. Only if $\overline{X}$ should be less than 1,000 pounds would a question arise concerning the validity of the hypothesis. It would then be appropriate to ask the question: if the mean of the population truly were 1,000 pounds or more, what is the probability of getting by chance a sample mean which falls below 1,000 pounds by as much as the one observed? That is to say, the particular sign of the observed difference now would have a bearing on the truth or falsity of the hypothesis as stated. It is appropriate in this case to test in but one

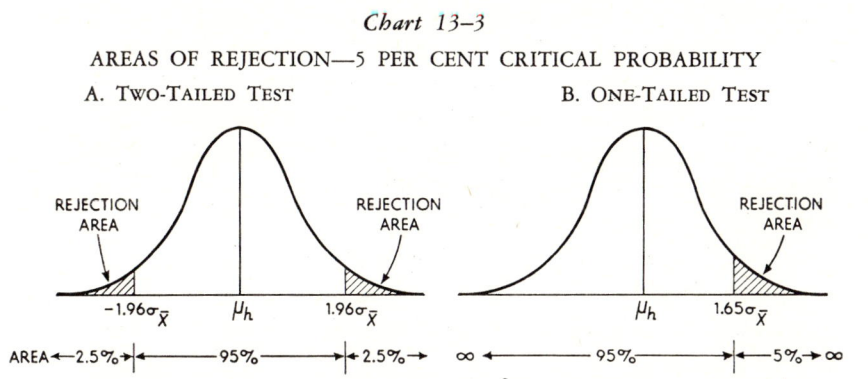

Chart 13–3

AREAS OF REJECTION—5 PER CENT CRITICAL PROBABILITY

A. TWO-TAILED TEST   B. ONE-TAILED TEST

direction, i.e., in terms of the probability of getting by chance a sample mean which lies below 1,000 pounds by an amount equal to or greater than that observed.

The judgment where to set the critical probability rests on the same grounds as before: a balancing of the practical consequence of an error of the first kind against the consequence of committing an error of the second kind. Again, the chance of a Type I error is identical with the value for the critical probability adopted. But the smaller this is made, the greater is the likelihood of committing a Type II error.

One important change is made, however, when applying a one-tailed test instead of a two-tailed test, namely, the multiple of the standard error which corresponds to any given critical probability. In a two-tailed test $1.96\sigma_{\overline{x}}$ corresponds to a 5 per cent critical probability, whereas $1.65\sigma_{\overline{x}}$ is the multiple of the standard error associated with 5 per cent in a one-tailed test. When testing in both directions, $2.58\sigma_{\overline{x}}$ goes with 1 per cent as the critical probability. But for testing in a single direction, the similar combination is 2.33 $\sigma_{\overline{x}}$ and 1 per cent. These can be read from Appendix E for various areas under the normal curve.

For a 5 per cent critical probability under a two-tailed test and one-tailed test, respectively, see Chart 13–3.

In any actual case of hypothesis testing two important judgments have to be made:

1. Which is really appropriate to the case, a two-tailed test or a one-tailed test?
2. What is the proper value to use for the critical probability?

TESTS OF DIFFERENCES BETWEEN ARITHMETIC MEANS

We now consider another important aspect of statistical inference, namely, tests of the significance of differences between sample means. This phase is concerned with the following problem: given an observed difference between the means of two random samples, each drawn from a different population, is this difference to be taken as signifying a real difference between the true means of the populations involved?

To handle this problem it is necessary to introduce the concept of a new sampling distribution, the sampling distribution of *differences* between means. We can think of this distribution as being formed in the following manner.

On the basis of random sampling from two separate populations the sampling distributions of the arithmetic means, $\overline{X}_1$ and $\overline{X}_2$, would be formed. Each of these sampling distributions is of the same type we have been discussing.

Now imagine that from each of these sampling distributions a sample mean is drawn at random, and that the difference between this pair of sample means is noted. Then a second pair of sample means is selected at random, each from its own sampling distribution. The difference between this second pair almost certainly would be different from that found between the first pair, due to chance alone. We can imagine the process carried on indefinitely. Then we would have an indefinitely large number of values representing the differences between all possible pairs of sample means which could be drawn at random from their respective sampling distributions. These differences would form a theoretical distribution known as the sampling distribution of the difference between two means.

We know the following things about this new distribution.

1. The sampling distribution of differences tends to be normal; which is to say that differences between pairs of sample means will be normally distributed, provided the sample size is large, or the original population is nearly normal.
2. The mean of the distribution of differences will be the true difference between the population means ($\mu_1 - \mu_2$). This follows

from the proposition that the mean of the differences between any two series of values is equal to the difference between their respective means.

3. The standard deviation of the distribution of differences may be estimated by the formula

$$s_{\bar{X}_1 - \bar{X}_2} = \sqrt{s_{\bar{X}_1}^2 + s_{\bar{X}_2}^2}$$

In this formula $s_{\bar{X}_1}$ is the standard error of the mean for the sampling distribution of $\bar{X}_1$ and $s_{\bar{X}_2}$ is the similar measure for the sampling distribution of $\bar{X}_2$. The value $s_{\bar{X}_1 - \bar{X}_2}$ is known as the *standard error of the difference between two means*.[2]

With this important new sampling distribution in mind, we can carry forward our discussion of the present phase of statistical inference in terms of specific examples.

Suppose two brands of cigarettes are tested for burning time with the purpose of deciding whether one brand is longer burning than the other. One hundred cigarettes of brand No. 1 are burned under test conditions, and the length of burning time noted; 144 cigarettes of brand No. 2 are similarly tested for length of burning time. (A difference in sample size is used in this example merely to emphasize that the two samples need not be equal in size for this method to be applicable.) The following means and standard deviations result (the subscripts referring to the brand number):

Cigarette No. 1
$n_1 = 100$
$\bar{X}_1 = 9.36$ min.
$s_1 = .83$ min.

Cigarette No. 2
$n_2 = 144$
$\bar{X}_2 = 9.23$ min.
$s_2 = 1.2$ min.

This test gives cigarette No. 1 an advantage of $\bar{X}_1 - \bar{X}_2 = .13$ minutes in average burning time. Nevertheless, because we are quite aware of chance variations that may occur in random sampling, we do not immediately jump to the conclusion that brand No. 1 is longer burning than brand No. 2. We are led to wonder if the difference in mean burning time observed in the samples arose by chance, or whether there is in fact a difference in average burning time between

---

[2] In this discussion s represents the standard error estimated from a sample; if the true population value were known, the symbol σ would be used, with appropriate subscript.

The variance (s^2) of the difference is the sum of the variances of the individual means. As a graphic check, the standard error of each mean can be laid off as a side of a right triangle; then the standard error of the difference can be read off as the hypotenuse.

all cigarettes of brand No. 1 and all cigarettes of brand No. 2. That is to say, we wish to know if the observed difference between the sample means indicates a real difference between the means of the two populations.

The Null Hypothesis

Our manner of solving this problem is to set up and test the so-called "null hypothesis." This means that we pose the hypothesis that there is *no* difference in average burning time between brand No. 1 and brand No. 2, and then proceed to test that hypothesis against the evidence found in the samples.

The null hypothesis states that the mean of the sampling distribution of differences is equal to zero. This is because the mean of the sampling distribution of differences is known to be $(\mu_1 - \mu_2)$, and the hypothesis is that there is no difference between these population means.

The observed difference of .13 minutes between the two random sample means is, in effect, one observation drawn at random from the sampling distribution of all possible differences between pairs of random sample means. We can therefore ask the question: if the mean of the sampling distribution of differences really were zero, what is the probability that we would get a difference between two sample means at least as large as .13?

Since the sampling distribution from which .13 came tends to be normal, we can answer this question as soon as we know the value for the standard error of the difference between means. This is computed as follows:

$$s_{\bar{x}_1} = \frac{.83}{\sqrt{100}} = .083 \qquad s_{\bar{x}_2} = \frac{1.2}{\sqrt{144}} = .10$$

$$s_{\bar{x}_1 - \bar{x}_2} = \sqrt{s_{\bar{x}_1}^2 + s_{\bar{x}_2}^2}$$

$$= \sqrt{(.083)^2 + (.10)^2}$$

$$= \sqrt{.0169}$$

$$s_{\bar{x}_1 - \bar{x}_2} = .13$$

Accepting the Null Hypothesis. Thus it turns out that the observed difference between the sample means is equal to one standard error of the difference. If the true difference between the population means really were zero, the probability is nevertheless $100 - 68 = 32$ per cent that a difference at least as large as .13 minutes would appear by chance. It would appear that there is no compelling evidence to be found in the samples that a real difference exists in average burning time between the two brands. In this case it is said that the difference between the sample means is too small to be significant—i.e., too small to signify an indisputable difference between the population means.

Rejecting the Null Hypothesis. Let us take the same case again, but assume $\overline{X}_2$ had come out 9.00 instead of 9.23 minutes. Now the observed difference between the sample means is $9.36 - 9.00 = .36$ minutes. This in turn is equal to 2.77 standard errors of such differences (i.e., $.36/.13 = 2.77$). Is the null hypothesis still tenable?

If there really were no difference between μ_1 and μ_2 the probability of getting an observed difference equal to or greater than 2.77 standard errors in either direction would be only .56 per cent. It appears highly unlikely, therefore, that the difference between the means of the samples could have appeared solely by chance in this case. The null hypothesis may very well be rejected. In this case the difference observed between the sample means is taken as significant of a difference between the means of the populations from which the samples were drawn. There is said to be a significant difference between the means of the samples.

The Choice between Acceptance and Rejection. What is to be taken as a significant difference and what is to be taken as a nonsignificant difference depends, of course, upon the critical probability chosen. The question is precisely the same as that treated earlier under tests of hypotheses. We should expect this to be true, for a test of the difference between means is also a test of a hypothesis, namely, the hypothesis that the mean of the sampling distribution of differences is equal to zero. Where the critical probability should be set in any particular case depends upon the relative consequences of rejecting a true hypothesis and of accepting a false hypothesis. We must strike an appropriate balance of risks of Type I and Type II errors as before.

A Type I error (rejecting a true null hypothesis) implies concluding that a difference is real when really it isn't. A Type II error (accepting a false null hypothesis) implies concluding no difference exists when really one does. In the present example, an error of the first kind would amount to concluding there was a real difference in burning time between the two brands when in fact no such difference existed. An error of the second kind would amount to concluding that the brands did not differ with regard to burning time when in fact they did.

If we were smokers who liked the two brands equally well on all other counts, and wanted to adopt the brand which was longer burning, we could afford to employ a high value for the critical probability. This is because we would suffer no consequences from an error of the first kind, since if no real difference existed in burning time it would be immaterial which brand we chose. But an error of the second kind might allow us to choose the shorter burning cigarette in the mistaken belief that it was no different from the other brand in this regard.

If, on the other hand, we were on the staff of the Federal Trade Commission investigating the advertising claims of brand No. 1, we might well employ a much lower value for the critical probability. We would then count it very serious to allow false claims to be made in advertising, and such would be the case if we made an error of the first kind in our statistical reasoning. We might think it much less serious to make an error of the second kind, for that would simply deprive brand No. 1 of one legitimate selling point it might otherwise have used.

In connection with tests of the significance of differences between sample means, the related problem of estimating the actual difference between population means often arises. If it is concluded that a real difference exists between the population means, how is the magnitude of this difference to be estimated?

The procedure is, in principle, identical with that employed earlier in estimating the mean of a population on the basis of the mean of a random sample drawn from that population. The only difference is that the sampling distribution of differences (and its associated measures) is employed in forming the appropriate confidence intervals in the present case.

We wish to estimate $(\mu_1 - \mu_2)$, which is known to be the mean of the sampling distribution of differences. From this sampling distribution we have one observation $(\overline{X}_1 - \overline{X}_2)$, based upon random sampling. Then 68 per cent of such observations would be expected to lie within $s_{\overline{x}_1 - \overline{x}_2}$ of the mean difference; 95 per cent would be expected to lie within $1.96 s_{\overline{x}_1 - \overline{x}_2}$ of $(\mu_1 - \mu_2)$; etc. Consequently, we should have a 68 per cent degree of confidence that an interval specified as $(\overline{X}_1 - \overline{X}_2) \pm s_{\overline{x}_1 - \overline{x}_2}$ would include the value $(\mu_1 - \mu_2)$, and a 95 per cent degree of confidence that the interval

$$(\overline{X}_1 - \overline{X}_2) \pm 1.96 s_{\overline{x}_1 - \overline{x}_2}$$

would include the true difference between the population means.

In the last example above, the observed difference is .36 minutes; with a standard error of .13 minutes. We may estimate, therefore, that the true difference between the population means lies within the interval .36 minutes $\pm$ .25 minutes (i.e., 1.96 times the standard error) and hold a 95 per cent degree of confidence that our estimate is correct. The 95 per cent confidence limits are then .11 minutes and .61 minutes for the superiority of cigarette No. 1 over cigarette No. 2 as regards length of burning.

If the confidence interval based upon $\pm 3 s_{\bar{x}_1 - \bar{x}_2}$ is computed to give a degree of confidence of 99.7 per cent that the true difference is located within its boundaries, the confidence limits work out to be minus .03 minutes to .75 minutes for the difference between brands No. 1 and No. 2 in average burning time. This result—the appearance of the negative sign for the lower limit of the confidence interval—might puzzle the student, but it really need not. All it means is that for us to be 99.7 per cent confident that we have located the real difference in average burning time between the two brands we should have to grant that superiority *might* lie to a small extent with brand No. 2.

SMALL SAMPLES

The foregoing discussion has been based upon the assumption that the sampling distribution of the arithmetic mean follows the normal curve. This is a valid assumption for samples of a size greater than about thirty items. When the size of sample employed is smaller than this, the sampling distribution of the arithmetic mean departs from the normal distribution because of sampling errors in the standard deviation (assuming the true value of σ is not known).[3]

This symmetric but nonnormal distribution is called the t distribution. The ratio t is defined as the deviation of the sample mean from the population mean expressed in standard error units.[4] That is,

$$t = \frac{\bar{X} - \mu}{s_{\bar{x}}}$$

where $s_{\bar{x}}$, the standard error of the mean, is computed from s, the standard deviation of a sample, by the formula $s_{\bar{x}} = s/\sqrt{n}$.

The sampling distribution of t differs for each size of sample. There is one t distribution for samples of size 10, another for size 11, and so on. Hence, the values of t corresponding to the 5 and 1 per cent probability levels are not 1.96 and 2.58, as in the normal curve, but depend on the sample size, as shown in Table 13–1.

---

[3] When the true value of σ is known, the means of small samples follow a normal distribution, just as in the case of large samples.

[4] The population from which we sample is here assumed to be normally distributed; this analysis is not strictly valid for nonnormal populations.

Table 13-1

VALUE OF *t* AT 5 AND 1 PER CENT PROBABILITY LEVELS

Degrees of Freedom	.05	.01
10	2.228	3.169
20	2.086	2.845
30	2.042	2.750
∞	1.960	2.576

Table 13-1 is abstracted from the more detailed *t* table in Appendix F. In this table the first column lists the "degrees of freedom" rather than sample size; that is, $n-1$ instead of n in the examples used thus far.[5] Since this column goes up to 30, we can define a small sample, for the purpose of using this table, as one in which n is 31 or less. The *t* distribution looks more and more like the normal distribution as n increases in size, so the *t* values approach the corresponding values for the normal distribution. These are listed in the last row of the table. The probabilities in the heading of the table refer to the sum of the two-tailed areas under the curve that lie outside the points $\pm t$. The values of *t* are listed in the body of the table. For a single-tailed area, divide the probability by 2.

As an example, for a sample of size 8, enter the row $n-1=7$; then 5 per cent of the area under the curve falls in the two tails outside the interval $t = \pm 2.365$. That is, 2½ per cent of the area falls in each tail, and 95 per cent of the area falls within the interval $t = \pm 2.365$. A *t* value of 2.365 should therefore be used in setting up a 95 per cent confidence interval for the mean when the sample size is 8.

Confidence Intervals

As an example, a manufacturer wishes to estimate the average weight of a large shipment of 20-gauge uncoated steel sheets received from a supplier. The estimate is to be expressed as a 95 per cent confidence interval centered on a sample mean. He selects eight pieces at random, and finds that the sample mean is 148.4 pounds per hundred square feet, while the standard deviation is 2.07 pounds. The standard error of the mean is then

---

[5] Gauss showed that "the number of observations is to be decreased by the number of unknowns estimated from the data, to serve as divisor in estimating the standard error." Here we use $n-1$ because one degree of freedom is lost when the standard deviation is computed from a sample. When all deviations from the arithmetic mean but one are determined, the last one is also determined.

$$s_{\bar{x}} = \frac{s}{\sqrt{n}} = \frac{2.07}{\sqrt{8}} = .73 \text{ pounds}$$

To find the 95 per cent confidence interval, he finds $t = 2.365$ in the t table as described above. The confidence interval is then

$$\overline{X} \pm t \cdot s_{\bar{x}} = 148.4 \pm 2.365(.73) = 148.4 \pm 1.7 \text{ pounds}$$

He can then state that the average weight of the whole shipment lies between 146.7 and 150.1 pounds, with a 95 per cent chance of being correct.

Testing Hypotheses

Alternatively, the manufacturer in the foregoing problem might wish to test whether the mean weight of the sample of steel sheets (148.4 pounds) differs significantly from the specification of 150 pounds called for in his purchase order. So he computes the deviation of the sample mean from this hypothetical mean in units of the estimated standard error (.73 pounds) as follows:

$$t = \frac{\overline{X} - \mu_h}{s_{\bar{x}}}$$

$$= \frac{148.4 - 150}{.73}$$

$$= -2.19$$

Appendix F shows that for 7 degrees of freedom the 5 per cent point of t is ± 2.365, as noted above. Hence the mean weight of 148.4 pounds does not differ significantly from the specified mean weight of 150 pounds at the 5 per cent level of significance. If the absolute value of t had exceeded 2.365, the difference would have been considered significant at the 5 per cent level.

The t test can be applied similarly to determine whether the *difference* between the means of two small samples is significant. This procedure will not be illustrated here.

In order to make inferences about the means of small samples, then, proceed as with large samples, except for using the t value in Appendix F in place of the corresponding value of x/σ in Appendix E.

SUMMARY

We can make a statistical inference either by constructing a *confidence interval* (as described in Chapter 12) or by *testing a hypothesis*. In the latter case we set up a hypothesis regarding the value of the parameter—say the mean. If the sample mean is close to the hypothetical mean, we accept the hypothesis; otherwise we reject it.

In the case of the razor-blade machine that was set to produce blades of average width .700 inches, a sample of 100 blades was tested, with $\overline{X} = .703$ inches and $s = .010$ inches, so $s_{\overline{X}} = s/\sqrt{n} = .001$ inches. Since the sample mean was three standard errors away from the hypothetical mean, the probability was only .3 per cent of getting such a discrepancy by chance, so the hypothesis was rejected. In a second trial, however, with $\overline{X} = .7005$ inches, the hypothesis ($\mu_h = .700$ inches) was accepted since such a discrepancy could easily occur by chance alone. A reasonable hypothesis is usually accepted unless the probability is quite low (say, under 5 per cent or even 1 per cent) that the discrepancy of the sample value could be attributed to chance. The problem is where to set this *critical probability* below which we will reject the hypothesis.

We can make two types of errors in testing hypotheses:

    Type I: rejecting a true hypothesis, or

    Type II: accepting a false hypothesis.

We can easily control the chance of making a Type I error, since this equals the critical probability that is set in advance. Unfortunately, for a given size of sample, we can reduce the chance of making a Type I error only at the cost of increasing the risk of making a Type II error. The chance of making the latter error is unknown, since it depends on how far the hypothetical mean is away from the true mean. The choice of the critical probability then must be determined by balancing the consequences of the two types of error. If a Type I error would be serious relative to a Type II error, the critical probability should be set relatively low. In practice, critical probabilities are often set at the arbitrary values of 5 per cent or 1 per cent.

By taking a larger sample, the combined chance of making either error can be reduced. In particular, if the critical probability is held constant, the chance of a Type I error also remains constant, in a larger sample, but the chance of a Type II error is reduced.

An operating characteristic or *OC* curve shows the probability of making a Type II error (that is, accepting the null hypothesis when it is false) for a given critical probability, depending on how far the true mean is from the hypothetical mean. The farther these means are apart, the smaller is the probability of a Type II error.

In testing hypotheses, we may make either a two-tailed or a one-tailed test. The *two-tailed test* takes into account the areas under both tails of the normal curve (Chart 13–3). It is appropriate in most prac-

Ch. 13]	TESTS OF HYPOTHESES	269

tical situations because we are concerned with discrepancies *either* above or below the hypothetical mean. In case we are concerned only with discrepancies in one direction from the hypothetical mean, however, it is appropriate to use the *one-tailed test,* which takes into account only the area under one tail of the normal curve. The decision rule is then to reject the hypothesis if $(\overline{X} - \mu_h)/s_{\overline{X}}$ exceeds the following values:

Critical Probability Chosen	Two-Tailed Test	One-Tailed Test
5 per cent	1.96	1.65
1 per cent	2.58	2.33

We can also test whether the *difference* between two sample means signifies a real difference between the population means, or whether the observed difference is merely due to chance. To do this, we find the standard error of the difference (theoretically, the standard deviation of a distribution of differences between many pairs of sample means). This is computed from the standard errors of the individual means. Then we can test the *null hypothesis* (that there is *no* difference between the population means) by expressing the difference between the sample means as a ratio of their standard error. If this ratio is small, we accept the null hypothesis; otherwise we reject it, depending on the probability that the difference could be due to chance (from Appendix E), and balancing the consequences of Type I and II errors as before. We can also set up a *confidence interval* around the difference between the sample means, based on its standard error, as was done earlier.

The means of small samples follow a *t distribution,* which differs more and more from the normal distribution as the sample size becomes smaller. If $n \leq 31$, therefore, we should look up $t = (\overline{X} - \mu)/s$ in Appendix F to find the appropriate multiple of the standard error for use in setting up confidence limits or testing hypotheses.

PROBLEMS

1. Distinguish between:
    a) Confidence intervals and tests of hypotheses.
    b) Type I and Type II errors.
    c) How to find the probability of Type I and Type II errors from an operating characteristic curve.
    d) One-tailed and two-tailed tests.
    e) Testing significance of means for large samples and for small samples.

2. A grocery chain store adopts a policy of issuing trading stamps on all purchases, the cost of the stamps being offset by an increase in average prices. Prior sales had averaged $15.50 per customer over the past year, with a

standard deviation of $4.80. At the end of a trial period with the new stamps, a random check of 400 customers shows average sales of $16.30. Are the stamps worthwhile, by this criterion?

3. A machine, when in adjustment, produces parts that have a mean diameter of .300 inches with a standard deviation of .006 inches. A random sample of nine parts yields a mean diameter of .297 inches. Is the machine probably still in adjustment or not? Give reasons.

4. If we change the critical probability from 5 per cent to 0.1 per cent, what is the effect on:
   a) The probability of rejecting a true hypothesis?
   b) The probability of accepting a false hypothesis?

5. *a)* Suppose the null hypothesis is $\mu_h = 14.0$; $n = 25$, $\sigma = 2.0$ and the critical probability is .05. Using Chart 13-2, what would be the probability of a Type II error if the actual μ of the population were 15.0? If the actual μ were 14.5?
   b) What would be the probability of a Type II error if the sample size were increased to 36 and the actual μ were 15.0? If the actual μ were 14.5?
   c) What would be the probability of a Type II error for $n = 25$, if a .01 critical probability were to be used and the actual μ were 15.0? If the actual μ were 14.5?

6. The Union Delivery Service is planning to purchase a fleet of Cord trucks, providing the average miles per gallon is not significantly smaller than 19. Sixty-four of these trucks have been tested under controlled driving conditions with $\overline{X} = 18.65$ and $s = 2.0$. Management is willing to subject the truck manufacturer to a 10 per cent risk of failing to make the sale, even if his trucks have satisfactory gasoline consumption. Should the Union Delivery Service buy the trucks?

7. Two brands of tires were used in road tests to compare their average service lives (in thousands of miles). For 100 brand A tires the mean was 35.0 and the standard deviation was 8.0, while for 100 brand B tires the mean was 38.5 and the standard deviation was 6.0.
   a) Test the significance of the difference between the two means.
   b) Construct a 99 per cent confidence interval for the difference (in thousands of miles) between expected service lives of the two brands of tires.

8. A random sample of 25 is drawn from the records of daily output of a large group of employees in order to estimate the population mean. The sample shows a mean of 136 units and a standard deviation of 24 units.
   a) Calculate a 98 per cent confidence interval for the mean output of all employees. (This is the same problem as Chapter 12, No. 6, except for the smaller sample.)
   b) Does the mean output of 136 units differ significantly from the standard output of 144 units set by management? Explain.

SELECTED READINGS
(See Chapter 14.)

14. INFERENCES INVOLVING PROPORTIONS

THE FOREGOING discussion of statistical inference has been applied to the arithmetic mean. This is an important measure of any variable. It should be noted, however, that many different statistical measures can be submitted to a similar type of statistical inference—medians, standard deviations, and so on. The three essential tools in such analysis are: (1) the designated measure as found within the sample, (2) the standard error of the measure involved, and (3) the sampling distribution of the measure.

An important type of statistical measure which also should be considered here is the *proportion*. A proportion represents an *attribute* of a population rather than the average value of a *variable*. In business and industrial statistics this might be the proportion of defective pieces in a lot of bolts produced, the proportion of stockholders favoring a particular executive compensation plan, the proportion of customers that plan to buy a color television set, and so on.

A proportion may be considered to be a special case of the arithmetic mean in which all the values are ones or zeros. Thus, if 20 out of 100 bolts inspected are defective, and we count the defectives as one and the others as zero, the *average* of the 20 ones and 80 zeros is .20, which is the same as the *proportion* defective. Our discussion about the sampling distribution of means thus applies for the most part to proportions also. In particular, the sample proportion is an unbiased estimate of the population proportion. That is, if all possible random samples were drawn from a population, the mean of the sample proportions, or the "expected value," would equal the population proportion. We will use the symbols p and P to denote the proportion of items in the sample and population, respectively, that have a given characteristic. Similarly, q and Q denote the proportion of items that do *not* have that characteristic. Hence $q = 1 - p$ and $Q = 1 - P$.

THE STANDARD ERROR OF A PROPORTION

The standard error of a proportion is the standard deviation of the p's in all samples that might be drawn from a population. As in the case of the mean, the standard error of a proportion equals the standard deviation of the population divided by the square root of the sample size. In the case of the proportion, however, the standard deviation $\sigma = \sqrt{PQ}$. Hence the standard error of a proportion is

$$\sigma_p = \sqrt{\frac{PQ}{n}}$$

For example, if $n = 100$ and $P = .20$,

$$\sigma_p = \sqrt{\frac{.20 \times .80}{100}} = \frac{.40}{10} = .04, \text{ or 4 per cent}$$

As in the case of the mean, the standard error of a proportion depends on the absolute size of the sample, n, rather than its relation to the size of population, n/N.[1]

For the moment, let us assume that the sampling distribution of p follows the normal curve, as in the case of the arithmetic mean. (In much practical work this is a valid assumption. Certain modifications of the assumption will be presented later.)

THE CONFIDENCE INTERVAL FOR A PROPORTION

Suppose that the management of a large grocery chain is interested in estimating what proportion of its customers would prefer a self-service display of pre-packaged meat to a meat counter serviced by a butcher. The market research department is assigned to make a study leading to such an estimate.

A random sample of 400 customers is taken, and it turns out that

---

[1] If the sample makes up a large part of the population, however, the same finite multiplier applies as in the case of the mean. The formula is then

$$\sigma_p = \sqrt{1 - \frac{n}{N}} \sqrt{\frac{PQ}{n}}$$

Thus, if the whole lot or population had a size of only $N = 500$ in the above example, we would have

$$\sigma_p = \sqrt{1 - \frac{100}{500}} \sqrt{\frac{.20 \times .80}{100}}$$
$$= .9 \times .04 = .036$$

220, or 55 per cent, are in favor of the self-service display. It is extremely unlikely that the population constituting *all* customers would divide in preference exactly in this proportion. How, then, do we estimate the interval in which the true proportion falls with, say, a 95 per cent degree of confidence? The analytical principles are the same as those used in constructing confidence intervals for the arithmetic mean. Only the measures are altered to fit the present case.

The standard error of a proportion, as we saw a moment ago, ideally requires the value of P for its calculation. This we do not know, or we would not be faced with the problem of estimating the interval within which it falls. The common practice is to assume that P has the value of p found in the sample, and to make the substitution accordingly. Hence the estimated standard error for the sample proportion is

$$s_p = \sqrt{\frac{pq}{n}}$$

$$= \sqrt{\frac{.55 \times .45}{400}}$$

$$= .0249 \text{ (rounded to .025)}$$

This formula is valid for large samples, provided neither p nor q is very small, as will be explained below.

The 95 per cent confidence interval is $p \pm 1.96 s_p$, or about two standard errors on each side of .55. Therefore, we are 95 per cent confident that the true proportion of customers favoring self-service meat counters lies somewhere between 50 and 60 per cent.

As in the case of the arithmetic mean, and for the same general reasons, we could construct intervals of varying degrees of confidence, based upon appropriate multiples of the standard error of the proportion laid off around the value for p observed in the sample.

Size of Sample

The *size* of a simple random sample needed to reduce the standard error to any desired level can be computed from the above formula in the same way as with the mean. Suppose we wish to determine the proportion of customers preferring self-service with a standard error s_p of only .02, or two percentage points. This corresponds to 95 per cent confidence limits of $p \pm 1.96(.02)$ or $p \pm .04$. From the trial survey cited above, p is tentatively .55. Then we solve for n in the equation $s_p = \sqrt{(pq)/n}$, as follows:

$$.02 = \sqrt{\frac{.55 \times .45}{n}}$$

Transposing, $\sqrt{n} = \dfrac{\sqrt{.55 \times .45}}{.02} = \dfrac{.4975}{.02} = 24.9$

Squaring, $n = 620$

It is necessary to sample about 620 customers, therefore (or 220 in addition to those already sampled), in order to obtain a value of p that has a standard error of only .02.

THE TEST OF A HYPOTHESIS FOR A PROPORTION

Let us suppose that the preceding problem had come up in a somewhat different way—and for purposes of exposition assume that we know nothing of the calculations made in the foregoing section.

Assume that a nation-wide survey by a grocery trade association had suggested that customers of chain stores were equally divided in their preference between self-service meat counters and counters serviced by butchers. The management of a regional chain is somewhat impressed by this finding, but recognizes that regional differences can exist. Management has decided that it will replace butcher-serviced counters if it can get compelling evidence that its particular group of customers favors self-service in a proportion greater than one half.

Now in this case the nation-wide survey has suggested the hypothesis that the true proportion is .50, and only if this is refuted by regional evidence will management decide otherwise. Further, management is interested only in the alternative hypothesis that the true proportion is *greater than* .50; therefore a one-tailed test is the appropriate one.

Let us assume that a random sample of 400 customers is drawn. From the hypothesis that the true population proportion is .50 (i.e., $P_h = .50$), we proceed to calculate the standard error of a sample proportion which would correspond to that hypothesis, namely,

$$\sigma_p = \sqrt{\frac{P_h Q_h}{n}}$$
$$= \sqrt{\frac{.50 \times .50}{400}}$$
$$= .025$$

Suppose that the proportion of customers favoring self-service in the sample turns out to be .55. Then the difference between the sample proportion (p) and the hypothetical proportion (P_h) is .05. In terms of multiples of the standard error, this is

$$\frac{p - P_h}{\sigma_p} = \frac{.55 - .50}{.025} = \frac{.05}{.025} = 2$$

Only 2.28 per cent of the area under a normal curve falls *above* 50 per cent by more than two standard errors in that one-tailed direction (see Appendix E). Hence the probability is only 2.28 per cent that such a large proportion could occur by chance if the true proportion were no greater than .50. We should have to make our decision on the grounds discussed earlier. But the probability of 2.28 that chance alone could have created this evidence is surely a low probability. And a conclusion that the true population proportion is greater than .50 is strongly indicated.

THE BINOMIAL DISTRIBUTION

The sampling distribution of p, like that of $\overline{X}$, is the distribution of its values that could be obtained from all possible random samples of size n taken from a population. The methods used in the preceding section to construct a confidence interval and to test a hypothesis for a proportion are based on the assumption that the distribution of p is *normal*. However, the sampling distribution of p actually follows a *binomial distribution*, which results from the expansion of the binomial $(P + Q)^n$. This distribution approaches the normal distribution when n, the sample size, is sufficiently large, or the value of P is not too far from one half, so our assumption is valid under these conditions.

The influence of sample size and value of P on the shape of the sampling distribution is illustrated in Chart 14–1 and discussed briefly in the next paragraph. The chart represents the sampling distributions of the number of "successes"—for example, number of customers favoring the self-service meat counter—for various combinations of values of n and P. The polygons show that the distribution of p is discrete rather than continuous. They also show how skewness depends on n, the size of sample and the population value of the proportion P. The skewness of a distribution is unaffected by multiplication by a constant such as n. Accordingly, the distribution of np, the number of successes, is chosen rather than that of p, the proportion of successes, chiefly because it is easier to present.

Chart 14–1

RELATIVE FREQUENCY POLYGONS FOR SAMPLING
DISTRIBUTIONS OF NUMBER OF SUCCESSES

A. Fixed Size of Sample, $n = 10$,
and Different Values of P

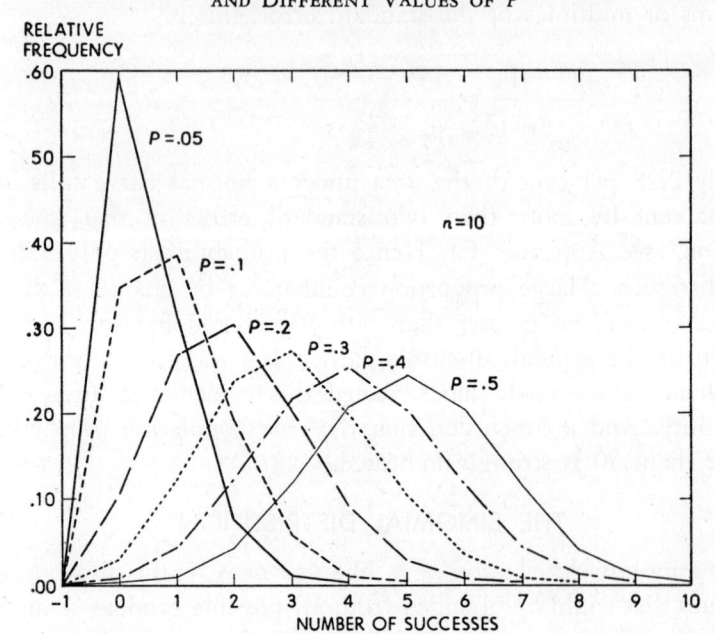

B. Fixed Value of Proportion, $P = .1$,
and Different Sizes of Sample

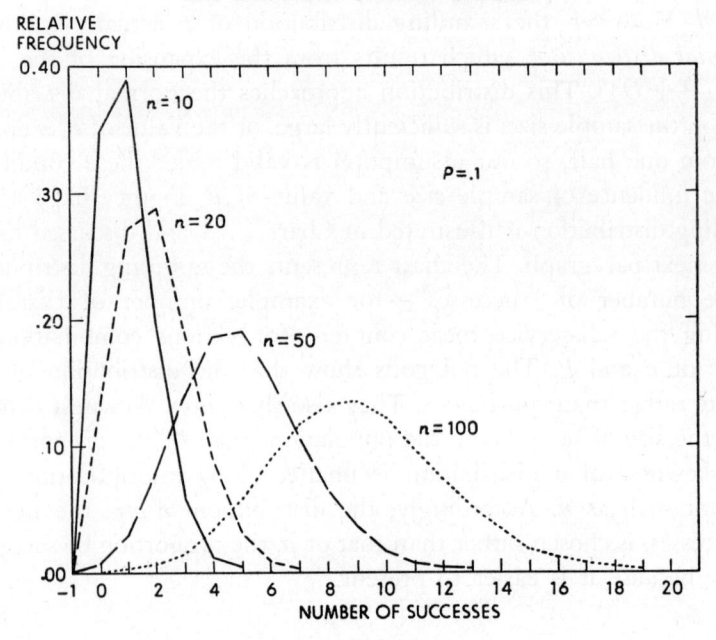

Effect of P on the Distribution

In panel A of Chart 14–1, relative frequency polygons for sampling distributions of number of successes are shown for samples of a fixed size—$n = 10$—but for varying values of P from .05 to .5. When $P = .05$, the distribution has a high degree of positive skewness. As the value of P approaches one half (.5), the skewness approaches zero, so that when $P = .5$ the distribution is perfectly symmetrical and nearly normal.

Effect of Sample Size

In panel B of Chart 14–1, frequency polygons are shown for a fixed value of a proportion ($P = .1$) but for varying sizes of sample from 10 to 100. For small values of n the skewness is large and positive; as n increases, the approach to the symmetrical normal curve is rather striking. The same curves apply to Q as for P, substituting "number of failures" for "number of successes."

These curves illustrate the fact that n should be large, or else P should be not far from one half, to justify the use of the methods presented above, since they are based on the assumption that the sampling distribution of a proportion is approximately normal. As a rule of thumb, both nP and nQ should be about 5 or more, for this assumption to be valid. Thus, if $n = 10$, P would have to be .5 to make $nP = 5$, as in the right-hand curve of panel A. On the other hand, if $P = .1$, n would have to be as large as 50 (panel B) for the distribution to be roughly normal. The assumption of normality is used here both because it is valid for most practical problems involving large samples and because it is simpler than using the binomial distribution.

THE TEST OF A DIFFERENCE BETWEEN TWO PROPORTIONS

Suppose that a manufacturer of farm implements is interested in whether farmers in state No. 1 differ significantly from farmers in state No. 2 with respect to the proportion preferring the make of tractor which he sells. He takes separately a random sample of 100 farmers in each state, and finds that the proportion preferring his make is .40 in state No. 1 and .30 in state No. 2. Should this difference in sample proportions be taken as signifying a difference in the true proportions?

The line of statistical reasoning by which this question is answered is already familiar from earlier discussions. Only the new, appropriate measures need to be introduced. The sampling distribution of

278 BUSINESS AND ECONOMIC STATISTICS [Ch. 14

$(p_1 - p_2)$ may be taken to be fairly normal, because of considerations discussed in the last section.

The *standard error of a difference* between two independent proportions p_1 and p_2 is

$$\sigma_{p_1-p_2} = \sqrt{\sigma_{p_1}^2 + \sigma_{p_2}^2}$$

Since the symbolism is going to be a little complicated, it will be more convenient to write this in squared form, which is known as the *sampling variance* of the difference between two proportions. Hence

$$\sigma_{p_1-p_2}^2 = \sigma_{p_1}^2 + \sigma_{p_2}^2$$

That is, the sampling variance of the difference between two independent proportions is the sum of their sampling variances.[2]

Since $\sigma_p^2 = PQ/n$ in each case, the above formula may be written

$$\sigma_{p_1-p_2}^2 = \frac{P_1 Q_1}{n_1} + \frac{P_2 Q_2}{n_2}$$

in which the subscripts 1 and 2 refer to the two states, respectively.

Now in the present case, we would set up and test the *null hypothesis* that there is *no* difference in the true population proportions involved. Our hypothesis states that $P_1 = P_2$; hence the observed difference between the sample proportions p_1 and p_2 is caused by sampling errors.

Since we do not know P_1 and P_2, the best estimate of their common value is the weighted mean of the sample proportions. Each proportion is weighted by its sample size. That is,

$$\overline{P} = \frac{n_1 p_1 + n_2 p_2}{n_1 + n_2}$$
$$= \frac{100 \times .40 + 100 \times .30}{100 + 100}$$
$$= \frac{70}{200} = .35$$

where $\overline{P}$ is the weighted mean of p_1 and p_2. $Q = 1 - \overline{P} = .65$. The value $\overline{P}$ is simply the proportion for the two samples combined; that is, 70 out of 200 farmers in the two states preferred the tractor.

The sampling variance then is

---

[2] As a graphic solution or check, lay off σ_{p_1} and σ_{p_2} as the sides of a right triangle; then $\sigma_{p_1-p_2}$ is the hypotenuse.

$$\sigma^2_{p_1-p_2} = \frac{\overline{PQ}}{n_1} + \frac{\overline{PQ}}{n_2}$$

$$= \frac{.35 \times .65}{100} + \frac{.35 \times .65}{100}$$

$$= .00455$$

To find the standard error of the difference we extract the square root, which gives

$$\sigma_{p_2-p_1} = .0675$$

In the way now familiar, we express the observed difference of the sample results from the null hypothesis as a ratio to the standard error of such differences. Since the null hypothesis assumes the true difference to be zero, the calculation which we want amounts to

$$\frac{p_1 - p_2}{\sigma_{p_1-p_2}} = \frac{.40 - .30}{.0675}$$

$$= 1.48$$

so that the observed difference differs from the null hypothesis by 1.48 standard errors.

Consultation of Appendix E shows that deviations of this size, regardless of sign, from a true value of zero, are expected to occur by chance alone in .1388 of all possible samples. In other words, the probability is about 14 per cent that this big a spread could occur by chance alone, were the null hypothesis true. This is not significant at the 5 or 10 per cent level. Therefore, based on the available evidence, we would probably "accept the null hypothesis," and attribute the sample results to mere chance. We do not have sufficient evidence to reject the null hypothesis, that is, to conclude that there is a real difference between the two states sampled. This does not prove that $P_1 = P_2$; the evidence is inconclusive. The manufacturer should consider increasing the size of the samples, so that, for any given critical probability chosen, the over-all likelihood of committing an error of inference would be reduced.

SUMMARY

Inferences may be made about sample proportions in much the same way as with means. In fact, a proportion may be considered a special case of a mean in which the attributes, such as defectives and non-defectives, are valued 1 and 0, respectively; and averaged to find the per cent defective.

The standard error of a proportion is $\sigma_p = \sqrt{(PQ)/n}$, where P is the population proportion, and $Q = 1 - P$. This is estimated as $s_p = \sqrt{(pq)/n}$ when sample values are used. The sampling distribution of p follows a *binomial distribution* which is discontinuous, and quite skewed when P or Q is small. However, when P is near .5, or when n is large (say, when $nP \geq 5$), the distribution is approximately normal, so we assume normality here for the sake of simplicity.

A 95 per cent *confidence interval* may be laid out around the sample proportion (i.e., $p \pm 1.96 s_p$) to include P, the population proportion, with a 95 per cent chance of being correct. Other degrees of confidence are handled similarly.

The *size* of sample needed to reduce the standard error s_p to any desired value can be obtained by solving for n in the formula $s_p = \sqrt{(pq)/n}$, using an estimated value of p.

Tests of hypotheses may be applied to proportions by computing the standard error, based on the hypothesized proportion P_h. Then the deviation of the sample proportion from this value ($p - P_h$) is divided by the standard error to determine whether it is large enough to be significant. Thus, if the standardized deviation is 1.96 or more (in a two-tailed test), it is significant at the 5 per cent level of confidence, and so on (Appendix E).

We can also test whether the *difference between two proportions* ($p_1 - p_2$) is significant by dividing the difference by its standard error, where $\sigma^2_{p_1 - p_2} = \sigma^2_{p_1} + \sigma^2_{p_2}$. If this standardized difference is 1.96 or more, it is significant at the 5 per cent level, etc., just as above. When we test the *null hypothesis* that there is no difference between p_1 and p_2, we use their average value, weighted by the size of the two samples, to compute the standard error of the difference.

The simple procedures described in this chapter are broadly useful in testing the significance of proportions found in sample surveys.

PROBLEMS

1. Explain:
    a) The concept of the proportion as a special case of the mean.
    b) The relation between the distribution of proportions and the normal distribution.
    c) A 90 per cent confidence interval for a proportion.
    d) How to test a hypothesis that a sample proportion .45 is significantly less than .50.
    e) The null hypothesis for the difference between two sample proportions.

2. A survey of consumer buying plans reports that 10 per cent of a sample of 2,500 families plan to buy a new refrigerator during the next year. Assume

that an unbiased simple random sample was used. Set up a 99 per cent confidence interval to estimate total refrigerator sales for the whole population of 50,000,000 families. Interpret this forecast.

3. The consumer research division of an automobile manufacturing firm has a budget of $3,000 for a survey to determine the proportion of consumers who prefer a new design for the radiator grill. The estimate should be correct to within 5 percentage points, with a 95 per cent confidence coefficient. Assume a simple random sample. Cost of the survey is $1,000 for overhead plus $5.00 an interview.

   Can this proportion be estimated with the required precision for $3,000, assuming $P = .50$? Explain.

4. A television distributor finds that about 22 per cent of the potential customers who enter his store buy a television set. Moving to another city, he wishes to estimate this percentage for the new location within ± 4 per cent, at the 90 per cent confidence level. How many observations should he take?

5. The median life of a certain electronic tube is claimed by the manufacturer to be 600 hours. You draw a random sample of 100 from a shipment of these tubes and find that only 23 last over 600 hours. Do you believe the manufacturer's claim? Why?

6. After finding that 23 out of 100 electronic tubes from manufacturer No. 1 outlast 600 hours, you order a shipment of similar tubes from manufacturer No. 2 and find that 52 out of a random sample of 200 outlast 600 hours. Is there a significant difference in the durability of the two manufacturers' tubes? Explain.

7. If, in a sample of 600 economics students drawn from schools throughout the country, 360 are sons of businessmen, what is the 90 per cent confidence interval for the proportion of *all* economics students who are sons of businessmen?

8. You wish to make a market survey to estimate the proportion of housewives who prefer your new product to competitors' products. You would like the error in estimating the proportion to be no greater than 4 percentage points, with a confidence coefficient of 95.45 per cent. The sales department offers a preliminary guess that about 20 per cent of housewives might prefer your product. If the survey costs $500 to set up, and $5.00 an interview, about how much should the whole survey cost?

SELECTED READINGS

CROXTON, FREDERICK E., and COWDEN, DUDLEY J. *Practical Business Statistics*. 3d ed. Englewood Cliffs. N.J.: Prentice-Hall, Inc., 1960.
   Chapter 12 introduces the range in making inferences; Chapters 19, 21–23 apply the general principles of statistical inference to business problems.

FREUND, JOHN E., and WILLIAMS, FRANK J. *Modern Business Statistics.* Englewood Cliffs, N.J.: Prentice-Hall, Inc., 1958.

    Chapters 7–12 contain a clear exposition of sampling distributions, estimation, and tests of hypotheses.

HANSEN, MORRIS H.; HURWITZ, WILLIAM N.; and MADOW, WILLIAM G. *Sample Survey Methods and Theory.* Vol. I, *Methods and Applications.* New York: John Wiley & Sons, Inc.; London: Chapman & Hall, Ltd., 1953.

    A comprehensive book treating a variety of sampling plans used in surveys of human populations, such as stratified and cluster sampling.

KENDALL, MAURICE G., and BUCKLAND, WILLIAM R. *A Dictionary of Statistical Terms.* New York: Hafner Publishing Co.; London and Edinburgh: Oliver & Boyd, Ltd., 1957.

    A useful reference book, with glossaries in French, German, Italian, and Spanish.

MCCARTHY, PHILIP J. *Introduction to Statistical Reasoning.* New York, Toronto, and London: McGraw-Hill Book Co., Inc., 1957.

    Treats inference in the form of conceptual models, with emphasis on the binomial distribution.

NATRELLA, MARY G. "The Relation between Confidence Intervals and Tests of Significance," *The American Statistician,* Vol. XIV (February 1960), pp. 20–22.

    Contrasts the two methods, and concludes that confidence intervals are the more often meaningful.

NEISWANGER, WILLIAM A. *Elementary Statistical Methods.* Rev. ed. New York: The Macmillan Co., 1956.

    Chapters 11 and 12 present a brief but clear introduction to sampling error and inference.

RICHMOND, SAMUEL B. *Principles of Statistical Analysis.* 2d ed. New York: The Ronald Press Co., 1964.

    Chapters 6–8 provide a rigorous treatment of statistical inference.

SCHLAIFER, ROBERT. *Probability and Statistics for Business Decisions.* New York, Toronto, and London: McGraw-Hill Book Co., Inc., 1959.

    Part Five presents a critical treatment of the classical theory of statistical inference, in contrast to the decision-theory approach.

SPROWLS, R. CLAY. *Elementary Statistics for Students of Social Science and Business.* New York, Toronto, and London: McGraw-Hill Book Co., Inc., 1955.

    Chapters 3–9 emphasize the role of testing hypotheses in decision making.

WALLIS, W. ALLEN, and ROBERTS, HARRY V. *Statistics: A New Approach.* Glencoe, Ill.: The Free Press, 1956.

    Part III treats a wide variety of topics in inference, with many examples.

15. INDEX NUMBERS

INDEX numbers express the *relative* changes in a variable compared with some base, which is taken as 100.[1] The variable may be a single series, such as electric power production, or an aggregate, such as a group of common stock prices. The index number usually represents a sample of such a group. The changes measured may be those occurring over a period of time or those between one place and another.

Many aspects of modern business are described by the use of index numbers. Both government and private agencies are devoting increasing efforts to the construction of index numbers as aids in management and in the interpretation of changes in general economic life. Many businesses use a variety of index numbers for their own internal administrative purposes. Certain statistical publications, notably the *Survey of Current Business* of the U.S. Department of Commerce and the *Statistics* bulletin of Standard and Poor's Corporation, contain hundreds of economic times series expressed in index number form.

ADVANTAGES OF INDEX NUMBERS

Index numbers are widely used because they have the following important advantages, in contrast with actual data:

1. They provide a simple method of comparing changes from time to time or from place to place. It is easy to compare 74 cents for a pound of butter with 25 cents for a quart of milk, but it is not so easy to compare price changes in the two articles over a period of time. Index numbers of the butter and milk prices would indicate the relative

---

[1] The term "index" is sometimes applied to a business indicator expressed in any unit. Thus, pig-iron production in tons may be referred to as an "index" of business activity. In this chapter, however, the term "index number" or "index" refers specifically to a ratio having some base as 100, or to a series of such ratios. The plural of "index" is either indexes" or "indices."

change in each price from some given price, and which of the two prices had shown the greater change (see Table 15–4). As the number of items increases, this advantage becomes even more apparent.

It is difficult, too, to compare price differences among several different places. However, by the use of the Bureau of Labor Statistics "City Worker's Family Budget" (*Monthly Labor Review,* August 1960), price indexes for various cities can be compared at a given time.

2. Index numbers facilitate comparison of changes in series of data expressed in a variety of units—e.g., dollars, tons, or gallons. Data pertaining to production, sales, inventories, costs, or other aspects of business may also be put into index number form and then compared.

3. They make possible the construction of composites that represent in a single figure some over-all measure of business. This simplifies comparisons with other types of data. In February 1961, the U.S. Bureau of Labor Statistics Index of Wholesale Prices stood at 120.0. This single figure indicates the average relation of prices in February 1961 to prices in 1947–49, the base period for this index, taken as 100. That is, it took $1.20 to buy the same amount of specified goods as could have been bought for $1.00 in 1947–49.

Even series expressed in different types of units can sometimes be combined into a meaningful aggregate, provided the combinations make sense. Many examples of such combinations appear throughout this chapter and the next.

4. They describe the typical seasonal patterns of business. The annual peak in department store sales, for instance, regularly occurs in December, while sales of soft drinks are greatest in midsummer. These "indexes of seasonal variation" are described in Chapter 19.

5. They permit the use of confidential information by concealing absolute values when necessary to safeguard the identity of data. This use of index numbers has arisen out of the desire of businessmen to have information about business in general without revealing data of specific firms. Some time ago an executive in Toledo, when asked if he would be willing to report his company's monthly sales in a co-operative reporting plan, responded: "Yes, but we'll only report them to you in index number form because we aren't permitted to reveal the dollar amounts."

KINDS OF INDEX NUMBERS

An examination of the financial section of a newspaper will reveal many different index numbers which describe changes in various

Table 15–1

SOURCES OF COMMONLY USED INDEXES*

Name of Index	Prepared by—	Frequency of Publication	Published Regularly in—
A. PRICE INDEXES			
1. Consumer Price Index	U.S. Bureau of Labor Statistics	M	*SCB, FRB, MLR, Business Week, S&P, Ec. Ind., NICB*
2. Wholesale Price Index	U.S. Bureau of Labor Statistics	W, M	*SCB, FRB, MLR, N.Y. Times, NICB Barron's, C&FC, S&P, Ec. Ind.*
3. Spot Market Prices of 22 Basic Commodities	U.S. Bureau of Labor Statistics	D, W, M	*Barron's, SCB*
4. Dow-Jones Commodities Futures	Dow-Jones & Co.	D	*Barron's*
5. Construction Cost Indexes	American Appraisal Co.	M	*SCB, S&P*
6. Stock Price Averages	Dow-Jones & Co.	H, D, W, M	*SCB, N.Y. Times, Barron's, S&P*
7. Stock Price Index, 500 Stocks	Standard and Poor's Corporation	W, M	*SCB, FRB, S&P, Ec. Ind., Business Week*
B. QUANTITY INDEXES			
1. Industrial Production	Federal Reserve Board	M	*SCB, FRB, N.Y. Times, S&P, Ec. Ind. NICB*
2. Business Activity	*New York Times*	W	*N.Y. Times*
3. Business Index	*Barron's*	W	*Barron's*
4. Manufacturing Production-Worker Employment	U.S. Bureau of Labor Statistics	M	*SCB, FRB, MLR, S&P, C&FC*
5. Steel Production	American Iron and Steel Institute	W, M	*SCB, FRB, Business Week, N.Y. Times, Barron's, C&FC, S&P*
6. Business Failures	Dun and Bradstreet	W, M	*NICB, C&FC, Barron's, S&P*
C. VALUE INDEXES			
1. Gross National Product	U.S. Department of Commerce	Q	*SCB, FRB, N.Y. Times, S&P, Ec. Ind., NICB, Barron's*
2. Department Store Sales	Federal Reserve Board	W, M	*SCB, FRB, N.Y. Times, Barron's, C&FC, S&P, NICB*
3. Retail Sales	U.S. Department of Commerce	M	*SCB*
4. Manufacturing Production-Worker Payrolls	U.S. Bureau of Labor Statistics	M	*SCB, FRB, MLR, S&P, C&FC*
5. Construction Contracts Awarded (Value)	Federal Reserve Board (from F. W. Dodge Corp. data)	M	*SCB, FRB, NICB, S&P, Ec. Ind.*
6. Measure of Personal Income (by states)	*Business Week*	M	*Business Week*

* Abbreviations:
H—hourly; D—daily; W—weekly; M—monthly; Q—quarterly.
SCB—*Survey of Current Business* (and weekly supplement)
FRB—*Federal Reserve Bulletin*
MLR—*Monthly Labor Review*
C&FC—*Commercial and Financial Chronicle*
S&P—Standard and Poor's *Trade and Securities Service*
Ec. Ind.—President's Council of Economic Advisers, *Economic Indicators*
NICB—National Industrial Conference Board, *Business Record*

aspects of business and economics. These index numbers may be classified as (1) price indexes, (2) quantity indexes, and (3) value indexes. Some of the most commonly used indexes of these three types are listed in Table 15–1. Most of these, but not all, are expressed in relative form.

Price Indexes

Some of the best-known indexes are those dealing with prices. Prices have been of widespread interest for centuries as sensitive barometers of industry and trade.

The necessary data for price index numbers arise from the exchange of commodities (1) at different stages of production—raw materials, semifinished goods, and completely fabricated products; (2) at several levels of distribution—industrial, wholesale, and retail; and (3) for a variety of groups of items—consumers' goods, producers' goods, stocks and bonds, durable and nondurable goods.

A *purchasing power index* is the reciprocal of a price index, when both indexes are expressed as ratios with base 1 rather than 100. Taking the wholesale price index of 120.0 for February 1961 as 1.200, its reciprocal is $1/1.200 = .833$, so the corresponding purchasing power index (with base 100) is 83.3. This means that for every dollar's worth of goods one could buy at 1947–49 wholesale prices, one could buy 83.3 cents' worth in February 1961. Hence the 1961 dollar was worth only 83.3 cents in comparison with the 1947–49 dollar.

Quantity Indexes

Quantity indexes measure the physical volume of production, construction, or employment. They are computed for (1) industry in general, (2) specific industries, or (3) specific operations or stages of production or distribution. The data may represent the country as a whole or local trading areas.

Because of the nature of the data, quantity index numbers are frequently less reliable than those based on dollar figures. Historically, business records were designed to include chiefly those aspects of business which could be expressed in monetary units, and consequently data in physical units for extended periods of time are difficult to obtain.

Value Indexes

Value indexes show the total dollar volume of income, payrolls, sales, and the like. Value is the result of multiplying quantity by price; index numbers of value therefore reflect changes in both quantity and price. The national income and national product estimates of the U.S. Department of Commerce are constructed much like other value indexes; but they are expressed in billions of dollars, rather than as percentages of a base, to avoid the "aura of normality" attached to a base period.

It will be noted that the *New York Times* and *Barron's* indexes of general business activity measure physical volume changes, such as tons of steel and kilowatts of electricity produced, while many regional indexes measure dollar volume, such as bank debits (i.e., checks cashed) and department store sales. Some regional business barometers even combine quantity and value measures, but these indexes are more difficult to interpret.

BASIC METHODS OF CONSTRUCTING INDEX NUMBERS

Simple Index Numbers

A simple index number is constructed from a single series of data which either extends over a period of time or simultaneously represents several different locations. In constructing such an index number, one particular period or place is selected as the base and the item for this base is taken as 100. The other items in the series are then expressed as percentages of this base. A simple index constructed in this manner is frequently called a price *relative,* quantity relative, or value relative.

As an example of a quantity relative, an airline executive may wish to compare the changes in air and automobile travel from 1955 to 1959. Since the volume of intercity automobile passenger-miles traveled is over 20 times that of air travel, the executive's purpose would not be accomplished by comparing the changes in actual passenger-miles. The two series can be more easily compared if they are expressed as percentages of passenger-miles traveled in the same base period—say 1955.

The construction of these simple indexes or quantity relatives is shown in Table 15–2. The three steps are: (1) choose the base period (1955); (2) divide the travel figure each year by the base figure;[2] and (3) multiply the result by 100 (i.e., move the decimal point two places to the right) to express it as a per cent or index

---

[2] Whenever it is necessary to divide a series by a constant divisor, as in this instance, it is usually easier to use the reciprocal of the divisor as a fixed multiplier, as described in Chapter 5. In this example, air passenger-miles can be simply multiplied by the reciprocal of 20 (found in Appendix C) $\times$ 100 = 5. This figure can be kept in the calculating machine without change throughout the entire computation, thus saving time and reducing the likelihood of error.

number. An index number is written just as a per cent, except that the per cent sign (%) is not used. Thus, the 1959 index for air travel is $29 \div 20 \times 100 = 145$.

This index means that air travel in 1959 was 145 per cent of its 1955 volume, an increase of 45 per cent. Hence, while automobile travel had increased more than air travel in passenger-miles during this period (84 versus 9 billion), its *relative* increase was only 14 per cent, compared with 45 per cent for air travel.

The increase in the air travel index from *1956* to 1959 was 35 index points, but this is not 35 per cent because the base is 110, not

Table 15–2

SIMPLE INDEX NUMBERS OF AIR TRAVEL
AND INTERCITY AUTOMOBILE TRAVEL
IN THE UNITED STATES, 1955–59

Year	Passenger-Miles (Billions) Air Travel	Passenger-Miles (Billions) Auto Travel	Index (1955 = 100) Air Travel	Index (1955 = 100) Auto Travel
1955	20	586	100	100
1956	22	618	110	105
1957	25	645	125	110
1958	25	664	125	113
1959	29	670*	145	114

* Estimated.
Source: *Air Transportation*, 1960, p. 27.

100. The *percentage* increase was $35 \div 110 = 32$ per cent. This is, of course, the same increase as that in the passenger-miles column ($7 \div 22 = 32$ per cent).

A simple index can be computed for any single series of data, such as the price of General Motors stock or a department store's sales. It can be computed for weeks, months, or any other period for which data are available. Statistical source books include many indexes of this type. The Bureau of Labor Statistics, for example, publishes monthly price relatives for each of about 1,900 commodities, as an aid in comparing individual price changes, in addition to its composite wholesale price indexes.[3]

Composite Index Numbers

Most index numbers in common use are composites. They are constructed according to the principles just described for simple indexes,

[3] See U.S. Department of Labor, *Wholesale Prices and Price Indexes, 1958*, Bulletin No. 1257 (July 1959).

but they combine several different sets of data. In the following pages, two basic methods of constructing composite index numbers are described: (1) the average of relatives index and (2) the aggregative index. Formulas for both types of indexes are presented on page 294, but it is not necessary to memorize them to understand the procedure involved.

Necessity of Weights. Whenever prices or other data are combined in an index number, the relative importance of each must be taken into account by assigning proper weights to each item. This is necessary because, in reality, no composite index is unweighted. If a set of weights is not explicitly applied, each element of the index *automatically* (or implicitly) receives *some* weight. For example, if unit prices of various foods are being added together in the preparation of a composite consumer price index, a given relative change in a higher-priced item, such as a pound of butter, will influence the total more than will the same relative change in a lower-priced item, such as a pound of bread. Bread, however, should really be weighted more heavily because people consume more; so a system of weights must be used in order to give bread its proper importance in the index. A composite index is thus a *weighted average*[4] of its components.

Average of Relatives Method. Many methods of constructing index numbers have been tried, but the average of relatives method is now used in most leading indexes, such as the Federal Reserve Board's index of industrial production and the Bureau of Labor Statistics' wholesale price indexes. In this method the individual series of price or quantity data are expressed as simple indexes, which are then multiplied by fixed value weights and totaled to yield the composite index.

To illustrate the construction of a *quantity* index, consider a manufacturer of light-weight airplane luggage and specially fitted car-top luggage for automobiles. About two thirds of his sales are typically airplane luggage and one third is car-top luggage. He wishes to construct a composite index of air and automobile travel, and project it into the future as a measure of the potential market for his products. The method is illustrated in Table 15–3. The steps are as follows:

---

[4] The weighted arithmetic mean is used almost universally in computing index numbers, although the weighted geometric mean is theoretically superior for averaging relatives, particularly since they tend to follow a logarithmic normal distribution, with a zero lower limit and infinite upper limit. The geometric mean also minimizes the influence of extremely large relatives, which may distort the arithmetic mean of a small number of items. Nevertheless, the arithmetic mean is used because it is easier to compute and easier to understand than the geometric mean. Also, an arithmetic price index represents changes in the total cost of a bill of goods more accurately than a geometric index, which reflects the average ratios of change in price. That is, the arithmetic mean makes more sense in this connection.

1. Express each individual series as a simple index or relative, by dividing through by the base value. This step is described above. (Cols. 1–3 in Table 15–3 are taken from Table 15–2.)
2. Select a dollar-value weight for each series as a measure of its importance in the base year or some other typical period. Divide these weights by their total to express them as *relative* weights

Table 15–3

CONSTRUCTION OF COMPOSITE INDEX
OF AIR AND AUTOMOBILE TRAVEL
BY AVERAGE OF RELATIVES METHOD
(1955 = 100)

Year	Simple Index (1955 = 100)		Weighted Index		Composite Index
	Air Travel	Auto Travel	Air Travel (Col. 2 × 2/3)	Auto Travel (Col. 3 × 1/3)	Air and Auto Travel
(1)	(2)	(3)	(4)	(5)	(6)
1955	100	100	67	33	100
1956	110	105	73	35	108
1957	125	110	84	37	121
1958	125	113	84	38	122
1959	145	114	97	38	135

Source: Table 15–2.

whose sum equals 1. In this case the relative importance of air and auto travel *to the manufacturer* is measured by the proportion of his dollar sales that go to each industry—2/3 and 1/3, respectively. As a more general example, the Federal Reserve Board weights its component indexes of manufacturing output by "value added by manufacture," from the Census of Manufactures, expressed as percentages of the total weight.
3. Multiply the simple indexes by the relative weights to obtain the weighted indexes (Table 15–3, cols. 4 and 5).
4. Add the weighted indexes to obtain the composite index (col. 6). This must equal 100 in the base year, since the simple indexes equal 100 and the weights total 1. (If the value weights are *not* adjusted to total 1, the sum of the weighted indexes can be divided through by its base-year value to obtain the same values as in column 6 of the Table.)

The composite index provides the manufacturer with a summary

Ch. 15] INDEX NUMBERS 291

measure of potential demand with which he can compare or predict his own sales.

A composite *price* index is constructed by this method in the same way as a quantity index. Table 15-4 illustrates the computation of a consumer price index for white bread, butter, and delivered milk in August 1953 (the base month) and August 1959, using the price

Table 15-4

CONSTRUCTION OF COMPOSITE INDEX
FOR THREE RETAIL FOOD PRICES
BY AVERAGE OF RELATIVES METHOD
(August 1953 = 100)

Month	Simple Index (August 1953 = 100)			Weighted Index			Composite Index
	Bread	Butter	Milk	Bread (Col.2 × .27)	Butter (Col.3 × .26)	Milk (Col.4 × .47)	(Total, Cols. 5-7)
(1)	(2)	(3)	(4)	(5)	(6)	(7)	(8)
August 1953	100.0	100.0	100.0	27.0	26.0	47.0	100.0
August 1959	125.0	94.9	108.7	33.7	24.7	51.1	109.5

Source of Price Data: U.S. Bureau of Labor Statistics, *Retail Food Prices by Cities.*

data in Table 15-5. Of course, actual indexes involve hundreds of commodities and many dates. The steps are similar to those cited above:

1. Divide each price series by its price in the base period (August 1953) to express it as a simple index (Table 15-4, cols. 2-4).
2. Measure the relative importance of each commodity in dollars for some normal period. The relative weights in the heading of columns 5-7 are based on a hypothetical consumer survey which showed that for every dollar the typical family spent on these foods $.27 went for white bread, $.26 for butter, and $.47 for delivered milk. The weights preferably apply to the base period, but this is not always feasible. Thus, the U.S. Bureau of Labor Statistics for years reported its Wholesale Price Index with the base 1947-49 = 100, but obtained its weights from sales values of commodities in the 1947 industrial censuses, and later in the 1954 censuses. (Note that *dollar values,* rather than prices or quantities, are used as weights in the weighted average of relatives method, for computing either price or quantity indexes. Also, the weight must be held constant over a period of years; otherwise changes in the weight would affect the level of the index itself.)

3. Multiply the simple indexes (cols. 2–4) by the weights to obtain the weighted indexes (cols. 5–7).
4. Add the weighted indexes for each period to get the composite index (col. 8). (If the weights are not adjusted to total 1, the last column must be divided by its base-period value to adjust this value to 100.)

Aggregative Method. The aggregative method is more direct than the average of relatives method in bypassing the calculation of simple indexes. Table 15–5 illustrates the construction of a *price* index by the aggregative method. The steps are:

Table 15–5

CONSTRUCTION OF COMPOSITE INDEX
FOR THREE RETAIL FOOD PRICES
BY AGGREGATIVE METHOD
(August 1953 = 100)

Month	Price per Unit			Cost of Week's Supply				Composite Index (Col. 8 ÷ 5.92)
	Bread (Lb.)	Butter (Lb.)	Milk (Qt.)	Bread (Col. 2 × 10)	Butter (Col. 3 × 2)	Milk (Col. 4 × 12)	Total (Cols. 5–7)	
(1)	(2)	(3)	(4)	(5)	(6)	(7)	(8)	(9)
August 1953	$.16	$.78	$.23	$1.60	$1.56	$2.76	$5.92	100.0
August 1959	.20	.74	.25	2.00	1.48	3.00	6.48	109.5

Source of Price Data: U.S. Bureau of Labor Statistics, *Retail Food Prices by Cities.*

1. Choose as weights the physical *quantities* of each commodity produced or consumed in a typical period. In this case, it is the quantity of each of three food items consumed by an average family in a week: 10 one-pound loaves of bread, 2 pounds of butter, and 12 quarts of milk.
2. Multiply each price (cols. 2–4) by its weight to obtain the weighted prices (cols. 5–7). The product of price times quantity gives the total cost of each commodity in the "market basket" as its price changes from time to time.
3. Total these products (col. 8) to get the cost of the whole market basket.
4. Select a base period (August 1953) and divide the totals by the total in the base period ($5.92). The results (col. 9) are aggregative index numbers. Here they indicate that in August 1959 the combined cost of the three commodities was 109.5 per cent of what it was in August 1953.

As a more realistic sample of the aggregative method, Standard and Poor's constructs its price index of 500 stocks by multiplying the current market price of each stock by the number of shares outstanding in the base period (modified by later capitalization changes). This weighted price, or aggregate market value of the original shares, is then totaled for all 500 stocks, and the grand total is divided by the aggregate market value in the base period to obtain the index.[5]

Quantity indexes are computed by the aggregative method in the same way as price indexes, except that quantity and price are interchanged. The varying quantities produced or consumed each month are multiplied by a fixed price in the base year or some other typical period. Hence, only changes in physical volume affect the movements of the index, and the fixed price serves to give each commodity its appropriate importance. Then the sum of the weighted quantities each month is divided by the sum in the average month of the base year to yield the weighted aggregative quantity index.

Dollar-value indexes (e.g., department store sales) reflect the movements of both price and quantity, so neither one need be held constant. Furthermore, the original data are already available in the form of dollar values. In the aggregative method, the estimated values for each component of the index are simply added each year. The totals themselves may then be reported, as in national income estimates; or they may be divided by a base-year value and reported as index numbers, as in the Federal Reserve Board Index of Department Store Sales or the U.S. Bureau of Labor Statistics Index of Manufacturing Production-Worker Payrolls.

The average of relatives method is used when the components are not comparable, as in bank debits and department store sales used in regional business indexes. Here the components are expressed as relatives and then multiplied by arbitrary weights to arrive at the final value indexes.

Formulas for the Basic Methods

The two basic methods of computing weighted index numbers can be expressed in the following symbols:
For an individual commodity:

p_0 = price in the base period (e.g., 1957–59 average),
p_n = price in current year of the series (e.g., 1962, 1963, etc.),
q_0 = quantity in the base period,

---

[5] The base is set at 1941–43 = 10 in order to make the current index approximate the average price of all stocks listed on the New York Stock Exchange.

q_n = quantity in current year of the series,

$\Sigma(p_n q_0)$ = sum of (price of first commodity in current year times base-period quantity) plus (price of second commodity in current year times base-year quantity), etc.

FORMULAS FOR COMPUTING COMPOSITE INDEXES*

	Average of Relatives Method	Aggregative Method
Price index	$\dfrac{\sum \left(\dfrac{p_n}{p_0}\right)(p_0 q_0)}{\Sigma(p_0 q_0)}$	$\dfrac{\Sigma(p_n q_0)}{\Sigma(p_0 q_0)}$
Quantity index	$\dfrac{\sum \left(\dfrac{q_n}{q_0}\right)(p_0 q_0)}{\Sigma(p_0 q_0)}$	$\dfrac{\Sigma(p_0 q_n)}{\Sigma(p_0 q_0)}$
Value index	$\dfrac{\sum \left(\dfrac{p_n q_n}{p_0 q_0}\right)(p_0 q_0)}{\Sigma(p_0 q_0)}$	$\dfrac{\Sigma(p_n q_n)}{\Sigma(p_0 q_0)}$

* These formulas, which use base-year weights, are variants of "Laspeyres' formula," as opposed to "Paasche's formula," which uses current-year weights, or Irving Fisher's "ideal" index, which is the geometric mean of the two.

The two formulas in each row are identical when the base-period price, quantity, or value is used as weight. That is, multiplying prices by base-year quantities gives the same algebraic result as multiplying price relatives by the same year's value, etc. This is the most common case in practice. If some other period is used as weight, the results will differ somewhat.

Formulas for quantity indexes are the same as for price indexes with p and q interchanged.

Comparison of Average Relatives and Aggregative Methods

The average of relatives and aggregative methods often yield identical results, as described above. Then which is the better one to use?

The aggregative method is the simpler and the more easily understandable of the two, so it may be used whenever appropriate weights (i.e., quantities for a price index) are available and when only the composite index is needed.

The average of relatives method, on the other hand, must be used when:

1. It is desired to compare the individual components in the form of relatives, as in the *New York Times* Index of Business Ac-

tivity. The first step in this method produces these relatives directly.
2. The available weights are in value form, as in the Federal Reserve Board index, which applies the "value added by manufacture" for a group of related items as a weight for the production of a single representative item. It is usually easier to obtain dollar values as weights than it is to find quantities or prices.
3. The component series are already in the form of relatives, as in combining several segments of the Federal Reserve Board Monthly Index of Industrial Production for comparison with a particular industry.

Since one or more of these conditions usually exist, the average of relatives method is more widely used than the aggregative method.

TESTS OF A GOOD INDEX NUMBER

It is important to understand the methods by which index numbers are constructed, but there are in addition a number of other problems which must be considered both by the producer and the user of index numbers. The user must be aware of these problems so that he may be able to appraise critically the indexes which he employs, and on that basis to judge their validity for his particular purpose. These major problems include: (1) the purpose of the index, (2) the items included, (3) the choice of the base period, and (4) the selection of weights.

Purpose of the Index

The purpose that an index number is intended to serve determines to a large extent its method of construction, the items to be included, the base period, and the weighting system. The user of an index number must therefore have some knowledge of its original purpose, and the producer of an index number must be able to state specifically what his purpose is before he starts his calculations.

For instance, the index of employment regularly computed by the Bureau of Business Research of Ohio State University has been developed to indicate the relative monthly changes in the number of persons employed in Ohio industries. Since it is based on the number of persons on company payrolls each month, it is an *employment* index only and cannot be used by itself as a measure either of unemployment, amount of payrolls, or man-hours worked. In similar fashion, the Federal Reserve Board index of construction contracts awarded was developed to indicate relative changes in the value of contract building. It cannot be used to measure changes in the physical volume of construction, nor changes in the value of construction put in place.

In looking for an index number appropriate to his purposes, the analyst must bear in mind that official names of indexes are often little more than general guides to their nature. Further investigation is necessary to ascertain their original purpose and to avoid the misinterpretation resulting from the use of the wrong index.

If a single index number proves inadequate, the use of several related indexes may fulfill a given need. For instance, in seeking a summary of the course of business during the past year in a certain area, it may be difficult to find a single index that will suffice. The general situation may be revealed, however, by the combined use of indexes of employment, payrolls, bank debits, construction contracts awarded, and carloadings. These should be compared with a composite index of business activity if there is one available for that area.

Items Included

The selection of the items to include in an index number presents two major questions for consideration: (1) how many different items should be included and (2) which items they should be. Although these are separate problems, they are so closely related that they will be treated simultaneously. In determining both the number and the specific items to include, there are three guides: (1) the purpose, (2) the location and accessibility of the data, and (3) the tenets of accepted sampling procedures.

The Purpose as a Guide. A comprehensive statement of the purpose should be drawn up as a guide to the kinds of items to be included in an index. This statement will indicate certain limitations, much the same as those involved in "defining the problem,"[6] as a first step in planning the investigation. It is not enough, for example, to decide that a retail food price index is to be prepared. That statement provides only three points of definition: it is to be a price index; the prices are to be at the retail level; and only food items are to be included. It is also necessary to know (1) the area to be covered, (2) the economic class of people to be represented, and (3) the time period to be covered.

Food habits vary widely in different geographical areas. The constituents of a retail food price index, therefore, should vary in accordance with the geographical section being represented; or, if the same

---

[6] Chapter 2, pp. 18–19.

items are included in all sections, their weights should be adjusted to correspond to the differences in consuming habits.

The economic class of people which the index number is to represent is an important criterion in selecting the food items to be included. An index intended to show changes in prices of food purchased by working-class families should contain only those items commonly used by that group. To determine what the common items are in various income groups is one of the main reasons for the recurrent studies of consumption habits conducted by the U.S. Bureau of Labor Statistics.

The time period covered is the final consideration because it is likely to depend on some of the other factors. In the United States during recent years, for instance, there has been a great increase in the number of food products which have become common in the diets of working families. It would probably be best, therefore, not to go back too many years in preparing a food price index, since it would be difficult to select a set of items that would be equally representative during the entire period. The recognition of these changes is one of the reasons which has led the Bureau of Labor Statistics to increase the number of items in its index of retail food prices at various times from 21 in 1920 to more than four times that number today.

Accessibility of Data. The data for an index number may have to be collected from widely scattered sources. When this is the situation, the amount of data included may be drastically limited by the cost of collection.

In many cases, data are already available but have been collected casually, or for some purpose which is foreign to subsequent needs. Such information may not be entirely satisfactory for index number construction. In fact, the desired index must sometimes be modified in order to utilize data which can be obtained quickly and economically.

The general form of such data may appear to be satisfactory, but they may prove unusable because of failure in the collection to adhere to rigid definitions, specifications, and standards, or because of unsatisfactory counting units. These deficiencies are usually of vital significance, and in any case they must be known before making a decision to disregard them.

For instance, if wheat prices are desired, it is important to know whether they are prices for the same kind and grade of wheat in different markets at each point in time. As this is being written, for example, winter wheat, No. 2 hard, is selling for $2.04 at Kansas City and $2.40 in the New York market; and spring wheat, No. 1 Dark Northern, is selling for $2.21 at Minneapolis. The same kinds of differences are found in almost every field. Lack of standards in naming and grading commodities, either from one place to another, or from time to time, may have an important bearing on the inclusion of available prices or quantities in an index number.

A further consideration is the speed with which certain data become available. If an index is being prepared to interpret current business conditions as promptly as possible, from month to month, only those items that are obtainable on the date required can be included.

Selecting the Sample. The third guide in choosing the items to include in an index arises from the statistical requirement that the data must provide a representative sample, unless, of course, they cover the entire field. The principles for selecting a sample have been treated in Chapter 4. It is of utmost importance that the data collected for constructing index numbers conform to these principles. Otherwise, no valid generalizations can be drawn from the results.

The following methods in particular may be useful in selecting a sample of items to include in an index number.

First, divide the commodities into a large number of small groups, or strata. Each group should comprise a closely related line of products that might be expected to move fairly uniformly in price, quantity, or value, as the case may be. Weights must be available for these groups. This stratification permits accurate weighting and flexible grouping into main categories as desired.

Then select from these groups a typical list of items to include not only all of the most important articles but also some that are typical of every category of goods in the group both in physical characteristics and price behavior, in the case of a price index. Each item must of course be precisely identified. The prices are then weighted and the products totaled to form group indexes, and the latter are again combined to provide the over-all index. The result may be called a highly *stratified, judgment sample.*

In groups or parts of groups where there is little basis for selection, as when there are many items of minor or relatively equal importance, each 10th, 20th, or some other numbered item may be taken from the list. This is a *systematic,* rather than a judgment, sample.

In any case, the proper selection of a typical cross section of items is the most crucial step in the entire process. Many regional "general business" indexes and others fail in this respect—they just don't measure what they purport to represent.

The number of items selected in each group may vary from one to twenty or more, depending on the group's importance and diversification. Thus, one item may represent a small group, and a very few items may accurately reflect the price behavior of a larger group if the products are similar in character and tend to move uniformly in price. On the other hand, large and diversified groups require larger samples.

For all groups combined, several hundred items should be priced to constitute a sample of adequate size. The Bureau of Labor Statistics, for example, includes about 300 items in its Consumer Price Index.[7] A smaller number might be used, however, for items that are fairly homogeneous as to type and price behavior.

Choice of a Base Period

The base of an index showing changes from time to time may be any period that provides the most suitable standard for comparison. There are a number of criteria for the selection of such a base. The most important of these are: (1) normality of the period, (2) the ease of recalling conditions at that time, (3) trustworthiness of the data in the period, (4) comparability with the base period used in existing index numbers, (5) inclusion of census years for bench-mark data, and (6) adequate length of period.

1. *Normality of Period.* It is frequently held that the base period should be one that is "normal" or "average"; that is, a period when the average of the data appears at a level about midway between the peaks and troughs of business cycles in that era. A period of very high prices, for instance, should not be used as the base because the influence of the most inflated components would be disproportionately low in other periods. In contrast, if a period of very low prices were used as the base, the influence of the most depressed components would be disproportionately high in other periods. Thus, neither the depression years 1931–34 nor the war years 1942–45 are as suitable base periods as are the more average levels of 1935–39, 1947–49, or 1957–59. There is never a time when every series included in an index is normal in this respect, so the base period should be one in which abnormal situations are at a minimum.

There is danger that readers will interpret "normal" as meaning the level at which the index *should* stand under proper conditions. In order to avoid this misconception, it is advisable to call the period chosen as the standard merely the base period, or 100 per cent.

2. *Ease of Recall.* A second criterion for choosing the base of an

---

[7] On the other hand, some 1,900 items are included in the Bureau's Wholesale Price Index in order to insure the reliability of its many component indexes. See Joint Economic Committee, *Economic Indicators, Historical and Descriptive Supplement,* 1957, pp. 51–55.

index is the ease with which readers will be able to recollect the conditions which existed during that time. If a period within easy memory is adopted as the base, the index is more meaningful. The use of this criterion suggests that the base period be changed about every ten years.

3. *Trustworthiness of Data.* Source materials have become generally more accurate and comprehensive in recent years, so that a recent period is more likely to provide a reliable base than an earlier period. The Bureau of Labor Statistics Wholesale Price and Consumer Price Indexes and the Federal Reserve Board Index of Industrial Production, for example, have all been revised since World War II to include new products developed since the war and to embody new weights reflecting changed production and consumption patterns. At the same time the older base periods (1926 for wholesale prices; 1935-39 for the others) were replaced by a 1947-49 base, which more nearly encompasses both the recently developed products and the particular years for which the weights are computed. Further revisions are being made in the early 1960's.

4. *Comparability with Other Index Numbers.* The base for a new index number is often chosen because it is used by existing index numbers with which the new one is most likely to be compared. Whatever the reasons for differences in base period, index numbers are not directly comparable unless their base periods are identical. For this reason the Office of Statistical Standards in the Bureau of the Budget has endeavored to standardize governmental indexes on a 1957-59 base.

5. *Inclusion of Census Years.* Since it is preferable to use base-year weights,[8] the base period should include census years for which bench-mark data are available as weights. The base period 1957-59, for example, includes the 1958 Census of Manufactures, the 1958 Census of Business, and the 1959 Census of Agriculture.

6. *Adequate Length of Period.* Single years such as 1947 and 1957, or even shorter periods, have sometimes been used as base, but an average of three to five years is generally considered preferable to iron out the irregularities in the constituent series. Hence the periods 1935-39, 1947-49, and 1957-59 have been more universally accepted as "normal" base periods in their respective epochs than the one-year bases.

---

[8] U.S. Bureau of the Budget, Division of Statistical Standards, *Recommendations on Post-war Base Period for Index Numbers,* March 14, 1951, p. 2.

Selection of Weights

Earlier in this chapter, weights were defined and used in calculating composite index numbers. Here the problems of selection of weights, type of weights, shifting weights, and weight bias are discussed.

Selection of Weights. Weights may be selected in such a way that they represent either the importance of a specific commodity or the importance of the entire economic group of which it is typical. In the latter case, one might include in a production index of house furnishings the relative for a standard type of domestic wool rug weighted by the total value of all sorts of similar rugs rather than to include a large number of different rugs and weight each one according to its own specific importance. This group weighting system is used in the Federal Reserve Board Index of Industrial Production, the Bureau of Labor Statistics Consumer Price Index, and others described in the next chapter.

Weights should also be appropriate to the purpose of an index. An average of relatives price index for a company's inventory, for example, should be weighted by inventory values; a price index of goods sold should be weighted by sales values; while a consumer price index should be weighted by consumer expenditures.

Weights may be rounded off to two or three significant figures, or even one figure for minor items, since an appreciable difference in weights will affect an index but little.[9]

Physical Quantities or Values as Weights. The factors used as weights for a given index number depend upon the method of construction and the kinds of data being employed. If it is an index number of prices and the aggregative method is used, i.e., a method which adds the actual weighted prices, the weights must be *quantity* data of some kind, never value. Value includes the effect of price, since it equals price times quantity. Its use as a weight in an aggregative index would actually have the effect of squaring the prices, which would give undue importance to changes in the larger prices. Conversely, an aggregative quantity index would be weighted by *prices*. For an average of either price or quantity relatives, on the other hand, *value* weights should be used, as illustrated in Table 15–4.

Whether the weights used will be quantities or values may, however, depend upon the availability of data. For most kinds of commodi-

---

[9] See Irving Fisher, *The Making of Index Numbers* (3d ed.; Boston: Houghton Mifflin Co., 1927), pp. 346, 432.

ties, exchange values in dollars are more likely to be available than quantities. Values must also be used for group weights, where the items are in different units. In these cases, the weighted average of relatives method should be used.

Constant or Variable Weights. Index numbers are designed to show changes only in the variable being measured—a price index, for instance, should isolate changes in price from changes which may be due to other factors. None of the factors in the computation except prices should be allowed to fluctuate. The weights, therefore, should usually be kept constant for an extended period. If prices and weights were allowed to vary simultaneously, the resulting index numbers would reflect changes due to both factors, and no one could tell what part of the final result was due to variations in prices and what part was due to variations in the weights.

This raises the question: If the weights are to be held constant for extended periods, which specific period should they represent? In the examples used as illustrations of method, the weights were quantities or values in the period used as the base of the index numbers, but this is not necessarily the best procedure to follow in every case.

The importance of commodities may change during relatively short periods so that, if weights of an early period are used, there is a danger that the current index number will not accurately reflect the present relative importance of its several constituents. For instance, the cost of purchasing and maintaining a television set is an important element in present-day cost of living that did not exist a few years ago. If data are available, therefore, weights should ordinarily be chosen from a period recent enough to be representative of current conditions.

When it is definitely known that the constituents of the index are changing in importance, and if current data are available to measure these changes, weights may be revised from time to time. Too frequent revisions, however, tend to impair the usefulness of an index number, so that ordinarily no change should be made as long as the weights are approximately correct. In long-established indexes the weights have been changed at intervals of about ten years.

Bias Due to Weighting. Bias due to methods of weighting is almost certain to occur in some degree. In this sense "bias" means that the index number tends to understate or overstate the degree of change because of the failure of the weights to represent accurately the relative importance of shifts in the items included. Price indexes are generally based on the cost of a fixed bill of goods, but people actually buy different quantities as prices change.

The U.S. Bureau of Labor Statistics Cost of Living Index, for example, was criticized during World War II because it did not reflect fully the increased costs due to quality deterioration, black markets, and shifts in consumption patterns characteristic of the war period. Most of these effects are impossible to measure accurately or to incorporate in a single index. One of the tangible results of the criticism was the change of name from Cost of Living Index to Consumers' Price Index (now called the Consumer Price Index). The probable bias of any index should be carefully considered before it is used in a major policy decision.

ADJUSTMENTS IN INDEX NUMBERS

Substitution of Items

Changes in production, distribution, habits of consumption, and a variety of other economic factors sometimes necessitate substitutions in the items included in an index, in its list of respondents, or in the specifications of the items included. For example, the change-over from oil to gas heating led the Bureau of Labor Statistics in 1958 to substitute a 30-gallon domestic hot water gas heater for a similar oil heater in computing its Wholesale Price Index. The availability of new and better data may also make it desirable to make adjustments in established index numbers, as described above.

When interpreting the movement of index numbers it is essential that these adjustments be kept in mind, for the particular method of adjustment may make a great deal of difference in the final result. During war periods, changing products and specifications are of particular importance in evaluating index numbers.

Changing the Base Period

The base period of an index number may need to be changed in either of the following situations: (1) When index numbers based on different periods are to be compared, it is necessary to shift one index to the same base period as the other, so that changes in the two will be measured from the same point in time. (2) It may be desired to shift the base of a series to some reference date such as prewar 1940 or 1949 in order to compare subsequent changes with conditions at that time.

A series can be shifted to a new base by multiplying each of its index numbers by $100/X$, where X is the index number for the period selected as the new base. That is, $X \cdot 100/X = 100$. Since each of the indexes is multipled by the same constant factor, the *relative* fluctuations of the series remain unchanged.

To illustrate, in Table 15–6 the base period for prices paid by farmers for family living items has been shifted from 1910–14 to 1947–49 for comparison with changes in the Consumer Price Index since that period. Since the original index of prices paid by farmers averaged 243.7 in 1947–49, the whole series has been multiplied by 100/243.7 to shift the 1947–49 average to 100 (col. 2), the same as for the Con-

Table 15–6

SHIFTING THE BASE OF PRICES PAID BY FARMERS FROM 1910–14 TO 1947–49 FOR COMPARISON WITH THE CONSUMER PRICE INDEX

	Prices Paid by Farmers for Family Living Items		Consumer Price Index
	1910–14 = 100 (1)	1947–49 = 100* (2)	1947–49 = 100 (3)
1947	237	97	95.5
1948	251	103	102.8
1949	243	100	101.8
1960	290	119	126.5

* Obtained by multiplying column 1 by 100/243.7 to shift the 243.7 value for the 1947–49 average to the 100 level.
Source: *Survey of Current Business.*

sumer Price Index. Note that index numbers for the base years must average 100. The last two columns show that from the 1947–49 average to 1960, prices paid by farmers advanced only 19 per cent as compared with 26.5 per cent for consumer prices generally, even though the original farm price index increased by more points than the Consumer Price Index.

Splicing Two Series

It is often necessary to splice two series to form a continuous series, as when the specifications of a commodity in a price index are changed. Any two series may be spliced provided they are both available for the same year. For example, the BLS Wholesale Price Index might be said to include everything but the kitchen sink. This is not true. It includes an enameled steel sink, but the price of a new reporting company was added to its sample in November 1958. As a result, the typical price had to be shifted from $13.39 (or an index of 91.1 on the 1947–49 base) to $13.13 in that month. Table 15–7 shows how to continue the original price index (col. 2) for the sink by splicing the new price (col. 3) onto it. The new price of $13.13 in the overlapping month November 1958 must be shifted not to 100 but to 91.1, the index for that month. The new price series is therefore multiplied by 91.1/$13.13 as shown in column 4. The spliced series in column 5 (combining cols. 2 and 4) now shows enameled steel sink prices continuously throughout the period, although the actual sample price shifts in November 1958.

Table 15–7

SPLICING TWO PRICE SERIES
REPRESENTING AN ENAMELED STEEL SINK
(Prices in Dollars; Indexes on 1947–49 Base)

	Original Sample of Reporting Companies		Enlarged Sample of Reporting Companies		Spliced Series
	Price (1)	Index (2)	Price (3)	Index (4)	Index (5)
September 1958	$13.194	89.8			89.8
November 1958	$13.39	91.1	$13.13	91.1	91.1
June 1959			$12.71	88.2	88.2

Source: U.S. Department of Labor, *Wholesale Prices and Price Indexes, 1958*, Bulletin No. 1257, (July 1959), pp. 225 and 230 (item #1053–11).

Strictly speaking, an index which is being shifted to a new base should be composed of the same items during the whole period of the index. Yet the most common use of base shifting is to link a current index containing one group of items to an earlier-period index containing a similar but not identical group of items. This procedure is legitimate if the old and new groups of items may be considered to be representative of the same population. This is true of the above example. In case the components of an index have changed more radically from time to time, however, as in the Cleveland Trust Company Index of Industrial Production from 1790 to date, the index loses its homogeneous character.

SUMMARY

Index numbers express the changes in a variable relative to some base taken as 100. They are particularly useful in comparing different series and in combining a group of series in a single summary figure. Most indexes are designed to show changes in price, quantity, or value (price times quantity), either from time to time or from place to place.

A simple index or relative is constructed by dividing a single series by its base figure, and multiplying by 100.

Composite indexes should ordinarily be weighted arithmetic means of their components. A composite price or quantity index may be constructed by two methods: (1) In the weighted average of relatives method, the relatives are first computed for each series as described above, and then multiplied by value weights expressed as decimal fractions of the total weight. The sum of the weighted relatives is the composite index. (2) In the aggregative method, the changing prices are multiplied by fixed quantity weights (or vice versa for a quantity index). The resulting products are then totaled, divided by the product in the base period or place, and multiplied by 100. The weights usually represent the importance of a component in the base years or some other normal period. In a *value* index the dollar values of each component are simply added in the aggregative method, or else the components are expressed as relatives and multiplied by arbitrary weights before being totaled.

The aggregative method is the simpler of the two, but the average of relatives method is preferable when individual series are to be compared, when available weights are in value form, or when the component series are expressed as relatives.

The following tests of a good index should be applied in appraising the validity of an index for some specific use: (1) The purpose of the index should be clearly defined. (2) The items included must be specifically related to the purpose and must be a representative sample of the population being measured. (3) The base period should be a fairly normal one, adequate in length, easy to recall, and one used by comparable indexes. Trustworthy data and census bench marks should be available for this period. (4) Appropriate quantity weights should be used in an aggregative price index, and vice versa, or value weights in an average of relatives index. Weights must be held constant, but should be revised every decade or so as the importance of the components changes appreciably. The probable bias due to weighting should also be considered.

Items may be substituted for others in an index, as necessary, by proper "linking." An index number may be changed to a new base or spliced onto a similar series by multiplying or dividing by a constant factor, without changing the relative movements of the index in any way.

PROBLEMS

1. *a*) Briefly describe three broad types of index numbers that are used to measure changes in business and economics.

Ch. 15] INDEX NUMBERS 307

   b) In your opinion, what is the one most important use of (1) simple index numbers and (2) composite indexes? Give reasons for your choice in each case.
   c) Cite the principal limitations of index numbers.

2. *a*) Compute a composite index of grain prices for the data below by the average of relatives method, with 1958 = 100, using base-year weights.
   b) Compute a composite price index by the aggregative method, using the same base.
   c) Compare the merits of the two methods in this case.

| | Price (Dollars per Bushel) || Production (Billions of Bushels) ||
	Wheat	Corn	Wheat	Corn
1958	$2.21	$1.10	1.46	3.80
1959	2.24	1.03	1.13	4.36

   Note: Price is wholesale, December average, all grades; production is crop estimate as of December 31, 1959.
   Source: *Survey of Current Business*, February 1960, p. S-27.

3. Using the data in Problem 2, above:
   a) Compute a composite index of grain *production* by the average of relatives method, with 1958 = 100, using base-year weights.
   b) Compute a composite production index by the aggregative method, on the same base.
   c) Compute an index of the *value* of grain production, on the same base.

4. The Bureau of Business Research of the University of Texas formerly published a monthly *Index of Texas Business Activity* with the following description: "1947–49 average = 100. Components: Retail sales, industrial electric power consumption, miscellaneous freight carloadings, building authorized, crude petroleum production, ordinary life insurance sales, crude oil runs to stills, total electric power consumption (weighted 46.8, 14.6, 10.0, 9.4, 8.1, 4.2, 3.9, and 3.0, respectively, and adjusted seasonally)." Each component was expressed as an index with 1947–49 = 100 before being weighted. Apply our tests of a good index number to give an appraisal of this index, listing its good and bad points.

5. Index numbers are ordinarily based on samples, so that care must be exercised to insure that the items included in the index are typical of the population.
   a) Describe the population represented by (1) an index of prices received by farmers, (2) an index of industrial building costs, (3) an index of manufacturing production, and (4) an index of retail sales in urban areas, for the United States in each case.
   b) Samples used in index numbers are usually stratified. Why?
   c) Compare the advantages of random, systematic, and judgment sampling in selecting items for a price index representing a comprehensive list of women's apparel items.

6. In 1959 the Office of Statistical Standards, Bureau of the Budget, proposed to other federal agencies the adoption of the base period 1957–59 for general-purpose index numbers, to replace the base 1947–49 then in use. Appraise the merits and drawbacks of choosing the 1957–59 period, according to the six criteria given in this chapter for choice of a base period.

7. Present a critical analysis of a composite business or economic index of interest to you (other than the Bureau of Labor Statistics price indexes or the Federal Reserve Board Index of Industrial Production), describing its (*a*) purpose, (*b*) method of construction, and (*c*) limitations. See Richard M. Snyder, *Measuring Business Changes,* as a finding aid.

8. *a*) Convert the index of railway employment, below, to the 1947–49 average as base.
   b) Discuss employment trends in the railway industry, as compared with those in manufacturing during this period.
   c) If the only available railway industry figure for 1945 was 1,448 thousand employees, compared with 1,382 thousand in 1947, splice these figures onto your new index in order to compute an index for 1945.

Year	Railway Employment (1935–39 = 100)	Manufacturing Production-Worker Employment (1947–49 = 100)
1947	132.5	103.4
1948	130.0	102.8
1949	116.7	93.8
1951	125.0	106.2
1953	118.4	111.8
1955	103.7	105.6
1956	102.8	106.7

SOURCE: U.S. Department of Commerce, *Business Statistics,* 1957, p. 63.

9. Compute a single composite LIFO inventory price index for December 31, 1964, with December 31, 1963 = 100, covering the following products of the Lockard Co. (see pp. 317–18):

	Dec. 31, 1963 Unit Price	Dec. 31, 1964 Unit Price	Dec. 31, 1964 Inventory Value
Product A	$10	$12	$3,000
Product B	20	22	5,000
Product C	5	4	2,000

SELECTED READINGS

(See Chapter 16.)

16. SOME IMPORTANT INDEXES

THE NATURE of business data and the problems of locating them are discussed in Chapter 2. Specific sources of information are listed in Appendix A. Index number construction is discussed in Chapter 15. In this chapter there is a brief description of a few important index numbers, an annotated list of other widely used business indicators, and an explanation of some of their specific uses. As in the last chapter, the term "index" is used for a series of data expressed as a percentage of the figures for some base period, while "indicator" is a term more generally applied to series expressed in the original units as well as to index numbers.

The development of index numbers is one of the great contributions of business statistics in the last forty years. There are currently many more business indexes and indicators than can be treated here, and so only the most widely used measures can be discussed. Price indexes, quantity indexes, and value indicators will be presented in order. Each of these indicators is usually available in newspaper releases of the organization that prepares them, as well as in the *Survey of Current Business, Economic Indicators,* the *Monthly Labor Review,* the *Federal Reserve Bulletin,* and many other periodicals and newspapers. Nineteen commonly used indexes and their principal sources are listed in Table 15–1, page 285.

Statistical ingenuity has developed an almost encyclopedic list of uses of business indicators. The most important of these are: (1) measures of the economic well-being of the economy, a geographic area, an industry, or a specific business; (2) comparisons of related series for administrative purposes; (3) the use of price indexes as deflators to express a value series in constant dollars; (4) the use of price indexes as escalators in wage and other contracts; (5) specific guides or "triggers" for the initiation of administrative business or government actions; and (6) the basis or orientation for forecasting.

The construction, uses, and limitations of four major indexes or indicators are first discussed in some detail. These are the wholesale and consumer price indexes of the Bureau of Labor Statistics, the industrial production index of the Federal Reserve Board, and the national income and product estimates of the Department of Commerce.

WHOLESALE PRICE INDEX

The Wholesale Price Index of the U.S. Bureau of Labor Statistics is the oldest American index number of prices. Started in 1902, this index was calculated monthly back to 1900 and annually back to 1890, and has subsequently been linked to other comparable data to provide a continuous index series back to 1749. In successive eras the base period has been set at the ten-year average 1890–1900 and the monthly average of 1913, 1926, 1947–49, and, prospectively, 1957–59.

This index measures the average rate and direction of movements in commodity prices at primary-market levels—that is, at the point of the first commercial transaction for each commodity—and specific price changes for individual commodities or groups of commodities.[1] The prices used in the index are those representing all sales of goods by or to manufacturers or producers, or those in effect on organized commodity exchanges. It therefore represents producers' prices or primary-market prices rather than those charged by wholesalers.

Prices for approximately 1,900 separate specifications of commodities are included in the index. To obtain "real" or "pure" price changes not influenced by changes in quality, quantity, terms of sale, etc., identical lists of commodities defined by precise specifications are priced from month to month. Prices are obtained from some 2,000 companies who are asked to quote the prices they actually charge for a specific commodity to a given type of buyer on a particular day, usually Tuesday of the week including the fifteenth of the month. Some quotations from trade journals and market reports are also used. Prices for each specification are obtained whenever possible from three reporters on a confidential basis.

Because the commodity population is so large, the index is based on a sample of commodities, a sample of specifications for the commodities, and a sample of reporting sources. The individual items are selected as the most important in each field and as those believed to rep-

---

[1] See U.S. Department of Labor, *Wholesale Prices and Price Indexes, 1958*, Bulletin No. 1257, 1959, pp. 4–18.

resent the price movements of other closely related commodities. The sample is thus a highly stratified, selected group, rather than a random sample. The broad coverage of 1,900 items permits the development of reliable subindexes for many small subdivisions of the economy.

The index is calculated fundamentally as a weighted average of

Chart 16–1

WHOLESALE PRICES

MONTHLY, 1947–49 = 100

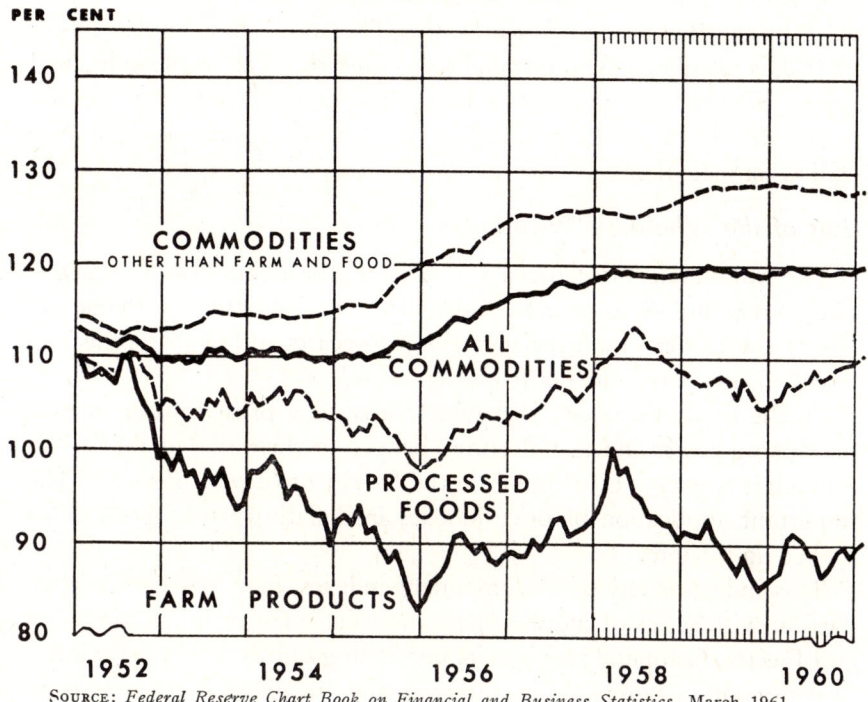

SOURCE: *Federal Reserve Chart Book on Financial and Business Statistics*, March 1961.

price relatives in which the weights are based on net sales values of commodities reported by the Census of Manufactures, the Census of Mineral Industries, and other sources for 1954. Each item has a weight which includes its own weight based on its sales in 1954 and the weight of the other items it represents in the index. The weights will be revised to reflect the relative importance of commodities in the 1958 industrial censuses, as well as in later censuses scheduled at five-year intervals.

The over-all index is divided into the broad categories of industrial commodities, and farm and food products, as shown in Chart 16–1. Special wholesale price indexes are reported by stage of processing and by durability of product. In addition, separate indexes are published each month for 15 major groups, 86 subgroups, about 250 product classes, and for most of the individual series.

The Bureau of Labor Statistics also prepares a Weekly Wholesale Price Index based on actual weekly prices of a sample of about 200 of the commodities included in the monthly index and on estimates of the prices of the other commodities. This index may be used to give interim estimates of the monthly index.

A Daily Index Number of Spot Primary Market Prices is also provided by the Bureau of Labor Statistics. This index, based on 1947–49 = 100, is calculated as an unweighted geometric mean of the individual price ratios for 22 commodities. It is not related in content or method to the weekly or monthly wholesale price indexes and should not be used to estimate them.

Uses of the Wholesale Price Index

The Wholesale Price Index is one of the basic business barometers used to measure the economic health of the nation. It is also frequently one of the factors employed in making forecasts, although forecasts of prices in any form are far from dependable.

Furthermore, the index is regularly used as a price deflator or as a purchasing-power index, reflecting changes in the value of the dollar. As such it is quoted each month in the *Survey of Current Business*. The important application of price indexes in deflating value series is described in Chapter 17.

This index, or any of its component indexes, may be used for comparison with series of individual business data. For example, the General Electric Company provides its purchasing offices with a price index of commodities purchased by the company, weighted by their importance to the company, and compares this with the BLS wholesale price index for industrial commodities.[2] A processed-food wholesaler keeps a monthly chart showing the wholesale price group index for processed foods and an index, on the same base, of his own company's purchase prices, to see whether his prices are moving like the average of those reported by the Bureau of Labor Statistics. Many manufacturers who purchase metal or metal products make similar comparisons as a regular procedure.

One of the most frequent uses of the Wholesale Price Index is as an escalator—that is, as the basis for adjusting contractual payments or

---

[2] C. Willard Bryant, "Planning to Meet Materials Shortages," *Purchasing*, August 1953, pp. 81–83.

values for changes in the value of the dollar. Long-term supply and production contracts include escalator clauses as guarantees against losses due to increases in the prices of materials and other costs. Rentals on long-term leases are also often adjusted by this index.

There are limitations to the wholesale price indexes which must be kept in mind when using them. (1) The indexes are based on quotations or prices that suppliers say they charge. They are not therefore necessarily the actual prices that purchasers pay. (2) They are not wholesalers' prices. (3) They relate to national coverage and hence should be used with caution in interpreting local or regional data. (4) Since they relate to changes of a given specification, they cannot be used with retail price indexes to calculate margins. (5) The index does not include any of the services, such as rent, transportation, or communications.

CONSUMER PRICE INDEX

The Consumer Price Index of the U.S. Bureau of Labor Statistics was known as the Cost of Living Index prior to 1946 and was called the Consumers' Price Index from 1946 to 1952. It is a "statistical measure of changes in prices of the goods and services bought by families of city wage earners and clerical workers." Published for the first time in 1918, the index was calculated quarterly back to 1913 and thereafter until early in World War II, when publication was initiated on a monthly basis.

Prior to the 1953 revision the index was expressed as a relative of the five-year 1935–39 average. The base was then shifted to 1947–49, and is planned to be expressed in terms of 1957–59 = 100 beginning about 1962.

The prices collected for this index are retail prices charged to consumers for "foods, clothing, house furnishings, fuel and other goods; the fees paid to doctors and dentists; prices in barber shops and other service establishments; rents; rates charged for transportation, electricity, gas and other utilities; and so on."[3] Sales and excise taxes are included in these prices. The goods and services represented are those included in the "market basket" of urban wage-earner and clerical-worker families of two or more persons living in towns, cities, and suburbs in the United States in 1950, adjusted to changes in 1952. These families represented about 64 per cent of the people living in urban places and about 40 per cent of the total United States population in

---

[3] See U.S. Department of Labor, *The Consumer Price Index,* Bulletin 1140, 1953; and *Monthly Labor Review,* September 1959, pp. 967 f. for further details.

314   BUSINESS AND ECONOMIC STATISTICS   [Ch. 16

1950. The index is designed to measure only changes in prices of the same market basket from time to time, not to measure changes in different market baskets or changes in consumers' standards of living.

Prices of about 300 items, "which together can be used to estimate the average change in prices of all items in the 'market basket,'" are collected from representative independent and chain stores and from

Chart 16–2

CONSUMER PRICES

1947–49 = 100

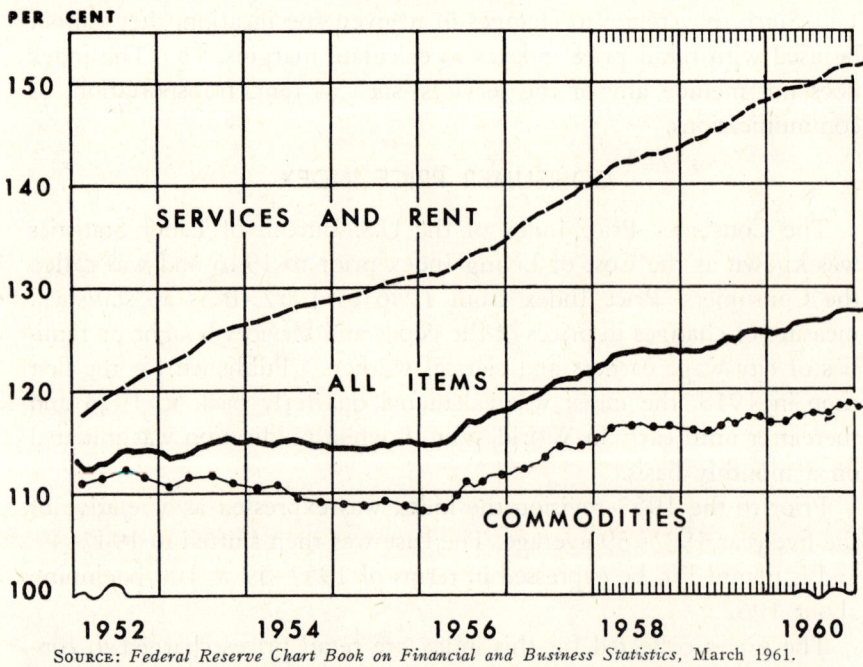

SOURCE: *Federal Reserve Chart Book on Financial and Business Statistics,* March 1961.

department and specialty stores patronized by wage and salary workers. Rents are collected from renting families. Prices are collected regularly in 46 cities, including the 12 largest in the United States, 9 other large cities, 9 medium-sized cities, and 16 small cities. Depending upon the difficulty of obtaining accurate information, prices are collected by trained representatives of the Bureau, or by mail with periodical personal checks.

For each of the 30 larger cities and for all of the 16 small cities combined, the percentage price change is calculated for each price collection period. This price percentage is multiplied by the expenditure weight of an item in the previous period to obtain the new expenditure weight. These are totaled to obtain a group expenditure weight for each of eight groups, which are summed to give the "All Items" total for the particular city or group of small cities. These totals are expressed as relatives of the previous period aggregates to obtain the group and "All Items" indexes. The indexes for each city and small city group are then combined by giving each a weight proportionate to the wage-earner and clerical-worker population it represents in the index. Chart 16–2 shows the changes in the index and its two major components from 1952 to 1960.

The Bureau of Labor Statistics is engaged in a five-year project to revise its Consumer Price Index. The number of items priced will be increased by 20 per cent. Consumer expenditure surveys will be conducted in about 66 cities during 1961 and 1962 to provide new weights for the component prices. Publication of the revised index, based on prices in about 50 cities, is planned for January 1964. Periodic revisions of indexes generally are necessary to reflect the rapidly changing technology and consumption patterns of American life.

Uses of the Consumer Price Index

The original Cost of Living Index was established at the close of World War I to aid in the adjustment of shipbuilders' wage rates. Since that time the index has served continuously as a deflator of money wages, as well as to evaluate the level of real wages, and has been used by labor and management frequently in the settlement of wage disputes. During World War II in particular, the index was established as a criterion by the National Labor Relations Board for allowable wage increases in the "Little Steel" case. Since that time the index has become an increasingly important aid to unions and management in adjusting wages to take account of changes in consumer prices.

The most important subsequent impetus to the use of the index for this purpose was its designation as a basis of wage-rate escalation in the contract signed by the United Automobile Workers and the General Motors Corporation in May 1948. This agreement, and its extension in 1950 for five years, provided for a quarterly adjustment of wage rates of 1 cent per hour for every change of 1.14 points in the Consumers' Price Index, 1935–39 = 100. In 1953, when the index was revised and shifted to a 1947–49 base, the escalator was changed to provide for a quarterly adjustment of 1 cent per hour for each .6 points in the new Consumer Price Index. Later agreements in the automobile industry followed a similar pattern. The Ford Motor Company agreement of September 1958, for example, provided for a 1-cent adjustment of hourly base pay for each .5 points in the index above 119.1, beginning with 1 cent for the index level of 119.2–119.6 (it was then 123.7), but no reduction in wages if the index dropped to 119.1 or below.

After each of these major agreements, many other contracts were signed on the same basis, frequently without any examination of the reasonableness of the relationship of wage-rate changes to index changes in each particular situation, or without full realization of the effects of arbitrarily accepting a ratio based on some other firm's or union's experience.

In some cases, other types of escalator relationships are used in an effort to maintain the basic wage-rate relationships more effectively. One such procedure provides for a quarterly adjustment of 1 per cent in wage rates for each 1 per cent change in the Consumer Price Index, both calculated from an agreed base date, as follows:

> Wage rates shall be adjusted automatically to the cost of living in the following manner: The basis shall be the quarterly cost of living index in (_date_), issued by the Bureau of Labor Statistics. Effective at pay period following publication of the index, wage rates shall be increased or decreased by the same percentage as the index has changed from quarter to quarter.

Whatever the type of escalator employed, however, it is important to both sides in a bargaining group that the procedure be adjusted to each particular situation.

The Consumer Price Index is also used as an economic indicator for many purposes in the same way as the Wholesale Price Index. It serves, for instance, to measure the purchasing power of the consumer's dollar, and as such is published monthly in the *Survey of Current Business*. In the words of the congressional Joint Committee on the Economic Report:[4]

> The value of the Index for certain uses is greatly enhanced if it is used as one among several measures rather than alone. For some problems it should be used as a first approximation to the truth, to be corrected by knowledge of the particular situation. A thermometer reading is useful to the physician if used in conjunction with other indicators of the health of the patient and as a guide to further diagnosis.

The Consumer Price Index also has limitations which should be carefully considered: (1) It measures changes only in a fixed bill of goods and services, but not changes in the standard or manner of living. (2) In wartime conditions of material shortages, it fails to reflect the full inflationary effect of black-market prices, quality deterioration,

---

[4] Staff of the Joint Committee on the Economic Report, *The Consumers' Price Index* (Washington, D.C.: U.S. Government Printing Office, 1949), p. 16.

and substitution of more expensive grades for cheaper grades of products. On the other hand, in peacetime the index does not always reflect gains due to gradual quality improvement. (3) While it measures changes in consumer prices from time to time, it cannot be used to compare prices between different places at a single point in time. Geographic differences may be measured by comparing the individual prices compiled for the Consumer Price Index (but not the index itself), or by referring to the Bureau of Labor Statistics "City Worker's Family Budget" (*Monthly Labor Review,* August 1960), which expresses prices in various cities in relation to the price level in Washington, D.C., as 100 per cent. (4) The index measures changes in prices only for the worker group in urban areas. It should not be used without modification for other income groups or for families living in rural areas. (5) Since the index represents an average family's consumption pattern, it may not represent the experience of any specific family or individual.

Inventory Price Indexes

A special product of the collection of prices for the Consumer Price Index by the Bureau of Labor Statistics is its *Department Store Inventory Price Indexes,* issued semiannually. These indexes, by agreement with the Bureau of Internal Revenue, may be used in the evaluation of inventories by department stores which use the last-in first-out (LIFO) method in calculating their federal income taxes. Companies other than department stores may compute their own price indexes for this purpose.

The LIFO method of valuing inventories has become popular in recent years[5] because it smooths out fluctuations in profits over the business cycle and reduces income taxes in time of inflation. Also, the U.S. Tax Court now permits the reporting of dollar values by departments of a company (rather than requiring the physical identification of individual items), and permits the use of index numbers to relate values in the opening and closing inventories.[6] The use of an index greatly simplifies the problem of pricing a complex inventory by the LIFO method.

A LIFO price index may be constructed by dividing the inventory into small uniform groups and selecting a sample of items in each

---

[5] American Institute of Accountants, *Accounting Trends and Techniques* (annual) shows the proportion of companies in each industry using LIFO.

[6] Hutzler Brothers case (8 TC 14), Edgar A. Basse (10 TC 328), and Treasury Decisions 5605 (March 4, 1948) and 5756 (November 2, 1949).

group. At the close of the fiscal year the price of each item is expressed as a relative of its beginning price as 100, and these relatives are weighted by the ending inventory value of all closely related items to arrive at a composite price index for each department of the company. This is a weighted average of relatives applied to a stratified sample of inventory items.[7]

The ending inventory at beginning prices is itself used as the LIFO closing inventory provided it is *less* than the beginning inventory. If it is *greater,* the difference is multiplied by the index and the product is added to the actual opening inventory to secure the LIFO closing inventory.[8]

INDUSTRIAL PRODUCTION INDEX

The Federal Reserve Board's Monthly Index of Industrial Production is one of the most widely used of the country's economic indicators. It measures changes in the physical volume of output of factories, mines, and utilities from 1919 to date. Major revisions and improvements of this index were completed in 1953 and 1959.[9] The latter project was facilitated by making use of electronic processing and charting machines, particularly in the revision of seasonal indexes.

The industrial production index includes 207 series expressed in physical terms—units, tons, yards, board feet, and the like—reflecting the production of American industries or data which represent such series. Electric and gas utility output was added to the index in the 1959 revision. Where physical output data are lacking, other series which are believed to fluctuate in the same way as output data are substituted. Such series include volume of shipments, production worker man-hours, materials consumed in production, etc. About 49 per cent of the weight of the monthly index is represented by man-hour data adjusted for estimated changes in output per man-hour. The balance is based on production and shipments data, and miscellaneous measures. The basic series are compiled by various organizations for other purposes and are adapted for the production index.

The component series of the index are combined with weights based on value added by manufacture in 1957 mainly as shown by the annual Census survey and the Census of Manufactures for 1954. The

---

[7] William A. Spurr, "Price Index for Lifo Inventory Valuation," in *Standard Handbook for Accountants* (New York: McGraw-Hill Book Co., Inc., 1956), pp. 9·212–9.

[8] J. Keith Butters, *Effects of Taxation—Inventory Accounting and Policies* (Boston: Harvard Graduate School of Business Administration, 1949).

[9] Federal Reserve Board, *Industrial Production: 1959 Revision,* 1960, or *Federal Reserve Bulletin,* "Revised Industrial Production Index," December 1959, pp. 1451–74.

composite index is calculated as a weighted average of relatives. It is expressed both in terms of 1957 as base and the 1947–49 average as base for comparability with other index numbers, pending adoption of a new base by federal agencies generally. The index is published for four broad classifications having the following relative importance in 1957: durable manufactures, 50%; nondurable manufactures, 37%; mining, 8%; and utilities, 5%. In the 1959 revision, a separate classification was made between the output of consumer goods, output of equipment (including ordnance) for business and government use, and materials. Indexes are also reported for some 25 major industrial groups, following the latest Standard Industrial Classification of the U.S. Bureau of the Budget, and for some 175 subgroups. This great number of industry series permits flexible grouping for most desired comparisons.

With the 1953 revision of the industrial production index the Federal Reserve Board for the first time provided an independent annual index based on many more actual production series than the monthly index. Also expressed in terms of its 1947–49 average, this annual index provides a useful bench mark to correct the level of the monthly indexes each year.

Uses of the Industrial Production Index

The major use of the Index of Industrial Production is as an indicator of the economy's output. It is the most sensitive and reliable indicator we have to answer the question: "Is production increasing or decreasing?" and "In which industries are major increases or decreases occurring?" Chart 16–3 shows the sensitivity of its movements in describing the pattern of business cycles from 1952 to 1960. The index is widely used in conjunction with other series for both forecasting and guidance in administrative decisions. For example, it is compared with figures on unemployment to obtain estimates of the country's total number of unemployed workers that may be associated with different levels of production. It is also compared with data on inventories and prices.

The detailed industry indexes serve as very useful comparisons or bench marks in studying the production of individual companies. The individual indexes are also useful in comparing growth rates in different sectors of the economy. For example, from the first half of 1947 to the first half of 1959, the production of all consumer goods expanded 58 per cent, but the output of air conditioners, television sets, clothes driers, and boats each increased over 400 per cent, while the output of home radios decreased 68 per cent.

320 BUSINESS AND ECONOMIC STATISTICS [Ch. 16

One limitation of the industrial production index is its restriction to manufacturing, mining, and utilities, which keeps it from serving as a measure of total production. Agriculture, construction, transportation, communication, and other services are not included. Another limitation is that changes in man-hours and other indirect measures of industrial

Chart 16-3

INDUSTRIAL PRODUCTION

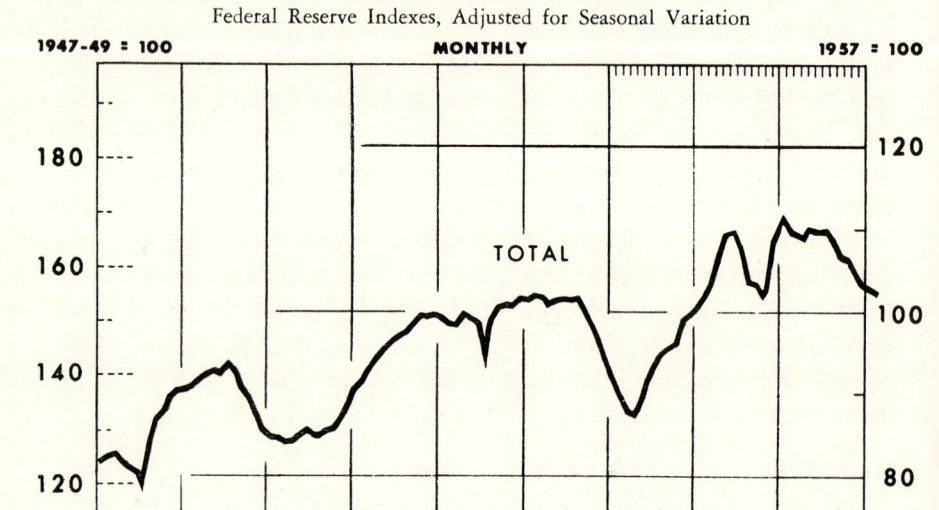

Federal Reserve Indexes, Adjusted for Seasonal Variation

SOURCE: *Federal Reserve Chart Book on Financial and Business Statistics,* March 1961.

activity sometimes do not reflect accurately the changes in physical volume of production, particularly in times of war and postwar reconversion.

NATIONAL INCOME AND PRODUCT

The statistical indexes so far discussed in this chapter are business indicators in the sense that they point the direction of business activity. They measure changes only in specific areas of the economy—i.e., prices or production. Estimates of national income and product are the broadest and most general indicators of changes in business and economic activity that have been constructed. These estimates were first developed by the National Bureau of Economic Research, and have been compiled and reported by the U.S. Department of Commerce since 1929.[10]

---

[10] See U.S. Department of Commerce, *U.S. Income and Output,* 1958, and the *National Income Number* of the *Survey of Current Business,* published in July each year, for data and detailed description.

National income and national product represent a summary of the receipts and expenditures of all governments, businesses, and individuals in the economy. An accounting framework is therefore basic to an understanding of this concept. National income is the sum of the money incomes accruing to all the factors of production, including labor, land, capital, and enterprise generally. The estimates include the following specific types of income: (1) compensation of employees, (2) proprietors' income, (3) rental income, (4) net interest, and (5) corporate profits. Since national income is in terms of dollars, it excludes the value of work done and not paid for. The value of a housewife's work in the home, for instance, or that of her husband in repairing the home is not included. On the other hand, the value of output consumed on farms, because of its magnitude, is included.

Gross national product, or GNP, represents the expenditure side of the accounts of all individuals, businesses, and governments in the nation. It is the total national output of goods and services at current prices, as measured by the expenditures made to acquire them. Estimates of national product include the following specific types of expenditures: (1) personal consumption expenditures, (2) gross private domestic investment, (3) net foreign investment, and (4) government purchases of goods and services.

National income and national product are the results of complicated estimating procedures and depend upon a wide variety of data supplied by various government agencies. The definitions, data, and procedures are described in detail in the 1954 *National Income* supplement to the *Survey of Current Business* and the *U.S. Income and Output* supplement, published in 1958. Current data appear in the *National Income Number* of the *Survey of Current Business*, published in July each year. National income and product are reported in billions of dollars at annual rates on a quarterly and yearly basis. Personal income, an important component of national income, is reported monthly for the nation and annually by states.

Gross national product and its major components are also estimated each quarter on a "real" or "constant-dollar" basis, in order to reflect the approximate changes in physical volume of output, without the influence of prices. Real GNP is expressed in dollars of 1954 purchasing power, but the figures can easily be shifted to current dollars by multiplying through by the ratio of the current price index (called "implicit price deflator" in the *Survey of Current Business*) divided by the 1954 index, which is 100. Chart 16–4 shows the quarterly fluctuations of gross national product since 1952 both in current dollars and in 1954 dollars.

Chart 16-4
GROSS NATIONAL PRODUCT
DEPARTMENT OF COMMERCE ESTIMATES, ADJUSTED FOR SEASONAL VARIATION

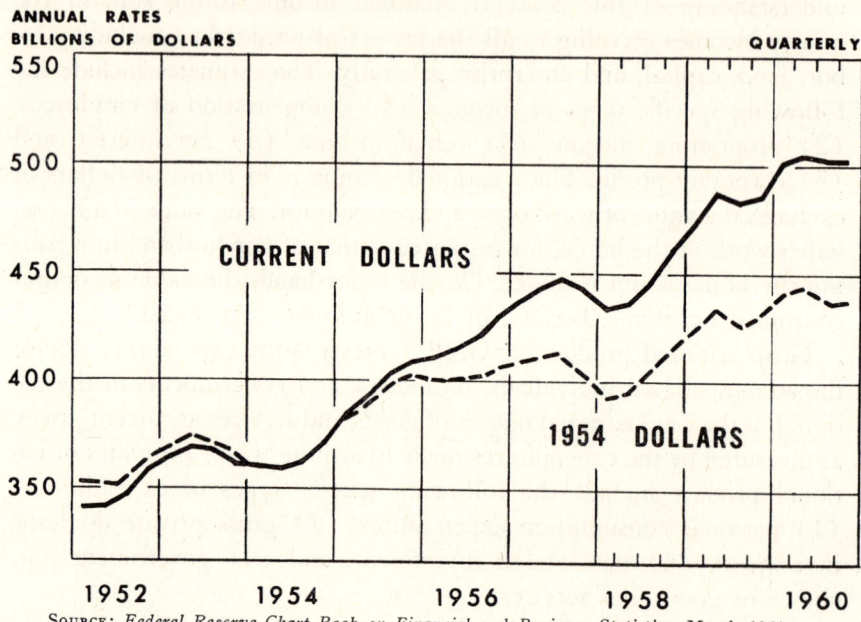

SOURCE: *Federal Reserve Chart Book on Financial and Business Statistics,* March 1961.

Uses of National Income and Product Estimates

The major value of both of these series is in their use as indicators of the income or expenditures related to current output. They provide independent estimates as checks on the national rate of production activity. More important probably is the analysis of components of these series and the study of their interrelationships with other indicators in appraising the economic activity of various sectors of the national economy. Specifically, it may be important from the merchandising point of view to know whether income of employees is rising more or less than corporate profits or to know how the income of a particular trade group compares with personal consumption expenditures.

There is not room here to describe in detail the various classifications of national income and national product data which are important to the study of economics and the interpretation of business activity. An examination of the business press will indicate how greatly business and economic analysts depend for current interpretation and forecasting upon the measurements of personal income, disposable personal income, income by industrial origin, income by distributive shares, consumer expenditures, and capital investment. All these measurements are closely related to and are products of the national income and national product estimates.

These two series share the serious limitation of complexity. The figures are large, the concepts are broad, and the estimates are necessarily rough in certain categories. Also, these are value indicators, in which it is difficult to separate the influence of price changes from those in physical volume. The major caution is to understand the definitions of the several components if appropriate use is to be made of the data.

OTHER NATIONAL INDEXES AND THEIR USES

Every economist, business analyst, or editor who regularly prepares interpretations of business activity develops combinations of business indicators which seem best to fit his particular needs. The variety of the component series in the lists of different analysts has been clearly shown by a number of polls on the subject conducted by statistical agencies and business publications.

In addition to the indicators detailed above, therefore, the nature and uses of ten other important national indexes are outlined briefly in the following section.[11] This will be followed by a brief reference to regional indexes. Note also the list of 19 important indexes and their sources on page 285, and the classification of 21 indicators by their leads and lags at business cycle turning points, on page 420.

Prices Paid and Received by Farmers, and Parity Ratio

U.S. Department of Agriculture, Agricultural Marketing Service. Indexes of the prices farmers pay and receive and their ratio are among the most important economic indicators in the United States. For a quarter of a century agricultural price policy has been closely related to them. Each year as new agricultural programs are discussed these indexes are subjected to careful scrutiny for the part they may play.

The Index of Prices Paid by Farmers, also called the Parity Index, and the prices which go into it are used in determining support prices for agricultural commodities. The ratio which results from dividing the Index of Prices Received by the Index of Prices Paid is known as the *Parity Ratio*. It is used to indicate changes in the economic well-being of farmers.

In addition to their use in establishing agricultural support prices, the indexes of prices paid and prices received by farmers frequently

---

[11] Summary descriptions of 2,600 series may be found in the footnote references of the biennial *Business Statistics* supplement to the *Survey of Current Business*.

serve as escalators, as in federal government contracts to buy sugar from Cuba during World War II, and as "triggers" for starting specific kinds of programs under federal legislation.

Construction Cost Indexes

U.S. Department of Commerce, E. H. Boeckh and Associates, Engineering News Record. Construction cost indexes are useful both as guides to the cost of new building construction and in appraising property for tax or financial purposes. The various index numbers of this type should be carefully examined in terms of the purposes for which they are to be used, for they differ in content. For instance, the *Engineering News Record* indexes are reported separately for building and construction. The Boeckh indexes are classified by type of building as well as geographic location. Since World War II, tax assessors have faced the demand for more objective methods of appraisal for tax purposes. When this need arises and it is desirable to express property values in terms of some base-period dollar, index numbers are essential. The Boeckh indexes have been widely used by tax assessors for this purpose.

Stock Price Indexes

Standard and Poor's Corporation Composite Index of 500 Stocks. Stock price indicators have become extremely important in the last forty years. They represent not only the general trend of security values but also the state of business confidence. Furthermore, stock price indexes serve as a barometer of future changes in general business activity. Finally, they are used as "triggers" in some investment systems, of which the "Dow Theory" is best known. That is, as certain predetermined levels of the Dow-Jones averages are reached, investors using such systems buy or sell common stocks. Standard and Poor's Corporation publishes the most complete index of common stock prices, together with indexes for numerous industry subgroups. Compiled hourly by electronic computer, it appears almost immediately on ticker tapes of brokerage houses throughout the country.

Indexes of Manufacturing Production-Worker Employment and Payrolls

U.S. Department of Labor, Bureau of Labor Statistics. These two monthly indexes are important measures of workers' welfare. It is desirable to study both indexes simultaneously, because employment may stay level or even increase while payrolls decline, if overtime is eliminated or if some workers are put on a part-time basis. The Bureau of Labor Statistics also publishes monthly figures on average weekly hours per worker, production-worker man-hours (i.e., employment times average weekly hours), average weekly earnings per worker, and average hourly earnings. The Department of Commerce publishes the Bureau of Labor Statistics indexes of employment adjusted for seasonal variation for better month-to-month comparisons.

Accurate interpretation of such figures can be very important to economists in appraising the general economic situation. Business analysts can also use these data by industry classification for comparison with their own company experience.

Monthly Report of the Labor Force

U.S. Department of Commerce, Bureau of the Census. Monthly estimates of the number of people in the total labor force and the civilian labor force (excluding the armed services) in the United States are important in appraising the significance of total employment and unemployment. For instance, in August 1953, unemployment dropped to 1,240,000, or 1.9 per cent of the civilian labor force of 64,931,000. In February 1961, on the other hand, unemployment reached 5,705,000, or 8.1 per cent of the labor force of 70,360,000. At the start of the depression in the 1930's, dependable data on the amount of unemployment did not exist. Unsuccessful attempts to estimate unemployment from employment data only emphasized the need for labor-force data.

Labor-force information is useful to employment offices in gauging the size of the labor supply, classified by age and sex. Total unemployment serves as a "trigger" figure in initiating government work projects.

Railway Freight Carloadings

Association of American Railroads. Railway freight carloadings provide a broad measure of transportation activity. The weekly reports are watched closely by business analysts to discern changes in traffic volume by major commodity groups as well as by local industrial areas. The long-term trend, however, is dampened by the gradual increase in traffic taken by competing forms of transportation and by the increasing capacity of the freight car itself. The merchandise and miscellaneous categories of the carloadings series are frequently used as measures of manufacturing distribution to avoid the erratic influences of farm and mine shipments.

Steel Ingot Production

American Iron and Steel Institute. Production of steel ingots is a basic business indicator which is very sensitive to changes in the activity of heavy industry. Indicators of steel ingot production are published weekly both in short tons and as index numbers on a 1957–59 base. Regional figures on production and operating rates are also published for major steel-mill areas.

Sales, Inventories, New Orders, and Unfilled Orders

U.S. Department of Commerce, Office of Business Economics. Each month the Department of Commerce issues figures on the estimated value of manufacturers', wholesalers', and retailers' sales and inventories, as well as new and unfilled orders by major manufacturing groups. These data have become widely used in recent years as measures of an important component of the economy. They serve the useful purpose of indicating whether new orders are keeping up with sales or whether inventories are gaining on sales. It should be clear, for instance, that if inventories increase more than sales for a substantial period, eventually shelves will be overstocked and production must slow down.

Construction Contracts—Number, Floor Area, and Value

F. W. Dodge Corporation. These monthly estimates of construction contracts awarded give an early indication of the direction of construction activity. The construction industry has a vital effect on the economy both because of its vast size and because of the magnitude of its fluctuations. In January 1956 the indexes were revised, and coverage was expanded from 37 states to 48 states. The data are classified (1) by regions, (2) according to public and private building, and (3) by the nature of the building—residential, nonresidential, public works, and utilities. The Census Bureau's estimates of the value of new construction activity and the number of private nonfarm dwelling units started are also invaluable in the analysis of this industry.

Business Failures—Number and Liabilities

Dun & Bradstreet, Inc. The number of business failures is a sensitive indicator of business health, and the dollar value of the liabilities reflects the size of the failures. These monthly series are used by business analysts as barometers of general business recovery and decline. An increase in the number indicates distress, while a decline indicates a business strengthening. For this reason these series are frequently inverted when they are shown with other business indicators.

The historical record of business failures by industry groups and by regions is useful to the businessman who intends entering a particular enterprise. An examination of the reasons for failure should provide a significant guide, especially for the smaller business.

REGIONAL BUSINESS INDEXES

Regional business indexes are published for many areas of the United States. For some areas, comprehensive collections of economic indicators are maintained by banks, bureaus of business research in universities, and other research agencies. In particular, each of the twelve Federal Reserve banks compiles a variety of indicators for its region and publishes a monthly bulletin dealing with regional business activity. University bureaus of business research also compile many kinds of local indicators of business activity—both individual series and composite indexes. Many regional indexes are constructed from bank debits, department store sales, and other retail sales data; so they serve as indicators of changes in consumer spending and in the dollar value of trade rather than in the physical volume of production.

The most comprehensive measures of regional business activity on a comparable basis are the Department of Commerce yearly data on personal income by states, published in the August issue of *Survey of Current Business*. These figures are estimated monthly by *Business Week*.[12]

SUMMARY

A knowledge and understanding of current index numbers is essential in business and economic analysis. This chapter describes the construction, uses, and limitations of four major business indexes, as currently revised, together with briefer sketches of twelve other national and regional indicators.

The wholesale and consumer price indexes of the Bureau of Labor Statistics represent broad samples of prices at the primary market and retail levels, respectively. They are widely used as economic indicators, as deflators of value series, and as escalators in contracts. The proper use of the Consumer Price Index in wage contracts is particularly important. LIFO price indexes are also coming into use for inventory valuation.

The Federal Reserve Monthly Index of Industrial Production is an important and sensitive measure of general industrial activity. It represents the physical volume of production, shipments, or man-hours in the manufacturing, mining, and utility industries.

The national income and product estimates of the Department of

---

[12] See U.S. Department of Commerce, *Personal Income by States Since 1929* (1956); and *Business Week* for March 30, 1959.

Commerce provide an elaborate national accounting of income and expenditures for all goods and services. These estimates are expressed in billions of dollars, in contrast to the price and production indexes mentioned above, which are expressed as index numbers. All of these indicators are broken down into numerous component parts for better comparability in specific situations.

The practical uses of a number of other national and regional indicators are cited to illustrate the value of understanding these statistical aids in interpreting the business scene.

PROBLEMS

1. If you were the economist of a national chain of drugstores and wished to compare the prices you pay with the Bureau of Labor Statistics Wholesale Price Index:
   a) Which subgroups of this index would you combine to meet your needs?
   b) What method, arithmetically, would you employ to combine them?

2. *a*) Why is the Bureau of Labor Statistics Wholesale Price Index, excluding farm products and foods, frequently used in place of the All Commodities Index as a measure of general price changes?
   b) How would you expect an index of wages and salaries in manufacturing to differ in its fluctuations from the index of manufacturing production?

3. Is the following procedure appropriate? If not, suggest improvements. In order to allow for changes in the cost of living, a wage contract is set up by the Ajax Machine Tool Company of Houston, Texas, providing that machine tool workers' wages will be adjusted upward or downward each month by 1 cent per hour for each one-point change in the Wholesale Price Index.

4. Find an article in *Monthly Labor Review* or elsewhere reporting on the Bureau of Labor Statistics' five-year program of revising the Consumer Price Index during fiscal 1960–64. Describe the principal steps in this program and explain how the resulting improvements justify the considerable expense involved.

5. Explain the differences in the effect of the following escalators on the wage-rate structure of a grocery chain:
   a) A *1-cent* change quarterly in wage rates at all levels for each .5-point change in a consumer price index above, but not below, the current level of 125.
   b) A *1 per cent* change quarterly in all wage rates for each successive change of 1 per cent in the same price index above, but not below, the 125 level.

6. What subindex or group of subindexes of the Federal Reserve Monthly Index of Industrial Production is appropriate for comparisons with the physical volume of production of:

a) A large integrated oil company?
b) A manufacturer of home laundry and kitchen appliances?
c) A household furniture factory?

7. Explain the change in gross national product, in the latest quarter available, that is attributable to each of its four principal expenditure components.

8. Considering the economic characteristics of your own state or area:
    a) List four business indicators that are most significant for this state, giving exact sources.
    b) Describe and appraise a general business index published for this state, other than those cited in this chapter.

SELECTED READINGS

FEDERAL RESERVE BOARD. *Industrial Production: 1959 Revision.* Washington, D.C.: Board of Governors of the Federal Reserve System, 1960.
    An authoritative discussion of principles and methods of constructing a quantity index.

JOINT ECONOMIC COMMITTEE, U.S. CONGRESS. *1960 Supplement to Economic Indicators.* Washington, D.C.: U.S. Government Printing Office, 1960.
    Contains brief descriptions of the series regularly included in *Economic Indicators* and describes uses and limitations of each.

MOORE, GEOFFREY H. (ed.). *Business Cycle Indicators.* New York: National Bureau of Economic Research, Inc., 1961, 2 vols.
    Twenty articles and basic data assessing the principal indicators of short-term business fluctuations in the United States and Canada.

NATIONAL BUREAU OF ECONOMIC RESEARCH. *The National Economic Accounts of the United States.* New York, 1958.
    A "Review, Appraisal and Recommendations" for improvement; presented before the congressional Joint Economic Committee.

SNYDER, RICHARD M. *Measuring Business Changes.* New York: John Wiley & Sons, Inc., 1955.
    A comprehensive analysis and description of American business indicators.

U.S. DEPARTMENT OF AGRICULTURE. *Major Statistical Series of the U.S. Department of Agriculture.* Agriculture Handbook No. 118. Washington, D.C.: U.S. Government Printing Office, 1958.
    Nine volumes covering farm prices, production, income, marketing costs, product utilization, land values, population, crop and livestock estimates, and co-operatives.

U.S. DEPARTMENT OF COMMERCE. *Business Statistics,* biennial supplement to the *Survey of Current Business.* Washington, D.C.: U.S. Government Printing Office, 1959, *et seq.*
    The "Explanatory Notes to the Statistical Series," referred to in the footnotes of the tables, cover 2,600 monthly or quarterly series, as of 1959.

U.S. DEPARTMENT OF COMMERCE. *U.S. Income and Output,* a supplement to the *Survey of Current Business.* Washington, D.C.: U.S. Government Printing Office, 1958.

A detailed discussion and tabulation of national income and product estimates.

U.S. DEPARTMENT OF LABOR. *Techniques of Preparing Major BLS Statistical Series.* Bulletin 1168. Washington, D.C.: U.S. Government Printing Office, 1954.

Contains description of data collection and methods of preparing all of the major Bureau of Labor Statistics series. The Bureau's *BLS Statistical Series —A Summary of Characteristics,* 1958, provides a more recent outline of 18 series.

See also Appendix A: "Selected Sources of Business Statistics."

17. ANALYSIS OF BUSINESS FLUCTUATIONS

MODERN business and economic affairs are intensely dynamic in nature. "The old order changeth," sometimes with bewildering rapidity, and the analyst must be alert to interpret the significance of the passing scene. The changes are of many types. The long-term growth of industrial production, the residential building cycle, seasonal swings in department store sales, the daily movements of stock prices, and countless other elements in the dynamics of enterprise must be measured and appraised as an aid in understanding the experience of the past and in formulating future policy. The importance of dynamic fluctuations, as opposed to static analysis, is reflected by the fact that the great bulk of data in business and economic publications (e.g., *Survey of Current Business, Economic Indicators*) is in the form of time series rather than being primarily classified by size, space, or other qualitative criteria at a given point of time.

TYPES OF BUSINESS FLUCTUATIONS

It is not sufficient for a businessman to observe merely the over-all behavior of an economic indicator. There are various factors at work, the combined effect of which produced this result. Suppose a company's sales increased 6 per cent over last month. Was this increase attributable to normal growth, a cyclical business boom, a pickup in seasonal demand, or an advertising campaign? What action should be taken as a result? Analysis of the data involves segregation of these factors so that their separate importance can be understood. The first necessity, then, is to know what factors are present in a time series. Next, how can the effect of each force be measured? Finally, how can it be predicted,

Chart 17-1
RESIDENTIAL BUILDING CONTRACTS, WITH THEIR SEASONAL, CYCLICAL TREND, AND IRREGULAR COMPONENTS, 1948-56

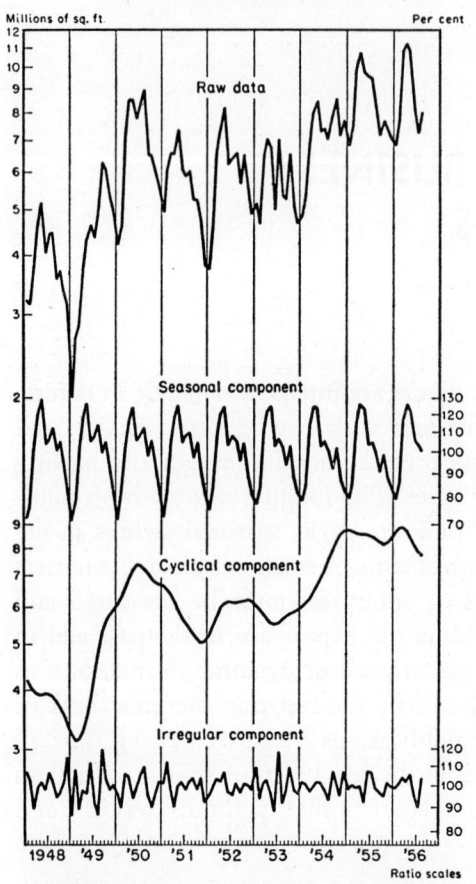

SOURCE: Julius Shiskin, *Electronic Computers and Business Indicators* (New York: National Bureau of Economic Research, Inc., 1957), p. 224.

as an aid to forward planning? The first of these problems is dealt with in this chapter; the others are deferred to succeeding chapters.

The principal component fluctuations in a time series are as follows:

1. Secular trend.
2. Cyclical fluctuations.
3. Seasonal variation.
4. Irregular movements.

To illustrate, Chart 17-1 shows monthly residential building contracts from 1948 to 1956, broken down into the seasonal component, the cyclical component combined with a rising secular trend, and the residual irregularities. Each of these types of movements will be described below.

Secular Trend

Secular trend is the gradual growth or decline of a series over a long period of time. The growth is ordinarily one of physical volume, like biological change; it does not strictly apply to long-term movements in prices, which do not grow in the biological sense. Hence secular trend analysis usually applies to physical volume series and "deflated" dollar value series (to be explained later in the chapter) rather than to dollar value or price series. However, trend curves are sometimes used to describe long-term movements in prices, as well as "secondary trends" or long cycles in other series, even though the rational basis of growth is absent.

"A long period of time" usually means several decades at least, in order to distinguish the basic growth trends from the short-term "trends" caused by the influence of cycles, wars, and other episodic factors. In some cases the purpose of the analysis determines the period to be used. Thus we speak of the trend of consumption since 1919, or the increase in productivity during the past century.

There are a number of circumstances in the development of the United States which have resulted in a rising trend in most of our economic measures. The growth of population, increasing industrialization, and the rising standard of living have combined to cause expansion of the production of both industrial and consumer goods, of services rendered by marketing, transportation, and financial agencies, as well as of personal services. Series such as pig-iron production, wheat production, cold-storage holdings, freight ton-miles, bank deposits, and hotel business all have increased with the expansion of the country.

Although this general relation of the growth component to the expansion of the country can be established readily, it does not follow that there is one rate of growth which is applicable to the fundamental forces in our economic system. It is necessary to study the growth component of each series separately. Some series will be found to be rising, others falling; some will change rapidly, others slowly. Most of them will vary in rate of growth over a long period of years.

There was a period in the development of statistical methods when it was generally believed that the trend component could be accurately described by a simple mathematical equation. Most frequently an arithmetic straight line was used. The dependence upon rigidly defined functions for the measurement of trend has proved to be unjustified, however, so that at the present time flexible, freehand methods are in wider use, and the arithmetic straight line has been replaced to a considerable extent by more rational types of curves, described in the next chapter.

The variations in the nature of the secular trend component can be seen in the three curves of Chart 17–2 (p. 334). Gross national product in constant dollars represents the physical volume of total production; aluminum production typifies a young industry, and bituminous coal an older one. The data have been plotted on identical ratio scales, and smooth trend curves have been fitted by the National Industrial Conference Board to indicate average growth tendencies. The slopes of these curves show how the per cent rates of change differ in each case.

Gross national product has maintained nearly a straight line or uniform per cent rate of growth since 1890. Aluminum production, on the

334   BUSINESS AND ECONOMIC STATISTICS   [Ch. 17

Chart 17–2

GROWTH PATTERNS IN AMERICAN INDUSTRY, 1890–1960

GROSS NATIONAL PRODUCT
(Constant Dollars)

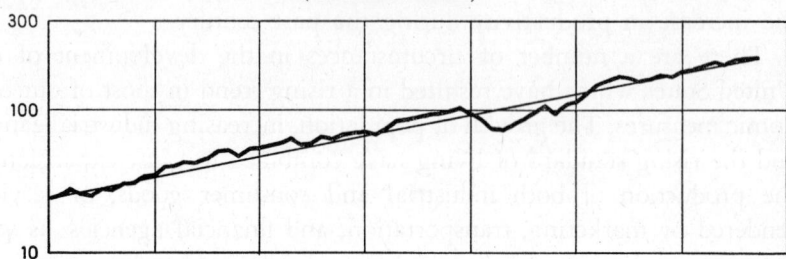

PRIMARY PRODUCTION OF ALUMINUM
MILLIONS OF POUNDS

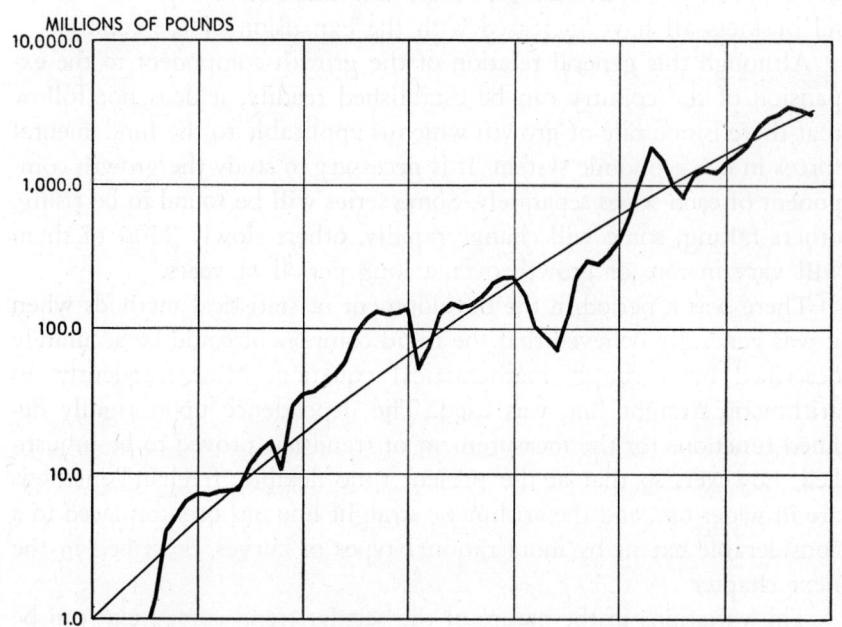

BITUMINOUS COAL PRODUCTION
MILLIONS OF SHORT TONS

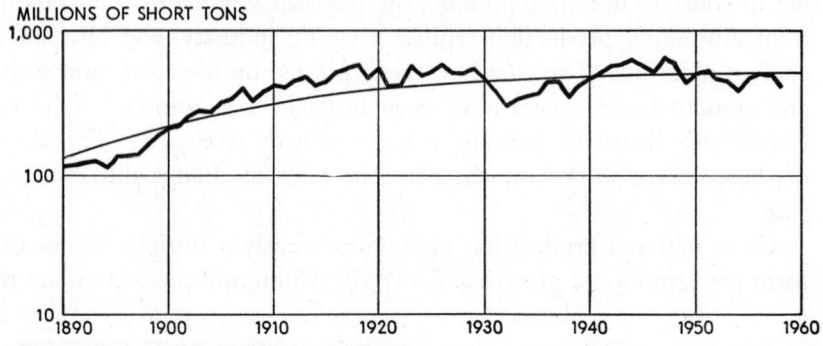

SOURCE: National Industrial Conference Board.

other hand, has shot up much more rapidly throughout its short life, although the trend curvature indicates that the rate of growth is slackening. The older bituminous coal industry developed at a more gradual rate from 1890 until World War I; since then it has matured and leveled off. Its course, however, has been steadier than that of aluminum. The three production series therefore exhibit marked differences in (1) shape of trend curve; (2) steepness of curve, or rate of growth; and (3) instability, measured in deviations from the curve. Trend analysis is most useful and reliable when growth is steady and steep, and the deviations about the trend curve are small. In this case the trend curve may even be projected into the future as a forecast if the factors affecting growth in the past may reasonably be expected to persist.

The trend types in Chart 17–2 illustrate the industrial application of a useful growth hypothesis popularly called the "law of growth." According to this principle, "If the population is expanding freely over unoccupied country, the percentage rate of increase is constant. If it is growing in a limited area, the percentage rate of increase must tend to get less and less as population grows . . ."[1] until it finally levels off as an upper limit is approached. The constant rate of growth is characteristic not only of young industries but of total production, which is a cumulation of individual growth curves. The "law of growth" principle will be applied to the measurement of industrial trends in the next chapter.

These examples are sufficient evidence that the growth factor may be described by a simple curve, although it differs for each series. The problem of trend measurement, however, is not merely the mechanical one of fitting a curve to the data; it also requires a knowledge of the background of the industry under consideration. With this knowledge, one can apply methods of time series analysis that are not only mechanically correct but logical as well.

Cyclical Fluctuations

Distinct from the growth component are those forces which cause fluctuations in a time series above and below the trend curve. The most important of these forces are those which cause cycles, or alternations between prosperity and depression.

---

[1] P. F. Verhulst, "Recherches mathematiques sur la loi d'accroissement de la population," *Nouveaux memoires de l'Academie Royale de Sciences et Belles-Lettres de Bruxelles*, Tome XVIII (1845). See also Raymond Pearl and Lowell J. Reed, "On the Rate of Growth of the Population of the United States since 1790 and Its Mathematical Representation," *Proceedings of the National Academy of Sciences*, June 15, 1920, pp. 275–88.

Business cycles are a type of fluctuation found in the aggregate economic activity of nations that organize their work mainly in business enterprises: a cycle consists of expansions occurring at about the same time in many economic activities, followed by similarly general recessions, contractions, and revivals which merge into the expansion phase of the next cycle; this sequence of changes is recurrent but not periodic; in duration business cycles vary from more than one year to ten or twelve years; they are not divisible into shorter cycles of similar character with amplitudes approximating their own.[2]

Business cycles have developed in modern industrialized countries having closely integrated business structures. The cycles are affected by factors outside business, such as wars, acts of government, and the size of crops; but it is the conditions within the business system itself that cause a protracted prosperity to give way to depression, and vice versa, in a roughly rhythmic fashion. Nearly all economic activities are affected by cyclical forces; but heavy industrial production and finance are most susceptible, and retail trade, personal service, and agricultural production are least affected.

The average length of business cycles in this country since 1919 has been about 4⅓ years, of which the expansion phase has been over twice as long as the contraction phase. Table 17–1 shows the turning points of the general business cycle, averaged from thousands of individual series by the National Bureau of Economic Research. It will be seen that the cycle averaged little over three years in length before 1929, but that a long depression and a long war have protracted the later moves.

In addition to the "short" cycle described above, some observers assert the existence of longer cycles, such as a nine-year intercrisis cycle and an 18-year residential building cycle. A conjunction of declines in these several cycles is said to cause major depressions. In any case, successive cycles vary so widely in amplitude (per cent rise and fall) and pattern, as well as in length, that their prediction is extremely difficult.

Cycles in individual series also differ markedly in these respects from the general business cycle. Chart 17–3 shows gross national product, aluminum, and coal production expressed in per cent deviations from the trend lines of Chart 17–2 to accentuate their cyclical movements. Gross national product is relatively insensitive to the cycle, since it contains many stable types of expenditures, such as interest payments, while aluminum production is extremely volatile, and coal is both moderate in amplitude and more sensitive to general business conditions than is

---

[2] This definition of Wesley C. Mitchell is used as the point of departure in the National Bureau of Economic Research studies in business cycles. See Arthur F. Burns and Wesley C. Mitchell, *Measuring Business Cycles* (New York: National Bureau of Economic Research, Inc., 1946), p. 3.

Table 17-1

TURNING POINTS OF BUSINESS CYCLES
IN THE UNITED STATES, 1919-61

Trough	Peak	Expansion	Contraction	Total
March 1919	January 1920	10	18	28
July 1921	May 1923	22	14	36
July 1924	October 1926	27	13	40
November 1927	August 1929	21	43	64
March 1933	May 1937	50	13	63
June 1938	February 1945	80	8	88
October 1945	November 1948	37	11	48
October 1949	July 1953	45	13	58
August 1954	July 1957	35	9	44
April 1958	May 1960	25	9	34
February 1961				
Mean duration		35	15	50
Median duration		31	13	44

SOURCE: *Business Cycle Developments*, App. A, April 1964. See Arthur F. Burns and Wesley C. Mitchell, *Measuring Business Cycles* (New York: National Bureau of Economic Research, Inc., 1946), p. 78, for earlier turning points, beginning in 1854.

aluminum. All three series, however, reflect the booms of the two world wars and the depressions of 1921 and 1932. The study of cycles is more crucial in "cyclical" or sensitive industries than in stable activities.

Seasonal Variation

The word "seasonal" implies that we are dealing with something related to the weather. This is partly but not entirely true. Seasonal variations are of two kinds: (1) those resulting from natural forces and (2) those resulting from man-made conventions. Some examples will clarify this distinction. In the northern part of the United States and in Canada, construction work is greatly curtailed during the winter season. Hence data concerning road construction, building activity, and the like have seasonal variations that are directly related to the weather. On the other hand, department store sales expand before Easter and Christmas, a circumstance related to man-made festivals rather than to the weather. Sales of ice cream is an example of a partial shift from one type of seasonality to the other. In an earlier day, sales were high in midsummer and sank to a small fraction of the summer volume during the winter months. At that time ice cream was considered a luxury to be enjoyed only in warm weather. More recently ice cream has become

Chart 17–3
CYCLICAL-IRREGULAR PATTERNS IN INDUSTRY
Gross National Product
(Constant Dollars)

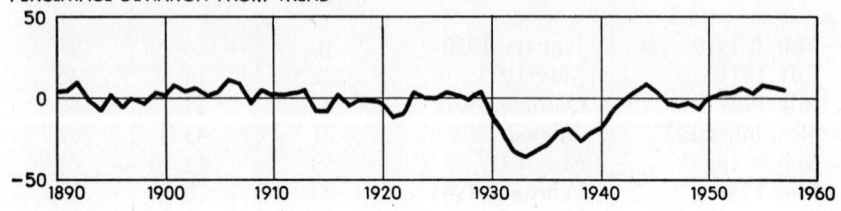

PERCENTAGE DEVIATION FROM TREND

Primary Production of Aluminum

PERCENTAGE DEVIATION FROM TREND

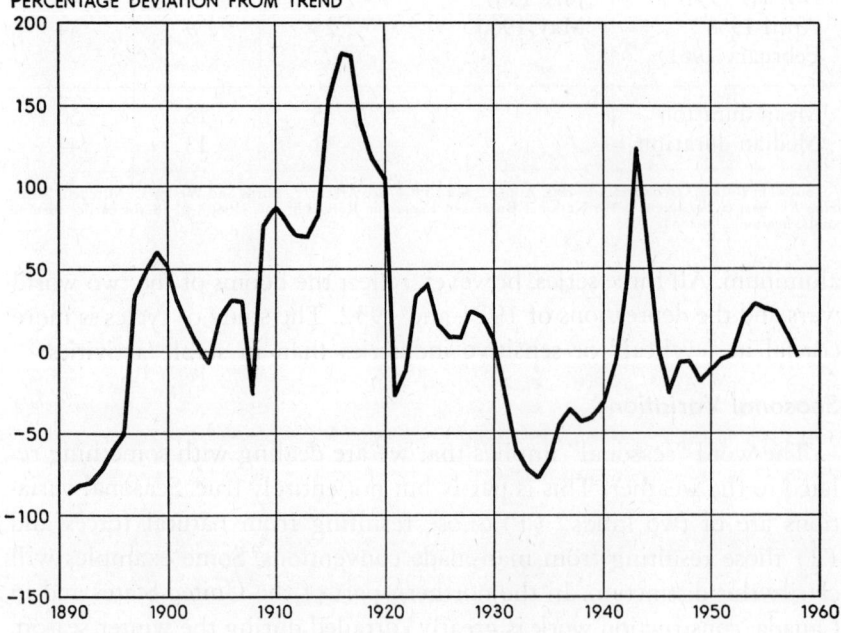

Bituminous Coal Production

PERCENTAGE DEVIATION FROM TREND

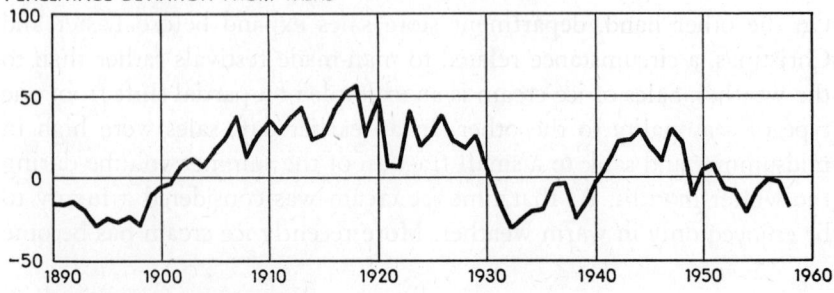

Source: National Industrial Conference Board.

a staple article of consumption. As a result the seasonal curve of sales has lost the greater part of its amplitude, albeit the peak is still in the summer months and the trough in the winter months.

Seasonal variations affect nearly all economic activities in this country.[3] The impact of seasonal influences is likely to be greatest at the point of origin and the point of consumption, and less in the intervening manufacturing process. The cotton crop, for example, is seasonal, and so are retail sales of cotton goods (in a different pattern); but textile mills manage to operate at a more stable rate by manufacturing for stock in the slack seasons. In some industries, however, only the supply is markedly seasonal (e.g., wheat versus bread) or the demand (consumer durable goods) or the fabrication process itself (building construction). Inventories in general are more seasonal, and prices less seasonal, than production or sales. The typical seasonal pattern includes either one peak and trough per year, as in the construction, ice cream, and cotton-crop examples, or else peaks in both spring and fall and troughs in midwinter and midsummer, as in retail trade generally. Seasonal analysis is most fruitful in cases where the seasonal movement is large and regular, and least worthwhile when it is small and irregular.

Chart 17-4 illustrates the seasonal behavior of four Mississippi business indicators. Cash farm income has a wide, regular seasonal swing, with a high peak following the harvest. Life insurance sales have a definite seasonal pattern, with peaks in the spring and in December, but the pattern is obscured by marked irregularities. Bank debits, or value of checks cashed, move in a more regular rhythm, with a year-end peak. Electric power consumption has a still smoother seasonal pattern, with a peak in early fall.

The seasonal pattern of retail trade in general is typified by the monthly sales of Sears, Roebuck & Company shown in Chart 19-2, page 395. The year starts with the midwinter slump, followed by a brisk spring trade, a June dip, a fall pickup, and a big Christmas rush. Accurate measures of seasonal behavior by products are invaluable to the management of such a firm in planning purchasing, inventory control, and selling programs.

Two important features of the seasonal rhythm should be noted: (1) it recurs year after year with a fixed period, and (2) the increases and decreases of sales occur at about the same time and in about the same percentage amount each year. The seasonal rhythm therefore has a fixed period and a fairly regular amplitude, whereas the cyclical

---

[3] See Simon Kuznets, *Seasonal Variations in Industry and Trade* (New York: National Bureau of Economic Research, Inc., 1933), chap. 1.

Chart 17-4

SEASONALITY IN MISSISSIPPI BUSINESS INDICATORS

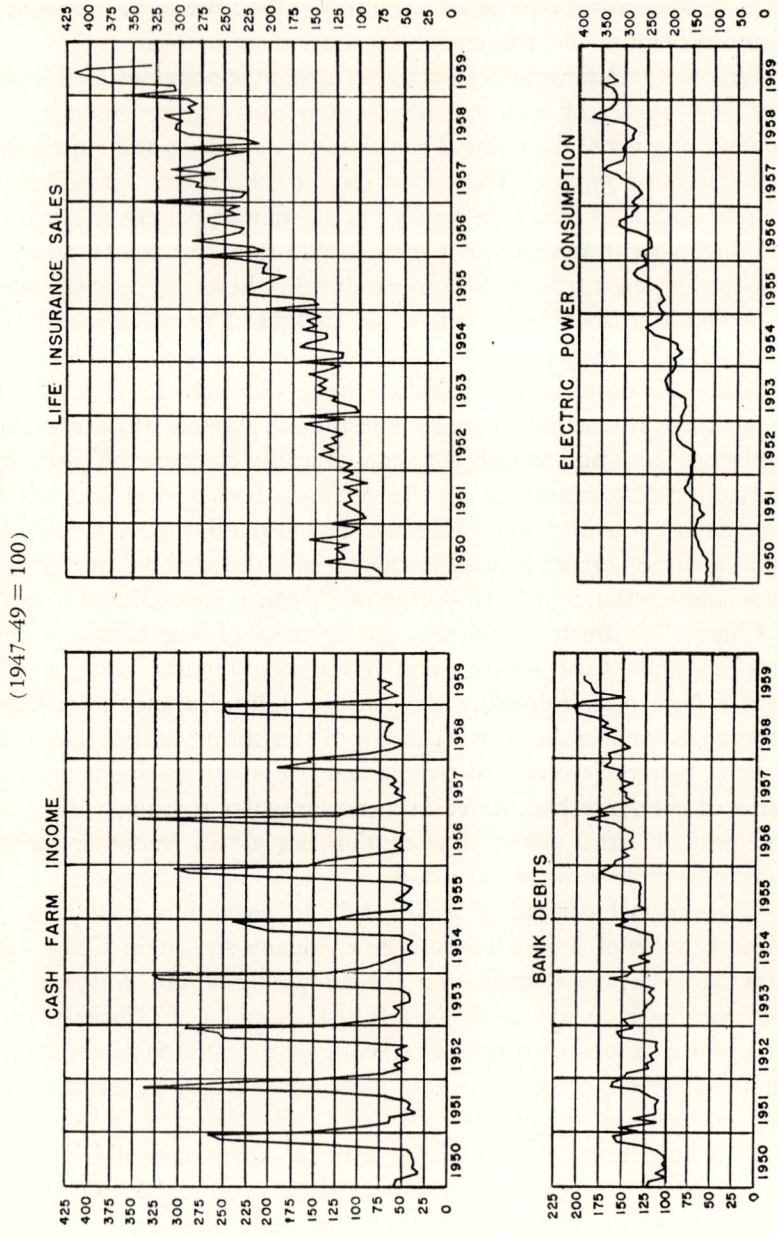

(1947–49 = 100)

SOURCE: Mississippi State University, *Mississippi Business Review*, September 1959.

rhythm is variable in both respects. Seasonal movements may consequently be measured and projected into the future much more accurately than cycles.

Other Rhythms. Many economic activities exhibit rhythmic movements having a shorter period than seasonal variations. Quarterly dividend and income tax payments and monthly payrolls cause regular fluctuations in the flow of funds through banks and in consumers' expenditures.

Weekly and daily rhythms may be illustrated by the volume of sales in a department store. Monday is apt to be light, except after a long holiday week end; then trade builds up gradually during the week to a peak on Saturday. The average sales on a number of Mondays may be compared with the averages for other weekdays (with separate norms for days before and after holidays), and a normal pattern of weekly variation worked out to aid in the timing of purchasing, advertising, and hiring of extra help. The typical day itself begins with a light volume that builds up during the forenoon; then a lunch-hour pause and a rising volume to a peak perhaps just before closing.

Daily rhythms occur in such data as the hourly number of messages crossing a telephone switchboard, the hourly number of riders on busses, or the hourly use of electric power. These and many similar series have such regular rhythms that engineers use them to determine the amount of equipment to be kept in service each hour of the day and night.

The rhythms having a shorter period than the seasonal may therefore be worth analyzing as an aid to short-term programing. Since they do not require the use of statistical techniques beyond averages, however, no further attention will be given to them here.

Calendar Variation. One cause of "seasonal" disturbances in monthly and weekly data is neither the weather nor customs, but the eccentricity of the calendar itself. The months are not uniform units of time; they vary, of course, from 28 to 31 days in length. But this is only one part of the variability. Some months have four Saturdays and Sundays; others have five. Some have one or several legal holidays; others have none. Further, some series of data arise from activities which operate five days a week; others 5½, 6, or even 7 days. All of these factors cause spurious movements in monthly data which are by no means negligible.[4] Weekly data, too, vary abruptly if one week contains a

---

[4] Several plans have been devised in recent years to eliminate some of the calendar irregularity by an adjustment of the lengths of the several months, as in the 12-month "World Calendar," or by the use of thirteen 28-day months. Some industrial concerns op-

holiday and others do not. For example, a regional newspaper ran a scare headline "Index Stages Big Retreat" over an article reporting that the New York Times Weekly Index of Business Activity had dropped to 207.3 in the week ended January 2, 1960, from 221.3 the week before. However, the article went on to say: "The major factor in the index's sharp drop was reduced production resulting from the New Year's holiday . . . ." The size of the corrections to be made for calendar irregularities and the methods of making such corrections are discussed later in this chapter.

Irregular Fluctuations

Irregular fluctuations in economic time series are caused by such forces as weather disasters, labor strife, war, government intervention, and all forms of unpredictable events. These forces are of two types. The first group serves as "originating forces" in inducing or altering business cycle movements. War and its aftermath, for example, tend to produce the familiar boom and bust phases of a major peacetime cycle. A government public-works program may stimulate a similar cycle on a smaller scale. A protracted steel strike, on the other hand, creates a condition similar to cyclical depression in that industry. These forces are generally unpredictable, although many Washington "services" advise business on what the government is likely to do, and whether there will be war, strikes, large or small crops, etc., with partial success.

The second group of irregular factors comprises the host of miscellaneous forces that act in a more or less random fashion to give a plotted curve its familiar zigzag contour. These factors are usually numerous, unidentifiable, and unpredictable. The random element varies widely in different series, from nothing in the Federal Reserve rediscount rate to a major influence in the value of building permits issued.

The irregular component in a time series represents the residue of fluctuations after secular trend, cyclical, and seasonal movements have been accounted for. In practice, however, the cycle itself is so erratic and is so interwoven with irregular movements that it is impossible to separate them, except in smoothing out some of the random factors of the second type. In the analysis of a series into its component fluctuations, therefore, secular trend and seasonal movements are usually measured directly, while cyclical and irregular fluctuations are left together after the other elements have been removed.

perate on a 13-period basis, but as a general rule the advantages of calendar reform have been given scant attention by businessmen.

THE PROBLEM OF TIME SERIES ANALYSIS

Some time series contain all of the foregoing components; others only some of them. Certain series are so largely controlled by one type of fluctuation that it is easily recognized from the original data. For example, seasonal movements dominate the recent fluctuations in cash farm income (Chart 17–4). Secular trend analysis is most useful for series in which the trend component dominates other types of fluctuations, and, similarly, cyclical and seasonal analysis are most worthwhile when these components dominate.

Usually the several components are not separately recognizable in the original data, but the businessman or economist needs to know the influence of each in order to understand the forces at work and the probable future behavior of the series. Therefore, the analyst's problem in dealing with time series is to identify the components and measure them separately.

The work of analysis can be divided into four parts: (1) preliminary adjustments, (2) measuring secular trend, (3) measuring seasonal variation, and (4) analyzing cyclical-irregular residuals.

The remainder of this chapter and the two which follow contain an explanation of the most useful methods for carrying out these four steps in the analysis of time series. In a particular application, only one or perhaps two of the steps may be needed, depending on the importance of the component and the purpose of the study. The various methods explained can be adapted readily to the form of partial analysis required in a particular case.

Preliminary Adjustments

Two preliminary adjustments are often made before a time series is analyzed into its components: (1) adjustment of monthly and weekly data for the effect of calendar variation and (2) adjustment of dollar value series for changes in the price level, when physical volume changes are needed.

Calendar Variation. The method of dealing with variations in the number of days in the month is to divide each monthly total by the number of operating days in that month to reduce it to a uniform average daily basis. The general rule is to count the number of days that the activity was carried on during the month. In some cases this will mean all of the days in the month; in others Sundays, or Saturdays and Sundays, will be excluded. If one day in the week is unusually light or heavy in volume, it may be weighted accordingly. Thus, the Federal

Reserve Board weights Sundays as 1½ days in adjusting monthly newspaper output—a component of the Industrial Production Index. Different holidays are observed in the several fields of business activity and in different communities. Consequently, the number of days to be used may differ for each series of data and for each area represented.[5]

Some examples will demonstrate the method of reducing a series to an average daily basis and the effect on its behavior. In Table 17-2, Part A, the monthly sales of a drugstore are listed. This store is open every day; hence the total number of days in each month has been divided into the sales to yield daily averages as shown in columns 2 and 3. In Part B of the table the amount of flour milled each month is also adjusted for calendar irregularities. In this case Sundays and six holidays —New Year's Day, Memorial Day, Independence Day, Labor Day, Thanksgiving, and Christmas—have been deducted from the number of days in the month to obtain the number of days flour mills were operated. In Part C the same computation is shown for bank clearings; but for this series, in addition to Sundays and holidays listed in Part B, the following bank holidays have been included: Lincoln's and Washington's birthdays, Columbus Day, Election Day, and Veterans Day.

To show the effect of these corrections the monthly totals and daily averages for each series are presented in Table 17-2 as index numbers, with the average month equal to 100 in each case. Thus in Part A, column 4 equals column 1 divided by 6,674, the average of column 1; and column 5 equals column 3 divided by 219, a weighted average of column 3 obtained by dividing the year's sales by the total operating days in the year.

The indexes are plotted in Chart 17-5. The drugstore sales show only slight changes due to calendar adjustment except in February. The effect on flour milling is more important because the operating days vary more from month to month than the calendar days. September, October, and November are particularly noteworthy because the monthly totals conceal irregularities that are brought to light by the daily averages. A reverse tendency appears in bank clearings, since the daily average curve eliminates some of the artificial irregularity introduced by the monthly total curve.

The method of reducing to a daily average basis should be used only for quantities that cumulate during the month. In the examples used, the drugstore sales, flour milled, and value of checks cleared all add up

---

[5] For a list of weekly working days in the principal manufacturing, mining, and utility industries, see Federal Reserve Board, *Industrial Production: 1959 Revision*, 1960, pp. S-4 to S-19.

Table 17-2
ADJUSTMENT FOR CALENDAR VARIATION
MONTHLY SALES OF A DRUGSTORE, FLOUR MILLED, AND BANK CLEARINGS

Month	A — Sales of a Drugstore						B — Flour Milled					C — Bank Clearings			
	(1) Monthly Totals (Dollars)	(2) No. of Working Days in Month	(3) Average Sales per Day (Dollars)	(4) Index of Monthly Sales	(5) Index of Average Daily Sales		(6) Monthly Totals (Thousand Barrels)	(7) No. of Working Days in Month	(8) Average Milled per Day (Thousand Barrels)	(9) Index of Flour Milled per Month	(10) Index of Flour Milled per Day	(11) Monthly Totals (Million Dollars)	(12) No. of Working Days per Month	(13) Average Clearings per Day (Million Dollars)	(14) Index of Clearings per Month	(15) Index of Clearings per Day
January	7,094	31	229	106	105		897	26	34.5	103	102	138.6	26	5.33	98	95
February	6,137	29	212	92	97		862	25	34.5	99	102	115.1	23	5.00	82	89
March	6,303	31	203	94	93		880	26	33.9	101	100	131.4	26	5.05	93	90
April	6,918	30	231	104	105		833	26	32.1	96	95	134.0	26	5.15	95	92
May	6,682	31	216	100	99		859	25	34.4	99	101	127.8	25	5.11	91	91
June	6,378	30	213	96	97		844	26	32.4	97	96	141.7	26	5.45	100	97
July	6,193	31	200	93	91		932	26	35.8	107	106	148.3	26	5.70	105	102
August	5,647	31	182	85	83		901	26	34.6	104	102	142.1	26	5.47	101	98
September	6,275	30	209	94	96		905	25	36.2	104	107	141.1	25	5.64	100	101
October	6,714	31	217	101	99		860	27	31.9	99	94	161.1	26	6.20	114	111
November	6,794	30	226	102	104		825	24	34.4	95	102	141.1	22	6.41	100	115
December	8,952	31	289	134	132		827	26	31.8	95	94	170.0	26	6.54	121	117
Average	6,674	...	219	...	...		869	...	33.8	...	...	141.0	...	5.59	...	...

SOURCE: University of Buffalo, Bureau of Business and Social Research.

Chart 17–5

ADJUSTMENT FOR CALENDAR VARIATION

MONTHLY SALES OF A DRUGSTORE, FLOUR MILLED, AND BANK CLEARINGS

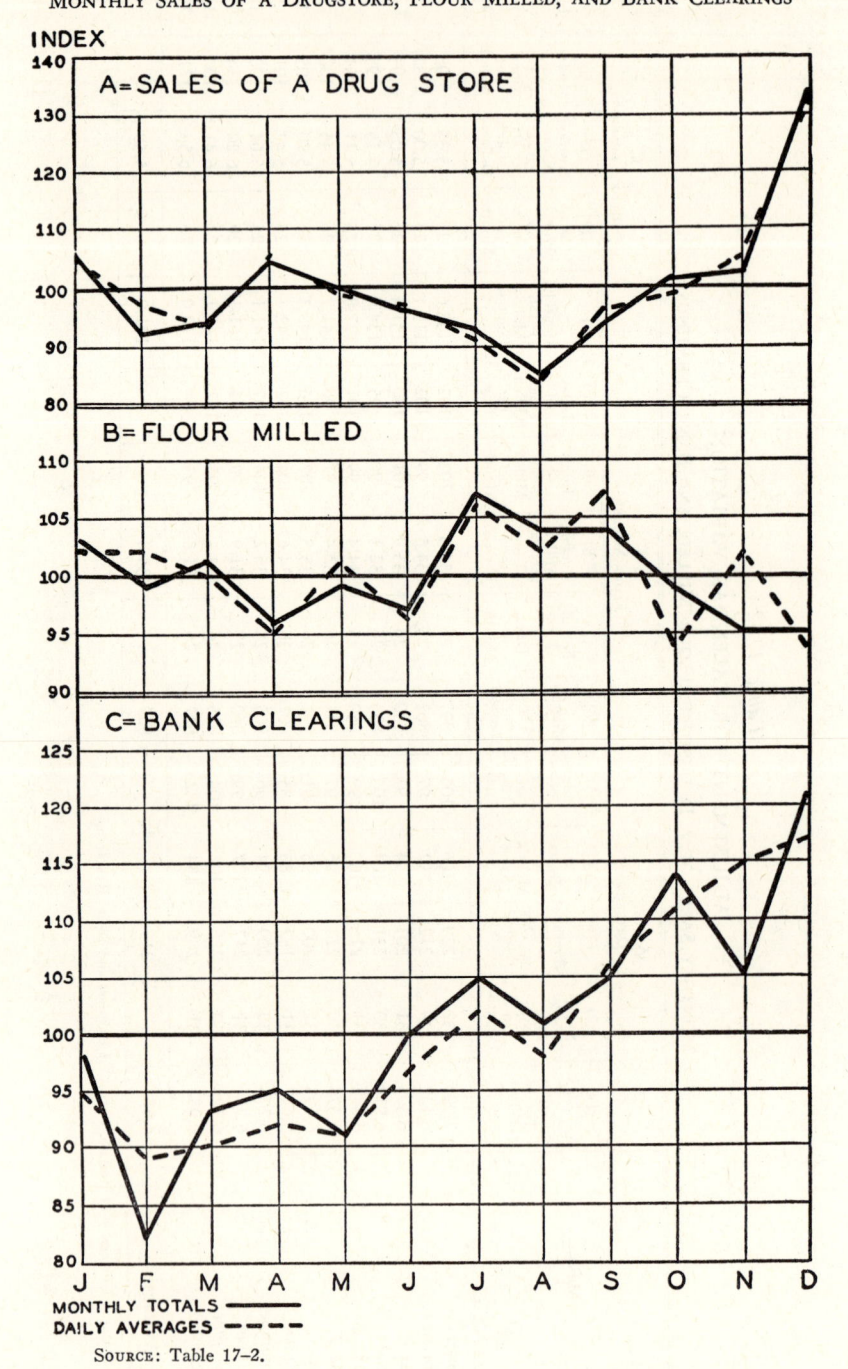

MONTHLY TOTALS ———
DAILY AVERAGES – – –

SOURCE: Table 17–2.

to larger amounts in long months than in short months. On the other hand, series such as the number of employees of drugstores, the capacity of flour mills, or the deposits of banks should not be reduced to an average daily basis, because they do not cumulate or build up to larger values in longer months. The same is true of prices and "point data" such as year-end balance sheet figures. Yearly and quarterly data in general are not adjusted for the calendar either, since the irregularity is negligible in these longer periods.

In the case of weekly data the number of weekdays is constant, and only holidays cause irregularities. These may be corrected by (1) adjusting weeks containing holidays to a full-time basis (e.g., adding $\frac{1}{5}$ to the figure for a five-day week to make it comparable with data for six-day weeks) or, (2) plotting curves for one year over the other on a tier chart so that weeks containing a given holiday are lined up vertically for direct comparability in different years.

When data are to be adjusted for seasonal variation, as described in Chapter 19, the calendar adjustment may sometimes be omitted, since the seasonal correction eliminates the difference between the *average* number of operating days in January and those in February. It does not, however, smooth out the differences in operating days between one January and the next.

Price Deflation. Many series on the volume of sales, production, and other economic activities are available only in the form of dollar values. These values are affected not only by the physical quantity of goods involved but also by their prices, and prices have varied widely in recent years. For many purposes it is necessary to know how much of the dollar value changes represents a real change in physical quantity, and how much is due to mere markups or markdowns in price tags. Physical quantities may be estimated by dividing the dollar values by the prices of the goods represented to eliminate the effect of price changes. (Price data are widely available.) That is, since value equals price times quantity, then value divided by price equals quantity. This adjustment is called price deflation or expressing a series in terms of constant dollars.

For example, suppose the sales in a shoe department increase from $10,000 in April to $10,450 in May. What was the change in physical volume? If we ascertain that the average price of shoes increased from $10 to $11 a pair in this period, we may divide the value by the price to learn that there has been an actual decline in shoes sold from 1,000 to 950 pairs, as shown below:

DEFLATION OF SHOE SALES

	April	*May*
1. Dollar sales	$10,000	$10,450
2. Average price per pair	$10	$11
3. Estimated number of pairs sold (1 ÷ 2)	1,000	950

Similarly, money wages may be deflated to find "real" wages, that is, wages in terms of the actual goods and services which can be purchased for a given amount of money. Suppose, for instance, an employee's wage rate increases from $60 to $120 a week during a period of inflation when a consumer price index, representing the goods and services he purchases, increases from 100 to 200. His deflated wages are $60/100 × 100 = $60 and $120/200 × 100 = $60, respectively. Hence, his real wage has failed to advance. A company analyst can deflate the average wages of employees each month in this way to measure changes in the purchasing power of wages.

The deflating process is a very simple one; but the major problem, the selection of the proper price index, is primarily a matter of good judgment. The rule to be followed is: Use an index number computed from the prices of the commodities whose values are to be deflated. For example, hardware store sales should be deflated by an index of hardware prices, not by a general price index.

In deflating dollar values that represent a variety of commodities, an appropriate price index may be pieced together from available sources to represent this particular "mix." For example, an investor may desire to study the long-term growth of Sears, Roebuck & Company. The secular trend curve should be fitted to the physical volume of sales, since the price changes reflected in dollar sales follow no consistent pattern and merely obscure the real growth. The dollar sales must therefore be divided by a price index of the goods sold by the company.

Such an index might be constructed by pricing a sample of important items sold by the store and weighting these prices by the sales volume of the departments represented. It is simpler, however, and adequate for the purpose, to use existing retail price indexes. The Consumer Price Index itself is not suitable, since it contains elements such as foods, rents, and personal services not sold by the store; but the apparel and house furnishings components of this index may be appropriate. An examination of an earlier study[6] and a Sears, Roebuck & Company catalog indicates that roughly half the sales are in apparel and other soft goods, one third in house furnishings and appliances, and one sixth

---

[6] Frederick C. Mills, "Movements of Mail-Order Prices," *Journal of the American Statistical Association*, March 1937, pp. 131–32.

Ch. 17] ANALYSIS OF BUSINESS FLUCTUATIONS 349

in farm implements and other hard goods. We may therefore weight the Consumer Price Index apparel component one half, the house furnishings component one third, and the Agricultural Marketing Service index of farm implement prices one sixth to get a combined price index appropriate for Sears, Roebuck & Company sales. These components may be expressed on the common base 1947–49 = 100 for comparability. Dividing actual sales in current dollars by this price index gives deflated sales in dollars of constant 1947–49 purchasing power, as shown in Table 17–3.

Chart 17–6 compares the actual and deflated sales, along with the price index, on a ratio grid. The deflated sales or physical volume of business held up much better than the dollar volume during the business collapse of 1929–32, and during the subsequent inflation has climbed at a more gradual but consistent rate. A secular trend curve will be fitted to the deflated series in the next chapter. Note that the use of the 1947–49 base in the price index brings the two curves to-

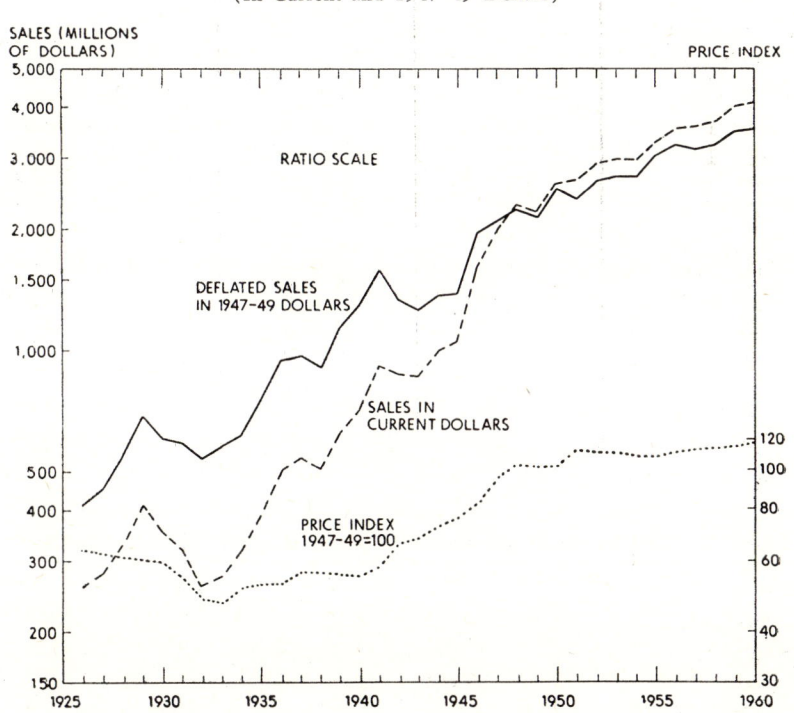

Chart 17–6

SEARS, ROEBUCK & COMPANY ANNUAL NET SALES, 1926–60
(In Current and 1947–49 Dollars)

Table 17-3
SEARS, ROEBUCK & COMPANY ANNUAL NET SALES, 1926–60

Year[a]	Net Sales[b] (Millions of Dollars)	Price Index[c] (1947–49 = 100)	Deflated Net Sales[d] (Millions of 1947–49 Dollars)
1926	258	63.19	408
1927	278	62.08	448
1928	329	61.11	538
1929	415	60.45	687
1930	355	59.18	600
1931	320	54.51	587
1932	260	48.68	534
1933	273	47.39	576
1934	318	51.47	618
1935	392	52.32	749
1936	495	52.90	936
1937	537	55.88	961
1938	502	55.86	899
1939	617	54.97	1,122
1940	704	54.92	1,282
1941	915	57.42	1,594
1942	868	65.37	1,328
1943	853	67.83	1,258
1944	989	72.43	1,365
1945	1,045	76.04	1,374
1946	1,613	82.55	1,954
1947	1,982	95.38	2,078
1948	2,296	102.93	2,231
1949	2,169	101.70	2,133
1950	2,556	101.71	2,513
1951	2,657	111.55	2,382
1952	2,932	110.63	2,650
1953	2,982	110.15	2,707
1954	2,965	109.42	2,710
1955	3,307	108.65	3,044
1956	3,556	110.10	3,230
1957	3,601	112.65	3,197
1958	3,721	113.03	3,292
1959	4,036	114.51	3,525
1960	4,134	116.06	3,562

[a] Calendar years 1926–32; years beginning February 1, 1933–60.
[b] Total net sales, less discounts, returns, and allowances, including outside sales by subsidiaries. 1932 sales estimated from 13 months report. Source: Stockholders' reports.
[c] Constructed from Bureau of Labor Statistics consumer price index for apparel (weight ½) and for house furnishings (weight ⅓), plus Agricultural Marketing Service index of prices paid by farmers for farm implements (weight ⅙).
[d] Net sales divided by price index times 100.

gether at the average level of these years. If a 1957–59 base had been used, the deflated sales curve would have been raised to match the other curve in these years, but its slope would not have been altered.

The effect of inflation on the economy as a whole is illustrated in Chart 16–4. Each component of gross national product has been divided by an "implicit price deflator" on the base $1954 = 100$, and the resulting GNP in 1954 dollars plotted with GNP in current dollars. It will be seen that much of the rise in GNP since 1954 represents inflation rather than a rise in real production. While output in current dollars increased 39 per cent from 1954 to 1960, "real" GNP advanced but 21 per cent.

SUMMARY

An understanding of the nature and causes of business fluctuations is essential in a dynamic economy. These fluctuations may best be understood by analyzing economic time series into their principal components—secular trend, cyclical fluctuations, seasonal variations, and irregular movements.

Secular trend is the gradual long-term increase or decrease in a series resulting from such basic factors as the growth of population, technology, and productivity. This development can be represented by a smooth trend curve fitted to the plotted data. Different series vary greatly in the shape and steepness of their trends, as well as in the variations of the data from the trend curve. Young industries and total production tend to grow at a constant percentage rate in this country. The rate of growth is often retarded as an industry matures, following the "law of growth" principle, and eventually tends to level off or even turn down.

Cyclical fluctuations are the rhythmic movements of alternating prosperity and depression that have developed in industrialized economies. The average length of the short cycle is about 4 years, although 9- and 18-year cycles are also believed to exist. Cycles vary widely in timing, pattern, and amplitude, both from one cycle to the next and from industry to industry. Major booms and depressions, however, affect nearly all economic activities.

Seasonal variations are regular rhythmic movements within a period of one year resulting from the weather and from man-made conventions such as holidays. They affect nearly all economic processes in varying degrees, particularly at the point of origin and the point of consumption. Seasonal variations may be wide and regular, or the reverse. They may also change in character over the years. However, seasonal fluctuations are much more regular than cycles, and so they can be measured and projected more accurately. Regular rhythms also occur within a quarterly, monthly, weekly, or daily period. Finally, the calendar itself causes quasi-seasonal variations in monthly and weekly data, since the number of operating days varies from one month or week to the next.

Irregular fluctuations are the residual component in a time series after secular trend, cyclical, and seasonal movements have been accounted for. It is usually impossible, however, to separate cyclical and irregular fluctuations satisfactorily. The irregular factors may be "originating forces" (such as wars and acts of government) that influence business cycles, or they may be miscellaneous unknown and unpredictable factors of a random nature.

The work of analyzing a time series includes preliminary adjustments for calendar variation and price changes when appropriate, and then the measurement of secular trend and seasonal variation. Cyclical-irregular movements are usually treated as a residual in combined form.

Adjustment for calendar variation in monthly data is made in order to eliminate fluctuations in the data caused by the varying length of the working month. The data are divided by the number of operating days in each month to place the series on a uniform daily average basis. The number of operating days must be determined separately for each industry and area. Weekly data are adjusted only for holidays, the number of weekdays being constant.

Price deflation is the process of dividing a dollar value series by a pertinent price index in order to reveal physical volume changes, expressed in "constant dollars." An appropriate price index may be compiled from segments of existing indexes, properly weighted, as in the Sears, Roebuck example. Price deflation is particularly necessary in times of wide price changes, since the "real" changes in output may differ drastically from the reported dollar figures.

PROBLEMS

1. *a*) As economist with the Polaroid Camera Company, manufacturers of camera and film, what would be the principal purpose of separating the company's monthly dollar sales into its component fluctuations? Give reasons to support your opinion.
   b) Briefly describe the causes of the four major components of this time series.
   c) Exactly how would you make two preliminary adjustments to this series before further analysis?

Ch. 17]   ANALYSIS OF BUSINESS FLUCTUATIONS   353

In Problems 2–4 graphs may be traced in pencil by placing a blank sheet of paper over a printed chart in the *Federal Reserve Chart Book, Economic Indicators,* or some other current publication. Do not use textbook examples.

2. *a)* Select and plot a series of annual data dominated by a steep secular trend, with mild short-term fluctuations.
   b) Describe the trend characteristics of this series: Is the trend a straight line, concave upward, or concave downward? What does this mean in terms of growth? Is the growth steady or erratic?

3. *a)* Select and plot a series of monthly data dominated by cyclical-irregular fluctuations rather than by secular or seasonal movements.
   b) Describe its cyclical characteristics: Is the amplitude wide or narrow? How does the timing of the peaks and troughs compare with the timing of turning points in general business (Table 17–1)? What is the current phase of the cycle—recovery, prosperity, recession, or depression?
   c) Describe the irregular movements: What was the behavior of this series during recent wars? What other major nonbusiness influences appear to have caused extended irregular movements? Are the month-to-month zigzag random forces marked or mild?

4. *a)* Select and plot a series of monthly data dominated by seasonal movements.
   b) Describe the seasonal characteristics: Is the seasonal amplitude wide or narrow? Is the seasonal pattern regular or irregular? What are the high and low months, and the seasonal tendency of other months? Give reasons for these movements.

5. Which of the following should be changed to an average daily basis, and which should not? Explain in each case.
   a) Monthly data on average sales per sales person in a chain of women's apparel stores.
   b) A monthly record of the stocks of a department store.
   c) The total loans of a commercial bank on the last day of each month.

6. *a)* List, from Moody's or Standard and Poor's Corporation reports, Sears, Roebuck & Company's sales for the first five months of this year or last year.
   b) Adjust these sales to a daily average basis, counting Saturday as 1½ days and omitting Sundays, January 1, and May 30. See calendar.
   c) Plot the actual sales and daily average sales on a small chart, using two scales.
   d) How does the calendar adjustment affect month-to-month movements?

7. Select in the *Survey of Current Business* a price index that might be appropriate for deflating the gross revenues of each of the following:
   a) A manufacturer of drugs and pharmaceuticals.

b) A St. Louis building contractor.
c) A clothing store.
d) A grocery supermarket.

8. Given the following data:

Year	Disposable Personal Income (Billions)	Consumer Price Index (1947–49 = 100)
1940	76.1	59.9
1947	170.1	95.5
1953	252.5	114.4
1959	334.6	124.6

Source: *Survey of Current Business.*

a) Deflate disposable personal income by the consumer price index and list the results.
b) Plot actual and deflated income on a small chart.
c) Explain the significance of the deflated data and compare the trends of the two curves.

9. The General Electric Company *1960 Annual Report* gives the following data:

Year	Net Sales Billed (Millions)	G. E. Product Price Index (1947–49 = 100)
1952	$2,994	114
1956	4,090	124
1960	4,198	129

a) Express net sales billed in terms of 1960 dollars.
b) Explain the meaning of this adjustment.

SELECTED READINGS

(See Chapter 19.)

18. SECULAR TREND

IN THE LAST chapter, secular trend was described as the gradual growth or decline in a series over a long period of time due to such fundamental forces as changes in population, technology, or productivity. The tremendous expansion in the economy in the past two decades has stimulated widespread interest in the problem of economic growth. In this chapter the various methods of measuring and projecting secular trend curves are described.

PURPOSES OF MEASURING TREND

There are three principal purposes of measuring secular trend:

1. The first purpose is to study the past growth or decline of a series. The secular trend curve describes the basic growth tendency of a product or industry, ignoring short-term fluctuations due to business cycles, seasons, wars, or other causes. The trend curve answers such questions as: Has the company maintained its historic rate of expansion in recent years, or is this rate tapering off? Has the company kept pace with its competitors or with the industry as a whole? Is the per cent rate of change constant as in many young industries, or is the rate a diminishing one as in the case of a mature industry? Is this a "growth" or a stable industry, or perhaps a declining one?

2. The second purpose of measuring secular trend is to project the curve into the future as a long-term forecast. If the past growth has been steady and if the conditions that determine this growth may reasonably be expected to persist in the future, a trend curve may be projected over five to ten years into the future as a preliminary forecast. Then a qualitative study of other factors, such as business cycles and specific demand and supply conditions, should be made to modify the statistical forecast.

A long-term forecast is desirable in making a decision to take a job with a given company or to invest in its stock. It is even more essential in the management's decision to expand its plant, develop a new product, or enter a new regional market, in order to justify the capital expansion. The projection of trend curves into the future is subject to considerable error, and is deplored by many because of its inexactness and dependence on subjective judgment. Nevertheless it is a necessary expedient, since any major business decision affecting future operations involves a forecast, whether explicit or implicit. In the effort to avoid explicit forecasting the assumption is too often made that present levels will continue unchanged. In a dynamic economy such as ours, this assumption is apt to lead to poorer planning than with the use of very crude extensions of past trend curves as forecasts.

3. The third purpose of measuring secular trend is to eliminate it, in order to clarify the cycles and other short-term movements in the data. A steep trend may obscure minor cycles. Dividing the data by the trend values yields ratios which make the curve fluctuate around a horizontal line, thus bringing the cycles into clear relief.

However, these cyclical relatives may be affected arbitrarily by the type of trend curve used and the period to which it is fitted. Also, cycles can usually be discerned without trend adjustment, since the trend component has rarely dominated short-term cyclical-irregular movements in recent times. Hence the trend is not so often eliminated in current practice as it was formerly. Most government indexes of business activity, for example, are expressed as percentages of some base, such as 1957–59 = 100, rather than as percentages of the trend values. These indexes show secular growth as well as short-term fluctuations.

The particular purpose of measuring trend affects the choice of a trend curve to some extent. (1) In measuring the past growth of an industry, any type of empirical trend curve that best describes the basic pattern of change may be used, although the logarithmic straight line is best for comparing the average per cent rate of change in different series. (2) In projecting trend curves, however, the trend must provide a rational preview of future tendencies as well as fitting the past data. Hence a decreasing rate of growth curve is often preferable. (3) Finally, in measuring the trend in order to eliminate it, any type of empirical curve that approximately bisects the cycles may be used. The various types of trend curves are described below.

PERIOD OF YEARS SELECTED

The following rules should be observed in selecting the period of years to be used in fitting a trend curve:

1. The period should be as long as possible, preferably at least 15 or 20 years. In a long period the trend curve is but little affected by short-term episodes such as wars and depressions; whereas in a short period a trend measurement may be distorted by these factors. Shorter periods are necessary, however, for some purposes, or because earlier data are lacking.
2. If the nature of a product or industry is abruptly changed by war, the introduction of a new product, or some other fundamental force, the series should be broken at this point and separate curves fitted to each segment. An examination of the graph of the data will be helpful in revealing such changes.
3. Each end of the series should represent the same phase of the business cycle. Thus, if recent years are prosperous, the series might go back to 1923 or 1925 to begin with the prosperous years of the mid-1920's. If the series began in 1932, the trend line would be tilted upward by the depression at the beginning and prosperity at the end of the period so that it would exaggerate the true basic growth. If the latest years are depressed, the series should begin with a depressed period.

Serious errors have occurred through fitting trend curves to short periods of years dominated by cycles and other temporary disturbances. In the late 1920's, "trend" curves were fitted from the first postwar year, 1919, through the following decade, a period dominated by the expansion phase of a major cycle. These trends were then projected forward to produce the illusory errors of the "new era." Conversely, pessimistic errors were made in the next decade by fitting curves over periods extending from the prosperous 1920's to the depressed 1930's, thus creating the illusion of a mature or stagnant economy.

Chart 18–1 shows trends fitted to various periods of years in output per man-hour, an important factor determining "productivity" or "improvement factor" increases in wage-rate contracts. Over short periods the average "trend" has varied from a growth of 4.1 per cent per year to a decline of more than 3 per cent. In particular, the United Auto Workers have cited the average annual growth of over 3 per cent since 1947 to support their demands for future wage-rate increases. On the other hand, the long-term growth since 1909 has averaged only 2.2 per cent per year, according to the Joint Economic Committee statisticians.

METHODS OF MEASURING TREND

A secular trend curve may be fitted to a series of data by means of (1) a graphic "freehand" fit, (2) moving averages, (3) the method of

Chart 18-1
ANNUAL RATES OF CHANGE IN OUTPUT PER MAN-HOUR IN THE TOTAL PRIVATE ECONOMY
(1947 = 100)

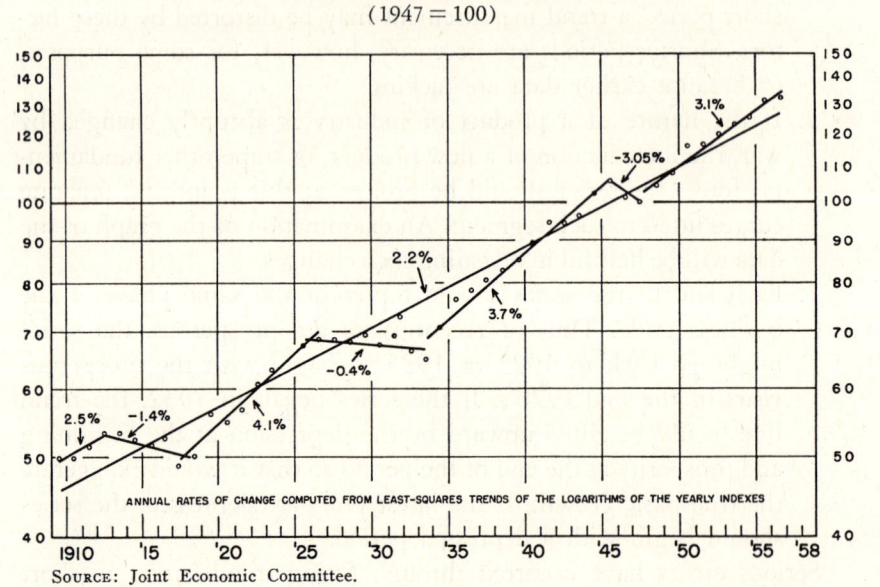

ANNUAL RATES OF CHANGE COMPUTED FROM LEAST-SQUARES TRENDS OF THE LOGARITHMS OF THE YEARLY INDEXES

SOURCE: Joint Economic Committee.

least squares, or (4) the method of three selected points used for "growth" curves. These will be described in turn. In each case the statistical technique must be supplemented by a knowledge of the economic forces involved and the rational nature of the growth factor represented.

Annual data are ordinarily used in secular trend analysis, rather than quarterly or monthly figures, because short-term movements are usually insignificant in measuring the broad sweep of an industry's growth or decline and because the use of such frequent data involves much extra work. However, the methods applied in this chapter to annual data can easily be adapted to quarterly or monthly figures if desired.

The series should first be plotted on a graph to provide a visual picture of the fluctuations in the data, and later the trend curve and the reasonableness of the fit. The arithmetic scale is somewhat easier to plot and simpler for the reader to understand than the ratio scale. Hence, an arithmetic vertical scale may be used for popular presentation or for fitting trend equations to the natural values of the data by least squares (to be explained below).

For trend analysis in general, however, it is recommended that the data be plotted on a ratio scale, since this grid shows the two most important types of trend curves in their simplest form: (1) The exponential curve, with a constant per cent rate of growth, appears as a straight line. This logarithmic straight line characterizes many young industries and affords easy comparison of average rates of change in different series. (2) The "growth" curve, with a decreasing rate of gain, appears as a simple curve bending over to the right, rather than as an elongated S on an arithmetic scale.

Graphic "Freehand" Measurement

The simplest method of fitting a trend curve is to draw it through the center of the plotted data by inspection.[1] If the general tendency of the data roughly follows a straight line, a transparent ruler or a piece of string may be used to locate the approximate central trend. If the trend is curved, a transparent French curve (such as Dietzgen No. 2217–48) or an engineer's flexible spline rule may be used. The term "freehand" is applied to any nonmathematical curve in statistical analysis, even when it is constructed with the aid of drafting instruments.

The trend line or curve should be drawn through the graph of the data in such a way that the areas above and below the trend are equal. They should be exactly equal for the series as a whole, and approximately equal for the first half and last half of the series separately, and as far as possible for each major cycle. That is, the vertical deviations of the data above the trend line must total the same as the vertical deviations below the line. These deviations may be marked off cumulatively on the edge of a strip of paper, one above the other, for comparison. In Chart 18–2, for example,[2] the total vertical deviations $(a+b+c)$ below the trend line must equal the total of those above $(d+e)$.

Use of Group Averages. The average values of groups of data may be plotted as guide points in drawing a smooth trend curve. These averages may be computed for successive three- or five-year periods; or

---

[1] For a more precise but detailed method of fitting a straight line, see S. I. Askovitz, "A Short-Cut Graphic Method for Fitting the Best Straight Line to a Series of Points According to the Criterion of Least Squares," *Journal of the American Statistical Association,* March 1957, pp. 13–17.

[2] Chart 18–2 also illustrates a graphic method of finding the mean deviation of the data around the trend line, as a measure of cyclical amplitude or instability of growth. Simply cumulate the total deviation $(a+b+c+d+e)$ on a paper strip, measure this distance in centimeters or inches, divide by the number of items (5), and lay off the average distance on the vertical scale of the chart to find the mean deviation. On a ratio scale, lay off the average distance above a base line as 100 per cent, as described on page 149. If it comes to 108.5, the mean deviation is $108.5 - 100 = 8.5$ *per cent.* Do not read off the total deviation on a ratio scale.

Chart 18-2

CHECKING THE FIT OF A FREEHAND TREND CURVE

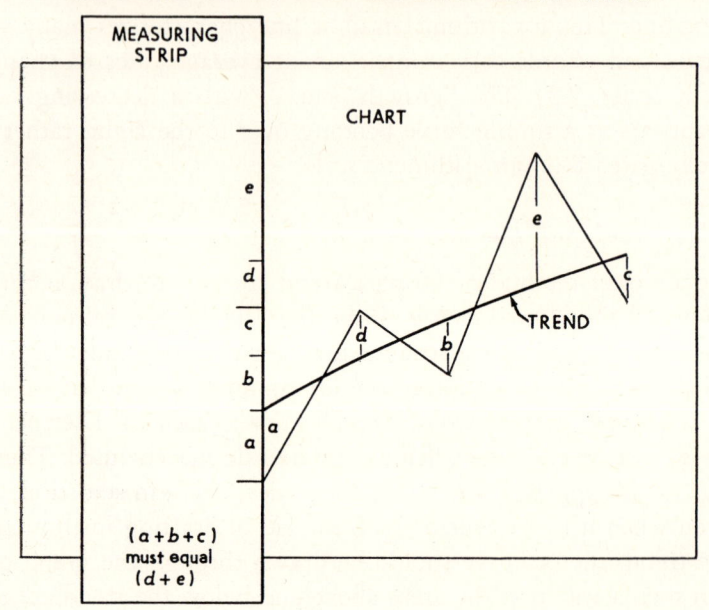

they may be computed for each cycle, marked off from trough to trough and plotted at the center year of the cycle. The trend is then drawn as a smooth curve between the plotted averages, but not necessarily through each one.

A special case of the method of plotting group averages in fitting a straight line trend is to use only two groups—the first half and the second half of the data. In case there is an odd number of years, the middle year may be omitted. The two averages are simply plotted on arithmetic graph paper at the center year of each period, and the two points connected by a straight line. This is called the *method of semi-averages*. It is an objective and simple method, but the trend line may be more affected by extreme deviations near the middle of the period than one drawn by inspection. Another special application of group averages is to use the averages of three groups in fitting growth curves, as described later in the chapter.

If there is a zone of uncertainty as to where the best trend line falls, several lines or curves may be drawn lightly in pencil by one or more analysts and an average of them selected as the most reasonable value.

An Example. Chart 18-3 shows two secular trend curves fitted by the graphic method to Sears, Roebuck sales from 1926 to 1956. Sales for the next four years 1957-60 have also been plotted as a check on

Chart 18–3

FREEHAND TRENDS FITTED TO SEARS, ROEBUCK & COMPANY DEFLATED NET SALES, 1926–56, AND PROJECTED TO 1960

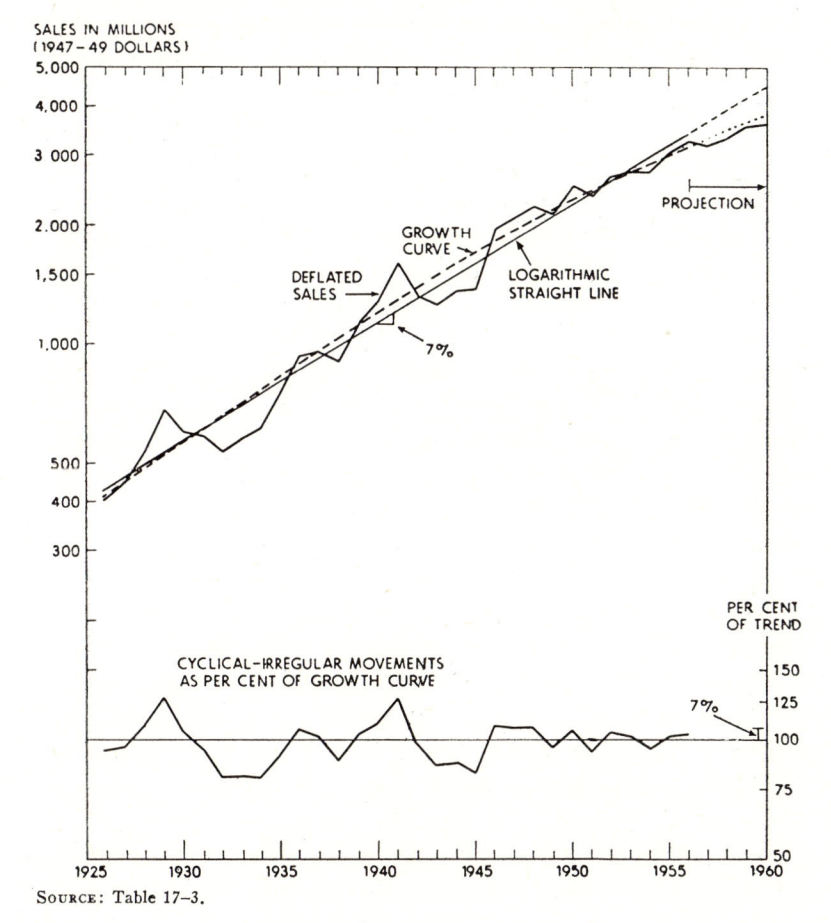

SOURCE: Table 17–3.

the validity of the trend projections. The sales have been deflated to remove the effect of price changes as described in the last chapter, and plotted on a ratio chart. The ratio scale is chosen because the percentage rate of growth has been nearly constant during this period, and so it can be represented by a simple straight line on this chart, whereas the trend would curve up more and more steeply on an arithmetic chart.

The period of years is long enough so that the trend growth dominates the short-term cyclical-irregular movements. This period also balances the high-level prosperity levels of 1926–29 and 1952–56 at its two extremes. Finally, it represents the era of the company's expansion in urban department stores, the first one of which was established in 1925. Earlier data would have reflected the growth of mail-order business alone.

The deflated sales data for 1926–56 show various cyclical-irregular fluctuations, but nevertheless the general growth tendency follows a nearly straight line. A linear trend or "logarithmic straight line" has therefore been drawn through the data with a transparent ruler so as to bisect approximately each of the major cycles, as far as possible. Then the vertical deviations above and below the line have been cumulated and the line adjusted slightly to equalize the sum of these deviations for the two halves of the series.

The average annual rate of growth has then been measured as described on pages 148–49. That is, the vertical rise in the trend line in any year (see 1940–41 in Chart 18–3) has been laid off by dividers on the right-hand per cent scale of the chart. This distance extends from 100 per cent upward to 107 per cent, indicating an average growth of 7 per cent per year in deflated sales over this period. This rate may be compared directly with that in deflated sales of other stores or real personal income, if desired.

The graphic measurement of average growth rate is subject to errors in drawing the slope of the trend line and in reading the result off the chart. The error in slope is small, however, if the trend is linear and the deviations from the trend line small. If these conditions do not hold, any measure of trend, whether graphic or mathematical, may be defective. The error in reading values from a chart is also small if the curve is drawn to a large vertical scale.

The straight line indicates that Sears, Roebuck has expanded at a fairly sustained rate over the past 30 years, although some flattening out is evident since 1947. A "growth" function has therefore been drawn with a French curve to embody a decreasing rate of gain. This curve is higher in the middle and lower at the ends than the straight line. In this case, the growth curve appears to describe the trend of sales somewhat better than the straight line, particularly in recent years. The growth curve may also be preferable for long-term projection since it follows the retardation-of-growth principle characteristic of many industries.

A logarithmic straight line may be projected for a limited period—say five or ten years—since the rate of expansion may be nearly constant for such a period, and the troublesome problem of curvature is avoided. In the very long run, however, the logarithmic straight line becomes too optimistic since it increases indefinitely at a geometric rate.

The 1957–60 sales plotted in Chart 18–3 show how the trend projections worked out for these years. The extended growth curve proved better than the straight line. On the other hand, a straight line fitted to the postwar years 1946–56 would have forecast 1957–60 sales fairly well. Of course, trend projections do not forecast cyclical-irregular fluctuations, and Sears, Roebuck sales were affected by the 1957–58 recession.

Eliminating Trend. The growth component of Sears, Roebuck & Company sales may be eliminated graphically on the ratio chart for the purpose of isolating cyclical-irregular movements as follows: Draw a horizontal line at some convenient level away from the original curve —say opposite the lower printed number 2. Then mark a percentage scale with 50, 100, and 150 per cent opposite the printed scale numbers 1, 2, and 3, respectively. Caption this scale "Per Cent of Trend." Now take the *vertical* distances from each point to the original trend (the growth curve in Chart 18–3) with a divider or paper strip, and lay these distances off in the same years above and below the horizontal 100 per cent line. Connect these points with straight lines.

The resulting curve, at the bottom of Chart 18–3, represents the cyclical-irregular movements in sales, since the trend is eliminated, or flattened out. (There are no seasonal fluctuations in annual data). The sales are now "adjusted for trend," or expressed as percentages of the trend values. This graphic adjustment is a short-cut method of dividing the sales data by the corresponding trend values and plotting the results.

The cyclical peak in 1929, the depression trough in 1932–34, the 1941 peak, the period of war shortages, and the mild postwar cycles are all clearly shown. The cyclical levels at the ends of the series, however, are somewhat uncertain, since the trend curve has a larger error where nearby past or future data are not known.

Graphic versus Mathematical Methods. Graphic "freehand" methods in statistical analysis have three major advantages over mathematical computations:

1. They usually save time and labor. For this reason they are widely used in business analysis where approximate results must be obtained in the minimum time.
2. Graphic curves are more flexible than rigid mathematical functions and hence may fit the data more closely. In Chart 18–4, for

Chart 18-4

FREEHAND AND GOMPERTZ CURVES FITTED TO OUTPUT
OF PORTLAND CEMENT, 1890–1958

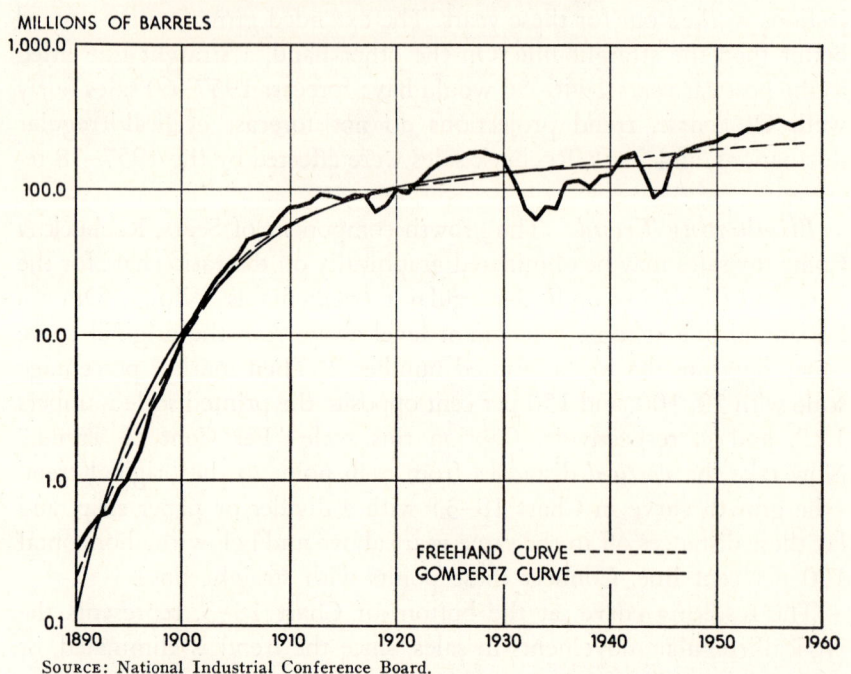

SOURCE: National Industrial Conference Board.

example, a Gompertz curve has been fitted mathematically to the output of Portland cement from 1890 to 1950. This is a fairly good fit, but the curve is clearly too high from about 1893 to 1902, too low from 1905 to 1915, and too nearly horizontal in 1950. A freehand trend drawn by inspection with a French curve (dashed line) appears to be a better fit during these periods. The Federal Reserve Board's trend-cycle curve used in measuring seasonal variation, described in the next chapter, also illustrates the flexibility of graphic curves.

3. Graphic methods afford a continuing picture of successive steps in analysis. Such a picture aids the observer in planning operations and judging the results. It also provides a visual aid in teaching or explaining the method to others.

Graphic methods, however, also have three major disadvantages:

1. They reflect the subjective errors of the analyst. His personal bias, mistakes in judgment, and optical errors all affect the results. As one writer expresses it: "The statistician determines what answer he wants and then proceeds to obtain it." The same writer,

however, later fits six different mathematical trend curves to the same data with the inconclusive result that "it is not easy to decide which of the trends brings out the cycles most accurately." Mathematical methods are no substitute for personal judgment.[3]

2. Because of the subjective element in graphic methods, a skilled analyst is required to draw curves with reasonable accuracy and good judgment. The amateur may be led astray. Also, since calculating machines can perform repetitive mathematical calculations rapidly, the cost of fitting a mathematical curve may be moderate.

3. Mathematical curves can be expressed by formulas that provide the "best" fit according to some stated criterion. Such results have at least the appearance of greater exactness than do hand-drawn curves, and hence may carry more conviction with the reader.

Most theoretical statisticians prefer mathematical methods of analysis for these reasons; but many practicing statisticians, particularly in business, lean toward graphic methods because of their speed, flexibility, and simplicity.

Graphic and mathematical methods may be used in combination to utilize the advantages of each. A graphic trend curve, for example, can be drawn to establish its general location and shape; then an appropriate mathematical equation can be selected for more objective measurement. The graphic curve also serves as a rough check on the accuracy and reasonableness of the mathematical equation. In a research department the director of research can sketch out a preliminary curve graphically, then set up the program for the proper mathematical computations to be performed on the calculating machine, and finally check the results against his own curves.

Moving Averages

A moving average is a series of overlapping averages that serves to approximate the trend of a series by canceling out the high and low values. Each average is an ordinary arithmetic mean of several values

---

[3] As Simon Kuznets puts it: "We must bear in mind the essential uncertainty of the whole process of separation or we shall be unduly influenced by mechanical methods of fitting. The method of least squares may save the investigator the trouble of decision in fitting to selected points and may seem more objective in the sense that identical results will be reached by different investigators. But mechanical arbitrariness is no whit better for being mechanical, and the method of least squares does not assure satisfaction of the two most obvious criteria of goodness of fit; namely, the balance and the minimizing of relative deviations from trend within each cycle" (*Secular Movements in Production and Prices* [New York: Houghton Mifflin Co., 1930], p. 62).

plotted at the center year. For example, in a three-year moving average the average of the data for the first three years is taken as the trend value for the second year; the average for the second to fourth years is taken as the trend value for the third year, etc. If the series contains uniform cycles of three years' duration, therefore, each three-year moving average will contain one complete cycle and the average will be free of cyclical influence, since the fluctuations in the two directions offset each other.

In Table 18–1, for example, a hypothetical series (col. 2) has been built up from a linear trend (col. 3) and a uniform three-year cycle (col. 4) expressed as deviations from the trend values. A three-year

Table 18–1

COMPUTATION OF THREE-YEAR MOVING AVERAGE

Year (1)	Hypothetical Series (2)	Trend (3)	Cycle (4)	3-Year Moving Total (5)	3-Year Moving Average (6)
1954	10	10	0	..	..
1955	12	11	+1	33	11
1956	11	12	−1	36	12
1957	13	13	0	39	13
1958	15	14	+1	42	14
1959	14	15	−1	45	15
1960	16	16	0	..	..

moving total is then computed (col. 5), beginning with 33 as the total for 1954–56, and 36 for 1955–57. Dividing these figures by 3 gives the moving average in column 6. These are seen to equal the true trend values (col. 3) except that no averages can be computed for the two end-years.

The period of years selected in computing the moving average should equal the median length of the cycles in the data. If the period is less than the length of the cycle, part of the cycle will remain in the moving average. If the number of years taken exceeds the length of the cycle, an inverse movement will be introduced into the moving average. An odd number of years is usually preferred to an even number so that the center of the period will fall on the middle year.

If a moving average is computed for an even number of years, an additional step in computation is required to center the average on the middle year. Thus, in Table 18–1, a four-year average for 1954–57 would be centered between 1955 and 1956, and the average for

1955–58 would be centered between 1956 and 1957; so these two averages must themselves be averaged to center the result at 1956. In this case the two averages are 11½ and 12¾; so their average centered on 1956 is 12⅛, the trend value for that year.

An application of moving averages in trend analysis is shown in Chart 18–5. Here Edward R. Dewey of the Foundation for the Study

Chart 18–5

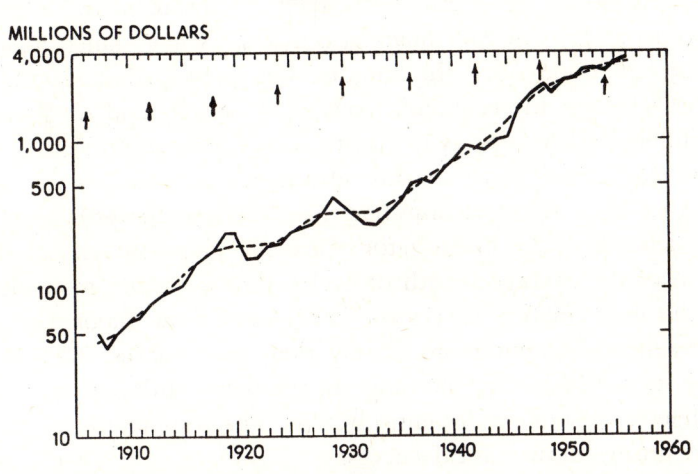

FIG. 1. Sears, Roebuck & Company Net Dollar Sales, 1907–56, together with a Six-Year Moving Average Trend (First Three and Last Three Values Estimated). Arrows Indicate Times of Ideal Highs of a Six-Year Cycle. Ratio Scale.

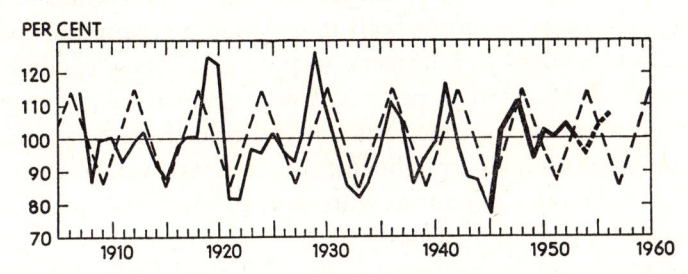

FIG. 2. The Six-Year Cycle in Sears, Roebuck & Company Net Dollar Sales as Percentages of Their Six-Year Moving Average. Bold Line Shows How the Forecast Has Worked Out.

SOURCE: Edward R. Dewey, "The 6-Year Cycle," *Cycles,* December 1952, p. 347, updated through 1956 by courtesy of Mr. Dewey.

of Cycles fits a six-year moving average to Sears, Roebuck & Company sales from 1907, the earliest date available, to 1951, on the premise that the average cycle length has been six years. It was not necessary to deflate sales for this purpose, since the study is concerned only with the *timing* of cyclical turning points, which are little affected by price changes. The moving average is fairly smooth, although it does not eliminate entirely two long cycles between 1914 and 1933. The moving-average values for the first and last three years are estimated. The arrows mark the timing of the crests in the average six-year cycle.

The lower panel shows the data adjusted for trend, i.e., divided by the moving averages. The cycles now stand out clearly, except the two noted above. A regular six-year cycle has been superimposed (dashed line) and projected upward to 1954, then downward to 1957, and upward again to 1960. Unfortunately, actual sales have failed to follow the projected cycle since the forecast was published in 1952. It is doubtful whether any economic cycle is so regular and so dominates other influences on sales as to justify such a precise projection.

Moving averages have several advantages as measures of secular trend: (1) They are more objective than freehand curves because they do not depend on the investigator's personal judgment, except in the selection of the average length of cycles. (2) They are more flexible than most mathematical curves and hence can follow major changes in the growth component more closely than such curves. The moving average stays well within the range of the data, while a mathematical curve may miss some cycles entirely. (3) The computation is simpler than in fitting mathematical curves.

Moving averages, however, also have several disadvantages as measures of secular trend:

1. They can represent trend accurately only if the cyclical-irregular fluctuations are uniform both in duration and amplitude, and if the true trend is an arithmetic straight line. These conditions, of course, do not hold in practice. Cycles and irregular movements are notoriously variable. Also, if the true trend curves upward from an arithmetic straight line, the moving average will be too high, unless elaborate weights are used; if the trend curves downward, the moving average will be too low.

2. Values cannot be computed at the ends of the series but must be drawn in freehand. Thus, in a five-year moving average no values are available for the last two years; yet these are the most important years of the series.

3. The most useful type of trend curve for summarizing past growth and for projection into the future is a smooth curve that represents a consistent and continuous development. The moving average fails in this respect. It may serve, therefore, to eliminate most of the trend component but is less useful than other curves for the study of trend itself.

Moving averages are sometimes used to measure "secondary trends" or "long cycles," the long-term drifts above and below the primary trend curve.[4] We are concerned here, however, with primary trends because they are more important and can be measured and projected more accurately. For this purpose the disadvantages of moving averages outweigh their advantages. Other measures of trends are to be preferred.

The Method of Least Squares

The mathematical equation of a smooth curve can often be used to describe the secular trend of a time series. Such an equation provides an objective and concise expression for the growth or decline of the series, but the form of the equation places certain limitations on the possible shapes of the fitted curve.

After the general equation of the trend curve has been selected, the curve is fitted by determining the constants (e.g., a and b in the equations below) so as to obtain the particular curve of the chosen type which fits best. Goodness of fit can be judged in several ways. For example, one might like to have the average trend values equal the corresponding averages of the data not only for the series as a whole but also for selected parts (e.g., halves or thirds), or one might prefer to have the fitted curve pass through certain key points, such as cycle averages.

The most widely used criterion is that of *least squares*. This criterion states that the best-fitting curve of a given type is the one from which the sum of the *squared* deviations of the data is least. Hence the "method of least squares." The deviations are measured *vertically* from the trend line, not perpendicularly. This criterion also requires that the sum of the deviations of the data (Y) above the trend line (Y_c) must equal the sum of the minus deviations below the line, so that the total deviations equal zero.

The method of least squares is applied here to the arithmetic straight line, the parabola, and the logarithmic straight line in turn. The sum of the squared deviations from the least-squares straight line is less than that from any other straight line. Similarly, the sum of the squared deviations from the least-squares parabola is less than that from any other curve described by a polynomial in X and X^2. Since the logarithmic straight line is fitted to the logarithms of the data, the sum of squares of logarithmic deviations is minimized. These usually cor-

---

[4] See Elmer C. Bratt, *Business Cycles and Forecasting* (5th ed.; Homewood, Ill.: Richard D. Irwin, Inc., 1961), pp. 19–20, 25–28, 98–101, for further discussion of secondary trends.

respond closely to percentage or relative deviations from trend, rather than to the absolute deviations.

The method of least squares is most appropriate for data having a uniform variance of deviations along the trend line, few extreme deviations, and deviations that are independent of each other, especially in adjacent periods. These conditions do not hold in time series. The deviations from trend are cyclical-irregular rather than random. Hence, one should attribute no special virtues to the method of least squares for fitting trends except simplicity from a practical point of view.

No matter what method is used to fit a trend, the equation type should be one which is capable of describing the basic tendency of the series. Straight lines are often fitted to series having curved trends, with ridiculous results. Even if a straight line or parabola fits the past growth accurately, it is a purely empirical description and will not necessarily fit future growth. There should be some logical justification for curves used in forecasting, such as the tendency of many industries to grow at a constant percentage rate in their youth and at a decreasing rate as they mature. These tendencies are described by logarithmic straight lines and growth curves, respectively. Trend curves should not be fitted and projected indiscriminately.

Arithmetic Straight Line. The general equation of an arithmetic straight line trend is $Y_c = a + bX$, where Y_c is the computed or trend value of the time series Y in the year numbered X. The constant a is the value of Y_c when $X = 0$, and the constant b is the slope of the trend line—the change in Y_c per unit change in X. In the method of least squares, the trend line is fitted by finding the values of a and b that minimize the sum of the squared deviations from the trend line. To do this, two conditions called the normal equations must be satisfied, since there are two constants in this equation. These equations are:

$$\Sigma Y = Na + b\Sigma X$$
$$\Sigma XY = a\Sigma X + b\Sigma X^2$$

where N is the number of items in the series.

The variable X can be measured from any point in time as the origin, such as the first year of the series. It is easier, however, to choose the origin at the *midpoint* in time because the negative values of X in the first half of the series balance out the positive values in the second half, so that $\Sigma X = 0$. In other words, the time variable is measured as a deviation from its mean. Accordingly, X is changed to the small letter x, where $x = X - \overline{X}$. Since $\Sigma x = 0$, the terms containing ΣX drop out of the normal equations, which become:

Ch. 18] SECULAR TREND 371

$$\Sigma Y = Na$$
$$\Sigma xY = b\Sigma x^2$$

Solving these equations for a and b,

$$a = \frac{\Sigma Y}{N}$$

$$b = \frac{\Sigma xY}{\Sigma x^2}$$

where x is measured from the middle year as origin. Here, the constant a is the arithmetic mean of the series, and b is a simple ratio.

A straight line trend can now be fitted by the method of least squares as follows:

1. Set up a table with columns for the year (x), the value of the time series (Y), the product xY, and x^2 for each year. (The column for x^2 may be omitted, if desired, by looking up Σx^2 in Appendix G.)
2. Add the columns and substitute the totals ΣY, ΣxY, and Σx^2 in the above formulas to find the constants a and b of the trend equation $Y_c = a + bx$.
3. Take any two values of x (preferably rather far apart), find the value Y_c from the trend equation in each case, plot the corresponding points, and draw a straight line through them. This is the trend line.

The computation is illustrated in Table 18–2 for a hypothetical series

Table 18-2

COMPUTATION OF A STRAIGHT LINE BY LEAST SQUARES
ODD NUMBER OF YEARS

Year	x	Y	xY	x^2	Y_c	Y/Y_c
1958	−2	3	−6	4	2	150%
1959	−1	2	−2	1	4	50
1960	0	8	0	0	6	133
1961	1	6	6	1	8	75
1962	2	11	22	4	10	110
Sum	0	30	20	10	30	...

having an odd number of years. This five-year period is of course too short for adequate trend analysis, but it serves to illustrate the method with a minimum of arithmetic detail. Taking the middle year 1960 as

0, the years go from -2 to 2 and the sum is 0. The given data (Y) are listed and the columns xY and x^2 computed for each year and totaled. Substituting the sums in the two normal equations, we have

$$a = \frac{\Sigma Y}{N} = \frac{30}{5} = 6 \quad \text{(the arithmetic mean)}$$

$$b = \frac{\Sigma xY}{\Sigma x^2} = \frac{20}{10} = 2 \quad \text{(the slope)}$$

The trend equation is therefore

$$Y_c = 6 + 2x \quad (x \text{ origin } 1960)$$

In 1958, $x = -2$; so $Y_c = 2$. In 1962, $x = +2$; so $Y_c = 10$. Plotting and connecting these two points gives the trend line, as shown in Chart 18–6. Note that a straight line fitted by least squares always passes through the means of the X and Y values.

If there is an *even* number of years in the series, the x origin must be placed midway between the two middle years in order to make $\Sigma x = 0$. In Table 18–3 this point is between 1960 and 1961. From this origin

Table 18-3

COMPUTATION OF STRAIGHT LINE BY LEAST SQUARES
EVEN NUMBER OF YEARS

Year	x*	Y	xY	x^2
1958	-5	3	-15	25
1959	-3	2	-6	9
1960	-1	8	-8	1
1961	1	6	6	1
1962	3	11	33	9
1963	5	12	60	25
Sum	0	42	70	70

* x unit is six months.

it is ½ year to the middle of 1961, 1½ years to the middle of 1962, and so on. In order to avoid fractions, therefore, let the x unit equal six months. Then mark the x values of the years following the origin 1, 3, 5, 7 . . . , and the x values going back from the origin -1, -3, -5, -7. . . . The computation then proceeds as above, and Σx^2 may again be found in Appendix G.

Chart 18–6
STRAIGHT LINE FITTED BY LEAST SQUARES
ODD NUMBER OF YEARS

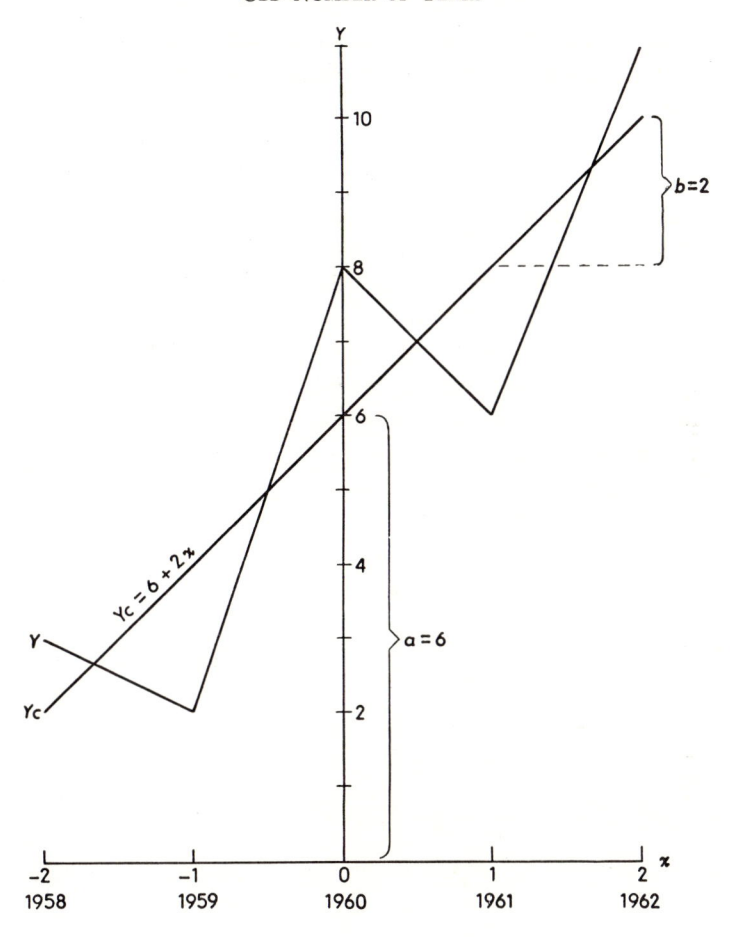

In Table 18–3,

$$a = \frac{\Sigma Y}{N} = \frac{42}{6} = 7$$

$$b = \frac{\Sigma xY}{\Sigma x^2} = \frac{70}{70} = 1$$

$$Y_c = 7 + 1x$$

This equation represents the same trend line as the equation $Y_c = 6 + 2x$ computed for 1958–62 (since the added 1963 value fell on that trend), but $a = 7$ is now the trend value at the new origin, and

$b = 1$ is now the increase in the trend in six months rather than in a year.

Another way to simplify calculations for an even number of years is to drop or add a year at the beginning of the period to make the number an odd one. This change will have little effect if the series is long enough for adequate trend measurement.

The trend values (Y_c) can be listed for each year, if desired, by computing the value for the first year and adding the b value successively on a calculating machine to get the other trend values. The results are shown in Table 18–2. Note that $\Sigma Y_c = \Sigma Y$ as a check.

Occasionally it is desired to eliminate trend, in order to clarify cyclical-irregular movements. To do this, compute and plot Y/Y_c for each year. As in other statistical adjustments, dividing by a factor ($Y_c =$ trend) eliminates the influence of that factor. The last column of Table 18–2 shows the cyclical-irregular movements (pretty violent in this case!) as percentages of the trend values.

As a more realistic example, a straight line trend is fitted by the same method to the deflated sales of Sears, Roebuck & Company from 1926 to 1956 in Table 18–4. The x origin is the middle year 1941. Here

$$a = \frac{\Sigma Y}{N} = \frac{45{,}496}{31} = 1{,}467.6 \quad \text{(i.e., the average sales in millions of dollars)}$$

$$b = \frac{\Sigma x Y}{\Sigma x^2} = \frac{229{,}640}{2{,}480} = 92.597 \quad \text{(i.e., the average increase per year in millions of dollars)}$$

and the trend equation is $Y_c = 1{,}467.6 + 92.597x$. This equation is plotted in Chart 18–7. It is a poor fit; the line is too high throughout the middle of the series and too low at the ends. Its projection to 1957–60 falls far below actual sales in those years, and its extension into the past goes below zero in 1925!

The indiscriminate use of the arithmetic straight line is a common error in trend analysis. For example, a large steel company featured this "standard" trend equation in a full-page magazine advertisement to emphasize the growth in per capita production of light steel products from 1901 to 1956. The result was similar to that in Chart 18–7: the production data curved more and more steeply upward, while the straight trend line touched this curve at only two points, and was far below it at the ends. An arithmetic straight line is a valid measure of trend for a series that tends to increase or decrease by constant abso-

Table 18-4
ARITHMETIC STRAIGHT LINE FITTED BY LEAST SQUARES TO SEARS, ROEBUCK & COMPANY DEFLATED NET SALES, 1926-56

(1) Year	(2) x	(3) Deflated Sales (Millions) Y	(4) xY	(5) x^2
1926	−15	408	−6,120	225
1927	−14	448	−6,272	196
1928	−13	538	−6,994	169
1929	−12	687	−8,244	144
1930	−11	600	−6,600	121
1931	−10	587	−5,870	100
1932	−9	534	−4,806	81
1933	−8	576	−4,608	64
1934	−7	618	−4,326	49
1935	−6	749	−4,494	36
1936	−5	936	−4,680	25
1937	−4	961	−3,844	16
1938	−3	899	−2,697	9
1939	−2	1,122	−2,244	4
1940	−1	1,282	−1,282	1
1941	0	1,594	0	0
1942	1	1,328	1,328	1
1943	2	1,258	2,516	4
1944	3	1,365	4,095	9
1945	4	1,374	5,496	16
1946	5	1,954	9,770	25
1947	6	2,078	12,468	36
1948	7	2,231	15,617	49
1949	8	2,133	17,064	64
1950	9	2,513	22,617	81
1951	10	2,382	23,820	100
1952	11	2,650	29,150	121
1953	12	2,707	32,484	144
1954	13	2,710	35,230	169
1955	14	3,044	42,616	196
1956	15	3,230	48,450	225
Total	0	45,496	229,640	2,480

SOURCE: Table 17-3.

lute increments, but it cannot describe the long-term growth of an industry that expands by bigger increments as the industry itself increases in size. A type of trend curve must be chosen that will follow the tendency of a series throughout its course, and will pass as nearly as possible through the center of individual cycles.

Chart 18–7
STRAIGHT LINE AND PARABOLA FITTED BY LEAST SQUARES
To Sears, Roebuck & Company Deflated Net Sales, 1926–56, and Projected to 1960

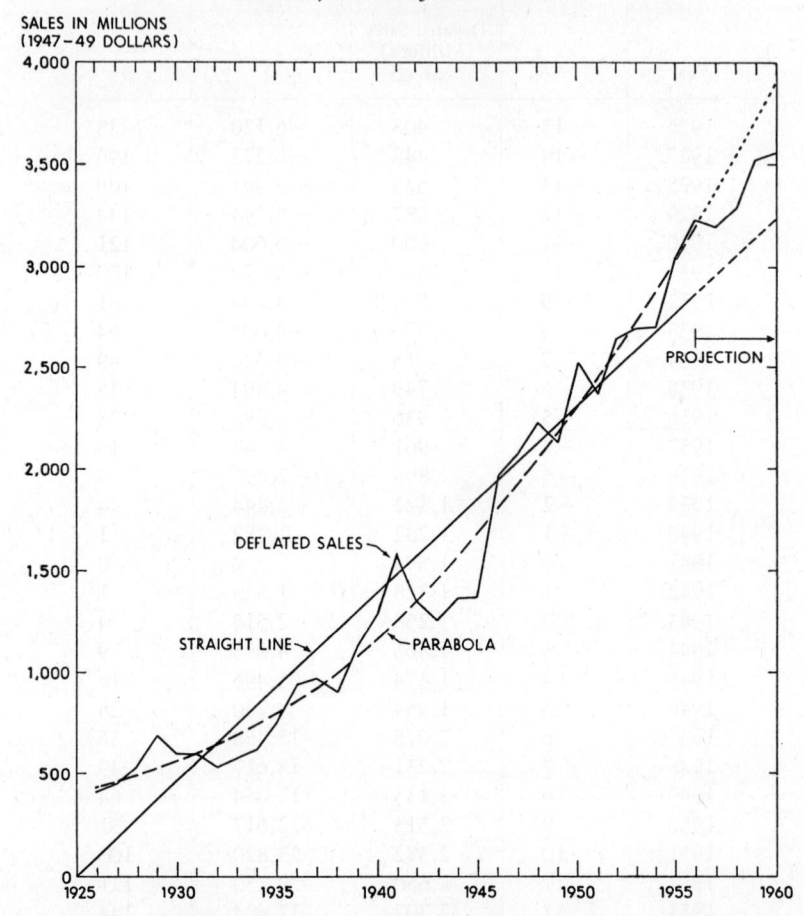

Parabola. The parabola is more flexible than the straight line as a measure of trend because of its curvature. The general shape of a parabola is that of an automobile headlight reflector, pointing either up or down in its usual form. The values of the data will determine automatically what segment of the parabola will be fitted.

The equation of the parabola which is useful in statistical work is $Y = a + bX + cX^2$, or $Y = a + bx + cx^2$ when the x origin is placed at the middle year. It is called a second-degree equation because X is raised to the second power. This equation contains the three constants, a, b, and c, which must be determined for a particular series of data by the least-squares method in order to obtain the best-fitting parabola for the series.[5] A parabola has been fitted to the Sears, Roebuck sales for 1926–56 in Table 18–4 with the following result:

$$Y_c = 1{,}268.01 + 92.597x + 2.495x^2$$

Here the x origin is centered at the middle year, 1941; a is the height of the curve in that year (but not the arithmetic mean); b is the slope of the curve at this point only; and c determines the amount and direction of curvature. The numerical values are in millions of dollars.

The parabola is plotted on Chart 18–7. It is seen to be a much better fit than the straight line. That is, it follows the data more closely, and roughly bisects most of the seven cycles in the period for which it was fitted.[6] On the other hand, the shape of the parabola might be influenced so greatly by cyclical or irregular fluctuations that it may not be a satisfactory description of trend even if it fits the data much better than does the straight line. In particular, the parabola is dangerous for use in forecasting, as it tends to become unreasonably steep when projected far into the future. Note its rise above the sales curve after 1956.

Third-degree polynomial trends of the form $Y_c = a + bX + cX^2 + dX^3$ and curves with still higher powers of X may also be fitted by the method of least squares, but these curves involve excessive labor and produce wavelike forms inconsistent with the concept of secular growth as a smooth curve. These curves are therefore seldom used for this purpose.

---

[5] Taking the middle year as the x origin, the three normal equations to be solved are:

    I. $\Sigma Y = Na + c\Sigma x^2$
    II. $\Sigma xY = b\Sigma x^2$
    III. $\Sigma x^2 Y = a\Sigma x^2 + c\Sigma x^4$

The same columns must be computed and totaled as in the straight line; and, in addition, columns must be computed for x^2Y and x^4. The terms Σx^2 and Σx^4, however, may be looked up directly in Appendix G without listing these columns. In the Sears, Roebuck example $\Sigma x^2 Y = 4{,}034{,}452$ and $\Sigma x^4 = 356{,}624$. The value of b is computed directly from equation II. Its value is the same as in a straight line. The constants a and c are found by solving equations I and III simultaneously. The values of a, b, and c are then substituted in the general equation as shown above, and values of Y_c are computed at five-year intervals of x to plot the trend on the chart.

[6] The goodness of fit could also be compared mathematically by computing the sum of the squared deviations $\Sigma(Y - Y_c)^2$ from each trend curve, and dividing by $(N - m)$, where m is the number of constants (a, b, c) in the trend equation—i.e., two in a straight line and three in a parabola. The trend with the smaller value of $\Sigma(Y - Y_c)^2 \div (N - m)$ is the better fit by this criterion. See Mordecai Ezekiel and Karl A. Fox, *Methods of Correlation and Regression Analysis* (3d ed.; New York: John Wiley & Sons, Inc., 1959), chap. 7, for a further discussion of this measure of goodness of fit.

Logarithmic Straight Line. A straight line drawn on a ratio chart (sometimes called an exponential or compound-interest curve) is often more useful for trend analysis than either the arithmetic straight line or parabola described above. Many younger industries tend to expand at a constant percentage rate of growth, rather than at a constant amount of growth per year which appears as a straight line on an arithmetic chart. Furthermore, the arithmetic straight line is often illogical in that the constant amount of growth each year is independent of the size of the industry itself. Finally, the slopes of logarithmic straight lines show average *per cent* rates of growth, and so they are comparable for series of different units or widely different size, whereas the slopes of trend lines on arithmetic scales are not comparable in such cases.

Even if the rate of growth tends to diminish over a long period, the logarithmic straight line can be used to average the rate over some shorter interval, such as a decade, when the rate of change may be nearly constant.

Measurements of this type . . . possess the advantages of simplicity and ease of calculation. They lend themselves readily, moreover, to comparison and combination, since they are expressed in percentage form. . . . This method yields, for each series, a single measurement which summarizes the direction and degree of change of that series during a stated period and which is directly comparable with similar measures derived from other series, regardless of the units of measurement in which the various series may have been expressed and of the magnitude of the figures in the various series.[7]

Two methods of fitting a logarithmic straight line are described below, and each is applied to the Sears, Roebuck & Company deflated sales shown in Chart 18–3 (p. 361).

In the *graphic method,* plot the data on a ratio chart, draw a straight line through the points with a transparent ruler in such a way as to equalize the areas above and below the line, and measure the vertical rise each year against the percentage scale of the chart, as described earlier in the chapter. The average annual growth in Sears, Roebuck & Company's sales from 1926 to 1956 was found to be 7 per cent. This method is quick and easy but is subject to personal errors in measurement, so that many prefer the following mathematical method.

In the *method of least squares,* look up the *logarithms* of the sales, then fit the equation $\log Y_c = a + bx$ exactly as in the least-squares solution for the arithmetic straight line, using $\log Y$ in place of Y.

In Table 18–5 (p. 379), the years (x) are listed in column 3 with

---

[7] Frederick C. Mills, *Economic Tendencies in the United States* (New York: National Bureau of Economic Research, Inc., 1932), p. 48.

Table 18-5
LOGARITHMIC STRAIGHT LINE FITTED BY LEAST SQUARES TO SEARS, ROEBUCK & COMPANY DEFLATED SALES, 1926–56

Year* (1)	Deflated Sales† Y (2)	x (3)	log Y (4)	x log Y (5)	log Y$_c$ (6)	Trend Y$_c$ (7)	Adjustment for Trend Y/Y$_c$ (Per Cent) (8)
1926	408	−15	2.6107	−39.1605	2.6338	430	94.9
1927	448	−14	2.6513	−37.1182	2.6639	461	97.2
1928	538	−13	2.7308	−35.5004	2.6940	494	108.9
1929	687	−12	2.8370	−34.0440	2.7241	530	129.6
1930	600	−11	2.7782	−30.5602	2.7541	568	105.6
1931	587	−10	2.7686	−27.6860	2.7842	608	96.5
1932	534	−9	2.7275	−24.5475	2.8143	652	81.9
1933	576	−8	2.7604	−22.0832	2.8444	699	82.4
1934	618	−7	2.7910	−19.5370	2.8745	749	82.5
1935	749	−6	2.8745	−17.2470	2.9046	803	93.3
1936	936	−5	2.9713	−14.8565	2.9347	860	108.8
1937	961	−4	2.9827	−11.9308	2.9648	922	104.2
1938	899	−3	2.9538	−8.8614	2.9949	988	91.0
1939	1,122	−2	3.0500	−6.1000	3.0249	1,059	105.9
1940	1,282	−1	3.1079	−3.1079	3.0550	1,135	113.0
1941	1,594	0	3.2025	0	3.0851	1,216	131.1
1942	1,328	1	3.1232	3.1232	3.1152	1,304	101.8
1943	1,258	2	3.0997	6.1994	3.1453	1,397	90.1
1944	1,365	3	3.1351	9.4053	3.1754	1,498	91.1
1945	1,374	4	3.1380	12.5520	3.2055	1,605	85.6
1946	1,954	5	3.2909	16.4545	3.2356	1,720	113.6
1947	2,078	6	3.3176	19.9056	3.2657	1,844	112.7
1948	2,231	7	3.3485	23.4395	3.2957	1,976	112.9
1949	2,133	8	3.3290	26.6320	3.3258	2,117	100.8
1950	2,513	9	3.4002	30.6018	3.3559	2,269	110.8
1951	2,382	10	3.3769	33.7690	3.3860	2,432	97.9
1952	2,650	11	3.4232	37.6552	3.4161	2,607	101.6
1953	2,707	12	3.4325	41.1900	3.4462	2,794	96.9
1954	2,710	13	3.4330	44.6290	3.4763	2,994	90.5
1955	3,044	14	3.4834	48.7676	3.5064	3,209	94.9
1956	3,230	15	3.5092	52.6380	3.5365	3,440	93.9
Total	45,496	0	95.6386	74.6215	95.6389		

* Calendar years 1926–32; years beginning February 1, 1933–56.
† Net sales, in millions of 1947–49 dollars.
Source: Table 17-3.

the origin centered in 1941, the logarithms of the sales (log Y) in column 4, and the product for each year (x log Y) in column 5. Columns 4 and 5 are then totaled, and Σx^2 is found from Appendix G. To determine a and b (which are both logarithms in this equation),

$$a = \frac{\Sigma \log Y}{N} = \frac{95.6386}{31} = 3.08512$$

$$b = \frac{\Sigma x \log Y}{\Sigma x^2} = \frac{74.6215}{2,480} = .030089$$

The trend equation is therefore:

$$\log Y_c = 3.08512 + .030089x$$

To graph the trend on a ratio chart, plot any two widely separated points, using natural values of Y_c, and draw a straight line through them.

In 1926,

$x = -15$, $\log Y_c = 3.08512 - .45134 = 2.6338$, so $Y_c = 430$

In 1956,

$x = +15$, $\log Y_c = 3.08512 + .45134 = 3.5365$, so $Y_c = 3,440$

Here, the trend practically coincides with the freehand line in Chart 18–3, and so it is not drawn in separately. The slope of the least-squares trend line is the logarithm b. This means that the ratio of each year's trend value to the preceding year's is antilog b, or 1.0717. The average rate of growth is then $1.0717 - 1 = .0717$, or 7.17 per cent.[8]

The trend may be eliminated, if desired, by computing and plotting Y/Y_c, or antilog ($\log Y - \log Y_c$), for each year. The computations are shown in Table 18–5, columns 6–8. The resulting curve resembles the graphically adjusted curve at the bottom of Chart 18–3 except that the trend base is the logarithmic straight line rather than the growth curve.

The parabola and logarithmic straight line appear to fit the trend of Sears, Roebuck sales about equally well through 1953, but thereafter both curves are too high. It would be better in this case to fit two

---

[8] The average rate of growth can be computed without using logarithms by the shortcut "method of moments," as follows: Take the first year as the origin (i.e., $X = 0$ in 1926), then compute XY for each year (where Y equals sales), and sum the Y and XY columns. Now compute the "mean value," $M = \Sigma XY/\Sigma Y$ and look up M and n (the number of years) in the Mean Value Table of James W. Glover's *Tables of Applied Mathematics* (Ann Arbor, Mich.: George Wahr, 1930), pp. 471 ff., to find the slope r. The a value may also be computed as described in Glover, p. 470.

This method minimizes the absolute deviations about the trend line rather than the logarithmic deviations, and so it gives more weight to larger values. The results of the method of moments and the logarithmic method do not differ appreciably, however, unless there are cyclical extremes at either end of the series. For further discussion, see Mills, *op. cit.*, pp. 46–49; and Arthur F. Burns, *Production Trends in the United States since 1870* (New York: National Bureau of Economic Research, Inc., 1934), pp. 42–44.

separate logarithmic straight lines to the periods before and after World War II. This trend type is generally preferable to the parabola because it is simpler, more comparable with other trends, and shows the average growth rate.

The graphic and least-squares methods of fitting a logarithmic straight line give nearly the same results in this case. The graphic method is recommended for quick, approximate results, and as a check on other methods; while the least-squares method is preferable for detailed, objective study, where computational assistance is available. The logarithmic least-squares method has the same merits and limitations as the arithmetic least-squares method described earlier in the chapter, except that the logarithmic straight line is more likely to be distorted by extreme *low* values than by extreme high values.

Chart 18-1, page 358, illustrates the use of the logarithmic straight line in economic analysis. The trend lines show that (1) output per man-hour has increased at the average rate of 2.2 per cent per year since 1909, but at a 3.1 per cent rate since 1948; (2) there is no evidence that the rate of growth is slowing down; (3) deviations from the trend "normal" have rarely exceeded 10 per cent, whichever trend is used; and (4) productivity can be projected over the next few years at an increase of from 2.2 to 3.1 per cent per year from the latest figure.

Growth Curves

Growth curves have come into widespread use in recent years for describing both past trends and probable future tendencies, since they embody the rational "law of growth" principle described in the last chapter. That is, an industry or population tends to grow at a nearly constant per cent rate during its youth; but as it matures, this rate tends to diminish.

There are several types of growth curves—the logistic (Pearl-Reed) and Gompertz being the most common[9]—but all have the general characteristics illustrated in Chart 18-8. Here the same logistic curve is plotted on an arithmetic scale in panel A and a ratio scale in panel B. During the period shown, the curve rises from 1 to 99 and approaches an upper limit of 100.

The elongated S curve in panel A shows the growth of a typical

---

[9] "The simple logistic and Gompertz curves, mostly the former, describe well the long-term movements of growing industries, and, with certain modifications, those of declining industries," Simon S. Kuznets, *Secular Movements in Production and Prices* (New York: Houghton Mifflin Co., 1930), p. 197.

Chart 18–8
THE LOGISTIC GROWTH CURVE
A. Arithmetic Vertical Scale

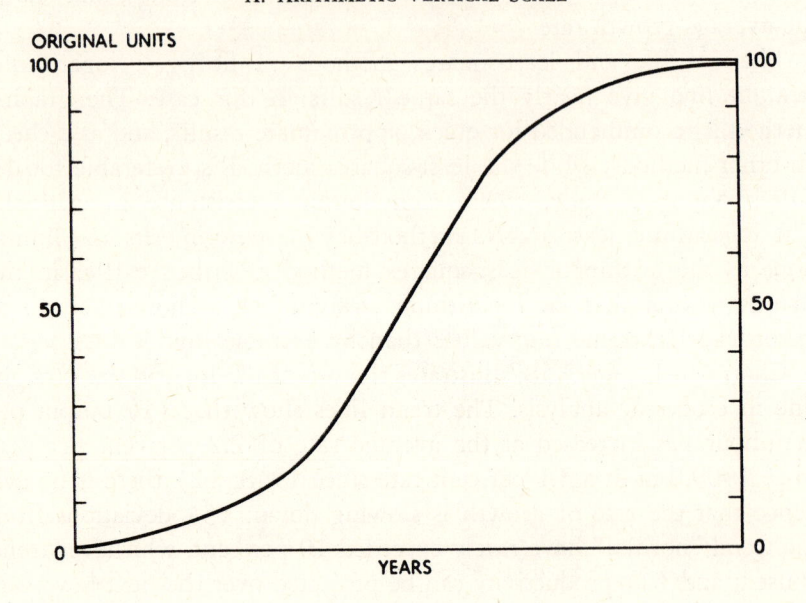

B. Logarithmic Vertical Scale

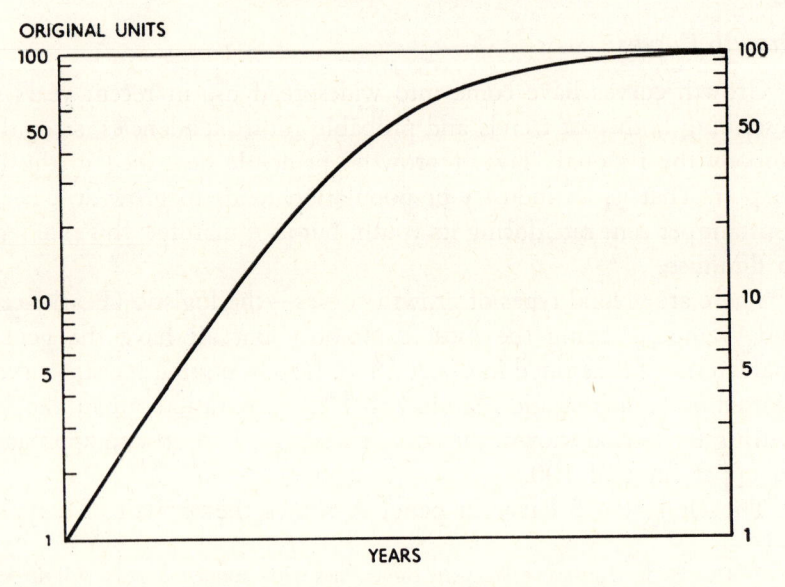

industry or product in absolute units. The first stage is one of experimentation and slow initial growth. Second, there is a period of rapid exploitation of the product, and third, a leveling off of growth with maturity and saturation of demand. The relative age of different industries may be determined by locating them on this curve. Thus the electronics and atomic energy industries would be located near its beginning; flour milling and railroads near the saturation level.

The same curve plotted on a ratio scale (panel B) is simpler in form, being concave downward throughout its length. This is the grid that best illustrates the growth principle of a nearly constant percentage rate of change at first, followed by smaller and smaller percentage gains as the industry ages. The data should be plotted on a ratio grid in any of the methods described below.

Before fitting a growth curve, two conditions should be satisfied: (*a*) The process represented should have the characteristics of biological growth to justify the use of this curve on logical grounds. Prices, ratios, business failures, or unemployment series would not qualify. (*b*) The data, when plotted on a ratio scale, must show a declining rate of growth or decline (i.e., must tend to flatten out) empirically, like this: growing series, ⌒; declining series ⌄. Otherwise a growth function cannot be fitted.

A growth curve may be fitted to a series of data in any of three ways:
1. The graphic "freehand" method was described earlier in the chapter. Plot the data on a ratio scale, and with a French curve draw a smooth trend that bends toward the horizontal, as in panel B, to fit the plotted points. As indicated, this method is easy and flexible, but it involves errors of personal judgment, particularly in projections into the future. Freehand growth curves are illustrated in Charts 18–3 and 18–4.
2. In the mathematical method the appropriate type of equation is fitted to three points which are selected at equal intervals of time to represent typical stages of early, middle, and recent development. These points are usually averages of several years to iron out cyclical-irregular influences. Three constants must then be computed to determine the trend equation. The procedure is too cumbersome to be presented here.[10]
3. A short-cut method may be used to fit a growth curve to three selected points, using a nomograph to determine the upper limit and a special grid on which the growth curve can be drawn as a

---

[10] See F. E. Croxton and D. J. Cowden, *Practical Business Statistics* (3d. ed.; Englewood Cliffs, N.J.: Prentice-Hall, Inc., 1960), chap. 38, for a description of mathematical methods of fitting logistic, Gompertz, and modified exponential curves.

straight line.[11] The result approximates that of the corresponding mathematical method, and much labor is saved.

A growth curve fitted to three points may be a poor fit if the analyst errs in his choice of the appropriate type of equation, the period of years covered, or the three points he believes to be typical. Different

Chart 18–9

PRODUCTION OF SYNTHETIC FIBERS, 1922–1960

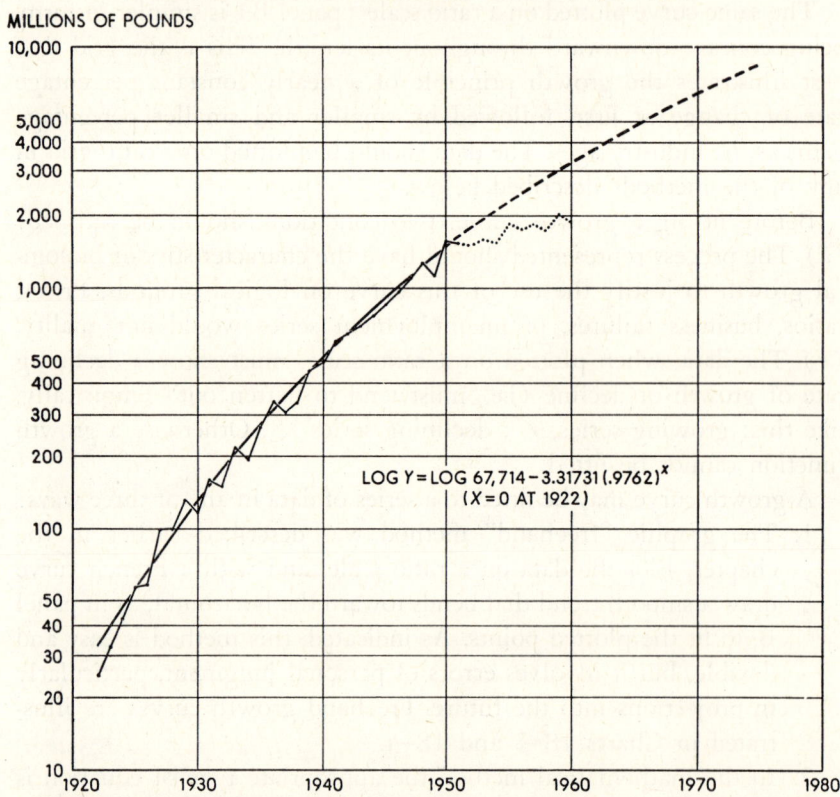

$$\text{LOG } Y = \text{LOG } 67{,}714 - 3.31731(.9762)^X$$
$$(X = 0 \text{ AT } 1922)$$

SOURCE: Raymond H. Ewell and Beth Scheuerman, "Forecasting in the Chemical Industry," *Chemical and Engineering News*, August 25, 1952, p. 3521; 1952–60 data added from Stanford Research Institute, *Chemical Economics Handbook*.

equation types and different selections of three points may therefore be tried to achieve an optimum fit in either the mathematical or the short-cut method, though such experimentation is easier in the latter case.

Chart 18–9 illustrates the use of growth curves in forecasting. Here, a Gompertz curve is fitted to the production of synthetic fibers (includ-

---

[11] See William A. Spurr and David R. Arnold, "A Short-Cut Method of Fitting a Logistic Curve," *Journal of the American Statistical Association*, March 1948, pp. 127–34; Eugene A. Rasor, "The Fitting of Logistic Curves by Means of a Nomograph," *ibid.*, December 1949, pp. 548–53; and Jack Sherman and W. J. Morrison, "Simplified Procedures for Fitting a Gompertz Curve and a Modified Exponential Curve," *ibid.*, March 1950, pp. 87–97.

ing rayon) from 1922 to 1951, and extended to 1975. The curve is a reasonably good fit. The forecast of 8 billion pounds in 1975 compares with estimates of 3.2 and 7.0 billion pounds, respectively, for the same year made by the President's Materials Policy Commission report *Resources for Freedom, 1952* (Vol. II, p. 105; Vol. IV, p. 200), and serves as a useful independent projection, supporting the higher of the two estimates.

Nevertheless, when we plot actual data for 1952 to 1960 (dotted line) as a test of the forecast, the projected curve proves to be much too high. The fact that the trend curve fitted the data in the past provides no assurance that its extrapolation will yield an accurate forecast. Many other factors affecting the industry's future development must also be considered.

SUMMARY

Secular trend may be measured for three purposes: (1) the study of past trends, (2) long-term forecasting, and (3) the elimination of trend to isolate cycles. The period of years selected for trend analysis should be as long as possible in order to minimize short-term disturbances; it should be broken at points of abrupt change; and it should begin and end at the same stage of the business cycle.

Trend may be measured by any of four methods: (1) a graphic "freehand" fit, (2) moving averages, (3) least squares, and (4) three selected points. Annual data are usually used—preferably plotted on a ratio chart.

1. To fit a trend curve by the graphic method, draw it with a transparent ruler or French curve so as to equalize the areas or vertical deviations above and below each major segment of the curve. Averages of groups of years may be plotted as aids in locating the trend. In the method of semiaverages the means of the two halves of the data, plotted on an arithmetic scale, are simply connected with a straight line. The average growth rate of a logarithmic straight line can be read off the percentage scale on the chart. To eliminate trend, lay off the vertical deviations from the trend line about a horizontal line on the ratio chart and label the scale "Per Cent of Trend."

Graphic methods are quick, flexible, and afford a continuous picture of successive steps, while mathematical methods are more objective and often more accurate; the latter can be performed by clerical labor, and the results can be expressed in concise form. The two methods may be combined for optimum effectiveness.

2. A moving average is a series of overlapping means that approximate the trend by canceling out any regular cycles having the same pe-

riod as the average. Moving averages are objective, flexible, and simple but cannot smooth out variable cyclical-irregular movements or fit curvilinear trends; they cannot be computed for the end-years and do not yield a consistent trend function. They are used more for secondary trends or long cycles than for basic trends.

3. The method of least squares fits a mathematical curve to the data such that the total of the squared deviations from the curve is less than that for any similar curve. The plus and minus deviations themselves total zero. This method is objective and reasonably accurate, provided the data follow the equation type chosen and are not too erratic. Unfortunately, however, the optimum conditions for the least-squares method do not occur in time series.

To fit a straight line by least squares, center the X origin at the middle year; set up a table of x, Y, xY, and x^2; and substitute the column totals in the given equations to find a and b in the equation $Y_c = a + bx$. To eliminate trend and isolate cyclical-irregular movements, compute and plot Y/Y_c for each year.

To fit a parabola, add columns for x^2Y and x^4 to the foregoing and substitute the totals in three equations to find a, b, and c in the equation $Y_c = a + bx + cx^2$. This is usually a better fit than a straight line, although it may be unduly affected by cyclical or irregular extremes.

The logarithmic straight line is superior to the other two in describing a rational growth tendency of young industries and in comparing relative rates of change. It may be drawn graphically as a straight line on a ratio chart, or computed by the method of least squares. The least-squares procedure is the same as in the arithmetic straight line, except that log Y is used in place of Y.

4. Growth curves of the logistic or Gompertz type represent the rational tendency of many industries and populations to grow at a declining percentage rate as they mature. A growth curve can be drawn graphically by using a transparent French curve on a ratio chart. It may also be fitted by selecting three typical points and computing the values of three constants in the appropriate equation, or by using a nomograph and special grid as a short cut. Although subjective in nature, these curves are widely used both in the study of past trends and in forecasting.

PROBLEMS

1. *a*) Is it valid to forecast by extrapolating a trend curve fitted to past data? Discuss briefly.
   b) Why may the particular purpose of measuring trend affect the choice of a trend curve?

Ch. 18] SECULAR TREND 387

  c) What factors determine the period of years used in fitting a secular trend curve to an industry's sales?

2. a) Describe the use of group averages in trend fitting.
   b) What is the one chief advantage of mathematical methods and of graphic methods, respectively, in trend analysis? Justify your selection.
   c) Why are moving averages more useful in measuring secondary trends than in measuring primary secular trends?

Problems 3–7 may be assigned either for full-length analysis, as given, or as short illustrative exercises covering only the years beginning 1951.

3. The annual production of electricity by electric utilities in the United States from 1935 to 1957 was as follows (in billions of kilowatt-hours):

Year	Electricity Production	Year	Electricity Production	Year	Electricity Production
1935	95	1943	218	1951	371
1936	109	1944	228	1952	399
1937	119	1945	222	1953	443
1938	114	1946	223	1954	472
1939	128	1947	256	1955	547
1940	142	1948	283	1956	601
1941	165	1949	291	1957	631
1942	186	1950	329		

Source: Federal Power Commission.

  a) Plot these figures on a two-cycle ratio chart, with the vertical scale beginning at 20 billion kilowatt-hours and the horizontal scale extended several years beyond 1957. (Choose a one-cycle ratio chart, with the vertical scale beginning at 200, for problems starting with the year 1951.) Use proper title, scale captions, and source reference.
  b) Draw a smooth freehand trend line or curve through the data, and project it several years beyond 1957, plotting group averages as guides and equalizing the deviations above and below the trend as described in the text.
  c) Describe the nature of growth in this industry. What has been the average annual per cent rate of growth since 1951? (Show on the chart how this value was obtained.)

4. a) Eliminate the trend in Problem 3 graphically, and plot the cyclical-irregular relatives in the lower part of the chart.
   b) Describe the cyclical timing and amplitude of electricity production, and the principal irregular forces at work during this period.

5. Plot the data in Problem 3 on an arithmetic chart, with the time scale extended several years beyond 1957, and compute an arithmetic straight line

by the method of least squares. Show computations and trend equation. Plot this curve on the arithmetic chart and project it into the future.

6. *a*) Fit a logarithmic straight line to the data in Problem 3 by least squares, plot it on the ratio chart, and extend it beyond 1957.
   b) What is the average annual per cent rate of growth?
   c) How does the least-squares criterion of goodness of fit differ in its application to the arithmetic straight line and the logarithmic straight line?
   d) Explain the meaning of the constants *a* and *b* in each of these equations.

7. *a*) Compare the goodness of fit of the freehand trend, the arithmetic straight line, and the logarithmic straight line in describing the growth of electricity production.
   b) Which of these three curves is the most logical for use in forecasting? Why?
   c) Find comparable up-to-date figures on electricity production and plot them on your two charts. What is the per cent error in your forecast for the latest year? What factors might explain this error?

8. *a*) Explain the "law of growth" principle implicit in the use of growth curves.
   b) Describe briefly one method of fitting a growth curve.
   c) What is the logical justification, if any, of fitting and projecting such a curve as a 20-year forecast of electricity production?

	1958	1959	1960	1961	1962	1963
GNP	401	429	440	448	475	493
FRB Index	94	106	109	110	118	124

SOURCE: *Survey of Current Business*, February 1964.

9. For Gross National Product (in billions of 1954 dollars):
   a) Fit a logarithmic straight line trend to the period 1958–62 (not 1963). Criticize the period of years chosen.
   b) What is the average annual per cent rate of growth for 1958–62?
   c) Forecast 1963 by extrapolating your trend. What is your per cent error in this forecast? Explain this error.

10. For the Federal Reserve Board Index of Industrial Production (1957–59 = 100) make the same analysis as in Problem 9.

SELECTED READINGS

(See Chapter 19.)

19. SEASONAL AND CYCLICAL VARIATIONS

THE PRINCIPAL types of fluctuations in economic activities were described in Chapter 17. Trend analysis was discussed in Chapter 18. In this chapter the purposes and principal methods of measuring seasonal variation and business cycles will be surveyed. These two are considered together because the cyclical component is usually considered as the residual after the seasonal variation has been eliminated.

In trend analysis, annual data are usually used. For the study of shorter-term seasonal and cyclical movements, however, quarterly, monthly, or weekly data are needed. Monthly figures are most common.

PURPOSES OF MEASURING SEASONALITY

There are three principal purposes of measuring seasonal movements: (1) to analyze past seasonal behavior, (2) to predict seasonal movements as an aid in short-term planning, and (3) to eliminate seasonality in order to reveal cyclical movements.

1. Measures of typical seasonal behavior in production, sales, inventories, and prices are indispensable in understanding the characteristic fluctuations of a business during the year, and in gauging the significance of current figures. Seasonal indexes serve to answer such questions as: Was the decline in sales last month more or less than the usual seasonal amount? How much does the price of a given product usually decline between July and August? What is the normal variation in inventories from month to month?

2. Seasonal measures are also useful in planning operations over the next year or two. Every successful business concern operates on a budget, in which the coming year's income and expense items are estimated,

and later checked against actual results. By means of seasonal indexes, next year's budget items may be allocated by months. Seasonal indexes are also particularly useful in scheduling purchases, inventory control, personnel requirements, seasonal financing, and selling and advertising programs.

Most major business decisions affect near-future operations rather than those in the more distant future. Hence short-term forecasting is even more often required than long-term projections. Seasonal fluctuations usually dominate the near-term outlook. Furthermore, these movements can usually be forecast more accurately than the trend or cycles, since they are more regular. Hence, seasonal forecasting is of great value in business planning. For example, according to the International Harvester Company *Annual Report* for 1956:

> There are strong seasonal factors that influence the sales of our products. We must produce our machines and service parts months ahead of the time they are sold at retail. Consequently, we must make [seasonal] estimates as to what the markets for our products will be, produce the machines and service parts, and have them in retail channels prior to the peak selling periods.

Seasonal movements, like cycles, are wasteful because the men and equipment needed in the peak season are idle in the slack season. An accurate knowledge of seasonal behavior is an aid in mitigating and ironing out seasonal movements through business policy. This may be done by introducing diversified products having different seasonal peaks, accumulating stocks in slack seasons in order to manufacture at a more regular rate, cutting prices in slack seasons, and advertising off-seasonal uses for products. While any veteran in a business will know the general nature of its seasonal fluctuations, a precise set of quantitative measures will produce better results.

3. Perhaps the principal purpose of measuring seasonal variations is to get rid of them. Business cycles are of utmost importance, but these cycles are frequently obscured by large seasonal movements. The latter must ordinarily be measured and eliminated to reveal the former. Many monthly statistical series in business and economic publications are "adjusted for seasonal variation" for this purpose. The *Survey of Current Business,* for example, lists the following data and many others on a seasonally adjusted or simply "adjusted" basis: national income, gross national product, industrial production, business sales and inventories, manufacturers' orders, new construction, advertising volume, retail sales, employment, and freight carloadings. A knowledge of seasonal adjustment and its effect on data is therefore essential for the business or economic analyst.

METHODS OF MEASURING SEASONAL VARIATION

Seasonal variation has been defined as a rhythmic movement which recurs each year with about the same relative intensity. This definition points the way to methods by which such variation can be measured. First, it recurs annually; all other rhythmic components of a series are eliminated except that regular one with a period of 12 months. Secondly, seasonal variation is rhythmic or periodic; irregular responses to weather factors or man-made conventions are excluded, and only amplitudes that are repeated each year are included. Finally, the same relative intensity means that a certain month, say March, is expected to vary in the same direction by the same per cent year after year because of seasonal influence.

All of these characteristics may be summarized by a seasonal pattern which is assumed to be typical of any year of a series, or which changes gradually from year to year. This pattern consists of twelve monthly indexes (or four quarterly indexes) whose average is 100 per cent. The problem of measuring seasonal variation is then one of determining these indexes for a given series.

A great many methods have been advanced for computing seasonal indexes.[1] Essentially, however, most refined methods arrive at a seasonal index for a given month by averaging its ratios to a trend-cycle base in several years (or fitting a trend curve to these ratios) to cancel out the nonseasonal factors. A simple method of averaging a given month's or quarter's unadjusted values will first be described and applied to data on sales of manufactured gas to residential consumers. Then more refined methods of averaging a month's ratio to a trend-cycle norm will be surveyed and applied to the sales of Sears, Roebuck & Company.

In any method of measuring seasonality the series is first plotted on a chart to show the general nature of the seasonal pattern and to aid in further analysis. Unless a fairly pronounced and regular rhythm is apparent, seasonal measurement may not be worthwhile. A ratio scale must be used in the graphic method described below, and is usually desirable in other methods as well, since seasonal movements in most economic data are more stable as percentages than in absolute amounts. Hence seasonal indexes themselves are expressed as percentages. The arithmetic scale, however, is frequently used in the moving-average method to simplify plotting.

---

[1] Twenty-seven methods are described in Mario de Vergottini, *Sul calcolo delle variazione stagionali dei fenomeni economici* (Trieste: R. Università di Trieste, 1935), but this list is by no means complete.

The period of time covered should be at least six or seven years for series having a regular seasonal pattern, and longer for irregular data, in order to average out the peculiarities in individual years. The conditions in this period should approximate those expected in the future if the seasonal indexes are to be used for forward planning. The normal seasonal rhythm may be disrupted by wars, strikes, government edicts, severe depressions, and abrupt changes in business policy. Such erratic periods should be excluded, as far as possible. Current analysis might well begin with the year 1947 or 1953 for many series, since the disruptions of World War II and the Korean War distorted normal seasonal behavior throughout the war periods. Sometimes the seasonal nature of a series will change gradually over the years. In this case a relatively long period of years should be used, as in trend analysis, and "progressive" indexes of seasonal variation should be computed as described later in the chapter.

Averages of Original Data

If the seasonal movements are regular and the trend and cyclical influences negligible, a very simple method of measuring seasonality may be used. This method is illustrated by the quarterly data on gas sales listed in Table 19–1 and plotted in Chart 19–1. As shown in the chart, there is a large and regular seasonal movement but little fluctuation of other types.

Table 19–1

SALES OF MANUFACTURED GAS
TO RESIDENTIAL CONSUMERS, 1953–58
(Millions of Therms)

Year	First	Second	Third	Fourth	Annual Average
1953	750	486	263	466	491
1954	804	508	283	552	537
1955	877	515	274	580	562
1956	954	593	189	410	537
1957	688	366	179	430	416
1958	756	396	181	444	444
Total	4,829	2,864	1,369	2,882	2,987
Quarterly average	805	477	228	480	498
Seasonal index	162	96	46	96	100

Source: American Gas Association, as reported in *Survey of Current Business*. Includes mixed gas.

Ch. 19] SEASONAL AND CYCLICAL VARIATIONS 393

Chart 19–1

AVERAGES-OF-ORIGINAL-DATA SEASONAL METHOD
SALES OF MANUFACTURED GAS TO RESIDENTIAL CONSUMERS
1953–58

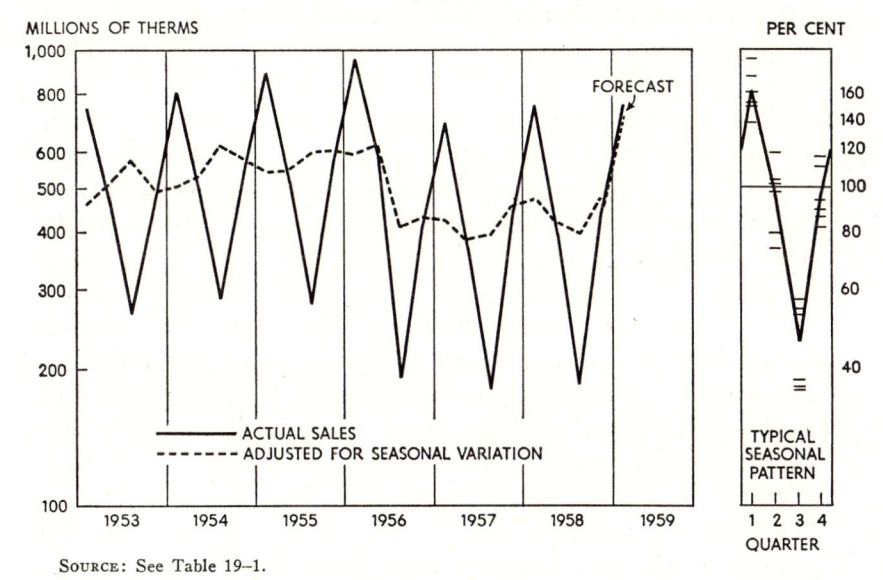

SOURCE: See Table 19–1.

The steps are: (1) Average the production in the first quarter for all years, and do the same for each of the other quarters. That is, add the columns in Table 19–1 and divide the sum by 6 (the number of years). (2) Divide each quarterly average (next to bottom row) by the annual average (498) to get the seasonal index (bottom row). For the first quarter, 805 ÷ 498 = 162 per cent, or an index of 162.

These indexes provide a concise, quantitative pattern of typical seasonal behavior for the six-year period. The index of 162 in the first quarter means that production in that quarter is typically 162 per cent of the average for all quarters, which is taken as 100 per cent. The normal decrease in gas sales between the first and second quarters is from 162 to 96. This is 66 index points, or 66/162 = 41 per cent. A decrease of less than 41 per cent in the second quarter is therefore favorable.

The four seasonal indexes are plotted on the right panel of Chart 19–1 on a per cent scale, with 100 per cent equal to the yearly average sales of 498. The dashes show the sales in each individual quarter. The vertical scatter of these dashes indicates the irregularity of the seasonal movement.

Gas sales may be *forecast* for the first quarter of 1959 by multiplying the 1958 average (444) by the first-quarter seasonal index (162 per cent), assuming no change in trend or cycle. The result is 719 million therms. This is fairly close to the actual reported figure of 748 million therms. Other future periods may be forecast similarly.

In order to *adjust for seasonal variation,* divide the data by the appropriate seasonal indexes.[2] For the first quarter of 1953, $750 \div 1.62 = 463$ million therms. For the second quarter, $486 \div 0.96 = 506$ million therms. These figures represent gas sales after eliminating average seasonal influences. The adjusted data appear as a dashed line in Chart 19–1. The seasonal seesaw is gone, and the basic trend-cyclical-irregular pattern is revealed.

The method of averaging original data is not satisfactory, however, for the great majority of series that have pronounced cycles or steep secular trends. The averaging process rarely cancels out plus and minus cyclical influences, and a strong upward trend will tilt the seasonal indexes of quarters or months later in the year above the earlier ones.

Two refinements of this method are sometimes used:

1. Instead of averaging the first-quarter values themselves, each quarterly value is divided by the annual average, and the ratios are then averaged. This "ratio-to-annual-average" method gives low-valued years the same influence as high-valued years in determining the seasonal indexes, but it still does not cancel out trend and cycle influences.
2. A secular trend curve may be computed and the original values divided by the trend ordinates before being averaged. This "ratio-to-trend" method eliminates the trend effect on the seasonal indexes but still does not cancel out the cyclical factor.[3] In most cases it is better to average the ratios of a given quarter or month to a *trend-cycle* base. This can be done either graphically or arithmetically, as described below.

Graphic Method

In the graphic method the seasonal factor is measured directly on a paper measuring sheet. Little or no calculation is required. This technique

---

[2] This may be done graphically on a ratio chart by lowering each first-quarter plot by the linear distance between 162 and 100 on the per cent scale of the chart, raising each second-quarter plot by the 96–100 interval, etc. Use dividers or mark the intervals on a paper strip. This is easier than division and involves only the small error of chart reading.

[3] This method was popular in the late 1920's but has since been replaced by ratio-to-trend-cycle methods. See H. D. Falkner and L. W. Hall in the *Journal of the American Statistical Association*, Vol. XIX (June 1924), pp. 156–66 and 171–79.

Ch. 19] SEASONAL AND CYCLICAL VARIATIONS 395

Chart 19–2

GRAPHIC SEASONAL METHOD
SEARS, ROEBUCK & COMPANY SALES, 1953–59
Ratio Chart

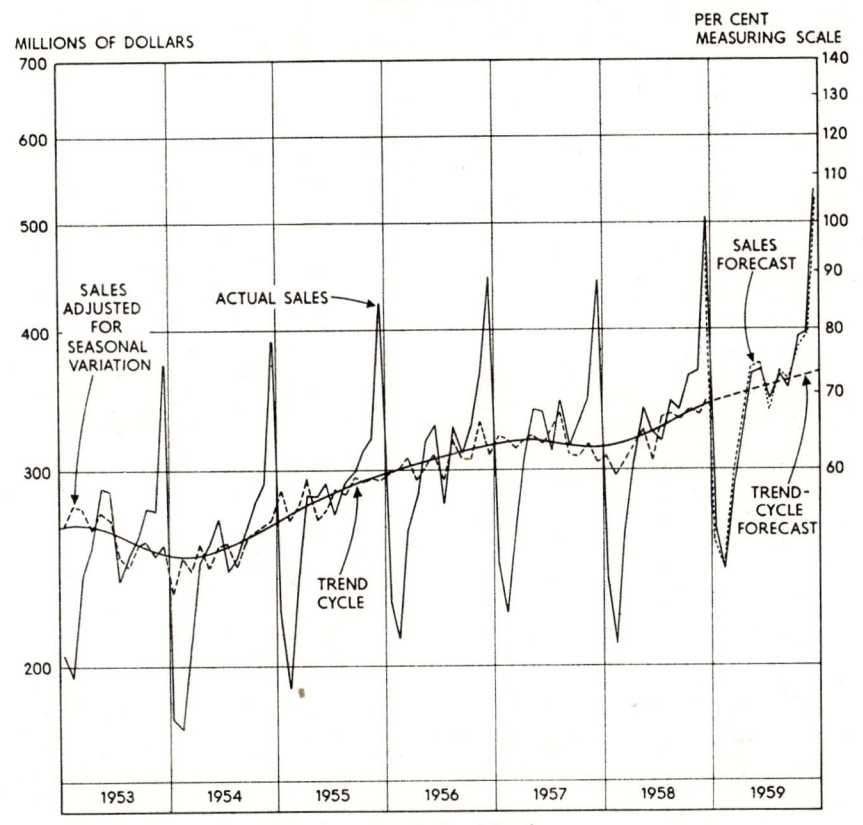

SOURCE: *Survey of Current Business;* Standard and Poor's.

will be applied to the monthly sales of Sears, Roebuck & Company from 1953 to 1958.[4] The steps are:

1. Plot the data on a ratio chart, preferably with a one-cycle scale. The large scale makes measurements more accurate than on a two- or three-cycle paper, and the ratio scale permits measuring and averaging percentages on the graph. As shown in Chart 19–2, Sears, Roebuck &

[4] Sears, Roebuck & Company sales have not been adjusted for calendar variation (except to reduce the 29-day February 1956 sales by 1/29 for comparability with other Februaries) because the seasonal indexes themselves will reflect the difference in average length of months and correct for this in the adjusted data. Slight variations due to the varying number of weekdays between one January and the next, etc., remain, and should be corrected by a separate calendar adjustment in a more refined study.

It is not necessary to deflate sales for price changes in seasonal analysis, since they have little effect on the seasonal rhythm and tend to cancel out in the averaging process.

Company sales have a pronounced seasonal rhythm, so that seasonal analysis is worthwhile.

2. Plot the annual average of monthly sales at the middle of each year (between June and July) and draw a freehand trend-cycle curve through these points (say, in green) by inspection. The curve should follow not only the trend but also cyclical and extended irregular movements such as those caused by war. A knowledge of economic conditions in this period will also help in locating the peaks and troughs of cycles. The fitting of this curve involves a subjective error, but part of the error is canceled in subsequent operations,[5] and the curve can be altered later to improve the fit, if necessary, as described under "Revision for Greater Accuracy" below. The trend-cycle curve in Chart 19–2 follows the general upward trend of sales, with cyclical dips in 1953 and 1957 and recoveries in 1954 and 1958, following the business cycle turning points shown in Table 17–1, page 337.

3. Fold a blank sheet of paper into twelve panels extending across the length of the sheet and draw a horizontal straight line in green across the middle, as in Chart 19–4, page 398. Mark it "Trend-Cycle = 100%" and label the twelve panels "Jan." to "Dec."

Now mark off each of the twelve panels as illustrated in Chart 19–3, panel A, for February. That is, fold the March–December part under, and place the February panel vertically on the chart with its right edge on the February point of the first year and its green center line on the green trend-cycle curve of the chart. Mark the February position on the edge of the panel with a dash, as indicated. Then move the panel along to the other Februaries, placing the green center line on the green trend-cycle curve in each case, and mark the other Februaries on the same vertical edge. Each of these marks represents a percentage of the trend-cycle base. The average distance of these marks from the center line of the strip represents the typical seasonal influence; the scatter of the marks reflects irregular factors. These may be averaged out as follows:

4. Locate the "center of gravity" of the central cluster of marks on the strip by inspection. First discard any extreme items as being unduly influenced by irregular factors. An objective rule is to discard just the highest and lowest mark for each month. The eye can then proceed from the median to the mean of the central cluster. Mark this point with a red arrow. This represents a modified geometric mean. Its purpose is to can-

---

[5] The error cancels out either if the average level of the freehand curve is too high or too low (since the seasonal indexes are adjusted to average 100 per cent) or if its positive and negative errors are equal (since the ratios for each month are averaged).

Ch. 19]   SEASONAL AND CYCLICAL VARIATIONS   397

Chart 19–3

USE OF MEASURING SHEET IN GRAPHIC SEASONAL METHOD
SEARS, ROEBUCK & COMPANY FEBRUARY SALES

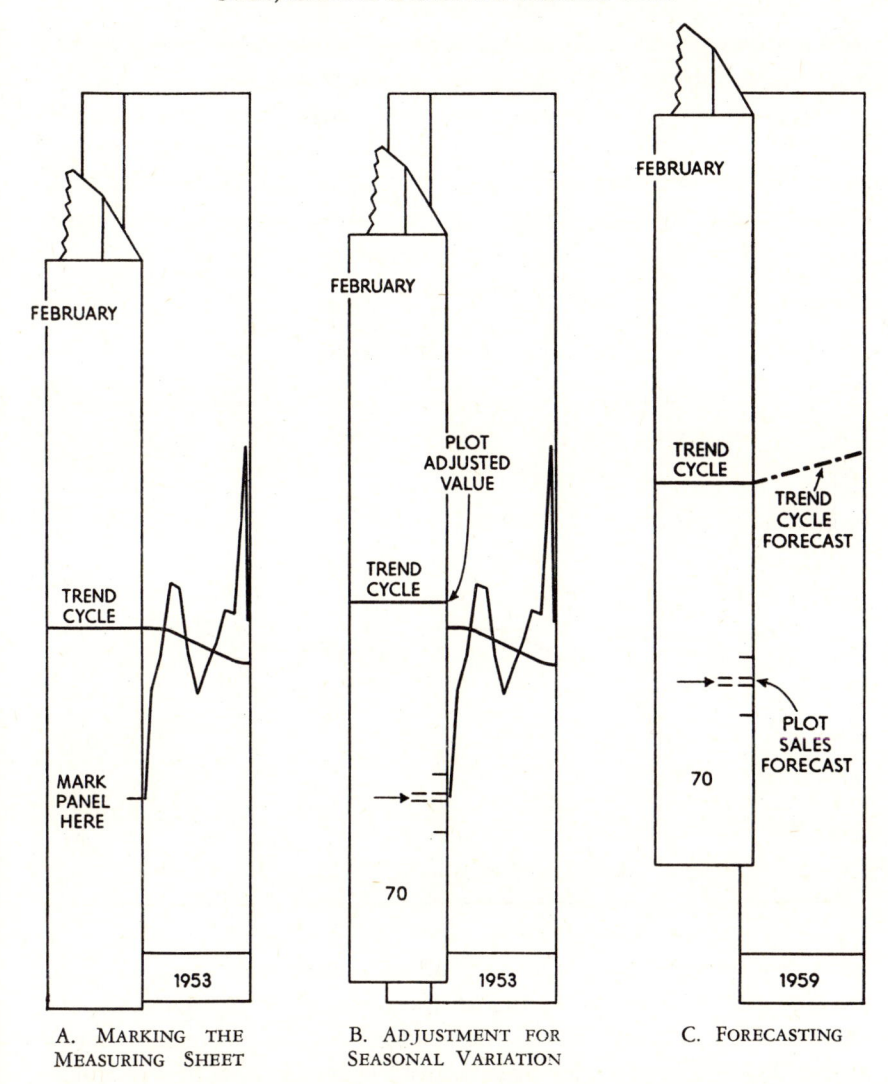

A. MARKING THE MEASURING SHEET

B. ADJUSTMENT FOR SEASONAL VARIATION

C. FORECASTING

cel out irregular factors and thus show the average level of February sales as a percentage of the trend-cycle base.

Mark a percentage scale on the right margin of the ratio chart (see Chart 19–2), placing 100 per cent opposite the number "5" printed on the graph paper (here labeled "500"), 120 per cent opposite "6," 80 per cent opposite "4," and the other numbers in the same proportion. Place the green center line of the strip on 100 per cent and read off the

398 BUSINESS AND ECONOMIC STATISTICS [Ch. 19

value of the arrow to find the preliminary seasonal index (see bottom of Chart 19–4).[6]

Mark the eleven other months and average them in the same way on the successive panels of the measuring sheet. Connect the twelve arrows by straight lines to show the typical seasonal pattern.

The concentration of marks about these arrows shows the degree of regularity of the seasonal movement and the reliability of the seasonal index. Where the marks are bunched closely, as in October and November, the seasonal movement has been more consistent than where

Chart 19–4

MEASURING SHEET FOR SEASONALITY
SEARS, ROEBUCK & COMPANY SALES, 1953–58

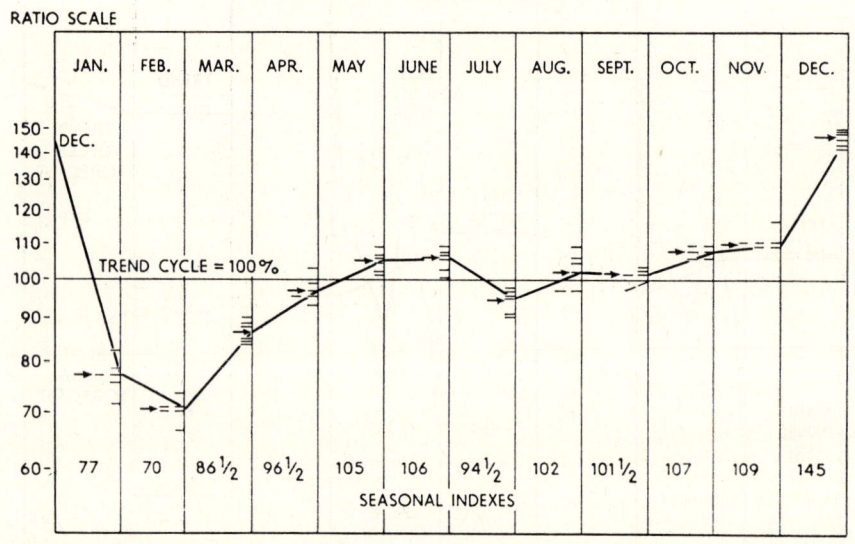

JAN.	FEB.	MAR.	APR.	MAY	JUNE	JULY	AUG.	SEPT.	OCT.	NOV.	DEC.
77	70	86½	96½	105	106	94½	102	101½	107	109	145

SEASONAL INDEXES

they are spread out, as in January. If all the scatters were centered about the 100 per cent line, as in August, there would be no significant seasonality. In this case, however, the average seasonal movement shown by the displacement of the clusters away from the base line is unmistakable.

5. Total the twelve preliminary seasonal indexes. If the total differs from 1,200 by more than 6 points (i.e., ½ of 1 per cent, since seasonal indexes are ordinarily accurate only to the nearest 1 per cent), multiply

---

[6] As an alternative step, the individual percentages on the measuring sheet can be read from the scale of the chart and averaged arithmetically to avoid the visual estimate of the modified mean. A piece of ratio paper can also be used as the measuring sheet to permit reading the percentages off the sheet itself.

each index by the quotient of 1,200 over this total. This will adjust the 12 figures so that their total equals 1,200 (subject to slight errors of rounding) and their average 100 per cent. The indexes on the measuring sheet (Chart 19–4) totaled 1,200½, so this adjustment was not necessary. (The ½ was dropped for February, which was slightly under 70½.) Adjust the arrows on the measuring sheet accordingly if necessary. This step is the same as that used in the moving-average method described later.

This adjustment can also be performed graphically by simply shifting the 100 per cent line on the measuring sheet by the interval between 1,200 and the sum of the twelve preliminary indexes taken from the vertical scale of the ratio chart. The line is raised if the sum exceeds 1,200; lowered if the sum is below 1,200. The adjusted seasonal indexes are then read off from the corrected base line.

These *seasonal indexes,* or indexes of seasonal variation, provide a quantitative measure of typical seasonal behavior and a basis for future planning as required in the first two purposes of measuring seasonality described at the beginning of the chapter. The typical seasonality in Sears, Roebuck & Company postwar sales can now be described precisely. The volume ranges from a low of 70 per cent of the average month—in February—to more than double that volume—145 per cent—in December. The normal seasonal rise from November to December is 33 per cent—i.e., $(145 - 109)/109$—the decline from December to January is 47 per cent, and so on.

6. If it is desired to adjust the data for seasonal variation (purpose 3, above), place the measuring sheet on the chart with the *arrow* of the February panel on the first February point, as shown in Chart 19–3, panel B. Then mark the *adjusted* February position on the chart (say, in red) opposite the green base line of the strip. Ignore the trend-cycle curve on the chart. Adjust the other Februaries by this identical amount. Then adjust the other months similarly, using appropriate panels. The seasonally low months are raised and the high months are lowered by the amount of their average seasonal displacement. Hence seasonality is eliminated. The effect of this adjustment is the same as that of dividing February sales by the seasonal index and plotting the result.

The resulting curve, drawn as a dashed line in Chart 19–2, is *adjusted for seasonal variation.* It reflects the trend, cycle, and irregular movements of the data, eliminating only the typical seasonal rhythm. In particular, the adjusted sales bring out clearly the recessions of 1953 and late 1957, as well as the recoveries of 1954–57 and 1958. Cyclical peaks occurred in February 1953 and August 1957, while troughs were reached in January 1954 and February 1958. These cyclical turns could not be seen in the unadjusted data.

Forecasting. As noted earlier, seasonal forecasting is invaluable in short-term business planning. Chart 19–2 shows how Sears, Roebuck sales can be forecast for each month of 1959 by extending the trend-cycle curve and laying off the seasonal deviations from the measuring strip above and below this curve. The same technique, of course, can be applied to individual products or departments, as well as to total sales.

The trend-cycle projection begins at the seasonally adjusted average of the last six months of 1958 (Chart 19–2) since this is a period of stable growth (see dashed line) which is long enough to iron out the irregularities of individual months. The average is obtained graphically by marking the center of the six deviations from any base line, and is plotted between September and October 1958. The trend-cycle curve is then drawn as a straight line through this point and a second point plotted 7 per cent higher (scaled from the chart) and a year later. This 7 per cent annual growth projection is based on two factors: (1) The 5.3 per cent average trend rise in nondeflated sales over the postwar period 1948–57 (not shown), omitting the readjustment years 1946–47 and the 1958 recession; and (2) the prospects in late 1958 for continued cyclical expansion through 1959, which justified raising the combined trend-cycle growth rate to 7 per cent, in line with the expansion rate in the last half of 1958.

The seasonal movements for 1959 are then laid off from the trend-cycle curve as in Chart 19–3, panel C. Place the February measuring strip with its trend-cycle line on the February trend-cycle point of the chart, and plot the sales forecast opposite the arrow of the strip. The sales forecast for all months of 1959 plotted in Chart 19–2 (dotted line) agrees fairly closely with the actual sales (solid line) that were drawn in later. The error of the forecast includes that of the trend-cycle projection (which increases with time) and that of the seasonal irregularity, which can be estimated from the scatter of the arrays in Chart 19–4. When seasonal fluctuations are large and regular, and short-term trend and cyclical movements are mild, as in retail trade generally, short-term forecasting is relatively accurate.

Revision for Greater Accuracy. The graphic method may be refined for more accurate results as follows: Draw a revised trend-cycle curve on the ratio chart so as to bisect the *seasonally adjusted* data, following the cyclical drift and ignoring only the month-to-month zigzag movements, as shown at the top of Chart 19–7, page 414. Then repeat steps 3 to 5 (and step 6 if the data are to be adjusted for seasonality) with a new measuring sheet. The revised trend-cycle curve is more sensitive to the cyclical positions of individual months than the trend-cycle curve in Chart 19–2. Hence the seasonal indexes are better. The correction in this case, however, does not seem to justify a revision. The revised curve is also probably more accurate than is the more commonly used 12-month moving average described in the next section.

Progressive Seasonality. Seasonal rhythm may change gradually over a period of years. Thus Sears, Roebuck & Company may cut prices and advertise new products to improve its sales in January and February. The seasonal swings in cement production have diminished with the development of year-round construction methods. New customs, such as giving gifts on Mother's and Father's days, boost retail sales in these seasons. This gradual change in seasonal behavior is called *progressive* (moving or changing) seasonality, as opposed to the "constant" seasonality discussed above.

Progressive seasonality may be measured graphically as follows: (1) Plot the data for a relatively long period of years on a ratio chart, and (2) draw a freehand trend-cycle curve as before. (3) Mark a time scale of years on each panel of the measuring sheet and plot the deviations for a given month (e.g., August) from the trend-cycle base chronologically on the panel instead of vertically in a ladder (see Chart 19–5).

Chart 19–5

MEASURING SHEET FOR PROGRESSIVE SEASONALITY

SEARS, ROEBUCK & COMPANY AUGUST AND SEPTEMBER SALES

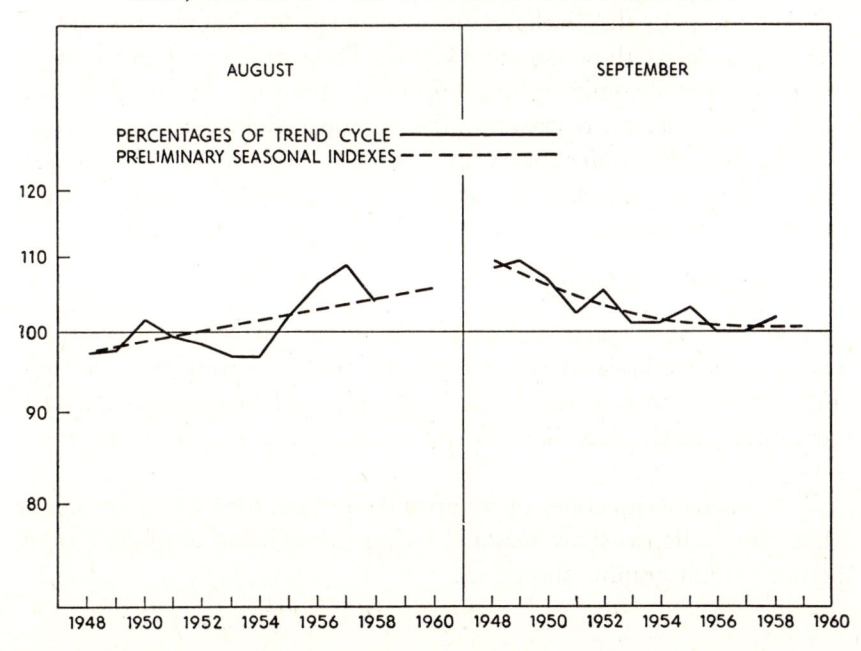

Do the same for each of the other 11 months. (4) Draw a smooth freehand trend curve through the plotted points on each panel. Then read off the preliminary seasonal indexes *from the trend curve*—a different index for August in each year. (5) Correct the twelve indexes in each year to average 100 per cent, if necessary, and (6) adjust the data for seasonality as described above.

The trend curves in Chart 19–5 represent contrasting drifts in the seasonal standings of Sears, Roebuck sales in August and September. The irregular fluctuations about the trend curve are canceled out in much the same way as in using a single average in all years. The single average might be considered a special case of progressive seasonality in which the trend line is horizontal.

In Chart 19–5 the August percentages of trend-cycle tend to rise over the years. If there were some known explanation (so as to be sure it wasn't merely a random run), a trend curve like the dashed line in Chart 19–5 could be drawn to represent the preliminary progressive seasonal indexes. Here the indexes for August rise from 97 in 1948 to a projected 106 in 1960. A similar plot for September shows a declining trend in earlier years that tends to flatten out near the 101½ level, which was obtained as the constant seasonal index for 1953–58 in Chart 19–4.

Progressive seasonal measurement is recommended for refined analysis, since it takes into account gradual changes in seasonal behavior. However, it still does not allow for cyclical changes in seasonality, such as the pickup in the slack season during cyclical booms, nor abrupt changes, such as those caused by war. These influences can best be avoided by simply omitting the abnormal periods in computing the seasonal indexes. Furthermore, progressive seasonal indexes are cumbersome because they differ for each month of each year. For ordinary purposes, therefore, the use of constant seasonal indexes for homogeneous periods of years should be adequate.

Moving-Average Method

The moving-average method of measuring seasonal variation involves the same basic steps as the graphic method except that the steps are performed arithmetically. This method will be illustrated by the same Sears, Roebuck & Company sales data as before. The steps are as follows:

1. Plot the series either on an arithmetic scale, for easier plotting, or on a ratio scale, to show seasonal swings of uniform amplitude or to permit certain graphic short cuts.

Ch. 19] SEASONAL AND CYCLICAL VARIATIONS 403

2. Compute a 12-month moving average to represent the trend-cycle base. This is simply a yearly average moved up a month at a time. A 12-month average includes both the high and low seasonal months during the year, and so the seasonal influences cancel out and the trend and cycle remain. The 12-month moving average is more objective than the freehand trend-cycle curve, although it tends to cut corners at cyclical turning points.[7]

To compute a 12-month moving average, first find the moving *total* as follows: Add the first 12 figures on an adding machine, list the total with the "subtotal" key on the tape, then add the next month and subtract the first month, list the subtotal again, and so on throughout the series. Check the last subtotal against an independent total of the last 12 months to verify all totals.

List each total in a table opposite the *seventh* of its 12 months.[8] Then divide the totals by 12 to get the moving averages. This may be done most easily by entering the reciprocal of 12—.083333—in a calculating machine and multiplying it successively by each of the totals without clearing the machine.[9]

In Table 19–2 below, Sears, Roebuck & Company sales are listed from July 1952 to May 1959 to determine the moving averages for the six-year period January 1953 to December 1958, since they cannot be computed for the end months. The total for the first 12 months, July 1952–June 1953, is listed in column 3 opposite the seventh month, January 1953. Moving up a month, the next 12-month total for August

---

[7] The 12-month moving average does not show the true trend-cycle position of its middle month but rather the average level of 12 adjoining months. Hence it cannot reach the peaks, valleys, and extremities of a series; it errs in the direction of curvature in either trend or cycle, and distorts the 12 months centered on a point of abrupt change.

[8] A 12-month total or average can be centered on either the sixth or seventh month, but the latter is a month more up to date. The exact center is midway between the two, so that sometimes two adjoining 12-month moving totals are themselves averaged in order to center exactly on a given month. Thus, a total of July 1952–June 1953 and August 1952–July 1953 would center precisely on January 1953. The steps are: (1) Compute a 12-month moving total, listing the first item opposite the sixth month. (2) Compute a two-item moving total of these totals, entering the first item opposite the seventh month of the original data. (3) Divide by 24. This is the centered moving average. However, since the moving average is only a rough approximation of trend-cycle at best, this very minor refinement in timing does not appear to justify the considerable extra labor. (See "Adjustment for Seasonal Variation," *Federal Reserve Bulletin*, June 1941, p. 5.)

[9] Twelve-month moving averages are used here to clarify the method, but the moving totals themselves can more easily be used in subsequent steps to save the labor of multiplying through by $1/12$, as follows: (1) Divide each month's sales by the moving total. The results will be just $1/12$ the percentages of moving averages. (2) Compute the modified mean of these ratios for each month and total the 12 means. (3) Multiply each mean by 1,200 over this total to arrive at seasonal indexes identical with those in the text, the final multiplication factors being just 12 times those in the text method.

Table 19–2
COMPUTATION OF 12-MONTH MOVING AVERAGES
SEARS, ROEBUCK & COMPANY SALES, 1953–58

Month (1)	Sales (Millions of Dollars) (2)	12-Month Moving Total (3)	12-Month Moving Average (4)	Per Cent of Moving Average (Col. 2 ÷ Col. 4) (5)	Month (1)	Sales (Millions of Dollars) (2)	12-Month Moving Total (3)	12-Month Moving Average (4)	Per Cent of Moving Average (Col. 2 ÷ Col. 4) (5)
1952:					1956:				
July	221.3	......	.....	.....	Jan.	228.1	3,554.4	296.2	77.0
Aug.	250.4	......	.....	.....	Feb.	210.1*	3,557.2	296.4	70.9
Sept.	271.3	......	.....	.....	Mar.	265.6	3,590.3	299.2	88.8
Oct.	300.6	......	.....	.....	Apr.	280.4	3,601.9	300.2	93.4
Nov.	283.0	......	.....	.....	May	317.6	3,617.8	301.5	105.3
Dec.	390.9	......	.....	.....	June	329.0	3,658.7	304.9	107.9
1953:					July	276.0	3,679.5	306.6	90.0
Jan.	205.5	3,190.6	265.9	77.3	Aug.	326.9	3,698.3	308.2	106.1
Feb.	196.3	3,206.6	267.2	73.5	Sept.	310.8	3,711.9	309.3	100.5
Mar.	240.0	3,206.7	267.2	89.8	Oct.	327.6	3,716.1	309.7	105.8
Apr.	254.7	3,195.9	266.3	95.6	Nov.	362.4	3,743.1	311.9	116.2
May	289.0	3,172.4	264.4	109.3	Dec.	445.0	3,763.8	313.6	141.9
June	287.6	3,164.9	263.7	109.1	1957:				
July	237.3	3,146.7	262.2	90.5	Jan.	246.9	3,770.6	314.2	78.6
Aug.	250.5	3,120.3	260.0	96.3	Feb.	223.7	3,803.1	316.9	70.6
Sept.	260.5	3,099.6	258.3	100.9	Mar.	269.8	3,820.7	318.4	84.7
Oct.	277.1	3,070.2	255.8	108.3	Apr.	307.4	3,824.8	318.7	96.5
Nov.	275.5	3,065.1	255.4	107.9	May	338.3	3,827.0	318.9	106.1
Dec.	372.7	3,033.7	252.8	147.4	June	335.8	3,809.3	317.4	105.8
1954:					July	308.5	3,805.8	317.1	97.3
Jan.	179.1	3,017.4	251.4	71.2	Aug.	344.5	3,795.5	316.3	108.9
Feb.	175.6	3,023.9	252.0	69.7	Sept.	314.9	3,780.6	315.0	100.0
Mar.	210.6	3,023.6	252.0	83.6	Oct.	329.8	3,775.5	314.6	104.8
Apr.	249.6	3,027.4	252.3	98.9	Nov.	344.7	3,771.8	314.3	109.7
May	257.6	3,032.5	252.7	101.9	Dec.	441.5	3,772.6	314.4	140.4
June	271.3	3,047.9	254.0	106.8	1958:				
July	243.8	3,066.4	255.5	95.4	Jan.	236.6	3,759.0	313.2	75.5
Aug.	250.2	3,100.2	258.3	96.9	Feb.	208.8	3,765.9	313.8	66.5
Sept.	264.3	3,115.2	259.6	101.8	Mar.	264.7	3,764.7	313.7	84.4
Oct.	282.2	3,147.4	262.3	107.6	Apr.	303.7	3,786.9	315.6	96.2
Nov.	290.9	3,185.2	265.4	109.6	May	339.1	3,820.8	318.4	106.5
Dec.	391.2	3,213.3	267.8	146.1	June	322.2	3,843.8	320.3	100.6
1955:					July	315.4	3,903.1	325.3	97.0
Jan.	212.9	3,235.1	269.6	79.0	Aug.	343.3	3,937.5	328.1	104.6
Feb.	190.6	3,264.5	272.0	70.1	Sept.	337.1	3,971.2	330.9	101.9
Mar.	242.8	3,308.1	275.7	88.1	Oct.	363.7	4,000.0	333.3	109.1
Apr.	287.4	3,343.0	278.6	103.2	Nov.	367.7	4,035.9	336.3	109.3
May	285.7	3,372.5	281.0	101.7	Dec.	500.8	4,061.7	338.5	147.9
June	293.1	3,403.1	283.6	103.3	1959:				
July	273.2	3,436.1	286.3	95.4	Jan.	271.0	......	.....	.....
Aug.	293.8	3,451.3	287.6	102.2	Feb.	242.5	......	.....	.....
Sept.	299.2	3,470.8	289.2	103.5	Mar.	293.5	......	.....	.....
Oct.	311.7	3,493.6	291.1	107.1	Apr.	339.6	......	.....	.....
Nov.	321.5	3,486.6	290.5	110.7	May	364.9	......	.....	.....
Dec.	424.2	3,518.5	293.2	144.7					

* February 1956 on 28-day basis.

Ch. 19] SEASONAL AND CYCLICAL VARIATIONS 405

```
    221.30
    250.40
    271.30
    300.60
    283.00
    390.90
    205.50
    196.30
    240.00
    254.70
    289.00
    287.60
  3,190.60 s
    237.30
    221.30 −
  3,206.60 s
    250.50
    250.40 −
  3,206.70 s
```

1952–July 1953 is computed as $3,190.6 + 237.3 - 221.3 = 3,206.6$ and listed opposite the seventh month, February 1953, and so on. A section of the adding machine tape is illustrated here. These totals are then multiplied by $\frac{1}{12} = .083333$ with a calculating machine. The resulting moving averages are listed in Table 19–2, column 4.

3. Divide each monthly item of original data by the corresponding 12-month moving average, and list the quotients as "Per Cent of Moving Average." In Table 19–2, column 2 divided by column 4 equals column 5. Division is preferable to subtraction here because seasonal variation tends to repeat itself from year to year with the same *relative* intensity. That is, a normal seasonal rise in a given month tends to remain at the same percentage as the enterprise grows, even though the dollar value rise in this month increases with the size of the business. Since the 12-month moving average roughly describes the path of the trend and cyclical fluctuations combined, the percentages of the original data divided by this average reflect primarily the effect of seasonal and irregular movements. By averaging these percentages for a given month (step 4) the irregular factors tend to cancel out and the average itself reflects the seasonal influence alone.

4. Compute a modified mean of the percentages of moving averages for each month in the different years, omitting the highest and lowest values as being unduly influenced by irregular factors such as strikes or war-scare buying.

The percentages in Table 19–2, column 5, are grouped in Table 19–3. The highest figure and the lowest figure in each column are then crossed out and the remaining four items totaled and divided by 4 to give the modified means shown in the next to the bottom row. These means are preliminary seasonal indexes. They should average 100 per cent, or total 1,200 for 12 months, by definition. The total in Table 19–3, however, is 1,202.0, because extreme values have been dropped before averaging the rest.

5. Therefore multiply each of the 12 modified means by the quotient of 1,200 over their total to yield the final *seasonal indexes*. Here, each mean is multiplied by 1,200/1,202.0 and the resulting indexes are listed in the last row. They total 1,200 and hence average 100 per cent.

The individual percentages and seasonal indexes in Table 19–3 show

Table 19-3
PERCENTAGES OF 12-MONTH MOVING AVERAGES AND COMPUTATION OF SEASONAL INDEXES
SEARS, ROEBUCK & COMPANY SALES, 1953–58

	Jan.	Feb.	Mar.	April	May	June	July	Aug.	Sept.	Oct.	Nov.	Dec.	Total
1953	77.3	~~73.5~~	~~89.8~~	95.6	~~109.3~~	~~109.1~~	90.5	~~96.5~~	100.9	108.3	~~107.9~~	147.4	
1954	~~71.2~~	69.7	~~83.6~~	98.9	101.9	106.8	95.4	96.9	101.8	107.6	109.6	146.1	
1955	~~79.0~~	70.1	88.1	~~103.2~~	~~101.7~~	103.3	95.4	102.2	~~103.5~~	107.1	110.7	144.7	
1956	77.0	70.9	88.8	~~93.4~~	105.3	107.9	~~90.0~~	106.1	100.5	105.8	~~116.2~~	141.9	
1957	78.6	70.6	84.7	96.5	106.1	105.8	~~97.5~~	~~108.9~~	~~100.0~~	~~104.8~~	109.7	~~140.4~~	
1958	75.5	~~66.5~~	84.4	96.2	106.5	~~100.6~~	97.0	104.6	101.9	~~109.1~~	109.3	~~147.9~~	
Total, middle four	308.4	281.3	346.0	387.2	419.8	423.8	378.3	409.8	405.1	428.8	439.3	580.1	4,807.9
Modified mean	77.1	70.3	86.5	96.8	105.0	106.0	94.6	102.4	101.3	107.2	109.8	145.0	1,202.0
Seasonal index	77.0	70.2	86.4	96.6	104.8	105.8	94.4	102.3	101.1	107.0	109.6	144.8	1,200.0

the seasonal pattern of Sears, Roebuck & Company sales in the same way as the measuring sheet (Chart 19-4) does in the graphic method. The slumps in January, February, and July, the autumn rise and the December peak are clearly evident. The seasonal index of 144.8 in December indicates that sales in this month are ordinarily about 144.8 per cent of those in the average month, as before.

The results of the graphic and moving-average methods are almost identical in this case. The two sets of seasonal indexes differ by only .2 per cent on the average, a negligible difference inasmuch as seasonal indexes are generally accurate only to the nearest 1 per cent.

The irregularities in seasonal behavior are shown by the scatter of the percentages of moving averages for a given month in Table 19-3. If the percentages are closely bunched, it means that the seasonal standing of the month is regular from year to year and the seasonal index is reliable for use in forecasting.

6. In order to adjust the sales for seasonal variation (i.e., eliminate seasonality to reveal the cycles), divide the actual sales by the seasonal indexes. Thus in January 1953, actual sales of 205.5 million (Table 19-2) divided by 77.0 per cent (Table 19-3) give adjusted sales of 266.9 million. This shows the nonseasonal level of sales, eliminating the effect of the normal January slump. The resulting graph is almost identical with the graphically "adjusted for seasonal variation" curve in Chart 19-2; so it is not presented separately.

If a given month's percentage of moving average tends to drift over a period of years, owing to some known cause, *progressive seasonal indexes* can be computed exactly as in the graphic method. That is, the percentages for August are plotted chronologically over the years, as in Chart 19-5. Either an arithmetic or a ratio scale may be used. A smooth freehand trend curve is drawn through these points, and the preliminary seasonal indexes are read off the trend line for each year and adjusted to average 100 per cent. (In the electronic computer method, a moving average is used in place of a freehand trend curve.) Similar graphs are drawn for each of the other 11 months. As in the graphic method, a fairly long period of years is required to establish reliable trends in these seasonal indexes.

Graphic versus Moving-Average Methods

While the averages-of-unadjusted-data method is adequate only for series with negligible trend and cycle, the graphic and moving-average methods are both useful for general-purpose analysis. These methods are compared below:

The graphic method has three major advantages: (1) It saves a great deal of labor by substituting graphic measurements for arithmetic computations. (2) The method is flexible, since the trend-cycle curve can follow cyclical movements more closely than the 12-month moving average provided it is drawn with skill and judgment. (3) The graphic medium also affords a continual visual check on successive operations, promptly revealing errors in measurement or judgment and allowing necessary variations in technique.

The method of moving averages, on the other hand, offers three different advantages: (1) The method is objective in that all analysts get the same answer. (2) The computations can be performed by clerical labor or by electronic computer as described below. (3) The results may be more convincing to the reader than those based on personal judgment, however acute this may be.

A method used by the Federal Reserve Board combines the graphic and moving-average methods, and adds other steps (fifteen in all) to refine the results, although at the cost of considerable additional labor.[10] In this method a 12-month moving average (or a formerly seasonally adjusted series) is plotted on an arithmetic scale between the sixth and seventh months. The moving average is then corrected by a freehand curve on the chart wherever it appears to depart significantly from the main nonseasonal movements of the series. (This procedure differs from the graphic method in that a yearly average is plotted as a check point every month instead of every year.) The original data are divided by these freehand trend-cycle values as read from the chart. The ratios are then plotted chronologically for each January, etc., and a freehand

---

[10] See H. C. Barton, Jr., "Adjustment for Seasonal Variation," *Federal Reserve Bulletin*, June 1941, pp. 518–28.

trend line drawn through these points to determine preliminary indexes of progressive seasonality. The indexes are corrected to average 100 per cent as in other methods. Several additional checks are used, including plotting the adjusted series for each year above each other to detect residual traces of seasonality.

Use of Electronic Computers

Electronic computer programs for measuring seasonal variation have been developed in recent years at the Bureau of the Census and the National Bureau of Economic Research.[11] These agencies have analyzed several thousand series and have made these programs available for use on machines in various parts of the country.

Electronic computers greatly reduce the burden of work in seasonal adjustment of time series, and consequently permit several refinements of technique. For most series, the results are claimed to be at least as good as those obtained by other methods.

The electronic computer programs now developed are based on the ratio-to-moving-average method. That is, the monthly data are first adjusted for calendar variation and then for seasonal variation, using progressive seasonal indexes computed as described above. Then, in the more refined of the two methods now in use, a 15-month weighted moving average of the seasonally adjusted data is computed. Like the freehand curve in the Federal Reserve method, this is a more refined approximation of the trend-cycle component than is the 12-month moving average. The original daily averages are then divided by this new moving average, and subsequent operations are repeated as before to arrive at progressive indexes of seasonal variation. Furthermore, the influence of extreme items among the seasonal-irregular ratios is automatically reduced by averaging them with the ratios immediately preceding and following. Finally, a *weighted* moving average is applied to the seasonal-irregular ratios of a given month in successive years to arrive at the progressive seasonal indexes.

The electronic computer therefore carries the ratio-to-moving-average method through more refinements than would otherwise be feasible. The computations require only two or three minutes for a ten-year monthly series on a large-scale computer of the UNIVAC class.

---

[11] For a detailed description, see Julius Shiskin and Harry Eisenpress, "Seasonal Adjustments by Electronic Computer Methods," *Journal of the American Statistical Association*, December 1957, pp. 415–49, reprinted as National Bureau of Economic Research Technical Paper 12, 1958.

Consequently, seasonality can be measured and adjusted for in far more economic time series than was formerly possible.

Electronic computers cannot handle certain problems such as gaps in the series, unrepresentative periods, and very extreme individual values such as arise from strikes. These situations should be adjusted by hand before the data are put into the computer. The new machines greatly speed and broaden the work of the analyst, but they still do not take the place of human judgment.

Which Method to Use? The following suggestions may be helpful in selecting an appropriate method for measuring seasonal variation:
1. The averages-of-original-data method is the simplest but should be used only if a seasonal rhythm dominates the data, and trend and cycle are negligible.
2. The graphic method is recommended for general use as a labor-saving device, provided a skilled analyst is available. For more refined results, draw a revised trend-cycle curve through the seasonally adjusted data and repeat the process.
3. The moving-average method may be used if a more objective procedure is preferred and sufficient staff and equipment are available.
4. Methods 2 and 3 may be combined and progressive seasonal indexes computed by the Federal Reserve Board method if additional accuracy is desired at the cost of extra labor.
5. Electronic computer methods may be preferable if many series are to be analyzed, and if programs and equipment are available.

Other Methods of Taking Seasonality into Account

There are several commonly used methods of allowing for seasonality without actually measuring it:

1. Seasonal movements are sometimes referred to merely in directional terms. For example, "Furniture sales made a seasonal gain in September over the August level." This statement, however, does not say whether the gain was more or less than the normal seasonal amount and how much it differed. It would be more meaningful to say: "Furniture sales gained 8 per cent in September over the August level, after allowance for the usual seasonal increase."

2. The common practice of comparing a month with the same month a year ago serves to eliminate the seasonal factor common to both months. This usage, however, may still distort the cyclical picture for either of two reasons: (*a*) The current month is judged in compari-

son with a single historic month that might have been erratic itself. Thus, the statement "Production in March was 3 per cent above a year ago" appears favorable, but it might represent an unfavorable situation if March last year was unduly depressed. (*b*) The comparison with a year ago ignores the trends of the past 11 months. For example, Sears, Roebuck & Company sales in August 1958 were below those a year ago. This report appears unfavorable, but it would have been more significant to note that seasonally adjusted sales had risen every month but one since February 1958, as shown in Chart 19–2 (p. 395).

3. Plotting weekly or monthly data for several years above each other on a tier chart with the horizontal scale extending from January to December enables one to compare current tendencies with those in the same seasons of other years without any calculations. But the comparison with several such years is apt to be confusing and offers no precise adjustment for the seasonal factor. In Chart 19–6, for example, the general level of 1961 truck production is obviously below that of the previous years, but the weekly nonseasonal comparisons are not clear. In particular, was the gain in production during the first quarter of 1961 more or less than the usual seasonal amount?

These methods are sometimes useful for simple presentation. For careful analysis, however, seasonal indexes should be computed as described earlier in the chapter.

BUSINESS CYCLES

Business cycles are perhaps the most important type of fluctuation in economic data; certainly they have received the most attention in economic literature. In order to understand cycles, they must be isolated and measured. There are three important purposes served by this analysis.

Reasons for Measuring Cycles

1. Measures of past cyclical behavior are valuable aids in studying the characteristic fluctuations of a business. These measures will answer such questions as: How sensitive is this business to general cyclical influences? What is the typical timing, amplitude, and general cyclical pattern of the company's production, sales, inventories, or raw material prices? How do these factors compare with those of other companies, or with the industry as a whole? Are there leads or lags compared with other series that would aid in forecasting?

The study of business cycles is also one of the major branches of economics. Today economists generally recognize the need not only of

Chart 19-6

MOTOR TRUCK PRODUCTION
WEEKLY, 1956-61

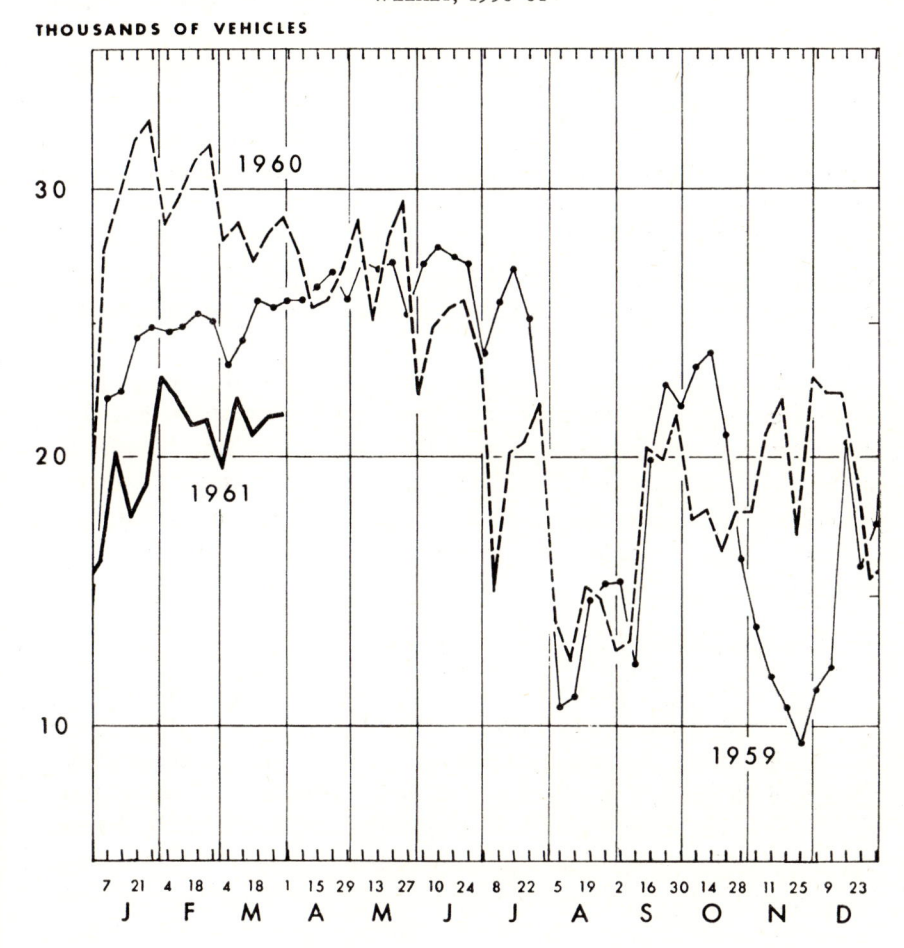

theory but also of accurate statistical measures in order to gain a clear understanding of this phenomenon. Hence the National Bureau of Economic Research and other agencies have devoted years of study to this measurement.

2. Successful businessmen plan ahead; planning requires forecasting; and forecasting involves a knowledge of both typical and recent cyclical behavior. Measures of *typical* cycles are used in the "economic rhythm" school of forecasting, which projects past cycles ahead in periodic fashion. Such measures also appear in the "specific historical analogy" method of relating present conditions to those in a comparable period of the past, and anticipating similar developments. Measures of

recent cyclical behavior are necessary as a starting point in any kind of forecast. Articles may be found in almost any business journal, particularly around the first of the year, containing forecasts based on cyclical indicators.

3. Cyclical measures are useful tools in formulating policy aimed to stabilize the level of business activity. Major efforts are being made by the federal government and by business to iron out the business cycle, since depressions are disastrous for the economy. The President's Council of Economic Advisers and the congressional Joint Economic Committee are important agencies that evaluate cyclical indicators as aids in devising safeguards against depression. Accurate cyclical measures are as necessary in planning preventive action as in anticipating what will happen without such action.

Despite the importance of business cycles, they are the most difficult type of economic fluctuation to measure. This is because successive cycles vary so widely in timing, amplitude, and pattern, and because the cyclical rhythm is inextricably mixed with irregular factors. Two methods of attempting to isolate cyclical fluctuations are described here: (1) the residual method and (2) the National Bureau of Economic Research method.

The Residual Method

This method consists of eliminating seasonal, secular, and irregular movements as far as possible, and plotting the residuals to show the cyclical fluctuations. Not all of these movements, however, need necessarily to be eliminated in practice. The more pronounced a noncyclical factor, the more it tends to obliterate the cyclical pattern and the greater the need for its elimination. Thus a wide seasonal swing, a steep trend, or a violently zigzag irregular contour requires adjustment more than if each of these factors were neutral. Ordinarily, the seasonal adjustment is the most important of the three. Frequently *only* this adjustment is made in the data, unless the resulting curve is so irregular as to require smoothing. This is because the secular trend does not ordinarily obscure short-term cycles, and the adjustment for trend introduces an error arising from the fitting of the trend curve itself. Furthermore, cycles cannot be successfully separated from the sustained irregular movements caused by originating forces.

Annual data need be adjusted only for secular trend, since seasonal and short-term irregular fluctuations tend to cancel out in the yearly totals. Chart 18–3 on page 361 shows the yearly deflated sales of Sears, Roebuck & Company from 1926 to 1956 adjusted for trend. The cycles in the annual data were described on page 363. However, since cycles are of short-term duration, monthly data are usually needed to give a more detailed picture.

Graphic Adjustment. Cycles may be isolated graphically by the residual method as follows:
1. Adjust the data for seasonal variation as described above. The seasonal adjustment raises or lowers the plotted data the distance from the arrow to the center line of the measuring strip.
2. Draw a freehand curve through the adjusted data, if necessary, to smooth out the zigzag irregularities. Consider the economic conditions of the period and the purpose of the study in so doing. The deviations above the curve should equal those below. This trend-cycle curve itself often suffices for cycle analysis. It may also be used in place of the preliminary freehand trend-cycle curve or 12-month moving average in recomputing the seasonal indexes, as described under "Revision for Greater Accuracy."
3. Adjust the resulting curve for secular trend as described in Chapter 18. That is, take the vertical deviations of the data from a trend curve on a ratio chart, and lay them off around a horizontal line.[12]

The graphic adjustments for isolating cycles by the residual method are illustrated in Chart 19-7.
1. The top curve, showing Sears, Roebuck & Company sales adjusted for seasonal variation, is reproduced from Chart 19-2.
2. A smooth curve had been drawn by inspection through the adjusted points. It shows the trend and cycle by averaging out the saw-tooth irregularities.
3. A straight trend line has been drawn through this curve. The trend was fitted to the nondeflated sales over the postwar period 1948-57, omitting the readjustment years 1946-47 and the 1958 recession. The deviations from this line were then marked on a paper strip and laid off around the horizontal 100 per cent line below, as described in the last chapter. The resulting curve shows the residual cycle, expressed as a per cent of the trend value as base. The cycle curve clearly shows the 1953 recession, the 1954 recovery, the 1955-57 prosperity plateau, and the milder recession and recovery of 1957-58, followed by prosperity in 1959.

---

[12] See William A. Spurr, "A Graphic Method of Measuring Seasonal Variation," *Journal of the American Statistical Association*, June 1937, p. 287, for a method of adjusting for seasonality and trend simultaneously.

414 BUSINESS AND ECONOMIC STATISTICS [Ch. 19

Chart 19–7

CYCLES IN SEARS, ROEBUCK & COMPANY SALES, 1953–59
RESIDUAL METHOD
Ratio Chart

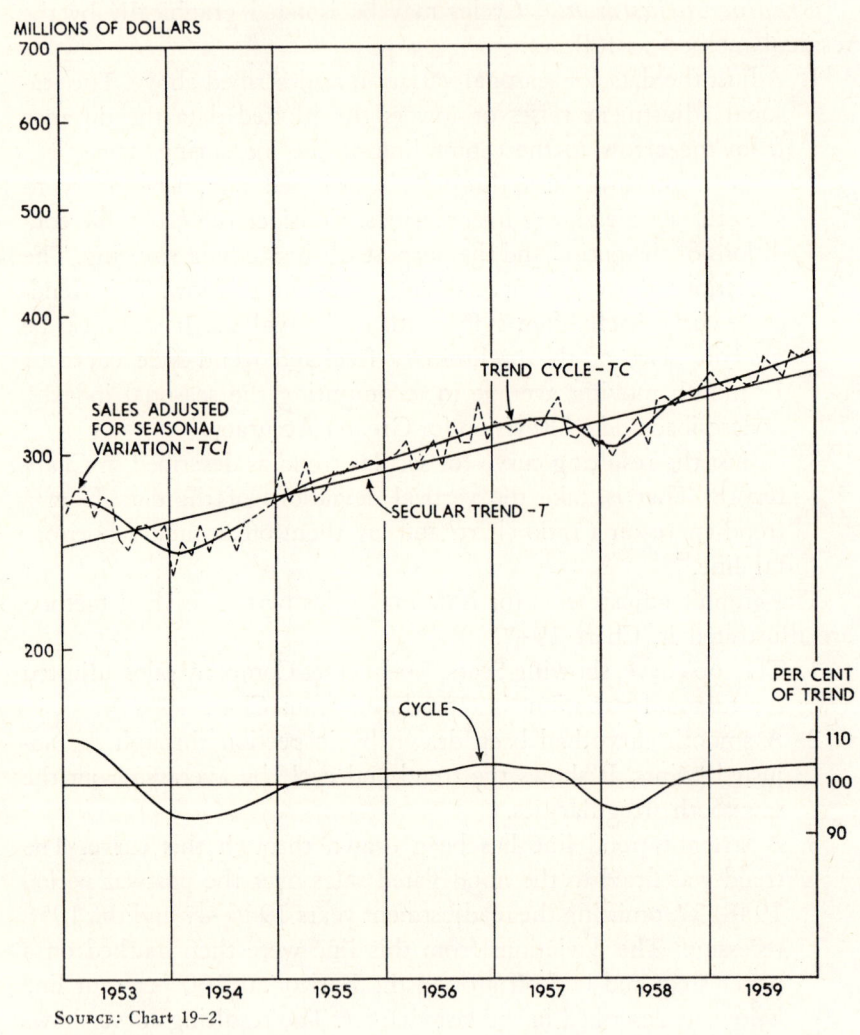

SOURCE: Chart 19–2.

Arithmetic Adjustment. Cycles may also be isolated arithmetically in three steps: (1) Divide the original data by the seasonal indexes to adjust for seasonal variation. (2) Compute a three- or five-month moving average, if necessary, to smooth out short-term irregular movements. These trend-cycle values themselves may be used for cycle analysis, as noted above. Thus, the *Federal Reserve Chart Book on Financial and Business Statistics* presents monthly charts of construction contracts as a "seasonally adjusted 3-month moving average." (3) If it is desired to adjust for trend, divide the seasonally adjusted data by the trend values before computing the three- or five-month moving averages. However, it makes little or no difference in what order the steps are performed. Methods of adjusting for seasonality and trend have already been described.

A series such as Sears, Roebuck & Company sales may be thought of as representing the combined influence of secular trend (T), cycles (C), seasonality (S), and irregular forces (I), or $T \times C \times S \times I$.[13] T is expressed in the original units (dollars), while the other components are in percentages. In order to isolate cycles, then, the effect of dividing by the seasonal index is $TCSI/S = TCI$. Then, dividing by the trend value, $TCI/T = CI$. Finally, a three- or five-month moving average cancels out part of the irregular movements to leave C as a residual.

Short-term irregular movements are usually smoothed by a three-month moving average. That is, the January–March average is plotted in the middle month, February; the February–April average is used for March; and so on. Sometimes a *weighted* moving average is used to give the middle month more influence in the result. This month has a weight of 2, and the sum (January + 2 February + March) is divided by 4 as the February moving average.

If the data are extremely erratic, a five-month moving average is preferable. This results in a smoother curve but one which is less sensitive to month-to-month movements than the three-month moving average. Of course, irregular movements do not exactly offset each other every three or five months, so some of the irregularities remain in the smoothed curve.

In an electronic computer method a moving average of from one to six months is used, depending on the relative amplitude of the month-to-month *irregular* changes as compared with the *cyclical* changes in a series.[14] The number of months used in computing the moving average is that in which the cumulative cyclical element in the series typically exceeds the irregular element. In a very irregular series such as liabilities of business failures, a six-month moving average is required for the cyclical element to dominate over the irregular movements. On the other hand, a single month's change in the Federal Reserve Board in-

---

[13] This is $TCSI$, not $T + C + S + I$, since C, S, and even I tend to be more constant as percentages than as absolute amounts. However, these factors can be added (or subtracted) on a ratio chart, since this operation is equivalent to adding the logarithms, or multiplying the natural values.

[14] Julius Shiskin, *Electronic Computers and Business Indicators*, Occasional Paper 57 (New York: National Bureau of Economic Research, Inc., 1957), pp. 235–43.

dex of industrial production typically contains a larger cyclical than irregular element, so the actual monthly figures are used without averaging several months.

Chart 19–8 illustrates the elimination of seasonality and the smoothing of irregularities in the sales of a major chemical company from 1948 to 1956, using the electronic computer methods described above. The four curves show: (1) the actual sales, (2) the gradually chang-

Chart 19–8

SALES OF A MAJOR CHEMICAL COMPANY
1948–56

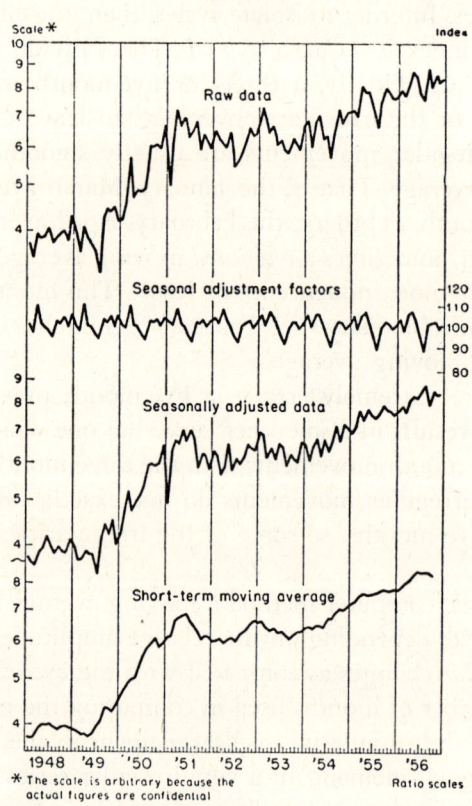

SOURCE: Julius Shiskin, *Electronic Computers and Business Indicators* (New York: National Bureau of Economic Research, Inc., 1957), p. 244.

ing pattern of seasonal indexes, (3) the sales divided by the seasonal indexes, and (4) the adjusted series smoothed by a short-term moving average to reveal the cycles, or more precisely the trend-cycle movements, since the trend has not been eliminated.

The arithmetic method of isolating cycles in Sears, Roebuck sales is not illustrated here because (1) the calculations are quite extensive and (2) the results would be quite similar to those shown in Chart

19–7 (p. 414). The chief difference is that a moving average would be somewhat more irregular (although more objective) than the graphic trend-cycle and cycle curves.

Comparing Cycles of Two Series. To compare the cyclical behavior of two or more series, plot the cyclical residuals on the same ratio chart so that both their turning points and their percentage rise and fall can be compared directly. If only the timing of turning points is to be compared, however, rather than differences in amplitude, the two series may be plotted on different arithmetic scales selected so that the apparent amplitudes are about the same.

Sometimes the cyclical residuals of each series are divided by their standard deviation, and the two curves plotted in common standard deviation units, rather than as percentages of trend, to equalize their average amplitudes. This procedure is not only cumbersome but destroys one of the purposes of cycle study—the comparison of amplitudes themselves—so it is not in common use.

The National Bureau of Economic Research Method

The residual method brings out the cyclical fluctuations in a series without any attempt to average the various cycles together to show their typical characteristics. Yet measures of *typical* behavior are invaluable in economic analysis. Wesley C. Mitchell, Arthur F. Burns, and others at the National Bureau of Economic Research have therefore developed a method of *averaging* the cycles of a series.[15]

In this method the monthly data are first adjusted for seasonal variation by the moving-average method. Then the cycles in the series, from one trough to the next, are averaged together so as to obtain a "specific-cycle pattern." This shows nine stages in the typical cycle expressed as percentages of the cycle average. The method is analogous to that of computing seasonal indexes by the ratio-to-annual-average method, with the Procrustean device of forcing long and short cycles into the same nine-point mold.

The series is also marked off at the months representing the troughs in general business activity (see Table 17–1, p. 337) rather than the troughs in the series itself. The same computations are then performed to yield a "reference-cycle pattern" showing the typical behavior of the series in the period of time occupied by a general business cycle.

Chart 19–9 shows the typical patterns in coke production from 1914

---

[15] See Arthur F. Burns and Wesley C. Mitchell, *Measuring Business Cycles* (New York: National Bureau of Economic Research, Inc., 1946), chap. 2; also Wesley C. Mitchell, *What Happens during Business Cycles: A Progress Report* (New York: National Bureau of Economic Research, Inc., 1951).

418   BUSINESS AND ECONOMIC STATISTICS   [Ch. 19

Chart 19–9
SAMPLE CHART OF CYCLICAL PATTERNS
NATIONAL BUREAU OF ECONOMIC RESEARCH

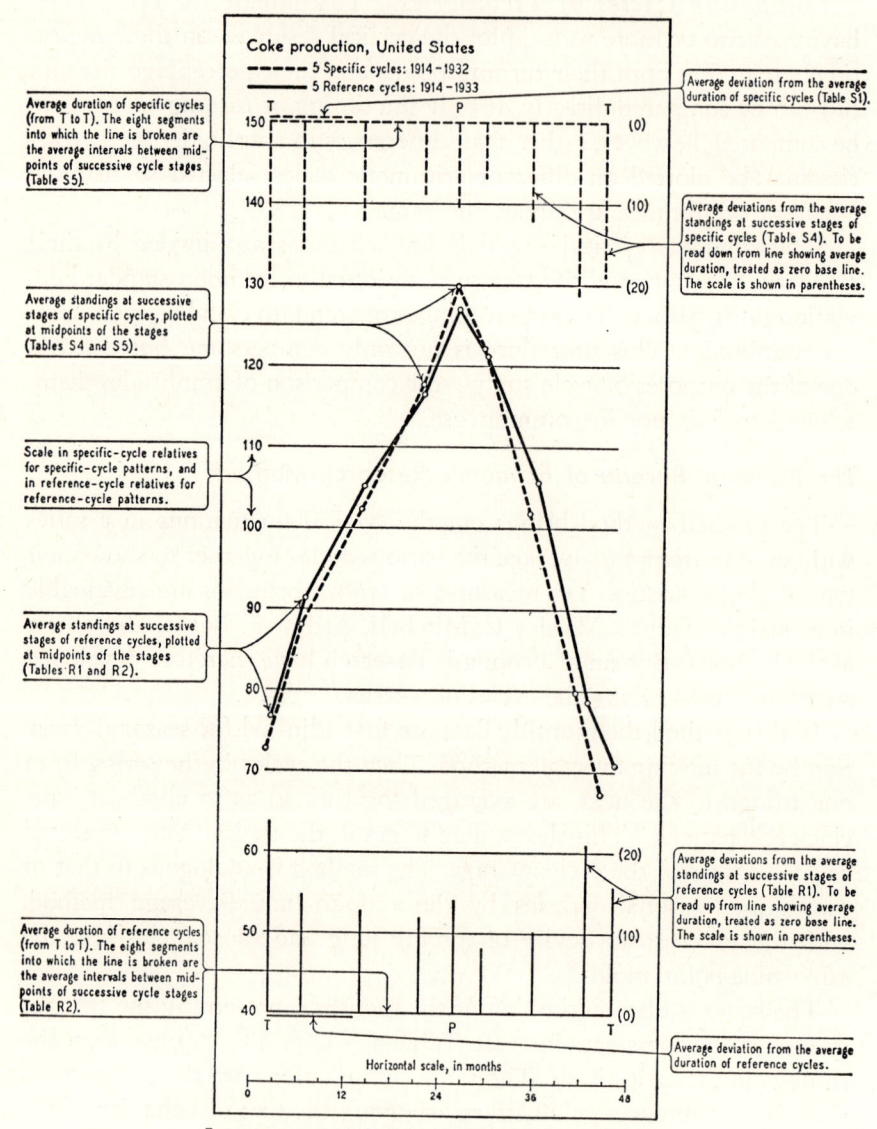

Coke production, United States
- - - - 5 Specific cycles: 1914–1932
———— 5 Reference cycles: 1914–1933

Average duration of specific cycles (from T to T). The eight segments into which the line is broken are the average intervals between midpoints of successive cycle stages (Table S5).

Average standings at successive stages of specific cycles, plotted at midpoints of the stages (Tables S4 and S5).

Scale in specific-cycle relatives for specific-cycle patterns, and in reference-cycle relatives for reference-cycle patterns.

Average standings at successive stages of reference cycles, plotted at midpoints of the stages (Tables R1 and R2).

Average duration of reference cycles (from T to T). The eight segments into which the line is broken are the average intervals between midpoints of successive cycle stages (Table R2).

Average deviation from the average duration of specific cycles (Table S1).

Average deviations from the average standings at successive stages of specific cycles (Table S4). To be read down from line showing average duration, treated as zero base line. The scale is shown in parentheses.

Average deviations from the average standings at successive stages of reference cycles (Table R1). To be read up from line showing average duration, treated as zero base line. The scale is shown in parentheses.

Average deviation from the average duration of reference cycles.

Horizontal scale, in months
0   12   24   36   48

T represents the trough stage (I or IX), P the peak stage (V). For explanation of how the line representing the average duration of specific cycles is placed in relation to the line representing the average duration of reference cycles, see Ch. 5, Sec. VIII.

SOURCE: Arthur F. Burns and Wesley C. Mitchell, *Measuring Business Cycles* (New York: National Bureau of Economic Research, 1946), p. 35.

to 1933. Since coke production follows general business activity closely in its cyclical turns, the specific- and reference-cycle curves are close together. The solid curve shows that coke production typically increases from about 77 per cent to 127 per cent of its cycle average during a typical expansion period in general business activity, and then drops somewhat more abruptly to about 71 per cent at the end. The dashed line shows the typical cycle in the expansion and contraction periods of coke production itself. The vertical lines at the top and bottom of the chart show the mean deviations of the individual cycle standings in each stage. These measures indicate considerable variation from cycle to cycle in most series. The wide discrepancies between different cycles of the same series make this method less precise than the measurement of seasonal variation.

Because of its complexity and limitations this method may not be feasible for the individual statistician's own use in analyzing cycles. However, the results of the National Bureau's comprehensive measures of cyclical behavior in hundreds of series provide an invaluable statistical picture of cycles that should be studied by all those working in this field.

Some Cyclical Indicators

Every economist, business analyst, or editor who regularly prepares interpretations of business activity develops combinations of cyclical indicators which seem best to fit his particular needs. In particular, the widespread desire to have the best possible forewarning of major turning points in the business cycle has led to the examination of various methods of classifying economic indicators according to their average leads or lags. No individual list of such indicators has been constructed on the basis of so detailed an investigation and study as that published by Geoffrey H. Moore of the National Bureau of Economic Research in *Statistical Indicators of Cyclical Revivals and Recessions* (1950), and in *Business Cycle Indicators* (1961).

Dr. Moore examined the timing of cyclical turning points in over 600 business indicators and selected 21 series which "warrant the attention of the business cycle analyst"—the man who would like to answer the frequently asked question, "Is another recession in the making?" The series are adjusted for seasonal variation as necessary, but not for trend or irregularities. He selected these 21 for two major reasons: "First, their cyclical swings regularly matched past business cycles—namely, before 1939. Second, they either led, coincided with, or lagged consistently behind general business movements. . ."

After careful analysis of these series he divided them into three groups according to the average timing of their turns relative to the general business cycle. The 8 series in the "leading group" usually turned down early in a recession and up early in revival. The 8 series in the "roughly coincident group" turned later than the leading group, and usually within several months of the peak or trough of the general business cycle. The remaining 5 series in the "lagging group" usually kept on going down after the revival had started and up after a recession had got under way.

In Table 19–4 the 21 series are listed by the three groups, and in the order of their average lead (−) or lag (+) with respect to the turn of cycles, as estimated in 1960. The first series, liabilities of business

Table 19–4

TIMING OF SELECTED STATISTICAL INDICATORS AT BUSINESS CYCLE TURNS

(Listed in Order of Average Lead)

Selected Indicator	Source	Median Lead (−) or Lag (+) in Months Peak	Median Lead (−) or Lag (+) in Months Trough
A. Leading Group			
1. Business failures, liabilities, industrial and commercial (inverted)	Dun & Bradstreet	−7	−7
2. Industrial common stock price index	Dow-Jones	−3	−7
3. New orders, durable goods industries, value*	U.S. Dept. of Com.	−6	−2
4. Residential building contracts, floor space	F. W. Dodge Corp.	−16	−5
5. Commercial and industrial building contracts, floor space	F. W. Dodge Corp.	−9	−1.5
6. Average hours worked per week, manufacturing	U.S. Bur. Lab. Stat.	−7	−4
7. New incorporations, number	Dun & Bradstreet	−2	−6
8. Wholesale price index, basic commodities	U.S. Bur. Lab. Stat.	−2	−1
B. Roughly Coincident Group			
9. Employment in nonagricultural establishments	U.S. Bur. Lab. Stat.	0	0
10. Unemployment	U.S. Dept. of Com.	−4	+1.5
11. Bank debits outside New York City	Fed. Reserve Board	+1.5	−3
12. Freight carloadings	Assn. of Am. Rrs.	−3	0
13. Industrial production index	Fed. Reserve Board	0	−1
14. Wholesale price index, excluding farm products and foods	U.S. Bur. Lab. Stat.	0	+1
15. Corporate profits, quarterly	U.S. Dept. of Com.	−4	−2
16. Gross national product, quarterly	U.S. Dept. of Com.	+.5	−1
C. Lagging Group			
17. Personal income	U.S. Dept. of Com.	+1	−2
18. Sales by retail stores	U.S. Dept. of Com.	+2.5	−0.5
19. Consumer installment debt	Fed. Reserve Board	+5.5	+3.5
20. Manufacturers' inventories, current prices	U.S. Dept. of Com.	+1.5	+3.5
21. Bank rates on business loans, quarterly	Fed. Reserve Board	+5	+5

* Average timing of new orders for southern pine lumber, oak flooring, architectural terra cotta, fabricated structural steel, and machine tools and forging machinery.

Note: All series except 2, 8, 14, and 21 are adjusted for seasonal variation.

Source: *The National Bureau's Research on Indicators of Cyclical Revivals and Recessions* (New York: National Bureau of Economic Research, Inc., August 1960), pp. 9–10.

failures, has reached its turning points about seven months ahead of the peaks and troughs in the general business cycle, on the average. At the other extreme, bank rates on business loans have lagged about five months behind the business cycle. However, the leads and lags in individual cycles differ widely from these averages.

These series foretold the business cycle peaks and troughs from 1948 through 1958 with a fair degree of accuracy, and should provide a useful guide to cyclical turning points in the future. The 21 indicators and many others are reported monthly by the U.S. Department of Commerce in *Business Cycle Developments*.

It is entirely possible for any of the series to give a false signal; but Dr. Moore says, "A substantial business recession or revival has seldom if ever been 'missed' by these curves" as a group. The fact that there is no assurance that these indicators will foretell the next recession or the subsequent recovery leaves with all statisticians the responsibility of attempting to improve our data and methods. There then remain the problems of alleviating the ills of business cycles.

SUMMARY

Seasonal variation is measured for the purpose of understanding past fluctuations, forecasting and budgeting, or adjusting data in order to reveal cycles. The seasonal pattern is best described by seasonal indexes that represent the average value for each month related to the average of all 12 months as 100 per cent. The period analyzed should be long enough to average out peculiarities in individual years, but abnormal periods should be omitted.

Several methods of computing seasonal indexes are described. In the averages-of-original-data method a given month or quarter is simply averaged for all years and the average divided by the annual average to get the seasonal index.

The graphic and moving-average methods, however, are usually preferable, since they eliminate trend and cycle more effectively. They are summarized in the table below, with symbols to indicate how the trend (T), cycle (C), and irregular (I) factors are eliminated to isolate the seasonal index (S).

If the seasonal pattern changes over the years, progressive or changing seasonal indexes may be computed in either method by plotting the ratios for each month in step 3 chronologically, and reading the preliminary indexes from freehand trend curves drawn through these plots.

To make a short-term forecast, multiply the trend-cycle projection by

Step	Graphic Method	Moving-Average Method	Shows
1	Plot on ratio chart	Plot on any chart	TCSI
2	Draw freehand TC curve	Compute 12-month moving average	TC
3	Mark deviations from TC on measuring sheet	Divide data by moving average	SI
4	Mark mean of central cluster on sheet with arrow	Compute modified means of ratios for each month	S (prelim.)
5	Adjust base line on sheet so that indexes average 100 per cent	Multiply indexes by 1,200 over their sum	S
6	To adjust for seasonality, shift plotted data the distance from arrow to base line on sheet	To adjust for seasonality, divide data by seasonal indexes	TCI

the seasonal index, or lay off the indexes around the TC projection on a ratio chart from the measuring sheet.

Graphic results can be improved by redrawing the trend-cycle curve through the seasonally adjusted data; the moving average can be improved by correcting it freehand at cyclical turning points. The Federal Reserve Board method of computing progressive seasonal indexes combines these methods and adds other steps for greater precision. Electronic computers greatly speed the necessary calculations, and permit several refinements in technique.

The methods compare as follows: The averages-of-original-data device is simplest but should be used only if trend and cycle are negligible. The graphic method is quick, flexible, and affords a continuous check on operations; while the moving-average method is objective, it can be performed by clerical labor, and the results are convincing. The Federal Reserve Board method combines the advantages of the two but is more laborious. Electronic computers may be preferable when a large number of series must be analyzed.

Seasonality is sometimes taken into account without actual measurement by means of (1) qualitative description, (2) comparing a month with the same month a year ago, or (3) plotting several years on a tier chart with the same monthly time scale. These devices are useful for simple presentation, but seasonal indexes are needed for refined analysis.

Measures of *business cycles* are important in the study of past cyclical behavior, in forecasting business activity, and in planning stabilization policy. Cycles, however, are difficult to separate from irregular movements, and still more difficult to average into a typical pattern, being quite variable.

In the residual method, trend and seasonality are eliminated by division or graphic adjustment, and irregularities are smoothed by a short-term moving average or freehand curve, leaving the cycle as a residual. Sometimes only the seasonal adjustment is necessary.

The National Bureau of Economic Research summarizes cyclical behavior by adjusting the data for seasonality, expressing the figures as percentages of the average cycle level between troughs, dividing each cycle into nine stages, and averaging each stage for all cycles. This yields a "specific-cycle pattern" of the typical cycle in the period of its own rise and fall, or a "reference-cycle pattern" in the period of the general business cycle. These studies are valuable for many types of business cycle analysis.

Finally, a method of combining a number of cyclical indicators to signal the imminence of recessions and recoveries is described.

PROBLEMS

1. *a*) Define "seasonal index."
   b) Having computed seasonal indexes, describe briefly how to make a seasonal forecast.
   c) A chart is captioned "Adjusted for Seasonal Variation." Explain.
   d) If you were to make a study today of seasonality in gasoline sales, what period of years would you use in computing (1) constant seasonal indexes and (2) progressive seasonal indexes? Why?

Problems 2–4 utilize the following data:

PRODUCTION OF TURPENTINE IN THE UNITED STATES, 1953–57
(Thousands of 50-Gallon Barrels)

Year	First	Second	Third	Fourth	Annual Average
1953	100.3	148.5	147.6	128.7	131.3
1954	111.5	162.9	164.6	147.2	146.6
1955	142.5	171.2	170.8	162.5	161.8
1956	151.0	174.8	167.6	155.1	162.1
1957	147.3	168.8	167.7	153.6	159.4
Total	652.6	826.2	818.3	747.1	761.2
Quarterly average	130.5	165.2	163.7	149.4	152.2

Source: U.S. Department of Agriculture. Includes gum and wood turpentine.

2. *a*) Compute indexes of seasonal variation for the turpentine production data above by the graphic method.
   b) Adjust this series graphically for seasonal variation.
   c) Forecast turpentine production graphically for the four quarters of 1958, extending your trend-cycle curve freehand.

3. *a*) Compute indexes of seasonal variation for the turpentine production data above by the moving-average method, centering the moving average on the third quarter. Use these additional production figures: 1952, third quarter, 156.0 thousand barrels; fourth quarter, 132.2; and 1958, first quarter, 137.3 thousand barrels.
  b) How much do these indexes differ from those of the graphic method? Give reasons for the differences.
  c) Adjust this series arithmetically for seasonal variation and plot the results. What is the purpose of this adjustment?
  d) Forecast turpentine production in the second quarter of 1958, assuming a trend-cycle decline of 2 per cent from the first quarter.

4. *a*) What factors determine whether indexes of constant or progressive seasonal variation should be computed?
  b) How does the computation of a progressive seasonal index differ from that of a constant seasonal index?
  c) Is there evidence of progressive seasonality in turpentine production (Problem 2 or 3 above)? Present small charts of each of the four quarters to support your answer.

5. *a*) Cite the one chief advantage of graphic methods and of arithmetic methods, respectively, in seasonal analysis, and explain your choice.
  b) In what type of series may the Federal Reserve Board method be preferable to the electronic calculator method described here?
  c) How could you measure the *irregularity* of seasonal fluctuations in your business?

6. *a*) Find a series of recent monthly data that is published both with and without seasonal adjustment, in *Survey of Current Business, Federal Reserve Bulletin,* or other source. Discuss the latest monthly figure in terms of (1) the per cent change in the unadjusted value over a year ago, and (2) the relation of the seasonally adjusted value to those of recent months. Compare these two methods of taking seasonality into account.
  b) Find a general business index that is adjusted for both seasonality and secular trend, and describe its recent behavior, indicating just what types of fluctuations are represented. See Richard M. Snyder, *Measuring Business Changes* (New York: John Wiley & Sons, Inc., 1955), as a finding aid.

7. *a*) Which of the three purposes of measuring cycles is most important, in your opinion? Explain your choice.
  b) Outline either the graphic or the arithmetic steps necessary to isolate cycles by the residual method.
  c) Just how does this procedure eliminate trend, seasonal, and irregular influences? What traces of these elements are likely to remain in the cyclical residuals?

8. *a*) Discuss the advantages and disadvantages of the National Bureau of Economic Research method of measuring cyclical behavior.
  b) How might these measures be used in forecasting a company's sales?

9. What is the present stage of the general business cycle—recovery, prosperity, recession, or depression—according to Geoffrey Moore's 21 indicators? Is a turning point in prospect? Cite the evidence supporting your view.

SELECTED READINGS

CROXTON, FREDERICK E., and COWDEN, DUDLEY J. *Practical Business Statistics.* 3d ed. Englewood Cliffs, N.J.: Prentice-Hall, Inc., 1960, chaps. 28–31, 34, 38.

    Explores numerous methods of isolating seasonal and cyclical fluctuations and trends, including the use of orthagonal polynomials and growth curves.

DEWHURST, J. F. *America's Needs and Resources—A New Survey.* New York: The Twentieth Century Fund, 1955.

    A detailed survey of trends in the economy, in some cases extending from 1850 to 2050.

MILLS, FREDERICK C. *Statistical Methods.* 3d ed. New York: Henry Holt & Co., Inc., 1955, chaps. 10–12 and Appendix F.

    An authoritative treatment of time series analysis.

MITCHELL, WESLEY C. *What Happens during Business Cycles: A Progress Report.* New York: National Bureau of Economic Research, Inc., 1951.

    Mitchell's works represent the most comprehensive statistical approach to business cycle analysis. See also his *Business Cycles: The Problem and Its Setting* (National Bureau of Economic Research, Inc., 1927); *Business Cycles and Their Causes* (Berkeley: University of California Press, 1942), Part III; and *Measuring Business Cycles,* with Arthur F. Burns (New York: National Bureau of Economic Research, Inc., 1946).

MOORE, GEOFFREY H. (ed.). *Business Cycle Indicators.* New York: National Bureau of Economic Research, Inc., 1961, 2 vols.

    A comprehensive evaluation of cyclical measures of business in the United States and Canada, including lead and lag indicators, diffusion indexes, seasonal measurement, and the use of computers.

NEISWANGER, WILLIAM A. *Elementary Statistical Methods.* Rev. ed. New York: Macmillan Co., 1956, chaps. 15–17 and Appendix F.

    A clear treatment of time series.

NETER, JOHN, and WASSERMAN, WILLIAM. *Fundamental Statistics for Business and Economics.* 2d ed. Boston: Allyn and Bacon, Inc., 1961.

    Chapters 15–17 cover time series analysis for forecasting, planning, and control.

SHISKIN, JULIUS, and EISENPRESS, HARRY. "Seasonal Adjustments by Electronic Computer Methods," *Journal of the American Statistical Association,* December 1957, pp. 415–49; reprinted as National Bureau of Economic Research Technical Paper 12, 1958.

    Describes the Census Bureau's UNIVAC (electronic computer) method of calculating progressive seasonal indexes by ratios to moving averages.

SMITH, JAMES G., and DUNCAN, ACHESON J. *Elementary Statistics and Applications.* New York: McGraw-Hill Book Co., Inc., 1944, chaps. 20–21.

    An excellent discussion of empirical versus rational trends, the latter including logarithmic straight lines and growth curves.

20. SIMPLE CORRELATION AND REGRESSION

Relationships between variables are fundamental in science. The physical sciences have been highly successful in establishing functional relationships or "laws" connecting variables such as temperature and pressure of gas in a closed container, the distance of an object from the earth and the gravitational pull exerted upon it, and so on. The biological and social sciences have had to deal with more complicated situations in which there is less reason to expect exact relationships between variables. The statistical tools of correlation and regression analysis were developed to estimate the closeness with which two or more variables were associated and the average amount of change in one variable that was associated with a unit increase in the value of another variable. It is important to explore both the applications and limitations of these powerful tools of analysis in the study of economic relationships.

In *simple* correlation and regression we relate a dependent variable to just one independent variable; in *multiple* correlation (Chapter 21) we relate the dependent variable to two or more independent variables. For example, correlating earnings per share and market price of common stocks in Chart 20-1, panel E, is simple correlation; correlating the combined influence of earnings per share and dividends on market price is multiple correlation.

PRELIMINARY ANALYSIS

As a first step in analyzing the relationship between two variables, it is often desirable to plot the observations on arithmetically ruled graph paper. The relationship between the two variables may be exact or statistical. The difference between these two types of relationship is shown in Chart 20–1. Panels A and B illustrate relationships that are exact.

Chart 20-1

RELATIONS BETWEEN TWO VARIABLES—
EXACT (PANELS A–B) AND STATISTICAL (PANELS C–F)

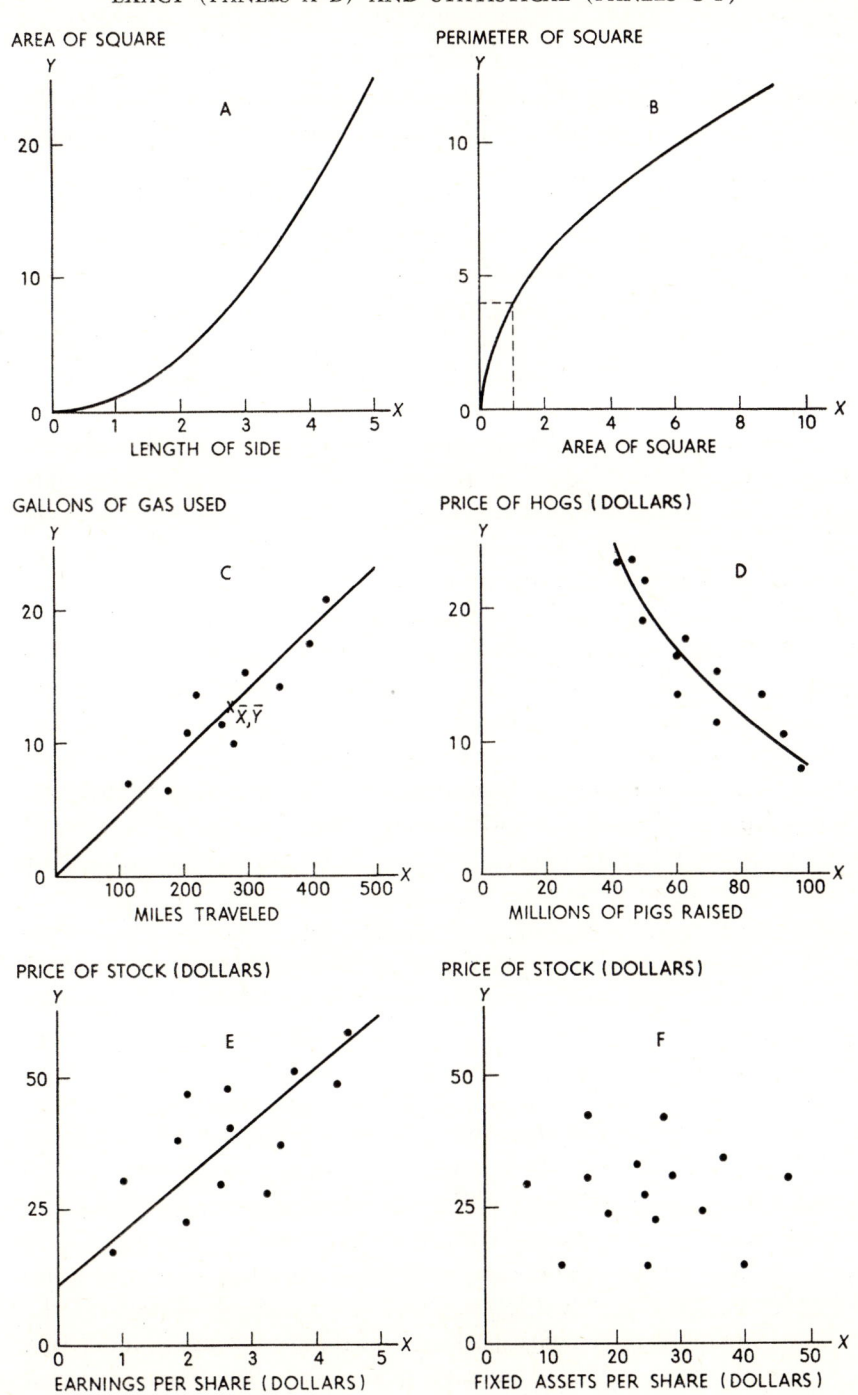

Panel A shows the relation between the area of a square (Y) and the length of one side (X). This relationship is defined by the formula $Y = X^2$ and is the mathematical definition of what is meant by a square. Panel B shows the length of the perimeter of a square (Y) as a function of its area (X). This relationship, $Y = 4\sqrt{X}$, also flows from the basic definition of a square. Thus, if the National Park Service decides to enclose a one-mile square of land, it follows from the formula that four miles of fence will be required (see dashed line).

Panels C–F are examples of statistical relationships. These graphs are often referred to as *scatter diagrams*. The scatter diagram may be defined as a dot chart showing the relationship between two variables: the *dependent variable*, which is to be predicted and is plotted on the vertical or Y axis; and the *independent variable* (plotted on the horizontal X axis), upon which the prediction is based. Panel C relates the number of gallons of gasoline consumed by a passenger automobile (Y) to the number of miles traveled (X). The dots represent the number of miles driven and the gallons of gasoline consumed on each of a number of different (hypothetical) trips. In this case, a straight line drawn through the origin of the graph and the "point of means" ($\overline{X}, \overline{Y}$) might be taken to describe the *average relationship* between gas consumption and mileage. If the car is not driven at all (zero mileage), gas consumption should also be zero. A trip of 400 miles should require just about twice as much gas as a trip of 200 miles. If we assume no errors of measurement, the deviations of the individual dots above and below the line of average relationship are attributable to "other factors," including the relative amount of driving through congested cities or over hilly terrain on the different trips, average speed maintained, and so on.

Panel D shows a line of average relationship between the number of pigs raised for slaughter and the market price of hogs. As the number of pigs available for market in a given year is known several months in advance of their actual sale, it is possible to use the number of pigs raised (X) as a variable with which to predict the market price of hogs (Y) during the period when this number of pigs is being marketed. The line of average relationship also indicates the extent to which the price of hogs might be raised *if* the number of pigs to be raised could be reduced by a specified amount. The deviations of the dots around the line of average relationship are attributable to other factors, including the supplies of cattle, the level of consumer income, and the various situations in the meat-packing and the food-retailing industries.

Panel E shows a line of average relationship between the current prices of a number of stocks (Y) in a given industry and their earnings per share during the previous year. The scatter of individual observations about the line of average relationship indicates that other factors in addition to earnings have important influences on the prices of stocks. In contrast, panel F shows little relation between the prices of stocks and the fixed assets per share, so that no line of relationship is shown.

In summary, the scatter diagram shows three aspects of the relationship by inspection: (1) Is the relationship close or not? When the dots lie close to the line drawn through them, as in Chart 20–1, panel C, the relationship is close and will provide fairly precise predictions. On the other hand, if the dots are scattered widely in buckshot fashion as in panel F, there is little or no correlation, and further analysis may not be worthwhile. (2) Is the correlation positive or negative? In *positive correlation* the dots move up to the right, as in panel E, where the rise in earnings is associated with a rise in price per share. In *negative correlation*, as one variable increases, e.g., number of pigs raised, in panel D, the other (price of hogs) tends to decrease. (3) Is the correlation *linear* or *curvilinear*? If the dots follow a straight line, as in panel E (a dollar increase in earnings per share tending to produce a constant increase in price), the relationship is said to be linear. If the dots follow a curved line (panel D), it is curvilinear or nonlinear.

All of the above cases may be significant, provided there is some logical relationship between the variables. Earnings per share are logically related to market price of stocks. On the other hand, while the consumption of beer might be said to be correlated with church attendance (both having increased over the years), there is no logical relationship, so correlation analysis would not be meaningful.

FUNDAMENTAL CONCEPTS

There are three basic measures used in simple correlation and regression analysis:

1. The line which expresses the relationship between the two variables is called the *line of average relationship* or, more briefly, the *regression line*. This may be a straight line of the form $Y_c = a + bX$, or a curved line.

The regression line is used in business and economics principally for two broad purposes: *control* and *prediction*. For example, consider Chart 20–1, panel E. As a control device, the chart might show the market price of one company's stock so far below its computed price, based on the regression line, that it might appear to be "out of control" and possibly a good buy. Or, as a prediction device, the price of the stock might be forecast to rise to the computed level, based on the typical relationship between earnings and price. For this reason, the line of average relationship is sometimes called the *estimating line,* since it provides a basis for estimating the value of the dependent variable if the independent variable is known.

2. The *standard error of estimate* (S_{YX}) is a measure of how scattered the individual observations are about the estimating line, or regression line. If the observations lie close to the line, S_{YX} is small. If the observations are widely scattered about the line, S_{YX} will be large. In effect, S_{YX} is the *standard deviation* of values of the dependent variable (Y) about the regression line. It is expressed in the units of the dependent variable (e.g., dollars per share in the chart cited).

3. The *coefficient of correlation, r,* is a pure number which expresses the degree of relationship between the two variables. It varies between 0, when there is no correlation (Chart 20–1, panel F), and 1 or — 1, when there is perfect correlation. In this case, all points are on the regression line.

REGRESSION ANALYSIS

The various techniques involved in correlation and regression analysis, as well as their limitations and use, can best be explained in terms of specific situations. In the examples that follow it will be assumed that appropriate sampling methods have been used in obtaining the data (see Chapter 4). In addition the student should keep in mind the cautions in the use of statistical data that were listed in Chapter 1. In the examples, samples smaller than might otherwise be desirable have been used, largely for purposes of simplifying computations and for ease in presentation. We will first take up the regression line, in both the linear and curvilinear cases.

Straight Line Relations

In most problems in business and economics involving simple correlation analysis, chief interest attaches to the average relationship between the two variables or to an analysis of the line of average relationship. Fortunately, the analysis of this line is not limited to situations in which the variables are normally distributed. In *controlled* or *designed* experiments, an agronomist, for example, might decide in advance the values of the independent variable (say, the amount of nitrogen fertilizer applied) in such a way as to obtain information about the average relationship between crop yields and fertilizer application over a wide range of values.

Suppose that a manufacturer is looking for a factual basis for promoting his brand of nitrogen fertilizer in an area where corn is the most important crop grown. The manufacturer wants to be reasonably sure that the claims made for his product by himself or his dealers will actually be borne out reasonably well by the performance of the product under field conditions.

He knows that the only active ingredient in his product is nitrogen, and he knows the percentage of nitrogen it contains. An obvious way to find out what his product will do in increasing corn yields is to try it. So he selects eight fields and has each one planted to corn. Four fields receive 40 pounds of nitrogen. The others receive no fertilizer at all.

The results of this experiment are shown in Chart 20–2 and Table 20–1 (page 434). Nitrogen, the independent variable, is plotted on the X axis, and corn yield, the dependent variable, on the Y axis. A regression line is then drawn to show the *average* relationship between corn yield and nitrogen.

The methods of fitting a regression line are analogous to those used in fitting a secular trend line (Chapter 18). In fact, trend analysis may be considered a special case of regression analysis in which the dependent variable is correlated with *time;* whereas in regression analysis the dependent variable is correlated with any other variable desired. Thus, Sears, Roebuck sales may be plotted against years in trend analysis or against personal disposable income in regression analysis.

Two methods of fitting a straight line are described below: the graphic "freehand" and the method of least squares. As in the case of trend analysis, the graphic method has the advantages of being simple and flexible in shape as well as permitting the skilled analyst to minimize the influence of extreme cases and otherwise follow the logical implications of the data. On the other hand, the method of least squares has the advantage of being objective and precise, and is easily adapted to large-scale machine computation. The graphic method is often used as a preliminary sketch to determine the general nature of the relationship whereupon the appropriate mathematical curve is fitted.

Graphic Method. The steps to be followed in the graphic method may be summarized as follows. Draw the line through the plotted points by inspection so that the *vertical* deviations of the dots above and below the line are exactly equal for the series as a whole, and approximately equal for each major segment of the plotted data. These deviations may be marked off accumulatively on the edge of a strip of paper, one above the other, for comparison.

When the dots in the scatter diagram are numerous or widely scattered, the average values of groups of data should be plotted to serve as objective guide points in drawing the regression line or curve. First, divide the data into several groups according to values of X; each group having about the same number of items. Using too many groups

Chart 20–2
NITROGEN FERTILIZER AND CORN YIELDS
Eight Fields

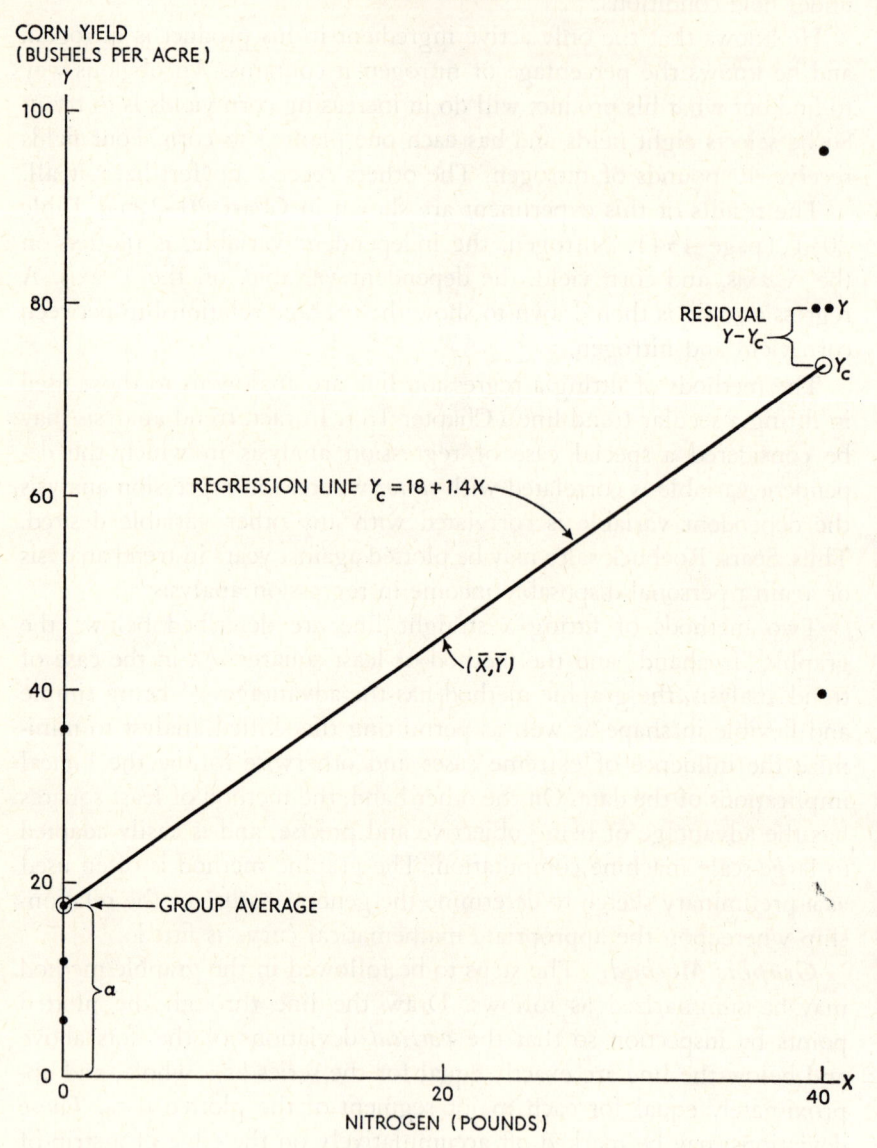

CORN YIELD (BUSHELS PER ACRE)

REGRESSION LINE $Y_c = 18 + 1.4X$

RESIDUAL $Y - Y_c$

$(\bar{X}, \bar{Y})$

GROUP AVERAGE

a

NITROGEN (POUNDS)

will lead to a zigzag pattern in the group averages; using too few groups will make the averages insensitive as guides to the shape of the estimating line.

Second, take the mean of the X and Y values in each group, and plot this group average on the scatter diagram.

Third, draw a smooth line or curve (using a transparent ruler or French curve) between the plotted averages, so that the vertical deviations of the averages above the line *exactly* equal those below the line over the whole range, and are approximately equal for each of several broad segments along the line. In particular, if the group averages follow a fairly straight line (except for zigzags), plot the over-all mean ($\overline{X}$, $\overline{Y}$) and draw a straight line through this point at such a slope as to equalize approximately the vertical deviations of the group averages on the left of this point and those on the right separately. A curve should be drawn only if the group averages follow an unmistakable curve which is supported by economic logic.

Most beginners have a tendency to draw graphic regression curves too steep because they judge goodness of fit by the shortest (or perpendicular) distance from the point to the line rather than by the vertical distance (the direction in which the dependent variable Y is measured) from the point to the line. Curvature of the regression aggravates this tendency, especially in the part of the chart where the regression is steepest. The use of group averages reduces this error.

In the corn-yield experiment, we need plot the averages of only two groups of data: when no nitrogen was applied, corn yield averaged 18 bushels per acre; and when 40 pounds of nitrogen were applied, corn yield averaged 74 bushels. The two group averages (shown as circles) are then connected by a straight line on Chart 20–2. (This also illustrates the method of semiaverages, described on page 360, since only two groups are used, each having the same number of points.)

The formula for a straight regression line is $Y_c = a + bX$, where Y_c is the computed value of Y (i.e., the value on the line for a given value of X). The constant a is the value of Y_c at the Y axis when $X = 0$, and b is the increase in Y_c for each unit increase in X. The value of b is therefore the slope of the regression line and is called the *regression coefficient*. ("Coefficient" means "multiplier" here.)

In the corn-yield example (Table 20–1) $a = 18$ bushels per acre, the average yield when no nitrogen is applied. Also, since the average yield increases from 18 to 74, or 56 bushels, when 40 pounds of nitrogen are applied, the average increase in yield for each pound of nitrogen is $56/40 = 1.4$ bushels per acre. This is the regression coefficient b. The regression equation is then

$$Y_c = 18 + 1.4X$$

The Method of Least Squares. A straight line fitted by the method of least squares gives a best fit to the data in the sense that it

Table 20-1

RELATIONSHIP OF NITROGEN FERTILIZER AND CORN YIELD
EIGHT FIELDS

Field	Nitrogen (Pounds) X	Corn Yield (Bu./Acre) Y	XY	X^2	Y^2
1	0	12	0	0	144
2	0	36	0	0	1,296
3	0	6	0	0	36
4	0	18	0	0	324
5	40	96	3,840	1,600	9,216
6	40	80	3,200	1,600	6,400
7	40	80	3,200	1,600	6,400
8	40	40	1,600	1,600	1,600
Sum	160	368	11,840	6,400	25,416
Mean	20	46			
Less mean times sum..................			−7,360	−3,200	−16,928
Equals adjusted sum.................			4,480	3,200	8,488
This is...........................			Σxy	Σx^2	Σy^2

makes the sum of the squared deviations from the line, $\Sigma(Y - Y_c)^2$, smaller than they would be from any other straight line. Also, if the observations can be regarded as a sample drawn from a definite population, the regression line yields the best estimate of the values of the dependent variable that will be associated with each specified value of the independent variable in any future observations drawn from the same population.

The values of a and b in the equation $Y_c = a + bX$ are found by solving the two normal equations

$$\Sigma Y = na + b\Sigma X$$
$$\Sigma XY = a\Sigma X + b\Sigma X^2$$

where n is the number of pairs of items.

The computations can be simplified in most problems, however, by measuring both X and Y as deviations from their means $\overline{X}$ and $\overline{Y}$. That is, the origin of the co-ordinates is moved up or "transformed" to the point $(\overline{X}, \overline{Y})$. These deviations are designated by the small letters x and y, where $x = X - \overline{X}$ and $y = Y - \overline{Y}$. It is not necessary, however, to subtract the mean from each value of X and Y. A simpler procedure is as follows:

1. Compute the product XY, and look up the squares X^2 and Y^2 in a table, for each original observation, as in Table 20–1.
2. Sum these columns.
3. Subtract from each sum the *mean times the sum* of the respective variables (grouped in the box under X and Y), to get the adjusted sums of the x's and y's expressed as deviations from their means. That is,

Sum	ΣXY	ΣX^2	ΣY^2
Less mean times sum	$-\overline{X}\Sigma Y$	$-\overline{X}\Sigma X$	$-\overline{Y}\Sigma Y$
Equals adjusted sum	$=\Sigma xy$	$=\Sigma x^2$	$=\Sigma y^2$

The sum of the deviations around the means, Σx and Σy, must equal zero, so they drop out of the two normal equations above, which reduce to

$$b = \frac{\Sigma xy}{\Sigma x^2}$$

$$a = \overline{Y} - b\overline{X}$$

where b derives from the second normal equation when $\Sigma x = 0$, and a is obtained by solving the first equation intact, to express it in the original units (a would be zero, measured from the new origin; the value of b is not affected by moving the origin).

In the corn-yield experiment,

$$b = \frac{4,480}{3,200} = 1.4$$

$$a = 46 - 1.4(20) = 18$$

The regression line is therefore

$$Y_c = 18 + 1.4X$$

as in the graphic solution. These figures are subject to error because they are derived from a sample and not from the total population. The sampling errors will be considered shortly.

Curvilinear Relations

Suppose the manufacturer cited above extends his experiment to determine the effect of larger amounts of fertilizer on corn yield. He has eight additional fields planted to corn: four fields receive 80 pounds of fertilizer, and the other four fields receive 120 pounds. The results for

Table 20-2

NITROGEN FERTILIZER AND CORN YIELD
SIXTEEN FIELDS

	Amount of Nitrogen (Pounds)			
	0	40	80	120
Corn yield (bushels per acre)	6	40	72	110
	12	80	112	122
	18	80	112	130
	36	96	128	142
Total yield..........	72	296	424	504
Average yield........	18	74	106	126

all 16 fields are shown in Table 20-2 and Chart 20-3. The average yields for the four groups of fields are listed at the bottom of the table and plotted as circles on the chart.

It now appears that the four group averages follow a *curved* line, concave downward. This is logical, since increasing amounts of fertilizer may well have successively smaller effects upon corn yield, until some level is reached at which corn yields stabilize or possibly even decline. A regression curve may be fitted by any of three methods: (1) drawing a "freehand" curve, (2) replotting the data on a logarithmic graph so that a straight line can be fitted, and (3) computing the equation of a parabola by least squares.

Graphic Method. A "freehand" regression curve has been drawn through the four group averages in Chart 20-3 with the aid of a French curve. If the relationship is really curvilinear, a hand-drawn curve is likely to be a better fit than a straight line fitted by least squares, however impressive the mathematical formulas and computer used. The analyst should always plot his data, check for curvilinearity, and consider whether the relationship is logically curvilinear rather than automatically using some straight line computer program.

Plotting on Logarithmic Scale. If the relationship appears curvilinear when plotted on an arithmetic grid, the data can be replotted on semilogarithmic graph paper (with either variable on the log scale) or on a double-logarithmic graph. Then, if the group averages follow approximately a *straight* line on any of these charts, the line can either be drawn graphically with a ruler or fitted by least squares.

In the least-squares method, the *logarithms* of the appropriate variable(s) are used in place of the original values, and a straight line is fitted just as described above. Thus, if the relationship is linear when

Chart 20-3
NITROGEN FERTILIZER AND CORN YIELDS
Sixteen Fields

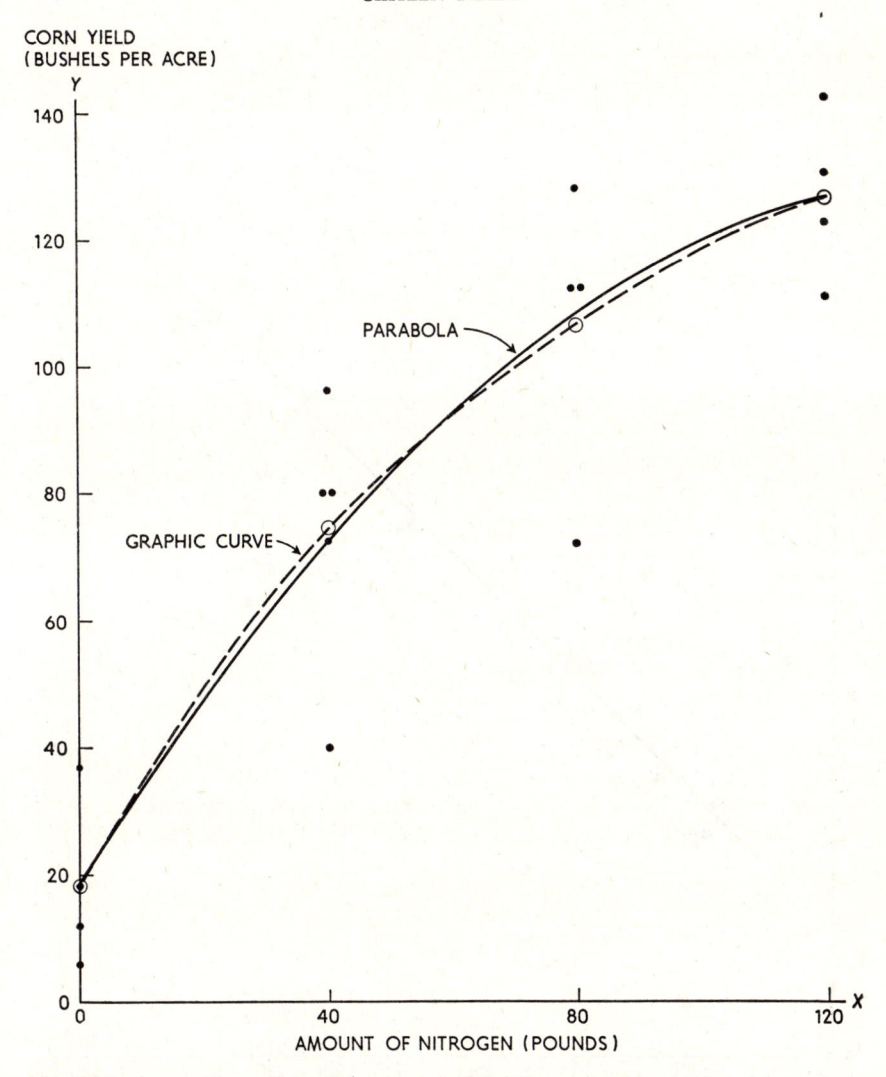

plotted on semilogarithmic paper (with Y on the log scale), the equation of the regression line is $\log Y_c = a + bX$. The method of fitting this equation in trend analysis was illustrated on pages 378–81. Conversely, a straight line on semilogarithmic paper with X on the log scale has the form $Y_c = a + b \log X$. Finally, if the relationship is linear when plotted on double-logarithmic paper, the equation is $\log Y_c = a + b \log X$. This equation is a reasonable one to use if Y tends to change by a constant *percentage* for each 1 per cent change in X,

438　BUSINESS AND ECONOMIC STATISTICS　[Ch. 20

Chart 20–4

PAPER CONSUMPTION AND DISPOSABLE PERSONAL INCOME
1929–57

(Double-Logarithmic Scale)

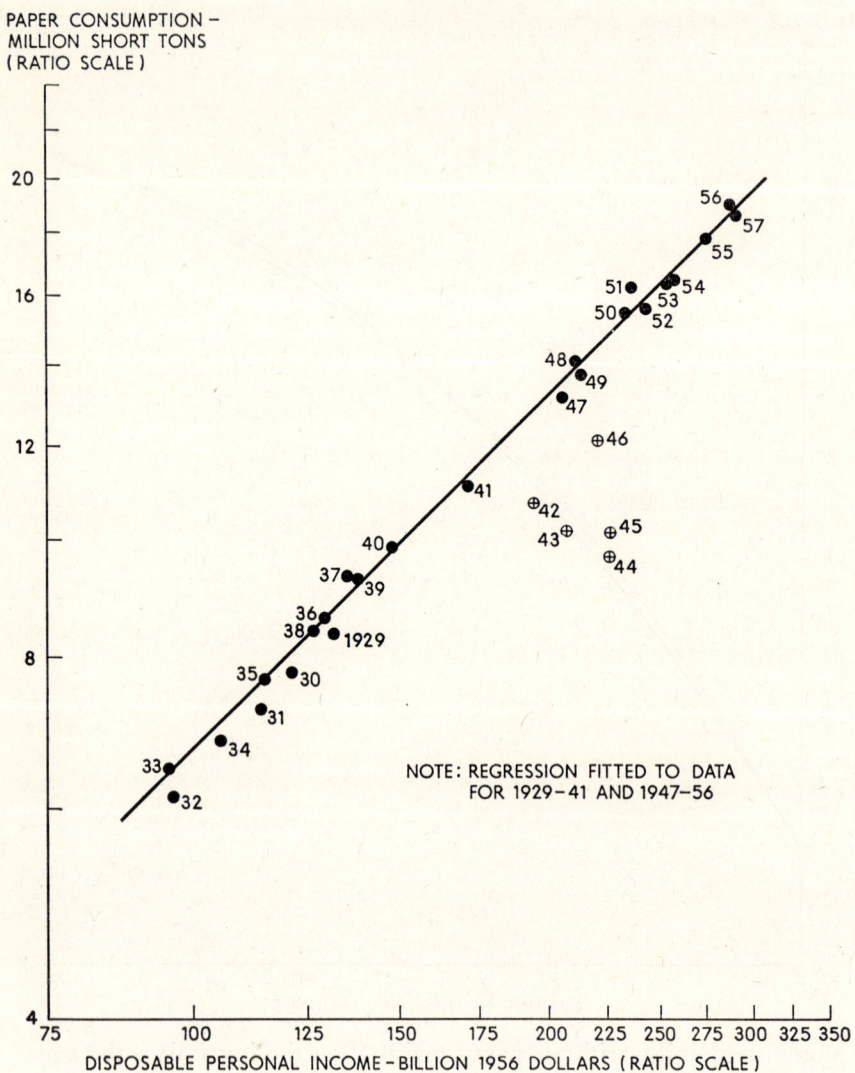

NOTE: REGRESSION FITTED TO DATA FOR 1929–41 AND 1947–56

SOURCE: U.S. Department of Commerce, *Survey of Current Business,* November 1957, p. 18.

over all X values. In Chart 20–4, for example, paper consumption is plotted against disposable personal income on a double-logarithmic scale. A straight line fitted to the nonwar years describes the relationship fairly closely.

In our example, plotting the corn yields on the log scale of a semilogarithmic graph fails to straighten out the group averages. (A curve has to be concave *upward* on an arithmetic graph to be linear on a semilogarithmic graph.) Nitrogen cannot be plotted on a log scale because some of its values are zero. Hence the method of transforming a curvilinear relationship to a linear one by replotting on a logarithmic scale cannot be used in the corn-yield experiment.

The Parabola. Various types of regression curves can be fitted by the method of least squares. This requires time and effort, and the type of curve chosen should be reasonably appropriate if the results are to be satisfactory. A wide knowledge of equations of types of curves which can easily be fitted by the method of least squares and an appreciation of the possible shapes of each type of curve are desirable preparations for one who is to choose the type of curve to fit to a given set of data.

The simplest curve is the parabola of the form $Y_c = a + bX + cX^2$. In this equation, a is the height of the curve at the Y axis, b is the slope of the curve at this point, and c determines the direction and degree of curvature.

A parabola has been fitted to the corn-yield data in Table 20–2 with the following result:[1]

$$Y_c = 18.6 + 1.565X - .005625X^2$$

The parabola is plotted in Chart 20–3. The curve does not pass precisely through the means of the four arrays, though it comes close to doing this. The parabola and graphic curves fit the data about equally well. The parabola is more objective, while the graphic curve is more flexible in being able to approximate types of functions that cannot be represented by simple mathematical formulas.

The Standard Error of Estimate

The usefulness of the regression line for purposes of prediction and control depends on the extent of the scatter of the observations about

---

[1] If we use x and y to represent deviations of X and Y from their means, we can solve the following two normal equations to determine the values of b and c:

$$\Sigma xy = b\Sigma x^2 + c\Sigma x^3$$
$$\Sigma x^2 y = b\Sigma x^3 + c\Sigma x^4$$

The constant term, a, can then be calculated from the formula:

$$a = \bar{Y} - b\bar{X} - \frac{c\Sigma X^2}{n}$$

Here, $\bar{X}, \bar{Y}, \Sigma x^2$, and Σxy have already been defined, and

$$\Sigma x^3 = \Sigma X^3 - \bar{X}\Sigma X^2$$
$$\Sigma x^4 = \Sigma X^4 - \frac{(\Sigma X^2)^2}{n}$$
$$\Sigma x^2 y = \Sigma X^2 Y - \bar{Y}\Sigma X^2$$

it. If the observed values of Y vary widely about the line, estimates of Y based on this line will not be very accurate. On the other hand, if the observed values of Y lie quite close to the line, the estimates based on this line may be very good. The measure of the scatter of the actual observations about the regression line is called the *standard error of estimate*. The standard error of estimate for the population may be approximated from a sample as follows:

$$S_{YX} = \sqrt{\frac{\Sigma(Y - Y_c)^2}{n - m}}$$

where n is the size of the sample and m is the number of constants in the regression equation.[2] For a straight line, $m = 2$; for a parabola, $m = 3$.

The value $\Sigma(Y - Y_c)^2$ can be obtained graphically by reading off the *vertical* (not perpendicular) deviation of each point (Y) from the regression line (Y_c) on the Y scale, squaring each deviation, and summing these squares. The value Y_c can also be computed from the regression equation for each given value of X, to find $\Sigma(Y - Y_c)^2$.

When a straight line regression has been fitted by least squares, however, it is usually simpler to compute the standard error of estimate by the formula:

$$S_{YX} = \sqrt{\frac{\Sigma y^2 - b\Sigma xy}{n - 2}}$$

Thus, in the first corn-yield experiment, with eight fields (Table 20–1):

$$S_{YX} = \sqrt{\frac{\Sigma y^2 - b\Sigma xy}{n - 2}}$$

$$= \sqrt{\frac{8{,}488 - 1.4(4{,}480)}{8 - 2}}$$

$$= \sqrt{369.3}$$

$$= 19.2 \text{ bushels per acre}$$

---

[2] The standard error of estimate for the sample itself is $\sqrt{\Sigma(Y - Y_c)^2/n}$. The use of $n - m$ adjusts for sample bias. This number represents the degrees of freedom around the regression line, just as $n - 1$ was used as the number of degrees of freedom around the mean in computing the standard deviation. Whereas the selection of the sample mean as a point from which to measure $Y - \overline{Y}$ uses up only one degree of freedom, the selection of a straight regression line as a base from which to measure the scatter uses up two degrees of freedom; one in requiring that the line pass through the point of means $(\overline{X}, \overline{Y})$, and the other in determining the slope of the regression line.

Essentially S_{YX} is the standard deviation of the "errors of estimate," or $Y - Y_c$ values, around the regression line. Therefore, if the deviations about the regression line follow something like a normal curve pattern, approximately two thirds of the actual Y values in a large sample will fall within one standard error of estimate above or below the line, and about 95 per cent of the observations will fall within twice this interval.

Is the Relationship Significantly Curvilinear? A curve will provide a more accurate estimate than a straight line only if its standard error of estimate is smaller. A curve might *appear* to be a better fit if we put enough twists in it, but the result might be meaningless. The factor m in the formula for the standard error serves to adjust for this bias.

In the second corn-yield experiment, with 16 fields (Chart 20-3), the standard error of estimate around the parabola was:

$$S_{YX} = \sqrt{\frac{\Sigma(Y - Y_c)^2}{n - m}} = \sqrt{\frac{4{,}521}{16 - 3}} = 18.6 \text{ bushels per acre}$$

A straight line (not shown) was also fitted by least squares to the same 16 observations. Its equation was $Y_c = 27.6 + .89X$, and its standard error was:

$$S_{YX} = \sqrt{\frac{\Sigma(Y - Y_c)^2}{n - m}} = \sqrt{\frac{5{,}817}{16 - 2}} = 20.4 \text{ bushels per acre}$$

It appears that the parabola *does* give more accurate estimates than the straight line, since the average scatter is smaller for the curve even after allowing for the increase in m. The underlying logic also justifies using a curve. The relationship therefore may be said to be significantly curvilinear.

Further Comments on Regression Results in a Controlled Experiment

The population from which the sample of 16 corn-yield observations was obtained has still not been defined very precisely. An agronomist would probably take a different set of experimental observations for each major type of soil on which corn is grown in the region in which the manufacturer operates. If the western portion of this region has lower rainfall than the eastern, he may also obtain separate sets of experimental observations in several areas with different average amounts of rainfall. These combinations of soil types and rainfall levels could be thought of as strata of a master sample for an entire region; alternatively each stratum could be thought of as a separate population, and no attempt would be made to extrapolate the results of fertilizer and yield experiments performed in one stratum to any other stratum.

Thus, the manufacturer would recommend different levels of fertilizer use on different soil types and in different subregions, and he would make somewhat different claims for his product when used on different soils or in more or less humid areas.

The problem of generalizing from relationships determined in one area to probable relationships between the same variables in other areas is quite similar to the problem that economists face in dealing with time series. An agronomist may be able to say without direct experimentation that soil types and climatic conditions in area B are sufficiently like those in area A, that results obtained in area A can be generalized to area B with perhaps a slight increase in the standard error of estimate. The business statistician or economist must try to make similar judgments about the applicability of results obtained for time period A to problems of prediction and control in time period B. A person who is thoroughly familiar with an industry or a sector of the economy may know that certain processes and products are changing only slowly; relationships between variables in such slowly changing areas may be projected for a year or two in advance with some degree of confidence. Certain other processes or products may be undergoing very rapid changes, and forecasts based upon several years of past history may be of little value.

Regression Analysis in a Sample Survey

The corn-yield example represented a controlled experiment in which the independent variable (nitrogen applied) was rigidly controlled. As a further example of regression analysis, consider a sample survey in which both X and Y are random variables.

The personnel manager in an electronic manufacturing company devises a manual dexterity test for job applicants to predict their production rating in the assembly department. In order to do this, he selects a random sample of 20 applicants. They are given the test and later assigned a production rating. It is a common practice to administer an aptitude test to applicants for jobs, especially for types of jobs which require similar skills and for which objective measures of success can be obtained later.

The results are shown in Table 20–3 and Chart 20–5, where each dot represents one employee. The test score is the independent variable. There seems to be a fairly close linear relationship, with the dots clustered along a straight line, and with no extreme deviations.

Table 20-3
CORRELATION BETWEEN SCORES ON MANUAL DEXTERITY TEST AND PRODUCTION RATINGS FOR 20 WORKERS

Worker	Test Score X	Production Rating Y	XY	X²	Y²
A	53	45	2,385	2,809	2,025
B	36	43	1,548	1,296	1,849
C	88	89	7,832	7,744	7,921
D	84	79	6,636	7,056	6,241
E	86	84	7,224	7,396	7,056
F	64	66	4,224	4,096	4,356
G	45	49	2,205	2,025	2,401
H	48	48	2,304	2,304	2,304
I	39	43	1,677	1,521	1,849
J	67	76	5,092	4,489	5,776
K	54	59	3,186	2,916	3,481
L	73	77	5,621	5,329	5,929
M	65	56	3,640	4,225	3,136
N	29	28	812	841	784
O	52	51	2,652	2,704	2,601
P	22	27	594	484	729
Q	76	76	5,776	5,776	5,776
R	32	34	1,088	1,024	1,156
S	51	60	3,060	2,601	3,600
T	37	32	1,184	1,369	1,024
Sum	1,101	1,122	68,740	68,005	69,994
Mean	55.05	56.10			
Less mean times sum............			−61,766	−60,610	−62,944
Equals adjusted sum............			6,974	7,395	7,050
This is....................			Σxy	Σx^2	Σy^2

The procedure then is to compute XY, X^2, and Y^2 for each worker, sum these, and subtract the respective mean times the sum to find Σxy, Σx^2, and Σy^2, as shown in Table 20–3. Then

$$b = \frac{\Sigma xy}{\Sigma x^2} = \frac{6,974}{7,395} = .943$$

$$a = \overline{Y} - b\overline{X} = 56.10 - .943(55.05) = 4.2$$

Chart 20–5
REGRESSION LINE AND STANDARD ERROR OF ESTIMATE
Test Scores and Production Ratings of 20 Workers

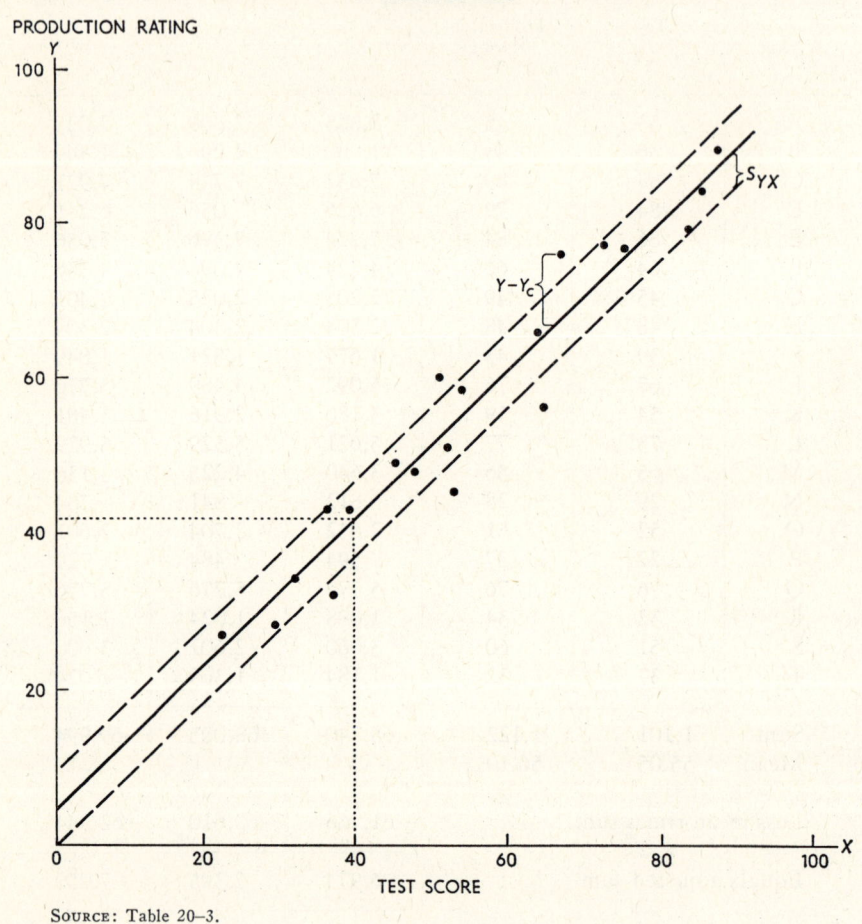

Source: Table 20–3.

Hence, the regression line is:

$$Y_c = 4.2 + .943X$$

If a job applicant from the same population received a test score of 40, therefore, his production rating could be estimated as

$$Y_c = 4.2 + .943(40) = 42$$

Alternatively, this value might be read from Chart 20–5 (dotted line). The standard error of this estimate is:

$$S_{YX} = \sqrt{\frac{\Sigma y^2 - b\Sigma xy}{n-2}} = \sqrt{\frac{7{,}050 - .943(6{,}974)}{20 - 2}} = 5.13$$

Hence, management could predict that the applicant's production rating will be 42 ± 5, or between 37 and 47, with two chances out of three of being correct. The standard error of estimate has been laid off above and below the regression line in Chart 20–5. (It will be seen that 15 dots, or three fourths, fell within this band, rather than two thirds, so the distribution is not quite normal.) This value can also be compared with the standard error of estimate based on the use of alternative aptitude tests as predictors, that is, mechanical aptitude, mathematical ability, etc. In this way, it is possible to compare the performance of various alternative tests as predictors of success on a given type of job.

This example will be used in the next section on statistical inference, since it illustrates the principles involved with a minimum of arithmetic. However, it should be emphasized that, in practice, a much larger sample would be needed to provide a really dependable basis for predicting production ratings. The present sample may be regarded simply as a pretest which appears promising enough to justify a broader survey from which regression measures can be estimated more accurately. For example, by increasing the sample size four times, we can cut the standard error of the regression coefficient about in half as will be explained in the next section.

REGRESSION ANALYSIS: STATISTICAL INFERENCE

We are only rarely interested in a regression equation solely as a description of a particular sample. Almost always we are really looking for a relationship that will enable us to control or predict new values of the dependent variable within limits of accuracy estimated from the original set of data.

Thus, regression analysis of business and economic statistics must be approached from the standpoint of (statistical) inference from a particular sample to a "parent population" or universe which includes the given sample and also such future or additional observations as we wish to control or predict. Both the given sample which we analyze and the actual future values or "drawings" we attempt to control or predict represent only a fraction of all of the possible values that might conceivably be drawn from the population in question. The application of statistical inference to regression analysis leads to the discovery and verification of relationships between variables. This is one of the most challenging and basic problems of scientific research in any discipline.

The regression line for a sample is only one of a family of regression lines for different samples that might be drawn from the same population. That is, regression measures are subject to sampling errors. Nevertheless, we can estimate within what limits the "true" regression line in the population is likely to fall. The theory of estimating population parameters from sample statistics was introduced in Chapters 12 and 13. This theory can now be applied in making statistical inferences about the true regression line.[3] The discussion will be confined to simple linear regression. We will begin with the regression coefficient.

Reliability of a Regression Coefficient

An inference about a regression coefficient can be made either as a test of significance or as a confidence interval, just as in the case of a mean or a proportion. Either type of inference depends on the standard error of the regression coefficient, as described below.

Testing the Significance of a Relationship. In the first place, it might be useful to know if there is *any* significant relationship between the variables X and Y. Some particular sample may indicate a relationship, even when none exists, by pure chance alone. Since the regression coefficient for the sample is b, let us call the true regression coefficient for the population β, or beta. If there is no relationship, then the β of the true regression line would be zero. This, then, is set up as the hypothesis, that is, $\beta = 0$. If the sample value b is significantly different from zero, we reject the hypothesis and assert that there is a definite relationship between the variables. To do all this, we compute the *standard error of the regression coefficient.* This is:

$$s_b = \frac{S_{YX}}{\sqrt{\Sigma x^2}}$$

Here, S_{YX} is the sample standard error of estimate, and Σx^2 describes the dispersion of X values around their mean. The value s_b is a measure of the amount of sampling error in b, just as $s_{\bar{x}}$ was a measure of the sampling error in the mean $\overline{X}$.

In the production rating example (Table 20–3):

$$s_b = \frac{5.13}{\sqrt{7,395}} = .060$$

---

[3] See M. Ezekiel and K. A. Fox, *Methods of Correlation and Regression Analysis* (3d ed.; New York: John Wiley & Sons, Inc., 1959), chaps. 17 and 19, for a more complete discussion of this topic.

SIMPLE CORRELATION AND REGRESSION

The procedure for deciding whether a positive relationship exists between corn yields and applications of fertilizer may be set forth as follows:

Null hypothesis: $\beta = 0$ (No relationship between corn yield and application of fertilizer)

Alternative hypothesis: $\beta > 0$ (Yield increases as amount of fertilizer increases)

Critical probability $= .05$

The value of b is .943. If the null hypothesis is true, $\beta = 0$ and b is .943 units from β. In terms of its standard error, this is $.943/s_b = .943/.06 = 16$. Thus b is 16 standard errors from $\beta = 0$.

If this analysis were based upon a large sample, the one-tailed probability associated with any given deviation could be found from the table of areas under the normal curve in Appendix E. For small samples such as this one (with $n < 33$) the t distribution in Table F must be used with $n - 2$ degrees of freedom. In either case a deviation of more than three standard errors is highly significant (except for very small samples). The chance is negligible, therefore, that a deviation as large as 16 standard errors could occur by chance. Hence we reject the null hypothesis and accept the alternative hypothesis that there is a significant relationship between the variables.

Confidence Intervals

A useful way to express the amount of sampling error in sample statistics is by use of confidence intervals. Confidence intervals will be illustrated here for:

1. The regression coefficient or slope of the population regression line (β).
2. The population value for any point on the regression line.
3. An individual forecast (Y).

The 95 per cent confidence interval will be illustrated here, but any other degree of confidence may be chosen instead, by reference to Appendix E or F.

The Regression Coefficient. The 95 per cent confidence interval for the regression coefficient in a large sample is:

$$b \pm 1.96 s_b \quad \text{(Appendix E)}$$

In the production rating example, however, with $n = 20$, we look up Appendix F with $n - 2 = 18$ degrees of freedom and $P = .05$ to find the confidence interval

$$b \pm 2.10 s_b$$
$$\text{This is } .943 \pm 2.10(.060)$$
$$= .943 \pm .126$$

The manufacturer could therefore make the statement that β is between .817 and 1.069, with a probability of .95 that this statement is correct.

The Regression Line. A regression line obtained from a sample will vary from the true regression line not only in its slope but also in its elevation. The average height of the line is best determined for the mean estimated value $\overline{Y}_c$, corresponding to the mean value of X. The standard error of the mean is:

$$s_{\overline{Y}_c} = \frac{S_{YX}}{\sqrt{n}}$$

The standard error for any point, Y_c, on the regression line may now be determined from the equations for $s_{\overline{Y}_c}$ and s_b. We can express the regression equation in the form $Y_c = \overline{Y}_c + bx$. The standard error of Y_c for any value of x (the deviation from the mean) will then include the standard errors of both $\overline{Y}_c$ and $b(x)$. Standard errors, like standard deviations, may be summed by adding their squares. The standard error of Y_c for any value of x is therefore derived as follows:

$$s_{Y_c}^2 = s_{\overline{Y}_c}^2 + (s_b x)^2$$
$$= \frac{S_{YX}^2}{n} + \frac{S_{YX}^2 x^2}{\Sigma x^2}$$

The standard error of a point on the regression line is therefore

$$s_{Y_c} = S_{YX} \sqrt{\frac{1}{n} + \frac{x^2}{\Sigma x^2}} \quad \text{for each value of } x = X - \overline{X}$$

In the production rating example, $S_{YX} = 5.13$, $n = 20$, and $\Sigma x^2 = 7,395$ (Table 20–3). Therefore,

$$s_{Y_c} = 5.13 \sqrt{\frac{1}{20} + \frac{x^2}{7,395}}$$

The standard error of the regression line is therefore smallest at $\overline{X}$, when $x = 0$, and increases in either direction. Its values are shown in Table 20–4, column 4, for selected values of the test score, X.

Table 20-4
STANDARD ERROR OF REGRESSION LINE AND STANDARD ERROR OF AN INDIVIDUAL FORECAST
Test Scores and Production Ratings of 20 Workers

Selected Value of X (1)	Deviation from Mean, x (2)	$\dfrac{x^2}{7{,}395}$ (3)	Standard Error of Regression Line, s_{Y_c} (4)	Standard Error of Forecast s_{Y-Y_c} (5)
15	−40	.2164	2.65	5.77
35	−20	.0541	1.65	5.39
55	0	0	1.15	5.26
75	20	.0541	1.65	5.39
95	40	.2164	2.65	5.77

Note: For 95 per cent confidence intervals multiply columns 4 and 5 by 2.10.
Source: Table 20-3.

The 95 per cent confidence interval for the regression line, when $n = 20$, is $Y_c \pm 2.10 s_{Y_c}$. This is shown by the dashed lines in Chart 20-6. The chances are 95 out of 100, therefore, that the true regression line for the population falls within these limits.

An Individual Forecast. It is often important to find within what limits a *new observation* may be expected to lie. For example, the regression line in Chart 20-5 was used to forecast the production rating for a new applicant who received a test score of 40. The estimated rating was 42 ± 5, where 5 was the standard error of estimate. This error, however, did not take into account the sampling error in the regression line itself.

The *standard error of forecast* (s_{Y-Y_c}) is a measure of the total sampling error for any new observation. It is obtained by combining the standard error of estimate (S_{YX}) and the standard error of the regression line (s_{Y_c}). The standard errors must be squared and added, as follows:

$$s^2_{Y-Y_c} = S^2_{YX} + s^2_{Y_c}$$

Substituting the value of s_{Y_c} found above, the formula for the standard error of forecast becomes:

$$s_{Y-Y_c} = S_{YX}\sqrt{1 + \frac{1}{n} + \frac{x^2}{\Sigma x^2}} \quad \text{for each value of } x = X - \overline{X}$$

This formula simply adds 1 under the radical to the formula for the standard error of the regression line.

Chart 20–6
CONFIDENCE INTERVALS FOR REGRESSION LINE AND INDIVIDUAL FORECAST
Test Scores and Production Ratings of 20 Workers

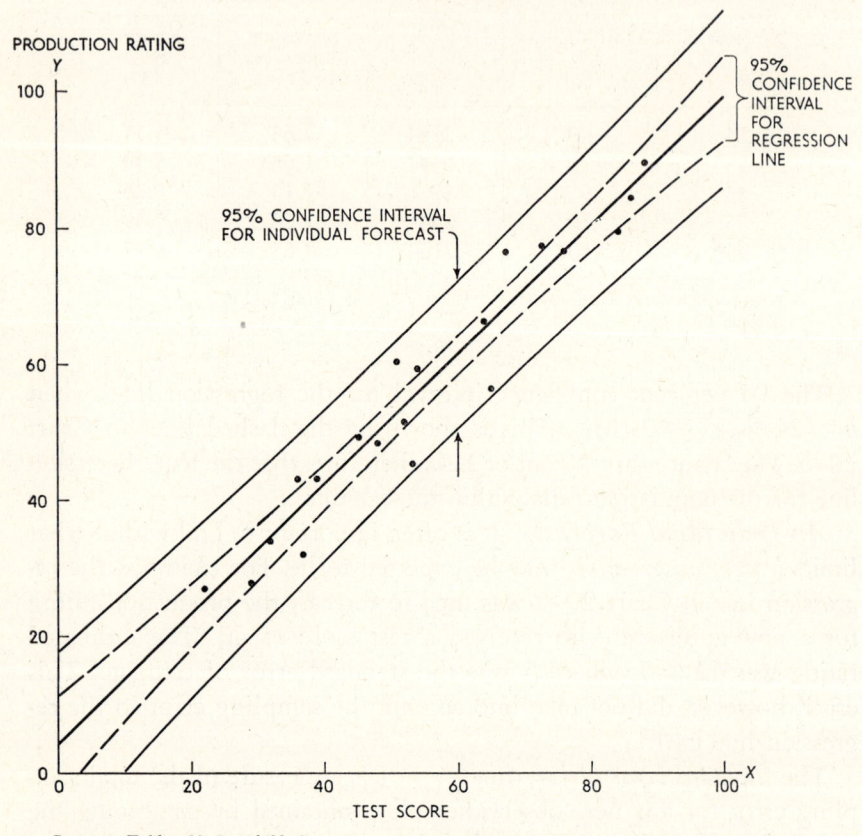

Source: Tables 20–3 and 20–4.

In the production rating case, the standard error of forecast is:

$$S_{Y-Y_c} = 5.13 \sqrt{1 + \frac{1}{20} + \frac{x^2}{7,395}}$$

The forecast errors for five selected test scores (X) are given in Table 20–4, column 5.

If the calculations for the forecast error are based upon a large sample and if the values are approximately normally distributed about the regression line, the chances are about 95 per cent that a new observation drawn from the same population will be within 1.96 forecast errors on either side of Y_c. That is to say, the 95 per cent confidence interval for a new observation (Y) is $Y \pm 1.96 s_{Y-Y_c}$.

In the present example, however, with sample size only 20, the 95 per cent confidence interval for a new observation is $Y \pm 2.10 s_{Y-Y_c}$. This interval is shown as the wide band in Chart 20-6. The chances are 95 out of 100, therefore, that a new applicant will achieve a production rating within these limits.

Certain characteristics of Chart 20-6 should be carefully observed. The boundaries of the confidence intervals are curved. The further the X values get from their arithmetic mean, the greater the width of the confidence intervals. This fact points up the danger of extrapolating for values of X that are a considerable distance from $\overline{X}$.

The forecast error is useful not only for *prediction* but also for *control*. If an observation falls outside the confidence limits, this is an indication that it is very likely "out of control" and should be investigated. As a control chart, Chart 20-6 serves much the same purpose as the statistical quality control charts described in Chapter 22. In the present example, management can not only *predict* that an applicant with test score of 40 will achieve a production rating between 31 and 53 (with probability 95 per cent), but they can use these points as *control* limits. If the applicant's actual production rating falls outside these limits, the chart warns the supervisor to investigate. If the employee's production is below 31, it may be possible to identify and remedy the cause of this deficiency; if it is above 53, the factors accounting for this superior performance should also be identified, either as a basis of rewarding the employee or of improving work practices generally.

Inferences about linear regression constants are valid when deviations around the regression line $(Y - Y_c)$ are independent and have the same normal distribution for all values of X. When these conditions are unrealistic in business research, lack of independence is usually more serious than lack of normality. Values of X must be normally distributed for making certain inferences about correlation coefficients, but this does not apply to regression studies. For example, in the corn-yield experiment, one is free to vary the amount of fertilizer, but he should be concerned as to whether yield per pound of fertilizer might be smaller for larger applications. Changing the amount from 40 to 80 pounds will increase the value of Σx^2, thus reducing the standard error of the regression coefficient.

COEFFICIENT OF CORRELATION

The coefficient of correlation is a relative measure of the relationship between two variables. It may be defined as:

$$r = \frac{s_{Y_{est}}}{s_Y}$$

where $s_{Y_{est}}$ is the standard deviation of the estimated values of the dependent variable, Y, on the regression line, for each value of X, and s_Y is the standard deviation of the actual values of Y; both standard deviations being measured from the mean value of Y.

The coefficient of correlation varies from zero (no correlation) to ± 1 (perfect correlation). The sign of r is the same as that of b in the regression equation. Thus, if $r = -1$, all dots are on a regression line sloping down to the right. This measure is called the *index* of correlation (i), if the regression line is curved. The index of correlation has no sign, since a curve may slope both up and down.

The coefficient of correlation may best be explained by considering r^2, which is called the *coefficient of determination*. Squaring the above equation, we have:

$$r^2 = \frac{s_{Y_{est}}^2}{s_Y^2} = \frac{\text{Explained variance}}{\text{Total variance}}$$

To illustrate these variances, note that the total deviation of any value Y from $\overline{Y}$ is the sum of the deviation $Y_c - \overline{Y}$ and the deviation $Y - Y_c$, as in Chart 20–7. We can add the squared standard deviations, or variances, of all such values in the same way. The *total variance* of the $Y - \overline{Y}$ values is the sum of the variance *explained* by the regression line (based on $Y_c - \overline{Y}$) and the variance *not explained* (based on $Y - Y_c$).

The coefficient of determination is therefore defined in the above equation as the proportion of the total variance in the dependent variable which is explained by the independent variable. The coefficient of determination is preferred to the coefficient of correlation for most applications in business and economics because it is a more clear-cut way of stating the proportion of the variance in Y which is associated with X. The coefficient of correlation may suggest a higher degree of correlation than really exists. Thus, if 50 per cent of the variance in Y is explained by X (and the other 50 per cent is not explained), $r^2 = .50$, but $r = \sqrt{.50} = .71$.

Chart 20-7
BASIC MEASURES FOR CORRELATION COEFFICIENT

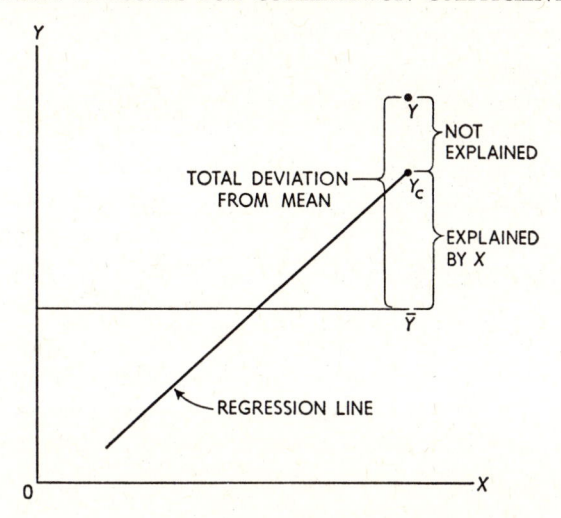

The coefficient of determination may also be expressed as 1 minus the proportion of total variance which is *not* explained. That is:

$$r^2 = 1 - \frac{S_{YX}^2}{S_Y^2} = 1 - \frac{\text{Unexplained variance}}{\text{Total variance}}$$

This formula is more convenient for computation than the first one, since the unexplained variance is the square of the standard error of estimate (S_{YX}), which we have already computed.

Thus, in the production rating case:

Unexplained variance is $\quad S_{YX}^2 = (5.13)^2 = 26.3 \quad$ (page 445)

Total variance is $\quad s_Y^2 = \dfrac{\Sigma y^2}{n-1} = \dfrac{7{,}050}{19} = 371 \quad$ (Table 20-3)

$$r^2 = 1 - \frac{26.3}{371} = .929$$

That is, 92.9 per cent of the variance in production ratings is explained, or accounted for, by the variance in test scores; only 7.1 per cent of the variance is not so explained. The above formulas give the estimated population value of the coefficient of determination, since the use of $n-2$ or $n-1$ instead of n in the basic formulas corrects for bias in the sample. These formulas may be used for either linear or curvilinear relationships.

Graphic Analysis

The coefficient of determination may also be estimated graphically by use of the above formula. The method is illustrated in Chart 20–8. This chart shows the effect of weight on handling time for 22 pieces of metal in a time study of an operation at a John Deere plant. The purpose of this study was to determine the best sizes of metal stock to use in feeding the bump gauge of a punch press.

The procedure is as follows: First, plot a large-scale scatter diagram and fit a freehand regression line, as described earlier in the chapter.

Chart 20–8

WEIGHT AND HANDLING TIME OF 22 PIECES OF METAL FED TO BUMP GAUGE OF NO. 13 PUNCH PRESS

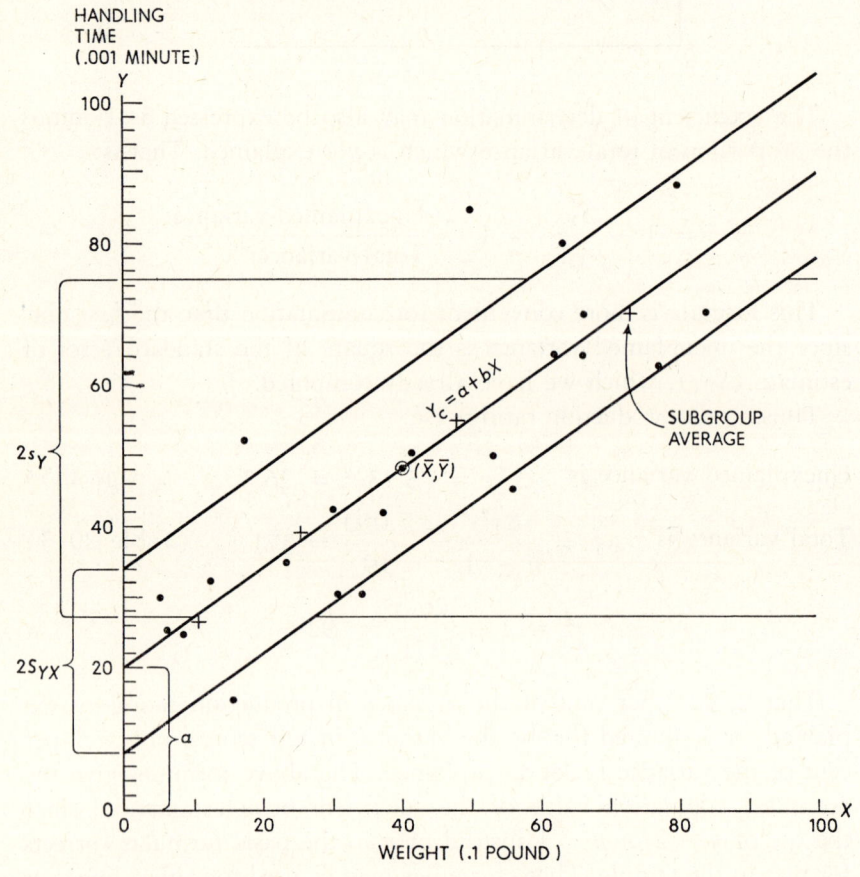

Note: The bands on the chart are drawn horizontally and parallel to the regression line so as to exclude one sixth of the points on either side.
SOURCE: John Deere and Company.

Ch. 20] SIMPLE CORRELATION AND REGRESSION 455

Second, draw two lines parallel to the regression line so that one sixth of the dots fall above and one sixth below this band. Thus, if there are 22 points as in Chart 20–8, the line may be drawn between the third and fourth dots from the top and bottom, measured toward the regression line. This may be done with a transparent ruler or parallel rules set along the regression line. In the case of a curved line, trace the curve and the Y axis on a transparent sheet, and move this sheet up and down along the Y axis until one sixth of the dots are excluded on either side.

Now measure the vertical width of this band on the Y axis. This value is roughly twice the standard error of estimate, $2S_{YX}$, since a range of S_{YX} above and below the regression line includes about two thirds of the items in a normal distribution. In Chart 20–6, $2S_{YX}$ is about 26, so S_{YX} is 13.

If gaps occur in the data near either of the points marked, the band may be drawn to exclude a fifth or some other fraction of the dots on either side, provided the same number of points falls outside the horizontal band in step 3, below. Since r^2 depends on the *ratio* of the two scatters, the proportion of points excluded might vary considerably without impairing the accuracy of this ratio.

Third, set the ruler on the scatter diagram *horizontally* and mark two straight lines separating off the top sixth of the items and the bottom sixth. Measure this spread, too, against the vertical scale of the chart. This is roughly $2s_Y$, or twice the standard deviation of the dependent variable, since a range of s_Y above and below the mean of the Y values includes about two thirds of the items in a normal distribution. Here, $2s_Y$ is about 47½, so $s_Y = 23¾$.

Finally, substitute these values in the above formula. In this example,

$$r^2 = 1 - \frac{S_{YX}^2}{s_Y^2}$$
$$= 1 - \frac{(13)^2}{(23.75)^2}$$
$$= .70$$

This measure of correlation is useful as a quick estimate of r^2, or as a check on the computed value. It is relatively accurate when r^2 is high. The chart also provides a visual picture of the degree of correlation: the smaller the *ratio* of the sloping band to the horizontal one, the higher the correlation.

Rapid Calculation Methods

When a straight line regression has been fitted by least squares, the coefficient of determination for the sample (r_s^2) may be computed by the short-cut formula:

$$r_s^2 = \frac{(\Sigma xy)^2}{\Sigma x^2 \Sigma y^2}$$

In the production rating case (Table 20–3, p. 443):

$$r_s^2 = \frac{(6{,}974)^2}{7{,}395 \times 7{,}050} = .933$$

However, this sample value must be adjusted downward to provide the unbiased population estimate of .929 given above.[4]

The calculation of all correlation and regression measures has been greatly facilitated in recent years by the wide availability of electronic computers and efficient programs for this purpose. If one wished to explore the demand structure for new automobile tires, for example, scores of regression equations could be run on an electronic computer—most of them multiple rather than simple regressions—in a matter of hours. Such computers can also be programmed to print off a complete set of estimates of the computed values of the dependent variable, Y_c, and each of the residuals from the regression.

Nevertheless, graphic methods are still valuable for exploratory analysis, for curvilinear regressions that do not follow a simple mathematical function, and as a running picture of operations and a check on final results. There is some danger that electronic computers will encourage slipshod logical analysis of problems simply because it is so easy to fit a large number of alternative regression forms and (in multiple regression) combinations of independent variables.

Reliability of Correlation Coefficients

The standard error of the correlation coefficient can be estimated from the formula

---

[4] The adjustment formula is

$$r^2 = 1 - (1 - r_s^2)\left(\frac{n-1}{n-2}\right)$$

In this example,

$$r^2 = 1 - (1 - .933)\left(\frac{19}{18}\right) = .929$$

$$s_r = \frac{1 - r^2}{\sqrt{n - 1}}$$

Unfortunately, this formula is not generally applicable; it is inadequate for small samples, and even for large samples the distribution of the sample r's is apt to be quite skewed when the true value of r is far from zero.[5]

The sampling variability of correlation coefficients may be illustrated graphically, however, in Chart 20-9. This chart shows the *minimum*

Chart 20-9

MINIMUM CORRELATION IN POPULATION, FOR VARYING OBSERVED CORRELATIONS AND SIZE OF SAMPLE

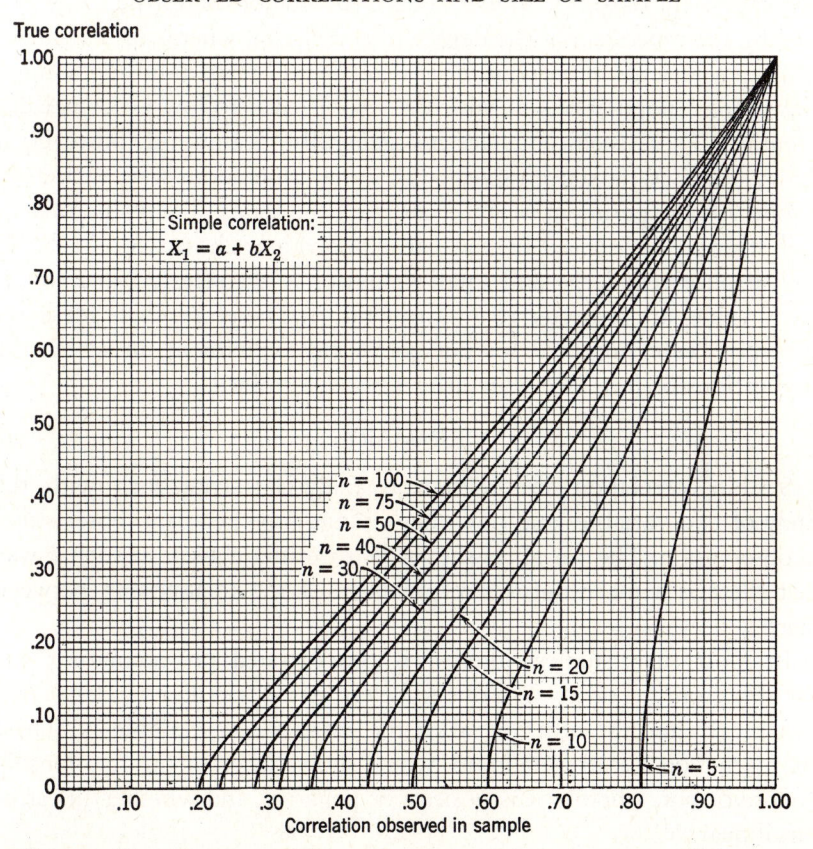

Under conditions of random sampling, one sample out of 20, on the average, will show a correlation coefficient with a ± value as high as that "observed in sample," when drawn from a population with the stated true correlation.

Reprinted with permission from M. Ezekiel, and K. A. Fox, *Methods of Correlation and Regression Analysis*, 3d ed. (New York: John Wiley & Sons, Inc., 1959), p. 294.

[5] The value r, however, can be transformed into a quantity called *Fisher's z*, whose sampling distribution is nearly normal. For a treatment of tests of hypotheses and confidence intervals using z, see the first edition of this book, pp. 492-93, and Appendix I.

value of the true correlation coefficient for any sample value of r, at the 95 per cent confidence level.

For example, in the production rating case, the coefficient of correlation for the sample of 20 workers is $\sqrt{.933}$, or .966. With this value on the X axis, use the $n = 20$ curve to find .93 on the Y axis. We can say, therefore, that the true correlation for the population is *at least .93*, with a 95 per cent chance of being correct.

If the sample r were .60, however, with $n = 10$, we could only say that the true value is at least zero, with the same degree of confidence. That is, even if there is *no* correlation in the population itself, 5 per cent of all possible samples of size 10 would still yield a correlation coefficient of .60 or higher. This chart demonstrates the danger of making inferences about the degree of correlation when r or n is small.

The coefficients of correlation or determination are valid for samples drawn from populations in which X and Y each follow a normal distribution. These coefficients are not generally meaningful, however, if the values of X have been selected in some nonrandom way, such as in a controlled experiment or an economic time series. The value of r or r^2 is strongly influenced by the particular values chosen for X, being high if only very large and small values of X are selected, and low if the X values are restricted to a narrow range. Therefore, these measures have not been computed for our corn-yield experiment, in which the applications of fertilizer were arbitrarily determined.

SUMMARY

Simple correlation and regression analysis is concerned with the study of two variables and how they change together from observation to observation. The variables should be carefully chosen in such a way that there is a meaningful interpretation of the relationship between them.

In most such studies, interest is concentrated on estimating one variable from the other. The one to be estimated is called the *dependent* variable Y, and the other is called the *independent* variable X. These are plotted on a scatter diagram, which shows whether the relationship is close or not, whether it is positive or negative, and whether linear or curvilinear.

The basic measures of relationship are the *regression line* or curve, which describes the average relationship between X and Y; the *standard error of estimate*, which is the standard deviation of the residuals $(Y - Y_c)$ around this line; and the *coefficient of correlation*, a relative measure of relationship which varies from 0 to ± 1.

Regression analysis is used in business and economics principally for the purposes of *prediction* and *control*. Thus, in correlating the earnings per share (X) with price per share (Y) for a number of stocks, we can predict the price of a stock from the regression line, based on estimated future earnings. Or, we can use the standard error of estimate to construct a confidence interval around this line, and consider the stock unduly high or low in price if it is outside these control limits.

Regression lines or curves can be fitted either graphically or mathematically. In graphic analysis, arrays are constructed by grouping observations for which values of X are approximately equal; a point of means for each array is estimated and indicated by a small cross or circle; and a smooth curve is drawn to fit the points of means. Such a curve should be relatively inflexible. If the regression is linear, the line is drawn through $(\overline{X}, \overline{Y})$, the point of means of all observations.

The regression of Y on X is said to be *linear* or *curvilinear*, depending on the shape of the curve determined by the means of arrays of Y values for various values of X. When the regression is linear, the two constants of the regression line are its *Y intercept a* and its *slope b*, the *regression coefficient*. When the regression curve is a parabola describing the mean value of Y as a second-degree function of X, a is the Y intercept, b is the slope at the Y axis, and c is the constant which determines the curvature.

The *method of least squares* is a means of computing the constants of the regression line so as to minimize the sum of squares of residuals from the line $(Y - Y_c)$. The equations which determine the required constants are called the *normal equations*. Shifting the origin to the point of means (that is, using x and y instead of X and Y as the variables) eliminates the constant a from the second normal equation, thus providing simpler formulas for b, r, and the other measures.

A regression *curve* can be drawn to fit points of means satisfactorily if the curvature of the regression is relatively slight. The task of drawing a satisfactory regression curve becomes more and more difficult as the curvature becomes greater. Fortunately, graph paper is available with various types of special ruling designed to straighten out trend and regression curves. Important types of special ruling are the semilogarithmic, for which only one scale is logarithmic, and the double-logarithmic graph. Parabolas and other curves can be fitted by least squares, by an extension of the methods used for a straight line.

The *standard error of estimate* measures the average error of the regression line in providing estimates of Y from given values of X. It may be computed as the standard deviation of the residuals $(Y - Y_c)$

around the regression line, or by means of a short-cut formula. A relationship is significantly curvilinear only if the standard error of estimate for a curve is smaller than that for a straight line, after taking into account the loss of degrees of freedom (m) in the curve.

We can apply *tests of significance* and *confidence intervals* to regression results from random samples in order to make statistical inferences about the parent population. Thus, we can determine whether there is any significant relationship between X and Y by testing the null hypothesis that the population regression coefficient β is zero. If the sample value b, divided by its standard error, is sufficiently large, according to a table of the normal or t distribution, the relationship is deemed to be significant.

The 95 per cent confidence interval for the regression coefficient in a large sample is $b \pm 1.96 s_b$. By adding $s_b x$ (squared) to the standard error of the mean $\overline{Y}_c$ (squared), we obtain the *standard error of the regression line*, or s_{Y_c} (squared). The curved 95 per cent confidence limits for the regression line are shown in Chart 20–6. We can state that the true regression line of the population falls within this interval, with 95 chances out of 100 of being correct.

By similarly combining the standard error of the regression line with the standard error of estimate, we obtain the *standard error of forecast*, which provides confidence limits within which any *new observation* may be expected to fall. The confidence bands for both the regression line and an individual forecast are narrowest at $\overline{X}$ (Chart 20–6); they widen out in either direction. This indicates the danger of estimating Y for values of X that are far from their mean. The forecast error is valuable both in predicting Y and in providing a control chart for Y.

The *coefficient of correlation* (or "index" of correlation in the curvilinear case) is a relative measure of relationship. Its square, the *coefficient of determination*, is the ratio of explained variance to total variance, or 1 minus the ratio of unexplained to total variance.

Total variance is the standard deviation (squared) of the Y values around their mean ($Y - \overline{Y}$). *Explained variance* is the standard deviation (squared) of the Y_c values around the mean ($Y_c - \overline{Y}$), since this part of the variation in Y can be explained by corresponding changes in X. *Unexplained variance* is the standard deviation (squared) of Y values around the regression line ($Y - Y_c$)—the variation in Y not explained by X. This is the standard error of estimate, squared. The coefficient of determination is a more direct and unequivocal measure of the proportion of variance in Y explained by X than is the higher-valued coefficient of correlation.

The coefficient of determination may be estimated graphically from the ratio of the vertical widths of two bands drawn horizontally and parallel to the regression line—each including the central two thirds of the dots. It may also be computed directly by a short-cut formula. All calculations in correlation and regression are greatly facilitated by the electronic computer programs now available. Confidence limits for r are shown in Chart 20–9. The chart illustrates the dangers of making inferences when r or n is small.

In conclusion, the regression coefficient b, the standard error of estimate S_{YX}, and the coefficient of determination r^2 each measure a different aspect of a given relationship. In the production rating example, the regression coefficient tells us the average *amount* of change in production for a given change in the test score; the standard error of estimate tells us how *accurate* our estimate of production is; and the coefficient of determination tells us what *proportion* of variance in production ratings is accounted for by the test scores. For many problems of control and prediction, the first two measures will suffice. The coefficient of determination is needed only if the problem calls for a measure of *proportionate* importance.

Regression analysis can be applied not only to controlled experiments and time series in which the X values are selected arbitrarily but also to surveys in which both X and Y are random variables. The measures of statistical inference and correlation, however, are valid only in the latter case, since they may be distorted by the arbitrary selection of X values.

PROBLEMS

1. Distinguish between:
   a) Regression and trend analysis.
   b) Linear and curvilinear regression.
   c) The standard error of estimate and the standard deviation of the dependent variable.
   d) The use of regression analysis for prediction and for control.
   e) The coefficient of regression and the coefficient of correlation.

2. Explain:
   a) The method of least squares, as applied to regression analysis.
   b) How to test whether there is any significant relationship between two variables.
   c) How to obtain a 99 per cent confidence interval for the regression coefficient, in a large sample.
   d) How the standard error of forecast is derived from the standard error of estimate and the standard error of the regression line.
   e) The coefficient of determination, in terms of explained variance, unexplained variance, and total variance.

3. Answer the following questions by inspection of Chart 20–8:
   a) Is the relationship between weight and handling time simple or multiple, linear or curvilinear, positive or negative, significant or negligible?
   b) Give the approximate regression equation. Explain the meaning of the a and b values in estimating handling time from weight.
   c) Give the estimated handling time (Y_c) for pieces weighing 80 tenths of a pound. What is the unexplained variation ($Y - Y_c$) for the piece that weighed this amount but actually required 88 thousandths of a minute to handle?
   d) Considering the sampling error of the regression line as well as the standard error of estimate, for what weight could you forecast handling time most accurately?

4. Assume that we conduct an experiment with eight fields planted to corn: four fields having no nitrogen fertilizer and four fields having 80 pounds of nitrogen fertilizer. The resulting corn yields are shown below, in bushels per acre.

Field	Nitrogen (Pounds)	Corn Yield Bu./Acre
1	0	12
2	0	36
3	0	6
4	0	18
5	80	128
6	80	112
7	80	112
8	80	72
Total	320	496

Note: This sample is too small to provide really valid inferences, but it serves to illustrate the methods involved with a minimum of computations.
   a) Plot the data as a scatter diagram on an arithmetic chart, and draw a regression line by the graphic method, using group averages as guides.
   b) Compute a linear regression equation by least squares. How does this compare with the graphic line when plotted on the chart? Explain the meaning of the regression equation in terms of fertilizer and corn yields.
   c) Compute the standard error of estimate and find the 95 per cent confidence limits around the regression line. That is, multiply S_{YX} by the factor in Appendix F under $P = .05$ for $n - 2$ degrees of freedom.
   d) Predict corn yield for a field treated with 60 pounds of fertilizer, and give the 95 per cent confidence limits for this prediction. (Assume a linear relationship and ignore sampling errors in the regression line itself.)
   e) Compute the estimated coefficient of determination for the population as one minus the unexplained variance over the total variance. What does

this figure tell you about the relationship of nitrogen fertilizer and corn yields in general?

5. *a*) How could you determine whether the regression between test scores and production ratings in Table 20–3 is significantly curvilinear?
   b) Since the formula for a straight line is merely a special case of that of a parabola in which $c = 0$, the parabola would seem to fit almost any set of data better than the less flexible straight line. Can you infer, then, that nearly all regressions are significantly curvilinear? Explain.

6. In the first corn-yield experiment described in the text (Table 20–1), where four fields had no fertilizer and four fields had 40 pounds, the regression equation was $Y_c = 18 + 1.4X$, with a standard error of estimate of 19.2 bushels per acre.
   a) Is there any significant relationship between nitrogen fertilizer and corn yields? That is, test the null hypothesis that $\beta = 0$ against the alternative hypothesis that $\beta > 0$, at a critical probability of, say, 5 per cent.
   b) Give the 95 per cent confidence interval for the regression coefficient.
   c) How is your interpretation of the results in (*a*) and (*b*) affected by the fact that the basic data represent a controlled experiment rather than a survey in which both X and Y are normally distributed? (Ignore the small size of sample.)

7. In the same corn-yield experiment (Table 20–1 and Problem 6):
   a) Compute the standard error of the regression line and its 95 per cent confidence limits for fertilizer applications of 0, 20, and 40 pounds, respectively.
   b) Compute the standard error of forecast and the 95 per cent confidence limits for individual forecasts of corn yield, assuming fertilizer applications of 0, 20, and 40 pounds, respectively.
   c) How is your interpretation of the results in (*a*) and (*b*) affected by the fact that the basic data represent a controlled experiment rather than a survey in which both X and Y are normally distributed? (Ignore the small size of sample.)

8. *a*) Estimate the coefficient of determination for test scores and production ratings in Chart 20–5 by the graphic method. How does this result compare with the computed value of $r^2 = .93$?
   b) If the sample value of r had been .60 in this example, with $n = 20$, what is the minimum value of the true correlation coefficient of the population, at the 95 per cent confidence level (Chart 20–9)?
   c) If the true correlation coefficient were zero, what sample value would be exceeded by 5 per cent of all random samples of size 20?

SELECTED READINGS
(See page 492.)

21. TIME SERIES AND MULTIPLE CORRELATION

THIS CHAPTER will first take up the correlation of business and economic data—particularly the correlation of time series and its use in forecasting. This is one of the most widespread and controversial applications of correlation and regression analysis. The latter part of the chapter will present an introduction to multiple correlation and regression analysis—a technique by which we can measure the simultaneous influence of any number of independent variables on a dependent variable.

REGRESSION ANALYSIS OF BUSINESS AND ECONOMIC DATA

Physical and biological scientists sometimes look askance at the efforts of economists and business statisticians to make statistical analyses and inferences on the basis of observations which were not obtained from a controlled experiment. But there are other sciences in which considerable knowledge has been obtained from nonexperimental observations—for example, astronomy and meteorology. Regression analyses of business or economic data cannot be regarded as unscientific just because many of them are based on nonexperimental data.

Suppose that the manufacturer in the corn-yield example (Chapter 20) did not want to wait a year or so for the results of a controlled experiment with nitrogen fertilizer and corn yields. He might instead hire some market research firm to make a sample survey of farmers in the region in which he is interested and ask them how much nitrogen fertilizer they used and what corn yields they obtained. Regression analyses could then be made of the results of the survey; standard errors and confidence intervals could be computed for these regressions, and the results could be made the basis of an advertising campaign.

As compared with a controlled experiment, the sample survey may be subject to substantial errors of measurement, as farmers try to recall how much fertilizer they applied and to estimate the corn yields they obtained. Even if yields and rates of nitrogen application were remembered perfectly, systematic factors might tend to bias the results. For example, the farmers applying above-average amounts of nitrogen fertilizer might be above average in their other cultural practices, so that their high yields could not be attributed solely to the greater amounts of fertilizer used.

Although there is something "scientific" about going out and collecting information from a random sample of a population of interest, the fact remains that it is not known precisely why the variables about which information is collected happen to be related as they are. If most of the possible sources of bias are foreseen, it is possible to collect from each farmer in the sample additional information that would help classify his level of managerial ability, the predominant soil type on his farm, whether or not he used supplemental irrigation or other practices that would have tended to raise corn yields on his farm relative to the amount of fertilizer applied, and so on. Such information can be used to stratify the sample into relatively homogeneous subgroups within which the factors other than nitrogen fertilizer show little variation. Or, stratifying factors as well as the rates of application of nitrogen fertilizer can be used as independent variables in a multiple regression analysis of factors affecting corn yields.

For present purposes, the main point is that in order to extract reliable information from nonexperimental data by means of regression analysis, there must be hypotheses or theories concerning the sorts of variables that cause fluctuations in the dependent variable. If variations in consumer purchases of a product are to be explained, the economic theory of consumer demand will give hypotheses as to what factors are pertinent. In analyzing fluctuations in stock prices, hypotheses might be set up concerning the motives which lead different classes of investors to buy or sell stocks.

An Example—Forecasting Tire Sales

As an example of the reasoning processes one must go through in interpreting nonexperimental data, consider the problem of forecasting industry-wide sales of new automobile tires for the coming year. There are two different types of demand. Quite a number of new tires will be sold to automobile manufacturers to become original equipment on new automobiles. Assuming that practically all new automobiles are sold with a spare tire, if the number of new cars to be produced next year were available, this figure could be multiplied by 5 to obtain the number of new tires that would be purchased by auto manufacturers. But if a dependable forecast of new automobile sales is not available, then a suitable forecast must be prepared. Plausible factors include the number of existing motor vehicles owned or registered at the end of the current year; the average age of existing automobiles; the total population 16 years of age or older; the level of disposable consumer income per capita; and the expected retail prices for new automobiles relative to the general price level for consumer goods and services. Here again, common sense (*and* economic theory) should indicate whether each of these variables has a positive or a negative effect upon the sales of new automobiles. It would appear that at least five independent variables would be necessary to explain or forecast variations in the sales of new automobiles.

Given an estimate of prospective sales of new automobiles, interest in the demand for new tires by automobile manufacturers might be refined along the following lines:

1. Interest might attach to the number of new automobiles *produced* during the next calendar year rather than the number sold.
2. Inventories of new automobiles in the hands of (*a*) manufacturers and (*b*) dealers at the beginning of the year should have some bearing upon the level of new car *production* relative to new car *sales*.
3. Inventories of tires owned by automobile manufacturers at the beginning of the year should have some influence upon the number of new tires purchased from rubber manufacturers relative to the number of new automobiles produced. Finally, *if* tires for foreign cars are produced exclusively in foreign countries, primary interest may be in estimating the purchases of new tires only for use on American-made cars. If so, the estimate of sales of new domestically produced automobiles must take some account of the probable competitive relationship between domestic and foreign cars.

The other major component of demand for new tires is the replacement demand. If most motorists drive less than 15,000 miles a year and if most new tires last more than 15,000 miles, replacement demand should not come significantly from new automobiles. Hence, an estimate of the number of motor vehicles registered at the beginning of the year, plus an estimate of the average number of miles driven per vehicle, should give a fairly accurate estimate of the amount of wear and tear on tires that will lead to replacement demand.

In estimating the number of new tires that will be sold through dealers and mail-order houses, a simple projection of time trend may be satisfactory—for example, the trend in total vehicle miles driven per year. In fact, with the increasing number of families owning two or more cars, it may be that the number of miles driven *per family* is more stable than the number of miles driven per car. At least, one might expect that when a family with two or more drivers shifts from one automobile to two the average number of miles *per car* will decrease even though the total mileage driven by the members of the family increases. The population 16 years of age and older and the level of disposable personal income per capita are factors that might logically influence the number of motor vehicles in existence, the average miles driven per car, and the product of these two variables—total vehicle miles driven—on a nation-wide basis.

CORRELATION OF TIME SERIES

The correlation of time series presents no new computational problems. The analysis of two series ordered in time may be carried out in a manner similar to that illustrated in the previous chapter. Problems of interpretation do arise, however, and there are some "booby traps" for the novice.

In the first place, much of the observed correlation between two economic time series may be due to the fact that both variables have strong upward trends. Any two linear trends will be perfectly correlated with one another, whether the series have any real connection or not. In appraising a high coefficient of determination obtained between total meat consumption and disposable income over a 40-year period, we should recognize that population growth is the most important component in the dependent variable and that it also accounts for about half of the increase in disposable income (if the latter is expressed in constant prices). This is a cheap and unenlightening victory; other things being equal, it is perfectly obvious that two people will consume twice as much meat as one. If *economic* relationships are important, these relationships should be investigated on a *per capita* basis. Further investigation may indicate that this relationship cannot be established satisfactorily by means of simple regression analysis but that it calls for multiple regression analysis.

In other cases, there may be trends in time series due to factors other than population growth or general growth of the economy. It must be decided whether interest is best served by (1) explaining the trend and ignoring the year-to-year fluctuations, as in Chapter 18, (2) eliminating the trend and explaining the year-to-year fluctuations, or (3) attempting to explain both simultaneously.

Methods of Correlating Time Series

There are four ways to correlate time series. The first two of these will be illustrated in the correlation of Sears, Roebuck sales and disposable personal income listed in Table 21–1. The following discussion applies to annual data; monthly data should be adjusted for calendar and seasonal variation before being correlated. Dollar value series may be correlated without price adjustment, as in our example, if it is wished to compare the combined effect of changes in price and physical volume. However, if it is desired to bring out the relationship in physical volume changes unobscured by price fluctuations, the dollar series should be deflated by dividing through by an appropriate price index. Unfortunately, however, each deflated series is affected by an unknown error in the price index itself. The four methods of correlating time series are:

1. *Correlate the actual annual data,* to show the combined effect of secular trend, and cyclical and irregular fluctuations. This method may be quite adequate for forecasting, particularly over the longer run. The pitfall here is that any two series that have nonhorizontal trends or that are affected by the general business cycle will *appear* to be correlated whether there is any real connection or not. The meat consumption example was a case in point. The remedy is to (1) choose only series that have a close logical relationship; (2) supplement this method with one of the following, in which trend is eliminated; and (3) avoid the coefficient of correlation or determination, which is spuriously high.

2. *Correlate first differences,* such as the per cent changes from a year ago listed in Table 21–1. The use of these percentages will eliminate all trend except that in a single year, and will avoid the errors involved in fitting a trend curve (method 3). This method is useful chiefly in short-term forecasting. Either the *relative* first differences (percentage changes) or *absolute* first differences (amounts of change) may be correlated. The amounts of change are obtained by *subtracting* each year's values from the next. It is usually better to correlate relative rather than absolute first differences, since percentages tend to have a more uniform dispersion over a period of time than do the absolute amounts. For example, the year-to-year changes in the dollar volume of

Sears sales tend to become larger in later years simply because the sales volume itself is so much greater. The later values thus have a disproportionate influence in determining the various measures of correlation.

3. *Correlate percentages of trend,* i.e., cyclical-irregular relatives. These values are shown in Chart 18–3, page 361, for Sears, Roebuck sales. Similar deviations would be used for disposable income. The results bring out the *cyclical* and other short-term relationships between the two series. This method is therefore useful for anticipating the effect of short-term business cycle changes. The trend line is a more stable base for computing percentages than is the previous year's level, so the scatter of percentages tends to be less erratic than in method 2. However, in the long run the projections obtained in method 3 are increasingly sensitive to errors in extrapolating the trend curve itself.

4. *Apply multiple regression analysis,* as described later in the chapter, with time as a separate independent variable. Thus we could correlate Sears sales with both disposable income and years. The regression coefficients then give the separate influence of income and trend (years) on sales, unless the independent variables are too closely correlated with each other to permit these influences to be segregated. If this is done, the equation form must be consistent with the secular trend function. Since we found in Chapter 18 that Sears sales followed a logarithmic straight line trend of the form $\log Y_c = a + bX$, it follows that the *logarithm* of sales should be used in a linear multiple regression if time is used as one of the independent variables. Otherwise the results will be distorted. If trends are present, logarithms are often used for *all* variables except time, in order to make the scatter of the residuals more uniform than would be the case if absolute values were used. By this device all correlation measures become more meaningful.

Correlating Actual Data. Suppose we are engaged in long-range planning for Sears, Roebuck & Company, and wish to establish a quantitative basis for projecting the company's future sales. Since the company distributes a wide variety of consumer products on a nationwide scale, its sales should move pretty closely with United States disposable personal income. Authoritative forecasts of the latter are available. We will therefore correlate the sales and income figures for 1947–58 shown in Table 21–1, and use this regression to forecast sales for 1959 and 1960. We will then check the forecasts against actual sales in these years. The period 1947–58 is rather short, but the relationship in earlier years was distorted by the depression of the 1930's and World War II.

The first step is to plot the data on an arithmetic scatter diagram, as

Table 21-1

SEARS, ROEBUCK NET SALES AND DISPOSABLE PERSONAL INCOME
1947–58 AND FORECAST YEARS 1959–60

Year	Disposable Income (Billions of Dollars) X	Sears Sales* (Billions of Dollars) Y	Per Cent Change from Previous Year X	Per Cent Change from Previous Year Y
1947	170.1	1.982	...	...
1948	189.3	2.296	11.3	15.8
1949	189.7	2.169	.2	−5.5
1950	207.7	2.556	9.5	17.8
1951	227.5	2.657	9.5	4.0
1952	238.7	2.932	4.9	10.4
1953	252.5	2.982	5.8	1.7
1954	256.9	2.965	1.7	−.6
1955	274.4	3.307	6.8	11.5
1956	292.9	3.556	6.7	7.5
1957	308.8	3.601	5.4	1.3
1958	317.9	3.721	2.9	3.3
Group Averages				
1947–50	189.2	2.251		
1951–54	243.9	2.884		
1955–58	298.5	3.546		
1947–58	243.9	2.894	5.88	6.11
Future Years (Actual)				
1959	337.3	4.036	6.1	8.5
1960	354.2	4.134	5.0	2.4

* Years beginning February 1.
SOURCE: *Survey of Current Business;* Sears, Roebuck *Annual Reports.*

in Chart 21–1. The dots tend to follow a straight line, so it is not necessary to replot the data on a semilogarithmic or double-logarithmic scale to achieve linearity. In order to fit a regression line graphically, we compute group averages for four-year periods (see table) as well as the over-all average $\overline{X}, \overline{Y}$. We chose four-year periods because the general business cycle averaged about four years in length during this era (Table 17–1, page 337), so each average should roughly balance out the ups and downs of one business cycle. The averages, when plotted as crosses on the chart, fall practically on a straight line. We therefore draw the line, with a transparent ruler, through the over-all mean $\overline{X}, \overline{Y}$, so as to equalize the vertical deviations of the group averages.

Ch. 21]　　　　　TIME SERIES AND MULTIPLE CORRELATION　　　471

Chart 21-1

SEARS, ROEBUCK NET SALES AND DISPOSABLE PERSONAL INCOME
1947–58, WITH FORECASTS FOR 1959 AND 1960
(Billions of Dollars)

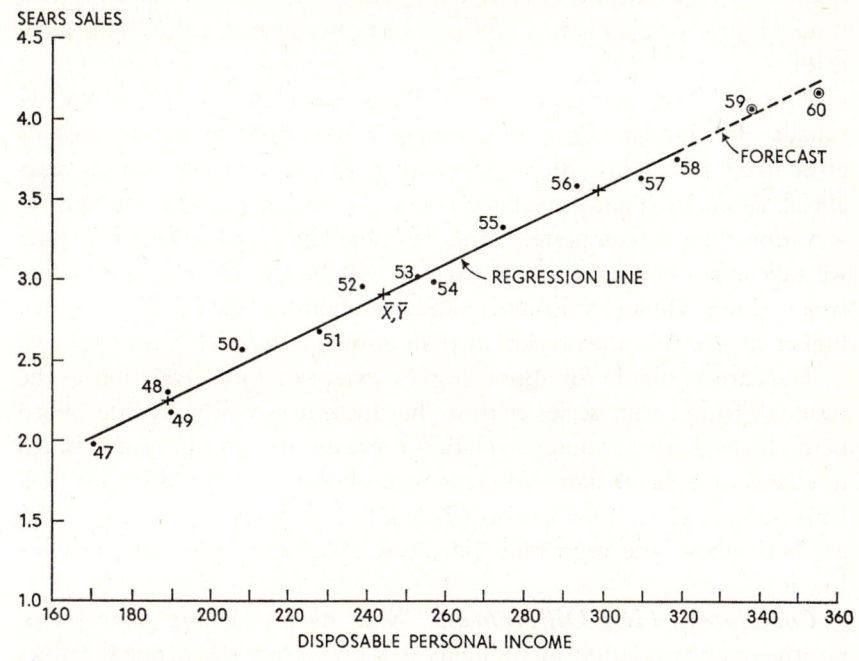

SOURCE: Table 21–1.

For more extended analysis, we would compute the least-squares regression line, the standard error of estimate, and confidence intervals for both the regression line and an individual forecast, exactly as we did for the production rating example in Chapter 20. The confidence interval for the regression line would apply if we were forecasting the general level or trend of sales over a number of future years, while the confidence interval for an individual forecast would apply if we were predicting sales for a particular year. We will not repeat this procedure here, as the graphic analysis will suffice to illustrate the peculiarities of correlating time series.

The measures of correlation described in this book are theoretically correct only if the residuals $(Y - Y_c)$ are randomly distributed, with uniform dispersion, around each section of the regression line. This is not true of time series. First, the presence of an extreme high or low value (occasioned, say, by a war scare or strike) influences the regression line in proportion to the *square* of its deviation, and so distorts the line. The war years were eliminated for this reason.

Second, the residuals tend to get bigger as the industry grows over the years. The use of logarithms or percentages to discount this tendency has been discussed.

Third, since most time series move in cycles rather than in purely random fashion, there are likely to be runs of several successive positive residuals or several negative residuals in a row. That is, each year's value is related to that of the adjoining year rather than being independent of it. This is called "autocorrelation." If autocorrelation exists in the residuals, the standard error of estimate will understate the amount of error likely to be encountered in making forecasts for one or two years ahead. Essentially, autocorrelated series give us less information per observation than do completely random ones. The closer together in time we take our observations, the greater will be the autocorrelation between them. Hence, seasonally adjusted monthly data will exhibit a higher degree of autocorrelation than annual data.

Tests are available for appraising the extent of autocorrelation in the residuals from a time series analysis, but these tests will not be described here.[1] If the degree of autocorrelation is greater than could be attributed to chance, the usual standard error formulas are inapplicable. There is little autocorrelation evident in Chart 21–1, although 1955 and 1956 are both above the regression line, and 1957 and 1958 are both below it.

Correlating First Differences. With most economic time series, positive autocorrelation in residuals is found when the original values of the variables are correlated. Positive autocorrelation can usually be reduced by using first differences, as in the last two columns of Table 21–1. If the regression equation is calculated in terms of first differences and the residuals from this equation are not significantly autocorrelated, then the standard errors of regression coefficients and the standard error of estimate are regarded as applicable and valid for the span of years covered. Use of this equation for forecasting in subsequent years still depends upon the study of future trends that would affect the relationship. This topic will be discussed later.

The relative first differences, or percentage changes from a year ago, are plotted in Chart 21–2 for Sears, Roebuck sales and disposable personal income. The point of means, $\overline{X}$, $\overline{Y}$, and the group averages for points to the left and right of this point are plotted as crosses. Since these three points fall in a straight line, a regression line has been drawn through them by the graphic method. The residuals in Chart

---

[1] The principal tests are the "coefficient of autocorrelation" and "von Neumann's ratio." For details, see M. Ezekiel and K. A. Fox, *Methods of Correlation and Regression Analysis* (3d ed.; New York: John Wiley & Sons, Inc., 1959), pp. 334–40.

Chart 21-2
PER CENT CHANGES FROM PREVIOUS YEAR IN SEARS, ROEBUCK SALES AND DISPOSABLE INCOME 1948–58, WITH FORECASTS FOR 1959 AND 1960

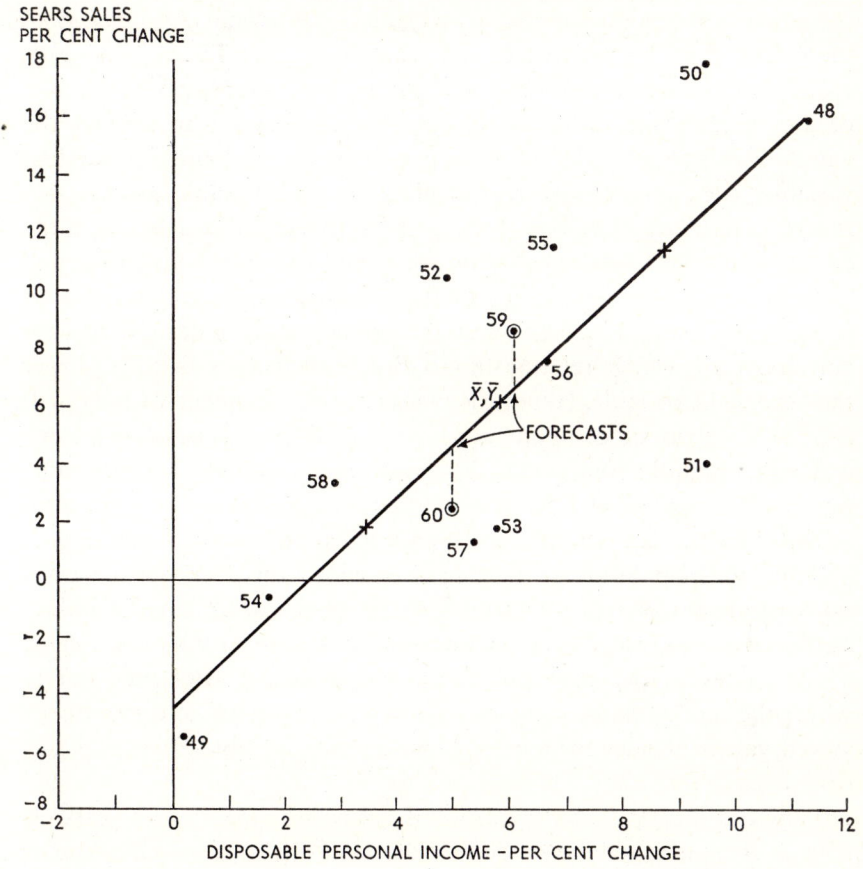

SOURCE: Table 21-1.

21–2 appear to be more randomly distributed than those in Chart 21–1, so there is less autocorrelation. For example, the pairs of years 1955–56 and 1957–58 no longer fall on the same side of the line. The various standard errors computed for these percentages, therefore, may be deemed more valid than those computed for the original values in Chart 21–1. This does not mean, of course, that a *forecast* based on first differences is necessarily more accurate than one based on original data.

Is the Correlation of Aggregates Valid for Forecasting?

The data used in this analysis were totals for the entire United States over the period 1947–58. Each variable—net sales and disposable personal income—is a population total, so there is no room for sampling errors in the variables although there may be some errors of measurement.

Do the data form a sample in any sense or do they simply describe a condition of the population in a particular time period? An analogy to the controlled experiment situation can be argued. Thus, each year's value of disposable income can be regarded as a "predetermined" value of the independent variable. No effort is made to try to explain the values of this variable. However, it may be assumed that the dependent variable, sales, is not perfectly correlated with disposable income, but is subject to a large number of more or less random disturbances in the economy. These forces may be too small and too numerous to list and measure separately; they are not predictable in advance, so that their net effect in the year just ahead is just as likely to raise the dependent variable above its average relationship to disposable income as it is to lower the dependent variable. Hence the values of the dependent variable will include a systematic component which is related to disposable income and also a random component. The systematic component is estimated by fitting a regression line; the random component will be reflected in the residual variation of the dependent variable around this line.

Thus, the population with respect to which the 1947–58 observations on disposable income and Sears, Roebuck sales have sampling significance is a rather peculiar one—a population in which the same set of values of disposable income is repeated time after time but in which the random economic disturbances will give rise to different observed values of sales for any given value of disposable income in successive samples.

How can the 1947–58 regression equation be used in later years? *If there is no reason for the random economic disturbances to increase or decrease in magnitude, we may tentatively assume that the standard error of estimate computed for 1947–58 will continue to apply. But will the regression equation hold good in these later years?* The equation is $Y_c = .008 + .0119X$, as determined graphically from Chart 21–1. For this relationship to remain valid, Sears, Roebuck will have to continue to get about 1.19 cents out of each new dollar of consumers' disposable income, as it has in the past. To test this assumption, a more detailed analysis of management policy, consumer preferences, and general economic conditions is needed, as described in the next section. If there is evidence that Sears' share of the consumer dollar will change in the future, the regression equation will have to be modified accordingly.

Attitudes toward extrapolation of regression curves differ greatly. Many writers insist that a regression function must not be applied beyond the range of the data on which it is based. On the other hand, estimates needed for practical purposes are sometimes obtained by reckless extrapolation of regression functions. Both extremes should be avoided. One of the major purposes of regression analysis is to provide the basis for estimates, and these sometimes involve extrapolation. At the same time, the analyst should be aware of difficulties associated with extrapolation and should support his statistical analysis with a good logical justification for any extension of a regression beyond the limits of the data on which it is based.

Forecasting Sales

Industrial output or company sales are often forecast by correlation with some basic measure of the economy—such as population or gross national product—for which relatively reliable projections are available. Chart 21–3 shows forecasts to 1960 for four industries, based on their relationship with industrial production, disposable income, or motor vehicle registrations.

In the Sears, Roebuck example, assume that we have accurate projections of disposable income—337.3 billion for 1959 and 354.2 billion for 1960. We can then forecast sales for these years from the regression line in Chart 21–1. Later on, in 1961, we can check these forecasts against actual sales. These are circled on the chart. The results are as follows (in billions of dollars):

Year	Forecast Sales	Actual Sales	Forecast Error
1959	4.006	4.036	− .7%
1960	4.207	4.134	1.8%

We can also forecast sales a year at a time from the projected *per cent* changes in disposable income shown in Chart 21–2. These forecasts compare with actual results as shown below:

Year	Increase in Disposable Income	Forecast Increase in Sales	Actual Increase in Sales	Resulting Sales Forecast (Billions)	Actual Sales (Billions)	Forecast Error
1959	6.1%	6.5%	8.5%	3.963	4.036	−1.8%
1960	5.0	4.5	2.4	4.218	4.134	2.0%

Chart 21-3
INDUSTRY FORECASTING BY REGRESSION ANALYSIS

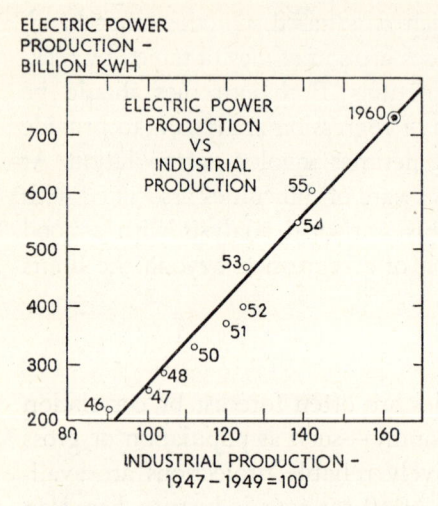

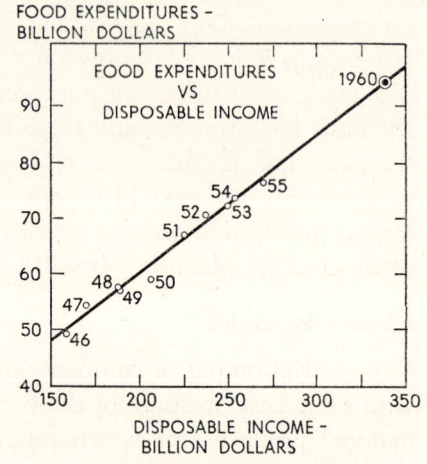

Electric power output may approach 750 billion K.W.H., an increase of close to 25 per cent, compared with an anticipated rise of 15 per cent in industrial production.

Food expenditures should rise more than twice as fast as population, thanks to the increasing popularity of convenience items.

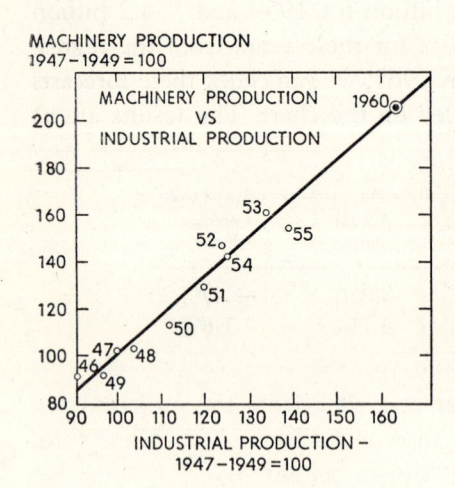

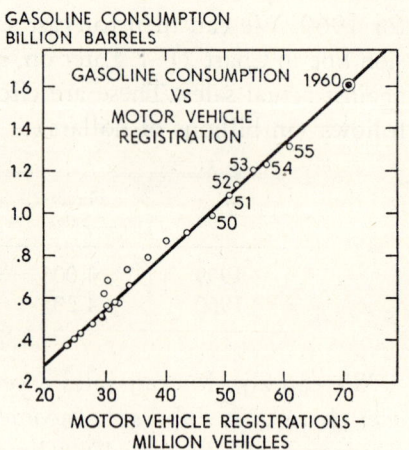

Output of industrial machinery will continue to outrun over-all production, as a result of new technologies and high defense spending.

Reflecting steady growth of motor vehicle registrations, gasoline consumption will continue to expand at better than a 4 per cent annual rate.

SOURCE: Brookmire's Investors Service, April 1958; reprinted from Standard and Poor's *The Outlook*, November 12, 1956, p. 520.

All these forecasts fell within 2 per cent of actual sales. Of course, this analysis does not include errors in projecting disposable income itself; such errors would either increase or decrease the error in the Sears sales forecast.

A simple regression forecast of total sales is useful for exploratory analysis (cf. Chart 21–3), but it will not suffice for management planning. For this purpose, sales should also be correlated with other related factors, preferably in a multiple regression analysis. The secular trend of sales should be projected, as described in Chapter 18. Management policy should be evaluated—such as its plans for opening new stores or taking on new types of merchandise. Any shifts in consumer preferences as between Sears, Roebuck and competing department stores or mail-order houses should be carefully gauged. Finally, the general economic outlook must be appraised. The Sears, Roebuck *Annual Report 1960* gives the following outlook for 1961:

The Year Ahead. There is reason to believe that the year 1961 will show some improvement over 1960 in retail sales. Although results during the first half year will be affected by the economic adjustment, it is anticipated that the general economy and retail trade will be on the up-grade by mid-year. Normal economic forces should bring about a reversal of inventory liquidation which, combined with rising outlays by the Federal and state governments for defense and other programs, should stimulate employment and help restore consumer confidence. The Company should benefit from this improvement in consumer attitude.

Furthermore, the analysis should be carried out for individual lines of merchandise, for different territories, and for the department store and mail-order branches of the business separately. It may then be possible to pinpoint with considerable assurance certain sources of demand for Sears, Roebuck products that will behave about the same in the early 1960's as they did in the 1950's and other sources of demand that may change drastically. Correlation analysis may be our basic tool in determining these more detailed relationships, and our forecasts of Sears, Roebuck sales as a whole could very well be the sum of forecasts of its individual components based on these several regression equations.

MULTIPLE CORRELATION AND REGRESSION

Multiple correlation and regression analysis is the study of the relationship between a dependent variable and two or more independent variables. It is useful in many problems of economic analysis and business management. Thus, we can predict the success of prospective employees not only by means of a placement test, as described in Chapter

20, but also by means of an interviewer's rating or other guides. A multiple regression equation based on several factors may provide a better basis for predicting job success than a simple equation based on a single test.

Multiple regression is often used in connection with forecasting. Such a forecast may be as broad as the general economic outlook for the nation as a whole, or it may be limited to the estimation of the price of a single stock. For example, the Value Line Investment Survey correlates the price of a stock in past years with its earnings per share and dividends (all in logarithms) to determine the estimated future value of the stock. Recommendations for stock purchase are based in part on this "value line" obtained by multiple regression analysis.

LINEAR RELATIONSHIPS

In most applications of multiple correlation analysis, only linear regression functions are used. This restriction is largely for simplicity, but there are other reasons as well. In many regression problems, the relationship is linear or nearly so. Even in a curvilinear relationship, it is often desirable to fit linear regression functions as the first step in the analysis. Under favorable conditions, it is even more effective to use logarithmic or other types of transformations to straighten out regression curves so as to permit the use of linear methods.

Important Multiple Correlation Measures

Just as in simple correlation, the most important measures of multiple correlation are (1) the regression equation, which describes the average relationship between the variables; (2) the standard error of estimate, which is essentially the standard deviation of the dependent variable from its computed values; and (3) the coefficient of correlation, which reflects the relative degree of relationship.

These measures are illustrated by an example for which the data are presented in Table 21–2. In multiple regression analysis, the dependent variable is usually designated by X_1, and the independent variables by X_2, X_3, and so on. Here we wish to predict job performance (X_1) of applicants for a given job based on the score of a placement test (X_2) and the interviewer's rating (X_3). The scales are arbitrary. We test a random sample of 18 new employees and later measure their job performance.

The regression of the dependent variable on two independent variables is said to be *linear* when the array means of X_1 values lie on a flat plane. In this context, an "array" is a set of observations in which

Table 21-2
RELATION OF TEST SCORES AND INTERVIEWER'S RATINGS TO JOB PERFORMANCE (18 EMPLOYEES)

Employee Number	Job Performance X_1	Test Score X_2	Interviewer's Rating X_3	X_1^2
1	5	10	5	25
2	13	10	5	169
3	9	20	5	81
4	17	20	5	289
5	13	30	5	169
6	21	30	5	441
7	14	10	20	196
8	22	10	20	484
9	18	20	20	324
10	26	20	20	676
11	22	30	20	484
12	30	30	20	900
13	20	10	30	400
14	28	10	30	784
15	24	20	30	576
16	32	20	30	1,024
17	28	30	30	784
18	36	30	30	1,296
Total	378	360	330	9,102
Mean	21	20	18.33	....

X_1 varies but both X_2 and X_3 are constant. In Table 21–2 it can be seen that each successive pair of observations provides an array of values of X_1 for which X_2 and X_3 are constant. Means of these arrays of X_1 values are presented in Table 21–3. When X_2 increases by 10, the

Table 21-3
MEANS OF ARRAYS OF THE DEPENDENT VARIABLE X_1

	$X_3 = 5$	$X_3 = 20$	$X_3 = 30$
$X_2 = 10$	9	18	24
$X_2 = 20$	13	22	28
$X_2 = 30$	17	26	32

Source: Table 21-2.

array mean of X_1 increases by 4 (four tenths as much as X_2); and as X_3 increases by 15 or 10, the array mean of X_1 increases by 9 or 6, respectively (six tenths of the change in X_3). Accordingly, the array means lie on a flat plane, and exactly satisfy the *linear multiple regression equation*

$$X_{1c} = a + b_2 X_2 + b_3 X_3$$
$$= 2 + .4 X_2 + .6 X_3$$

Here the subscript c is used to distinguish computed from observed values of X_1 and the constant a is the X_1 intercept (value of X_{1c} when X_2 and X_3 are both equal to zero). Each of the coefficients b_2 and b_3 has the same subscript number as that of the independent variable to which it applies, and is called a *net regression coefficient*.

The net regression coefficient b_2 shows the average effect of a one-unit increase in X_2 (test score) on X_1 (job performance), *holding X_3 constant*. That is, b_2 indicates how the test score predicts job performance for men rated alike by the interviewer. The net regression coefficient thus differs from the *gross* regression coefficient b in simple correlation between test scores and job performance in that b shows the *combined* effect of test score and the intercorrelated effect of interviewer's rating in predicting job performance.

Each of the X_1 values is four units above or below its array mean, so the *standard error of estimate* $S_{1.23}$ for the sample (the standard deviation of residuals from the regression plane) is also 4. The *unexplained variance* $S_{1.23}^2$ is then $4^2 = 16$.

The *total variance* (or standard deviation squared) of the dependent variable X_1, measured from its mean, is

$$s_1^2 = \frac{\Sigma x_1^2}{n}$$
$$= \frac{1{,}164}{18}$$
$$= 64.67$$

for the sample, where $x_1 = X_1 - \overline{X}_1$. Accordingly, the *coefficient of multiple determination*, which is the proportion of variance explained, or 1 minus the proportion of variance unexplained, is

$$R^2 = 1 - \frac{S_{1.23}^2}{s_1^2}$$
$$= 1 - \frac{16}{64.67}$$
$$= .75$$

Taking the square root, the *coefficient of multiple correlation* is

$$R = \sqrt{.75} = .87$$

This completes the list of multiple correlation measures which will be discussed in this chapter. For simplicity the standard error of estimate and following values above apply to the sample only (strictly speaking, the symbols should be modified accordingly); they have not been adjusted to provide unbiased estimates of the population values.

In the next section we will determine the multiple regression equation in an actual case by the method of least squares. We will then compute unbiased estimates of the standard error of estimate and the coefficient of determination for the population.

Finding the Regression Equation by Least Squares

Just as in the case of simple regression analysis, the constants of the linear multiple regression equation are determined by the method of least squares by solving a system of simultaneous linear equations, called the *normal equations,* in which the unknowns are the constants of the regression equation. The method of determining these constants for practical problems will be illustrated for the following study of effects of weight and length on the amount of time required to handle pieces of metal. The time required to handle a piece of flat metal stock to the bump gauge of a No. 13 Williams and White Punch Press varies with the weight and length of the piece. To determine the relative influence of weight as compared with that of length when both characteristics vary simultaneously, a multiple regression study was made of data on handling time, weight of piece, and length of piece from one of the John Deere farm machinery plants.

Twenty-five observations on X_1 time (in thousandths of a minute), X_2 weight (in tenths of a pound), and X_3 length (in tenths of an inch) are presented in Table 21–4. In order to find the constants in the three-variable linear multiple regression,

$$X_{1c} = a + b_2 X_2 + b_3 X_3$$

the following three normal equations must be solved:

$$\Sigma X_1 = Na + b_2 \Sigma X_2 + b_3 \Sigma X_3$$
$$\Sigma X_1 X_2 = a \Sigma X_2 + b_2 \Sigma X_2^2 + b_3 \Sigma X_2 X_3$$
$$\Sigma X_1 X_3 = a \Sigma X_3 + b_2 \Sigma X_2 X_3 + b_3 \Sigma X_3^2$$

These equations can be solved directly, but it is usually simpler to move the origin to the point of means, as we did in simple regression,

Table 21-4

HANDLING TIME X_1, WEIGHT X_2, AND LENGTH X_3 OF 25 PIECES OF METAL WITH ESTIMATES, RESIDUALS, AND SQUARES OBTAINED FROM LEAST-SQUARES REGRESSION EQUATION

Item	Time (.001 Min.) X_1	Weight (.1 Lb.) X_2	Length (.1 In.) X_3	Estimated X_{1c}	Residual $X_1 - X_{1c}$	Square of Residual $(X_1 - X_{1c})^2$
1	30	5	35	22.05	7.95	63
2	32	12	46	25.03	6.97	49
3	15	15	63	28.53	−13.53	183
4	30	31	67	31.50	− 1.50	2
5	25	6	70	28.55	− 3.55	13
6	25	8	83	31.20	− 6.20	38
7	42	37	88	36.16	5.84	34
8	35	23	104	37.10	− 2.10	4
9	42	30	134	43.54	− 1.54	2
10	30	34	151	47.19	−17.19	295
11	52	17	153	45.17	6.83	47
12	50	53	164	52.26	− 2.20	5
13	45	56	173	54.20	− 9.26	86
14	50	41	191	55.43	− 5.43	29
15	70	84	196	62.35	7.65	59
16	64	62	198	59.63	4.37	19
17	64	66	204	61.28	2.72	7
18	70	66	208	62.01	7.99	64
19	80	63	238	67.05	12.95	168
20	88	80	295	79.78	8.22	68
21	105	154	308	92.48	12.52	158
22	85	50	310	78.33	6.67	44
23	85	184	319	98.67	−13.67	187
24	105	186	324	99.86	5.14	26
25	84	122	394	103.65	−19.65	386
Total	1,403	1,485	4,516	1,403	0	2,036
Mean	56.12	59.40	180.64			

SOURCE: A John Deere farm machinery plant.

and measure each variable as a deviation from its mean (small x), where $x_1 = X_1 - \overline{X}_1$, etc. This is done most easily by totaling the squares and products of the original X's, as called for in the above formula, and then subtracting the *mean times the sum* of the respective variables to get the sums of the small x's, as follows:

$$\begin{aligned}\Sigma X_1^2 & & \Sigma X_2^2 & & \Sigma X_3^2 & & \Sigma X_1 X_2 & & \Sigma X_1 X_3 & & \Sigma X_2 X_3 \\ -\bar{X}_1 \Sigma X_1 & & -\bar{X}_2 \Sigma X_2 & & -\bar{X}_3 \Sigma X_3 & & -\bar{X}_1 \Sigma X_2 & & -\bar{X}_1 \Sigma X_3 & & -\bar{X}_2 \Sigma X_3 \\ =\Sigma x_1^2 & & =\Sigma x_2^2 & & =\Sigma x_3^2 & & =\Sigma x_1 x_2 & & =\Sigma x_1 x_3 & & =\Sigma x_2 x_3\end{aligned}$$

In the present example, these values are:

	X_1^2	X_2^2	X_3^2	$X_1 X_2$	$X_1 X_3$	$X_2 X_3$
Total	95,373	152,857	1,058,726	111,392	312,216	372,933
Less mean times sum*	78,736	88,209	815,770	83,338	253,438	268,250
Equals adjusted total	16,637	64,648	242,956	28,054	58,778	104,683

* From Table 21-4, last two rows (e.g., $\bar{X}_1 \Sigma X_1 = 56.12 \times 1,403 = 78,736$).

The individual squares and products of the X's are not shown because they are usually cumulated in a calculating machine and only the totals need be recorded.[2]

The value of a is found in terms of b_2 and b_3 by solving the first normal equation above to obtain the formula

$$a = \bar{X}_1 - b_2 \bar{X}_2 - b_3 \bar{X}_3$$

from which the value of a can be obtained after the values of b_2 and b_3 have been found.

When we express the second and third normal equations in small x's, the terms ΣX_2 and ΣX_3 equal zero, and the equations become:

$$\Sigma x_1 x_2 = b_2 \Sigma x_2^2 + b_3 \Sigma x_2 x_3$$
$$\Sigma x_1 x_3 = b_2 \Sigma x_2 x_3 + b_3 \Sigma x_3^2$$

Substituting the numerical values above,

$$28,054 = 64,648 b_2 + 104,683 b_3$$
$$58,778 = 104,683 b_2 + 242,956 b_3$$

These equations can be solved simultaneously to find b_2 and b_3, as

---

[2] Since the normal equations for a three-variable problem involve quite a number of sums of squares and products, it is important to choose a system of internal checks. In this connection a sum variable,

$$X_S = X_1 + X_2 + X_3$$

is extremely useful. In addition to the comparatively simple check,

$$\Sigma X_S = \Sigma X_1 + \Sigma X_2 + \Sigma X_3$$

the sum of squares of X_S provides the check

$$\Sigma X_S^2 = \Sigma X_1^2 + \Sigma X_2^2 + \Sigma X_3^2 + 2\Sigma X_1 X_2 + 2\Sigma X_1 X_3 + 2\Sigma X_2 X_3$$

follows: Multiply the first equation by 104,683/64,648, the ratio of the b_2 coefficients. The result is:

$$45{,}427 = 104{,}683 b_2 + 169{,}511 b_3$$

Subtract this from the second normal equation to eliminate b_2. Then

$$13{,}351 = 73{,}445 b_3, \text{ and}$$
$$b_3 = .1818$$

Substitute this value of b_3 in the first normal equation. Solving,

$$b_2 = .1396$$

Finally, substitute both values in the second normal equation, as a check on arithmetic.

The value of the constant a is:

$$\begin{aligned} a &= \overline{X}_1 - b_2 \overline{X}_2 - b_3 \overline{X}_3 \\ &= 56.12 - (.1396)(59.40) - (.1818)(180.64) \\ &= 14.99 \end{aligned}$$

Now substitute the three constants in the multiple regression equation

$$\begin{aligned} X_{1c} &= a + b_2 X_2 + b_3 X_3 \\ &= 14.99 + .1396 X_2 + .1818 X_3 \end{aligned}$$

Thus, if the plant manager decided to handle uniform metal pieces of weight 100 and length 200 units, the average handling time could be predicted as

$$\begin{aligned} X_{1c} &= 14.99 + .1396(100) + .1818(200) \\ &= 65.3 \text{ thousandths of a minute} \end{aligned}$$

Standard Error of Estimate

The estimated value X_{1c} has been computed for each of the 25 pieces of metal and listed in Table 21–4. The residuals $X_1 - X_{1c}$ and their squares are also shown, for use in computing the standard error of estimate.

Just as in simple correlation, the standard error of estimate is in effect the standard deviation of the residuals, $X_1 - X_{1c}$. It measures the average scatter of X_1 values around the regression plane. The standard error of estimate is:

$$S_{1.23} = \sqrt{\frac{\Sigma (X_1 - X_{1c})^2}{n - m}}$$

where n is the size of sample and m is the number of constants in the regression equation. Here $n = 25$ and $m = 3$.

The numerator $\Sigma(X_1 - X_{1c})^2$ is 2,036 from the last column of Table 21–4, so

$$S_{1.23} = \sqrt{\frac{2{,}036}{25 - 3}}$$
$$= \sqrt{92.55}$$
$$= 9.6$$

That is, the actual handling time of the metal pieces should fall within 9.6 thousandths of a minute around the estimated value in two cases out of three, for this size of sample. If pieces of weight 100 and length 200 were used, the estimated time would be 65.3 ± 9.6, or between 55.7 and 74.9 thousandths of a minute, for two cases out of three.

Tests of significance and confidence intervals can be applied to multiple regression measures by finding their standard errors through an extension of methods used in simple correlation. In particular, the standard errors of the net regression coefficients b_2 and b_3 are sensitive to the presence of high correlation *between* the independent variables. There is a high correlation between weight and length in the present example, as shown below. Hence the sample value of b_2 is subject to a wide error, since it is difficult to separate out the effect of weight on handling time when length is so closely related to weight.

Confidence intervals can also be computed for any value X_{1c} in the multiple regression equation, and for any individual forecast. Correlation results may be particularly unreliable if many independent variables are used, or if the sample size is small. The treatment of these measures of reliability, however, is beyond the scope of this book.

Coefficient of Multiple Determination

As in simple correlation, the coefficient of multiple determination may be expressed as 1 minus the unexplained variance over the total variance. That is,

$$R^2 = 1 - \frac{S_{1.23}^2}{s_1^2}$$

In handling time example, $S_{1.23}^2$, the unexplained variance (or standard error of estimate squared) was found to be 92.55. The estimated total variance (or standard deviation of X_1, squared) for the population, is

$$s_1^2 = \frac{\Sigma x_1^2}{n-1} = \frac{16{,}637}{25-1} = 693.2$$

Therefore,

$$R^2 = 1 - \frac{92.55}{693.2} = .866$$

About 86.6 per cent of the variance in handling time, therefore, is explained by the variances in the weight and length of the metal pieces handled.

The coefficient of multiple correlation is:

$$R = \sqrt{.866} = .931$$

Charts are available that show the lower confidence limits for various values of the sample R and n. Such charts provide a quick check on the reliability of the sample correlation coefficient.[3]

The coefficient of multiple determination .866 in the handling-time case is greater than the simple coefficient of X_1 with either $X_2 (r_{12}^2 = .720)$ or $X_3 (r_{13}^2 = .848)$. That is, we can explain the variations in handling time more completely by considering both weight and length than by taking either one alone. On the other hand, the excess of R over r_{13} is rather small in this problem, mainly because the two independent variables are closely correlated ($r_{23}^2 = .685$). Therefore, if it were desirable to simplify control chart procedures, the length factor might be used alone to control handling time, without great loss of accuracy.

CURVILINEAR RELATIONSHIPS

One of the most effective devices for dealing with curvilinear relationships is that of transformations which straighten out regression curves. This is especially true whenever graph paper with appropriate ruling is available, but transformations can be used with computational methods just as in simple two-variable regression analysis. The regression in the handling-time problem, for example, would be more linear if logarithms had been used in place of natural numbers.

---

[3] See Ezekiel and Fox, *op. cit.*, pp. 296–98, for examples of these charts with 3, 5, and 7 independent variables.

Just as in simple regression analysis, it is possible to fit a curvilinear regression function by least squares, but the problem of choosing the algebraic form of the regression function is much more complicated. Because of the interrelations among the independent variables, it is difficult to tell from the scatter diagrams of pairs of variables what the approximate shape of any net regression curve should be.

After the main characteristics of the various net regression curves have been decided upon, it is sometimes difficult to think of an algebraic equation which describes the form of these curves adequately. In addition, each term added to the regression equation not only increases the complexity of the normal equations already needed but also adds another equation to the system to be solved. For all of these reasons, it is usually better to use appropriate transformations or to use graphic methods [4] than to complicate the form of the regression function with terms in squares and higher powers of the independent variables introduced to take care of possible curvature of regressions.

SUMMARY

Correlation techniques are applicable to time series and other economic data provided there is a rational hypothesis supporting the relationship. There are four methods of correlating time series, of which the first two are illustrated in this chapter.

1. *Correlate the actual annual data* (or deseasonalized monthly data) to show the combined effects of secular trend, and cyclical and irregular fluctuations.
2. *Correlate relative or absolute first differences* (percentages or amounts of change from year to year) to partially eliminate trend.
3. *Correlate percentages of trend,* using secular trend values as base. Methods 2 and 3 show the relationships of cyclical and other short-term fluctuations.
4. *Apply multiple regression analysis,* with time as one independent variable. Logarithms may be used for all variables except time, to achieve a more uniform scatter of residuals.

Sears, Roebuck sales are correlated with disposable personal income for 1947–58, and the regression is used to forecast 1959 and 1960 sales. The results are then checked against the actual sales for these years. Plotting the original data in Chart 21–1, we find a close linear relationship. However, there is danger that the residuals around the line

---

[4] See the first edition of this book, pp. 433–40, for a discussion of graphic methods in multiple regression analysis.

may be autocorrelated (i.e., successive years' values may be alike) so the standard error formulas may be inapplicable. In order to reduce autocorrelation and eliminate trend, which produces a spuriously high correlation, we plot the year-to-year percentage changes in Chart 21–2. The relative scatter here is wider, but the various standard error formulas are more valid than in correlating original data.

To determine whether regression relationships will apply in the future, one must make a careful study of management policy, consumer preferences, and general economic trends. Extrapolation of regression curves is dangerous, but it is nevertheless necessary and widely used in forward planning. The forecasts of Sears, Roebuck sales based on the regression with disposable income proved to be fairly accurate for 1959 and 1960. For management planning purposes, however, more elaborate correlation and trend analysis is needed, as well as a careful appraisal of intangible factors. This analysis should be applied to individual products, territories, and departments of the business.

Multiple correlation and regression analysis is a means of relating a dependent variable to two or more independent variables. The regression relationship may be linear or curvilinear.

A *linear multiple regression equation* of the form $X_{1c} = a + b_2 X_2 + b_3 X_3 + \cdots$ may be fitted by the method of least squares. It is necessary to solve a set of normal equations to find values of the constants $a, b_2, b_3, \cdots$ that minimize the sum of squares of residuals. By transforming the origin to the point of means, and expressing all values as deviations from the mean (small x's), calculations can be simplified. Programs for this procedure are available on electronic calculators. The *net regression coefficient* b_2 measures the average influence of X_2 on X_1, holding X_3 constant; thus showing the separate effect of the independent variable on the dependent variable.

The *standard error of estimate* is the standard deviation of actual X_1 values from their computed values. It is calculated and interpreted much as in simple correlation. Tests of significance and confidence intervals can be computed for the regression coefficients, the regression equation, and for individual forecasts by an extension of methods explained in Chapter 20. The results may be unreliable if many independent variables are used, or if the sample size is small.

The *coefficient of multiple determination* is the proportion of variance in X_1 explained by all independent variables. This relative measure of relationship is analogous to the coefficient of simple determination in its calculation and interpretation.

Multiple curvilinear regressions are best measured by appropriate

TIME SERIES AND MULTIPLE CORRELATION

transformations (e.g., the use of logarithms) to produce linearity, or by graphic methods, in most cases, rather than by employing more complex mathematical equations.

PROBLEMS

1. As an oil company economist you wish to forecast United States gasoline consumption, in barrels, for each of the next five years, by correlation with some basic economic factors for which forecasts are available. One such factor—motor vehicle registrations—is illustrated in Chart 21-3 (lower right). Give two other factors that you might logically choose to correlate with gasoline consumption as a basis for prediction. Support your choice.

2. The regression line in Chart 21-3, lower right, was fitted to data through 1955 and extended to provide a forecast for 1960. This forecast proved to be too high. As shown in the chart below, the regression line for 1955–60 was flatter than that for earlier years.

GASOLINE DOMESTIC DEMAND
AND
UNITED STATES MOTOR VEHICLE REGISTRATIONS

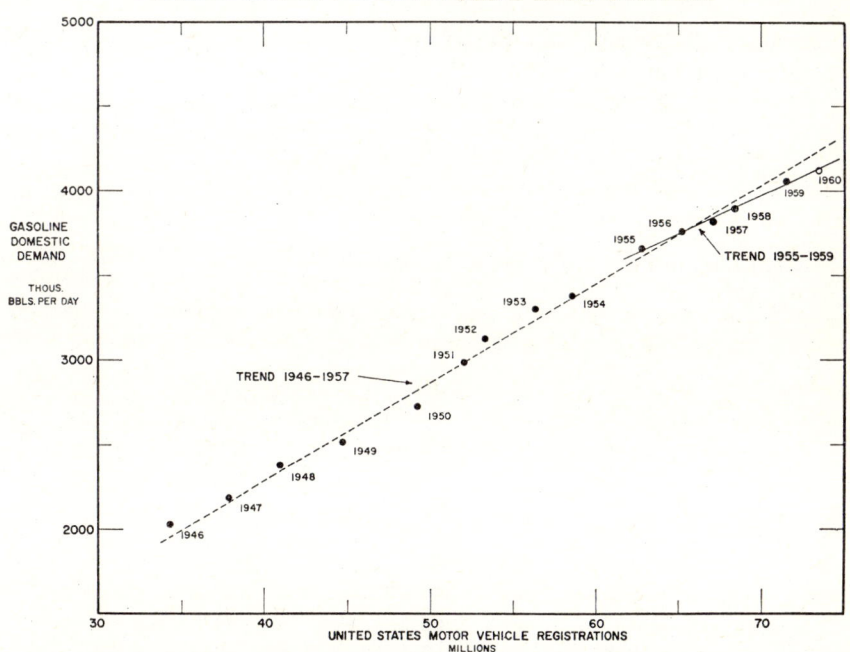

Source: Economics and Statistics Division, Ohio Oil Co.; data from Bureau of Mines, American Petroleum Institute.

   a) What economic developments in 1955–60 might have caused this shift in the regression line?
   b) What economic assumptions would you have to make in order to justify using the 1955–60 line to forecast 1965 gasoline demand, based on an available estimate of motor vehicle registrations for that year?

490   BUSINESS AND ECONOMIC STATISTICS   [Ch. 21

c) Is the period 1955–60 long enough on which to base a regression forecast to 1965? If not, how could you proceed?

3. As an experiment, Sears, Roebuck sales were correlated with disposable personal income for the years 1947–56 by each of the four methods described on pages 468–73, with the following results:

Factors Correlated	Standard Error of Estimate	Coefficient of Determination
(1) Actual annual data	$110 million	.93
(2) Relative first differences (% changes)	6.74%	.40
(3) Percentages of log straight line trends	3.25%	.43
(4) Multiple regression between actual sales, disposable income, and number of stores	$115 million	.93

Sears sales in 1956 were $3,601 million, while the 1957 trend value was about $3,700 million.

a) In the light of this information, which of these four methods would have been preferable for use in forecasting 1957 sales, based on an available estimate of 1957 disposable income? Why?

b) Is disposable income satisfactory as a predictor of short-run changes in Sears sales? Explain your answer.

4. Retail sales in the 1950's were as follows:

RETAIL SALES IN THE UNITED STATES, 1951–59
(Billions of Dollars)

Year	Durable Goods	Nondurable Goods
1951	54.5	102.1
1952	55.3	107.1
1953	60.4	108.7
1954	58.1	111.0
1955	67.0	116.9
1956	65.8	123.9
1957	68.5	131.5
1958	63.4	136.9
1959	71.7	143.7

SOURCE: U.S. Department of Commerce.

a) Plot retail sales of either durable goods or nondurable goods, as assigned, against disposable personal income (Table 21–1, p. 470) for 1951–59 on an arithmetic scatter diagram.

b) Fit a regression line by the graphic method or by least squares, as assigned, and draw a band one standard error of estimate above and below it, as a rough 65 per cent confidence interval. Describe the relationship in these years and the probable reason for the deviation of points from the line.
c) Forecast 1960 retail sales of durable or nondurable goods, and give the $\pm 1 S_{YX}$ limits, based on estimated 1960 disposable income of $354.2 billion.
d) Compare this forecast with actual 1960 sales of $71.5 billion for durables or $148.3 billion for nondurables (annual rate through October, estimated in Standard & Poor's *Industry Survey—Retail Trade,* December 15, 1960). Explain the probable reason for your error of forecast.

5. The personnel director of the Acme Insurance Company wishes to determine whether the selling ability of salesmen can be predicted from their education and age. If so, these criteria would provide a valuable aid in selecting the most promising candidates for employment. As a start, ten salesmen are selected at random, and are rated by their supervisor as to sales ability, education, and age. The rating on sales ability covers a seven-point scale, from "Poor" (0) to "Excellent" (6). The education scale varies from "Did not finish high school" (0) to "Has master's degree" (4). The age scale extends from "Age 20–29" (0) to "Age 60–69" (4). The results are shown below.

Salesman	Sales Ability X_1	Education X_2	Age X_3
A	1	0	3
B	1	1	4
C	1	0	2
D	2	2	4
E	2	1	3
F	3	3	1
G	4	2	0
H	4	4	2
I	6	3	0
J	6	4	1
Sum	30	20	20

a) Compute the multiple linear regression equation by the method of least squares to estimate sales ability from education and age. Show all computations.
b) What is the meaning of the net regression coefficient b_2 in this particular case? How would this value differ in meaning from the regression coefficient in simple correlation between sales ability and education alone?
c) How would the reliability of b_2 be affected if the younger men generally had more education than the older men?

6. *a*) Compute the standard error of estimate in Problem 5, and interpret its meaning as applied to predicting the sales ability of future salesmen.
   b) Compute the coefficient of multiple determination, and interpret its meaning in describing the relationship between sales ability, education, and age for salesmen of this type.

7. The Value Line Investment Survey computes a multiple regression equation for each common stock showing the typical relationship between its price (X_1), earnings per share (X_2), and dividends per share (X_3) in past years. The following equation was reported for Boeing Airplane Company on May 1, 1961:

   Log normal average value next 12 months
   $= 1.355 + .440 \log (.22 \times \text{earnings} + 1.00 \times \text{dividends})$

   a) Explain the meaning of this equation and its use for an investor.
   b) What type of linear transformation does this equation illustrate?
   c) What other measures or qualifications would be desirable in this Survey to aid the investor in appraising the reliability of the equation?

SELECTED READINGS

CROXTON, FREDERICK E., and COWDEN, DUDLEY J. *Practical Business Statistics.* 3d ed. Englewood Cliffs, N.J.: Prentice-Hall, Inc., 1960, chaps. 24–27, 35–37.

   Treats a wide variety of topics in simple and multiple correlation.

EZEKIEL, MORDECAI, and FOX, KARL A. *Methods of Correlation and Regression Analysis.* 3d ed. New York and London: John Wiley & Sons, Inc., 1959.

   This is the standard book in the field. In the third edition, its major emphasis has been shifted from correlation to regression. Graphic analysis of curvilinear relationships is stressed.

LEWIS, EDWARD E. *Methods of Statistical Analysis in Economics and Business.* Boston: Houghton Mifflin Co., 1953.

   Chapters 12–14 provide a clear introduction to simple and multiple correlation.

SPURR, WILLIAM A. "A Short-Cut Measure of Correlation," *Journal of the American Statistical Association,* Vol. XLVI (March 1951), pp. 89–94.

   Describes the graphic estimation of the correlation coefficient *r*.

WILLIAMS, E. J. *Regression Analysis.* New York and London: John Wiley & Sons, Inc., 1959.

   Provides the practical statistician with a compendium of the classical techniques associated with regression analysis.

YULE, G. UDNY, and KENDALL, M. G. *An Introduction to the Theory of Statistics.* 14th ed. London: Charles Griffin & Co., Ltd., 1950.

   Chapters 9–14 present a broad survey of correlation theory, with emphasis on the correlation coefficient.

22. STATISTICAL QUALITY CONTROL

AMERICAN industry in recent years has adopted a new management technique based on the principles of statistics. This technique is known as statistical quality control or, more simply, quality control. The methods employed had their origin in the 1920's, but World War II led to their widespread adoption by producers of war matériel. Manufacturers were faced with demands for vast quantities of acceptable products in a short time. Specifications were more exacting than ever before required. The quality control techniques developed to meet this need proved outstandingly successful in speeding work, reducing manufacturing waste, improving product quality, and bettering product designs. Today, these methods have become an integral and permanent part of management controls.

Quality control methods are applied to two distinct phases of plant operation: (1) the control of a process during manufacture, and (2) the inspection of materials to determine their acceptability, whether they be in the raw, semifinished, or completed state. The principal emphasis here will be on the first phase, the control of a process.

TYPES OF VARIATION IN QUALITY

No two objects are exactly alike. Variation is present everywhere, although it may not always be immediately evident. Modern methods of production have succeeded in producing thousands of items which possess a great degree of uniformity, but differences can always be detected provided measurement is sufficiently precise.

Ordinarily, in a manufacturing process there is a tendency to disregard variation until it causes trouble. If the customer complains of a defective product; if waste, scrap, rejects, or rework increases costs materially; or if sales are lost because a competitor has a more uniform product, a search is instituted in an effort to detect the causes of variability in the product. In the past, and frequently today, such a search has been conducted on the basis of trial and error, and the process is corrected accordingly.

Statistical quality control has demonstrated, however, that such trial-and-error methods waste time and money (1) because of the lack of a systematic procedure for detection of trouble and (2) because such methods do not become operative until a great many defective parts are discovered by the plant inspector or by the customer. As a consequence, losses are sustained in producing defectives, in excessive inspection costs, in sales, and in goodwill. Manufacturing processes have become so complex and so many things can happen to make them go wrong that it is imperative to have a systematic method of detecting or predicting trouble. Only in this way can prompt corrective action be instituted.

It is evident, then, that any manufacturer must distinguish between permissible variation and excessive variation. His ability to eliminate the latter will be a determining factor in his success or failure.

Statistical quality control permits the partitioning of the total variation of a quality characteristic into two components: (1) *Chance variation* is that which results from many minor causes that behave in a random manner. This type of variation is permissible, and indeed inevitable, in manufacturing. (2) *Assignable variation* is a relatively large variation that can be attributed to special nonrandom causes. It may be excessive in amount so as to require correction. These two types of variation are described below. A *quality characteristic* is simply any measurable variable (such as the thickness of a shingle) or any attribute (such as color) of a part which must be controlled in order that the resulting product be acceptable.

The meaning of *chance variation* may be illustrated by a game of chance. A tossed coin shows a head. You ascribe the result to chance, meaning that the factors actually responsible for the result are so numerous and complex that it is impossible to explain the effect of each on the final result.

Similarly, one can express the idea of the *probability* that this event will happen if *chance only* is operative. The probability in this case is 1/2, since the occurrence of a head or tail is equally likely. If you tossed the coin ten times, the most probable result is five heads and five tails; but if six heads and four tails turned up, you would still doubtless ascribe the result to chance. If, however, ten heads showed, you would wonder whether the method of tossing or the coin was faulty. Such a result could possibly come about purely by chance, but the probability is only $1/2^{10}$, or one chance in 1,024. When a result which has a very small probability of occurring by chance actually happens, the assumption is made that nonchance (nonrandom) factors cause the particular outcome. The occurrence of ten heads in ten tosses would therefore lead to the inference that the game is not fair (nonrandom factors present).

Manufacturing processes are similar to games of chance. The process is subject to numerous small influences which combine to give a pattern of chance variation. This pattern cannot be altered without a change in the process. From time to time other causes of variation enter the process to produce *assignable variation.* Tool wear, a change in the raw material, a new operator, improper machine setting—all can produce assignable variations. The value of quality control lies in its power to detect quickly the assignable variations in a process; in fact, these variations are often discovered before the product becomes defective.

Once the assignable variation in a process has been eliminated by taking corrective action, only the unavoidable chance variation remains. It is possible to measure this chance variation. Then, if the average value of the quality characteristic is set by the engineering specification, it is possible to determine whether the process can conform to these specifications.

CONTROL CHARTS FOR VARIABLES

Control charts are used to distinguish the assignable variation from the chance variation of a process. There are two principal types of control charts: (1) charts for variables and (2) charts for attributes. As indicated above, variables are quality characteristics that can be measured and expressed in numbers, such as the diameter of a bushing. Attributes usually refer to the classification of a quality characteristic into one of two classes, either conforming or not conforming to specifications, as in "accept" or "reject" by visual inspection, or a "go not-go" gauge test. Sometimes quality characteristics which can be measured as variables are actually checked as attributes. Attributes may be judged either by the proportion of units that are defective or by the number of defects per unit. This section is devoted to control of a variable. Control of attributes will be treated later.

Two charts are commonly used in control of variables, the $\overline{X}$ chart and the R chart.

$\overline{X}$ Charts

The $\overline{X}$ chart, or chart for averages, shows variations in the "level" of the process, i.e., the arithmetic mean of a quality characteristic being measured. If a process contains no assignable variation in the characteristic controlled, the mean value of the characteristic is the mean of a population of its values, the population being generated by conceiving the process to run ad infinitum without change. It is apparent that the actual level of a process cannot be determined, but an accurate estimate of this level can be made by averaging the means of a number of samples—say 20 or more.[1] This estimate of the population mean μ is designated $\overline{\overline{X}}$.

This same hypothetical population would contain random variation, which may be measured by the standard deviation σ. Since σ, the population standard deviation, is usually unknown, it is necessary to estimate it from data secured by sampling. Such an estimate may be made by the use of either the average range or the average standard deviation of a number of samples. If the sample size is small (about 15 or less), sample range values provide a good estimate of σ. If, however, the sample size is greater than 15, standard deviation values should be employed instead for this purpose.

Sample sizes of only 4 or 5 are typical in control charts for $\overline{X}$. Furthermore, ranges are much easier to calculate than standard deviations. Therefore, R charts are much more commonly used than σ charts in control procedure, and only the former will be included in the following discussion.

The control chart for averages is an excellent application of the distribution of sample means. If, from a population with mean μ and standard deviation σ, all possible random samples of size n are drawn and the averages (arithmetic means) of these samples are placed in a frequency distribution, the resulting distribution will be approximately *normal* with mean μ. The distribution of means is nearly normal even for small samples if the population is normal and the true σ is known. Furthermore, the standard deviation of these means (i.e., $\sigma_{\overline{x}}$, the standard error of the mean) will equal $\sigma/\sqrt{n}$. The normal distribution pattern permits one to predict the proportion of sample means which will fall within a certain distance of the population mean. In particular, 99.73 per cent of the means of small samples should fall in an interval defined by $\mu \pm 3\sigma_{\overline{x}}$, assuming a normal distribution, with σ known.

The distribution of sample means is the foundation of the control chart for averages. When used on a control chart, $\overline{\overline{X}}$, the estimated value of μ, is made the central line and the values $\overline{\overline{X}} + 3\sigma_{\overline{x}}$ and

---

[1] Walter A. Shewhart recommends using at least 25 samples (assuming a size of 4) whose means fall within control limits, in order to set up a valid control chart. (*Statistical Method from the Viewpoint of Quality Control* [Washington, D.C.: Graduate School, Department of Agriculture, 1939], p. 37.)

Ch. 22] STATISTICAL QUALITY CONTROL 497

$\overline{X} - 3\sigma_{\overline{X}}$ are termed the upper and lower control limits, respectively. The use of 3σ limits is standard practice for control charts in the United States.

Ordinarily, the value of σ is estimated from a sample, or group of samples, and hence should be represented by the symbol s, as has been done throughout this book. The symbol σ will be used in this chapter, however, in accordance with the almost universal practice among quality control engineers. Therefore, it should be borne in mind that whenever "σ" is computed from a sample, it is in reality the estimate s, which is subject to sampling errors.

Chart 22–1, panel A, is an $\overline{X}$ chart, or control chart for averages.

Chart 22–1
CONTROL CHARTS FOR VARIABLES

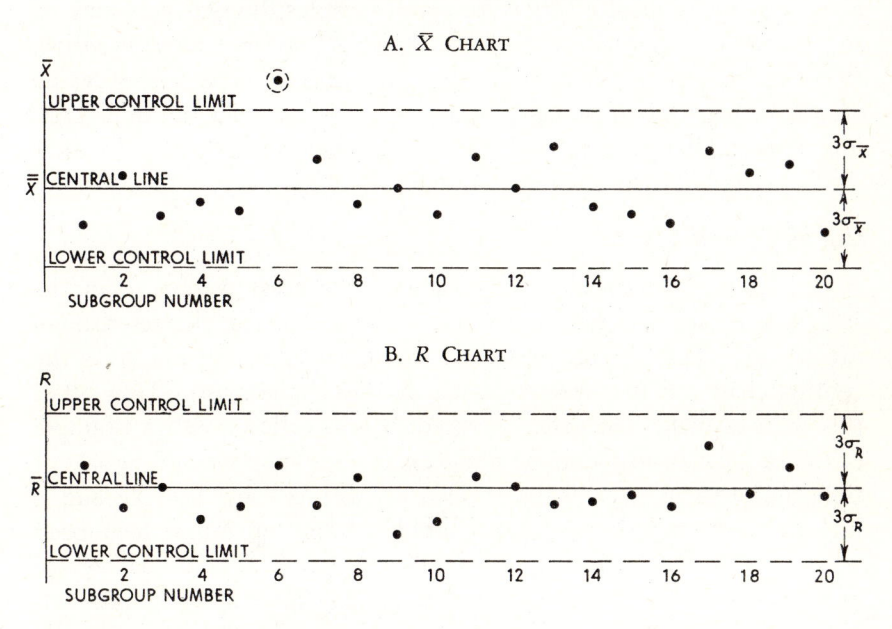

A. $\overline{X}$ CHART

B. R CHART

Note that the horizontal scale is designated by subgroup number. In industrial work it is customary to term the sample a "subgroup." Subgroups are samples taken in a certain order. The ordering may be on the basis of time or by lot number or some other plan, but it is important to maintain the order of sampling. The vertical scale is labeled $\overline{X}$. At the point $\overline{\overline{X}}$ on the vertical scale a horizontal central line is drawn. On either side of this line at a distance of $3\sigma_{\overline{X}}$, parallel dashed lines are drawn. These are the control limits.

R Charts

The R chart shows variations in the ranges of samples. It is similar to the chart for averages in its construction, as shown in Chart 22–1, panel B. The vertical scale is labeled R. A horizontal control line is drawn at $\overline{R}$, the average of a number of sample ranges. The control limits are dashed and set at a distance of $3\sigma_R$ from the central line, where σ_R is the standard deviation of the sample ranges. (The method of computation will be described later.)

The distribution of the ranges of all possible samples drawn from a normal population is not normal but is skewed in a positive direction. Therefore, as many as 1 per cent of the cases may exceed the upper $3\sigma_R$ limit. Nevertheless, it works reasonably well to use $3\sigma_R$ limits about the average range, $\overline{R}$, as control limits, and this is the usual practice. The chief difficulty is that for small samples the skewness may be so great as to cause the lower control limit ($\overline{R} - 3\sigma_R$) to be negative. In such a case the lower control limit is set at zero, since a range value cannot be negative. If no assignable variation is present in the process, it is expected that practically all the sample range values will fall within the $3\sigma_R$ band about the average range.

Use of Control Charts

$\overline{X}$ *Charts.* Assume that the value of the process average μ, and its standard deviation, σ, have been estimated for a certain characteristic—say, the thickness of shingles—and that Chart 22–1, panel A, is the control chart for the average value of this characteristic. How shall this chart be used? The general procedure is as follows: Select a sample of the product from the manufacturing process at specified intervals of time. (The sample size is determined in advance—say $n = 5$—and is used in calculation of the control limits.) Subgroup 1 may have been taken at 8:00 A.M., subgroup 2 at 8:30 A.M., etc. Calculate the average of each subgroup. Plot these averages on the chart at equal intervals along the horizontal axis. If chance variation *only* is present, virtually all of the sample means should fall inside the control limits defined as $\overline{X} \pm 3\sigma_{\overline{X}}$.

If a point should fall beyond the control limits, the presumption is that assignable causes have affected the process, since the probability of getting such an extreme value by chance is very small. The process is no longer "in control," but is "out of control." The importance of ordering the samples is here evident: a point beyond limits indicates that trouble has occurred in the process since the taking of the last sample. The procedure is to investigate immediately to determine the source of this variation. The process may then be shut down until the trouble is located and corrected. Note the average for subgroup 6 on Chart 22–1, panel A, which is out of control, indicating assignable variation.

The fact that sample averages follow the normal distribution when assignable variation is absent can be used to detect trouble in a process even though no points may have gone beyond the control limits. With trouble absent, the sample averages should be distributed at random about the central line, with more points near the line than far from it. If, then, an excessively long run—say, 7 points or more—occurs on one side of the central line, as in Chart 22–2, the evidence is that as-

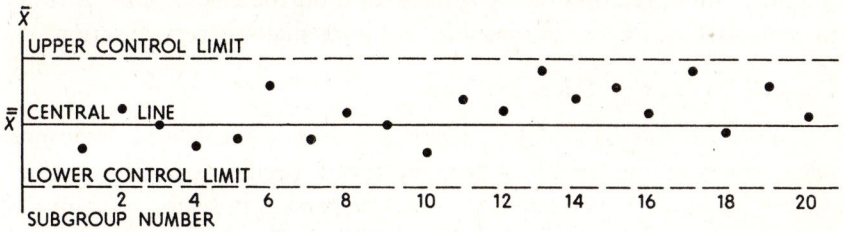

Chart 22–2

$\bar{X}$ CHART SHOWING SHIFT IN PROCESS AVERAGE

signable variation has entered the process, causing a shift in process level, even though no points may have fallen beyond the control limits.

Furthermore, if an upward or downward trend is noted in the points on the average chart, as in Chart 22–3, the evidence also indicates that

Chart 22–3

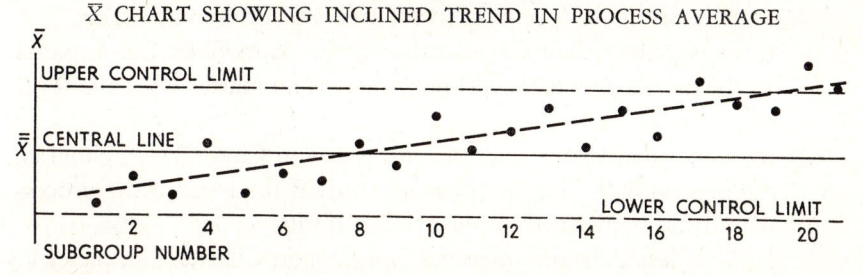

$\bar{X}$ CHART SHOWING INCLINED TREND IN PROCESS AVERAGE

assignable variation is present. This is frequently the result of uniform tool wear. Thus it is evident that in many cases the control chart for averages, if properly interpreted, can give an indication of impending trouble even though no points have actually exceeded limits. Corrective action can then be taken to avoid production of unsatisfactory items.

R *Charts.* The plotting of the points on a range chart is similar to that on an X chart. The sample range values are plotted at the appropriate subgroup numbers. A point outside limits indicates that the variability of the process has changed and that a search should be instituted immediately to locate the source of the trouble.

The points on a range chart should also be distributed at random in the absence of assignable variation, except that the positive skewness of these distributions means that a few more values should fall below the central line than above it. Any suspicious deviation from such a pattern (even though no points fall outside limits) should be regarded as evidence of a change in the variability of the process.

In summary, control charts for variables provide a basis for action with respect to both the average level and the variability of a process. The charts provide a continuous check on consistency of performance. A proper interpretation of the information on the charts often permits the detection of impending trouble and immediate corrective action.

Control Charts and Specifications

Once a process is brought under control, it is possible to determine whether or not it is capable of meeting stated specifications. The method is as follows: First, estimate the process dispersion measure, σ, from the average range, $\overline{R}$ (or average standard deviation), of the items sampled. The estimated σ equals $\overline{R}/d_2$, where d_2 is a factor found in Table 22-2 below (p. 505). Second, on the assumption that the characteristic under control is distributed normally, one can say that nearly all (99.73 per cent) of its values should fall within the range $\overline{X} \pm 3\sigma$. This interval of 6σ can then be compared with the tolerance range (upper specification limit minus lower specification limit) to determine whether the process can meet these specifications. Three situations may occur:

1. If 6σ is greater than the tolerance range, as in Chart 22-4, panel A, the process cannot meet specifications no matter what the level of the process is.
2. If 6σ is equal to the tolerance range, as in Chart 22-4, panel B, the process will meet specifications only if the level of the process is midway between the specification limits.
3. If 6σ is less than the tolerance range, as in Chart 22-4, panel C, the process will meet specifications even if the level of the process is allowed to shift within certain limits.

In this way it is possible to judge whether there is excessive variation in the product. Any variation outside specifications is excessive. There

Chart 22–4

A. PROCESS NOT CAPABLE OF MEETING SPECIFICATIONS

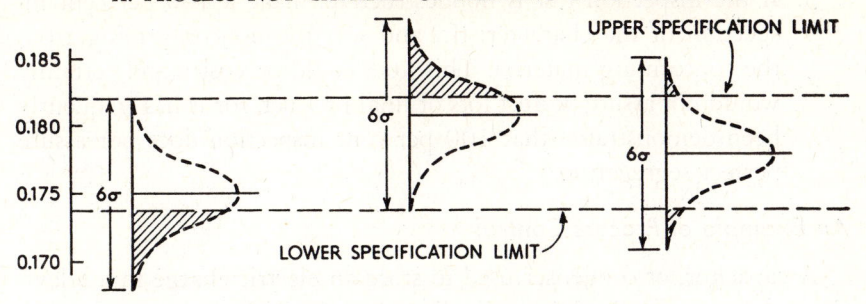

B. PROCESS JUST CAPABLE OF MEETING SPECIFICATIONS

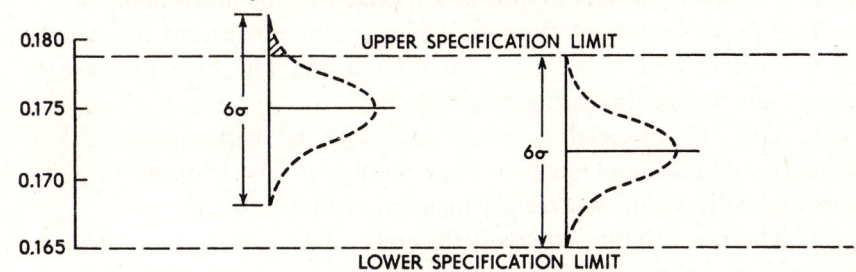

C. PROCESS MORE THAN CAPABLE OF MEETING SPECIFICATIONS

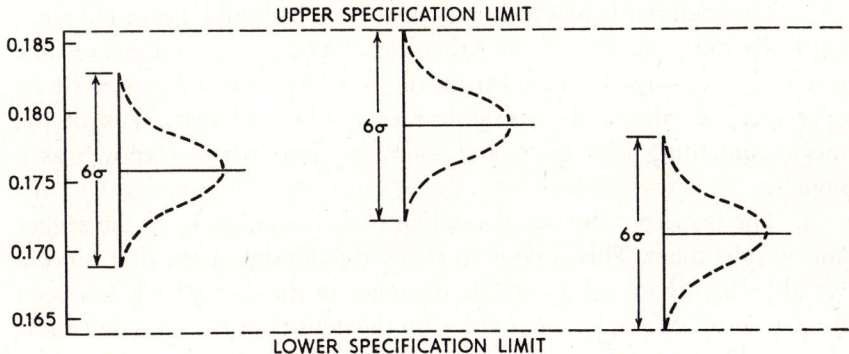

are, in general, three corrective actions which may be taken in this case:

1. Revise the specifications, relaxing tolerances so that the process can meet the new limits.
2. If specifications as written *must* be met, change the process if possible. This may be a minor change, such as resetting a machine or tightening and repairing existing equipment; or it can be an extremely expensive job, involving a change in the raw material, a

complete revision of the process, or installation of new machines.
3. If the inspection test is nondestructive, make a 100 per cent inspection of the characteristic, and sort the nonconforming from the conforming material. This, too, could be costly and certainly would not assure perfect lots of final product, for it has frequently been demonstrated that 100 per cent inspection does not assure perfect segregation.

An Example of Process Control

A capacitor, or condenser used to store an electric charge in a television set, is composed of a ceramic disc which is silvered on each face, attached to two leads, and dipped in a special wax for protection.

The Manufacturing Process. This example concerns the control of the diameter of the ceramic disc after firing. The steps involved in the production of this part are as follows:

1. The raw material is mixed and blended with various fillers, binders, and moisture agents in huge revolving vats by means of agitators and rollers, and is screened manually to uniform size.

2. The raw mixture is passed through a large drier designed to reduce the moisture content to 1 per cent. The material is then stored in metal barrels until needed.

3. The material is placed in a hopper on a hydraulic press, fed automatically into a die the shape of the disc, and subjected to pressure. The resulting green disc is ejected from the die, inspected for defects by an operator, and placed on a ceramic rack holding 15 discs. Ten of the racks, containing 150 discs, are assembled into what is known as a sagger.

4. The inspector chooses at random five green discs from the sagger and weighs them. This is done to check the density of the disc, since a variable density means a variable diameter in the disc after it has been fired. Control charts are maintained on the density of the discs, but these charts will not be discussed here.

5. If the inspector finds the density of the discs acceptable, ten saggers are placed on a cart. The cart is then passed through an electric kiln on a track at a uniform speed.

6. The carts emerge from the firing operation at ten-minute intervals. The inspector takes five fired discs from each sagger and measures the diameter of each. These readings are entered on an appropriate form, and the average and range of each subgroup are calculated. The values are then plotted on control charts, and, if in limits, the sagger is accepted.

7. After acceptance, the fired discs are inspected for defects (pits, cracks, chips, warp) and prepared for shipment to the customer.

Sources of Variation. This process is subjected to numerous sources of variation. Some of these are: (1) raw material may vary as a result of its composition, mixing and sizing, drying, or storage; (2) variations may occur in the setting of machines, in level of material in hoppers, in hydraulic pressure applied, and in operation of presses by workers; and (3) kilns may vary in firing time or in temperature.

The most troublesome variations occur in the density of the disc, for wide density variation causes nonuniform shrinkage of the disc when fired. Density is affected by all preliminary operations—particularly the state of the raw material, the level of material in the hopper, and the pressure applied by the press. Also, if the discs are fired too quickly, the rapid rise in temperature causes them to warp, chip, or crack.

Control of the Fired Diameter of the Disc. For purposes of illustration assume that this process is just being put under control. Nothing is known about the variability of the process other than that the green discs are controlled by weight before entering the kilns.

The characteristic to be controlled is the fired diameter, which is specified on the drawing as 500 ± 10 thousandths of an inch. The inspector takes 20 subgroups of 5 each, one subgroup from each sagger, and records the readings in thousandths of an inch as deviations from .500 inch. See Table 22–1.

1. *Calculation of Trial Control Limits.* Add the 20 sample means and divide by 20 to secure the over-all mean:

$$\overline{\overline{X}} = \Sigma \overline{X}/n = -2.4/20 = -.12$$

Take this value tentatively as the best approximation of the population mean, μ (process level). Now compute the average range from the sample ranges in the same way:

$$\overline{R} = \Sigma R/n = 113/20 = 5.65$$

The calculation of control limits for the $\overline{X}$ chart requires an estimate of $3\sigma_{\overline{x}}$. Tables have been prepared which simplify this task materially. Enter Table 22–2 at sample size 5 and choose the value of A_2. It is .577. Then $3\sigma_{\overline{x}}$ may be estimated as $A_2\overline{R}$:

$$3\sigma_{\overline{x}} = A_2\overline{R} = .577 \times 5.65 = 3.26$$

The upper and lower control limits for the $\overline{X}$ chart are therefore

$$UCL_{\overline{x}} = -.12 + 3.26 = 3.14$$
$$LCL_{\overline{x}} = -.12 - 3.26 = -3.38$$

Table 22-1
MEASUREMENT OF FIRED DIAMETER OF CERAMIC DISC

Specification: 500 ± 10 Thousandths of an Inch
Kiln No. 5—Shift 2   *Characteristic:* Fired Diameter
(Deviations from .500 Inch in Thousandths of an Inch)

Sagger Number	Disc Number 1	2	3	4	5	Total	Mean	Range
1	2	3	4	0	−5	4	.8	9
2	−3	1	−5	1	1	−5	−1.0	6
3	−2	−1	1	3	−4	−3	− .6	7
4	−4	−2	1	−3	−4	−12	−2.4	5
5	−1	4	3	−2	6	10	2.0	8
6	3	4	0	1	2	10	2.0	4
7	4	2	4	2	3	15	3.0	2
8	−3	−3	2	2	0	−2	− .4	5
9	1	2	−3	−2	2	0	0	5
10	1	2	−1	2	−6	−2	− .4	8
11	−2	2	1	2	1	4	.8	4
12	−5	−8	−8	0	−4	−25	−5.0	8
13	−2	4	−1	−1	2	2	.4	6
14	0	−2	−2	−2	1	−5	−1.0	3
15	2	1	1	0	0	4	.8	2
16	2	0	−4	−5	−1	−8	−1.6	7
17	0	−5	1	−1	−4	−9	−1.8	6
18	−1	0	2	0	1	2	.4	3
19	2	5	3	−6	2	6	1.2	11
20	−1	−1	3	0	1	2	.4	4
Total	...	...	...	...	...	−12	−2.4	113

Source: Confidential.

The control limits for the *range* chart may be estimated as easily as those for the $\overline{X}$ chart. The upper control limit is $D_4\overline{R}$, where D_4 is found in Table 22–2, for sample size 5. D_4 is 2.114. Then

$$UCL_R = \overline{R} + 3\sigma_R = D_4\overline{R} = 2.115 \times 5.65 = 11.95$$

Similarly, the lower control limit is $D_3\overline{R}$, where D_3 is 0 in Table 22–2:

$$LCL_R = \overline{R} - 3\sigma_R = D_3\overline{R} = 0 \times 5.65 = 0$$

Here, because of the small sample size, the computed value of LCL_R is negative, and so the limit is placed at zero, since it is not possible to have a negative range value.

2. *Interpretation of the Charts.* In the chart for averages (Chart 22–5, panel A) all points are within the control limits except subgroup 12. No trend is apparent, and there is no indication of excessively long runs. It is concluded that, with the exception of subgroup 12, the process is free of assignable variation. (In this case, an investigation dis-

Table 22–2

FACTORS USEFUL IN CONSTRUCTION OF CONTROL CHARTS*

Number of Items in Sample, n	Chart for Averages — Factors for Control Limits A_2	Chart for Averages — Factors for Central Line d_2	Chart for Ranges — Factors for Control Limits D_3	Chart for Ranges — Factors for Control Limits D_4
2	1.880	1.128	0	3.267
3	1.023	1.693	0	2.575
4	.729	2.059	0	2.282
5	.577	2.326	0	2.115
6	.483	2.534	0	2.004
7	.419	2.704	.076	1.924
8	.373	2.847	.136	1.864
9	.337	2.970	.184	1.816
10	.308	3.078	.223	1.777
11	.285	3.173	.256	1.744
12	.266	3.258	.284	1.716
13	.249	3.336	.308	1.692
14	.235	3.407	.329	1.671
15	.223	3.472	.348	1.652

* *Note:* These factors assume a normal distribution, with true value of σ known.

SOURCE: American Society for Testing Materials, *Manual on Quality Control of Materials*, Table B2, p. 115. For more detailed table and explanation, see Acheson J. Duncan, *Quality Control and Industrial Statistics* (rev. ed.; Homewood, Ill.: Richard D. Irwin, Inc., 1959), Table M, p. 886.

closed that the sagger from which subgroup 12 was drawn had been red-tagged, i.e., rejected, because it didn't meet green-density standards but had been processed through error.) The chart for ranges (Chart 22–7, panel B) also shows an "in control" condition with respect to process variability.

3. *Revision of Limits.* Since the $\overline{X}$ chart contains a subgroup outside limits, it would not be proper to use the value of $\overline{\overline{X}} = -.12$ as the best estimate of the process level (average) under control. As a better

Chart 22-5
CONTROL CHARTS FOR FIRED DIAMETER OF CERAMIC DISCS
A. $\overline{X}$ Chart

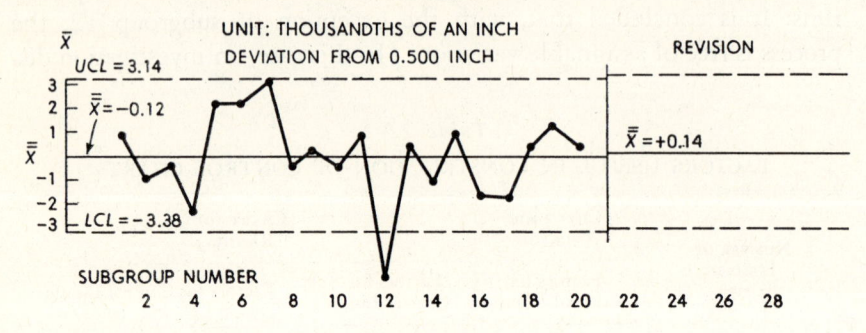

UNIT: THOUSANDTHS OF AN INCH
DEVIATION FROM 0.500 INCH

UCL = 3.14
$\overline{\overline{X}} = -0.12$
LCL = -3.38
REVISION
$\overline{\overline{X}} = +0.14$

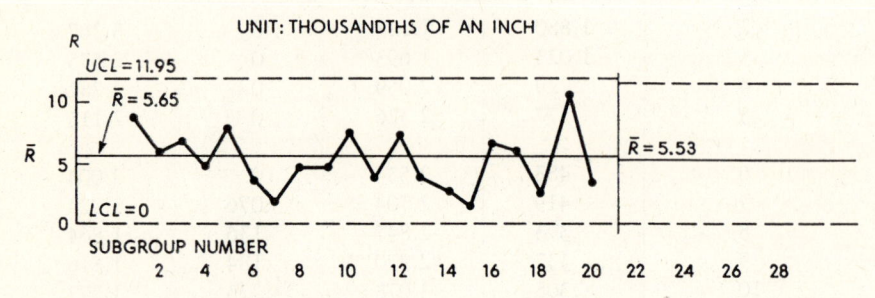

B. R Chart
UNIT: THOUSANDTHS OF AN INCH

UCL = 11.95
$\overline{R} = 5.65$
LCL = 0
$\overline{R} = 5.53$

approximation, eliminate subgroup 12 and compute a revised $\overline{X}$ from the remaining 19 groups:

$$\overline{\overline{X}}_{rev.} = \frac{\Sigma \overline{X}}{n} = \frac{-2.4 - (-5.0)}{20 - 1} = \frac{+2.6}{19} = +.14$$

Although the range chart shows control, it will give a better estimate of normal process variability if subgroup 12 (from the rejected sagger) is eliminated. Revised values of $\overline{R}$ and $A_2\overline{R}$ for the remaining 19 groups are:

$$\overline{R}_{rev.} = \frac{\Sigma R}{n} = \frac{113 - 8}{20 - 1} = \frac{105}{19} = 5.53$$

$$A_2\overline{R}_{rev.} = .577 \times 5.53 = 3.19$$

Revised control limits for the $\overline{X}$ chart are:

$$UCL_{\overline{X}} = .14 + 3.19 = 3.33$$
$$LCL_{\overline{X}} = .14 - 3.19 = -3.05$$

Revised control limits for the R chart are:

$$UCL_R = \overline{R} + 3\sigma_R = D_4\overline{R} = 2.115 \times 5.53 = 11.70$$
$$LCL_R = \overline{R} - 3\sigma_R = D_3\overline{R} = 0 \quad \times 5.53 = 0$$

The revised central lines and control limits are drawn on the right side of Chart 22–5. The points on the two charts still lie within the new control limits, except for subgroup 12 which is expected to fall outside the limits on the $\overline{X}$ chart. The revised values of $\overline{\overline{X}}$ and $\overline{R}$ are the best estimates of the true process average and range which are possible on the basis of 20 subgroup readings. As additional data are secured, it may be desirable to revise these estimates.

4. *Ability of Process to Meet Specifications.* Since the R chart exhibits control, it is possible to estimate the value of σ, the process variation measure, as follows:

$$\sigma = \frac{\overline{R}}{d_2} = \frac{5.53}{2.326} = 2.38$$

where d_2 is a factor secured for subgroup size 5 in Table 22–2. The range 6σ is then $6 \times 2.38 = 14.28$. According to specifications, the tolerance range is 20. Since 6σ is less than the tolerance range, this process can meet the specifications if the process level is satisfactory. If the characteristic follows the normal pattern, nearly all of the fired diameters will fall between $\overline{X} \pm 3\sigma$ or $.14 \pm 7.14$. Specifications are 0 ± 10. It is evident that this process will meet specifications if it is controlled at the present level.

5. *Future Use of Charts.* For the next period, the two control charts will have new central lines and new control limits, as indicated above. The inspector will compute and plot the values of $\overline{X}$ and R immediately upon measuring the five members of the subgroup. In this way, he can detect trouble promptly and undertake an investigation at once to determine the cause.

In summary, the ceramic disc diameters are shown to be adhering to a level of $+.14$ thousandths (specification: 0) with a variation of 2.38 (σ), on the basis of the first 20 subgroups. This process seems capable of control and will meet specifications if controlled at the present level.

CONTROL OF ATTRIBUTES

As mentioned earlier, the control of *variables* employs the $\overline{X}$ and R chart technique. Control of *attributes* is achieved by use of either the p chart or the c chart, the first for proportion of units that are defective, and the second for number of defects per unit. A defect is any imperfection which will render the article or part unfit for the purpose originally intended. For example, if white enamel panels are inspected visually, a chip, black spot, crack, imperfect coverage of enamel, off color, or bend in the panel is an imperfection which will cause the article to be rejected and is consequently termed a defect. If a panel has one or more of these defects, it is counted as one *defective* panel, while a count must be made to determine the number of *defects*.

Fraction Defective Chart or p Chart

The p chart is used to control the *proportion of units that are defective* in a given attribute. This chart has its theoretical basis in the binomial distribution, and generally gives best results when the sample size is large—say, at least 50.

The central line is placed at $\bar{p}$, the average fraction defective, where $\bar{p}$ is the number of defectives divided by the total number inspected. The control limits are $3\sigma_p$ from the central line, where $\sigma_p = \sqrt{\bar{p}\bar{q}/n}$ for sample size n, and $\bar{q} = 1 - \bar{p}$. As in the case of the $\bar{X}$ chart, the value of $\bar{p}$ is subject to revision as more data are secured. The following case illustrates the application of this chart.

An inspection procedure in the manufacture of spark plugs calls for an inspection for defectives on finished plugs in lots of 200 each. The

Table 22–3

INSPECTION DATA ON COMPLETED SPARK PLUGS
(4,800 Spark Plugs in 24 Lots of 200 Spark Plugs Each)

Lot Number	Number Defectives	Fraction Defective	Lot Number	Number Defectives	Fraction Defective
1	10	.050	13	8	.040
2	7	.035	14	6	.030
3	14	.070	15	10	.050
4	4	.020	16	13	.065
5	20	.100	17	7	.035
6	11	.055	18	5	.025
7	14	.070	19	3	.015
8	8	.040	20	4	.020
9	6	.030	21	1	.005
10	12	.060	22	3	.015
11	15	.075	23	2	.010
12	5	.025	24	4	.020
			Total	192	....

check is visual and can be made rapidly by experienced operators. The data in Table 22–3 show the number of defectives found in the inspection of 24 lots of 200 each. The computations are as follows:

$$\text{Average fraction defective: } \bar{p} = \frac{192}{4{,}800} = .040$$

$$\sigma_p = \sqrt{\frac{\bar{p}\bar{q}}{n}} = \sqrt{\frac{.040 \times .960}{200}} = .0138$$

$3\sigma_p = 3 \times .0138 = .041$
Upper control limit: $\bar{p} + 3\sigma_p = .040 + .041 = .081$
Lower control limit: $\bar{p} - 3\sigma_p = .040 - .041 = -.001$
LCL set at 0.

Chart 22–6

p CHART FOR SPARK PLUG INSPECTION
(24 Lots of 200 Spark Plugs Each)

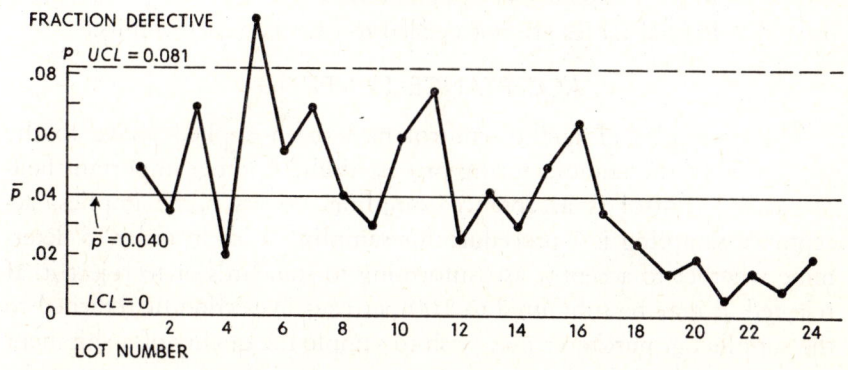

Chart 22–6 is the control chart for these lots. Note that there is one point above the upper control limit, indicating one lot which had more defectives than expected. The last eight lots are all below the central line, indicating that the fraction defective has changed to a lower level during this period. If this trend continues, it will be desirable to revise the value of $\bar{p}$ and to establish new, closer control limits. The introduction of a p chart frequently results in a rapid decrease in number of defectives, since it sounds the alarm for immediate action in case of trouble.

In most cases, the number of items inspected varies from lot to lot, causing the upper and lower control limits to vary. Although this requires more computations, the interpretation of such a chart is precisely the same as one with constant control limits.

Chart for Number of Defects per Unit or c Chart

This chart is employed to control the actual *number of defects per unit,* rather than the number of defective units. The theoretical basis of the chart is the Poisson distribution, or law of improbable events. The *c* chart is most frequently used where (1) a natural unit does not exist, as in defects per 100 square yards of cloth, the unit of area being arbitrary; or (2) where the unit is quite complex (e.g., aircraft instruments) so that almost all units have some defects. The so-called area of opportunity (e.g., 100 square yards of an identical type of cloth) for the occurrence of a defect must be held constant from part to part for this chart to be effective as a control. The number of units inspected, however, may still vary from sample to sample.

The *c* chart is similar to the *p* chart in its construction and interpretation. The central line is placed at $\bar{c}$, the average number of defects per unit. The upper and lower control limits are placed at $\bar{c} \pm 3\sigma_c$, where $\sigma_c = \sqrt{\bar{c}}$. Special tables are not needed to calculate these limits.

ACCEPTANCE SAMPLING

The principles of quality control have been applied above to the regulation of the manufacturing process itself. Another important field of quality control is acceptance sampling. As its name implies, acceptance sampling is a procedure for sampling a lot in order to determine whether to accept it as conforming to standards or to reject it. If rejected, it may be submitted to 100 per cent inspection or returned to the supplier. A purchaser may wish to sample the quality of a shipment of goods received, or a manufacturer may submit his own output to acceptance sampling at various stages of production. The purpose of acceptance sampling is therefore to determine whether to accept or reject a product. It does not attempt to control quality during the manufacturing process, as do the techniques described earlier in the chapter.

It is often preferable to inspect only a sample, rather than the entire lot, to determine its acceptability. This is particularly true when inspection is very costly or destructive. Even if 100 per cent inspection is feasible, a carefully worked out sampling plan may produce equally good or better results at lower cost. An acceptance sampling plan will improve the quality of the product through rejecting defective lots and bringing pressure to bear on suppliers to improve quality. The lot can be judged promptly, with a known probability of making a mistake.

Acceptance sampling methods were perfected during World War II to meet military needs for quick and accurate inspection of vast supplies of matériel. These methods have since been adopted in industry generally.

While the theory is complex, acceptance sampling is simple in practice and can be applied by inspectors without advanced statistical training. The techniques will not be described here but may be found in Eugene L. Grant, *Statistical Quality Control* (2d ed.; New York: McGraw-Hill Book Co., Inc., 1952), Part IV; Acheson J. Duncan, *Quality Control and Industrial Statistics* (rev. ed.; Homewood, Ill.: Richard D. Irwin, Inc., 1959), Parts II and III; or Dudley J. Cowden, *Statistical Methods in Quality Control* (Englewood Cliffs, N.J.: Prentice-Hall, Inc., 1957), chaps. 30–40.

The three principal types of acceptance sampling plans now in use are as follows:

1. The single-sampling plan specifies the sample size and the number of defective units in the sample that will cause the entire lot to be rejected. If a smaller number of defectives is found, the lot is accepted.

2. In a double-sampling plan a smaller sample can be taken to begin with. If it contains a specified number c_1 or fewer defective units, the lot is immediately accepted; if it contains more than c_2, a larger number, the lot is rejected. In the intermediate case, however, a second larger sample is taken. Then, if the combined number of defectives in the two samples is c_2 or less, the lot is accepted; otherwise it is rejected. Double sampling is preferable to single sampling in reducing the total amount of inspection on very good or very poor lots that can be judged on the first sample. It also has the psychological advantage of giving a tentatively rejected lot a second chance. When many second samples are required, however, double sampling may be more complicated and expensive than single sampling.

3. In sequential sampling the size of sample is not determined in advance. Instead, a decision is made after each observation or group of observations to (1) accept, (2) reject, or (3) suspend judgment and continue sampling until a decision is ultimately reached. Sequential methods permit reaching a decision on the basis of even fewer observations than other plans in the case of very good or very bad lots, but the procedure is relatively complex in operation.

SUMMARY

Quality control methods have come into widespread use in recent years both for the control of a process during manufacture and for determining the acceptability of a product. This chapter is primarily devoted to process control.

All products vary in quality. Control charts are used to separate the normal *chance* variation from *assignable* variation (attributable to nonrandom causes) so that the latter can be promptly recognized and remedied. The principal types of control charts are for *variables,* or measurable characteristics, and for *attributes,* or traits that are either present or absent (e.g., passing a "go not-go" gauge test) or nonmeasurable (e.g., color).

The $\overline{X}$ chart for variables is used to control the average value or "level" of a quality characteristic. To construct an $\overline{X}$ chart, draw horizontal lines at the estimated population mean on the vertical scale, and at $3\sigma_{\overline{x}}$ control limits on either side. These limits are usually estimated from the average of sample ranges. Plot subgroup averages at equal intervals along the horizontal axis.

The R chart for variables is used to control the variability of the process. To construct an R chart, draw horizontal lines at $\overline{R}$ and at the $3\sigma_R$ limits. If the lower control limit is negative, place it at zero. Then plot the subgroup ranges as in the $\overline{X}$ chart.

Nearly all of the points should fall within the control limits of an $\overline{X}$ or R chart if chance variation alone is present. If a point falls outside the limits, or if about seven or more consecutive points fall on one side of the central line, or if they show an upward or downward trend, assignable variation is probably present. This should be corrected promptly.

The range 6σ must be less than or equal to the specified tolerance range, as shown in Chart 22–4, for the process to meet specifications. If it cannot, the manufacturer can revise specifications, change the process, or resort to 100 per cent inspection unless inspection is too costly or destructive.

The example of the ceramic disc illustrates how process control works—i.e., how to calculate trial control limits with the aid of tables, how to interpret the charts, revise the limits, and gauge the ability of the process to meet specifications.

The control of attributes is achieved through the use of either p charts for proportion of units that are defective or c charts for number of defects per unit. The latter are used where no natural unit exists or where the unit is so complex that virtually all units have some defects. These charts are constructed and interpreted in much the same way as the control charts for variables summarized above.

Acceptance sampling is an economical and efficient method of determining whether to accept or reject a shipment or stock of material, based on a sample. This may be a single or double sample, or a sequential plan in which the amount of sampling depends on the results of successive tests. Quality control and acceptance sampling have come into widespread use in industrial management, since they help produce a better product at a lower cost.

PROBLEMS

1. Distinguish between:
    a) Process control and acceptance sampling.
    b) Chance variation and assignable variation.
    c) Variables and attributes, as applied to quality characteristics.
    d) $\bar{X}$ and R charts for variables.
    e) p and c charts for attributes.

2. a) Describe two situations in which the pattern of points on a control chart would indicate trouble even if no points actually fall outside control limits.
    b) Explain how to determine whether or not a process is capable of meeting specifications.
    c) If a process cannot meet specifications, what corrective action can be taken?

3. One of the critical component parts of a product manufactured by your company is a size $5/16''$ carbon steel bolt. In order to meet product specifications this bolt must have a hardness rating between 77.5 and 89.5 on the Rockwell "B" Hardness Scale. Following a heat treatment designed to produce the desired hardness, a sample of four bolts is drawn at random from each lot, and each bolt is tested for hardness. Ten of these samples, taken in consecutive order, test as follows on the Rockwell "B" Scale:[2]

1	2	3	4	5
85.0	87.0	82.0	82.5	89.0
84.5	81.0	93.0	83.0	81.5
85.0	80.5	85.0	85.0	82.0
87.0	79.0	84.5	82.5	84.0

6	7	8	9	10
83.0	84.5	89.0	85.5	89.0
89.0	85.0	88.0	89.5	85.5
83.0	85.0	85.0	89.0	87.0
81.5	88.0	83.5	82.5	89.0

a) Set up $\bar{X}$ and R charts to control the hardness of these bolts. Show all calculations, and plot results.

---
[2] Ten samples are used here to minimize computations. In practice, however, at least 20 or 25 samples are needed for reliable results.

b) Does the heat-treating process appear to be in statistical control? If so, what is your best estimate of the average hardness rating of all bolts produced by this process?

c) If any points are out of control, revise the limits accordingly, and plot the results on the charts.

d) Can this process meet specifications? Explain.

4. Following are mean net weights (expressed as deviations from 1,000 grains) and ranges, both in grains, of 20 subgroups, each consisting of five bottles of sodium bicarbonate. These are filled by machine and labeled "100 ten-grain tablets."

Subgroup Number	$\bar{X}$	R	Subgroup Number	$\bar{X}$	R
1	4.6	5	11	.4	2
2	4.4	3	12	8.0	6
3	4.0	9	13	2.2	5
4	5.0	6	14	5.6	13
5	.8	2	15	7.2	11
6	2.4	9	16	2.2	8
7	7.2	10	17	4.6	5
8	4.4	4	18	−1.8	6
9	1.8	8	19	7.4	6
10	3.2	11	20	6.0	4

a) Set up $\bar{X}$ and R charts to control the operation of the bottle-filling machine. Show all calculations, and plot results.

b) Is this process in control? Cite evidence to support your conclusion.

c) If any points are out of control, revise the limits accordingly, and plot the results on the charts.

d) If specifications are 4 ± 8 (i.e., tolerance range 16), can this process meet specifications? Explain.

5. Following are the number of defective electric-shaver motors inspected during each of 23 working days of October, in daily samples of 100.

October	Number Defective	October	Number Defective	October	Number Defective
1	5	11	2	23	2
2	9	12	1	24	3
3	10	15	2	25	5
4	10	16	2	26	5
5	13	17	3	29	3
8	10	18	6	30	2
9	13	19	3	31	3
10	2	22	3		

a) Construct a p chart to control the quality of the motors.

b) It is reported that a faulty machine used in assembling the motors was repaired during the month. If there is evidence that the fraction defective changed to a lower level during this period, discard earlier observations, revise $\bar{p}$, compute closer control limits, and plot the results for future use.

6. A test of 2,000 transistors, in 20 lots, each containing 100 transistors, shows 10 per cent defective on the average. What is the maximum per cent defective the inspector should allow on the next lot, for it to be within $3\sigma_p$ control limits?

SELECTED READINGS

ASTM Manual on Quality Control of Materials. Philadelphia: American Society for Testing Materials, 1951.

A concise manual, with illustrations in Part 3 of control charts for a wide variety of single-sampling, single-variable problems.

BOWKER, ALBERT H., and LIEBERMAN, GERALD J. *Engineering Statistics.* Englewood Cliffs, N.J.: Prentice-Hall, Inc., 1959.

Contains a readable and authoritative treatment of quality control.

COWDEN, DUDLEY J. *Statistical Methods in Quality Control.* Englewood Cliffs, N.J.: Prentice-Hall, Inc., 1957.

A broad treatise on statistical techniques in process control and product control, including economic considerations, with a minimum of mathematics in the text sections.

DUNCAN, ACHESON J. *Quality Control and Industrial Statistics.* Rev. ed. Homewood, Ill.: Richard D. Irwin, Inc., 1959.

A broad survey of statistics useful in industrial research. Parts II and III cover acceptance sampling, and Part IV covers control charts.

GRANT, EUGENE L. *Statistical Quality Control.* 2d ed. New York: McGraw-Hill Book Co., Inc., 1952.

A very readable, nontechnical working manual, designed for use by production and inspection supervisors, engineers, and management.

JURAN, J. M. (ed.). *Quality Control Handbook.* New York: McGraw-Hill Book Co., Inc., 1951.

An encyclopedia on managerial aspects of quality control and applications of quality control principles in specific industries, with less emphasis on statistical techniques.

APPENDIXES

A. SELECTED SOURCES OF BUSINESS STATISTICS

(*Revised to August 17, 1961*)

THE PRINCIPAL sources of business statistics relating to the American and Canadian economies are listed below. The most useful of these are starred (*). The items are grouped into United States government sources, classified by government agency; Canadian government sources; and nongovernment sources. The latter are grouped into statistical source books and general business periodicals.

For more detailed lists of sources, see:

Andriot, John L., *Guide to U.S. Government Statistics* (3d ed.; Arlington 10, Va., 1961).

Carpenter, Robert N., *Guidelist for Marketing Research and Economic Forecasting* (New York: American Management Association, Inc., 1961).

Chamber of Commerce of the United States, *What's the Answer? A Brief Guide to Sources of Business Statistics* (Washington 6, D.C., 1959).

Cole, Arthur H., *Measures of Business Change* (Homewood, Ill.: Richard D. Irwin, Inc., 1952).

Gunther, Edgar, and Goldstein, Frederick A., *Current Sources of Marketing Information* (Chicago: American Marketing Association, 1960).

Hausdorfer, Walter, *Handbook of Commercial, Financial and Information Services* (5th ed.; New York: Special Libraries Association, 1956 and later supplements).

Hauser, Philip M., and Leonard, William R., *Government Statistics for Business Use* (2d ed.; New York: John Wiley & Sons, Inc., 1956).

Manley, Marian C., *Business Information—How to Find and Use It* (New York: Harper & Bros., 1955).

Snyder, Richard M., *Measuring Business Changes* (New York: John Wiley & Sons, Inc., 1955).

520 BUSINESS AND ECONOMIC STATISTICS

U.S. Government, Bureau of the Budget, *Statistical Services of the United States Government* (rev. ed.; Washington, D.C.: U.S. Government Printing Office, 1959). Some of the summaries of government sources listed below are taken from this manual.

U.S. Government, Department of Commerce, *United States Department of Commerce Publications* (Washington, D.C.: U.S. Government Printing Office, 1952 and later supplements).

Wasserman, Paul, *Information for Administrators* (Ithaca, N.Y.: Cornell University Press, 1956).

UNITED STATES GOVERNMENT SOURCES

Department of Commerce—Office of Business Economics

1. *Survey of Current Business* (monthly, with supplements)

    The monthly issues present articles and charts on current business trends, and about 2,500 statistical series for the past 13 months on national income and other business indexes, commodity prices, construction, domestic trade, employment and wages, finance, foreign trade, transportation, production, prices, and shipments. The annual review appears in February, national income data in July, and state income figures in the August issue.

    The *Weekly Supplement* brings many of the monthly figures up to date and gives weekly data for a few important series.

    Statistical supplements, now called *Business Statistics* (*), have been issued in 1932 and biennially 1936–42 and 1947–59. These include complete monthly figures for past years and a full explanation of sources and methods of computation.

    U.S. Income and Output, a supplement to the *Survey of Current Business* (1958), gives complete national income and product accounts from 1929 through 1957.

    Personal Income by States, another supplement (1956), contains detailed income data by years from 1929 to 1955; especially useful in market analysis.

Department of Commerce—Bureau of the Census

2. *Statistical Abstract of the United States* (annual)

    Summarizes a large mass of annual data on economic, social, and political subjects, from governmental and nongovernmental sources, with detailed explanatory notes.

    Historical Statistics of the United States, from Colonial Times to 1957, a supplement to the *Statistical Abstract,* includes about 3,000 time series, largely annual, extending back to the earliest year for which the data are available, with specific source notes, definitions of terms, and descriptive text.

    County and City Data Book, 1956, another supplement to the *Statistical Abstract,* presents hundreds of series for each county and city, mostly drawn from recent censuses.

3. *U.S. Census of Population, 1960* (decennial since 1790)

Covers number and characteristics of the population, including nativity, labor force, occupation, industry, income, internal migration, and family data, classified by states, counties, metropolitan areas, minor civil divisions, and census tracts.

4. *Current Population Reports*

    Monthly and special releases obtained from the Current Population Survey, including estimates and characteristics of the population and labor force.

5. *U.S. Census of Housing, 1960* (decennial since 1940)

    Housing characteristics, residential financing, and block statistics, including number of dwelling units by occupancy and tenure, classified by states, cities, and metropolitan areas.

6. *U.S. Census of Agriculture, 1959* (quinquennial)

    Number, acreage, and value of farms; uses, irrigation, and drainage of farm lands; acreage, production, and value of specified crops and livestock; as well as data on mortgage debt, taxes, and farm employment, classified by counties and state economic areas.

7. **U.S. Census of Manufactures, 1958* (quinquennial after 1958)

    Number and size of establishments, employment and payrolls, inventories, cost of material and fuel used, value of product and value added by manufacture; by industries, products, states, and industrial areas. Previous censuses were quinquennial 1899–1919, biennial 1921–39, 1947, and 1954.

8. *Annual Survey of Manufactures*

    Beginning 1949, this interim report includes value added, value of shipments, cost of materials, fuel and electric energy consumed, employment, man-hours, payrolls, and capital expenditures.

9. *Current Industrial Reports* (formerly *Facts for Industry*)

    Monthly, quarterly, and annual releases on shipments, production, stocks, and orders for more than 60 commodities.

10. **U.S. Census of Business, 1958* (quinquennial after 1958)

    Retail and wholesale trade statistics, including employment and payrolls, number and size of establishments, operating expenses and sales by merchandise and commodity lines for counties and metropolitan areas. Also covers service establishments including personal and business service, transportation, automotive and other repair, banking and insurance, places of amusement, and hotels and motels. Earlier censuses of distribution were taken in 1929, 1933, 1935, 1939, 1948, and 1954. Separate series of bulletins summarize the census data for specific fields.

11. Monthly Trade Reports

    Information on the trends in sales, receipts, and inventories of wholesale and retail trade by kind of business for selected large cities and the country as a whole.

12. *County Business Patterns* (published every two or three years)

    Employment, taxable payrolls, and reporting units by size for business establishments covered under the old-age and survivors insurance program, by industry groups. Covers first quarter of each year since 1946. Published jointly with U.S. Department of Health, Education and Welfare.

13. *Catalog of United States Census Publications*

The base book covering 1790–1945 was released in 1950. A *Monthly Supplement* and quarterly and cumulative-to-annual issues bring the catalog up to date.

Department of Labor—Bureau of Labor Statistics

14. **Monthly Labor Review,* with *Statistical Supplement* (annual)

Covers labor economics, prices and construction, including employment and payrolls, labor turnover, wages and hours, work stoppages, consumer price indexes by commodities and large cities, retail prices of foods by cities, wholesale prices by groups of commodities, and construction contracts and costs.

15. *Consumer Price Index and Retail Food Prices* (monthly)

Gives index numbers of retail prices by major groups of commodities and services in the consumers' budget, and index numbers of retail food prices by major groups of commodities and by cities.

16. *Wholesale Price Index* (monthly)

Gives price indexes by groups, and actual prices and price relatives for about 2,000 commodities included in the wholesale price index. The monthly data are also presented in the annual *Wholesale Prices*.

17. Other reports

Separate reports, presenting more detailed data on subjects covered in the *Monthly Labor Review,* are issued monthly for employment and payrolls, labor turnover, current wage developments, hours and earnings, labor-management disputes and construction.

18. *Handbook of Labor Statistics, 1950 Edition* (Bulletin No. 1016, 1951) and later supplements

A statistical source book on employment and payrolls, labor turnover, wage rates, cost of living, industrial relations, output per man-hour, work injuries, housing and construction, social security, and consumers' co-operatives.

19. *Publications of the Bureau of Labor Statistics* (monthly)

Lists all current and forthcoming publications, with semiannual cumulative issues.

Board of Governors of the Federal Reserve System

20. **Federal Reserve Bulletin* (monthly)

Current data on money and banking and selected economic series, including the Federal Reserve indexes of industrial production by industries, consumer credit, department store sales and stocks, and international financial statistics. Articles include annual surveys of consumer finances and buying plans.

APPENDIXES

21. *Federal Reserve Chart Book on Financial and Business Statistics* (monthly, with annual *Historical Supplement*)

    Large-scale charts on banking, currency, credit, security markets, foreign trade, industrial production, building construction, department store sales, and other economic indicators.

22. Monthly publications of Federal Reserve Banks

    The Federal Reserve Bank of each of the twelve districts publishes a monthly bulletin summarizing business conditions in that region.

Executive Office of the President—Council of Economic Advisers

23. *The Economic Report of the President* (annual)

    Analysis of current developments in employment, production, and purchasing power, with recommendations for policy action, and statistical appendixes.

24. *Economic Indicators* (monthly)

    Summarizes basic statistical series on prices, employment and wages, production, national income, purchasing power, money, credit, and federal finance. Prepared by the Council but published by the congressional Joint Economic Committee.

Department of Agriculture—General

25. *Agricultural Statistics* (annual)

    Presents detailed tables covering a series of years on acreage, yield, and production of crops; prices received by farmers; livestock, poultry, and dairy production; market supplies and prices; foreign trade in agricultural products; and some data on world production.

26. Statistical Bulletins

    Handbooks, some on a periodic and others on an occasional basis, present all available data on specific fields such as food consumption, cotton, wool, dairy products, and feed.

Department of Agriculture—Agricultural Marketing Service

27. *Agricultural Situation* and *Agricultural Outlook Digest* reports

    A series of monthly, quarterly, or annual reports providing summaries and tables on supply, demand, price, and other economic factors affecting agriculture. Separate reports are issued on specific subjects such as farm income, demand and price, marketing and transportation, farm costs, and major commodities, including livestock and meat, poultry and eggs, dairy products, fruit, vegetables, sugar, and tobacco.

28. *Agricultural Prices* (monthly)

    Prices received by farmers for principal crops and livestock products, index numbers and prices received and paid by farmers, and parity prices.

29. *Checklist of Reports and Charts Issued by the Agricultural Marketing Service* (monthly)

A listing of all periodical and special reports issued during the month by the Agricultural Marketing Service.

Treasury Department—Office of the Secretary

30. *Annual Report of the Secretary of the Treasury on the State of the Finances*
    Statistical data for fiscal years ended June 30 on receipts, expenditures, budget, deficit, public debt, and money in circulation. Lists outstanding obligations and securities of the United States government, as well as assets and liabilities of government corporations and credit agencies.
31. *Treasury Bulletin* (monthly)
    "Analysis of receipts and expenditures, composition of the public debt, prices and yields of government securities, and other treasury statistics."

Department of the Treasury—Office of the Comptroller of the Currency

32. *Annual Report of the Comptroller of the Currency*
    Compilation of financial reports for the calendar year on national banks and all banks in the United States.

Department of the Treasury—Bureau of Internal Revenue

33. *Statistics of Income* (annual)
    Detailed data on income tax returns by individuals, partnerships, and corporations, and estate and gift tax returns, by states. Part 1 covers individual returns; Part 2, corporate returns. County and city figures are available in separate mimeographed bulletins.

Interstate Commerce Commission

34. *Transport Statistics in the United States* (annual)
    Covers traffic, operations, equipment, finances, and employment of railways, motor and water carriers, oil pipelines and related agencies.

Department of the Interior—Bureau of Mines

35. *Minerals Yearbook* (annual)
    General tables show yearly quantity and value of mineral production by states; also employment and injuries. Separate chapters on each mineral give production and shipments, principal mines, value, prices, consumption, stocks, foreign trade, reserves, employment, and world production by country.
36. *Mineral Industry Surveys* and other current reports on minerals
    Weekly, monthly, or quarterly statistics on production, consumption, shipments, and stocks of important minerals and mineral products.

Federal Trade Commission and Securities and Exchange Commission

37. *Quarterly Financial Report—United States Manufacturing Corporations*
    Current income and balance sheet statements for all manufacturing industries, classified by major industry group, beginning in 1947.

Federal Power Commission

38. *Electric Power Statistics* (monthly)

    Production of electric energy and capacity of plants by states, classes of ownership, and types of prime movers; consumption of fuel for production of electric energy; electric power requirements and supply showing actual and forecast peak demands, together with existing and scheduled generating capacity.

39. *Statistics of Electric Utilities in the United States, Classes A and B, Privately Owned Companies* (annual)

    Gives comprehensive financial and operating information, as well as rate data, on privately owned electric utilities.

40. *Statistics of Natural Gas Companies* (annual)

    Composite financial and operating statements for the natural gas industry, including Class C and Class D Companies.

Federal Communications Commission

41. *Statistics of the Communications Industry in the United States* (annual)

    Financial and operating data on telephone, wire-telegraph, ocean-cable, and radiotelegraph carriers and controlling companies; employment, accidents and compensation, and number of telephones in homes, by states and principal cities.

Department of Health, Education and Welfare—Social Security Administration

42. *Social Security Bulletin* (monthly)

    Covers benefits and beneficiaries under old-age and survivors insurance, recipients and payments under public assistance programs, by state, and selected data for unemployment insurance, railroad, civil service, veterans and related programs. An *Annual Statistical Supplement* is published separately.

Department of Defense—Corps of Engineers, Department of the Army

43. *Statistics of Water-Borne Commerce*

    Tonnage of domestic and foreign water traffic, both freight and passenger, by ports, rivers, canals, and by commodity.

Securities and Exchange Commission

44. *Statistical Bulletin* (monthly)

    Security offerings, security trading on exchanges, and related data on stock and bond markets.

45. *Working Capital of U.S. Corporations* (quarterly)

    Principal items of current assets and current liabilities for all corporations, beginning 1939.

526   BUSINESS AND ECONOMIC STATISTICS

46. *Volume and Composition of Individuals' Saving* (quarterly)

Summarizes factors affecting corporate and individual savings, such as changes in securities, cash, insurance, consumers' indebtedness, and consumers' durable goods.

47. *Business Plant and Equipment Expenditure Programs* (quarterly)

Actual and anticipated expenditures on new plant and equipment, by industry groups, including manufacturing, mining, transportation, and public utilities. Compiled jointly with the Office of Business Economics in the Department of Commerce.

CANADIAN GOVERNMENT SOURCES

Dominion Bureau of Statistics

48. *Current Publications of the Dominion Bureau of Statistics, Including Memoranda and Reference Papers* (annual)

Lists publications of the Bureau by division and section.

49. **Canadian Statistical Review* (monthly, with weekly and biennial supplements)

Successor to the *Monthly Review of Business Statistics.* Presents a wide variety of monthly data on current economic conditions. The biennial supplements, beginning 1953, present important economic series back to 1926.

50. *Census of Canada, 1951, Ninth* (1953)

Eleven volumes presenting comprehensive statistics on population, industry, and agriculture. Supplemented by *Canada Year Book.*

51. *Quarterly Bulletin of Agricultural Statistics*

Summaries of current statistics on agriculture published in permanent record form. Back data for field crops from 1908 appear in the *Handbook of Agricultural Statistics, Part I: Field Crops* (D.B.S. Reference Paper No. 25, 1951).

52. *Prices & Price Indexes* (monthly)

Contains wholesale price indexes by industries and commodities, consumer price indexes by cities, average weekly wages, and security price indexes.

NONGOVERNMENT SOURCES

Statistical Source Books

53. **Current Statistics Combined with Basic Statistics* (annual) and *Current Statistics* (monthly), published by Standard & Poor's Corporation, *Trade and Securities Statistics* service, New York

The only reference book giving a complete record of *monthly* data concerning business and financial operations running back as far as the data are available. The basic series are kept up to date in the monthly *Current Statistics.* Statistical summaries are also published by industries.

54. *Moody's Manual of Investments* (annual) by Moody's Investors Service, New York

   Contains financial and operating data for each of several thousand corporations, including a brief history, balance sheet and income statements, security analyses, and a statistical "Special Features Section." There are five volumes each year—industrials, transportation, public utilities, banks and finance, and governments and municipals. Data are brought up to date in loose-leaf binders.

55. *Handbook of Basic Economic Statistics* (annual, with monthly and quarterly supplements) by Economic Statistics Bureau of Washington, D.C.

   General compilation of monthly data on industry, commerce, labor, and agriculture.

56. National Industrial Conference Board, Inc., New York

   a) *Economic Almanac* (annual)

   Detailed statistics on every type of business, economic, labor, and government activity.

   b) *Management Record* (monthly)

   Contains statistics prepared by the Conference Board on wages, earnings, hours, and employment by individual industries, salaries of clerical workers, and cost-of-living data for fifty cities.

   c) *Conference Board Business Record* (monthly)

   Contains special articles on business conditions in specific industries, with statistical data from other sources and a table of "Selected Business Indicators."

   d) *Statistics of Manufacturing Industries*

   A series of volumes with detailed annual and census data, by industries.

   e) Other reports, such as *Chartbook of Current Business Trends* and several weekly services, describe the current business situation.

57. *World Almanac* (annual) by New York World-Telegram

   A "book of facts," including summary statistics and articles on innumerable economic subjects.

58. *Basic Economic Data of the American Economy* by William N. Peach and Walter Krause (4th ed.; Homewood, Ill.: Richard D. Irwin, Inc., 1955)

   Summary tables and charts showing long-term trends in national income, population and labor force, natural resources, money and banking, international trade, government expenditures, prices, manufacturing, and agriculture. Designed to supplement economics textbooks.

59. *Commodity Yearbook* by Commodity Research Bureau, New York

   Statistical records, charts, and supplementary information on prices, supplies, production, and consumption of 86 basic commodities.

60. *Statistical Yearbook* and *Monthly Bulletin of Statistics* of the United Nations Statistical Office

   A summary of international statistics, formerly published by the League of Nations, on population, agriculture, mining, manufacturing, finance, and trade. Annual data back to 1928 and current monthly figures.

61. *Bibliography of Selected Statistical Sources of the American Nations* (Washington, D.C.: Inter-American Statistical Institute, 1947)

    "A guide to the principal statistical materials of the 22 American nations, including data, analyses, methodology, and laws and organization of statistical agencies." Includes about 2,500 publications.

62. *Annual Statistical Report of the American Iron and Steel Institute,* New York

    Data concerning all iron and steel products, classified by types and by states, including prices, foreign trade, and production.

63. *Year Book of the American Bureau of Metal Statistics,* New York

    Production, consumption, operations, trade, and prices of nonferrous metals.

64. *Metal Statistics* (annual) by American Metal Market, New York

    A compendium of annual data on all metals.

65. *Chemical Economics Handbook* by Stanford Research Institute, Menlo Park, California

    A seven-volume statistical encyclopedia, with graphs, emphasizing long-term trends.

66. *Automobile Facts and Figures* (annual) and *Motor Truck Facts* (annual) by Automobile Manufacturers Association, Detroit

    These yearbooks cover production, sales, registrations, taxation, financing, exports, used-car sales, and allied data, by years and by states.

67. *Aerospace Facts and Figures* (annual) by Aeroscope Industries Association of America, Inc., Washington, D.C.

    Summarizes annual traffic, production, etc., for aircraft and missiles.

68. *Petroleum Facts and Figures* (annual) by American Petroleum Institute, New York

    Gives annual data on United States and world production, consumption, imports and exports, prices, marketing, taxes, and stocks of various products.

69. *Gas Facts* (annual) and *Historical Statistics of the Gas Industry* (1956, with later supplements) by American Gas Association, New York

    These publications cover all aspects of the gas utility industry.

70. *Electric Light and Power Industry in the United States, Statistical Bulletin* (annual) by the Edison Electric Institute, New York

    Gives detailed data on production, fuel consumption, and sales of electric consumption and electric power, as well as financial and employment statistics of the industry.

71. *Life Insurance Fact Book* (annual) by the Institute of Life Insurance, New York

    Provides basic facts about life insurance, including sales, amount and types of insurance in force, benefit payments, annuities, and company assets.

72. *Industrial Marketing, Market Data and Directory Number* (annual), Chicago

   General data on manufacturing and distribution. Includes a list of virtually all yearbooks in the business field.

73. *Sales Management, Survey of Buying Power* (annual), New York

   Yearly estimates of personal income and retail and wholesale sales for all counties in the United States. Useful in marketing studies.

74. *Market Guide* (annual) by Editor and Publisher

   Detailed information by states, counties, and cities on population, bank deposits, auto registrations, gas and electric meters, principal industries, chain stores, transportation facilities, and department stores.

75. *Dodge Statistical Research Service* (bimonthly) by F. W. Dodge Corporation, New York

   Construction contracts awarded, by type and region, and other building data affecting many types of business.

General Business Periodicals

   This category includes statistical services, bank letters, financial and business magazines and newspapers.

76. *Outlook* (weekly) by Standard & Poor's Corporation, New York

   Analyses of stocks and bonds, principal industries, and general business conditions, with supporting statistics.

77. *Stock Survey* (weekly) and *Bond Survey* (weekly) by Moody's Investors Service, New York

   Analyses and statistics on individual securities, industries, and the general business outlook.

78. *United Business Service* (weekly), Boston

   Analyses of investments, industries, general business and commodity prices, with summary opinions of other investment services.

79. *Business and Economic Conditions* (monthly) by First National City Bank of New York

   Articles and statistics on general business conditions, credit, federal finance, and corporate earnings.

80. *Business in Brief* (quarterly) by Chase Manhattan Bank of New York

   Graphic analyses of strategic economic developments.

81. *Morgan Guaranty Survey* (monthly) by Morgan Guaranty Trust Company of New York

   Review of general business and credit conditions.

82. *Business Bulletin* (monthly) by Cleveland Trust Company

   Brief surveys of industrial production, security markets, and general business.

83. *Barron's* (weekly) by Barron's Publishing Company, Inc., New York

   Gives stock and bond quotations, banking and financial data, corporation statements, and general industrial, trade, and commodity data, including several original indexes.

84. *Business Week* by McGraw-Hill Publishing Company, Inc., New York

Presents brief articles on current business topics, a page of weekly indicators entitled "Figures of the Week," and monthly income estimates by states.

85. *Commercial and Financial Chronicle* (two issues weekly: statistical issue, and general news and advertising issue) by William B. Dana Company, New York

Gives general corporation and investment news, including stock and bond quotations, banking and financial data, corporation statements, general industrial, trade, and commodity data, news and comments, with quarterly indexes.

86. *Dun's Review and Modern Industry* (monthly) by Dun & Bradstreet, Inc., New York

General analysis of business conditions. Includes Dun's index of business failures by industry group and Dun's daily wholesale price index.

87. *Journal of Commerce* (daily), New York

Covers current business and financial news, including detailed daily quotations and other information on commodities, stocks, and bonds.

88. *Wall Street Journal* (daily) by Dow, Jones & Company, Inc., New York

Reports current events of economic and financial interest. Gives detailed price quotations on stocks, bonds, and commodities, and indexes of security, commodity, and retail prices, dividend payments, and industrial data.

89. *Exchange* (monthly) by New York Stock Exchange

Presents summary data on the activities of the New York Stock Exchange, number and volume of sales, etc.

90. *New York Times* (daily) by New York Times Company

The Business and Financial Section, particularly on Sundays, contains detailed price quotations and other economic data, including the New York Times Weekly Index of Business Activity.

91. *Economist* (weekly) by Economist Newspaper, Ltd., London

Authoritative articles and statistics on business conditions in all major countries.

B. GLOSSARY OF SYMBOLS

a	Value of Y_c (ordinate of trend or regression line or curve) when $X = 0$; value of X_{1c} in multiple regression equation when X_2, $X_3 \cdots$ equal zero.
b	Slope of trend line; regression coefficient for a sample; slope of higher degree curve at Y axis.
$b_2, b_3 \cdots$	Coefficients in multiple regression equation.
β	Regression coefficient for a population (beta).
C	Cyclical component in time series, expressed as per cent of trend (T).
c	Constant determining curvature in second-degree equation.
c_1, c_2	Acceptance numbers in double sampling.
d	Deviation of class midpoint from assumed mean of frequency distribution in class interval units.
df	Degrees of freedom.
F	Cumulative frequency for all classes below median or quartile interval.
f	Frequency or number of items in any class ($\Sigma f = n$).
G	Geometric mean.
I	Irregular component in time series expressed as per cent of $T \times C \times S$.
i	Class interval in a frequency distribution.
L	Lower limit of class interval in a frequency distribution.
LCL	Lower control limit in quality control chart.
$\log$	Logarithm.
m	Number of constants in an equation.
M.D.	Mean deviation.
Md	Median.
μ	Arithmetic mean of a population (mu).
μ_h	Hypothetical population mean.
N	Number of items in a population.
n	Number of items in a sample.
n	Subscript for any year.
o	Subscript for base period.

P	Probability; population proportion.
p	Price; sample proportion.
$\bar{p}, \bar{q}$	Average of several sample proportions.
P_h, Q_h	Hypothetical population proportions.
Q	Quartile deviation; population proportion, where $Q = 1 - P$.
Q_1, Q_3	First and third quartiles (Q_2 = median).
q	Quantity; sample proportion, where $q = 1 - p$.
R	Range; coefficient of multiple correlation.*
$\bar{R}$	Arithmetic mean of several sample ranges.
R^2	Coefficient of multiple determination.*
r	Coefficient of simple correlation.*
r^2	Coefficient of simple determination.*
r_s	Coefficient of simple correlation for a sample.
S	Seasonal index.
Sk	Coefficient of skewness.
S_{YX}	Standard error of estimate from a simple regression line or curve.
$S_{1.23}\ldots$	Standard error of estimate in multiple regression analysis.
Σ	Sum (capital sigma).
s	Standard deviation.*
s^2	Variance.*
$s_{\bar{X}}$	Standard error of the mean;* s is used with other subscripts for standard errors of other measures.
s_{Y-Y_c}	Standard error of an individual forecast.
σ	Standard deviation (small sigma) of a population; or, in quality control, its estimated value.
$\sigma_{\bar{X}}$, etc.	Standard error of mean; σ is used with other subscripts for standard errors of other measures.
T	Trend ordinate in time series ($T = Y_c$).
t	Deviation of sample mean, etc., from population mean, expressed in standard error units. The t distribution applies to small samples.
UCL	Upper control limit in quality control chart.
X, Y	Independent and dependent variables measured from zero.
$\bar{X}, \bar{Y}$	Arithmetic means of X and Y in a sample. (Subscripts 1, 2, etc., refer to different samples.)
$\bar{\bar{X}}$	Arithmetic mean of several sample means.
$\bar{X}_a$	Assumed mean of X.
X_1	Dependent variable in multiple correlation.
X_{1c}	Value of X_1 computed from multiple regression equation.
$X_2, X_3 \cdots$	Independent variables in multiple correlation.
x, y	Variables measured from means: $(x = X - \bar{X})\quad (y = Y - \bar{Y})$
$|x|$	Deviation of X from the mean $\bar{X}$, ignoring sign.
Y_c	Value of Y computed from trend or regression equation.

* Population value as estimated from a sample.

C. LOGARITHMS

HOW TO USE THE TABLE OF LOGARITHMS

LOGARITHMS are used to simplify the operations of multiplication, division, raising numbers to powers, and extracting roots. They are especially valuable in constructing ratio charts, in computing the geometric mean, and in fitting certain types of secular trend curves.

The common logarithm of a number is the power of 10 which is equal to that number. For example, the third power of 10 is 1,000, so

$$\log 1{,}000 = 3$$

That is, the logarithm of 1,000 is 3 because $10^3 = 1{,}000$. Similarly, log $100 = 2$, log $10 = 1$, log $1 = 0$, log $0.1 = -1$, log $0.01 = -2$, etc. For intermediate numbers the logarithm is a whole number, as above, followed by a decimal fraction.

The whole number part of a logarithm (to the left of the decimal point) is called the *characteristic,* and the fractional part (to the right of the decimal point) is called the *mantissa.* To find the logarithm of any number, determine the characteristic from the following rules and look up the mantissa in the accompanying table.

Rules for Determining the Characteristic

1. The characteristics of the logarithms of all numbers greater than one are positive, and their numerical values are one unit less than the number of digits to the left of the decimal point in the numbers themselves.

534   BUSINESS AND ECONOMIC STATISTICS

Examples:

Number	Characteristic of Logarithm
286.	2
12,769.	4
1,008.73	3
1.827	0

2. The characteristics of the logarithms of all numbers between zero and one are negative, and their numerical values are one unit greater than the number of zeros between the decimal point and the first significant digit of the numbers themselves. A negative value is indicated either by a minus sign written above the characteristic or as a positive number followed by -10, as shown below.

Examples:

Number	Characteristic of Logarithm
0.764	$\bar{1}$, or 9.... -10
0.031	$\bar{2}$, or 8.... -10
0.02793	$\bar{2}$, or 8.... -10
0.00004	$\bar{5}$, or 5.... -10

3. The number zero and negative numbers have no logarithms.

How to Find the Mantissa

The following table (pp. 536–37) shows four-place mantissas of logarithms for three-digit numbers. This table is accurate enough for most business and economic data. For convenience in printing, decimal points are omitted, but each entry in the table must be interpreted as a four-place decimal. Mantissas are always positive.

The mantissa of any number of three digits or less can be read directly from the table. The first two digits are found in the column labeled "N" at the left of the page, and the third digit is found at the top of the page. Thus, to find the logarithm of 316, write down the characteristic 2 from Rule 1 above, followed by the mantissa .4997 from the table. This is found by moving down the column on the left to 31 and going to the right under the column headed 6. The log of 316 therefore is 2.4997.

Examples:

$$\log 3.160 = 0.4997$$
$$\log 0.316 = \bar{1}.4997, \text{ or } 9.4997 - 10$$
$$\log 180,000 = 5.2553$$
$$\log 0.031 = \bar{2}.4914, \text{ or } 8.4914 - 10$$

The logarithms of four-place numbers may be determined by interpolation. Thus, to find the log of 3.162, go two tenths of the way from log 3.160 (i.e., 0.4997) to log 3.170 (i.e., 0.5011). This is 0.4997 + 0.2 × 0.0014 = 0.5000.

Antilogarithms

To find the antilogarithm or natural number corresponding to a logarithm, find the nearest logarithm in the table and read the first two digits of the corresponding natural number from the left-hand column and the third digit from the top row. Thus, to get the antilog of 3.3101, find 3096, the nearest mantissa in the table, and read across and up to the number 204. Then from the rules on characteristics the answer is 2,040. This value may also be interpolated if four-place accuracy is desired.

Rules for Using Logarithms

1. To multiply numbers add their logarithms. Then look up the antilogarithm of their sum. The fact that numbers may be multiplied by adding their logarithms is the most basic property of logarithms.

Example: Multiply 19 by 28:

log 19	=	1.2788
log 28	=	1.4472
log product	=	2.7260
product	=	antilog 2.7260 = 532

2. To divide one number by another, subtract the logarithm of the latter from that of the former. Then look up the antilogarithm of the difference.

Example: Divide 532 by 28:

log 532	=	2.7259
log 28	=	1.4472
log difference	=	1.2787
quotient	=	antilog 1.2787 = 19.0

3. To raise a number to a given power, multiply the logarithm of the number by the exponent of the power and look up the antilogarithm of the product.

4. To extract any root of a number, divide its logarithm by the index of the root and look up the antilogarithm of the quotient.

FOUR-PLACE LOGARITHMS

N	0	1	2	3	4	5	6	7	8	9
10	0000	0043	0086	0128	0170	0212	0253	0294	0334	0374
11	0414	0453	0492	0531	0569	0607	0645	0682	0719	0755
12	0792	0828	0864	0899	0934	0969	1004	1038	1072	1106
13	1139	1173	1206	1239	1271	1303	1335	1367	1399	1430
14	1461	1492	1523	1553	1584	1614	1644	1673	1703	1732
15	1761	1790	1818	1847	1875	1903	1931	1959	1987	2014
16	2041	2068	2095	2122	2148	2175	2201	2227	2253	2279
17	2304	2330	2355	2380	2405	2430	2455	2480	2504	2529
18	2553	2577	2601	2625	2648	2672	2695	2718	2742	2765
19	2788	2810	2833	2856	2878	2900	2923	2945	2967	2989
20	3010	3032	3054	3075	3096	3118	3139	3160	3181	3201
21	3222	3243	3263	3284	3304	3324	3345	3365	3385	3404
22	3424	3444	3464	3483	3502	3522	3541	3560	3579	3598
23	3617	3636	3655	3674	3692	3711	3729	3747	3766	3784
24	3802	3820	3838	3856	3874	3892	3909	3927	3945	3962
25	3979	3997	4014	4031	4048	4065	4082	4099	4116	4133
26	4150	4166	4183	4200	4216	4232	4249	4265	4281	4298
27	4314	4330	4346	4362	4378	4393	4409	4425	4440	4456
28	4472	4487	4502	4518	4533	4548	4564	4579	4594	4609
29	4624	4639	4654	4669	4683	4698	4713	4728	4742	4757
30	4771	4786	4800	4814	4829	4843	4857	4871	4886	4900
31	4914	4928	4942	4955	4969	4983	4997	5011	5024	5038
32	5051	5065	5079	5092	5105	5119	5132	5145	5159	5172
33	5185	5198	5211	5224	5237	5250	5263	5276	5289	5302
34	5315	5328	5340	5353	5366	5378	5391	5403	5416	5428
35	5441	5453	5465	5478	5490	5502	5514	5527	5539	5551
36	5563	5575	5587	5599	5611	5623	5635	5647	5658	5670
37	5682	5694	5705	5717	5729	5740	5752	5763	5775	5786
38	5798	5809	5821	5832	5843	5855	5866	5877	5888	5899
39	5911	5922	5933	5944	5955	5966	5977	5988	5999	6010
40	6021	6031	6042	6053	6064	6075	6085	6096	6107	6117
41	6128	6138	6149	6160	6170	6180	6191	6201	6212	6222
42	6232	6243	6253	6263	6274	6284	6294	6304	6314	6325
43	6336	6345	6355	6365	6375	6385	6395	6405	6415	6425
44	6435	6444	6454	6464	6474	6484	6493	6503	6513	6522
45	6532	6542	6551	6561	6571	6580	6590	6599	6609	6618
46	6628	6637	6646	6656	6665	6675	6684	6693	6702	6712
47	6721	6730	6739	6749	6758	6767	6776	6785	6794	6803
48	6812	6821	6830	6839	6848	6857	6866	6875	6884	6893
49	6902	6911	6920	6928	6937	6946	6955	6964	6972	6981
50	6990	6998	7007	7016	7024	7033	7042	7050	7059	7067
51	7076	7084	7093	7101	7110	7118	7126	7135	7143	7152
52	7160	7168	7177	7185	7193	7202	7210	7218	7226	7235
53	7243	7251	7259	7267	7275	7284	7292	7300	7308	7316
54	7324	7332	7340	7348	7356	7364	7372	7380	7388	7396

FOUR-PLACE LOGARITHMS (*Continued*)

N	0	1	2	3	4	5	6	7	8	9
55	7404	7412	7419	7427	7435	7443	7451	7459	7466	7474
56	7482	7490	7497	7505	7513	7520	7528	7536	7543	7551
57	7559	7566	7574	7582	7589	7597	7604	7612	7619	7627
58	7634	7642	7649	7657	7664	7672	7679	7686	7694	7701
59	7709	7716	7723	7731	7738	7745	7752	7760	7767	7774
60	7782	7789	7796	7803	7810	7818	7825	7832	7839	7846
61	7853	7860	7868	7875	7882	7889	7896	7903	7910	7917
62	7924	7931	7938	7945	7952	7959	7966	7973	7980	7987
63	7993	8000	8007	8014	8021	8028	8035	8041	8048	8055
64	8062	8069	8075	8082	8089	8096	8102	8109	8116	8122
65	8129	8136	8142	8149	8156	8162	8169	8176	8182	8189
66	8195	8202	8209	8215	8222	8228	8235	8241	8248	8254
67	8261	8267	8274	8280	8287	8293	8299	8306	8312	8319
68	8325	8331	8338	8344	8351	8357	8363	8370	8376	8382
69	8388	8395	8401	8407	8414	8420	8426	8432	8439	8445
70	8451	8457	8463	8470	8476	8482	8488	8494	8500	8506
71	8513	8519	8525	8531	8537	8543	8549	8555	8561	8567
72	8573	8579	8585	8591	8597	8603	8609	8615	8621	8627
73	8633	8639	8645	8651	8657	8663	8669	8675	8681	8686
74	8692	8698	8704	8710	8716	8722	8727	8733	8739	8745
75	8751	8756	8762	8768	8774	8779	8785	8791	8797	8802
76	8808	8814	8820	8825	8831	8837	8842	8848	8854	8859
77	8865	8871	8876	8882	8887	8893	8899	8904	8910	8915
78	8921	8927	8932	8938	8943	8949	8954	8960	8965	8971
79	8976	8982	8987	8993	8998	9004	9009	9015	9020	9025
80	9031	9036	9042	9047	9053	9058	9063	9069	9074	9079
81	9085	9090	9096	9101	9106	9112	9117	9122	9128	9133
82	9138	9143	9149	9154	9159	9165	9170	9175	9180	9186
83	9191	9196	9201	9206	9212	9217	9222	9227	9232	9238
84	9243	9248	9253	9258	9263	9269	9274	9279	9284	9289
85	9294	9299	9304	9309	9315	9320	9325	9330	9335	9340
86	9345	9350	9355	9360	9365	9370	9375	9380	9385	9390
87	9395	9400	9405	9410	9415	9420	9425	9430	9435	9440
88	9445	9450	9455	9460	9465	9469	9474	9479	9484	9489
89	9494	9499	9504	9509	9513	9518	9523	9528	9533	9538
90	9542	9547	9552	9557	9562	9566	9571	9576	9581	9586
91	9590	9595	9600	9605	9609	9614	9619	9624	9628	9633
92	9638	9643	9647	9652	9657	9661	9666	9671	9675	9680
93	9685	9689	9694	9699	9703	9708	9713	9717	9722	9727
94	9731	9736	9741	9745	9750	9754	9759	9763	9768	9773
95	9777	9782	9786	9791	9795	9800	9805	9809	9814	9818
96	9823	9827	9832	9836	9841	9845	9850	9854	9859	9863
97	9868	9872	9877	9881	9886	9890	9894	9899	9903	9908
98	9912	9917	9921	9926	9930	9934	9939	9943	9948	9952
99	9956	9961	9965	9969	9974	9978	9983	9987	9991	9996

D. SQUARES, SQUARE ROOTS, AND RECIPROCALS 1–1,000

HOW TO FIND A SQUARE ROOT

SQUARE ROOTS can be read from the following table by any of three methods:

1. For any whole number from 1 to 1,000, listed in the N column, find the square root in the same row of the $\sqrt{N}$ column. Thus, the square root of 458 (in the N column) is 21.4+ (in the $\sqrt{N}$ column).

2. For any multiple of 10 from 10 to 10,000, move the decimal point one place to the left, look up this number in the N column, and find the square root in the $\sqrt{10N}$ column. For example, to get the square root of 8,670, look up 867 in the N column and find 93.1 + in the $\sqrt{10N}$ column.

3. When a problem calls for the square root of a number not given in the N column, it may be possible to find that number in the N^2 column. If the number is located in the N^2 column, its square root is given in the N column. Thus, to obtain the square root of 1,225, find this number under N^2 and read the square root, 35, to the left in the N column.

The square root of other numbers may also be read from the table in any of these methods by observing the rule that moving the decimal point *two* places to the left or right in the number moves it *one* place in the square root. As an example, the number 123,201 is given in the N^2 column of the table. Then,

$$\text{The square root of } 123{,}201. = 351.$$
$$\text{The square root of } 1{,}232.01 = 35.1$$
$$\text{The square root of } 12.3201 = 3.51$$

The square root of any number not shown in the table may be estimated by interpolating between values which are included. For example, the square root of 65.12 must be between the square root of 65 and the square root of 66. Since 65.12 stands at a point .12 of the way from

65 to 66, its square root should be approximately .12 of the way from the square root of 65 to the square root of 66. The following procedure is used:

Number	Root
66	8.124
65.12	?
65	8.062
Difference	.062

$$\sqrt{65.12} = 8.062 + .12(.062) = 8.069+$$

More detailed values of square roots may be obtained without interpolation by the use of *Barlow's Tables,* published by the Chemical Publishing Co., Inc., 234 King Street, Brooklyn, New York, which gives the squares, cubes, square roots, cube roots, and reciprocals of all integer numbers up to 12,500.

THE USE OF RECIPROCALS

Multiplication and division can often be facilitated by the use of reciprocals.* Instead of multiplying, one can divide one number by the reciprocal of the second, if the reciprocal is a simple number. For example:

$$1{,}582 \times 25 = \frac{158{,}200}{4} = 39{,}550$$

$$220 \times 50 = \frac{22{,}000}{2} = 11{,}000$$

$$17{,}228 \times 125 = \frac{17{,}228{,}000}{8} = 2{,}153{,}500$$

Similarly, instead of dividing, it may be easier to multiply the numerator by the reciprocal of the denominator. Thus,

$$5{,}725 \div 25 = 5{,}725 \times .04 = 57.25 \times 4 = 229$$
$$280{,}400 \div 50 = 2{,}804 \times 2 = 5{,}608$$
$$245{,}925 \div 125 = 245.925 \times 8 = 1{,}967.4$$

This short cut is particularly useful in computing a series of per cents on a common base, such as per cents of various asset accounts to total assets in a balance sheet. Simply place the reciprocal of the base (e.g., total assets) in a calculating machine, and *multiply* by each of the other items in turn, without clearing the machine. Reciprocals may be found in the last column of the following table.

---

* The reciprocal of a number is defined as unity divided by the number; i.e., the reciprocal of 5 is $1 \div 5 = .2$. The reciprocal of .25 is $1 \div .25 = 4$.

SQUARES, SQUARE ROOTS, AND RECIPROCALS 1–1,000*

N	N^2	$\sqrt{N}$	$\sqrt{10N}$	$1/N$	N	N^2	$\sqrt{N}$	$\sqrt{10N}$	$1/N$ .0
					50	2 500	7.071 068	22.36068	2000000
1	1	1.000 000	3.162 278	1.0000000	51	2 601	7.141 428	22.58318	1960784
2	4	1.414 214	4.472 136	.5000000	52	2 704	7.211 103	22.80351	1923077
3	9	1.732 051	5.477 226	.3333333	53	2 809	7.280 110	23.02173	1886792
4	16	2.000 000	6.324 555	.2500000	54	2 916	7.348 469	23.23790	1851852
5	25	2.236 068	7.071 068	.2000000	55	3 025	7.416 198	23.45208	1818182
6	36	2.449 490	7.745 967	.1666667	56	3 136	7.483 315	23.66432	1785714
7	49	2.645 751	8.366 600	.1428571	57	3 249	7.549 834	23.87467	1754386
8	64	2.828 427	8.944 272	.1250000	58	3 364	7.615 773	24.08319	1724138
9	81	3.000 000	9.486 833	.1111111	59	3 481	7.681 146	24.28992	1694915
10	100	3.162 278	10.00000	.1000000	60	3 600	7.745 967	24.49490	1666667
11	121	3.316 625	10.48809	.09090909	61	3 721	7.810 250	24.69818	1639344
12	144	3.464 102	10.95445	.08333333	62	3 844	7.874 008	24.89980	1612903
13	169	3.605 551	11.40175	.07692308	63	3 969	7.937 254	25.09980	1587302
14	196	3.741 657	11.83216	.07142857	64	4 096	8.000 000	25.29822	1562500
15	225	3.872 983	12.24745	.06666667	65	4 225	8.062 258	25.49510	1538462
16	256	4.000 000	12.64911	.06250000	66	4 356	8.124 038	25.69047	1515152
17	289	4.123 106	13.03840	.05882353	67	4 489	8.185 353	25.88436	1492537
18	324	4.242 641	13.41641	.05555556	68	4 624	8.246 211	26.07681	1470588
19	361	4.358 899	13.78405	.05263158	69	4 761	8.306 624	26.26785	1449275
20	400	4.472 136	14.14214	.05000000	70	4 900	8.366 600	26.45751	1428571
21	441	4.582 576	14.49138	.04761905	71	5 041	8.426 150	26.64583	1408451
22	484	4.690 416	14.83240	.04545455	72	5 184	8.485 281	26.83282	1388889
23	529	4.795 832	15.16575	.04347826	73	5 329	8.544 004	27.01851	1369863
24	576	4.898 979	15.49193	.04166667	74	5 476	8.602 325	27.20294	1351351
25	625	5.000 000	15.81139	.04000000	75	5 625	8.660 254	27.38613	1333333
26	676	5.099 020	16.12452	.03846154	76	5 776	8.717 798	27.56810	1315789
27	729	5.196 152	16.43168	.03703704	77	5 929	8.774 964	27.74887	1298701
28	784	5.291 503	16.73320	.03571429	78	6 084	8.831 761	27.92848	1282051
29	841	5.385 165	17.02939	.03448276	79	6 241	8.888 194	28.10694	1265823
30	900	5.477 226	17.32051	.03333333	80	6 400	8.944 272	28.28427	1250000
31	961	5.567 764	17.60682	.03225806	81	6 561	9.000 000	28.46050	1234568
32	1 024	5.656 854	17.88854	.03125000	82	6 724	9.055 385	28.63564	1219512
33	1 089	5.744 563	18.16590	.03030303	83	6 889	9.110 434	28.80972	1204819
34	1 156	5.830 952	18.43909	.02941176	84	7 056	9.165 151	28.98275	1190476
35	1 225	5.916 080	18.70829	.02857143	85	7 225	9.219 544	29.15476	1176471
36	1 296	6.000 000	18.97367	.02777778	86	7 396	9.273 618	29.32576	1162791
37	1 369	6.082 763	19.23538	.02702703	87	7 569	9.327 379	29.49576	1149425
38	1 444	6.164 414	19.49359	.02631579	88	7 744	9.380 832	29.66479	1136364
39	1 521	6.244 998	19.74842	.02564103	89	7 921	9.433 981	29.83287	1123596
40	1 600	6.324 555	20.00000	.02500000	90	8 100	9.486 833	30.00000	1111111
41	1 681	6.403 124	20.24846	.02439024	91	8 281	9.539 392	30.16621	1098901
42	1 764	6.480 741	20.49390	.02380952	92	8 464	9.591 663	30.33150	1086957
43	1 849	6.557 439	20.73644	.02325581	93	8 649	9.643 651	30.49590	1075269
44	1 936	6.633 250	20.97618	.02272727	94	8 836	9.695 360	30.65942	1063830
45	2 025	6.708 204	21.21320	.02222222	95	9 025	9.746 794	30.82207	1052632
46	2 116	6.782 330	21.44761	.02173913	96	9 216	9.797 959	30.98387	1041667
47	2 209	6.855 655	21.67948	.02127660	97	9 409	9.848 858	31.14482	1030928
48	2 304	6.928 203	21.90890	.02083333	98	9 604	9.899 495	31.30495	1020408
49	2 401	7.000 000	22.13594	.02040816	99	9 801	9.949 874	31.46427	1010101
50	2 500	7.071 068	22.36068	.02000000	100	10 000	10.00000	31.62278	1000000

* From Frederick E. Croxton and Dudley J. Cowden, *Practical Business Statistics* (2d ed.; New York: Prentice-Hall, Inc., 1948), pp. 524–33. Reprinted by permission of the publisher.

SQUARES, SQUARE ROOTS, AND RECIPROCALS 1–1,000 (*Continued*)

N	N^2	$\sqrt{N}$	$\sqrt{10N}$	1/N .0	N	N^2	$\sqrt{N}$	$\sqrt{10N}$	1/N .00
100	10 000	10.00000	31.62278	10000000	150	22 500	12.24745	38.72983	6666667
101	10 201	10.04988	31.78050	09900990	151	22 801	12.28821	38.85872	6622517
102	10 404	10.09950	31.93744	09803922	152	23 104	12.32883	38.98718	6578947
103	10 609	10.14889	32.09361	09708738	153	23 409	12.36932	39.11521	6535948
104	10 816	10.19804	32.24903	09615385	154	23 716	12.40967	39.24283	6493506
105	11 025	10.24695	32.40370	09523810	155	24 025	12.44990	39.37004	6451613
106	11 236	10.29563	32.55764	09433962	156	24 336	12.49000	39.49684	6410256
107	11 449	10.34408	32.71085	09345794	157	24 649	12.52996	39.62323	6369427
108	11 664	10.39230	32.86335	09259259	158	24 964	12.56981	39.74921	6329114
109	11 881	10.44031	33.01515	09174312	159	25 281	12.60952	39.87480	6289308
110	12 100	10.48809	33.16625	09090909	160	25 600	12.64911	40.00000	6250000
111	12 321	10.53565	33.31666	09009009	161	25 921	12.68858	40.12481	6211180
112	12 544	10.58301	33.46640	08928571	162	26 244	12.72792	40.24922	6172840
113	12 769	10.63015	33.61547	08849558	163	26 569	12.76715	40.37326	6134969
114	12 996	10.67708	33.76389	08771930	164	26 896	12.80625	40.49691	6097561
115	13 225	10.72381	33.91165	08695652	165	27 225	12.84523	40.62019	6060606
116	13 456	10.77033	34.05877	08620690	166	27 556	12.88410	40.74310	6024096
117	13 689	10.81665	34.20526	08547009	167	27 889	12.92285	40.86563	5988024
118	13 924	10.86278	34.35113	08474576	168	28 224	12.96148	40.98780	5952381
119	14 161	10.90871	34.49638	08403361	169	28 561	13.00000	41.10961	5917160
120	14 400	10.95445	34.64102	08333333	170	28 900	13.03840	41.23106	5882353
121	14 641	11.00000	34.78505	08264463	171	29 241	13.07670	41.35215	5847953
122	14 884	11.04536	34.92850	08196721	172	29 584	13.11488	41.47288	5813953
123	15 129	11.09054	35.07136	08130081	173	29 929	13.15295	41.59327	5780347
124	15 376	11.13553	35.21363	08064516	174	30 276	13.19091	41.71331	5747126
125	15 625	11.18034	35.35534	08000000	175	30 625	13.22876	41.83300	5714286
126	15 876	11.22497	35.49648	07936508	176	30 976	13.26650	41.95235	5681818
127	16 129	11.26943	35.63706	07874016	177	31 329	13.30413	42.07137	5649718
128	16 384	11.31371	35.77709	07812500	178	31 684	13.34166	42.19005	5617978
129	16 641	11.35782	35.91657	07751938	179	32 041	13.37909	42.30839	5586592
130	16 900	11.40175	36.05551	07692308	180	32 400	13.41641	42.42641	5555556
131	17 161	11.44552	36.19392	07633588	181	32 761	13.45362	42.54409	5524862
132	17 424	11.48913	36.33180	07575758	182	33 124	13.49074	42.66146	5494505
133	17 689	11.53256	36.46917	07518797	183	33 489	13.52775	42.77850	5464481
134	17 956	11.57584	36.60601	07462687	184	33 856	13.56466	42.89522	5434783
135	18 225	11.61895	36.74235	07407407	185	34 225	13.60147	43.01163	5405405
136	18 496	11.66190	36.87818	07352941	186	34 596	13.63818	43.12772	5376344
137	18 769	11.70470	37.01351	07299270	187	34 969	13.67479	43.24350	5347594
138	19 044	11.74734	37.14835	07246377	188	35 344	13.71131	43.35897	5319149
139	19 321	11.78983	37.28270	07194245	189	35 721	13.74773	43.47413	5291005
140	19 600	11.83216	37.41657	07142857	190	36 100	13.78405	43.58899	5263158
141	19 881	11.87434	37.54997	07092199	191	36 481	13.82027	43.70355	5235602
142	20 164	11.91638	37.68289	07042254	192	36 864	13.85641	43.81780	5208333
143	20 449	11.95826	37.81534	06993007	193	37 249	13.89244	43.93177	5181347
144	20 736	12.00000	37.94733	06944444	194	37 636	13.92839	44.04543	5154639
145	21 025	12.04159	38.07887	06896552	195	38 025	13.96424	44.15880	5128205
146	21 316	12.08305	38.20995	06849315	196	38 416	14.00000	44.27189	5102041
147	21 609	12.12436	38.34058	06802721	197	38 809	14.03567	44.38468	5076142
148	21 904	12.16553	38.47077	06756757	198	39 204	14.07125	44.49719	5050505
149	22 201	12.20656	38.60052	06711409	199	39 601	14.10674	44.60942	5025126
150	22 500	12.24745	38.72983	06666667	200	40 000	14.14214	44.72136	5000000

APPENDIXES 541

SQUARES, SQUARE ROOTS, AND RECIPROCALS 1–1,000 (*Continued*)

N	N^2	$\sqrt{N}$	$\sqrt{10N}$	1/N .00	N	N^2	$\sqrt{N}$	$\sqrt{10N}$	1/N .00
200	40 000	14.14214	44.72136	5000000	250	62 500	15.81139	50.00000	4000000
201	40 401	14.17745	44.83302	4975124	251	63 001	15.84298	50.09990	3984064
202	40 804	14.21267	44.94441	4950495	252	63 504	15.87451	50.19960	3968254
203	41 209	14.24781	45.05552	4926108	253	64 009	15.90597	50.29911	3952569
204	41 616	14.28286	45.16636	4901961	254	64 516	15.93738	50.39841	3937008
205	42 025	14.31782	45.27693	4878049	255	65 025	15.96872	50.49752	3921569
206	42 436	14.35270	45.38722	4854369	256	65 536	16.00000	50.59644	3906250
207	42 849	14.38749	45.49725	4830918	257	66 049	16.03122	50.69517	3891051
208	43 264	14.42221	45.60702	4807692	258	66 564	16.06238	50.79370	3875969
209	43 681	14.45683	45.71652	4784689	259	67 081	16.09348	50.89204	3861004
210	44 100	14.49138	45.82576	4761905	260	67 600	16.12452	50.99020	3846154
211	44 521	14.52584	45.93474	4739336	261	68 121	16.15549	51.08816	3831418
212	44 944	14.56022	46.04346	4716981	262	68 644	16.18641	51.18594	3816794
213	45 369	14.59452	46.15192	4694836	263	69 169	16.21727	51.28353	3802281
214	45 796	14.62874	46.26013	4672897	264	69 696	16.24808	51.38093	3787879
215	46 225	14.66288	46.36809	4651163	265	70 225	16.27882	51.47815	3773585
216	46 656	14.69694	46.47580	4629630	266	70 756	16.30951	51.57519	3759398
217	47 089	14.73092	46.58326	4608295	267	71 289	16.34013	51.67204	3745318
218	47 524	14.76482	46.69047	4587156	268	71 824	16.37071	51.76872	3731343
219	47 961	14.79865	46.79744	4566210	269	72 361	16.40122	51.86521	3717472
220	48 400	14.83240	46.90416	4545455	270	72 900	16.43168	51.96152	3703704
221	48 841	14.86607	47.01064	4524887	271	73 441	16.46208	52.05766	3690037
222	49 284	14.89966	47.11688	4504505	272	73 984	16.49242	52.15362	3676471
223	49 729	14.93318	47.22288	4484305	273	74 529	16.52271	52.24940	3663004
224	50 176	14.96663	47.32864	4464286	274	75 076	16.55295	52.34501	3649635
225	50 625	15.00000	47.43416	4444444	275	75 625	16.58312	52.44044	3636364
226	51 076	15.03330	47.53946	4424779	276	76 176	16.61325	52.53570	3623188
227	51 529	15.06652	47.64452	4405286	277	76 729	16.64332	52.63079	3610108
228	51 984	15.09967	47.74935	4385965	278	77 284	16.67333	52.72571	3597122
229	52 441	15.13275	47.85394	4366812	279	77 841	16.70329	52.82045	3584229
230	52 900	15.16575	47.95832	4347826	280	78 400	16.73320	52.91503	3571429
231	53 361	15.19868	48.06246	4329004	281	78 961	16.76305	53.00943	3558719
232	53 824	15.23155	48.16638	4310345	282	79 524	16.79286	53.10367	3546099
233	54 289	15.26434	48.27007	4291845	283	80 089	16.82260	53.19774	3533569
234	54 756	15.29706	48.37355	4273504	284	80 656	16.85230	53.29165	3521127
235	55 225	15.32971	48.47680	4255319	285	81 225	16.88194	53.38539	3508772
236	55 696	15.36229	48.57983	4237288	286	81 796	16.91153	53.47897	3496503
237	56 169	15.39480	48.68265	4219409	287	82 369	16.94107	53.57238	3484321
238	56 644	15.42725	48.78524	4201681	288	82 944	16.97056	53.66563	3472222
239	57 121	15.45962	48.88763	4184100	289	83 521	17.00000	53.75872	3460208
240	57 600	15.49193	48.98979	4166667	290	84 100	17.02939	53.85165	3448276
241	58 081	15.52417	49.09175	4149378	291	84 681	17.05872	53.94442	3436426
242	58 564	15.55635	49.19350	4132231	292	85 264	17.08801	54.03702	3424658
243	59 049	15.58846	49.29503	4115226	293	85 849	17.11724	54.12947	3412969
244	59 536	15.62050	49.39636	4098361	294	86 436	17.14643	54.22177	3401361
245	60 025	15.65248	49.49747	4081633	295	87 025	17.17556	54.31390	3389831
246	60 516	15.68439	49.59839	4065041	296	87 616	17.20465	54.40588	3378378
247	61 009	15.71623	49.69909	4048583	297	88 209	17.23369	54.49771	3367003
248	61 504	15.74802	49.79960	4032258	298	88 804	17.26268	54.58938	3355705
249	62 001	15.77973	49.89990	4016064	299	89 401	17.29162	54.68089	3344482
250	62 500	15.81139	50.00000	4000000	300	90 000	17.32051	54.77226	3333333

SQUARES, SQUARE ROOTS, AND RECIPROCALS 1–1,000 (*Continued*)

N	N^2	$\sqrt{N}$	$\sqrt{10N}$	$1/N$ .00	N	N^2	$\sqrt{N}$	$\sqrt{10N}$	$1/N$ .00
300	90 000	17.32051	54.77226	3333333	350	122 500	18.70829	59.16080	2857143
301	90 601	17.34935	54.86347	3322259	351	123 201	18.73499	59.24525	2849003
302	91 204	17.37815	54.95453	3311258	352	123 904	18.76166	59.32959	2840909
303	91 809	17.40690	55.04544	3300330	353	124 609	18.78829	59.41380	2832861
304	92 416	17.43560	55.13620	3289474	354	125 316	18.81489	59.49790	2824859
305	93 025	17.46425	55.22681	3278689	355	126 025	18.84144	59.58188	2816901
306	93 636	17.49286	55.31727	3267974	356	126 736	18.86796	59.66574	2808989
307	94 249	17.52142	55.40758	3257329	357	127 449	18.89444	59.74948	2801120
308	94 864	17.54993	55.49775	3246753	358	128 164	18.92089	59.83310	2793296
309	95 481	17.57840	55.58777	3236246	359	128 881	18.94730	59.91661	2785515
310	96 100	17.60682	55.67764	3225806	360	129 600	18.97367	60.00000	2777778
311	96 721	17.63519	55.76737	3215434	361	130 321	19.00000	60.08328	2770083
312	97 344	17.66352	55.85696	3205128	362	131 044	19.02630	60.16644	2762431
313	97 969	17.69181	55.94640	3194888	363	131 769	19.05256	60.24948	2754821
314	98 596	17.72005	56.03570	3184713	364	132 496	19.07878	60.33241	2747253
315	99 225	17.74824	56.12486	3174603	365	133 225	19.10497	60.41523	2739726
316	99 856	17.77639	56.21388	3164557	366	133 956	19.13113	60.49793	2732240
317	100 489	17.80449	56.30275	3154574	367	134 689	19.15724	60.58052	2724796
318	101 124	17.83255	56.39149	3144654	368	135 424	19.18333	60.66300	2717391
319	101 761	17.86057	56.48008	3134796	369	136 161	19.20937	60.74537	2710027
320	102 400	17.88854	56.56854	3125000	370	136 900	19.23538	60.82763	2702703
321	103 041	17.91647	56.65686	3115265	371	137 641	19.26136	60.90977	2695418
322	103 684	17.94436	56.74504	3105590	372	138 384	19.28730	60.99180	2688172
323	104 329	17.97220	56.83309	3095975	373	139 129	19.31321	61.07373	2680965
324	104 976	18.00000	56.92100	3086420	374	139 876	19.33908	61.15554	2673797
325	105 625	18.02776	57.00877	3076923	375	140 625	19.36492	61.23724	2666667
326	106 276	18.05547	57.09641	3067485	376	141 376	19.39072	61.31884	2659574
327	106 929	18.08314	57.18391	3058104	377	142 129	19.41649	61.40033	2652520
328	107 584	18.11077	57.27128	3048780	378	142 884	19.44222	61.48170	2645503
329	108 241	18.13836	57.35852	3039514	379	143 641	19.46792	61.56298	2638522
330	108 900	18.16590	57.44563	3030303	380	144 400	19.49359	61.64414	2631579
331	109 561	18.19341	57.53260	3021148	381	145 161	19.51922	61.72520	2624672
332	110 224	18.22087	57.61944	3012048	382	145 924	19.54483	61.80615	2617801
333	110 889	18.24829	57.70615	3003003	383	146 689	19.57039	61.88699	2610966
334	111 556	18.27567	57.79273	2994012	384	147 456	19.59592	61.96773	2604167
335	112 225	18.30301	57.87918	2985075	385	148 225	19.62142	62.04837	2597403
336	112 896	18.33030	57.96551	2976190	386	148 996	19.64688	62.12890	2590674
337	113 569	18.35756	58.05170	2967359	387	149 769	19.67232	62.20932	2583979
338	114 244	18.38478	58.13777	2958580	388	150 544	19.69772	62.28965	2577320
339	114 921	18.41195	58.22371	2949853	389	151 321	19.72308	62.36986	2570694
340	115 600	18.43909	58.30952	2941176	390	152 100	19.74842	62.44998	2564103
341	116 281	18.46619	58.39521	2932551	391	152 881	19.77372	62.52999	2557545
342	116 964	18.49324	58.48077	2923977	392	153 664	19.79899	62.60990	2551020
343	117 649	18.52026	58.56620	2915452	393	154 449	19.82423	62.68971	2544529
344	118 336	18.54724	58.65151	2906977	394	155 236	19.84943	62.76942	2538071
345	119 025	18.57418	58.73670	2898551	395	156 025	19.87461	62.84903	2531646
346	119 716	18.60108	58.82176	2890173	396	156 816	19.89975	62.92853	2525253
347	120 409	18.62794	58.90671	2881844	397	157 609	19.92486	63.00794	2518892
348	121 104	18.65476	58.99152	2873563	398	158 404	19.94994	63.08724	2512563
349	121 801	18.68154	59.07622	2865330	399	159 201	19.97498	63.16645	2506266
350	122 500	18.70829	59.16080	2857143	400	160 000	20.00000	63.24555	2500000

SQUARES, SQUARE ROOTS, AND RECIPROCALS 1–1,000 (*Continued*)

N	N^2	$\sqrt{N}$	$\sqrt{10N}$	1/N .00	N	N^2	$\sqrt{N}$	$\sqrt{10N}$	1/N .00
400	160 000	20.00000	63.24555	2500000	450	202 500	21.21320	67.08204	2222222
401	160 801	20.02498	63.32456	2493766	451	203 401	21.23676	67.15653	2217295
402	161 604	20.04994	63.40347	2487562	452	204 304	21.26029	67.23095	2212389
403	162 409	20.07486	63.48228	2481390	453	205 209	21.28380	67.30527	2207506
404	163 216	20.09975	63.56099	2475248	454	206 116	21.30728	67.37952	2202643
405	164 025	20.12461	63.63961	2469136	455	207 025	21.33073	67.45369	2197802
406	164 836	20.14944	63.71813	2463054	456	207 936	21.35416	67.52777	2192982
407	165 649	20.17424	63.79655	2457002	457	208 849	21.37756	67.60178	2188184
408	166 464	20.19901	63.87488	2450980	458	209 764	21.40093	67.67570	2183406
409	167 281	20.22375	63.95311	2444988	459	210 681	21.42429	67.74954	2178649
410	168 100	20.24846	64.03124	2439024	460	211 600	21.44761	67.82330	2173913
411	168 921	20.27313	64.10928	2433090	461	212 521	21.47091	67.89698	2169197
412	169 744	20.29778	64.18723	2427184	462	213 444	21.49419	67.97058	2164502
413	170 569	20.32240	64.26508	2421308	463	214 369	21.51743	68.04410	2159827
414	171 396	20.34699	64.34283	2415459	464	215 296	21.54066	68.11755	2155172
415	172 225	20.37155	64.42049	2409639	465	216 225	21.56386	68.19091	2150538
416	173 056	20.39608	64.49806	2403846	466	217 156	21.58703	68.26419	2145923
417	173 889	20.42058	64.57554	2398082	467	218 089	21.61018	68.33740	2141328
418	174 724	20.44505	64.65292	2392344	468	219 024	21.63331	68.41053	2136752
419	175 561	20.46949	64.73021	2386635	469	219 961	21.65641	68.48357	2132196
420	176 400	20.49390	64.80741	2380952	470	220 900	21.67948	68.55655	2127660
421	177 241	20.51828	64.88451	2375297	471	221 841	21.70253	68.62944	2123142
422	178 084	20.54264	64.96153	2369668	472	222 784	21.72556	68.70226	2118644
423	178 929	20.56696	65.03845	2364066	473	223 729	21.74856	68.77500	2114165
424	179 776	20.59126	65.11528	2358491	474	224 676	21.77154	68.84766	2109705
425	180 625	20.61553	65.19202	2352941	475	225 625	21.79449	68.92024	2105263
426	181 476	20.63977	65.26868	2347418	476	226 576	21.81742	68.99275	2100840
427	182 329	20.66398	65.34524	2341920	477	227 529	21.84033	69.06519	2096436
428	183 184	20.68816	65.42171	2336449	478	228 484	21.86321	69.13754	2092050
429	184 041	20.71232	65.49809	2331002	479	229 441	21.88607	69.20983	2087683
430	184 900	20.73644	65.57439	2325581	480	230 400	21.90890	69.28203	2083333
431	185 761	20.76054	65.65059	2320186	481	231 361	21.93171	69.35416	2079002
432	186 624	20.78461	65.72671	2314815	482	232 324	21.95450	69.42622	2074689
433	187 489	20.80865	65.80274	2309469	483	233 289	21.97726	69.49820	2070393
434	188 356	20.83267	65.87868	2304147	484	234 256	22.00000	69.57011	2066116
435	189 225	20.85665	65.95453	2298851	485	235 225	22.02272	69.64194	2061856
436	190 096	20.88061	66.03030	2293578	486	236 196	22.04541	69.71370	2057613
437	190 969	20.90454	66.10598	2288330	487	237 169	22.06808	69.78539	2053388
438	191 844	20.92845	66.18157	2283105	488	238 144	22.09072	69.85700	2049180
439	192 721	20.95233	66.25708	2277904	489	239 121	22.11334	69.92853	2044990
440	193 600	20.97618	66.33250	2272727	490	240 100	22.13594	70.00000	2040816
441	194 481	21.00000	66.40783	2267574	491	241 081	22.15852	70.07139	2036660
442	195 364	21.02380	66.48308	2262443	492	242 064	22.18107	70.14271	2032520
443	196 249	21.04757	66.55825	2257336	493	243 049	22.20360	70.21396	2028398
444	197 136	21.07131	66.63332	2252252	494	244 036	22.22611	70.28513	2024291
445	198 025	21.09502	66.70832	2247191	495	245 025	22.24860	70.35624	2020202
446	198 916	21.11871	66.78323	2242152	496	246 016	22.27106	70.42727	2016129
447	199 809	21.14237	66.85806	2237136	497	247 009	22.29350	70.49823	2012072
448	200 704	21.16601	66.93280	2232143	498	248 004	22.31591	70.56912	2008032
449	201 601	21.18962	67.00746	2227171	499	249 001	22.33831	70.63993	2004008
450	202 500	21.21320	67.08204	2222222	500	250 000	22.36068	70.71068	2000000

SQUARES, SQUARE ROOTS, AND RECIPROCALS 1–1,000 (*Continued*)

N	N^2	$\sqrt{N}$	$\sqrt{10N}$	1/N .00	N	N^2	$\sqrt{N}$	$\sqrt{10N}$	1/N .00
500	250 000	22.36068	70.71068	2000000	550	302 500	23.45208	74.16198	1818182
501	251 001	22.38303	70.78135	1996008	551	303 601	23.47339	74.22937	1814882
502	252 004	22.40536	70.85196	1992032	552	304 704	23.49468	74.29670	1811594
503	253 009	22.42766	70.92249	1988072	553	305 809	23.51595	74.36397	1808318
504	254 016	22.44994	70.99296	1984127	554	306 916	23.53720	74.43118	1805054
505	255 025	22.47221	71.06335	1980198	555	308 025	23.55844	74.49832	1801802
506	256 036	22.49444	71.13368	1976285	556	309 136	23.57965	74.56541	1798561
507	257 049	22.51666	71.20393	1972387	557	310 249	23.60085	74.63243	1795332
508	258 064	22.53886	71.27412	1968504	558	311 364	23.62202	74.69940	1792115
509	259 081	22.56103	71.34424	1964637	559	312 481	23.64318	74.76630	1788909
510	260 100	22.58318	71.41428	1960784	560	313 600	23.66432	74.83315	1785714
511	261 121	22.60531	71.48426	1956947	561	314 721	23.68544	74.89993	1782531
512	262 144	22.62742	71.55418	1953125	562	315 844	23.70654	74.96666	1779359
513	263 169	22.64950	71.62402	1949318	563	316 969	23.72762	75.03333	1776199
514	264 196	22.67157	71.69379	1945525	564	318 096	23.74868	75.09993	1773050
515	265 225	22.69361	71.76350	1941748	565	319 225	23.76973	75.16648	1769912
516	266 256	22.71563	71.83314	1937984	566	320 356	23.79075	75.23297	1766784
517	267 289	22.73763	71.90271	1934236	567	321 489	23.81176	75.29940	1763668
518	268 324	22.75961	71.97222	1930502	568	322 624	23.83275	75.36577	1760563
519	269 361	22.78157	72.04165	1926782	569	323 761	23.85372	75.43209	1757469
520	270 400	22.80351	72.11103	1923077	570	324 900	23.87467	75.49834	1754386
521	271 441	22.82542	72.18033	1919386	571	326 041	23.89561	75.56454	1751313
522	272 484	22.84732	72.24957	1915709	572	327 184	23.91652	75.63068	1748252
523	273 529	22.86919	72.31874	1912046	573	328 329	23.93742	75.69676	1745201
524	274 576	22.89105	72.38784	1908397	574	329 476	23.95830	75.76279	1742160
525	275 625	22.91288	72.45688	1904762	575	330 625	23.97916	75.82875	1739130
526	276 676	22.93469	72.52586	1901141	576	331 776	24.00000	75.89466	1736111
527	277 729	22.95648	72.59477	1897533	577	332 929	24.02082	75.96052	1733102
528	278 784	22.97825	72.66361	1893939	578	334 084	24.04163	76.02631	1730104
529	279 841	23.00000	72.73239	1890359	579	335 241	24.06242	76.09205	1727116
530	280 900	23.02173	72.80110	1886792	580	336 400	24.08319	76.15773	1724138
531	281 961	23.04344	72.86975	1883239	581	337 561	24.10394	76.22336	1721170
532	283 024	23.06513	72.93833	1879699	582	338 724	24.12468	76.28892	1718213
533	284 089	23.08679	73.00685	1876173	583	339 889	24.14539	76.35444	1715266
534	285 156	23.10844	73.07530	1872659	584	341 056	24.16609	76.41989	1712329
535	286 225	23.13007	73.14369	1869159	585	342 225	24.18677	76.48529	1709402
536	287 296	23.15167	73.21202	1865672	586	343 396	24.20744	76.55064	1706485
537	288 369	23.17326	73.28028	1862197	587	344 569	24.22808	76.61593	1703578
538	289 444	23.19483	73.34848	1858736	588	345 744	24.24871	76.68116	1700680
539	290 521	23.21637	73.41662	1855288	589	346 921	24.26932	76.74634	1697793
540	291 600	23.23790	73.48469	1851852	590	348 100	24.28992	76.81146	1694915
541	292 681	23.25941	73.55270	1848429	591	349 281	24.31049	76.87652	1692047
542	293 764	23.28089	73.62065	1845018	592	350 464	24.33105	76.94154	1689189
543	294 849	23.30236	73.68853	1841621	593	351 649	24.35159	77.00649	1686341
544	295 936	23.32381	73.75636	1838235	594	352 836	24.37212	77.07140	1683502
545	297 025	23.34524	73.82412	1834862	595	354 025	24.39262	77.13624	1680672
546	298 116	23.36664	73.89181	1831502	596	355 216	24.41311	77.20104	1677852
547	299 209	23.38803	73.95945	1828154	597	356 409	24.43358	77.26578	1675042
548	300 304	23.40940	74.02702	1824818	598	357 604	24.45404	77.33046	1672241
549	301 401	23.43075	74.09453	1821494	599	358 801	24.47448	77.39509	1669449
550	302 500	23.45208	74.16198	1818182	600	360 000	24.49490	77.45967	1666667

SQUARES, SQUARE ROOTS, AND RECIPROCALS 1–1,000 (*Continued*)

N	N^2	$\sqrt{N}$	$\sqrt{10N}$	1/N .00	N	N^2	$\sqrt{N}$	$\sqrt{10N}$	1/N .00
600	360 000	24.49490	77.45967	1666667	650	422 500	25.49510	80.62258	1538462
601	361 201	24.51530	77.52419	1663894	651	423 801	25.51470	80.68457	1536098
602	362 404	24.53569	77.58866	1661130	652	425 104	25.53429	80.74652	1533742
603	363 609	24.55606	77.65307	1658375	653	426 409	25.55386	80.80842	1531394
604	364 816	24.57641	77.71744	1655629	654	427 716	25.57342	80.87027	1529052
605	366 025	24.59675	77.78175	1652893	655	429 025	25.59297	80.93207	1526718
606	367 236	24.61707	77.84600	1650165	656	430 336	25.61250	80.99383	1524390
607	368 449	24.63737	77.91020	1647446	657	431 649	25.63201	81.05554	1522070
608	369 664	24.65766	77.97435	1644737	658	432 964	25.65151	81.11720	1519757
609	370 881	24.67793	78.03845	1642036	659	434 281	25.67100	81.17881	1517451
610	372 100	24.69818	78.10250	1639344	660	435 600	25.69047	81.24038	1515152
611	373 321	24.71841	78.16649	1636661	661	436 921	25.70992	81.30191	1512859
612	374 544	24.73863	78.23043	1633987	662	438 244	25.72936	81.36338	1510574
613	375 769	24.75884	78.29432	1631321	663	439 569	25.74879	81.42481	1508296
614	376 996	24.77902	78.35815	1628664	664	440 896	25.76820	81.48620	1506024
615	378 225	24.79919	78.42194	1626016	665	442 225	25.78759	81.54753	1503759
616	379 456	24.81935	78.48567	1623377	666	443 556	25.80698	81.60882	1501502
617	380 689	24.83948	78.54935	1620746	667	444 889	25.82634	81.67007	1499250
618	381 924	24.85961	78.61298	1618123	668	446 224	25.84570	81.73127	1497006
619	383 161	24.87971	78.67655	1615509	669	447 561	25.86503	81.79242	1494768
620	384 400	24.89980	78.74008	1612903	670	448 900	25.88436	81.85353	1492537
621	385 641	24.91987	78.80355	1610306	671	450 241	25.90367	81.91459	1490313
622	386 884	24.93993	78.86698	1607717	672	451 584	25.92296	81.97561	1488095
623	388 129	24.95997	78.93035	1605136	673	452 929	25.94224	82.03658	1485884
624	389 376	24.97999	78.99367	1602564	674	454 276	25.96151	82.09750	1483680
625	390 625	25.00000	79.05694	1600000	675	455 625	25.98076	82.15838	1481481
626	391 876	25.01999	79.12016	1597444	676	456 976	26.00000	82.21922	1479290
627	393 129	25.03997	79.18333	1594896	677	458 329	26.01922	82.28001	1477105
628	394 384	25.05993	79.24645	1592357	678	459 684	26.03843	82.34076	1474926
629	395 641	25.07987	79.30952	1589825	679	461 041	26.05763	82.40146	1472754
630	396 900	25.09980	79.37254	1587302	680	462 400	26.07681	82.46211	1470588
631	398 161	25.11971	79.43551	1584786	681	463 761	26.09598	82.42272	1468429
632	399 424	25.13961	79.49843	1582278	682	465 124	26.11513	82.58329	1466276
633	400 689	25.15949	79.56130	1579779	683	466 489	26.13427	82.64381	1464129
634	401 956	25.17936	79.62412	1577287	684	467 856	26.15339	82.70429	1461988
635	403 225	25.19921	79.68689	1574803	685	469 225	26.17250	82.76473	1459854
636	404 496	25.21904	79.74961	1572327	686	470 596	26.19160	82.82512	1457726
637	405 769	25.23886	79.81228	1569859	687	471 969	26.21068	82.88546	1455604
638	407 044	25.25866	79.87490	1567398	688	473 344	26.22975	82.94577	1453488
639	408 321	25.27845	79.93748	1564945	689	474 721	26.24881	83.00602	1451379
640	409 600	25.29822	80.00000	1562500	690	476 100	26.26785	83.06624	1449275
641	410 881	25.31798	80.06248	1560062	691	477 481	26.28688	83.12641	1447178
642	412 164	25.33772	80.12490	1557632	692	478 864	26.30589	83.18654	1445087
643	413 449	25.35744	80.18728	1555210	693	480 249	26.32489	83.24662	1443001
644	414 736	25.37716	80.24961	1552795	694	481 636	26.34388	83.30666	1440922
645	416 025	25.39685	80.31189	1550388	695	483 025	26.36285	83.36666	1438849
646	417 316	25.41653	80.37413	1547988	696	484 416	26.38181	83.42661	1436782
647	418 609	25.43619	80.43631	1545595	697	485 809	26.40076	83.48653	1434720
648	419 904	25.45584	80.49845	1543210	698	487 204	26.41969	83.54639	1432665
649	421 201	25.47548	80.56054	1540832	699	488 601	26.43861	83.60622	1430615
650	422 500	25.49510	80.62258	1538462	700	490 000	26.45751	83.66600	1428571

SQUARES, SQUARE ROOTS, AND RECIPROCALS 1–1,000 (*Continued*)

N	N^2	$\sqrt{N}$	$\sqrt{10N}$	$1/N$ .00	N	N^2	$\sqrt{N}$	$\sqrt{10N}$	$1/N$ .00
700	490 000	26.45751	83.66600	1428571	750	562 500	27.38613	86.60254	1333333
701	491 401	26.47640	83.72574	1426534	751	564 001	27.40438	86.66026	1331558
702	492 804	26.49528	83.78544	1424501	752	565 504	27.42262	86.71793	1329787
703	494 209	26.51415	83.84510	1422475	753	567 009	27.44085	86.77557	1328021
704	495 616	26.53300	83.90471	1420455	754	568 516	27.45906	86.83317	1326260
705	497 025	26.55184	83.96428	1418440	755	570 025	27.47726	86.89074	1324503
706	498 436	26.57066	84.02381	1416431	756	571 536	27.49545	86.94826	1322751
707	499 849	26.58947	84.08329	1414427	757	573 049	27.51363	87.00575	1321004
708	501 264	26.60827	84.14274	1412429	758	574 564	27.53180	87.06320	1319261
709	502 681	26.62705	84.20214	1410437	759	576 081	27.54995	87.12061	1317523
710	504 100	26.64583	84.26150	1408451	760	577 600	27.56810	87.17798	1315789
711	505 521	26.66458	84.32082	1406470	761	579 121	27.58623	87.23531	1314060
712	506 944	26.68333	84.38009	1404494	762	580 644	27.60435	87.29261	1312336
713	508 369	26.70206	84.43933	1402525	763	582 169	27.62245	87.34987	1310616
714	509 796	26.72078	84.49852	1400560	764	583 696	27.64055	87.40709	1308901
715	511 225	26.73948	84.55767	1398601	765	585 225	27.65863	87.46428	1307190
716	512 656	26.75818	84.61678	1396648	766	586 756	27.67671	87.52143	1305483
717	514 089	26.77686	84.67585	1394700	767	588 289	27.69476	87.57854	1303781
718	515 524	26.79552	84.73488	1392758	768	589 824	27.71281	87.63561	1302083
719	516 961	26.81418	84.79387	1390821	769	591 361	27.73085	87.69265	1300390
720	518 400	26.83282	84.85281	1388889	770	592 900	27.74887	87.74964	1298701
721	519 841	26.85144	84.91172	1386963	771	594 441	27.76689	87.80661	1297017
722	521 284	26.87006	84.97058	1385042	772	595 984	27.78489	87.86353	1295337
723	522 729	26.88866	85.02941	1383126	773	597 529	27.80288	87.92042	1293661
724	524 176	26.90725	85.08819	1381215	774	599 076	27.82086	87.97727	1291990
725	525 625	26.92582	85.14693	1379310	775	600 625	27.83882	88.03408	1290323
726	527 076	26.94439	85.20563	1377410	776	602 176	27.85678	88.09086	1288660
727	528 529	26.96294	85.26429	1375516	777	603 729	27.87472	88.14760	1287001
728	529 984	26.98148	85.32292	1373626	778	605 284	27.89265	88.20431	1285347
729	531 441	27.00000	85.38150	1371742	779	606 841	27.91057	88.26098	1283697
730	532 900	27.01851	85.44004	1369863	780	608 400	27.92848	88.31761	1282051
731	534 361	27.03701	85.49854	1367989	781	609 961	27.94638	88.37420	1280410
732	535 824	27.05550	85.55700	1366120	782	611 524	27.96426	88.43076	1278772
733	537 289	27.07397	85.61542	1364256	783	613 089	27.98214	88.48729	1277139
734	538 756	27.09243	85.67380	1362398	784	614 656	28.00000	88.54377	1275510
735	540 225	27.11088	85.73214	1360544	785	616 225	28.01785	88.60023	1273885
736	541 696	27.12932	85.79044	1358696	786	617 796	28.03569	88.65664	1272265
737	543 169	27.14774	85.84870	1356852	787	619 369	28.05352	88.71302	1270648
738	544 644	27.16616	85.90693	1355014	788	620 944	28.07134	88.76936	1269036
739	546 121	27.18455	85.96511	1353180	789	622 521	28.08914	88.82567	1267427
740	547 600	27.20294	86.02325	1351351	790	624 100	28.10694	88.88194	1265823
741	549 081	27.22132	86.08136	1349528	791	625 681	28.12472	88.93818	1264223
742	550 564	27.23968	86.13942	1347709	792	627 264	28.14249	88.99438	1262626
743	552 049	27.25803	86.19745	1345895	793	628 849	28.16026	89.05055	1261034
744	553 536	27.27636	86.25543	1344086	794	630 436	28.17801	89.10668	1259446
745	555 025	27.29469	86.31338	1342282	795	632 025	28.19574	89.16277	1257862
746	556 516	27.31300	86.37129	1340483	796	633 616	28.21347	89.21883	1256281
747	558 009	27.33130	86.42916	1338688	797	635 209	28.23119	89.27486	1254705
748	559 504	27.34959	86.48699	1336898	798	636 804	28.24889	89.33085	1253133
749	561 001	27.36786	86.54479	1335113	799	638 401	28.26659	89.38680	1251564
750	562 500	27.38613	86.60254	1333333	800	640 000	28.28427	89.44272	1250000

SQUARES, SQUARE ROOTS, AND RECIPROCALS 1–1,000 (*Continued*)

N	N²	√N	√10N	1/N .00	N	N²	√N	√10N	1/N .00
800	640 000	28.28427	89.44272	1250000	850	722 500	29.15476	92.19544	1176471
801	641 601	28.30194	89.49860	1248439	851	724 201	29.17190	92.24966	1175088
802	643 204	28.31960	89.55445	1246883	852	725 904	29.18904	92.30385	1173709
803	644 809	28.33725	89.61027	1245330	853	727 609	29.20616	92.35800	1172333
804	646 416	28.35489	89.66605	1243781	854	729 316	29.22328	92.41212	1170960
805	648 025	28.37252	89.72179	1242236	855	731 025	29.24038	92.46621	1169591
806	649 636	28.39014	89.77750	1240695	856	732 736	29.25748	92.52027	1168224
807	651 249	28.40775	89.83318	1239157	857	734 449	29.27456	92.57429	1166861
808	652 864	28.42534	89.88882	1237624	858	736 164	29.29164	92.62829	1165501
809	654 481	28.44293	89.94443	1236094	859	737 881	29.30870	92.68225	1164144
810	656 100	28.46050	90.00000	1234568	860	739 600	29.32576	92.73618	1162791
811	657 721	28.47806	90.05554	1233046	861	741 321	29.34280	92.79009	1161440
812	659 344	28.49561	90.11104	1231527	862	743 044	29.35984	92.84396	1160093
813	660 969	28.51315	90.16651	1230012	863	744 769	29.37686	92.89779	1158749
814	662 596	28.53069	90.22195	1228501	864	746 496	29.39388	92.95160	1157407
815	664 225	28.54820	90.27735	1226994	865	748 225	29.41088	93.00538	1156069
816	665 856	28.56571	90.33272	1225490	866	749 956	29.42788	93.05912	1154734
817	667 489	28.58321	90.38805	1223990	867	751 689	29.44486	93.11283	1153403
818	669 124	28.60070	90.44335	1222494	868	753 424	29.46184	93.16652	1152074
819	670 761	28.61818	90.49862	1221001	869	755 161	29.47881	93.22017	1150748
820	672 400	28.63564	90.55385	1219512	870	756 900	29.49576	93.27379	1149425
821	674 041	28.65310	90.60905	1218027	871	758 641	29.51271	93.32738	1148106
822	675 684	28.67054	90.66422	1216545	872	760 384	29.52965	93.38094	1146789
823	677 329	28.68798	90.71935	1215067	873	762 129	29.54657	93.43447	1145475
824	678 976	28.70540	90.77445	1213592	874	763 876	29.56349	93.48797	1144165
825	680 625	28.72281	90.82951	1212121	875	765 625	29.58040	93.54143	1142857
826	682 276	28.74022	90.88454	1210654	876	767 376	29.59730	93.59487	1141553
827	683 929	28.75761	90.93954	1209190	877	769 129	29.61419	93.64828	1140251
828	685 584	28.77499	90.99451	1207729	878	770 884	29.63106	93.70165	1138952
829	687 241	28.79236	91.04944	1206273	879	772 641	29.64793	93.75500	1137656
830	688 900	28.80972	91.10434	1204819	880	774 400	29.66479	93.80832	1136364
831	690 561	28.82707	91.15920	1203369	881	776 161	29.68164	93.86160	1135074
832	692 224	28.84441	91.21403	1201923	882	777 924	29.69848	93.91486	1133787
833	693 889	28.86174	91.26883	1200480	883	779 689	29.71532	93.96808	1132503
834	695 556	28.87906	91.32360	1199041	884	781 456	29.73214	94.02127	1131222
835	697 225	28.89637	91.37833	1197605	885	783 225	29.74895	94.07444	1129944
836	698 896	28.91366	91.43304	1196172	886	784 996	29.76575	94.12757	1128668
837	700 569	28.93095	91.48770	1194743	887	786 769	29.78255	94.18068	1127396
838	702 244	28.94823	91.54234	1193317	888	788 544	29.79933	94.23375	1126126
839	703 921	28.96550	91.59694	1191895	889	790 321	29.81610	94.28680	1124859
840	705 600	28.98275	91.65151	1190476	890	792 100	29.83287	94.33981	1123596
841	707 281	29.00000	91.70605	1189061	891	793 881	29.84962	94.39280	1122334
842	708 964	29.01724	91.76056	1187648	892	795 664	29.86637	94.44575	1121076
843	710 649	29.03446	91.81503	1186240	893	797 449	29.88311	94.49868	1119821
844	712 336	29.05168	91.86947	1184834	894	799 236	29.89983	94.55157	1118568
845	714 025	29.06888	91.92388	1183432	895	801 025	29.91655	94.60444	1117318
846	715 716	29.08608	91.97826	1182033	896	802 816	29.93326	94.65728	1116071
847	717 409	29.10326	92.03260	1180638	897	804 609	29.94996	94.71008	1114827
848	719 104	29.12044	92.08692	1179245	898	806 404	29.96665	94.76286	1113586
849	720 801	29.13760	92.14120	1177856	899	808 201	29.98333	94.81561	1112347
850	722 500	29.15476	92.19544	1176471	900	810 000	30.00000	94.86833	1111111

SQUARES, SQUARE ROOTS, AND RECIPROCALS 1–1,000 (*Continued*)

N	N^2	$\sqrt{N}$	$\sqrt{10N}$	$1/N$ .00	N	N^2	$\sqrt{N}$	$\sqrt{10N}$	$1/N$ .00
900	810 000	30.00000	94.86833	1111111	950	902 500	30.82207	97.46794	1052632
901	811 801	30.01666	94.92102	1109878	951	904 401	30.83829	97.51923	1051525
902	813 604	30.03331	94.97368	1108647	952	906 304	30.85450	97.57049	1050420
903	815 409	30.04996	95.02631	1107420	953	908 209	30.87070	97.62172	1049318
904	817 216	30.06659	95.07891	1106195	954	910.116	30.88689	97.67292	1048218
905	819 025	30.08322	95.13149	1104972	955	912 025	30.90307	97.72410	1047120
906	820 836	30.09983	95.18403	1103753	956	913 936	30.91925	97.77525	1046025
907	822 649	30.11644	95.23655	1102536	957	915 849	30.93542	97.82638	1044932
908	824 464	30.13304	95.28903	1101322	958	917 764	30.95158	97.87747	1043841
909	826 281	30.14963	95.34149	1100110	959	919 681	30.96773	97.92855	1042753
910	828 100	30.16621	95.39392	1098901	960	921 600	30.98387	97.97959	1041667
911	829 921	30.18278	95.44632	1097695	961	923 521	31.00000	98.03061	1040583
912	831 744	30.19934	95.49869	1096491	962	925 444	31.01612	98.08160	1039501
913	833 569	30.21589	95.55103	1095290	963	927 369	31.03224	98.13256	1038422
914	835 396	30.23243	95.60335	1094092	964	929 296	31.04835	98.18350	1037344
915	837 225	30.24897	95.65563	1092896	965	931 225	31.06445	98.23441	1036269
916	839 056	30.26549	95.70789	1091703	966	933 156	31.08054	98.28530	1035197
917	840 889	30.28201	95.76012	1090513	967	935 089	31.09662	98.33616	1034126
918	842 724	30.29851	95.81232	1089325	968	937 024	31.11270	98.38699	1033058
919	844 561	30.31501	95.86449	1088139	969	938 961	31.12876	98.43780	1031992
920	846 400	30.33150	95.91663	1086957	970	940 900	31.14482	98.48858	1030928
921	848 241	30.34798	95.96874	1085776	971	942 841	31.16087	98.53933	1029866
922	850 084	30.36445	96.02083	1084599	972	944 784	31.17691	98.59006	1028807
923	851 929	30.38092	96.07289	1083424	973	946 729	31.19295	98.64076	1027749
924	853 776	30.39737	96.12492	1082251	974	948 676	31.20897	98.69144	1026694
925	855 625	30.41381	96.17692	1081081	975	950 625	31.22499	98.74209	1025641
926	857 476	30.43025	96.22889	1079914	976	952 576	31.24100	98.79271	1024590
927	859 329	30.44667	96.28084	1078749	977	954 529	31.25700	98.84331	1023541
928	861 184	30.46309	96.33276	1077586	978	956 484	31.27299	98.89388	1022495
929	863 041	30.47950	96.38465	1076426	979	958 441	31.28898	98.94443	1021450
930	864 900	30.49590	96.43651	1075269	980	960 400	31.30495	98.99495	1020408
931	866 761	30.51229	96.48834	1074114	981	962 361	31.32092	99.04544	1019368
932	868 624	30.52868	96.54015	1072961	982	964 324	31.33688	99.09591	1018330
933	870 489	30.54505	96.59193	1071811	983	966 289	31.35283	99.14636	1017294
934	872 356	30.56141	96.64368	1070664	984	968 256	31.36877	99.19677	1016260
935	874 225	30.57777	96.69540	1069519	985	970 225	31.38471	99.24717	1015228
936	876 096	30.59412	96.74709	1068376	986	972 196	31.40064	99.29753	1014199
937	877 969	30.61046	96.79876	1067236	987	974 169	31.41656	99.34787	1013171
938	879 844	30.62679	96.85040	1066098	988	976 144	31.43247	99.39819	1012146
939	881 721	30.64311	96.90201	1064963	989	978 121	31.44837	99.44848	1011122
940	883 600	30.65942	96.95360	1063830	990	980 100	31.46427	99.49874	1010101
941	885 481	30.67572	97.00515	1062699	991	982 081	31.48015	99.54898	1009082
942	887 364	30.69202	97.05668	1061571	992	984 064	31.49603	99.59920	1008065
943	889 249	30.70831	97.10819	1060445	993	986 049	31.51190	99.64939	1007049
944	891 136	30.72458	97.15966	1059322	994	988 036	31.52777	99.69955	1006036
945	893 025	30.74085	97.21111	1058201	995	990 025	31.54362	99.74969	1005025
946	894 916	30.75711	97.26253	1057082	996	992 016	31.55947	99.79980	1004016
947	896 809	30.77337	97.31393	1055966	997	994 009	31.57531	99.84989	1003009
948	898 704	30.78961	97.36529	1054852	998	996 004	31.59114	99.89995	1002004
949	900 601	30.80584	97.41663	1053741	999	998 001	31.60696	99.94999	1001001
950	902 500	30.82207	97.46794	1052632	1000	1 000 000	31.62278	100.00000	1000000

E. AREAS UNDER THE NORMAL CURVE

EACH ENTRY in this table is the proportion of the total area under a normal curve which lies under the segment between the mean and x/σ standard deviations from the mean. Example: $x = X - \mu = 31$ and $\sigma = 20$, so $x/\sigma = 1.55$. Then the required area is .4394.

x/σ	.00	.01	.02	.03	.04	.05	.06	.07	.08	.09
0.0	.0000	.0040	.0080	.0120	.0160	.0199	.0239	.0279	.0319	.0359
0.1	.0398	.0438	.0478	.0517	.0557	.0596	.0636	.0675	.0714	.0753
0.2	.0793	.0832	.0871	.0910	.0948	.0987	.1026	.1064	.1103	.1141
0.3	.1179	.1217	.1255	.1293	.1331	.1368	.1406	.1443	.1480	.1517
0.4	.1554	.1591	.1628	.1664	.1700	.1736	.1772	.1808	.1844	.1879
0.5	.1915	.1950	.1985	.2019	.2054	.2088	.2123	.2157	.2190	.2224
0.6	.2257	.2291	.2324	.2357	.2389	.2422	.2454	.2486	.2518	.2549
0.7	.2580	.2612	.2642	.2673	.2704	.2734	.2764	.2794	.2823	.2852
0.8	.2881	.2910	.2939	.2967	.2995	.3023	.3051	.3078	.3106	.3133
0.9	.3159	.3186	.3212	.3238	.3264	.3289	.3315	.3340	.3365	.3389
1.0	.3413	.3438	.3461	.3485	.3508	.3531	.3554	.3577	.3599	.3621
1.1	.3643	.3665	.3686	.3708	.3729	.3749	.3770	.3790	.3810	.3830
1.2	.3849	.3869	.3888	.3907	.3925	.3944	.3962	.3980	.3997	.4015
1.3	.4032	.4049	.4066	.4082	.4099	.4115	.4131	.4147	.4162	.4177
1.4	.4192	.4207	.4222	.4236	.4251	.4265	.4279	.4292	.4306	.4319
1.5	.4332	.4345	.4357	.4370	.4382	.4394	.4406	.4418	.4429	.4441
1.6	.4452	.4463	.4474	.4484	.4495	.4505	.4515	.4525	.4535	.4545
1.7	.4554	.4564	.4573	.4582	.4591	.4599	.4608	.4616	.4625	.4633
1.8	.4641	.4649	.4656	.4664	.4671	.4678	.4686	.4693	.4699	.4706
1.9	.4713	.4719	.4726	.4732	.4738	.4744	.4750	.4756	.4761	.4767
2.0	.4772	.4778	.4783	.4788	.4793	.4798	.4803	.4808	.4812	.4817
2.1	.4821	.4826	.4830	.4834	.4838	.4842	.4846	.4850	.4854	.4857
2.2	.4861	.4864	.4868	.4871	.4875	.4878	.4881	.4884	.4887	.4890
2.3	.4893	.4896	.4898	.4901	.4904	.4906	.4909	.4911	.4913	.4916
2.4	.4918	.4920	.4922	.4925	.4927	.4929	.4931	.4932	.4934	.4936
2.5	.4938	.4940	.4941	.4943	.4945	.4946	.4948	.4949	.4951	.4952
2.6	.4953	.4955	.4956	.4957	.4959	.4960	.4961	.4962	.4963	.4964
2.7	.4965	.4966	.4967	.4968	.4969	.4970	.4971	.4972	.4973	.4974
2.8	.4974	.4975	.4976	.4977	.4977	.4978	.4979	.4979	.4980	.4981
2.9	.4981	.4982	.4982	.4983	.4984	.4984	.4985	.4985	.4986	.4986
3.0	.49865	.4987	.4987	.4988	.4988	.4989	.4989	.4989	.4990	.4990
3.1	.49903	.4991	.4991	.4991	.4992	.4992	.4992	.4992	.4993	.4993
3.2	.4993129	.4993	.4994	.4994	.4994	.4994	.4994	.4995	.4995	.4995
3.3	.4995166	.4995	.4995	.4996	.4996	.4996	.4996	.4996	.4996	.4997
3.4	.4996631	.4997	.4997	.4997	.4997	.4997	.4997	.4997	.4998	.4998
3.5	.4997674	.4998	.4998	.4998	.4998	.4998	.4998	.4998	.4998	.4998
3.6	.4998409	.4998	.4999	.4999	.4999	.4999	.4999	.4999	.4999	.4999
3.7	.4998922	.4999	.4999	.4999	.4999	.4999	.4999	.4999	.4999	.4999
3.8	.4999277	.4999	.4999	.4999	.4999	.4999	.4999	.5000	.5000	.5000
3.9	.4999519	.5000	.5000	.5000	.5000	.5000	.5000	.5000	.5000	.5000
4.0	.4999683									
4.5	.4999966									
5.0	.4999997133									

SOURCE: Frederick E. Croxton and Dudley J. Cowden, *Practical Business Statistics* (2d ed.; New York: Prentice-Hall, Inc., 1948), p. 511. Reprinted by permission of the publisher.

Through $x/\sigma = 2.99$, from Rugg's *Statistical Methods Applied to Education*, by arrangement with the publishers, Houghton Mifflin Company. A much more detailed table of normal curve areas is given in Federal Works Agency, Work Projects Administration for the City of New York, *Tables of Probability Functions* (New York: National Bureau of Standards, 1942), Vol. II, pp. 2–238. In this appendix values for $x/\sigma = 3.00$ through 5.00 were computed from the latter source.

F. VALUES OF t

THE VALUE t describes the sampling distribution of a deviation from a population value divided by the standard error.

Probabilities in the heading refer to the sum of the two-tailed areas under the curve that lie outside the points $\pm t$. (For a single tail divide the probability by 2.) Degrees of freedom are listed in the first column.

Example: In the distribution of the means of samples of size $n = 10$, $df = n - 1 = 9$; then .05 of the area under the curve falls in the two tails outside the interval $t = \pm 2.262$. The last row shows the corresponding areas under the normal curve.

PROBABILITY (P)

df	.20	.10	.05	.02	.01
1	3·078	6·314	12·706	31·821	63·657
2	1·886	2·920	4·303	6·965	9·925
3	1·638	2·353	3·182	4·541	5·841
4	1·533	2·132	2·776	3·747	4·604
5	1·476	2·015	2·571	3·365	4·032
6	1·440	1·943	2·447	3·143	3·707
7	1·415	1·895	2·365	2·998	3·499
8	1·397	1·860	2·306	2·896	3·355
9	1·383	1·833	2·262	2·821	3·250
10	1·372	1·812	2·228	2·764	3·169
11	1·363	1·796	2·201	2·718	3·106
12	1·356	1·782	2·179	2·681	3·055
13	1·350	1·771	2·160	2·650	3·012
14	1·345	1·761	2·145	2·624	2·977
15	1·341	1·753	2·131	2·602	2·947
16	1·337	1·746	2·120	2·583	2·921
17	1·333	1·740	2·110	2·567	2·898
18	1·330	1·734	2·101	2·552	2·878
19	1·328	1·729	2·093	2·539	2·861
20	1·325	1·725	2·086	2·528	2·845
21	1·323	1·721	2·080	2·518	2·831
22	1·321	1·717	2·074	2·508	2·819
23	1·319	1·714	2·069	2·500	2·807
24	1·318	1·711	2·064	2·492	2·797
25	1·316	1·708	2·060	2·485	2·787
26	1·315	1·706	2·056	2·479	2·779
27	1·314	1·703	2·052	2·473	2·771
28	1·313	1·701	2·048	2·467	2·763
29	1·311	1·699	2·045	2·462	2·756
30	1·310	1·697	2·042	2·457	2·750
∞	1·28155	1·64485	1·95996	2·32634	2·57582

Reprinted from Table IV, p. 174, of R. A. Fisher, *Statistical Methods for Research Workers* (11th ed.), published by Oliver and Boyd, Ltd. Edinburgh, by permission of the author and publishers.

G. SUMS OF SQUARES AND FOURTH POWERS USED IN TREND FITTING

THIS TABLE gives the values of Σx^2 and Σx^4 needed to find the constants in secular trend equations fitted by least squares, where the x origin is centered at the midpoint in time. Use the left half of the table for an odd number of years, where the x unit is one year. Use the right half of the table for an even number of years, where the x unit is six months, and the years are numbered 1, 3, 5, $\cdots$ and $-1, -3, -5$ $\cdots$ from the origin. The sum includes the powers of negative as well as positive values of x. For example, $N = 51$ includes integer values of x from -25 to 25, and $N = 50$ includes odd-numbered values of x from -49 to 49.

\multicolumn{3}{c	}{For Odd Number of Years x Unit Is 1 Year}	\multicolumn{3}{c}{For Even Number of Years x Unit Is 6 Months}
N	Σx^2	Σx^4	N	Σx^2	Σx^4
3	2	2	2	2	2
5	10	34	4	20	164
7	28	196	6	70	1 414
9	60	708	8	168	6 216
11	110	1 958	10	330	19 338
13	182	4 550	12	572	48 620
15	280	9 352	14	910	105 742
17	408	17 544	16	1 360	206 992
19	570	30 666	18	1 938	374 034
21	770	50 666	20	2 660	634 676
23	1 012	79 948	22	3 542	1 023 638
25	1 300	121 420	24	4 600	1 583 320
27	1 638	178 542	26	5 850	2 364 570
29	2 030	255 374	28	7 308	3 427 452
31	2 480	356 624	30	8 990	4 842 014
33	2 992	469 696	32	10 912	6 689 056
35	3 570	654 738	34	13 090	9 060 898
37	4 218	864 690	36	15 540	12 062 148
39	4 940	1 125 332	38	18 278	15 810 470
41	5 740	1 445 332	40	21 320	20 437 352
43	6 622	1 834 294	42	24 682	26 088 874
45	7 590	2 302 806	44	28 380	32 926 476
47	8 628	2 862 488	46	32 430	41 127 726
49	9 800	3 526 040	48	36 848	50 887 088
51	11 050	4 307 290	50	41 650	62 416 690
53	12 402	5 221 242	52	46 852	75 947 092
55	13 860	6 284 124	54	52 470	91 728 054
57	15 428	7 513 436	56	58 520	110 029 304
59	17 110	8 927 998	58	65 018	131 141 306
61	18 910	10 547 998	60	71 980	155 376 028

INDEX

INDEX

INDEX

A
Acceptance sampling, 510–13
Accuracy of economic data, 82–87, 233n.
    spurious, 13
American Iron and Steel Institute, 325–26
American Society of Mechanical Engineers, 118n.
Analysis, statistical
    in business, 4–6
    in decision making, 3–4
    definition, 1–2
    in economics, 6–8
    misuses of, 8–16
Arithmetic mean; *see* Averages
Arnold, David R., 384n.
Array, 156–57
Askovitz, S. I., 359n.
Association of American Railways, 325
Attributes, vs. variables, 271
Average deviation; *see* Dispersion measures, mean deviation
Averages, 179–97, 200–203
    arithmetic mean, 179–86, 189–90, 193–95
    characteristics, 194–96
    factors governing choice, 193–94
    geometric mean, 191–94, 196, 312
    median, 179, 186–90, 193–96, 204–6
    mode, 179, 190–91, 193–96, 218
    modified mean, 186, 189–90, 196, 405
    weighted mean, 181

B
Barlow's Tables, 209, 539
Barton, H. C., Jr., 407n.
Bias, 8–9, 40, 49, 233
Bibliographies, sources of, 22, 519–20
Binomial distribution, 275–77
Boeckh and Associates, E. H., 324
Bratt, Elmer C., 369n.
Brumbaugh, Martin A., 50n.
Bryant, C. Willard, 312n.
Burns, Arthur F., 189n., 207n., 336n., 337n., 380n., 417n., 418n.
Business cycles; *see* Cyclical fluctuations
Business indicators; *see* Index numbers
Butters, J. Keith, 318n.

C
Calendar variation, 341–47, 352, 395n.
Census (complete enumeration), 38–39

Central tendency, 172, 179n.; *see also* Averages
Charts, 97–98, 113–28, 130–51
    analysis by use of, 113–14
    arithmetic line charts, 114–28, 130–32
    bar charts, 130–39
    circle charts, 139–40
    comparing series, 122–24, 146–48
    construction of, 118–27
    Gantt charts, 134
    pictographs, 136–37
    planning, 115–18
    purposes of, 113–14
    ratio charts, 124, 140–51
    scatter diagrams, 426–29
    telling a story, 127–28
    tier charts, 410–11
Class interval; *see* Frequency distributions
Coefficient of correlation; *see* Correlation and regression
Coefficient of determination; *see* Correlation and regression
Coefficient of dispersion, 217–18
Coefficient of regression; *see* Correlation and regression
Coefficient of skewness, 219
Collection of data, 18–35, 38–61; *see also* Data, statistical
    consumer panels, 41
    editing schedules, 50–52
    mail questionnaires, 40–42
    personal interviews, 39–40
    questionnaires, preparation of, 42–50
    telephone interviews, 42
Confidence interval; *see* Inference, statistical
Consumer panels, 41, 77–78
Consumer Price Index; *see* Index numbers
Control charts; *see* Quality control
Correlation and regression, 426–89
    assuming causation from, 12
    coefficient of correlation
        multiple, 478, 481, 486
        simple, 452, 456–58
    coefficient of determination
        multiple, 480, 485–86
        simple, 452–56
    control, use in, 429, 451
    in controlled experiment, 430–42
    first differences, 468–69, 472–73
    in forecasting, 465–67, 469–77
    index of correlation, 452

556 INDEX

Correlation and regression—*Cont.*
  line of average relationship; *see* regression analysis
  multiple, 426, 477–89
  percentages of trend, 469
  prediction, use in, 429, 445, 451
  regression analysis, 429–51, 464–84
    business and economic data, 464–67
    multiple curvilinear, 486–87
    multiple linear, 469, 478–84
    simple curvilinear, 435–39, 441
    simple linear, 430–35, 442–44, 448–49
      graphic method, 431–33, 469–70
      least squares, 433–35
    statistical inference, 445–51
      confidence intervals, 447–51
      testing hypotheses, 446–47
  regression coefficient, 433, 446–48, 480
  reliability of correlation coefficient, 456–58
  in sample survey, 442–51, 453, 456, 458
  scatter diagram, 426–29
  simple, 426–61, 464–77, 487–88
  standard error of estimate, 430, 439–41, 444–45
    multiple correlation, 478, 480, 484–85
    simple correlation, 430, 439–41, 444–45
  standard error of forecast, 449–50
  standard error of regression line, 448–50
  in time series, 467–77
  in time study, 454–55
  variance, explained and unexplained, 452–53, 480
Cowden, D. J., 232n., 383n., 511
Croxton, F. E., 232n., 383n.
Cyclical fluctuations, 14, 331–32, 335–38, 356, 366–68, 390, 411–23
  comparing cycles, 417
  conjuncture analysis, 336
  forecasting turning points, 419–21
  methods of measuring
    arithmetic adjustment, 414–17
    graphic adjustment, 413–14
    National Bureau of Economic Research, 189, 207, 417–19
    residual, 412–17
  reasons for measuring cycles, 411–12
  types of, 332, 336, 369
Cyclical indicators, 419–21; *see also* Index numbers

D

Data, statistical
  accuracy of, 82–87
  correct use of, 29–35

Data—*Cont.*
  counting and measurement, 84–85
  criterion of usefulness of published data, 19–21
  definition, 1
  noncomparable, 10–11
  significant figures, 85–87
  sources of, 18–35, 519–30
  steps in finding source, 22–24
  testing for accuracy, 29–33
  testing for validity, 33–35
Deduction, faulty, 10
Defining the problem, 18–19
Degrees of freedom, 266–67, 440n., 447–48, 551
Dewey, Edward R., 367–68
Dewey Decimal System, 24
Differences, significance of; *see* Inference, statistical
Dispersion measures, 200–220
  characteristics, 216–17
  mean deviation, 206–8, 214–17
  purposes of, 202–3
  quartile deviation, 204–6, 214–17
  range, 203–4, 216, 496, 498
  relation between, 214–16
  relative, 217–18
  standard deviation, 208–18
  uses of, 219–20
Dodge, F. W., Corp., 326
Dow Theory, 324
Dun & Bradstreet, 326–27
Duncan, Acheson J., 505n., 511
Dun's Review and Modern Industry, 204n.

E

Editing schedules, 50–52
Efficient estimators, 232–33
Eisenpress, Harry, 408n.
Electronic data processing, 58–60
Elgin National Watch Co., 243
Engineering News Record, 324
Escalator clause, using index numbers, 309, 312–13, 315–16
Ewell, Raymond H., 384n.
Expected value of statistic, 233
Exponential curve; *see* Trend, secular
Extrapolation; *see* Forecasting
Ezekiel, Mordecai, 377n., 446n., 457n.

F

Fabricant, Solomon, 3n.
Falkner, H. D., 394n.
Federal Reserve Board, 318–20, 407–8; *see also* Index numbers
Finite multiplier, 235–36
Fisher, Irving, 294n., 301n.
Fisher's z-transformation, 457n.

Fluctuations, business; *see* Time series, Trend, Seasonal variation, Cyclical fluctuations, Irregular movements
Forecasting, 5, 14, 310, 400, 410–11
 cyclical, 419–21
 by regression analysis, 429, 445, 449–51, 465–67, 469–77
 seasonal, 389–90, 393–95, 400
 trend, 355–56, 361–63, 376–77, 384–85
Fox, Karl A., 377n., 446n., 457n.
Freehand curves; *see* Graphic analysis
Frequency curves, 166–74, 200–202
 normal curve, 169–70
 ogive, 173–74
Frequency distributions, 155–75
 charts, 164–72
 class intervals, 155, 157–64
 comparison of two distributions, 168, 170
 cumulative, 172–74
 errors of grouping, 183
 J-shaped, 169, 171–72
 percentage, 163–64
 skewed, 169, 171, 194–95
 symmetrical, 169–71
 U-shaped, 169, 172
Frequency polygon, 166–67

G

Generalization, faulty, 9–10
Geometric mean; *see* Averages
Glover, James W., 380n.
Gompertz curve; *see* Trend, secular
Grant, Eugene L., 511
Graph, definition of, 113n.; *see also* Charts
Graphic analysis, 113–14, 140, 148–50
 correlation and regression, 431–33, 454–55, 469–70
 cyclical, 413–14
 seasonal, 394–402, 407–9
 trend, 359–65, 383–86
Gross national product; *see* Index numbers
Growth curve; *see* Trend, secular
Gutenberg, Arthur W., 57n.

H

Hall, L. W., 394n.
Hansen, M. H., 235n., 243
Histogram, 164–67
Hurwitz, W. N., 235n., 243
Hypotheses; *see* Tests of hypotheses

I

Index numbers, 192, 283–328, 419–21
 adjustments, 303–5
  changing the base, 303–4
  splicing two series, 304–5
  substitution of items, 303
 advantages of, 283–84

Index numbers—*Cont.*
 illustrations, 309–28
  business activity, 287, 294–95
  business failures, 326–27
  city worker's family budget, 284, 317
  construction contracts, 295–96, 326
  construction costs, 324
  consumer prices, 299–301, 313–17, 348–49
  employment and payrolls, 293, 295–96, 324–25
  farm prices, 323–24, 349
  gross national product, 287, 320–23, 333–36, 338, 349
  industrial production, 289, 290, 295, 300, 305, 318–20
  inventories, 326
  inventory prices, 317–18
  labor force, 325
  national income, 320–23
  new orders, 326
  railway freight carloadings, 325
  regional activity, 287, 293, 327
  retail food prices, 291–92
  sales, 293, 326
  steel production, 325–26
  stock prices, 324
  unfilled orders, 326
  wholesale prices, 39, 284, 300, 303, 310–13
 kinds of, 284–87
  price, 285–86, 291–94
  quantity, 285–86, 289–90, 293–94
  value, 285–87, 293–94
 methods of constructing, 287–95
  base period, 299–300
  composite indexes, 288–95
   aggregative, 292–95
   average of relatives, 289–92, 311
  formulas for basic methods, 293–94
  items included, 296–99
  selecting sample, 298–99
  simple indexes, 287–88
  weights, 289, 301–3
 purposes of, 295–96
 tests of, 295–303
 uses of, 124, 147, 309–10
Index of correlation; *see* Correlation
Indicators, business; *see* Index numbers
Industrial Production Index; *see* Index numbers
Inference, statistical; *see also* Sampling, Tests of Hypotheses
 arithmetic means, 227–45
  confidence coefficient, 238, 240–41
  confidence interval, 238–41, 247, 266–67, 269
  confidence limits, 238–39
  difference between means, 260–65, 269

INDEX

Inference—*Cont.*
   sampling distribution, 227–33
   size of sample, 241–43, 245
   standard error, 233–38
   testing hypotheses, 247–69
  central limit theorum, 232
  interval estimate, 224
  point estimate, 224
  proportions, 271–80
   binomial distribution, 275–77
   confidence interval, 272–73, 280
   difference between proportions, 277–80
   size of sample, 273–74, 277, 280
   standard error, 272, 280
   testing hypotheses, 274–75, 280
  standard normal deviate, 225
Inspection, 100 per cent, 502, 510
International Business Machines Corp., 56n.
Interviewing; *see* Collection of data
Irregular movements, 332, 342, 412–16

J

Joint Economic Committee, 316, 358n., 412

K

Kellogg, Lester S., 50n.
Kurtosis, 170–71, 200–202
Kuznets, Simon S., 339n., 365n., 381n.

L

"Law of growth," 335
Leabo, D. A., 257n.
Leading and lagging series, 411, 419–21
Least squares, method of
  regression analysis, 433–36, 439, 442–44, 481–84
  trend analysis, 365n., 369–81
LIFO, use of index numbers, 317–18
Livingston, J. A., 127n.
Logarithms, 141, 143, 533–37
Long, C. D., 85n.

M

Madow, W. G., 235n., 243
Market research, 38, 73–75
McGraw-Hill Publishing Co., 73–74
Mean deviation; *see* Dispersion measures
Median; *see* Averages
Median class, 187
Mills, Frederick C., 85n., 348n., 378n., 380n.
Mississippi Business Review, 340
Misuses of statistics, 8–16
Mitchell, Wesley C., 189n., 207n., 336n., 337n., 417n., 418n.
Modal class, 164, 191
Mode; *see* Averages
Modified mean; *see* Averages

Moore, Geoffrey H., 419–21
Morrison, W. J., 384n.
Moving averages
  cyclical-irregular analysis, 414–16
  seasonal analysis, 402–9
  trend analysis, 365–69

N

National Bureau of Economic Research, 189, 207, 411, 417–20
National income; *see* Index numbers
National Industrial Conference Board, 204, 333–34, 338n., 364n.
Newbury, Frank D., 5n.
Nielsen, A. C., Company, 77
Nomograph, 114, 383–84
Normal curve, 169–71, 200–201, 214–15, 244
  areas under, table of, 225–27, 550
Normal deviate; *see* Inference, statistical
Normal distribution, 194, 214–15, 225–27, 236–37, 244
Normal equations
  regression analysis, 434–35, 439n., 481–84
  trend analysis, 370–71, 377n., 380
Null hypothesis; *see* Tests of hypotheses

O

Ogive, 173–74, 188–89, 206
Ohio State University, Bureau of Business Research, 295

P

Pacific Telephone and Telegraph Co., 98
Parabola, 376–77, 439
Parameter, 224
Pearl, Raymond, 335n.
Percentages, 87–93
  errors in, 14–15
Pie charts; *see* Charts, circle
Polls, election, 74–75
Polynomials, 376–77, 439
Population, statistical, 65; *see also* Inference, statistical
Precision of sample estimates, 233
Presentation of data; *see* Tables, Charts
Price deflation, 312, 315, 347–52
Progressive seasonality; *see* Seasonal variation
Punch cards, 54–58

Q

Quality control, 203, 218, 493–513
  acceptance sampling, 510–13
  assignable variation, 494–95
  chance variation, 494–95
  control charts for attributes, 507–10
   fraction defective or p chart, 508–10

Quality control—*Cont.*
number of defects per unit or *c* chart, 510
control charts for variables, 495–507
R charts, 496, 498, 500, 503–7
X̄ charts, 495–99, 503–6
example, 502–7
specifications, meeting, 500–502, 506
use of, 498–502
Quartile deviation; *see* Dispersion measures
Quartiles, 174, 204–6
Questionnaires; *see* Collection of data

R

Railway freight carloadings, 325
Random numbers; *see* Sampling
Random sampling; *see* Sampling
Range; *see* Dispersion measures
Range chart; *see* Quality control
Rasor, Eugene A., 384n.
Ratios, 87–93
cautions in the use of, 90–92
importance of including original data, 92–93
selection of base, 88–90
use of, in tables, 101
Reciprocals, 539
table of, 540–49
Reed, Lowell J., 335n.
Regression; *see* Correlation and regression
Relative dispersion, 217–18
Relatives; *see* Index numbers
Reliability of sample estimates, 233n.; *see also* Inference, statistical
Research sources, 18–35, 519–30
Roberts, H. V., 235n.
Rounding off numbers, 83–84, 108

S

Sampling, 38–39, 64–79
area, 71–73
cluster, 71–73
consumer panels, 41, 77–78
controlled or purposive, 74n.
double, 511
judgment, 75–76
nonprobability, 73–76
nontypical samples, 9–10
probability, 66–73
proportional and nonproportional, 69–70
quota, 73–75
random, 66–69
recurrent surveys, 76–78
sequential, 511
stratified, 68–70
systematic, 70–72
Scatter diagram, 426–29
Scheuerman, Beth, 384n.

Sears, Roebuck & Company, 348–50, 360–63, 367–68, 374–80, 395–406, 412–15, 468–75, 477
Seasonal variation, 284, 331–32, 337–41, 389–411, 421–22
adjusting for, 390, 394, 399, 406, 416
calendar influence, 341–42
characteristics, 337, 339–41, 391–92
cyclical influence, 402
forecasting, 389–90, 400
methods of measuring, 391–411
averages of original data, 392–94
electronic computer, 408–9
Federal Reserve Board, 407–8
graphic method, 394–402, 407–9
moving-average method, 402–9
other methods, 394, 409–11
progressive seasonality, 401–2, 406–7
purposes of measuring, 389–90
seasonal indexes, 393, 399, 405–6
Secondary trend, 332, 369
Secular trend; *see* Trend, secular
Semantics, errors in, 11
Semilogarithmic charts; *see* Charts, ratio
Sheppard's adjustment, 213n.
Sherman, Jack, 384n.
Shiskin, Julius, 408n., 415n., 416n.
Significance, tests of; *see* Tests of hypotheses
Significant figures, 83–87, 108
Skewness, 171, 193–95, 200–202, 216, 218–19, 275–77, 500
Slide rule, 140, 143
Smith, C. Frank, 257n.
Sources of data, 18–35, 519–30
Splicing index numbers, 304–5
Spurr, William A., 318n., 384n., 413n.
Squares, square roots, 538–39
table of, 540–49
Squares, sums of, 552
Standard deviation; *see* Dispersion measures
Standard error; *see* Inference, Tests of hypotheses
Standard error of estimate; *see* Correlation and regression
Standard and Poor's Corporation, 324
Statistic, 224
Statistical Abstract of the United States, 30, 34, 105n., 123n., 147n.
Statistical analysis; *see* Analysis, statistical
Statistical data; *see* Data, statistical
Statistical inference; *see* Inference, statistical
Statistical quality control; *see* Quality control
Sturges, H. A., 159n.
Subgroup, use of, in quality control, 497

560 INDEX

Survey of Current Business, 31, 85, 102n., 138n., 139n., 149n., 321, 390
Symbols, glossary of, 531–32

T

t-distribution, *see* Tests of hypotheses
  table of, 551
Tables, 97–110
  classification of data, 98–100, 102–4
  construction, 101–9
  reference, 100–101
  summary, 100–101, 108–9
Tabulation, 44, 52–61
  coding, 52
  electronic data processing, 58–60
  preliminary tables, 52–60
  preparing returns, 52
  punch cards, 54–58
  sorting-counting, 53
  tally sheets, 53–54
Tests of hypotheses, 247–69
  critical probability, 251–54, 257
  difference between means, 260–65, 269
    standard error, 261
  errors of first and second kind, 251–57, 259
  example, 247–51
  null hypothesis, 262–63, 269, 278–80
  one-tailed tests, 257–60, 268–69
  operating characteristic curves, 255–57
  proportions, 274–75
  risk, level of, 252
  size of sample, 254–55, 257
  small samples, 265–67, 269
  t-ratio, 265–67, 269, 551
  two-tailed tests, 257–60, 268–69
  type I and type II errors, 251–57, 259
Time series, 331–52; *see also* Cyclical fluctuations, Irregular movements, Seasonal variation, Trend
  analysis, 343–52
    calendar variation, 341–47, 352, 395n.
    price deflation, 347–52
  charts, 114–18, 120–27, 132–38, 145–48
  components, 331–42
  correlation of, 467–77
Trend, secular, 332–35, 343, 355–86
  causes of, 332–35
  effect on correlation, 467–69
  elimination from series, 363, 374

Trend—*Cont.*
  graphic methods, 359–65, 378, 381, 383–86
  least squares method, 365n., 369–81
  moving averages, 365–69
  period of years selected, 356–57
  purposes of measuring, 355–56
  secondary, 332, 369
  semiaverages, 360
  types of trend curves
    arithmetic straight line, 369–76
    empirical, 356–65, 383
    growth, 334–35, 358–59, 381–86
      Gompertz, 363–64, 381, 384–86
      logistic, 381–86
    logarithmic straight line (exponential curve), 145n., 356, 359, 361–63, 378–81, 436–37
    parabola, 369–70, 376–77
Trend-cycle curve, 395–97, 400–402

U

Unbiased estimators, 232–33
U.S. Department of Agriculture, Agricultural Marketing Service, 323–24
U.S. Department of Commerce
  Bureau of the Census, 52, 84–85, 241, 325
  Office of Business Economics, 287, 320–23, 324, 326, 438n.
U.S. Department of Labor, Bureau of Labor Statistics, 284, 310–18, 324–25
Universe, statistical, 65
University of Buffalo, Bureau of Business and Social Research, 345n.

V

Variance, 209, 452–53, 480
Variation; *see* Dispersion measures
Vergottini, Mario de, 391n.
Verhulst, P. F., 335n.

W

Walker, Helen M., 82
Wallis, W. A., 235n.
Weighted mean, 181
Weighting index numbers, 289–92
Weights in sampling, 70
Wholesale Price Index; *see* Index numbers
"World Calendar," 341n.

This book has been set on the Linotype in 12 and 10 point Garamond #3, leaded 1 point. Chapter titles and numbers are in 18 point Lydian Bold. The size of the type page is 27 x 46½ picas.